HTML5 Canvas

HTML5 Canvas
Native Interactivity and Animation for the Web

Steve Fulton and Jeff Fulton

O'REILLY®

Beijing · Cambridge · Farnham · Köln · Sebastopol · Tokyo

HTML5 Canvas

by Steve Fulton and Jeff Fulton

Copyright © 2011 8bitrocket Studios. All rights reserved.
Printed in the United States of America.

Published by O'Reilly Media, Inc., 1005 Gravenstein Highway North, Sebastopol, CA 95472.

O'Reilly books may be purchased for educational, business, or sales promotional use. Online editions are also available for most titles (*http://my.safaribooksonline.com*). For more information, contact our corporate/institutional sales department: (800) 998-9938 or *corporate@oreilly.com*.

Editors: Mike Loukides and Simon St.Laurent
Production Editor: Kristen Borg
Copyeditor: Marlowe Shaeffer
Proofreader: Sada Preisch

Indexer: Ellen Troutman Zaig
Cover Designer: Karen Montgomery
Interior Designer: David Futato
Illustrator: Robert Romano

Printing History:

May 2011:   First Edition.

To Flash.

Table of Contents

Preface

HTML5 Canvas offers developers the chance to create animated graphics in ordinary web browsers using common tools: HTML and JavaScript. Canvas is one of the most visible parts of HTML5, fueling demo after demo, game after game. It offers interactivity with great visuals, and provides tremendous freedom to do whatever you want in the browser window. However, it differs enough from typical JavaScript development (as well as Flash and Silverlight development) that it needs careful exploration!

Running the Examples in the Book

The best part about programming HTML5 Canvas is that the entry barrier is very low—all you need is a modern web browser and a text editor.

As far as compatibility, we suggest you download and/or use the latest version of the web browsers as ordered below.

1. Chrome
2. Safari
3. Opera
4. Firefox
5. Internet Explorer (version 9 or higher)

Every example in this book was tested with Google Chrome, Safari, and Opera. Late in the development of the example code, Firefox started causing issues. While we made every attempt to ensure these examples worked across as many browsers as possible, we recommend you use Google Chrome or Safari for the best results until Canvas support improves.

Please note that if you are using the .pdf version of this book to cut and paste the code, there may be instances where minus ("-") signs are represented by another character, such as a hyphen. You may need to replace the other character with a minus sign ("-") to get the code to work properly.

We suggest that if you have purchased the electronic version of this book, you should use the printed code samples as a guide only, and instead download the code from the book distribution. With that code, you will also get all the images, libraries, and assets necessary to make all the examples work in a web browser.

What You Need to Know

Ideally, you know your way around programming in some kind of modern language, such as C, C++, C#, ActionScript 2, ActionScript 3, Java, or JavaScript. However, if you're new to this space, we will introduce Canvas in a way that should familiarize you with web programming at the same time.

Web developers with a foundation in HTML and JavaScript should easily be able to pick up this book and run with it.

If you are a Flash developer, JavaScript and ActionScript 1 are essentially the same language. While Adobe took some liberties with ActionScript 2, you should be very comfortable with JavaScript. If you only have experience with ActionScript 3, JavaScript might feel like a step backward.

If you are a Silverlight or C# developer, take a deep breath and think about a time before ASP.NET/C# when you might have had to develop web apps in VBScript. You are about to enter a similar space.

How This Book Is Organized

This book is organized into 11 chapters. The first four chapters walk you through the HTML Canvas API by example. The topics covered include text, images, and drawing. These chapters contain a few finished apps, but mainly consist of demos designed to show you the facets of the Canvas API. The following six chapters build upon the Canvas API by expanding the scope of the examples to application length. In these chapters, we discuss math and physics applications, video, audio, games, and mobile. The final chapter introduces a couple experimental areas: 3D and multiplayer.

What you won't get in this book is a simple rundown and retelling of the published W3C Canvas API. While we cover portions of the API in detail, some of it is not applicable to games. Furthermore, you can just read the documentation here:

   http://dev.w3.org/html5/2dcontext

Our goal is to feature the ways Canvas can be used to create animation, games, and entertainment applications for the Web.

Conventions Used in This Book

The following typographical conventions are used in this book:

Plain text
> Indicates menu titles, menu options, menu buttons, and keyboard accelerators (such as Alt and Ctrl).

Italic
> Indicates new terms, URLs, email addresses, filenames, file extensions, pathnames, directories, and Unix utilities.

`Constant width`
> Indicates commands, options, switches, variables, attributes, keys, functions, types, classes, namespaces, methods, modules, properties, parameters, values, objects, events, event handlers, XML tags, HTML tags, macros, the contents of files, or the output from commands.

`Constant width bold`
> Shows commands or other text that should be typed literally by the user.

`Constant width italic`
> Shows text that should be replaced with user-supplied values.

 This icon signifies a tip, suggestion, or general note.

 This icon indicates a warning or caution.

Using Code Examples

This book is here to help you get your job done. In general, you may use the code in this book in your programs and documentation. You do not need to contact us for permission unless you're reproducing a significant portion of the code. For example, writing a program that uses several chunks of code from this book does not require permission. Selling or distributing a CD-ROM of examples from O'Reilly books does require permission. Answering a question by citing this book and quoting example code does not require permission. Incorporating a significant amount of example code from this book into your product's documentation does require permission.

We appreciate, but do not require, attribution. An attribution usually includes the title, author, publisher, and ISBN. For example: "*HTML5 Canvas* by Steve Fulton and Jeff Fulton (O'Reilly). Copyright 2011 8bitrocket Studios, 978-1-4493-9390-8."

If you feel your use of code examples falls outside fair use or the permission given above, feel free to contact us at *permissions@oreilly.com*.

We'd Like to Hear from You

Please address comments and questions concerning this book to the publisher:

O'Reilly Media, Inc.
1005 Gravenstein Highway North
Sebastopol, CA 95472
(800) 998-9938 (in the United States or Canada)
(707) 829-0515 (international or local)
(707) 829-0104 (fax)

We have a web page for this book, where we list errata, examples, and any additional information. You can access this page at:

http://www.oreilly.com/catalog/9781449393908

To comment or ask technical questions about this book, send email to:

bookquestions@oreilly.com

For more information about our books, courses, conferences, and news, see our website at *http://www.oreilly.com*.

Find us on Facebook: *http://facebook.com/oreilly*

Follow us on Twitter: *http://twitter.com/oreillymedia*

Watch us on YouTube: *http://www.youtube.com/oreillymedia*

Safari® Books Online

Safari Safari Books Online is an on-demand digital library that lets you easily search over 7,500 technology and creative reference books and videos to find the answers you need quickly.

With a subscription, you can read any page and watch any video from our library online. Read books on your cell phone and mobile devices. Access new titles before they are available for print, and get exclusive access to manuscripts in development and post feedback for the authors. Copy and paste code samples, organize your favorites, download chapters, bookmark key sections, create notes, print out pages, and benefit from tons of other time-saving features.

O'Reilly Media has uploaded this book to the Safari Books Online service. To have full digital access to this book and others on similar topics from O'Reilly and other publishers, sign up for free at *http://my.safaribooksonline.com*.

Acknowledgments

First, Steve would like to thank his beautiful wife, Dawn, for the amazing patience, guidance, and support she lovingly provided before, during, and after this book was written. Steve would also like to thank his girls—Rachel, Daphnie, and Katie—for all their enthusiastic support and for not getting too frustrated every time they asked him to play and Daddy said, "Sure, yeah, in just a couple minutes" because his head was buried in these pages. He'd also like to thank his mom and dad, plus his sisters, Mari and Carol for everything they taught us; and his uncle Richard and cousin John for all their love and support. Also thanks to Sue, Morgan, and Lauren Miller; Jen, Eric, Sarah, and Paige Garnica; Dietrich; Chantal Martin; and Ryan and Justin Fulton.

Jeff would like to thank his amazing wife, Jeanne, and his two wonderful boys, Ryan and Justin, for putting up with him writing this second book in two years. The writing process is a time- and energy-consuming endeavor that demands patience and understanding from those in close proximity to the temperamental author. Jeff would also like to thank his mom and dad, as well as sisters Mari and Carol, for the morale and babysitting support that was needed during the crucial writing times. Also, special thanks to the Perry and Backlar clans for all of their love and support.

The authors would also like to acknowledge all the fine people at O'Reilly, especially Mike Loukides, who took the chance on us for this book; and Simon St.Laurent, who led us out of the wilderness; our copyeditor, Marlowe Shaeffer, who made the text sparkle in her own special way; and our production editor, Kristen Borg, for finishing the job.

We'd also like to thank our technical reviewers, Raffaele Cecco, Shelley Powers, and Andres Pagella.

Thanks to everyone at Electrotank, especially Jobe Makar, Matthew Weisner, and Teresa Carrigan; as well as our friends at Jett Morgan, Creative Bottle, Producto Studios, Mattel, Mochi, Adobe, Microsoft, Zynga, The SPIL Group, Giles Thomas from Learningwebgl.com, Ari Feldman, and Terry Paton, plus Ace The Super Villain, Bas Alicante, egdcltd, Tony Fernando, SeuJogo, Hayes, Jose Garay, Richard Davey (@PhotonStorm), Squize and nGfx (@GamingYourWay), and all our other friends at 8bitrocket.com. We would also like to give a huge shout out to the simply outstanding team at 444 Deharo, especially the entire FV team and the Foo Fighters pod!

Finally, we'd like to thank all of our friends who helped along the way, including Ian Legler, Brandon Crist, Eric Barth, Wesley Crews, Kenny Brown, Mike Foti, Evan Pershing, Scott Johnson, Scott Lunceford, Kurt Legler, Ryan Legler, John Little, Matt Hyatt, Varun Tandon, Mark Hall, Jason Neifeld, Mike Peters and The Alarm.

...and, last but not least, thanks to the W3C for coming up with such a kickass spec for HTML5 Canvas.

CHAPTER 1

Introduction to HTML5 Canvas

HTML5 is the current iteration of HTML, the *HyperText Markup Language*. HTML was first standardized in 1993, and it was the fuel that ignited the World Wide Web. HTML is a way to define the contents of a web page using tags that appear within pointy brackets, < >.

HTML5 Canvas is an *immediate mode* bitmapped area of the screen that can be manipulated with JavaScript. Immediate mode refers to the way the canvas renders pixels on the screen. HTML5 Canvas completely redraws the bitmapped screen on every frame using Canvas API calls from JavaScript. As a programmer, your job is to set up the screen display before each frame is rendered so that the correct pixels will be shown.

This makes HTML5 Canvas very different from Flash, Silverlight, or SVG, which operate in *retained mode*. In this mode, a display list of objects is kept by the graphics renderer, and objects are displayed on the screen according to attributes set in code (i.e., the *x* position, *y* position, and alpha transparency of an object). This keeps the programmer away from low-level operations, but gives her less control over the final rendering of the bitmapped screen.

The basic HTML5 Canvas API includes a 2D context that allows a programmer to draw various shapes, render text, and display images directly onto a defined area of the browser window. You can apply colors; rotations; alpha transparencies; pixel manipulations; and various types of lines, curves, boxes, and fills to augment the shapes, text, and images you place onto the canvas.

In itself, the HTML5 Canvas 2D context is a display API used to render graphics on a bitmapped area, but there is very little in that context to create applications using the technology. By adding cross-browser-compatible JavaScript functionality for keyboard and mouse inputs, timer intervals, events, objects, classes, sound, math functions, etc., you can learn to take HTML5 Canvas and create stunning animations, applications, and games.

Here's where this book comes in. We are going to break down the Canvas API into digestible parts and then put it back together, demonstrating how to use it to create applications. Many of the techniques you will learn in this book have been tried and used successfully on other platforms, and now we are applying them to this exciting new technology.

Browser Support for HTML5 Canvas

With the exception of Internet Explorer 8, HTML5 Canvas is supported in some way by most modern web browsers, with specific feature support growing on an almost daily basis. The best support seems to be from Google Chrome, followed closely by Safari, Firefox, and Opera. We will utilize a JavaScript library named *modernizr.js* that will help us figure out which browsers support which Canvas features. At the same time, if you are worried about Internet Explorer, version 9 promises to have support for Canvas. In the meantime, you can check out Google Chrome Frame (*http://code .google.com/chrome/chromeframe/*), which delivers Canvas support for IE.

The Basic HTML Page

Before we get to Canvas, we need to talk a bit about the HTML5 standards we will be using to create our web pages.

HTML is the standard language used to construct pages on the World Wide Web. We will not spend much time on HTML, but it does form the basis of <canvas>, so we cannot skip it entirely.

A basic HTML page is divided into sections, commonly <head> and <body>. The new HTML5 specification adds a few new sections, such as <nav>, <article>, <header>, and <footer>.

The <head> tag usually contains information that will be used by the HTML <body> tags to create the HTML page. It is a standard convention to put JavaScript functions in the <head>, as you will see later when we discuss the <canvas> tag. There may be reasons to put some JavaScript in the <body>, but we will make every attempt to keep things simple by having all JavaScript in the <head>.

Basic HTML for a page might look like Example 1-1.

Example 1-1. A basic HTML page

```
<!doctype html>
<html lang="en">
<head>
<meta charset="UTF-8">
<title>CH1EX1: Basic Hello World HTML Page</title>
</head>
<body>
Hello World!
</body>
</html>
```

<!doctype html>

This tag informs the web browser to render the page in standards mode. According to the HTML5 spec from W3C, this is required for HTML5 documents. This tag simplifies a long history of oddities when it came to rendering HTML in different browsers. This should always be the first line of HTML in a document.

<html lang="en">

This is the <html> tag with the language referenced: for example, "en" = English. Some of the more common language values are:

Chinese – lang = "zh"
French – lang = "fr"
German – lang = "de"
Italian – lang = "it"
Japanese – lang = "ja"
Korean – lang = "ko"
Polish – lang = "pl"
Russian – lang = "ru"
Spanish (Castilian) – lang = "es"

<meta charset="UTF-8">

This tag tells the web browser which character-encoding method to use for the page. Unless you know what you're doing, there is no need to change it. This is a required element for HTML5 pages.

<title>...</title>

This is the title that will be displayed in the browser window for the HTML page. This is a very important tag, as it is one of the main pieces of information a search engine uses to catalog the content on the HTML page.

A Simple HTML5 Page

Now let's look at this page in a web browser (this would be a great time to get your tools together to start developing code). Open your chosen text editor, and get ready to use your preferred web browser: Safari, Firefox, Opera, Chrome, or IE.

1. In your text editor, type in the code from Example 1-1.
2. Save the code as *CH1EX1.html* in a directory of your choosing.

3. Under the File menu in Chrome, Safari, or Firefox, you should find the option Open File. Click that selection. You should then see a box to open a file. (On Windows using Chrome, you might need to press Ctrl+O to open a file.)

4. Locate the *CH1EX1.html* that you just created.

5. Click Open.

You should see something similar to Figure 1-1.

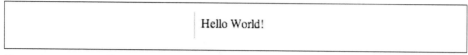

Figure 1-1. HTML Hello World!

 This is one of only two examples in this entire book that will work with Internet Explorer 8 or earlier.

Basic HTML We Will Use in This Book

Many HTML tags can be used to create an HTML page. In past versions of HTML, tags that specifically instructed the web browser on how to render the HTML page (e.g., `<font>` and `<center>`) were very popular. However, as browser standards have become more restrictive in the past decade, those types of tags have been pushed aside, and the use of CSS (Cascading Style Sheets) has been adopted as the primary way to style HTML content. Because this book is not about creating HTML pages (i.e., pages that don't have Canvas in them), we are not going to discuss the inner workings of CSS.

We will focus on only two of the most basic HTML tags: `<div>` and `<canvas>`.

`<div>`

This is the main HTML tag that we will use in this book. We will use it to position `<canvas>` on the HTML page.

Example 1-2 uses a `<div>` tag to position the words "Hello World!" on the screen, as shown in Figure 1-2.

Hello World!

Figure 1-2. HTML5 Hello World! with a <div>

Example 1-2. HTML5 Hello World!

```
<!doctype html>
<html lang="en">
<head>
<meta charset="UTF-8">
<title>CH1EX2: Hello World HTML Page With A DIV </title>
</head>
<body>
<div style="position: absolute; top: 50px; left: 50px;">
Hello World!
</div>
</body>
</html>
```

The `style="position: absolute; top: 50px; left: 50px;"` code is an example of inline CSS in an HTML page. It tells the browser to render the content at the `absolute` position of 50 pixels from the top of the page, and 50 pixels from the left of the page.

`<canvas>`

Our work with `<canvas>` will benefit from using the absolute positioning method with `<div>`. We will place our `<canvas>` inside the `<div>` tag, and it will help us retrieve information, such as the relative position of the mouse pointer when it appears over a canvas.

The Document Object Model (DOM) and Canvas

The Document Object Model represents all the objects on an HTML page. It is language- and platform-neutral, allowing the content and style of the page to be updated after it is rendered in the web browser. The DOM is accessible through JavaScript, and has been a staple of JavaScript, DHTML, and CSS development since the late 1990s.

The `canvas` element itself is accessible through the DOM in a web browser via the Canvas 2D context, but the individual graphical elements created on Canvas are not accessible to the DOM. As we stated earlier, this is because Canvas works in immediate mode and does not have its own objects, only instructions on what to draw on any single frame.

Our first example will use the DOM to locate the `<canvas>` tag on the HTML5 page so that we can manipulate it with JavaScript. There are two specific DOM objects we will need to understand when we start using `<canvas>`: `window` and `document`.

The `window` object is the top level of the DOM. We will need to test this object to make sure all the assets and code have loaded before we can start our Canvas applications.

The `document` object contains all the HTML tags that are on the HTML page. We will need to look at this object to find the instance of `<canvas>` that manipulates with JavaScript.

JavaScript and Canvas

JavaScript, the programming language we will use to create Canvas applications, can be run inside nearly any web browser in existence. If you need a refresher on the topic, read Douglas Crockford's *JavaScript: The Good Parts* (O'Reilly), which is a very popular and well-written reference on the subject.

JavaScript Frameworks and Libraries

There are many popular JavaScript frameworks that developers use to help get their JavaScript off the ground, including libraries such as jQuery, Processing.js, and others. We expect these frameworks to add robust support for Canvas in the next 6–12 months. In the meantime, we will focus on straight JavaScript to control the canvas. However, where appropriate, we will introduce you to frameworks and JavaScript libraries that will help augment Canvas development (e.g., Modernizr, JSColor, and WebGL).

Where Does JavaScript Go and Why?

Because we will create the programming logic for the Canvas in JavaScript, a question arises: where does that JavaScript go in the pages we have already created?

It's a good idea to place your JavaScript in the <head> of your HTML page because it makes it easy to find. However, placing JavaScript there means that the entire HTML page needs to load before your JavaScript can work with the HTML. This also means that the JavaScript code will start to execute before the entire page loads. As a result, you will need to test to see whether the HTML page has loaded before you run your JavaScript program.

There has been a recent move to put JavaScript right before the </body> at the end of an HTML document to make sure the whole page loads before the JavaScript runs. However, because we are going to test to see whether the page has loaded in JavaScript before we run our <canvas> program, we will put our JavaScript in the traditional <head> location. If you are not comfortable with this, you can adapt the style of the code to your liking.

No matter where you put the code, you can place it inline in the HTML page or load an *external* *.js* file. The code for loading an external JavaScript file might look like this:

```
<script type="text/javascript" src="canvasapp.js"></script>
```

To make things simple, we will code our JavaScript inline in the HTML page. However, if you know what you are doing, saving an external file and loading it will work just as well.

In HTML5 you no longer have to specify the script type.

HTML5 Canvas "Hello World!"

As we just mentioned, one of the first things we need to do when putting Canvas on an HTML5 page is test to see whether the entire page has loaded and all HTML elements are present before we start performing any operations. This will become essential when we start working with images and sounds in Canvas.

To do this, you need to work with *events* in JavaScript. Events are dispatched by objects when a defined event occurs. Other objects listen for events so they can do something based on the event. Some common events that an object in JavaScript might listen for are key presses, mouse movements, and when something has finished loading.

The first event we need to listen for is a `window` object's `load` event, which occurs when the HTML page has finished loading.

To add a *listener* for an event, use the `addEventListener()` method that belongs to objects that are part of the DOM. Because `window` represents the HTML page, it is the top level of the DOM.

The `addEventListener()` function accepts three arguments:

Event: `load`
> This is the named event for which we are adding a listener. Events for existing objects like `window` are already defined.

Event handler function: `eventWindowLoaded()`
> Call this function when the event occurs. In our code, we will then call the `canvasApp()` function, which will start our main application execution.

`useCapture:` `true` *or* `false`
> This sets the function to capture this type of event before it propagates lower in the DOM tree of objects. We will always set this to `false`.

Below is the final code we will use to test to see whether the `window` has loaded:

```
window.addEventListener("load", eventWindowLoaded, false);
function eventWindowLoaded () {
    canvasApp();
}
```

Alternatively, you can set up an event listener for the `load` event in a number of other ways:

```
window.onload = function()
    {
        canvasApp();
    }
```

or:

```
window.onload = canvasApp();
```

We will use the first method throughout this book.

Encapsulating Your JavaScript Code for Canvas

Now that we have created a way to test to see whether the HTML page has loaded, we can start creating our JavaScript application. Because JavaScript runs in an HTML page, it could be running with other JavaScript applications and code simultaneously. Usually, this does not cause any problems. However, there is a chance that your code might have variables or functions that conflict with other JavaScript code on the HTML page.

Canvas applications are a bit different from other apps that run in the web browser. Because Canvas executes its display in a defined region of the screen, its functionality is most likely self-contained, so it should not interfere with the rest of the page, and vice versa. You might also want to put multiple Canvas apps on the same page, so there must be some kind of separation of JavaScript when defining the code.

To avoid this issue, you can encapsulate your variables and functions by placing them inside another function. Functions in JavaScript are objects themselves, and objects in JavaScript can have both properties and methods. By placing a function inside another function, you are making the second function local in scope to the first function.

In our example, we are going to have the canvasApp() function that is called from the window load event contain our entire Canvas application. This "Hello World!" example will have one function named drawScreen(). As soon as canvasApp() is called, we will call drawScreen() immediately to draw our "Hello World!" text.

The drawScreen() function is now local to canvasApp(). Any variables or functions we create in canvasApp() will be local to drawScreen(), but not to the rest of the HTML page or other JavaScript applications that might be running.

Here is the sample code for how we will encapsulate functions and code for our Canvas applications:

```
function canvasApp() {
    drawScreen();

    ...

    function drawScreen() {

        ...

    }

}
```

Adding Canvas to the HTML Page

In the <body> section of the HTML page, add a <canvas> tag using code such as the following:

```
<canvas id="canvasOne" width="500" height="300">
 Your browser does not support HTML5 Canvas.
 </canvas>
```

Now, let's break this down to understand what we are doing. The <canvas> tag has three main *attributes*. In HTML, attributes are set within pointy brackets of an HTML tag. The three attributes we need to set are:

id

 The id is the name we will use to reference this <canvas> tag in our JavaScript code. canvasOne is the name we will use.

width

 The width, in pixels, of the canvas. The width will be 500 pixels.

height

 The height, in pixels, of the canvas. The height will be 300 pixels.

 HTML5 elements, including canvas, have many more attributes: tabindex, title, class, accesskey, dir, draggable, hidden, etc.

Between the opening <canvas> and closing </canvas> tags, you can put text that will be displayed if the browser executing the HTML page does not support Canvas. For our Canvas applications, we will use the text "Your browser does not support HTML5 Canvas." However, you can adjust this text to say anything.

Using document to reference the canvas element in JavaScript

We will now make use of the DOM to reference the <canvas> we defined in HTML. Recall that the document object represents every element of an HTML page after it has loaded.

We need a reference to the Canvas object so that we will know where to display the Canvas API calls we will make from JavaScript.

First, we will define a new variable named theCanvas that will hold the reference to the Canvas object.

Next, we retrieve a reference to canvasOne by calling the getElementById() function of document, and passing the name canvasOne, which we defined as the id of the <canvas> tag we created in the HTML page:

```
var theCanvas = document.getElementById("canvasOne");
```

Testing to See Whether the Browser Supports Canvas

Now that we have a reference to the canvas element on the HTML page, we need to test to see whether it contains a *context*. The Canvas context refers to the drawing surface defined by a web browser to support Canvas. Simply put, if the context does not exist, neither does the canvas. There are several ways to test this. This first test looks to see whether the getContext method exists before we call it using Canvas, as we have already defined it in the HTML page:

```
if (!theCanvas || !theCanvas.getContext) {
    return;
}
```

Actually, this tests two things. First, it tests to see whether theCanvas does not contain false (the value returned by document.getElementById() if the named id does not exist). Then, it tests whether the getContext() function exists.

The return statement breaks out and stops execution if the test fails.

Another method—popularized by Mark Pilgrim on his HTML5 website, *http://divein tohtml5.org*—uses a function with a test of a dummy canvas created for the sole purpose of seeing whether browser support exists:

```
function canvasSupport () {
    return !!document.createElement('testcanvas').getContext;
}
function canvasApp() {
    if (!canvasSupport) {
        return;
    }

}
```

Our favorite method is to use the *modernizr.js* library, which you can find here: *http://www.modernizr.com/*. Modernizr—an easy-to-use, lightweight library for testing support for various web-based technologies—creates a set of static Booleans that you can test against to see whether Canvas is supported.

To include *modernizr.js* in your HTML page, download the code from *http://www.modernizr.com/* and then include the *external .js* file in your HTML page:

```
<script src="modernizr-1.6.min.js"></script>
```

To test for Canvas, change the canvasSupport() function to look like this:

```
function canvasSupport () {
    return Modernizr.canvas;
}
```

We are going to use the *modernizr.js* method because we think it offers the best approach for testing whether Canvas is supported in web browsers.

Retrieving the 2D Context

Finally, we need to get a reference to the 2D context so we can manipulate it. HTML5 Canvas is designed to work with multiple contexts, including a proposed 3D context. However, for the purposes of this book, we only need to get the 2D context:

```
var context = theCanvas.getContext("2d");
```

The drawScreen() Function

It's time to create actual Canvas API code. Every operation we perform on Canvas will be through the `context` object, as it references the object on the HTML page.

We will delve into writing text, graphics, and images to HTML5 Canvas in later chapters, so for now, we will only spend a very short time on the code of the `drawScreen()` function.

The "screen" here is really the defined drawing area of the canvas, not the whole browser window. We refer to it as such because within the context of the games and applications you will write, it is effectively the "window" or "screen" into the canvas display that you will be manipulating.

The first thing we want to do is clear the drawing area. The following two lines of code draw a yellow box on the screen that is the same size as the canvas. `fillStyle()` sets the color, and `fillRect()` creates a rectangle and puts it on the screen:

```
context.fillStyle = "#ffffaa";
context.fillRect(0, 0, 500, 300);
```

 Notice that we are calling functions of the `context`. There are no screen objects, color objects, or anything else. This is an example of the immediate mode we described earlier.

Again, we will discuss the text functions of Canvas in the next chapter, but here is a short preview of the code we will use to put the text "Hello World!" on the screen.

First, we set the color of the text in the same way we set the color of the rectangle:

```
context.fillStyle  = "#000000";
```

Then we set the font size and weight:

```
context.font = "20px _sans";
```

Next, we set the vertical alignment of the font:

```
context.textBaseline = "top";
```

Finally, we print our test on the screen by calling the `fillText()` method of the context object. The three parameters of this method are text string, x position, and y position:

```
context.fillText  ("Hello World!", 195, 80);
```

Let's add some graphics to our "Hello World!" text. First, let's load in an image and display it. We will dive into images and image manipulation in Chapter 4, but for now, let's just get an image on the screen. To display an image on the canvas, you need to create an instance of the Image() object, and set the Image.src property to the name of the image to load.

You can also use another canvas or a video as the image to display. We will discuss these topics in Chapters 4 and 6.

Before you display it, you need to wait for the image to load. Create a `callback()` function for the Image load event by setting the onload function of the Image object. `callback()` will be executed when the onload event occurs. When the image has loaded, you then call `context.drawImage()`, passing three parameters to put it on the canvas: Image object, x position, and y position:

```
var helloWorldImage = new Image();
helloWorldImage.src = "helloworld.gif";
helloWorldImage.onload = function () {
    context.drawImage(helloWorldImage, 160, 130);
}
```

Finally, let's draw a box around the text and the image. To draw a box with no fill, use the `context.StrokeStyle()` method to set a color for the stroke (the border of the box), and then call the `context.strokeRect()` method to draw the rectangle border. The four parameters for the `strokeRect()` method are the upper left x and y coordinates, and the lower right x and y coordinates:

```
context.strokeStyle = "#000000";
context.strokeRect(5,  5, 490, 290);
```

The full code for the HTML5 Hello World! application is shown in Example 1-3, and its results are illustrated in Figure 1-3.

Example 1-3. HTML5 Canvas Hello World!

```
<!doctype html>
<html lang="en">
<head>
<meta charset="UTF-8">
<title>CH1EX3: Your First Canvas Application </title>
<script src="modernizr-1.6.min.js"></script>
<script type="text/javascript">
window.addEventListener("load", eventWindowLoaded, false);
```

```
var Debugger = function () { };
Debugger.log = function (message) {
    try {
        console.log(message);
    } catch (exception) {
        return;
    }
}

function eventWindowLoaded () {
    canvasApp();
}

function canvasSupport () {
    return Modernizr.canvas;
}

function canvasApp () {

        if (!canvasSupport()) {
          return;
        }

    var theCanvas = document.getElementById("canvasOne");
    var context = theCanvas.getContext("2d");

    Debugger.log("Drawing Canvas");

      function drawScreen() {
      //background
      context.fillStyle = "#ffffaa";
      context.fillRect(0, 0, 500, 300);

      //text
      context.fillStyle  = "#000000";
      context.font = "20px _sans";
      context.textBaseline = "top";
      context.fillText  ("Hello World!", 195, 80 );

      //image
      var helloWorldImage = new Image();
      helloWorldImage.src = "helloworld.gif";
      helloWorldImage.onload = function () {
          context.drawImage(helloWorldImage, 160, 130);
      }

      //box
      context.strokeStyle = "#000000";
      context.strokeRect(5,  5, 490, 290);

    }

    drawScreen();
```

```
    }

</script>
</head>
<body>
<div style="position: absolute; top: 50px; left: 50px;">
<canvas id="canvasOne" width="500" height="300">
 Your browser does not support HTML5 Canvas.
</canvas>
</div>
</body>
</html>
```

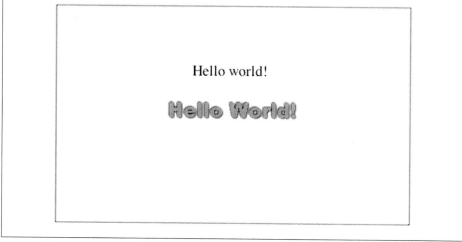

Figure 1-3. HTML5 Canvas Hello World!

Debugging with Console.log

There is one more thing to discuss before we explore bigger and better things beyond "Hello World!" In this book, we have implemented a very simple debugging methodology using the `console.log` functionality of modern web browsers. This function lets you log text messages to the JavaScript console to help find problems (or opportunities!) with your code. Any browser that has a JavaScript console (Chrome, Opera, Safari, Firefox with Firebug installed) can make use of `console.log`. However, browsers without `console.log` support throw a nasty error.

To handle this error, we use a wrapper around `console.log` that only makes the call if the function is supported. The wrapper creates a class named `Debugger`, and then creates a static function named `Debugger.log` that can be called from anywhere in your code, like this:

```
Debugger.log("Drawing Canvas");
```

Here is the code for the `console.log()` functionality:

```
var Debugger = function () { };
Debugger.log = function (message) {
    try {
        console.log(message);
    } catch (exception) {
        return;
    }
}
```

The 2D Context and the Current State

The HTML5 2D context (the `CanvasRenderingContext2D` object), retrieved by a call to the `getContext()` method of the `Canvas` object, is where all the action takes place. The `CanvasRenderingContext2D` contains all the methods and properties we need to draw onto the canvas. The `CanvasRenderingContext2D` (or context, as we will call it hereafter) uses a Cartesian coordinate system with 0,0 at the upper left and corner of the canvas, and coordinates increasing in value to the left and down.

However, all of these properties and methods are used in conjunction with *current state*, a concept that must be grasped before you can really understand how to work with HTML5 Canvas. The current state is actually a stack of drawing states that apply globally to the entire canvas. You will manipulate these states when drawing on the canvas. These states include:

Transformation matrix
    Methods for scale, rotate, transform, and translate

Clipping region
    Created with the `clip()` method

Properties of the context
    Properties include `strokeStyle`, `fillStyle`, `globalAlpha`, `lineWidth`, `lineCap`, `line Join`, `miterLimit`, `shadowOffsetX`, `shadowOffsetY`, `shadowBlur`, `shadowColor`, `global CompositeOperation`, `font`, `textAlign`, and `textBaseline`.

Don't worry; these should not look familiar to you just yet. We will discuss these properties in depth in the next three chapters.

Remember earlier in this chapter when we discussed immediate mode versus retained mode? The canvas is an immediate mode drawing surface, which means everything needs to be redrawn every time something changes. There are some advantages to this; for example, global properties make it very easy to apply effects to the entire screen. Once you get your head around it, the act of redrawing the screen every time there is an update makes the process of drawing to the canvas straightforward and simple.

On the other hand, retained mode is when a set of objects is stored by a drawing surface and manipulated with a display list. Flash and Silverlight work in this mode. Retained mode can be very useful for creating applications that rely on multiple objects with their own independent states. Many of the same applications that could make full use of the canvas (games, activities, animations) are often easier to code with a retained mode drawing surface, especially for beginners.

Our challenge is to take advantage of the immediate mode drawing surface, while adding functionality to our code to help it act more like it works in retained mode. Throughout this book we will discuss strategies that will help take this immediate mode operation and make it easier to manipulate through code.

The HTML5 Canvas Object

Recall that the Canvas object is created by placing the <canvas> tag in the <body> portion of an HTML page. You can also create an instance of a canvas in code like this:

```
var theCanvas = document.createElement("canvas");
```

The Canvas object has two associated properties and methods that can be accessed through JavaScript: width and height. These tell you the current width and height of the canvas rendered on the HTML page. It is important to note that they are *not* read-only; i.e., they can be updated in code and changed on an HTML page. What does this mean? It means you can dynamically resize the canvas on the HTML page without reloading.

You can also use CSS styles to change the scale of the canvas. Unlike resizing, scaling takes the current canvas bitmapped area and resamples it to fit into the size specified by the width and height attributes of the CSS style. For example, to scale the canvas to a 400×400 area, you might use this CSS style:

```
style="width: 400px; height:400px"
```

We include an example of scaling the Canvas with a transformation matrix in Chapter 3.

There are also two public methods for the Canvas object. The first is getContext(), which we used earlier in this chapter. We will continue to use it throughout this book to retrieve a reference to the Canvas 2D context so we can draw onto the canvas. The second property is toDataURL(). This method will return a string of data that represents the bitmapped image of the Canvas object as it is currently rendered. It's like a snapshot of the screen. By supplying different MIME types as a parameter, you can retrieve the data in different formats. The basic format is an *image/png*, but *image/jpeg* and other formats can be retrieved. We will use the toDataURL() in the next application to export an image of the canvas into another browser window.

Another Example: Guess The Letter

Now we will take a quick look at a more involved example of a "Hello World!"-type application, the game "Guess The Letter." We've included this example to illustrate how much more Canvas programming is done in JavaScript than in the Canvas API.

In this game, shown in Figure 1-4, the player's job is to guess the letter of the alphabet the computer has chosen randomly. The game keeps track of how many guesses the player has made, lists the letters he has already guessed, and tells the player whether he needs to guess higher (toward Z) or lower (toward A).

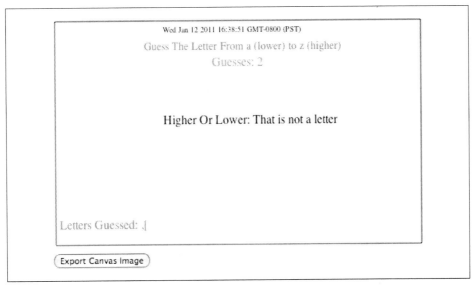

Figure 1-4. HTML5 Canvas "Guess The Letter" game

How the Game Works

This game is set up with the same basic structure as "Hello World!" canvasApp() is the main function, and all other functions are defined as local to canvasApp(). We use a drawScreen() function to render text on the canvas. However, there are some other functions included as well, which are described next.

The "Guess The Letter" Game Variables

Here is a rundown of the variables we will use in the game. They are all defined and initialized in canvasApp(), so they have scope to the encapsulated functions that we define locally.

guesses

This variable holds the number of times the player has pressed a letter. The lower the number, the better he has done in the game.

message

The content of this variable is displayed to give the user instructions on how to play.

letters

This array holds one of each letter of the alphabet. We will use this array to both randomly choose a secret letter for the game, and to figure out the relative position of the letter in the alphabet.

today

This variable holds the current date. It is displayed on the screen but has no other purpose.

letterToGuess

This variable holds the current game's secret letter that needs to be guessed.

higherOrLower

This variable holds the text "Higher" or "Lower" depending on where the last guessed letter is in relation to the secret letter. If the secret letter is closer to "a," we give the "Lower" instruction. If the letter is closer to "z," we give the "Higher" instruction.

lettersGuessed

This array holds the current set of letters the player has guessed already. We will print this list on the screen to help the player remember what letters he has already chosen.

gameOver

This variable is set to `false` until the player wins. We will use this to know when to put the "You Win" message on the screen, and to keep the player from guessing after he has won.

Here is the code:

```
var guesses = 0;
var message = "Guess The Letter From a (lower) to z (higher)";
var letters = [
        "a","b","c","d","e","f","g","h","i","j","k","l","m","n","o",
        "p","q","r","s","t","u","v","w","x","y","z"
        ];
var today = new Date();
var letterToGuess = "";
var higherOrLower = "";
var lettersGuessed;
var gameOver = false;
```

The initGame() Function

The `initGame()` function sets up the game for the player. The two most important blocks of code are as follows. This code finds a random letter from the letters array and stores it in the `letterToGuess` variable:

```
var letterIndex = Math.floor(Math.random() * letters.length);
letterToGuess = letters[letterIndex];
```

This code adds an event listener to the `window` object of the DOM to listen for the keyboard `keyup` event. When a key is pressed, the `eventKeyPressed` event handler is called to test the letter pressed:

```
window.addEventListener("keyup",eventKeyPressed,true);
```

Here is the full code for the function:

```
function initGame() {
    var letterIndex = Math.floor(Math.random() * letters.length);
    letterToGuess = letters[letterIndex];
    guesses = 0;
    lettersGuessed = [];
    gameOver = false;
    window.addEventListener("keyup",eventKeyPressed,true);
    drawScreen();
}
```

The eventKeyPressed() Function

This function, called when the player presses a key, contains most of the action in this game. Every event handler function in JavaScript is passed an **event** object that has information about the event that has taken place. We use the **e** argument to hold that object.

The first test we make is to see whether the **gameOver** variable is **false**. If so, we continue to test the key that was pressed by the player; the next two lines of code are used for that purpose. The first line of code gets the key-press value from the event, and converts it to an alphabetic letter that we can test with the letter stored in `letterToGuess`:

```
var letterPressed = String.fromCharCode(e.keyCode);
```

The next line of code converts the letter to lowercase so that we can test uppercase letters if the player unintentionally has Caps Lock on:

```
letterPressed = letterPressed.toLowerCase();
```

Next, we increase the **guesses** count to display, and use the **Array.push()** method to add the letter to the `lettersGuessed` array:

```
guesses++;
lettersGuessed.push(letterPressed);
```

Now it is time to test the current game state to give feedback to the player. First, we test to see whether `letterPressed` is equal to `letterToGuess`. If so, the player has won the game:

```
if (letterPressed == letterToGuess) {
    gameOver = true;
```

If the player has not won, we need to get the index of `letterToGuess` and the index of `letterPressed` in the `letters` array. We are going to use these values to figure out whether we should display "Higher," "Lower," or "That is not a letter." To do this, we use the `indexOf()` array method to get the relative index of each letter. Because we alphabetized the letters in the array, it is very easy to test which message to display:

```
} else {
    letterIndex = letters.indexOf(letterToGuess);
    guessIndex = letters.indexOf(letterPressed);
```

Now we make the test. First, if `guessIndex` is less than zero, it means that the call to `indexOf()` returned `-1`, and the key press was not a letter. We then display an error message:

```
if (guessIndex < 0) {
    higherOrLower = "That is not a letter";
```

The rest of the tests are simple. If `guessIndex` is greater than `letterIndex`, we set the `higherOrLower` text to "Lower." Conversely, if `guessIndex` is less than `letterIndex`, we set the `higherOrLower` test to "Higher":

```
} else if (guessIndex > letterIndex) {
    higherOrLower = "Lower";
} else {
    higherOrLower = "Higher";
}

}
```

Finally, we call `drawScreen()` to paint the screen:

```
drawScreen();
```

Here is the full code for the function:

```
function eventKeyPressed(e) {
    if (!gameOver) {
        var letterPressed = String.fromCharCode(e.keyCode);
        letterPressed = letterPressed.toLowerCase();
        guesses++;
        lettersGuessed.push(letterPressed);

        if (letterPressed == letterToGuess) {
            gameOver = true;
        } else {

            letterIndex = letters.indexOf(letterToGuess);
            guessIndex = letters.indexOf(letterPressed);
            Debugger.log(guessIndex);
```

```
        if (guessIndex < 0) {
            higherOrLower = "That is not a letter";
        } else if (guessIndex > letterIndex) {
            higherOrLower = "Lower";
        } else {
            higherOrLower = "Higher";
        }

    }
    drawScreen();
    }
}
```

The drawScreen() Function

Now we get to drawScreen(). The good news is that we have seen almost all of this before—there are only a few differences from "Hello World!" For example, we paint multiple variables on the screen using the Canvas Text API. We only set context.text Baseline = 'top'; once for all the text we are going to display. Also, we change the color using context.fillStyle, and the font with context.font.

The most interesting thing we display here is the content of the lettersGuessed array. On the canvas, the array is printed as a set of comma-separated values, like this:

```
Letters Guessed: p,h,a,d
```

To print this value, all we do is use the toString() method of the lettersGuessed array, which prints out the values of an array as—you guessed it—comma-separated values:

```
context.fillText  ("Letters Guessed: " + lettersGuessed.toString(), 10, 260);
```

We also test the gameOver variable. If it is true, we put *You Got It!* on the screen in giant 40px text so the user knows he has won.

Here is the full code for the function:

```
function drawScreen() {
    //Background
    context.fillStyle = "#ffffaa";
    context.fillRect(0, 0, 500, 300);
    //Box
    context.strokeStyle = "#000000";
    context.strokeRect(5,  5, 490, 290);

    context.textBaseline = "top";
    //Date
    context.fillStyle = "#000000";
    context.font = "10px _sans";
    context.fillText  (today, 150 ,10);
    //Message
    context.fillStyle = "#FF0000";
    context.font = "14px _sans";
    context.fillText  (message, 125, 30);
```

```
  //Guesses
  context.fillStyle = "#109910";
  context.font = "16px _sans";
  context.fillText ('Guesses: ' + guesses, 215, 50);
  //Higher Or Lower
  context.fillStyle = "#000000";
  context.font = "16px _sans";
  context.fillText ("Higher Or Lower: " + higherOrLower, 150,125);
  //Letters Guessed
  context.fillStyle = "#FF0000";
  context.font = "16px _sans";
  context.fillText ("Letters Guessed: " + lettersGuessed.toString(), 10, 260);
  if (gameOver) {
     context.fillStyle = "#FF0000";
     context.font = "40px _sans";
     context.fillText ("You Got It!", 150, 180);
  }
}
```

Exporting Canvas to an Image

Earlier, we briefly discussed the toDataUrL() property of the Canvas object. We are going to use that property to let the user create an image of the game screen at any time. This acts almost like a screen-capture utility for games made on Canvas.

We need to create a button in the HTML page that the user can press to get the screen capture. We will add this button to <form> and give it the id createImageData:

```
<form>
<input type="button" id="createImageData" value="Export Canvas Image">
</form>
```

In the init() function, we retrieve a reference to that form element by using the getElementById() method of the document object. We then set an event handler for the button "click" event as the function createImageDataPressed():

```
var formElement = document.getElementById("createImageData");
formElement.addEventListener('click', createImageDataPressed, false);
```

In canvasApp(), we define the createImageDataPressed() function as an event handler. This function calls window.open(), passing the return value of the Canvas.toDataUrl() method as the source for the window. Since this data forms a valid *PNG*, the image is displayed in the new window:

```
function createImageDataPressed(e) {

    window.open(theCanvas.toDataURL(),"canvasImage","left=0,top=0,width=" +
    theCanvas.width + ",height=" + theCanvas.height +",toolbar=0,resizable=0");
    }
```

We will discuss this process in depth in Chapter 3.

The Final Game Code

Example 1-4 shows the full code for the Guess The Letter game.

Example 1-4. Guess The Letter game

```
<!doctype html>
<html lang="en">
<head>
<meta charset="UTF-8">
<title>CH1EX4: Guesss The Letter Game</title>
<script src="modernizr-1.6.min.js"></script>
<script type="text/javascript">

window.addEventListener('load', eventWindowLoaded, false);

var Debugger = function () { };
Debugger.log = function (message) {
    try {
        console.log(message);
    } catch (exception) {
        return;
    }
}

function eventWindowLoaded() {

    canvasApp();
}

function canvasSupport () {
    return Modernizr.canvas;
}

function eventWindowLoaded() {

    canvasApp();
}

function canvasApp() {
    var guesses = 0;
    var message = "Guess The Letter From a (lower) to z (higher)";
    var letters = [
            "a","b","c","d","e","f","g","h","i","j","k","l","m","n","o",
            "p","q","r","s","t","u","v","w","x","y","z"
            ];
    var today = new Date();
    var letterToGuess = "";
    var higherOrLower = "";
```

```
var lettersGuessed;
var gameOver = false;

if (!canvasSupport()) {
      return;
    }

var theCanvas = document.getElementById("canvasOne");
var context = theCanvas.getContext("2d");

initGame();

function initGame() {
   var letterIndex = Math.floor(Math.random() * letters.length);
   letterToGuess = letters[letterIndex];
   guesses = 0;
   lettersGuessed = [];
   gameOver = false;
   window.addEventListener("keyup",eventKeyPressed,true);
   var formElement = document.getElementById("createImageData");
   formElement.addEventListener('click', createImageDataPressed, false);
   drawScreen();
}

function eventKeyPressed(e) {
   if (!gameOver) {
      var letterPressed = String.fromCharCode(e.keyCode);
      letterPressed = letterPressed.toLowerCase();
      guesses++;
      lettersGuessed.push(letterPressed);

      if (letterPressed == letterToGuess) {
         gameOver = true;
      } else {

         letterIndex = letters.indexOf(letterToGuess);
         guessIndex = letters.indexOf(letterPressed);
         Debugger.log(guessIndex);
         if (guessIndex < 0) {
            higherOrLower = "That is not a letter";
         } else if (guessIndex > letterIndex) {
            higherOrLower = "Lower";
         } else {
            higherOrLower = "Higher";
         }

      }
      drawScreen();
    }
}

function drawScreen() {
   //Background
   context.fillStyle = "#ffffaa";
   context.fillRect(0, 0, 500, 300);
```

```
            //Box
            context.strokeStyle = "#000000";
            context.strokeRect(5,   5, 490, 290);
            context.textBaseline = "top";
            //Date
            context.fillStyle = "#000000";
            context.font = "10px _sans";
            context.fillText  (today, 150 ,10);
            //Message
            context.fillStyle = "#FF0000";
            context.font = "14px _sans";
            context.fillText  (message, 125, 30);
            //Guesses
            context.fillStyle = "#109910";
            context.font = "16px _sans";
            context.fillText  ('Guesses: ' + guesses, 215, 50);
            //Higher Or Lower
            context.fillStyle = "#000000";
            context.font = "16px _sans";
            context.fillText  ("Higher Or Lower: " + higherOrLower, 150,125);
            //Letters Guessed
            context.fillStyle = "#FF0000";
            context.font = "16px _sans";
            context.fillText  ("Letters Guessed: " + lettersGuessed.toString(), 10, 260);
            if (gameOver) {
                context.fillStyle = "#FF0000";
                context.font = "40px _sans";
                context.fillText  ("You Got It!", 150, 180);
            }
        }

    function createImageDataPressed(e) {

        window.open(theCanvas.toDataURL(),"canvasImage","left=0,top=0,width=" +
        theCanvas.width + ",height=" + theCanvas.height +",toolbar=0,resizable=0");
    }

}

</script>
</head>
<body>
<div style="position: absolute; top: 50px; left: 50px;">
<canvas id="canvasOne" width="500" height="300">
 Your browser does not support HTML5 Canvas.
</canvas>
<form>
<input type="button" id="createImageData" value="Export Canvas Image">
</form>
</div>
</body>
</html>
```

What's Next

So now you should have a basic understanding of the HTML and JavaScript we will use to render and control HTML5 Canvas on an HTML page. In the next chapter, we will take this information and expand on it to create an interactive application that uses the canvas to render information on the screen.

CHAPTER 2

Drawing on the Canvas

Using HTML5 Canvas effectively requires a strong foundation in drawing, coloring, and transforming basic two-dimensional shapes. While the selection of built-in shapes is relatively limited, we can draw any shape we desire using a series of line segments called *paths*, which we will discuss in the upcoming section "Using Paths to Create Lines" on page 30.

 The HTML5 Canvas API is well covered in many online forms. The W3C site has an exhaustive and constantly updated reference that details the features of the Canvas 2D Drawing API. It can be viewed at *http://dev.w3.org/html5/canvas-api/canvas-2d-api.html*.

However, this online reference lacks concrete examples on using the API. Rather than simply reprinting this entire specification, we will spend our time creating examples to explain and explore as many features as we have space to cover.

The Basic File Setup for This Chapter

As we proceed through the Drawing API, all the examples in this chapter will use the same basic file setup, shown below. Use this code as the basis for all of the examples we create. You will only have to change the contents of the `drawScreen()` function:

```
<!doctype html>
<html lang="en">
<head>
<meta charset="UTF-8">
<title>Ch2BaseFile - Template For Chapter 2 Examples</title>
<script src="modernizr-1.6.min.js"></script>
<script type="text/javascript">
window.addEventListener('load', eventWindowLoaded, false);
function eventWindowLoaded() {

    canvasApp();
```

```
    }

    function canvasSupport () {
        return Modernizr.canvas;
    }

    function canvasApp(){

    if (!canvasSupport()) {
            return;
        }else{
          var theCanvas = document.getElementById("canvas");
          var context = theCanvas.getContext("2d");
        }

        drawScreen();

        function drawScreen() {
            //make changes here.
            context.fillStyle = '#aaaaaa';
            context.fillRect(0, 0, 200, 200);
            context.fillStyle  = '#000000';
            context.font = '20px _sans';
            context.textBaseline = 'top';
            context.fillText  ("Canvas!", 0, 0);

        }
    }

</script>
</head>
<body>
<div style="position: absolute; top: 50px; left: 50px;">
<canvas id="canvas" width="500" height="500">
 Your browser does not support HTML5 Canvas.
</canvas>
</div>
</body>
</html>
```

The Basic Rectangle Shape

Let's get our feet wet by looking at the single primitive, built-in geometric shape on Canvas—the rectangle. On Canvas, basic rectangle shapes can be drawn in three different ways: filling, stroking, or clearing. We can also build rectangles (or any other shape) by using paths, which we will cover in the next section.

First, let's look at the API functions used for these three operations:

fillRect(x,y,width,height)
> Draws a filled rectangle at position x,y for width and height.

strokeRect(x,y,width,height)

    Draws a rectangular outline at position x,y for width and height. This makes use of the current `strokeStyle`, `lineWidth`, `lineJoin`, and `miterLimit` settings.

clearRect(x,y,width,height)

    Clears the specified area and makes it fully transparent (using transparent black as the color) starting at position x,y for width and height.

Before we can use any of these functions, we will need to set up the fill or stroke style that will be used when drawing to the canvas.

The very basic way to set these styles is to use a color value represented by a 24-bit hex string. Here is an example from our first demonstration:

```
context.fillStyle = '#000000';
context.strokeStyle = '#ff00ff';
```

In Example 2-1, the fill style is simply set to be the RGB color black, while the stroke style is a classic purple color. The results are shown in Figure 2-1:

Example 2-1. Basic rectangles

```
function drawScreen() {
    context.fillStyle   = '#000000';
    context.strokeStyle = '#ff00ff';
    context.lineWidth   = 2;
    context.fillRect(10,10,40,40);
    context.strokeRect(0, 0,60,60);
    context.clearRect(20,20,20,20);

}
```

Figure 2-1. Basic rectangles

The Canvas State

When we draw on the Canvas context, we can make use of a stack of so-called drawing *states*. Each of these states stores data about the Canvas context at any one time. Here is a list of the data stored in the stack for each state:

- Transformation matrix information such as rotations or translations using the `context.rotate()` and `context.setTransform()` methods
- The current clipping region

- The current values for canvas attributes, such as (but not limited to):
  —globalAlpha
  —globalCompositeOperation
  —strokeStyle
  —textAlign, textBaseline
  —lineCap, lineJoin, lineWidth, miterLimit
  —fillStyle
  —font
  —shadowBlur, shadowColor, shadowOffsetX, and shadowOffsetY

We will cover these states later in this chapter.

What's Not Part of the State?

The current path (which we will explore later in this chapter) and current bitmap (see Chapter 4) being manipulated on the Canvas context are *not* part of the saved state. This very important feature will allow us to draw and animate individual objects on the canvas. The section "Simple Canvas Transformations" on page 41 utilizes the Canvas state to apply transformations to only the current shape being constructed and drawn, leaving the rest of the canvas not transformed.

How Do We Save and Restore the Canvas State?

To save (push) the current state to the stack, call:

```
context.save()
```

To restore the canvas by "popping" the last state saved to the stack, use:

```
context.restore()
```

Using Paths to Create Lines

Paths are a method we can use to draw any shape on the canvas. A path is simply a list of points, and lines to be drawn between those points. A Canvas context can only have a single "current" path, which is not stored as part of the current drawing state when the context.save() method is called.

Context for paths is a critical concept to understand, because it will enable you to transform only the current path on the canvas.

Starting and Ending a Path

The beginPath() function call starts a path, and the closePath() function call ends the path. When you connect two points inside a path, it is referred to as a *subpath*. A subpath is considered "closed" if the final point connects to the first point.

 The current transformation matrix will affect everything drawn in this path. As we will see when we explore the upcoming section on transformations, we will always want to set the transformation matrix to the identity (or reset) if we do not want any transformation applied to a path.

The Actual Drawing

The most basic path is controlled by a series of moveTo() and lineTo() commands, as shown in Example 2-2.

Example 2-2. A simple line path

```
function drawScreen() {
    context.strokeStyle = "black"; //need list of available colors
    context.lineWidth  = 10;
    context.lineCap  = 'square';
    context.beginPath();
    context.moveTo(20, 0);
    context.lineTo(100, 0);
    context.stroke();
    context.closePath();

}
```

Figure 2-2 shows an example of this output.

Figure 2-2. A simple line path

Example 2-2 simply draws a 10-pixel-wide horizontal line (or stroke) from position 20,0 to position 100,0.

We have also added the lineCap and strokeStyle attributes. Let's take a brief look at the various attributes we can apply to a line before we move on to some more advanced drawing.

lineCap attributes

context.lineCap. The `lineCap` is the end of a line drawn on the context. It can be one of three values:

`butt`
> The default; a flat edge that is perpendicular to the edge of the line.

`round`
> A semicircle that will have a diameter that is the length of the line.

`square`
> A rectangle with the length of the line width and the width of half the line width placed flat perpendicular to the edge of the line.

lineJoin attributes

context.lineJoin. The `lineJoin` is the "corner" that is created when two lines meet. This is called a *join*. A filled triangle is created at the join, and we can set its basic properties with the `lineJoin` Canvas attribute.

`miter`
> The default; an edge is drawn at the join. The `miterLimit` is the maximum allowed ratio of miter length to line width (the default is 10).

`bevel`
> A diagonal edge is drawn at the join.

`round`
> A round edge is drawn at the join.

lineWidth

The `lineWidth` (default = 1.0) depicts the thickness of the line.

strokeStyle

The `strokeStyle` defines the color or style that will be used for lines and around shapes (as we saw with the simple rectangles in Example 2-2).

Examples of More Advanced Line Drawing

Example 2-3 shows these attributes in action; the results are depicted in Figure 2-3. There are a few oddities when drawing lines on the canvas, which we will point out along the way.

Example 2-3. Line cap and join

```
function drawScreen() {

    // Sample 1: round end, bevel join, at top left of canvas
    context.strokeStyle  = "black"; //need list of available colors
    context.lineWidth  = 10;
    context.lineJoin  = 'bevel';
    context.lineCap  = 'round';
    context.beginPath();
    context.moveTo(0, 0);
    context.lineTo(25, 0);
    context.lineTo(25,25);
    context.stroke();
    context.closePath();

    // Sample 2: round end, bevel join, not at top or left of canvas
    context.beginPath();
    context.moveTo(10, 50);
    context.lineTo(35, 50);
    context.lineTo(35,75);
    context.stroke();
    context.closePath();

    // Sample 3: flat end, round join, not at top or left of canvas
    context.lineJoin  = 'round';
    context.lineCap = 'butt';
    context.beginPath();
    context.moveTo(10, 100);
    context.lineTo(35, 100);
    context.lineTo(35,125);
    context.stroke();
    context.closePath();

}
```

Figure 2-3. Line cap and join

These three line and join samples should help illustrate some of the combinations of attributes we can use to draw paths on the canvas.

The first sample attempts to draw starting at the top left of the canvas, resulting in a strange image. Canvas paths are drawn outward in both the *x* and *y* directions from the center of the pixel it begins on. For this reason, the top line in Sample 1 seems to be thinner than the 10 pixels we specified. In addition, the "round" end of the top-left horizontal line segment cannot be seen because both of these were drawn off the screen in the "negative" value areas of the screen coordinates. Furthermore, the diagonal "bevel" at the lineJoin is not drawn.

Sample 2 rectifies the problems in Sample 1 by offsetting the beginning of the drawing away from the top left. This allows the entire horizontal line to be drawn, as well as the "round" lineCap and the "bevel" lineJoin.

Sample 3 shows us eliminating the extra lineCap in favor of the default "butt," and changing the lineJoin to "round."

Advanced Path Methods

Let's take a deeper look at some of the other methods we can use to draw paths on the canvas, including arcs and curves that can be combined to create complex images.

Arcs

There are four functions we can use to draw arcs and curves onto the canvas. An arc can be a complete circle or any part of a circle

context.arc()

```
context.arc(x, y, radius, startAngle, endAngle, anticlockwise)
```

The x and y values define the center of our circle, and the radius will be the radius of the circle upon which our arc will be drawn. startAngle and endAngle are in radians, not degrees. anticlockwise is a true or false value that defines the direction of the arc.

For example, if we want to draw a circle with a center point at position 100,100 and with a radius of 20, as shown in Figure 2-4, we could use the code below for the contents of drawScreen():

```
context.arc(100, 100, 20, (Math.PI/180)*0, (Math.PI/180)*360, false);
```

Example 2-4 illustrates the code necessary to create a simple circle.

Example 2-4. A circle arc

```
function drawScreen() {

        context.beginPath();
        context.strokeStyle = "black";
        context.lineWidth = 5;
        context.arc(100, 100, 20, (Math.PI/180)*0, (Math.PI/180)*360, false);

        //full circle
        context.stroke();
        context.closePath();

}
```

Figure 2-4. A basic circle arc

Notice that we have to convert our start angle (0) and our end angle (360) into radians by multiplying them by (Math.PI/180). By using 0 as the start angle and 360 as the end, we create a full circle.

We can also draw a segment of a circle by not specifying the entire 0 to 360 start and stop angles. This code for drawScreen() will create one-quarter of a circle drawn clockwise, as shown in Figure 2-5:

```
context.arc(100, 200, 20, (Math.PI/180)*0, (Math.PI/180)*90, false);
```

Figure 2-5. A one-quarter circle arc

If we want to draw everything *but* the 0–90 angle, as shown in Figure 2-6, we can employ the anticlockwise argument and set it to true:

```
context.arc(100, 200, 20, (Math.PI/180)*0, (Math.PI/180)*90, true);
```

Figure 2-6. A three-fourths circle arc

context.arcTo()

```
context.arcTo(x1, y1, x2, y2, radius)
```

The arcTo method has only been implemented in the latest browsers—perhaps because its capabilities can be replicated by the arc() function. It takes in a point (x1,y1) and draws a straight line from the current path position to this new position. Then it draws an arc from that point to the y1,y2 point using the given radius.

The context.arcTo method will work only if the current path has at least one subpath. So, let's start with a line from position 0,0 to position 100,200. Then we will build our small arc. It will look a little like a bent wire coat hanger (for lack of a better description), as shown in Figure 2-7:

```
context.moveTo(0,0);
context.lineTo(100, 200);
context.arcTo(350,350,100,100,20);
```

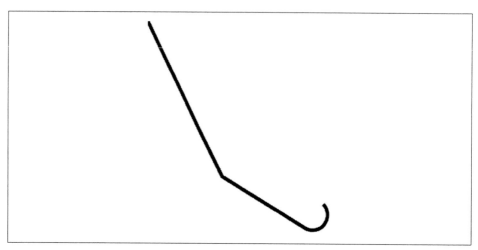

Figure 2-7. An arcTo() example

Bezier Curves

Bezier curves, which are far more flexible than arcs, come in both the cubic and quadratic types:

- context.bezierCurveTo(*cp1x, cp1y, cp2x, cp2y, x, y*)
- context.quadraticCurveTo(*cpx, cpy, x, y*)

The Bezier curve is defined in 2D space by a "start point," an "end point," and one or two "control" points, which determine how the curve will be constructed on the canvas. A normal cubic Bezier curve uses two points, while a quadric version uses a single point.

The quadratic version, shown in Figure 2-8, is the simplest, only needing the end point (last) and a single point in space to use as a control point (first):

```
context.moveTo(0,0);
context.quadraticCurveTo(100,25,0,50);
```

Figure 2-8. A simple quadratic Bezier curve

This curve starts at 0,0 and ends at 0,50. The point in space we use to create our arc is 100,25. This point is roughly the center of the arc vertically. The 100 value for the single control point pulls the arc out to make an elongated curve.

The cubic Bezier curve offers more options because we have two control points to work with. The result is that curves—such as the classic "S" curve shown in Figure 2-9—are easier to make:

```
context.moveTo(150,0);
context.bezierCurveTo(0,125,300,175,150,300);
```

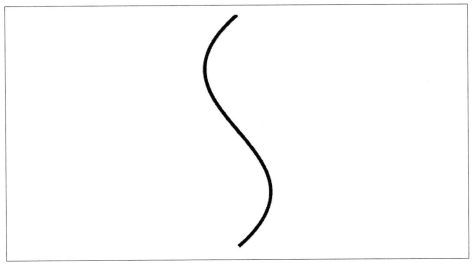

Figure 2-9. A Bezier curve with two control points

The Canvas Clipping Region

Combining the `save()` and `restore()` functions with the Canvas clip region limits the drawing area for a path and its subpaths. We do this by first setting `rect()` to a rectangle that encompasses the region we would like to draw in, and then calling the `clip()` function. This will set the clip region to be the rectangle we defined with the `rect()` method call. Now, no matter what we draw onto the current context, it will only display the portion that is in this region. Think of this as a sort of mask that you can use for your drawing operations. Example 2-5 shows how this works, producing the clipped result shown in Figure 2-10.

Example 2-5. The Canvas clipping region

```
function drawScreen() {

    //draw a big box on the screen
    context.fillStyle = "black";
    context.fillRect(10, 10, 200, 200);
    context.save();
    context.beginPath();
```

```
//clip the canvas to a 50x50 square starting at 0,0
context.rect(0, 0, 50, 50);
context.clip();

//red circle
context.beginPath();
context.strokeStyle = "red"; //need list of available colors
context.lineWidth = 5;
context.arc(100, 100, 100, (Math.PI/180)*0, (Math.PI/180)*360, false);
//full circle
context.stroke();
context.closePath();

context.restore();

//reclip to the entire canvas
context.beginPath();
context.rect(0, 0, 500, 500);
context.clip();

//draw a blue line that is not clipped
context.beginPath();
context.strokeStyle = "blue"; //need list of available colors
context.lineWidth = 5;
context.arc(100, 100, 50, (Math.PI/180)*0, (Math.PI/180)*360, false);
//full circle
context.stroke();
context.closePath();


}
```

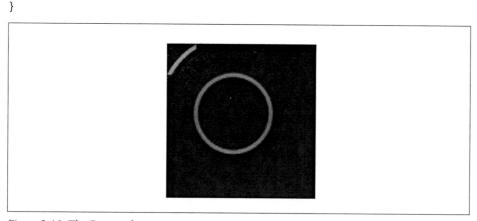

Figure 2-10. The Canvas clipping region

Example 2-5 first draws a large 200×200 black rectangle onto the canvas. Next, we set our Canvas clipping region to rect(0,0,50,50). The clip() call then clips the canvas to those specifications. When we draw our full red circle arc, we only see the portion inside this rectangle. Finally, we set the clipping region back to rect(0,0,500,500) and draw a new blue circle. This time, we can see the entire circle on the canvas.

Other Canvas methods can be used with the clipping region. The most obvious is the `arc()` function:

```
arc(float x, float y, float radius, float startAngle,
    float endAngle, boolean anticlockwise)
```

This can be used to create a circular clipping region instead of a rectangular one.

Compositing on the Canvas

Compositing refers to how finely we can control the transparency and layering effects of objects as we draw them to the canvas. There are two attributes we can use to control Canvas compositing operations: `globalAlpha` and `globalCompositeOperation`.

globalAlpha
> The `globalAlpha` Canvas property defaults to `1.0` (completely opaque) and can be set from `0.0` (completely transparent) through `1.0`. This Canvas property must be set before a shape is drawn to the canvas.

globalCompositeOperation
> The `globalCompositeOperation` value controls how shapes are drawn into the current Canvas bitmap after both `globalAlpha` and any transformations have been applied (see the next section, "Simple Canvas Transformations" on page 41, for more information).

In the following list, the "source" is the shape we are about to draw to the canvas, and the "destination" refers to the current bitmap displayed on the canvas.

copy
> Where they overlap, displays the source and not the destination.

destination-atop
> Destination atop the source. Where the source and destination overlap and both are opaque, displays the destination image. Displays the source image wherever the source image is opaque but the destination image is transparent. Displays transparency elsewhere.

destination-in
> Destination in the source. Displays the destination image wherever both the destination image and source image are opaque. Displays transparency elsewhere.

destination-out
> Destination out source. Displays the destination image wherever the destination image is opaque and the source image is transparent. Displays transparency elsewhere.

destination-over

> Destination over the source. Displays the destination image wherever the destination image is opaque. Displays the source image elsewhere.

lighter

> Source plus destination. Displays the sum of the source image and destination image, with color values approaching 1.0 as a limit.

source-atop

> Source atop the destination. Displays the source image wherever both images are opaque. Displays the destination image wherever the destination image is opaque but the source image is transparent. Displays transparency elsewhere.

source-in

> Source in the destination. Displays the source image wherever both the source image and destination image are opaque. Displays transparency elsewhere.

source-out

> Source out destination. Displays the source image wherever the source image is opaque and the destination image is transparent. Displays transparency elsewhere.

source-over

> (Default.) Source over destination. Displays the source image wherever the source image is opaque. Displays the destination image elsewhere.

xor

> Source xor destination. Exclusive OR of the source image and destination image.

Example 2-6 shows how some of these values can affect how shapes are drawn to the canvas, producing Figure 2-11.

Example 2-6. Canvas compositing example

```
function drawScreen() {

    //draw a big box on the screen
    context.fillStyle = "black"; //
    context.fillRect(10, 10, 200, 200);

    //leave globalCompositeOperation as is
    //now draw a red square
    context.fillStyle = "red";
    context.fillRect(1, 1, 50, 50);

    //now set it to source-over
    context.globalCompositeOperation = "source-over";
    //draw a red square next to the other one
    context.fillRect(60, 1, 50, 50);
```

```
//now set to destination-atop
context.globalCompositeOperation = "destination-atop";
context.fillRect(1, 60, 50, 50);

//now set globalAlpha
context.globalAlpha = .5;

//now set to source-atop
context.globalCompositeOperation = "source-atop";
context.fillRect(60, 60, 50, 50);

}
```

Figure 2-11. Canvas compositing example

As you can see in this example, we have toyed a little with both the `globalComposite` `Operation` and the `globalAlpha` Canvas properties. When we assign the string `source-over`, we are essentially resetting the `globalCompositeOperation` back to the default. We then create some red squares to demonstrate a few of the various compositing options and combinations. Notice that `destination-atop` switches the newly drawn shapes under the current Canvas bitmap, and that the `globalAlpha` property only affects shapes that are drawn after it is set. This means we don't have to `save()` and `restore()` the Canvas state to set the next drawn shape to a new transparency value.

In the next section, we will look at some transformations that affect the entire canvas. As a result, if we want to transform only the newly drawn shape, we will have to use the `save()` and `restore()` functions.

Simple Canvas Transformations

Transformations on the canvas refer to the mathematical adjustment of physical properties of drawn shapes. The two most commonly used shape transformations are scale and rotate, which we will focus on in this section.

Under the hood, a mathematical matrix operation applies to all transformations. Luckily, you do not need to understand this to use simple Canvas transformations. We will discuss how to apply rotation, translation, and scale transformations by changing simple Canvas properties.

Rotation and Translation Transformations

An object on the canvas is said to be at the 0 angle rotation when it is facing to the left (this is important if an object has a facing; otherwise, we will use this as a guide). Consequently, if we draw an equilateral box (all four sides are the same length), it doesn't have an initial facing other than one of the flat sides facing to the left. Let's draw that box for reference:

```
//now draw a red square
context.fillStyle = "red";
context.fillRect(100,100,50,50);
```

Now, if we want to rotate the entire canvas 45 degrees, we need to do a couple simple steps. First, we always set the current Canvas transformation to the "identity" (or "reset") matrix:

```
context.setTransform(1,0,0,1,0,0);
```

Because Canvas uses radians, not degrees, to specify its transformations, we need to convert our 45-degree angle into radians:

```
var angleInRadians = 45 * Math.PI / 180;
context.rotate(angleInRadians);
```

Lesson 1: Transformations are applied to shapes and paths drawn after the setTransform() or other transformation function is called

If you use this code verbatim, you will see a funny result...*nothing*! This is because the setTransform() function call only affects shapes drawn to the canvas *after* it is applied. We drew our square first, then set the transformation properties. This resulted in no change (or transform) to the drawn square. Example 2-7 gives the code in the correct order to produce the expected result, as illustrated in Figure 2-12.

Example 2-7. Simple rotation transformation

```
function drawScreen() {

    //now draw a red square
    context.setTransform(1,0,0,1,0,0);
    var angleInRadians = 45 * Math.PI / 180;
    context.rotate(angleInRadians);
    context.fillStyle = "red";
    context.fillRect(100,100,50,50);

}
```

Figure 2-12. Simple rotation transformation

We get a result this time, but it will probably differ from what you expect. The red box is rotated, but it looks like the canvas was rotated with it. The entire canvas did not rotate, only the portion drawn after the context.rotate() function was called. So, why did our square both rotate and move off to the left of the screen? The origin of the rotation was set at the "nontranslated" 0,0 position, resulting in the square rotating from the top left of the entire canvas.

Example 2-8 offers a slightly different scenario: draw a black box first, then set the rotation transform, and finally draw the red box again. See the results in Figure 2-13.

Example 2-8. Rotation and the Canvas state

```
function drawScreen() {

        //draw black square
        context.fillStyle = "black";
        context.fillRect(20,20,25,25);

        //now draw a red square
        context.setTransform(1,0,0,1,0,0);
        var angleInRadians = 45 * Math.PI / 180;
        context.rotate(angleInRadians);
        context.fillStyle = "red";
        context.fillRect(100,100,50,50);

    }
```

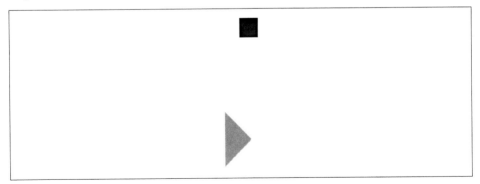

Figure 2-13. Rotation and the Canvas state

The small black square was unaffected by the rotation, so you can see that only the shapes drawn after the context.rotate() function was called were affected.

Again, the red box was moved far off to the left. To reiterate, this occurred because the canvas did not know what origin to use for the rotation. In the absence of an actual translated origin, the 0,0 position setting is applied, resulting in the context.rotate() function rotating "around" the 0,0 point, which brings us to our next lesson.

Lesson 2: We must "translate" the point of origin to the center of our shape to rotate it around its own center

Let's change Example 2-8 to rotate the red square 45 degrees while keeping it in its current location.

First, we take the numbers we applied to the fillRect() function call to create a few variables to hold the red square's attributes. This is not necessary, but it will make the code much easier to read and change later:

```
var x = 100;
var y = 100;
var width = 50;
var height = 50;
```

Next, using the context.translate() function call, we must change the origin of the canvas to be the center of the red square we want to rotate and draw. This function moves the origin of the canvas to the accepted x and y locations. The center of our red square will now be the desired top-left corner x location for our object (100), plus half the width of our object. Using the variables we created to hold attributes of the red square, this would look like:

```
x+0.5*width
```

Next, we must find the y location for the origin translation. This time, we use the y value of the top-left corner of our shape and the height of the shape:

```
y+.05*height
```

The translate() function call looks like this:

```
context.translate(x+.05*width, y+.05*height)
```

Now that we have translated the canvas to the correct point, we can do our rotation. The code has not changed:

```
context.rotate(angleInRadians);
```

Finally, we need to draw our shape. We cannot simply reuse the same values from Example 2-8 because the canvas origin point has moved to the center of the location where we want to draw our object. You can now consider 125,125 as the starting point for all draw operations. We get 125 for x by taking the upper-left corner of the square (100) and adding half its width (25). We do the same for the y origin position. The translate() method call accomplishes this.

We will need to draw the object starting with the correct upper-left coordinates for x and y. We do this by subtracting half the width of our object from the origin x, and half the height of our object from the origin y:

```
context.fillRect(-0.5*width,-0.5*height, width, height);
```

Why do we do this? Figure 2-14 illustrates the situation.

Consider that we want to draw our square starting at the top-left corner. If our origin point is at 125,125, the top left is actually 100,100. However, we have translated our origin so the canvas now considers 125,125 to be 0,0. To start our box drawing at the nontranslated canvas, we have to start at −25,−25 on the "translated" canvas.

This forces us to draw our box as though the origin is at 0,0, not 125,125. Therefore, when we do the actual drawing of the box, we must use these coordinates, as shown in Figure 2-15.

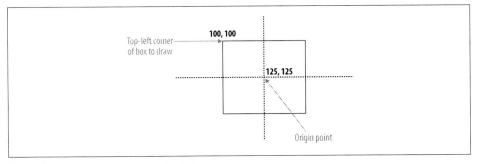

Figure 2-14. The newly translated point

Figure 2-15. Drawing with a translated point

In summary, we needed to change the point of origin to the center of our square so it would rotate around that point. But when we draw the square, we need our code to act as though the (125,125) point is actually (0,0). If we had not translated the origin, we could have used the (125,125) point as the center of our square (as in Figure 2-14). Example 2-9 demonstrates how this works, creating the result shown in Figure 2-16.

Example 2-9. Rotation around the center point

```
function drawScreen() {

        //draw black square
        context.fillStyle = "black";
        context.fillRect(20,20 ,25,25);

        //now draw a red square
        context.setTransform(1,0,0,1,0,0);
        var angleInRadians = 45 * Math.PI / 180;
        var x = 100;
        var y = 100;
        var width = 50;
        var height = 50;
        context.translate(x+.5*width, y+.5*height);
        context.rotate(angleInRadians);
        context.fillStyle = "red";
        context.fillRect(-.5*width,-.5*height , width, height);

}
```

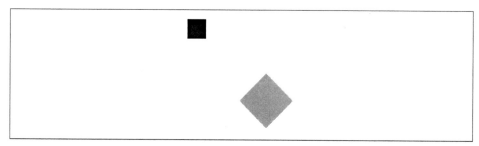

Figure 2-16. Rotation around the center point

Let's look at one final rotation example. Example 2-10 takes Example 2-9 and simply adds four separate 40×40 squares to the canvas, rotating each one slightly. The result is shown in Figure 2-17.

Example 2-10. Multiple rotated squares

```
function drawScreen() {

        //now draw a red square
        context.setTransform(1,0,0,1,0,0);
        var angleInRadians = 45 * Math.PI / 180;
        var x = 50;
        var y = 100;
        var width = 40;
        var height = 40;
        context.translate(x+.5*width, y+.5*height);
        context.rotate(angleInRadians);
        context.fillStyle = "red";
        context.fillRect(-.5*width,-.5*height , width, height);
```

```
        context.setTransform(1,0,0,1,0,0);
        var angleInRadians = 75 * Math.PI / 180;
        var x = 100;
        var y = 100;
        var width = 40;
        var height = 40;
        context.translate(x+.5*width, y+.5*height);
        context.rotate(angleInRadians);
        context.fillStyle = "red";
        context.fillRect(-.5*width,-.5*height , width, height);

        context.setTransform(1,0,0,1,0,0);
        var angleInRadians = 90 * Math.PI / 180;
        var x = 150;
        var y = 100;
        var width = 40;
        var height = 40;
        context.translate(x+.5*width, y+.5*height);
        context.rotate(angleInRadians);
        context.fillStyle = "red";
        context.fillRect(-.5*width,-.5*height , width, height);
        context.setTransform(1,0,0,1,0,0);
        var angleInRadians = 120 * Math.PI / 180;
        var x = 200;
        var y = 100;
        var width = 40;
        var height = 40;
        context.translate(x+.5*width, y+.5*height);
        context.rotate(angleInRadians);
        context.fillStyle = "red";
        context.fillRect(-.5*width,-.5*height , width, height);

}
```

Figure 2-17. Multiple rotated squares

Next, we will examine scale transformations.

Scale Transformations

The context.scale() function takes in two parameters: the first is the scale attribute for the x-axis, and the second is the scale attribute for the y-axis. The value 1 is the normal scale for an object. Therefore, if we want to double an object's size, we can set both values to 2. Using the code below in drawScreen() produces the red square shown in Figure 2-18:

```
context.setTransform(1,0,0,1,0,0);
context.scale(2,2);
context.fillStyle = "red";
context.fillRect(100,100 ,50,50);
```

Figure 2-18. A simple scaled square

If you test this code, you will find that scale works in a similar manner as rotation. We did not translate the origin of the scale point to double the size of the square; rather, we used the top-left corner of the canvas as the origin point. The result is that the red square appears to move farther down and to the left. What we would like is for the red square to remain in place and to scale from its center. We do this by translating to the center of the square before we scale, and by drawing the square around this center point (just as we did in Example 2-9). Example 2-11 produces the result shown in Figure 2-19.

Example 2-11. Scale from the center point

```
function drawScreen() {

    //now draw a red square
    context.setTransform(1,0,0,1,0,0);
    var x = 100;
    var y = 100;
    var width = 50;
    var height = 50;
    context.translate(x+.5*width, y+.5*height);
    context.scale(2,2);
    context.fillStyle = "red";
    context.fillRect(-.5*width,-.5*height , width, height);

}
```

Figure 2-19. Scale from the center point

Combining Scale and Rotation Transformations

If we want to both scale and rotate an object, Canvas transformations can easily be combined to achieve the desired results (as shown in Figure 2-20). Let's look in Example 2-12 at how we might combine them by using scale(2,2) and rotate(angleIn Radians) from our previous examples.

Example 2-12. Scale and rotation combined

```
function drawScreen() {
    context.setTransform(1,0,0,1,0,0);
    var angleInRadians = 45 * Math.PI / 180;
    var x = 100;
    var y = 100;
    var width = 50;
    var height = 50;
    context.translate(x+.5*width, y+.5*height);
    context.scale(2,2);
    context.rotate(angleInRadians);
    context.fillStyle = "red";
    context.fillRect(-.5*width,-.5*height , width, height);

}
```

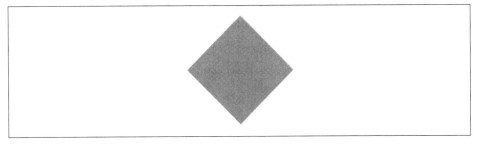

Figure 2-20. Scale and rotation combined

Example 2-13 also combines rotation and scale, this time using a rectangle. Figure 2-21 reveals what it creates.

Example 2-13. Scale and rotate a nonsquare object

```
function drawScreen() {

    //now draw a red rectangle
    context.setTransform(1,0,0,1,0,0);
    var angleInRadians = 90 * Math.PI / 180;
    var x = 100;
    var y = 100;
    var width = 100;
    var height = 50;
    context.translate(x+.5*width, y+.5*height);
    context.rotate(angleInRadians);
    context.scale(2,2);
```

```
    context.fillStyle = "red";
    context.fillRect(-.5*width,-.5*height , width, height);

}
```

Figure 2-21. Scale and rotate a nonsquare object

Finding the Center of Any Shape

The rotation and scale of a rectangle or any other shape we draw on the canvas acts much like that of a square. In fact, as long as we are sure to translate to the center of our shape before we scale, rotate, or scale and rotate, we will see the results we expect from our simple transformations. Keep in mind that the "center" of any shape will be the x value that is half its width, and the y value that is half its height. We need to use the *bounding box theory* when we attempt to find this center point.

Figure 2-22 demonstrates this theory. Even though the shape is not a simple square, we have been able to find a bounding box that encompasses each point of the object. Figure 2-22 is roughly square, but the same theory holds for rectangle-shaped bounding boxes.

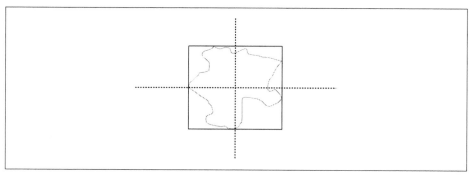

Figure 2-22. The bounding box of a complex shape

Filling Objects with Colors and Gradients

In this chapter, we have quickly looked at color and fill styles as we proceeded through the discussions of basic and complex shape construction. In this section, we will take a deeper look at coloring and filling shapes we draw on the canvas. In addition to these simple colors and fills, there are a number of different gradient styles that we can employ. Furthermore, Canvas also has a method to fill shapes with bitmap images (see Chapter 4).

Setting Basic Fill Colors

The Canvas `fillStyle` property is used to set a basic color for filling shapes on the canvas. We saw this earlier in the chapter when we used simple color names for our `fillStyle`. An example is:

```
context.fillStyle = "red";
```

Below is a list of the usable color string values from the HTML4 specification. As of this writing, the HTML5 color specification has not been set. In the absence of any additional HTML5-specific colors, the HTML4 colors will work properly in HTML5:

Black = #000000
Green = #008000
Silver = #C0C0C0
Lime = #00FF00
Gray = #808080
Olive = #808000
White = #FFFFFF
Yellow = #FFFF00
Maroon = #800000
Navy = #000080
Red = #FF0000
Blue = #0000FF
Purple = #800080
Teal = #008080
Fuchsia = #FF00FF
Aqua = #00FFFF

 All these color values will work with the `strokeStyle` as well as the `fillStyle`.

Of course, using a string for the color name is not the only available method of specifying a solid color fill. The list below includes a few other methods:

Setting the fill color with the `rgb()` *method*

The `rgb()` method lets us use the 24-bit RGB value when specifying our fill colors:

```
context.fillStyle = rgb(255,0,0);
```

This will result in the same red color as the string value above.

Setting the fill color with a hex number string

We can also set the `fillStyle` color with a hex number in a string:

```
context.fillStyle = "#ff0000";
```

Setting the fill color with the `rgba()` *method*

The `rgba()` method allows us to specify a 32-bit color value with the final 8 bits representing the alpha value of the fill color:

```
context.fillStyle = rgba(255,0,0,1);
```

The alpha value can be from 1 (opaque) to 0 (transparent).

Filling Shapes with Gradients

There are two basic options for creating gradient fills on the canvas: linear and radial. A *linear* gradient creates a horizontal, vertical, or diagonal fill pattern; the *radial* variety creates a fill that "radiates" from a central point in a circular fashion. Let's look at some examples of each.

Linear gradients

Linear gradients come in three basic styles: horizontal, vertical, and diagonal. We control where colors change in our gradient by setting *color stops* at points along the length of the object we wish to fill.

Linear horizontal gradients. Example 2-14 creates a simple horizontal gradient, as shown in Figure 2-23.

Example 2-14. A linear horizontal gradient

```
function drawScreen() {

    // horizontal gradient values must remain 0
    var gr = context.createLinearGradient(0, 0, 100, 0);

    // Add the color stops.
    gr.addColorStop(0,'rgb(255,0,0)');
    gr.addColorStop(.5,'rgb(0,255,0)');
    gr.addColorStop(1,'rgb(255,0,0)');

    // Use the gradient for the fillStyle.
    context.fillStyle = gr;
    context.fillRect(0, 0,100,100);

}
```

Figure 2-23. A linear horizontal gradient

To create the horizontal gradient, we must first create a variable (gr) to reference the new gradient. Here's how we set it:

```
var gr = context.createLinearGradient(0,0,100,0);
```

The four parameter values in the createLinearGradient method call are the top-left *x* and *y* coordinates to start the gradient, as well as the two bottom-right points to end the gradient. Our example starts at 0,0 and goes to 100,0. Notice that the *y* values are both 0 when we create a horizontal gradient; the opposite will be true when we create a vertical gradient.

Once we have defined the size of our gradient, we then add in color stops that take two parameter values. The first is a relative position origin point along the gradient to start with color, and the second is the color to use. The relative position must be a value from 0.0 to 1.0:

```
gr.addColorStop(0,'rgb(255,0,0)');
gr.addColorStop(.5,'rgb(0,255,0)');
gr.addColorStop(1,'rgb(255,0,0)');
```

Therefore, in Example 2-14, we have set a red color at 0, a green color at .5 (the center), and another red color at 1. This will fill our shape with a relatively even red to green to red gradient.

Next, we need to get the context.fillStyle to be the gradient we just created:

```
context.fillStyle = gr;
```

Finally, we create a rectangle on the canvas:

```
context.fillRect(0, 0, 100, 100);
```

Notice that we created a rectangle that was the exact size of our gradient. We can change the size of the output rectangle like this:

```
context.fillRect(0, 100, 50, 100);
context.fillRect(0, 200, 200, 100);
```

Example 2-15 adds these two new filled rectangles to Example 2-14 to create Figure 2-24. Notice that the gradient fills up the available space, with the final color filling out the area larger than the defined gradient size.

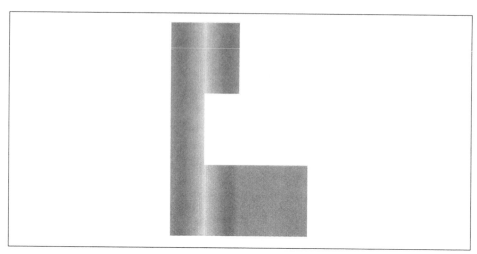

Figure 2-24. Linear horizontal gradient on multiple objects

Example 2-15. Multiple gradient-filled objects

```
function drawScreen() {

    var gr = context.createLinearGradient(0, 0, 100, 0);

    // Add the color stops.
    gr.addColorStop(0,'rgb(255,0,0)');
    gr.addColorStop(.5,'rgb(0,255,0)');
    gr.addColorStop(1,'rgb(255,0,0)');

    // Use the gradient for the fillStyle.
    context.fillStyle = gr;
    context.fillRect(0, 0, 100, 100);
    context.fillRect(0, 100, 50, 100);
    context.fillRect(0, 200, 200, 100);

    }
```

Applying a horizontal gradient to a stroke. Gradients can be applied to any shape—even the stroke around a shape. Example 2-16 takes the filled rectangles from Example 2-15 and creates a strokeRect shape instead of a filled rectangle. Figure 2-25 shows the very different result.

Example 2-16. A horizontal stroke gradient

```
function drawScreen() {

    var gr = context.createLinearGradient(0, 0, 100, 0);

    // Add the color stops.
    gr.addColorStop(0,'rgb(255,0,0)');
    gr.addColorStop(.5,'rgb(0,255,0)');
    gr.addColorStop(1,'rgb(0,0,0)');
```

```
// Use the gradient for the fillStyle.
context.strokeStyle = gr;
context.strokeRect(0, 0, 100, 100);
context.strokeRect(0, 100, 50, 100);
context.strokeRect(0, 200, 200, 100);

}
```

Figure 2-25. Horizontal stroke gradients

Applying a horizontal gradient to a complex shape. We can also apply a linear gradient to a "closed" shape made up of points, as shown in Example 2-17. A shape is considered closed when the final point is the same as the starting point.

Example 2-17. Horizontal gradient on a complex shape

```
function drawScreen() {

    var gr = context.createLinearGradient(0, 0, 100, 0);

    // Add the color stops.
    gr.addColorStop(0,'rgb(255,0,0)');
    gr.addColorStop(.5,'rgb(0,255,0)');
    gr.addColorStop(1,'rgb(255,0,0)');

    // Use the gradient for the fillStyle.
    context.fillStyle = gr;
    context.beginPath();
    context.moveTo(0,0);
    context.lineTo(50,0);
    context.lineTo(100,50);
    context.lineTo(50,100);
    context.lineTo(0,100);
```

```
context.lineTo(0,0);
context.stroke();
context.fill();
context.closePath();

}
```

In this example, we use the `context.fill()` command to fill in our shape with the current `fillStyle`, creating the output shown in Figure 2-26.

Figure 2-26. A horizontal gradient on a complex shape

Figure 2-26 shows the new shape we have created with points. As long as the points are closed, the fill will work as we expect.

Vertical gradients. Vertical gradients are created in a very similar manner as the horizontal variety. The difference is that we must specify a y value that is not 0, and the x values must both be 0. Example 2-18 shows the shape from Example 2-17 created with a vertical rather than a horizontal gradient to produce the output in Figure 2-27.

Example 2-18. Vertical gradients

```
function drawScreen() {

    var gr = context.createLinearGradient(0, 0, 0, 100);

    // Add the color stops.
    gr.addColorStop(0,'rgb(255,0,0)');
    gr.addColorStop(.5,'rgb(0,255,0)');
    gr.addColorStop(1,'rgb(255,0,0)');

    // Use the gradient for the fillStyle.
    context.fillStyle = gr;
    context.beginPath();
    context.moveTo(0,0);
    context.lineTo(50,0);
    context.lineTo(100,50);
    context.lineTo(50,100);
    context.lineTo(0,100);
    context.lineTo(0,0);
    //context.stroke();
    context.fill();
    context.closePath();

}
```

Figure 2-27. A vertical gradient example

The only difference between Example 2-18 and Example 2-17 is the line creating the linear gradient.

The horizontal version (Example 2-17):

```
var gr = context.createLinearGradient(0, 0, 100, 0);
```

The new vertical version (Example 2-18):

```
var gr = context.createLinearGradient(0, 0, 0, 100);
```

All of the same rules for strokes on horizontal gradients apply to vertical ones. Example 2-19 takes the shape from Example 2-18, stroking it with the gradient instead of filling it, producing the outline shown in Figure 2-28.

Example 2-19. A vertical gradient stroke

```
function drawScreen() {

    var gr = context.createLinearGradient(0, 0, 0, 100);

    // Add the color stops.
    gr.addColorStop(0,'rgb(255,0,0)');
    gr.addColorStop(.5,'rgb(0,255,0)');
    gr.addColorStop(1,'rgb(255,0,0)');

    // Use the gradient for the fillStyle.
    context.strokeStyle = gr;
    context.beginPath();
    context.moveTo(0,0);
    context.lineTo(50,0);
    context.lineTo(100,50);
    context.lineTo(50,100);
    context.lineTo(0,100);
    context.lineTo(0,0);
    context.stroke();
    context.closePath();

}
```

Diagonal gradients. You can easily create a diagonal gradient by varying both the second x and second y parameters of the createLinearGradient() function:

```
var gr= context.createLinearGradient(0, 0, 100, 100);
```

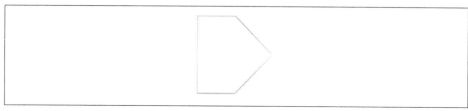

Figure 2-28. A vertical gradient stroke

To create a perfect diagonal gradient, as shown in Figure 2-29, fill a square that is the same size as the diagonal gradient. The code is provided in Example 2-20.

Example 2-20. A diagonal gradient

```
function drawScreen() {

    var gr = context.createLinearGradient(0, 0, 100, 100);

    // Add the color stops.
    gr.addColorStop(0,'rgb(255,0,0)');
    gr.addColorStop(.5,'rgb(0,255,0)');
    gr.addColorStop(1,'rgb(255,0,0)');

    // Use the gradient for the fillStyle.
    context.fillStyle = gr;
    context.beginPath();
    context.moveTo(0,0);
    context.fillRect(0,0,100,100)
    context.closePath();

}
```

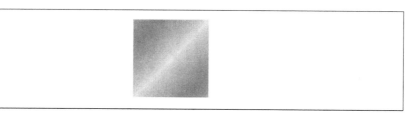

Figure 2-29. A diagonal gradient example

Radial gradients

The definition process for radial and linear gradients is very similar. Although a radial gradient takes six parameters to initialize rather than the four needed for a linear gradient, it uses the same color stop idea to create the color changes.

The six parameters are used to define the center point and the radii of two circles. The first circle is the "start" circle, and the second circle is the "end" circle. Let's look at an example:

```
    var gr = context.createRadialGradient(50,50,25,50,50,100);
```

The first circle has a center point of 50,50 and a radius of 25; the second has a center point of 50,50 and a radius of 100. This will effectively create two concentric circles.

We set color stops the same way we did with the linear gradients:

```
gr.addColorStop(0,'rgb(255,0,0)');
gr.addColorStop(.5,'rgb(0,255,0)');
gr.addColorStop(1,'rgb(255,0,0)');
```

Example 2-21 puts this together to create the result shown in Figure 2-30.

Example 2-21. A simple radial gradient

```
function drawScreen() {

    var gr = context.createRadialGradient(50,50,25,50,50,100);

    // Add the color stops.
    gr.addColorStop(0,'rgb(255,0,0)');
    gr.addColorStop(.5,'rgb(0,255,0)');
    gr.addColorStop(1,'rgb(0,0,0)');

    // Use the gradient for the fillStyle.
    context.fillStyle = gr;
    context.fillRect(0, 0, 200, 200);

}
```

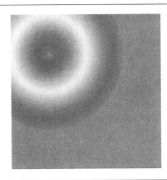

Figure 2-30. A simple radial gradient

Example 2-22 offsets the second circle from the first to create the effects shown in Figure 2-31.

Example 2-22. A complex radial gradient

```
function drawScreen() {

    var gr = context.createRadialGradient(50,50,25,100,100,100);

    // Add the color stops.
    gr.addColorStop(0,'rgb(255,0,0)');
```

```
gr.addColorStop(.5,'rgb(0,255,0)');
gr.addColorStop(1,'rgb(255,0,0)');

// Use the gradient for the fillStyle.
context.fillStyle = gr;
context.fillRect(0, 0, 200, 200);
}
```

Figure 2-31. A complex radial gradient

As with the linear gradients, we can also apply the radial gradients to complex shapes. Example 2-23 takes an arc example from earlier in this chapter, but applies a radial gradient to create Figure 2-32.

Example 2-23. A radial gradient applied to a circle

```
function drawScreen() {

    var gr = context.createRadialGradient(50,50,25,100,100,100);

    // Add the color stops.
    gr.addColorStop(0,'rgb(255,0,0)');
    gr.addColorStop(.5,'rgb(0,255,0)');
    gr.addColorStop(1,'rgb(255,0,0)');

    // Use the gradient for the fillStyle.
    context.fillStyle = gr;
    context.arc(100, 100, 100, (Math.PI/180)*0, (Math.PI/180)*360, false);
    context.fill();

}
```

Example 2-23 takes the radial gradient from Example 2-22 and applies it to a circle shape rather than a rectangle shape. This removes the red square from the background of the shape.

We can also apply our radial gradient to the stroke of our arc rather than the fill, as shown in Example 2-24 and Figure 2-33.

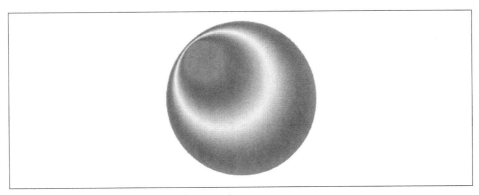

Figure 2-32. A radial gradient applied to a circle

Example 2-24. An arc stroke gradient

```
function drawScreen() {

    var gr = context.createRadialGradient(50,50,25,100,100,100);

    // Add the color stops.
    gr.addColorStop(0,'rgb(255,0,0)');
    gr.addColorStop(.5,'rgb(0,255,0)');
    gr.addColorStop(1,'rgb(255,0,0)');

    // Use the gradient for the fillStyle.
    context.strokeStyle = gr;
    context.arc(100, 100, 50, (Math.PI/180)*0, (Math.PI/180)*360, false)
    context.stroke();

}
```

Figure 2-33. An arc stroke gradient

Example 2-24 created a circle that is smaller than the version in Example 2-23, so the radial gradient would show up on the stroke of the arc. If we left it the same size as Example 2-23, we would have a solid red fill because the radial gradient is solid red at the diameter edge of the circle.

Filling Shapes with Patterns

We will cover using bitmap images on the canvas in Chapter 4, but for now, let's take a quick look at how images can be used as fill patterns for shapes we draw.

Fill patterns are initialized with the `createPattern()` function, which takes two parameters. The first is an `Image` object instance, and the second is a `String` representing how to display the `repeat` pattern inside the shape. We can use a loaded image file or an entire other canvas as a fill pattern for a drawn shape.

There are currently four types of image fills:

- `repeat`
- `repeat-x`
- `repeat-y`
- `no-repeat`

Modern browsers have implemented these four types to various degrees, but standard `repeat` seems to be the most common. Let's look at it now and then we will take a brief look at the other three.

Figure 2-34 shows a simple bitmap fill pattern that we can use to test this functionality. It is a 20×20 green circle on a transparent background, saved as a *.gif* file named *fill_20x20.gif*.

Figure 2-34. The fill_20x20.gif image for our fill

Example 2-25 tests this first with the `repeat` string to create a box full of little green circles, as shown in Figure 2-35.

Example 2-25. Filling with an image file using repeat

```
function drawScreen() {

        var fillImg = new Image();
        fillImg.src = 'fill_20x20.gif';
        fillImg.onload = function(){

           var fillPattern = context.createPattern(fillImg,'repeat');
           context.fillStyle = fillPattern;
           context.fillRect(0,0,200,200);

        }

    }
```

It is best not to use `Image` instances until they have loaded completely. We will cover this in detail in Chapter 4, but for now, we simply create an inline `onload` event handler function that will be called when `Image` is ready to be used. The `repeat` pattern string does a good job of completely filling the 200×200 square. Let's see the code for how the other repeat strings perform (in Example 2-26), and view the results in Figures 2-36 through 2-38.

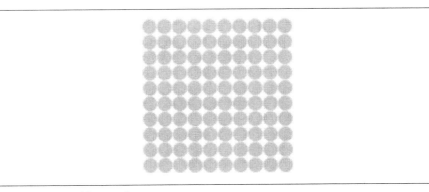

Figure 2-35. repeat fill example

Example 2-26. Using the no-repeat, repeat-x, and repeat-y strings

```
function drawScreen() {

    var fillImg = new Image();
    fillImg.src = 'fill_20x20.gif';

    fillImg.onload = function(){

        var fillPattern1 = context.createPattern(fillImg,'no-repeat');
        var fillPattern2 = context.createPattern(fillImg,'repeat-x');
        var fillPattern3 = context.createPattern(fillImg,'repeat-y');

        context.fillStyle = fillPattern1;
        context.fillRect(0,0,100,100);

        context.fillStyle = fillPattern2;
        context.fillRect(0,110,100,100);

        context.fillStyle = fillPattern3;
        context.fillRect(0,220,100,100);

    }

}
```

 Each browser will show these patterns in a different manner.

Only Firefox seems to show anything of significance when the `repeat-x` and `repeat-y` strings are used in the `repeat` parameter. We will cover more examples of filling, as well as many other uses for bitmap images, in Chapter 4.

Figure 2-36. no-repeat, repeat-x, and repeat-y in Safari

Figure 2-37. no-repeat, repeat-x, and repeat-y in Firefox

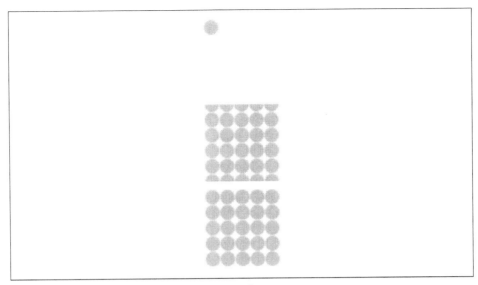

Figure 2-38. no-repeat, repeat-x, and repeat-y in Chrome

Creating Shadows on Canvas Shapes

We can add shadows to shapes we draw on the canvas using four parameters. As with the tiled fill patterns in the previous section, this feature has not been fully implemented on all HTML5-compliant browsers.

We add a shadow by setting four Canvas properties:

- shadowOffsetX
- shadowOffsetY
- shadowBlur
- shadowColor

The shadowOffsetX and shadowOffsetY values can be positive or negative. Negative values will create shadows to the left and top rather than to the bottom and right. The shadowBlur property sets the size of the blurring effect on the shadow. None of these three parameters is affected by the current Canvas transformation matrix. The shadow Color can be any color set via HTML4 color constant string—rgb() or rgba()—or with a string containing a hex value.

Example 2-27 and Figure 2-39 show a few different boxes drawn with various shadow settings.

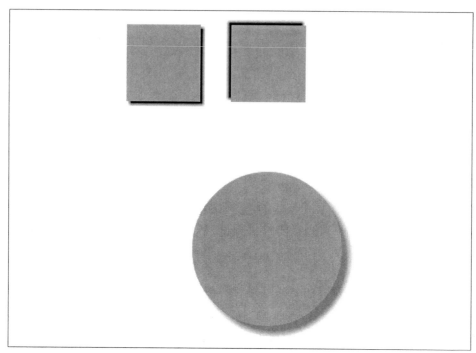

Figure 2-39. Adding shadows to drawn objects

Example 2-27. Adding shadows to drawn objects

```
function drawScreen() {

    context.fillStyle = 'red';

    context.shadowOffsetX = 4;
    context.shadowOffsetY = 4;
    context.shadowColor = 'black';
    context.shadowBlur = 4;
    context.fillRect(10,10,100,100);

    context.shadowOffsetX = -4;
    context.shadowOffsetY = -4;
    context.shadowColor = 'black';
    context.shadowBlur = 4;
    context.fillRect(150,10,100,100);

    context.shadowOffsetX = 10;
    context.shadowOffsetY = 10;
    context.shadowColor = 'rgb(100,100,100)';
    context.shadowBlur = 8;
    context.arc(200, 300, 100, (Math.PI/180)*0, (Math.PI/180)*360, false)
    context.fill();
}
```

As you can see, if we adjust the shadowOffset values along with the shadowBlur value, we create various shadows. We can also create shadows for complex shapes drawn with paths and arcs.

What's Next

We covered a lot of ground in this chapter, introducing the ways to construct primitive and complex shapes, and how we can draw and transform them on the canvas. We also discussed how to composite, rotate, scale, translate, fill, and create shadows on these shapes. But we've only just begun exploring HTML5 Canvas. In the next chapter, we will look at how to create and manipulate text objects on the canvas.

CHAPTER 3

The HTML5 Canvas Text API

The HTML5 Canvas Text API allows developers to render text on an HTML page in ways that were either tricky or next to impossible before its invention.

We are providing an in-depth analysis of the HTML5 Canvas Text API because it is one of the most basic ways to interact with the canvas. However, that does not mean it was the first Canvas API feature developed. In fact, for many browsers, it was one of the last parts implemented.

There was a time in the recent past when HTML5 Canvas Text API support in browsers was spotty at best. Back then, using *modernizr.js* to test for text support would have been a good idea. However, at this historic moment, all modern browser versions (besides IE) support the HTML5 Canvas Text API in some way.

This chapter will create an application named "Text Arranger" to demonstrate the features and interdependencies of the HTML5 Canvas Text API. This application will display a single line of text in an almost infinite number of ways. This is also a useful tool to see whether support for text is common among web browsers. Later in this chapter you will see that some text features are incompatible when drawn on the canvas at the same time.

Displaying Basic Text

Displaying text on HTML5 Canvas is simple. In fact, we covered the very basics in Chapter 1. First, we will review these basics, and then we will show you how to make them work with the Text Arranger application.

Basic Text Display

The simplest way to define text to be displayed on the canvas is to set the `context.font` style using standard values for CSS font style attributes: `font-style`, `font-weight`, `font-size`, and `font-face`.

We will discuss each of these attributes in detail in the upcoming section "Setting the Text Font" on page 78. All you need to know now is that a font designation of some type is required. Here is a simple example of setting a 50-point serif font:

```
context.font = "50px serif";
```

You also need to set the color of the text. For filled text, you would use the context.fillStyle attribute and set it using a standard CSS color, or with a Canvas Gradient or CanvasPattern object. We will discuss the latter two options later in the chapter.

Finally, you call the context.fillText() method, passing the text to be displayed and the x and y positions of the text on the canvas.

Below is an example of all three basic lines of code required to display filled text on HTML5 Canvas:

```
context.font = "50px serif"
context.fillStyle = "#FF0000";
context.fillText ("Hello World", 100, 80);
```

If you do not specify a font, the default 10px sans-serif will be used automatically.

Handling Basic Text in Text Arranger

For Text Arranger, we are going to allow the user to set the text displayed by the call to context.fillText(). To do this, we will create a variable named message where we will store the user-supplied text. We will later use that variable in our call to context.fillText(), inside the standard drawScreen() method that we introduced in Chapter 1 and will continue to use throughout this book:

```
var message = "your text";
...

function drawScreen() {
  ...
  context.fillStyle = "#FF0000";
  context.fillText (message, 100, 80);
}
```

To change the text displayed on the canvas to the text entered by the user, we need to create an event handler for the text box keyup event. This means that whenever someone changes text in the box, the event handler function will be called.

To make this work, we are going to name our text box in our HTML <form> using an <input> form element. Notice that the id is set to the value textBox. Also notice that we have set the placeholder="" attribute. This attribute is new to HTML5, so it might not work in every browser. You can also substitute it with the value="" attribute, which will not affect the execution of this application:

```
<form>
  Text: <input id="textBox" placeholder="your text"/>
  <br>
</form>
```

Communicating Between HTML Forms and the Canvas

Back in our JavaScript code, we need to create an event handler for the keyup event of textBox. We do this by finding the form element using the document.getElement ById() function of the DOM document object, and storing it in the formElement variable. Then we call the addEventListener() method of formElement, setting the event to keyup and the event handler to the function textBoxChanged, which we have yet to define:

```
var formElement = document.getElementById("textBox");
formElement.addEventListener('keyup', textBoxChanged, false);
```

The final piece of the puzzle is to define the textBoxChanged() event handler. This function works like the event handlers we created in Chapter 1. It is passed one parameter when it is called, an event object that we universally name e because it's easy to remember.

The event object contains a property named target that holds a reference to the HTML form element that created the change event. In turn, the target contains a property named value that holds the newly changed value of the form element that caused the event to occur (i.e., textBox). We retrieve this value, and store it in the message variable we created in JavaScript. It is the very same message variable we use inside the drawScreen() method to paint the canvas. Now, all we have to do is call draw Screen(), and the new value of message will appear "automagically" on the canvas:

```
function textBoxChanged(e) {
    var target = e.target;
    message = target.value;
    drawScreen();
}
```

We just spent a lot of time describing how we will handle changes in HTML form controls with event handlers in JavaScript, and then display the results on an HTML5 Canvas. We will repeat this type of code several more times while creating Text Arranger. However, we will refrain from explaining it in depth again, instead focusing on different ways to render and capture form data and use it with Canvas.

Using measureText

The HTML5 Canvas context object includes a useful method, measureText(). When supplied with a text string, it will return some properties about that text based on the current context settings (font face, size, etc.) in the form of a TextMetrics object. Right now the TextMetrics object has only a single property: width. The width property of a

TextMetrics object gives you the exact width in pixels of the text when rendered on the canvas. This can be very useful when attempting to center text.

Centering text using width

For the Text Arranger application, we will use the TextMetrics object to center the text the user has entered in the textBox form control on the canvas. First, we retrieve an instance of TextMetrics by passing the message variable (which holds the text we are going to display) to the measureText() method of the 2D context, and storing it in a variable named metrics:

```
var metrics = context.measureText(message);
```

Then, from the width property of metrics, we get the width of the text in pixels and store it in a variable named textWidth:

```
var textWidth = metrics.width;
```

Next, we calculate the center of the screen by taking the width of the canvas and dividing it in half (theCanvas.width/2). From that, we subtract half the width of the text (textWidth/2). We do this because text on the canvas is vertically aligned to the left when it is displayed without any alignment designation (more on this a bit later). So, to center the text, we need to move it half its own width to the left, and place the center of the text in the absolute center of the canvas. We will update this in the next section when we allow the user to select the text's vertical alignment:

```
var xPosition = (theCanvas.width/2) - (textWidth/2);
```

What about the height of the text?

So, what about finding the height of the text so you can break text that is longer than the width of the canvas into multiple lines, or center it on the screen? Well, this poses a problem. The TextMetrics object does not contain a height property. The text font size does not give the full picture either, as it does not take into account font glyphs that drop below the baseline of the font. While the font size will help you estimate how to center a font vertically on the screen, it does not offer much if you need to break text onto two or more lines. This is because the spacing would also need to be taken into account, which could be very tricky.

For our demonstration, instead of trying to use the font size to vertically center the text on the canvas, we will create the yPosition variable for the text by simply placing it at one-half the height of the canvas. The default baseline for a font is middle, so this works great for centering on the screen. We will talk more about baseline in the next section:

```
var yPosition = (theCanvas.height/2);
```

 In the chat example in Chapter 11, we will show you an example of breaking up text onto multiple lines.

fillText and strokeText

The context.fillText() function (as shown in Figure 3-1) will render solid colored text to the canvas. The color used is set in the context.fillColor property. The font used is set in the context.font property. The function call looks like this:

```
fillText([text],[x],[y],[maxWidth]);
```

where:

text
> The text to render on the canvas.

x
> The x position of the text on the canvas.

y
> The y position of the text on the canvas.

maxWidth
> The maximum width of the text as rendered on the canvas. At the time of this writing, support for this property was just being added to browsers.

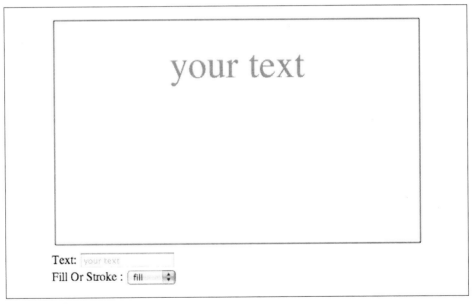

Figure 3-1. fillText in action

The context.strokeText() function (as shown in Figure 3-2) is similar, but it specifies the outline of text strokes to the canvas. The color used to render the stroke is set in the context.strokeColor property; the font used is set in the context.font property. The function call looks like:

```
strokeText([text],[x],[y],[maxWidth])
```

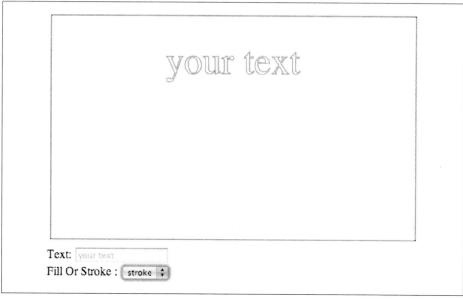

Figure 3-2. strokeText setting outline properties

where:

text
> The text to render on the canvas.

x
> The x position of the text on the canvas.

y
> The y position of the text on the canvas.

maxWidth
> The maximum width of the text as rendered on the canvas. At the time of this writing, this property does not appear to be implemented in any browsers.

The next iteration of Text Arranger adds the ability for the user to select fillText, strokeText, or both. Selecting both will give the fillText text a black border (the strokeText). In the HTML <form>, we will add a <select> box with the id fillOr Stroke, which will allow the user to make the selections:

```
Fill Or Stroke:
<select id = "fillOrStroke">
  <option value = "fill">fill</option>
  <option value = "stroke">stroke</option>
   <option value = "both">both</option>
</select>
```

In the `canvasApp()` function, we will define a variable named `fillOrStroke` that we will use to hold the value selected by the user on the HTML `<form>`. The default value will be `fill`, which means Text Arranger will always show `fillText` first:

```
var fillOrStroke = "fill";
```

We will also create the event listener for a change in the `fillOrStroke` form element...

```
formElement = document.getElementById("fillOrStroke");
formElement.addEventListener('change', fillOrStrokeChanged, false);
```

...and create the function `fillOrStrokeChanged()` to handle the event:

```
function fillOrStrokeChanged(e) {
    var target = e.target;
    fillOrStroke = target.value;
    drawScreen();
}
```

---

eval()

While we created a separate function for each event handler for the applications in this chapter, in reality many of them work in an identical way. However, some developers might be inclined to use an **eval()** function, such as the following, as their event handler for changes made to the HTML element that controls Text Arranger:

```
var formElement = document.getElementById("textBox");
    formElement.addEventListener('keyup', function(e) {
        applyChange('message', e) }, false);
formElement = document.getElementById("fillOrStroke");
formElement.addEventListener('change', function(e) {
    applyChange('fillOrStroke', e) }, false);
function applyChange (variable, e) {
    eval(variable + ' = e.target.value');
    drawScreen();
}
```

The code above uses **eval()** to create and execute JavaScript code on the fly. It dynamically creates the name of the HTML element so that the multiple event handler functions do not need to be created individually. However, many developers are wary of using **eval()** because it opens up security holes, and makes debugging code more difficult. Use at your own risk.

In the `drawScreen()` function, we test the `fillOrStroke` variable to see whether it contains the value `fill`. Since we have three states (`fill`, `stroke`, or `both`), we use a `switch` statement to handle the choices. If the choice is `both`, we set the `strokeStyle` to black (#000000) as the highlight for the colored `fillText`.

If we use the `xPosition` and `yPosition` calculated using the width and height of the canvas, the `message` variable that contains the default or user-input text, and the `fill Or Stroke` variable to determine how to render the text, we can display the text as configured by the user in `drawScreen()`:

```
      var metrics = context.measureText(message);
      var textWidth = metrics.width;
      var xPosition = (theCanvas.width/2) - (textWidth/2);
      var yPosition = (theCanvas.height/2);

   switch(fillOrStroke) {
      case "fill":
         context.fillStyle = "#FF0000";
         context.fillText (message,  xPosition,yPosition);
         break;
      case "stroke":
         context.strokeStyle = "#FF0000";
         context.strokeText (message, xPosition,yPosition);
         break;
      case "both":
         context.fillStyle = "#FF0000";
         context.fillText (message, xPosition,yPosition);
         context.strokeStyle = "#000000";
            context.strokeText (message, xPosition,yPosition);
            break;
      }
```

Example 3-1 shows the full code for Text Arranger. Test it out to see how the user
controls in HTML affect the canvas. There are not many ways to change the text here,
but you can see the difference between fillText and strokeText. In the next section,
we will update this application to configure and render the text in multiple ways.

Example 3-1. Text Arranger 1.0

```
<!doctype html>
<html lang="en">
<head>
<meta charset="UTF-8">
<title>CH3EX1: Text Arranger Version 1.0</title>
<script src="modernizr-1.6.min.js"></script>
<script type="text/javascript">

window.addEventListener("load", eventWindowLoaded, false);
function eventWindowLoaded() {

   canvasApp();
}

function canvasSupport () {
   return Modernizr.canvas;
}

function eventWindowLoaded() {

   canvasApp();
}

function canvasApp() {
```

```
var message = "your text";
var fillOrStroke ="fill";

if (!canvasSupport()) {
      return;
    }

var theCanvas = document.getElementById("canvasOne");
var context = theCanvas.getContext("2d");

var formElement = document.getElementById("textBox");
formElement.addEventListener("keyup", textBoxChanged, false);

formElement = document.getElementById("fillOrStroke");
formElement.addEventListener("change", fillOrStrokeChanged, false);

drawScreen();

function drawScreen() {

    //Background
    context.fillStyle = "#ffffaa";
    context.fillRect(0, 0, theCanvas.width, theCanvas.height);

    //Box
    context.strokeStyle = "#000000";
    context.strokeRect(5,   5, theCanvas.width-10, theCanvas.height-10);

    //Text
    context.font = "50px serif"

    var metrics = context.measureText(message);
    var textWidth = metrics.width;
    var xPosition = (theCanvas.width/2) - (textWidth/2);
    var yPosition = (theCanvas.height/2);

    switch(fillOrStroke) {
       case "fill":
          context.fillStyle = "#FF0000";
              context.fillText (message, xPosition,yPosition);
          break;
       case "stroke":
          context.strokeStyle = "#FF0000";
          context.strokeText (message, xPosition,yPosition);
          break;
       case "both":
          context.fillStyle = "#FF0000";
              context.fillText (message, xPosition ,yPosition);
          context.strokeStyle = "#000000";
          context.strokeText (message, xPosition,yPosition);
          break;
    }

}
```

```
    function textBoxChanged(e) {
        var target = e.target;
        message = target.value;
        drawScreen();
    }

    function fillOrStrokeChanged(e) {
        var target = e.target;
        fillOrStroke = target.value;
        drawScreen();
    }

}

</script>
</head>
<body>
<div style="position: absolute; top: 50px; left: 50px;">
<canvas id="canvasOne" width="500" height="300">
 Your browser does not support HTML5 Canvas.
</canvas>

<form>

  Text: <input id="textBox" placeholder="your text" />
  <br>

  Fill Or Stroke :
  <select id="fillOrStroke">
  <option value="fill">fill</option>
  <option value="stroke">stroke</option>
  <option value="both">both</option>
  </select>
  <br>

</form>

</div>
</body>
</html>
```

Setting the Text Font

Now that we have placed text on the canvas, it's time to explore some of the basics of setting the context.font property. As you will see, specifying the font for displaying basic text on Canvas is really no different from doing the same thing in HTML and CSS.

Font Size, Face Weight, and Style Basics

It is very easy to style text that will be rendered on the canvas. It requires you to set the size, weight, style, and font face in a CSS-compliant text string that is applied to the context.font property. The basic format looks like this:

```
[font style] [font weight] [font size] [font face]
```

An example might be:

```
context.font = "italic bold 24px serif";
```

or:

```
context.font = "normal lighter 50px cursive";
```

Once the `context.font` property is set, it will apply to *all* text that is rendered afterward—until the `context.font` is set to another CSS-compliant string.

Handling Font Size and Face in Text Arranger

In Text Arranger, we have implemented only a subset of the available font options for displaying text. We have chosen these to make the application work in as many browsers as possible. Here is a short rundown of the options we will implement.

Available font styles

CSS defines the valid font styles as:

```
normal | italic | oblique | inherit
```

In Text Arranger, we have implemented all but `inherit`.

Here is the markup we used to create the font style `<select>` box in HTML. We made the id of the form control equal to `fontStyle`. We will use this id when we listen for a `change` event, which is dispatched when the user updates the value of this control. We will do this for all the controls in this version of Text Arranger:

```
<select id="fontStyle">
 <option value="normal">normal</option>
 <option value="italic">italic</option>
 <option value="oblique">oblique</option>
</select>
```

Available font weights

CSS defines the valid font weights as:

```
normal | bold | bolder | lighter | 100 | 200 | 300 | 400 | 500 | 600 | 700 | 800 | 900 |
inherit | auto
```

We have used only `normal`, `bold`, `bolder`, and `lighter` in Text Arranger. You can add the other values as you see fit.

Here is the markup we used to create the font weight `<select>` box in HTML:

```
<select id="fontWeight">
 <option value="normal">normal</option>
 <option value="bold">bold</option>
 <option value="bolder">bolder</option>
```

```
<option value="lighter">lighter</option>
</select>
```

Generic font faces

Because we cannot be sure which font will be available in the browser at any time, we have limited the font face choices in Text Arranger to those that are defined as "generic" in the CSS specification: serif, sans-serif, cursive, fantasy, and monospace.

Here is the markup we used to create the font face <select> box in HTML:

```
<select id="textFont">
<option value="serif">serif</option>
<option value="sans-serif">sans-serif</option>
<option value="cursive">cursive</option>
<option value="fantasy">fantasy</option>
<option value="monospace">monospace</option>
</select>
```

Font size and HTML5 range control

To specify the size of the font, we have implemented the new HTML5 range form control. range is an <input> type that creates a slider on the HTML page to limit the numerical input to that specified in the range. A range is created by specifying range as the type of a form input control. range has four properties that can be set:

min
> The minimum value in the range

max
> The maximum value in the range

step
> The number of units to step when the range slider is moved

value
> The default value of the range

Here is the markup we used to specify the range in the Text Arranger HTML:

```
<input type="range" id="textSize"
min="0"
max="200"
step="1"
value="50"/>
```

If the browser does not support this range control, it will be rendered as a text box.

 At the time of this writing, range did not render in Firefox.

Creating the necessary variables in the canvasApp() function

In the `canvasApp()` container function, we need to create four variables—`fontSize`, `fontFace`, `fontWeight`, and `fontStyle`—that will hold the values set by the HTML form controls for Text Arranger. We create a default value for each so that the canvas can render text the first time the `drawScreen()` function is called. After that, `drawScreen()` will be called only when a change event is handled by one of the event handler functions we will create for each form control:

```
var fontSize = "50";
var fontFace = "serif";
var fontWeight = "normal";
var fontStyle = "normal";
```

Setting event handlers in canvasApp()

Just like we did in version 1.0 of Text Arranger, we need to create event listeners and the associated event handler functions so changes on the HTML page form controls can interact with HTML5 Canvas. All of the event listeners below listen for a change event on the form control:

```
formElement = document.getElementById("textSize");
formElement.addEventListener('change', textSizeChanged, false);

formElement = document.getElementById("textFont");
formElement.addEventListener('change', textFontChanged, false);

formElement = document.getElementById("fontWeight");
formElement.addEventListener('change', fontWeightChanged, false);

formElement = document.getElementById("fontStyle");
formElement.addEventListener('change', fontStyleChanged, false);
```

Defining event handler functions in canvasApp()

Below are the event handlers we need to create for each form control. Notice that each handler updates the variable associated with part of the valid CSS font string, and then calls `drawScreen()` so the new text can be painted onto the canvas:

```
function textSizeChanged(e) {
   var target = e.target;
   fontSize = target.value;
   drawScreen();
}

function textFontChanged(e) {
   var target = e.target;
   fontFace = target.value;
   drawScreen();
}

function fontWeightChanged(e) {
   var target = e.target;
```

```
        fontWeight = target.value;
        drawScreen();
    }

    function fontStyleChanged(e) {
        var target = e.target;
        fontStyle = target.value;
        drawScreen();
    }
```

Setting the font in the drawScreen() function

Finally, in the `drawScreen()` function, we put all of this together to create a valid CSS font string that we apply to the `context.font` property:

```
context.font = fontWeight + " " + fontStyle + " " + fontSize + "px " + fontFace;
```

Figures 3-3 and 3-4 show the results.

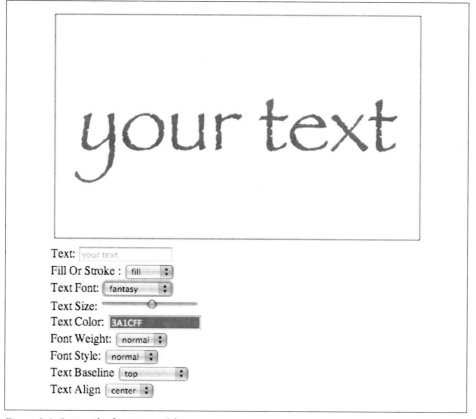

Figure 3-3. Setting the font size and face

Figure 3-4. Setting the font as bold and italic

Font Color

Setting the font color for text rendered on HTML5 Canvas is as simple as setting the `context.fillStyle` or `context.strokeStyle` property to a valid CSS RGB color. Use the format "#RRGGBB", where RR is the red component hexadecimal value, GG is the green component hexadecimal value, and BB is the blue component hexadecimal value. Here are some examples:

`context.fillStyle = "#FF0000";`
    Sets the text fill to red.

`context.strokeStyle = "#FF00FF";`
    Sets the text stroke to purple.

`context.fillStyle = "#FFFF00";`
    Sets the text fill to yellow.

Handling font color with JSColor

For Text Arranger, we will allow the user to select the text color. We could have made this a drop-down or a text box, but instead, we want to use the new HTML5 <input> type of color. This handy new form control works directly in the web browser, allowing users to visually choose a color from a beautifully designed color picker. At the time of this writing, only Opera has implemented the color <input> object of the HTML5 specification.

However, since we could really use a nice color picker for Text Arranger, we will implement a third-party color picker, JSColor (*http://jscolor.com/*). The jsColor control creates a nice color picker in JavaScript (see Figure 3-5), similar to the one that will someday grace browsers supporting HTML5.

To implement jsColor and the color picker for Text Arranger, first download the *jscolor.js* library and put it in the same folder as Text Arranger. Then, add this line of code in the <head> to include jsColor in the HTML page:

```
<script type="text/javascript" src="jscolor/jscolor.js"></script>
```

Then add a new <input> element to the ever-growing HTML <form> on the Text Arranger HTML page, and give it the CSS class designation color:

```
<input class="color" id="textFillColor" value="FF0000"/>
```

When you pick a color with jsColor, it creates a text value that looks like "FF0000", representing the color value chosen. However, we already know that we need to append the pound (#) sign to the front of that value to work with HTML5 Canvas. The textFillColorChanged event handler does this by appending "#" to the value of the textFillColor form control:

```
function textFillColorChanged(e) {
    var target = e.target;
    textFillColor = "#" + target.value;
    drawScreen();
}
```

Oh yes, and let's not forget the event listener we must create so that we can direct and "change" events from the textFillColor <input> element to the textFillColor Changed() event handler:

```
formElement = document.getElementById("textFillColor");
formElement.addEventListener('change', textFillColorChanged, false);
```

Finally, in the canvasApp() function, we need to create the textFillColor variable:

```
var textFillColor = "#ff0000";
```

We do this so that the variable can be updated by the aforementioned event handler, and then implemented when that event handler calls the drawScreen() function:

```
switch(fillOrStroke) {
  case "fill":
      context.fillStyle = textFillColor;
```

```
            context.fillText (message, xPosition,yPosition);
            break;
      case "stroke":
            context.strokeStyle = textFillColor;
            context.strokeText (message, xPosition,yPosition);
            break;
      case "both":
            context.fillStyle = textFillColor;
            context.fillText (message, xPosition ,yPosition);
            context.strokeStyle = "#000000";
            context.strokeText (message, xPosition,yPosition);
            break;
   }
```

Notice that we needed to update the switch() statement created for Text Arranger version 1.0 so that it used textFillColor instead of hardcoded values. However, when both a stroke and a fill are chosen, we still render the stroke as black ("#000000"). We could have added an additional color picker for the strokeColor, but that is something you can do if you want to start expanding the application. Figure 3-5 illustrates what it looks like now.

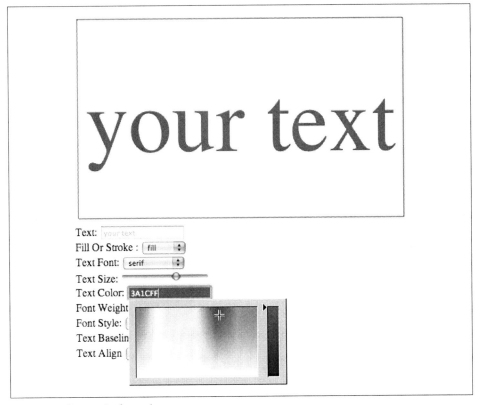

Figure 3-5. Setting the font color

Font Baseline and Alignment

You have options to align text on HTML5 Canvas both vertically and horizontally. These alignments affect the text in relation to Canvas itself, but only to the invisible bounding box that would surround the text's topmost, bottommost, rightmost, and leftmost sides. This is an important distinction because it means these alignments affect the text in ways that might be unfamiliar to you.

Vertical alignment

The font baseline is the vertical alignment of the font glyphs based on predefined horizontal locations in a font's `em square` (the grid used to design font outlines) in relation to font descenders. Basically, font glyphs, like lowercase *p* and *y* that traditionally extend "below the line," have *descenders*. The baseline tells the canvas where to render the font based on how those descenders relate to other glyphs in the font face.

The HTML5 Canvas API online has a neat graphic that attempts to explain baseline. We could copy it here, but in reality, we think it's easier to understand by *doing*, which is one of the main reasons we wrote the Text Arranger application.

The options for the `context.textBaseline` property are:

top
> The top of the text `em square` and the top of the highest glyph in the font face. Selecting this baseline will push the text the farthest down (highest y position) the canvas of all the baselines.

hanging
> This is a bit lower than the `top` baseline. It is the horizontal line from which many glyphs appear to "hang" from near the top of their face.

middle
> The dead vertical center baseline. We will use `middle` to help us vertically center the text in Text Arranger.

alphabetic
> The bottom of vertical writing script glyphs such as Arabic, Latin, and Hebrew.

ideographic
> The bottom of horizontal writing script glyphs such as Han Ideographs, Katakana, Hiragana, and Hangul.

bottom
> The bottom of the `em square` of the font glyphs. Choosing this baseline will push the font the farthest up (lowest y position) the canvas.

So, for example, if you want to place your text with a `top` baseline, you would use the following code:

```
context.textBaseline = "top";
```

All text displayed on the canvas afterward would have this baseline. To change the baseline, you would change the property:

```
context.textBaseline = "middle";
```

In reality, you will probably choose a single baseline for your app and stick with it, unless you are creating a word-processing or design application that requires more precise text handling.

Horizontal alignment

The context.textAlign property represents the horizontal alignment of the text based on its x position. These are the available textAlign values:

center
> The dead horizontal center of the text. We can use this alignment to help center our text in Text Arranger.

start
> Text is displayed directly after the text y position.

end
> All text is displayed before the text y position.

left
> Text is displayed starting with the y position of the text in the leftmost position (just like start).

right
> Text is displayed with the y position in the rightmost position of the text (just like end).

For example, to set the text alignment to center, you would use the code:

```
context.textAlign = "center";
```

After this property is set, all text would be displayed with the y value of the text as the center point. However, this does not mean the text will be "centered" on the canvas. To do that, you need to find the center of the canvas, and use that location as the y value for the text position. We will do this in Text Arranger.

These values can also be modified by the dir attribute of the Canvas object (inherited from the DOM document object). dir changes the direction of how text is displayed; the valid values for dir are rtl ("right to left") and ltr ("left to right").

Handling text baseline and alignment

We are going to handle the text baseline and alignment much like we handled the other text properties in Text Arranger. First, we will add some variables to the canvasApp() function in which Text Arranger operates that will hold the alignment values. Notice that we have set the textAlign variable to center, helping us simplify centering the text on the canvas:

```
var textBaseline = "middle";
var textAlign = "center";
```

Next, we add the <select> form elements for each new attribute to the HTML portion of the page:

```
Text Baseline <select id="textBaseline">
  <option value="middle">middle</option>
  <option value="top">top</option>
  <option value="hanging">hanging</option>
  <option value="alphabetic">alphabetic</option>
  <option value="ideographic">ideographic</option>
  <option value="bottom">bottom</option>
</select>
<br>
Text Align <select id="textAlign">
  <option value="center">center</option>
  <option value="start">start</option>
  <option value="end">end</option>
  <option value="left">left</option>
  <option value="right">right</option>

</select>
```

We then add event listeners and event handler functions so we can connect the user interaction with the HTML form elements to the canvas display. We register the event listeners in the canvasApp() function:

```
formElement = document.getElementById("textBaseline");
formElement.addEventListener('change', textBaselineChanged, false);

formElement = document.getElementById("textAlign");
formElement.addEventListener('change', textAlignChanged, false);
```

Next, we need to create the event handler functions inside canvasApp():

```
function textBaselineChanged(e) {
  var target = e.target;
  textBaseline = target.value;
  drawScreen();
}

function textAlignChanged(e) {
  var target = e.target;
  textAlign = target.value;
  drawScreen();
}
```

We then apply the new values in the drawScreen() function:

```
context.textBaseline = textBaseline;
context.textAlign = textAlign;
```

Finally, we change the code that centers the text horizontally on the screen. Because we used the center alignment for context.textAlign, we no longer need to subtract half the width of the text that we retrieved through `context.measureText()` like we did previously in Text Arranger 1.0:

```
var metrics = context.measureText(message);
var textWidth = metrics.width;
var xPosition = (theCanvas.width/2) - (textWidth/2);
```

Instead, we can simply use the center point of the canvas:

```
var xPosition = (theCanvas.width/2);
```

Remember, `center` is only the default alignment for the text. Because you can change this with Text Arranger, the text can still be aligned in different ways while you are using the application.

Figure 3-6 shows how a font set to `start` alignment with a `middle` baseline might appear on the canvas.

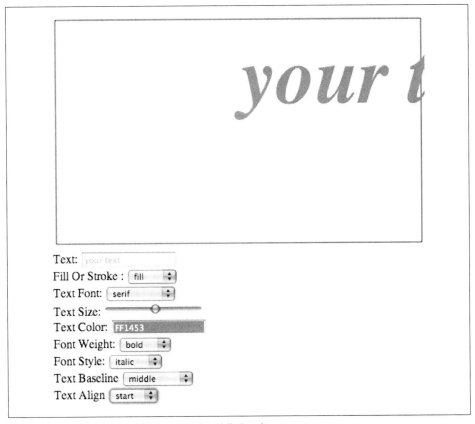

Figure 3-6. Font with start alignment and middle baseline

Text Arranger Version 2.0

Now, try the new version of Text Arranger, shown in Example 3-2. You can see that we have added a ton of new options that did not exist in version 1.0. One of the most striking things is how fluidly the text grows and shrinks as the font size is updated. Now, imagine scripting the font size to create animations. How would you do that? Could you create an application to record the manipulations the user makes with Text Arranger, and then play them back in real time?

Also, notice how all the alignment options affect one another. Experiment with how changing the text direction affects the vertical alignment. Choose different font faces and see how they affect the baseline. Do you see how an application like Text Arranger can help you understand the complex relationships of all the text properties on HTML5 Canvas in an interactive and—dare we say—fun way?

Example 3-2. Text Arranger 2.0

```
<!doctype html>
<html lang="en">
<head>
<meta charset="UTF-8">
<title>CH3EX2: Text Arranger Version 2.0</title>
<script src="modernizr-1.6.min.js"></script>
<script type="text/javascript" src="jscolor/jscolor.js"></script>
<script type="text/javascript">

window.addEventListener("load", eventWindowLoaded, false);
function eventWindowLoaded() {

    canvasApp();
}

function canvasSupport () {
    return Modernizr.canvas;
}

function eventWindowLoaded() {

    canvasApp();
}

function canvasApp() {

    var message = "your text";
    var fillOrStroke = "fill";

    var fontSize = "50";
    var fontFace = "serif";
    var textFillColor = "#ff0000";
    var textBaseline = "middle";
    var textAlign = "center";
    var fontWeight = "normal";
    var fontStyle = "normal";
```

```
if (!canvasSupport()) {
      return;
   }

var theCanvas = document.getElementById("canvasOne");
var context = theCanvas.getContext("2d");

var formElement = document.getElementById("textBox");
formElement.addEventListener('keyup', textBoxChanged, false);

formElement = document.getElementById("fillOrStroke");
formElement.addEventListener('change', fillOrStrokeChanged, false);

formElement = document.getElementById("textSize");
formElement.addEventListener('change', textSizeChanged, false);

formElement = document.getElementById("textFillColor");
formElement.addEventListener('change', textFillColorChanged, false);

formElement = document.getElementById("textFont");
formElement.addEventListener('change', textFontChanged, false);

formElement = document.getElementById("textBaseline");
formElement.addEventListener('change', textBaselineChanged, false);

formElement = document.getElementById("textAlign");
formElement.addEventListener('change', textAlignChanged, false);

formElement = document.getElementById("fontWeight");
formElement.addEventListener('change', fontWeightChanged, false);

formElement = document.getElementById("fontStyle");
formElement.addEventListener('change', fontStyleChanged, false);

drawScreen();

function drawScreen() {

    //Background
    context.fillStyle = "#ffffaa";
    context.fillRect(0, 0, theCanvas.width, theCanvas.height);

    //Box
    context.strokeStyle = "#000000";
    context.strokeRect(5,  5, theCanvas.width-10, theCanvas.height-10);

    //Text
    context.textBaseline = textBaseline;
    context.textAlign = textAlign;
    context.font = fontWeight + " " + fontStyle + " " + fontSize + "px " + fontFace;

    var xPosition = (theCanvas.width/2);
    var yPosition = (theCanvas.height/2);
```

```
    switch(fillOrStroke) {
        case "fill":
            context.fillStyle = textFillColor;
                context.fillText (message, xPosition,yPosition);
            break;
        case "stroke":
            context.strokeStyle = textFillColor;
            context.strokeText (message, xPosition,yPosition);
            break;
        case "both":
            context.fillStyle = textFillColor;
                context.fillText (message, xPosition ,yPosition);
            context.strokeStyle = "#000000";
            context.strokeText (message, xPosition,yPosition);
            break;
    }

}

function textBoxChanged(e) {
    var target = e.target;
    message = target.value;
    drawScreen();
}

function fillOrStrokeChanged(e) {
    var target = e.target;
    fillOrStroke = target.value;
    drawScreen();
}

function textSizeChanged(e) {
    var target = e.target;
    fontSize = target.value;
    drawScreen();
}

function textFillColorChanged(e) {
    var target = e.target;
    textFillColor = "#" + target.value;
    drawScreen();
}

function textFontChanged(e) {
    var target = e.target;
    fontFace = target.value;
    drawScreen();
}

function textBaselineChanged(e) {
    var target = e.target;
    textBaseline = target.value;
    drawScreen();
}
```

```
      function textAlignChanged(e) {
         var target = e.target;
         textAlign = target.value;
         drawScreen();
      }

      function fontWeightChanged(e) {
         var target = e.target;
         fontWeight = target.value;
         drawScreen();
      }

      function fontStyleChanged(e) {
         var target = e.target;
         fontStyle = target.value;
         drawScreen();
      }

   }

</script>
</head>
<body>
<div style="position: absolute; top: 50px; left: 50px;">
<canvas id="canvasOne" width="500" height="300">
 Your browser does not support HTML5 Canvas.
</canvas>

<form>
  Text: <input id="textBox" placeholder="your text" />
  <br>

  Fill Or Stroke :
  <select id="fillOrStroke">
  <option value="fill">fill</option>
  <option value="stroke">stroke</option>
  <option value="both">both</option>
  </select>
  <br>
  Text Font: <select id="textFont">
  <option value="serif">serif</option>
  <option value="sans-serif">sans-serif</option>
  <option value="cursive">cursive</option>
  <option value="fantasy">fantasy</option>
  <option value="monospace">monospace</option>
  </select>
  <br>
  Text Size: <input type="range" id="textSize"
       min="0"
       max="200"
       step="1"
       value="50"/>
  <br>
  Text Color: <input class="color" id="textFillColor" value="FF0000"/>
  <br>
```

```
Font Weight:
<select id="fontWeight">
<option value="normal">normal</option>
<option value="bold">bold</option>
<option value="bolder">bolder</option>
<option value="lighter">lighter</option>
</select>
<br>
Font Style:
<select id="fontStyle">
<option value="normal">normal</option>
<option value="italic">italic</option>
<option value="oblique">oblique</option>
</select>
<br>
Text Baseline <select id="textBaseline">
<option value="middle">middle</option>
<option value="top">top</option>
<option value="hanging">hanging</option>
<option value="alphabetic">alphabetic</option>
<option value="ideographic">ideographic</option>
<option value="bottom">bottom</option>
</select>
<br>
Text Align <select id="textAlign">
<option value="center">center</option>
<option value="start">start</option>
<option value="end">end</option>
<option value="left">left</option>
<option value="right">right</option>

</select>

</div>
</body>
</html>
```

Text and the Canvas Context

We've already discussed a couple Canvas context properties that affect the canvas in a global fashion: fillStyle and strokeStyle. However, there are two areas that visually demonstrate how changes to the properties of the context can affect the entire HTML5 Canvas: alpha transparencies and shadows.

Global Alpha and Text

Using alpha is a cool way to make objects seem to be partially or fully transparent on HTML5 Canvas. The globalAlpha property of the Canvas context is used for this purpose. After globalAlpha is applied, it affects all drawing on the canvas, so you need to be careful when setting it.

The valid values for `context.globalAlpha` are numbers between 0.0 (transparent) and 1.0 (opaque), and they act as a percentage for the alpha value. For example, a 50% alpha value would be coded like this:

```
context.globalAlpha = 0.5;
```

A 100% alpha (no transparency) would be coded like this:

```
context.globalAlpha = 1.0;
```

Handling globalAlpha transparencies

Besides the now-familiar elements that we included for most of the other configurable options in Text Arranger, the `globalAlpha` property requires us to think a bit more about when we use it and how it will affect the rest of the canvas.

First, we create a variable named `textAlpha` in the `canvasApp()` function and initialize it with 1, which means the text will have no transparency when it is first displayed:

```
var textAlpha = 1;
```

Next, in the `drawImage()` function, we need to set the `globalAlpha` property twice: once before we draw the background and the bounding box frame...

```
function drawScreen() {
        //Background

        context.globalAlpha = 1;
```

...and then again to the value stored in `textAlpha`, just before rendering the text to the canvas:

```
        context.globalAlpha = textAlpha;
```

This will reset `globalAlpha` so we can draw the background, but it will still allow us to use a configurable alpha value for the displayed text.

We will use another HTML5 `range` control in our form, but this time we set the value range with a min of 0.0 and a max of 1.0, stepping 0.01 every time the range is moved:

```
Alpha: <input type="range" id="textAlpha"
        min="0.0"
        max="1.0"
        step="0.01"
        value="1.0"/>
```

The `textAlphaChanged()` function works just like the other event handler functions we created in this chapter:

```
function textAlphaChanged(e) {
        var target = e.target;
        textAlpha = (target.value);
        drawScreen();
    }
```

Also, don't forget the event listener for the `textAlpha` range control:

```
formElement = document.getElementById("textAlpha");
formElement.addEventListener('change', textAlphaChanged, false);
```

The results will look like Figure 3-7.

Figure 3-7. Text with globalAlpha applied

Global Shadows and Text

HTML5 Canvas includes a unique set of properties for creating a shadow for drawings. The `context.shadow` functions are not unique to text, but they can make some very good text effects with very little effort.

To create a shadowEffect, there are four properties of the Canvas context that need to be manipulated:

context.shadowColor
> The color of the shadow. This uses the same "#RRGGBB" format of the fill Style and strokeStyle properties.

context.shadowOffsetX
> The x offset of shadow. This can be a positive or negative number.

context.shadowOffsetY
> The y offset of shadow. This can be a positive or negative number.

context.shadowBlur
> The blur filter diffusion of the shadow. The higher the number, the more diffusion.

For example, if you want to create a red shadow that is 5 pixels to the right and 5 pixels down from your text, with a blur of 2 pixels, you would set the properties like this:

```
context.shadowColor = "#FF0000";
context.shadowOffsetX = 5;
context.shadowOffsetY = 5;
context.shadowBlur = 2;
```

Handling global shadows

Just like we saw with globalAlpha, we must reset the shadow properties before we draw the background for textArranger; otherwise, the shadow will apply to the entire image. First, in the canvasApp() function, we create a set of variables to hold the shadow values:

```
var textAlpha = 1;
var shadowX = 1;
var shadowY = 1;
var shadowBlur = 1;
var shadowColor = "#707070";
```

We then make sure to turn off the shadow before we render the background for textArranger in the drawScreen(). We don't have to reset the shadowColor, but we think it is good practice to update all the relative properties relating to any global change to the Canvas context:

```
context.shadowColor = "#707070";
context.shadowOffsetX = 0;
context.shadowOffsetY = 0;
context.shadowBlur = 0;
```

Later in drawScreen(), we render the shadow based on the settings in the four variables we created:

```
context.shadowColor = shadowColor;
context.shadowOffsetX = shadowX;
context.shadowOffsetY = shadowY;
context.shadowBlur = shadowBlur;
```

We also need to create the HTML to allow the user to update the shadow settings. We do this with three range controls, as well as another color picker using jsColor:

```
Shadow X:<input type="range" id="shadowX"
        min="-100"
        max="100"
        step="1"
        value="1"/>
<br>
Shadow Y:<input type="range" id="shadowY"
        min="-100"
        max="100"
        step="1"
        value="1"/>
<br>
Shadow Blur: <input type="range" id="shadowBlur"
        min="1"
        max="100"
        step="1"
        value="1" />
<br>
Shadow Color: <input class="color" id="shadowColor" value="707070"/>
```

Finally, we need to add the event listeners and event handler functions so the HTML form elements can communicate with the canvas. See the results in Figure 3-8:

```
formElement = document.getElementById("shadowX");
formElement.addEventListener('change', shadowXChanged, false);

formElement = document.getElementById("shadowY");
formElement.addEventListener('change', shadowYChanged, false);

formElement = document.getElementById("shadowBlur");
formElement.addEventListener('change', shadowBlurChanged, false);

formElement = document.getElementById("shadowColor");
formElement.addEventListener('change', shadowColorChanged, false);
function shadowXChanged(e) {
    var target = e.target;
    shadowX = target.value;
    drawScreen();
}

function shadowYChanged(e) {
    var target = e.target;
    shadowY = target.value;
    drawScreen();
}

function shadowBlurChanged(e) {
    var target = e.target;
    shadowBlur = target.value;
    drawScreen();
}
```

```
function shadowColorChanged(e) {
    var target = e.target;
    shadowColor = target.value;
    drawScreen();
}
```

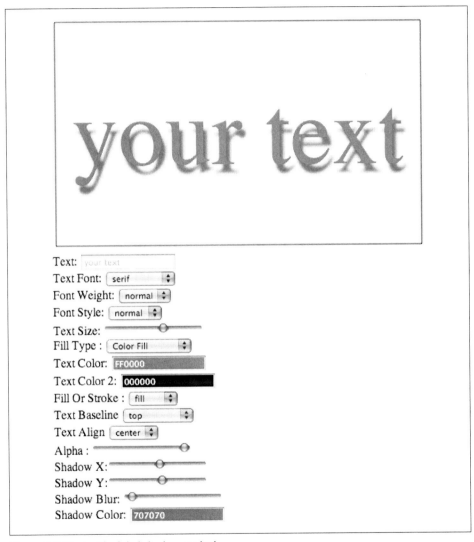

Figure 3-8. Text with global shadow applied

Text with Gradients and Patterns

We've already explored the fillColor and strokeColor properties of the Canvas context by setting those value to CSS-compliant colors. However, those very same properties can be set to refer to a few other objects defined in the Canvas API to create some stunning text effects. The objects are:

Linear gradient
> A linear color gradient with two or more colors

Radial gradient
> A circular color gradient with two or more colors

Image pattern
> An Image object used as a fill pattern

Linear Gradients and Text

To create a linear gradient, make a call to the context's createLinearGradient() method to create a Gradient object. The createLinearGradient() method accepts four parameters that all define the line of the linear gradient. The *x0* and *y0* parameters are the starting point of the line, and *x1* and *y1* represent the ending point of the line:

```
var gradient = context.createLinearGradient( [x0],[y0],[x1],[y1]);
```

For example, if you want to create a linear gradient that starts at the beginning of the text (located at 100,100), and has an endpoint that is the width of your text as displayed on the canvas, you might write the following code:

```
var metrics = context.measureText(message);
var textWidth = metrics.width;
var gradient = context.createLinearGradient(100, 100, textWidth, 100);
```

After you have created the line that represents the gradient, you need to add colors that will form the gradations of the gradient fill. This is done with the addColorStop() method, which requires two arguments: offset and color:

```
gradient.addColorStop([offset],[color]);
```

offset
> This is the offset on the gradient line to start the color gradation. The entire gradient is represented by the numbers between 0.0 and 1.0. The offset will be a decimal that represents a percentage.

color
> A valid CSS color in the format "#RRGGBB".

So, if you want black to be the first color in the gradient, and then red to be the second color that starts halfway down the gradient line, you would create two calls to add ColorStop():

```
gradient.addColorStop(0, "#000000");
gradient.addColorStop(.5, "#FF0000");
```

 If you fail to add colors with `addColorStop()`, the text will be rendered invisible.

The results are shown in Figure 3-9.

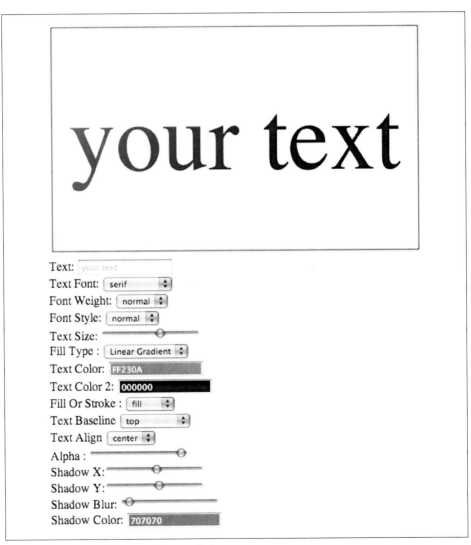

Figure 3-9. Text with linear gradient applied

Radial Gradients and Text

A radial gradient is created much like a linear gradient, except that it represents a cone—not a line. The cone is created by defining the center points and the radii of two different circles when calling the createRadialGradient() function of the Canvas context:

```
var gradient = context.createRadialGradient([x0],[y0],[radius0],[x1],[y1],[radius1]);
```

Let's say you want to create a radial gradient based on a cone. It starts with a circle that has its center point at 100,100 and a radius of 20, and ends at a circle with its center point at 200,100 and a radius of 5. The code would look like this:

```
var gradient = context.createRadialGradient(100,100,20,200,100,5);
```

Adding color stops to a radial gradient works the same as with a linear gradient, except the color moves along the cone instead of the line:

```
gradient.addColorStop(0, "#000000 ");
gradient.addColorStop(.5, "#FF0000");
```

Image Patterns and Text

Another option for filling text on HTML5 Canvas is to use an Image object. We will devote all of Chapter 4 to using the Image API, so here we will only discuss the basics of how to use one as a pattern for a text fill.

To create an image pattern, call the createPattern() method of the Canvas context, passing a reference to an Image object, and an option for repetition:

```
var pattern = context.createPattern([image], [repetition]);
```

image
> A valid Image object that has been loaded with an image by setting the pattern .src property and waiting for the image to load by setting an event listener for the Image onload event. The Canvas specification also allows for a video element or another <canvas> to be used here as well.

repetition
> The "tiling" of the image. This can have one of four values:

> repeat
>> The image is tiled on both the x and y axes.

> repeat-x
>> The image is tiled only on the x-axis (horizontally).

> repeat-y
>> The image is tiled only on the y-axis (vertically).

> no-repeat
>> The image is not tiled.

To use the image pattern, apply it to the `fillColor` and `strokeColor` properties of the context, just as you would apply a color:

```
context.fillStyle = pattern;
```

or:

```
context.strokeStyle = pattern;
```

For example, to load an image named *texture.jpg* and apply it to the `fillStyle` so that it tiles on both the x and y axes, you would write code like this:

```
var pattern = new Image();
pattern.src = "texture.jpg"
pattern.onload = function() {
 var pattern = context.createPattern("texture.jpg", "repeat");
 context.fillStyle = pattern;
 ...
}
```

Patterns with Video: The Bad News

The HTML5 Canvas API specifies that an HTML5 `video` element can be used as the source for `createPattern()` instead of an image. However, all of our attempts to do so emitted the following JavaScript error:

```
Uncaught Error: TYPE_MISMATCH_ERR: DOM Exception 17
```

According to the DOM reference at www.gnu.org, DOM Exception 17, TYPE _MISMATCH_ERR occurs "if the type of an object is incompatible with the expected type of the parameter associated to the object."

So it appears that most browsers have not included support for using video as the pattern for `createPattern()`. However, you can still load and play video on Canvas, which we will discuss in depth in Chapter 6.

Handling Gradients and Patterns in Text Arranger

Text Arranger 3.0 includes many changes that were implemented to support using gradients and image patterns with text on HTML5 Canvas. To see these changes in action, we first need to make sure that we have preloaded the *texture.jpg* image, which we will use for the `context.createPattern()` functionality. To do this, we will create a new function named `eventAssetsLoaded()` that we will set as the event handler for the `onload` event of the `Image` object that will hold the pattern. When that image has loaded, we will call `canvasApp()` in the same way we called it from `eventWindowLoaded()`:

```
function eventWindowLoaded() {
    var pattern = new Image();
    pattern.src = "texture.jpg";
    pattern.onload = eventAssetsLoaded;
}
```

```
function eventAssetsLoaded() {

    canvasApp();
}
```

 We are not going to use the pattern variable we created in this function, as it does not have scope in the canvasApp() function. We are merely using it to make sure that the image is available before we use it.

In the canvasApp() function, we will create three variables to support this new functionality. fillType describes how the text will be filled (a regular color fill, a linear gradient, a radial gradient, or a pattern). The textColorFill2 variable is the second color we will use for the gradient color stop. Finally, the pattern variable holds the Image object we preloaded, which we now need to create an instance of in canvasApp():

```
var fillType = "colorFill";
var textFillColor2 = "#000000";
var pattern = new Image();
...
pattern.src = "texture.jpg";
```

Now, let's jump to the HTML of our <form>. Since we have created different ways to fill the text we are displaying, we need to build a selection that allows for this choice. We will create a <select> box with the id of fillType for this purpose:

```
Fill Type: <select id="fillType">
  <option value="colorFill">Color Fill</option>
  <option value="linearGradient">Linear Gradient</option>
  <option value="radialGradient">Radial Gradient</option>
  <option value="pattern">pattern</option>
</select>
```

We need to add a second color selection that we can use for the gradient fills. We will use the jsColor picker and the id textColorFill2:

```
Text Color 2: <input class="color" id="textFillColor2" value ="000000"/>
  <br>
```

Back in canvasApp(), we need to create the event listeners for our two new form elements:

```
formElement = document.getElementById("textFillColor2");
formElement.addEventListener('change', textFillColor2Changed, false);

formElement = document.getElementById("fillType");
formElement.addEventListener('change', fillTypeChanged, false);
```

We also need to create the associated event handler functions for the new form elements:

```
function textFillColor2Changed(e) {
    var target = e.target;
    textFillColor2 = "#" + target.value;
```

```
        drawScreen();
    }

    function fillTypeChanged(e) {
        var target = e.target;
        fillType = target.value;
        drawScreen();
    }
```

We need to add support to drawScreen() for this new functionality. First, we use the measureText() method of the context to get the width of the text, which we will use to create the gradients:

```
var metrics = context.measureText(message);
var textWidth = metrics.width;
```

Then, we need to decide how to format our "color" for the fillStyle or strokeStyle of the context. In this instance, it can be a CSS color, a gradient, or an image pattern; the list below provides more information.

Color fill
> If we are doing a simple color fill, we operate just like in previous versions of Text Arranger. All we need to do is make tempColor equal to the value of y.

Linear gradient
> For the linear gradient, we need to decide what line we are going to create for the gradient. Our line will start at the beginning of the text (xPosition-textWidth/2 because the text uses the center alignment), and runs horizontally to the end of the text (textWidth). We also add two color stops (at 0 and 60%)—the colors are textFillColor1 and textFillColor2.

Radial gradient
> For the radial gradient, we are going to create a cone that starts at the center of the text (xPosition,yPosition) with a radius the size of the font (fontSize). The cone will extend horizontally the width of the text (textWidth) with a radius of 1.

Pattern
> For this option, we create a pattern using the pattern image variable we previously created. We designate it to repeat so it will tile horizontally and vertically.

Here's the code:

```
var tempColor;
if (fillType == "colorFill") {
    tempColor = textFillColor;
} else if (fillType == "linearGradient") {
    var gradient = context.createLinearGradient(xPosition-
        textWidth/2, yPosition, textWidth, yPosition);
    gradient.addColorStop(0,textFillColor);
    gradient.addColorStop(.6,textFillColor2);
    tempColor = gradient;
} else if (fillType == "radialGradient") {
    var gradient = context.createRadialGradient(xPosition, yPosition,
        fontSize, xPosition+textWidth, yPosition, 1);
```

```
        gradient.addColorStop(0,textFillColor);
        gradient.addColorStop(.6,textFillColor2);
        tempColor = gradient;
    } else if (fillType == "pattern") {
        var tempColor = context.createPattern(pattern,"repeat");
    } else {
        tempColor = textFillColor;
    }
```

Now, when we set our `fillStyle` or `strokeStyle`, we use `tempColor` instead of `textFill Color`. This will set the proper text fill choice that will be displayed on the canvas, as shown in Figure 3-10:

```
    context.fillStyle = tempColor;
```

Width, Height, Scale, and toDataURL() Revisited

In Chapter 1, we briefly discussed that you can set the width and height of the canvas, as well as the scale (style `width` and `height`) of the canvas display area, dynamically in code. We also showed you an example of using the `Canvas` object's `toDataURL()` method to export a "screenshot" of the Canvas application. In this section, we will revisit those functions as they relate to Text Arranger 3.0.

Dynamically Resizing the Canvas

In the code we developed in this chapter, we created a reference to the `Canvas` object on the HTML page—with the id `canvasOne`—and used it to retrieve the 2D context of the `Canvas` object:

```
    var theCanvas = document.getElementById("canvasOne");
    var context = theCanvas.getContext("2d");
```

While the 2D context is very important because we used it to draw directly onto the canvas, we did not spend any time discussing the `Canvas` object itself. In this chapter, we use the `width` property of the `Canvas` object to center text on the canvas. However, the `Canvas` object also includes another property named `height`, and both of these properties can be used to dynamically resize the `Canvas` object on demand. Why would you want to do this? There could be many uses, such as:

- Updating the canvas to the exact size of a loaded `video` object
- Dynamically animating the canvas after the page is loaded
- Other, more creative uses like the one we will experiment with next

Resizing the canvas on the fly is quite easy. To do it, simply set the `width` and `height` properties of the `Canvas` object, and then redraw the canvas contents:

```
    Canvas.width = 600;
    Canvas.height = 500;
    drawScreen();
```

Figure 3-10. Text with image pattern applied

The Canvas 2D API describes this function as a way to "scale" the canvas, but in practice, this does not appear to be true. Instead, the contents of the canvas are simply redrawn at the same size and same location on a larger canvas. Furthermore, if you don't redraw the canvas content, it appears to be invalidated, blanking the canvas back to white. To properly scale the canvas, you need to use the CSS `width` and `height` attributes, as described in the next section. We discuss using a matrix transformation to scale the Canvas in both Chapters 2 and 4.

Dynamically resizing in Text Arranger

We will add the ability for the canvas to be resized at will, giving you a good example of how resizing works and what it does to your drawn content.

First, we will add a couple new range controls to the HTML <form>. As you might have already guessed, we really like this new HTML5 range control, so we've tried to find as many uses as possible for it—even though it's only tangentially related to HTML5 Canvas.

We will give the controls the ids canvasWidth and canvasHeight:

```
Canvas Width:  <input type="range" id="canvasWidth"
       min="0"
       max="1000"
       step="1"
       value="500"/>
  <br>

  Canvas Height:
  <input type="range" id="canvasHeight"
       min="0"
       max="1000"
       step="1"
       value="300"/>
  <br>
```

Next, we add event listeners for the new form elements in the canvasApp() function:

```
formElement = document.getElementById("canvasWidth");
formElement.addEventListener('change', canvasWidthChanged, false);

formElement = document.getElementById("canvasHeight");
formElement.addEventListener('change', canvasHeightChanged, false);
```

Finally, we add the event handlers. Notice that we set the width and height of the Canvas (the variable we created that represents the Canvas object on screen) right inside these functions. We also need to make sure that we call drawScreen() in each function so that the canvas is redrawn on the newly resized area. If we did not do this, the canvas on the page would blank back to white:

```
function canvasWidthChanged(e) {
    var target = e.target;
    theCanvas.width = target.value;
    drawScreen();
}

function canvasHeightChanged(e) {
    var target = e.target;
    theCanvas.height = target.value;
    drawScreen();
}
```

We also need to change the way we draw the background for the application in the drawScreen() function so it supports a resized canvas. We do this by using the width and height attributes of theCanvas to create our background and bounding box:

```
context.fillStyle = '#ffffaa';
context.fillRect(0, 0, theCanvas.width, theCanvas.height);
//Box
context.strokeStyle = '#000000';
context.strokeRect(5,  5, theCanvas.width-10, theCanvas.height-10);
```

Dynamically Scaling the Canvas

Besides resizing the canvas using theCanvas.width and theCanvas.height attributes, you can also use CSS styles to change its scale. Unlike resizing, scaling takes the current canvas bitmapped area and resamples it to fit into the size specified by the width and height attributes of the CSS style. For example, to scale the canvas to a 400×400 area, you might use this CSS style:

```
style = "width: 400px; height:400px"
```

To update the style.width and style.height properties of the canvas in Text Arranger, we first create two more range controls in the HTML page:

```
Canvas Style Width:  <input type="range" id="canvasStyleWidth"
        min="0"
        max="1000"
        step="1"
        value="500"/>
  <br>

  Canvas Style Height:
  <input type="range" id="canvasStyleHeight"
        min="0"
        max="1000"
        step="1"
        value="300"/>
  <br>
```

Next, we set the event handler for each range control. However, this time we are using the same handler —canvasStyleSizeChanged()—for both:

```
formElement = document.getElementById("canvasStyleWidth");
formElement.addEventListener("change", canvasStyleSizeChanged, false);
formElement = document.getElementById("canvasStyleHeight");
formElement.addEventListener("change", canvasStyleSizeChanged, false);
```

In the event handler, we use the document.getElementById() method to get the values from both range controls. We then create a string that represents the style we want to set for the canvas:

```
"width:" + styleWidth.value + "px; height:" + styleHeight.value +"px;";
```

Finally, we use the `setAttribute()` method to set the "style":

```
function canvasStyleSizeChanged(e) {

    var styleWidth = document.getElementById("canvasStyleWidth");
    var styleHeight = document.getElementById("canvasStyleHeight");
    var styleValue = "width:" + styleWidth.value + "px; height:" +
        styleHeight.value +"px;";
    theCanvas.setAttribute("style", styleValue );
    drawScreen();
}
```

 While trying to change `theCanvas.width` and `theCanvas.height` attributes, you might notice some oddities if you try to change the scale with CSS at the same time. It appears that once you change the scale with CSS, the `width` and `height` attributes update the canvas in relation to that scale, which might not be the effect you are expecting. Experiment with Text Arranger 3.0 to see how these different styles and attributes interact.

The toDataURL() Method of the Canvas Object

As we briefly explained in Chapter 1, the `Canvas` object also contains a method named `toDataURL()`, which returns a string representing the canvas' image data. A call with no arguments will return a string of image data of MIME type *image/png*. If you supply the *image/jpg* as an argument, you can also supply a second argument between the numbers 0.0 and 1.0 that represents the quality/compression level of the image.

We are going to use `toDataURL()` to output the image data of the canvas into a `<textarea>` on our form, and then open a window to display the actual image. This is just a simple way to show that the function is working.

The first thing we do is create our last two form controls in HTML for Text Arranger. We start by creating a button with the id of `createImageData` that, when pressed, will create the image data with a call to an event handler named `createImageDataPressed()`.

We also create a `<textarea>` named `imageDataDisplay` that will hold the text data of the image after the `createImageData` button is pressed:

```
<input type="button" id="createImageData" value="Create Image Data">
<br>

<br>
<textarea id="imageDataDisplay" rows=10 cols=30></textarea>
```

Next, we set up the event listener for the `createImageData` button:

```
formElement = document.getElementById("createImageData");
formElement.addEventListener('click', createImageDataPressed, false);
```

Then, in the `createImageDataPressed()` event handler, we call the `toDataURL()` method of the Canvas object (`theCanvas`), and set the value of the imageDataDisplay `<textarea>`

to the data returned from `toDataURL()`. Finally, using the image data as the URL for the window, we call `window.open()`. When we do this, a window will pop open, displaying the actual image created from the canvas (see Figure 3-11). You can right-click and save this image, just like any other image displayed in an HTML page. Pretty cool, eh?

```
function createImageDataPressed(e) {

    var imageDataDisplay = document.getElementById('imageDataDisplay');
    imageDataDisplay.value = theCanvas.toDataURL();
    window.open(imageDataDisplay.value,"canvasImage","left=0,top=0,width=" +
        theCanvas.width + ",height=" + theCanvas.height +
        ",toolbar=0,resizable=0");
}
```

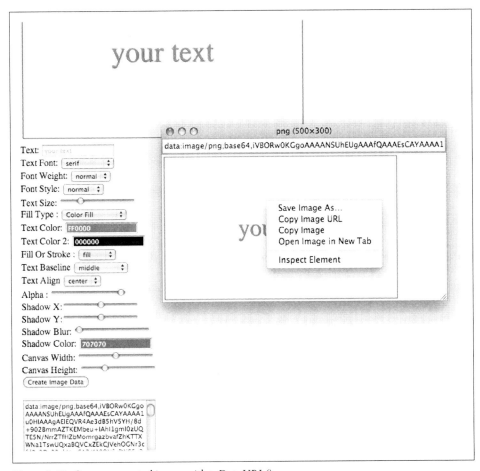

Figure 3-11. Canvas exported image with toDataURL()

Final Version of Text Arranger

The final version of Text Arranger (3.0) brings together all the HTML5 Text API features we have discussed in this chapter (see Example 3-3). Play with the final app, and see how the different options interact with one another. Here are a couple things you might find interesting:

- Shadows don't work with patterns or gradients.
- Increasing the text size with a pattern that is the size of the canvas changes the pattern on the text (it acts like a mask or window into the pattern itself).
- Canvas width and height are affected by the style width and height (scaling).

Example 3-3. Text Arranger 3.0

```
<!doctype html>
<html lang="en">
<head>
<meta charset="UTF-8">
<title>CH3EX3: Text Arranger 3.0</title>
<script src="modernizr-1.6.min.js"></script>
<script type="text/javascript" src="jscolor/jscolor.js"></script>
<script type="text/javascript">

window.addEventListener("load", eventWindowLoaded, false);
function eventWindowLoaded() {

    canvasApp();
}

function canvasSupport () {
    return Modernizr.canvas;
}

function eventWindowLoaded() {
   var pattern = new Image();
   pattern.src = "texture.jpg";
   pattern.onload = eventAssetsLoaded;
}

function eventAssetsLoaded() {
```

```
        canvasApp();
}

function canvasApp() {

    var message = "your text";
    var fontSize = "50";
    var fontFace = "serif";
    var textFillColor = "#ff0000";
    var textAlpha = 1;
    var shadowX = 1;
    var shadowY = 1;
    var shadowBlur = 1;
    var shadowColor = "#707070";
    var textBaseline = "middle";
    var textAlign = "center";
    var fillOrStroke ="fill";
    var fontWeight = "normal";
    var fontStyle = "normal";
    var fillType = "colorFill";
    var textFillColor2 = "#000000";
    var pattern = new Image();

    if (!canvasSupport()) {
            return;
        }

    var theCanvas = document.getElementById("canvasOne");
    var context = theCanvas.getContext("2d");

    var formElement = document.getElementById("textBox");
    formElement.addEventListener("keyup", textBoxChanged, false);

    formElement = document.getElementById("fillOrStroke");
    formElement.addEventListener("change", fillOrStrokeChanged, false);

    formElement = document.getElementById("textSize");
    formElement.addEventListener("change", textSizeChanged, false);

    formElement = document.getElementById("textFillColor");
    formElement.addEventListener("change", textFillColorChanged, false);

    formElement = document.getElementById("textFont");
    formElement.addEventListener("change", textFontChanged, false);

    formElement = document.getElementById("textBaseline");
    formElement.addEventListener("change", textBaselineChanged, false);

    formElement = document.getElementById("textAlign");
    formElement.addEventListener("change", textAlignChanged, false);

    formElement = document.getElementById("fontWeight");
    formElement.addEventListener("change", fontWeightChanged, false);
```

```
formElement = document.getElementById("fontStyle");
formElement.addEventListener("change", fontStyleChanged, false);

formElement = document.getElementById("shadowX");
formElement.addEventListener("change", shadowXChanged, false);

formElement = document.getElementById("shadowY");
formElement.addEventListener("change", shadowYChanged, false);

formElement = document.getElementById("shadowBlur");
formElement.addEventListener("change", shadowBlurChanged, false);

formElement = document.getElementById("shadowColor");
formElement.addEventListener("change", shadowColorChanged, false);

formElement = document.getElementById("textAlpha");
formElement.addEventListener("change", textAlphaChanged, false);

formElement = document.getElementById("textFillColor2");
formElement.addEventListener("change", textFillColor2Changed, false);

formElement = document.getElementById("fillType");
formElement.addEventListener("change", fillTypeChanged, false);

formElement = document.getElementById("canvasWidth");
formElement.addEventListener("change", canvasWidthChanged, false);

formElement = document.getElementById("canvasHeight");
formElement.addEventListener("change", canvasHeightChanged, false);

formElement = document.getElementById("canvasStyleWidth");
formElement.addEventListener("change", canvasStyleSizeChanged, false);

formElement = document.getElementById("canvasStyleHeight");
formElement.addEventListener("change", canvasStyleSizeChanged, false);

formElement = document.getElementById("createImageData");
formElement.addEventListener("click", createImageDataPressed, false);

pattern.src = "texture.jpg";

drawScreen();

function drawScreen() {

  //Background
  context.globalAlpha = 1;
  context.shadowColor = "#707070";
  context.shadowOffsetX = 0;
  context.shadowOffsetY = 0;
  context.shadowBlur = 0;
  context.fillStyle = "#ffffaa";
  context.fillRect(0, 0, theCanvas.width, theCanvas.height);
```

```
//Box
context.strokeStyle = "#000000";
context.strokeRect(5,   5, theCanvas.width-10, theCanvas.height-10);

//Text
context.textBaseline = textBaseline;
context.textAlign = textAlign;
context.font = fontWeight + " " + fontStyle + " " + fontSize + "px " + fontFace;
context.shadowColor = shadowColor;
context.shadowOffsetX = shadowX;
context.shadowOffsetY = shadowY;
context.shadowBlur = shadowBlur;
context.globalAlpha = textAlpha;

var xPosition = (theCanvas.width/2);
var yPosition = (theCanvas.height/2);

var metrics = context.measureText(message);
var textWidth = metrics.width;

var tempColor;
if (fillType == "colorFill") {
   tempColor = textFillColor;
} else if (fillType == "linearGradient") {

   var gradient = context.createLinearGradient(xPosition-
      textWidth/2, yPosition, textWidth, yPosition);
   gradient.addColorStop(0,textFillColor);
   gradient.addColorStop(.6,textFillColor2);
   tempColor = gradient;
} else if (fillType == "radialGradient") {
   var gradient = context.createRadialGradient(xPosition, yPosition,
      fontSize, xPosition+textWidth, yPosition, 1);
   gradient.addColorStop(0,textFillColor);
   gradient.addColorStop(.6,textFillColor2);
   tempColor = gradient;
} else if (fillType == "pattern") {
   var tempColor = context.createPattern(pattern,"repeat")
} else {
   tempColor = textFillColor;
}

switch(fillOrStroke) {
   case "fill":
      context.fillStyle = tempColor;
         context.fillText  (message, xPosition,yPosition);
      break;
   case "stroke":
      context.strokeStyle = tempColor;
      context.strokeText  (message, xPosition,yPosition);
      break;
   case "both":
      context.fillStyle = tempColor;
         context.fillText  (message, xPosition,yPosition);
      context.strokeStyle = "#000000";
```

```
                context.strokeText  (message, xPosition,yPosition);
                break;
        }


    }

    function textBoxChanged(e) {
        var target = e.target;
        message = target.value;
        drawScreen();
    }

    function textBaselineChanged(e) {
        var target = e.target;
        textBaseline = target.value;
        drawScreen();
    }

    function textAlignChanged(e) {
        var target = e.target;
        textAlign = target.value;
        drawScreen();
    }

    function fillOrStrokeChanged(e) {
        var target = e.target;
        fillOrStroke = target.value;
        drawScreen();
    }

    function textSizeChanged(e) {
        var target = e.target;
        fontSize = target.value;
        drawScreen();
    }

    function textFillColorChanged(e) {
        var target = e.target;
        textFillColor = "#" + target.value;
        drawScreen();
    }

    function textFontChanged(e) {
        var target = e.target;
        fontFace = target.value;
        drawScreen();
    }

    function fontWeightChanged(e) {
        var target = e.target;
        fontWeight = target.value;
        drawScreen();
    }
```

```
function fontStyleChanged(e) {
    var target = e.target;
    fontStyle = target.value;
    drawScreen();
}

function shadowXChanged(e) {
    var target = e.target;
    shadowX = target.value;
    drawScreen();
}

function shadowYChanged(e) {
    var target = e.target;
    shadowY = target.value;
    drawScreen();
}

function shadowBlurChanged(e) {
    var target = e.target;
    shadowBlur = target.value;
    drawScreen();
}

function shadowColorChanged(e) {
    var target = e.target;
    shadowColor = target.value;
    drawScreen();
}

function textAlphaChanged(e) {
    var target = e.target;
    textAlpha = (target.value);
    drawScreen();
}

function textFillColor2Changed(e) {
    var target = e.target;
    textFillColor2 = "#" + target.value;
    drawScreen();
}

function fillTypeChanged(e) {
    var target = e.target;
    fillType = target.value;
    drawScreen();
}

function canvasWidthChanged(e) {
    var target = e.target;
    theCanvas.width = target.value;
    drawScreen();
}
```

```
      function canvasHeightChanged(e) {
         var target = e.target;
         theCanvas.height = target.value;
         drawScreen();
      }

      function canvasStyleSizeChanged(e) {

         var styleWidth = document.getElementById("canvasStyleWidth");
         var styleHeight = document.getElementById("canvasStyleHeight");
         var styleValue = "width:" + styleWidth.value + "px; height:" +
             styleHeight.value +"px;";
         theCanvas.setAttribute("style", styleValue );
         drawScreen();
      }


      function createImageDataPressed(e) {

         var imageDataDisplay = document.getElementById("imageDataDisplay");
         imageDataDisplay.value = theCanvas.toDataURL();
         window.open(imageDataDisplay.value,"canvasImage","left=0,top=0,width=" +
            theCanvas.width + ",height=" + theCanvas.height +
            ",toolbar=0,resizable=0");

      }

}

</script>
</head>
<body>
<div style="display:none">
      <video id="theVideo" autoplay="true" loop="true">
         <source src="spaceeggs.ogg" type="video/ogg"/>
      </video>

</div>

<div style="position: absolute; top: 50px; left: 50px;">
<canvas id="canvasOne" width="500" height="300">
 Your browser does not support HTML5 Canvas.
</canvas>
<form>
  Text: <input id="textBox" placeholder="your text" />
  <br>
  Text Font: <select id="textFont">
  <option value="serif">serif</option>
  <option value="sans-serif">sans-serif</option>
  <option value="cursive">cursive</option>
  <option value="fantasy">fantasy</option>
  <option value="monospace">monospace</option>
  </select>
  <br>
```

```
Font Weight:
<select id="fontWeight">
<option value="normal">normal</option>
<option value="bold">bold</option>
<option value="bolder">bolder</option>
<option value="lighter">lighter</option>
</select>
<br>
Font Style:
<select id="fontStyle">
<option value="normal">normal</option>
<option value="italic">italic</option>
<option value="oblique">oblique</option>
</select>
<br>
Text Size: <input type="range" id="textSize"
      min="0"
      max="200"
      step="1"
      value="50"/>
 <br>
 Fill Type: <select id="fillType">
<option value="colorFill">Color Fill</option>
<option value="linearGradient">Linear Gradient</option>
<option value="radialGradient">Radial Gradient</option>
<option value="pattern">pattern</option>
</select>
<br>
Text Color: <input class="color" id="textFillColor" value="FF0000"/>
<br>
Text Color 2: <input class="color" id="textFillColor2" value ="000000"/>
<br>
Fill Or Stroke: <select id="fillOrStroke">
<option value="fill">fill</option>
<option value="stroke">stroke</option>
<option value="both">both</option>
</select>
<br>
Text Baseline <select id="textBaseline">
<option value="middle">middle</option>
<option value="top">top</option>
<option value="hanging">hanging</option>
<option value="alphabetic">alphabetic</option>
<option value="ideographic">ideographic</option>
<option value="bottom">bottom</option>
</select>
<br>
Text Align <select id="textAlign">
<option value="center">center</option>
<option value="start">start</option>
<option value="end">end</option>
<option value="left">left</option>
<option value="right">right</option>
</select>
<br>
```

```
Alpha: <input type="range" id="textAlpha"
      min="0.0"
      max="1.0"
      step="0.01"
      value="1.0"/>
<br>
Shadow X:<input type="range" id="shadowX"
      min="-100"
      max="100"
      step="1"
      value="1"/>
<br>
Shadow Y:<input type="range" id="shadowY"
      min="-100"
      max="100"
      step="1"
      value="1"/>
<br>
Shadow Blur: <input type="range" id="shadowBlur"
      min="1"
      max="100"
      step="1"
      value="1" />
<br>
Shadow Color: <input class="color" id="shadowColor" value="707070"/>
<br>
Canvas Width:  <input type="range" id="canvasWidth"
      min="0"
      max="1000"
      step="1"
      value="500"/>
<br>
Canvas Height:
 <input type="range" id="canvasHeight"
      min="0"
      max="1000"
      step="1"
      value="300"/>
<br>
Canvas Style Width:  <input type="range" id="canvasStyleWidth"
      min="0"
      max="1000"
      step="1"
      value="500"/>
<br>
Canvas Style Height:
 <input type="range" id="canvasStyleHeight"
      min="0"
      max="1000"
      step="1"
      value="300"/>
<br>
<input type="button" id="createImageData" value="Create Image Data">
<br>
```

```
<br>
<textarea id="imageDataDisplay" rows=10 cols=30></textarea>
</form>

</div>
</body>
</html>
```

What's Next

In this chapter, we introduced you to the fundamentals of the HTML5 Canvas Text API, offered some general concepts relating to drawing on the canvas, and explained how to communicate with HTML form controls. As you can now see, the basic concept of writing text to HTML5 Canvas can be taken to very complex (and some might argue ludicrous) levels. The final application, Text Arranger 3.0, allows you to modify a single line of text in an almost infinite number of ways. In the next chapter, we move on to displaying and manipulating images on the canvas.

CHAPTER 4

Images on the Canvas

Like the Canvas Drawing API, the Canvas Image API is very robust. With it, we can load in image data and apply it directly to the canvas. This image data can also be cut and spliced to display any desired portion. Furthermore, Canvas gives us the ability to store arrays of pixel data that we can manipulate and then draw back to the canvas.

There are two primary Canvas functions we can perform with images. We can display images, and we can modify them pixel by pixel and paint them back to the canvas. There are only a few Image API functions, but they open up a world of pixel-level manipulation that gives the developer the power to create optimized applications directly in the web browser without needing any plug-ins.

The Basic File Setup for This Chapter

All the examples in this chapter will use the same basic file setup for displaying our demonstrations as we proceed through the Drawing API. Use the following as the basis for all the examples we create—you will only need to change the contents of the drawScreen() function:

```
<!doctype html>
<html lang="en">
<head>
<meta charset="UTF-8">
<title>Ch4BaseFile - Template For Chapter 4 Examples</title>
<script src="modernizr-1.6.min.js"></script>
<script type="text/javascript">
window.addEventListener('load', eventWindowLoaded, false);
function eventWindowLoaded() {

    canvasApp();

}

function canvasSupport () {
    return Modernizr.canvas;
}
```

```
function canvasApp(){

    if (!canvasSupport()) {
            return;
      }else{
        var theCanvas = document.getElementById("canvas");
        var context = theCanvas.getContext("2d");
    }

drawScreen();

    function drawScreen() {
        //make changes here
        context.fillStyle = '#aaaaaa';
        context.fillRect(0, 0, 200, 200);
        context.fillStyle = '#000000';
        context.font = '20px _sans';
        context.textBaseline = 'top';
        context.fillText  ("Canvas!", 0, 0);
    }
}
</script>
</head>
<body>
<div style="position: absolute; top: 50px; left: 50px;">
<canvas id="canvas" width="500" height="500">
 Your browser does not support HTML5 Canvas.
</canvas>
</div>
</body>
</html>
```

Image Basics

The Canvas API allows access to the DOM-defined Image object type through the use of the drawImage() method. The image can be defined in HTML, such as:

```
<img src="ship1.png" id="spaceship">
```

Or it can be defined in JavaScript. We create a new JavaScript Image instance like this:

```
var spaceShip = new Image();
```

We can then set the file source of the image by assigning a URL to the src attribute of our newly created Image object:

```
spaceShip.src = "ship1.png";
```

Preloading Images

Before an image can be called in code, we must ensure that it has properly loaded and is ready to be used. We do this by creating an event listener to fire off when the `load` event on the image occurs:

```
spaceShip.addEventListener('load', eventShipLoaded , false);
```

When the image is fully loaded, the `eventShipLoaded()` function will fire off. Inside this function we will then call `drawScreen()`, as we have in the previous chapters:

```
function eventShipLoaded() {
    drawScreen();
}
```

 In practice, we would not create a separate event listener function for each loaded image. This code example works fine if your application contains only a single image. In Chapter 9, we will build a game with multiple image files (and sounds) and use a single listener function for all loaded resources.

Displaying an Image on the Canvas with drawImage()

Once we have an image loaded in, we can display it on the screen in a number of ways. The `drawImage()` Canvas method is used for displaying image data directly onto the canvas. `drawImage()` is *overloaded* and takes three separate sets of parameters, each allowing varied manipulation of both the image's source pixels and the destination location for those pixels on the canvas. Let's first look at the most basic:

```
drawImage(Image, dx, dy)
```

This function takes in three parameters: an `Image` object, and x and y values representing the top-left corner location to start painting the image on the canvas.

Here is the code we would use to place our spaceship image at the 0,0 location (the top-left corner) of the canvas:

```
context.drawImage(spaceShip, 0, 0);
```

If we want to place another copy at 50,50, we would simply make the same call but change the location:

```
context.drawImage(spaceShip, 50, 50);
```

Example 4-1 shows the full code for what we have done so far.

Example 4-1. Load and display an image file

```
var spaceShip = new Image();
spaceShip.addEventListener('load', eventShipLoaded , false);
spaceShip.src = "ship1.png";
```

```
function eventShipLoaded() {
   drawScreen();
}

function drawScreen() {

   context.drawImage(spaceShip, 0, 0);
   context.drawImage(spaceShip, 50, 50);

}
```

Figure 4-1 shows the 32×32 *ship1.png* file.

Figure 4-1. Load and display an image file

In practice, we would probably not put all of our drawing code directly into a function such as `drawScreen()`. It almost always makes more sense to create a separate function, such as `placeShip()`, shown here:

```
function drawScreen() {
   placeShip(context, spaceShip, 0, 0);
   placeShip(context, spaceShip, 50, 50);
}

function placeShip(ctx, obj, posX, posY, width, height) {
   if (width && height) {
      context.drawImage(obj, posX, posY, width, height);
   } else {
      context.drawImage(obj, posX, posY);
   }
}
```

The `placeShip()` function accepts the context, the image object, the x and y positions, and a height and width. If a height and width are passed in, the first version of the `drawScreen()` function is called. If not, the second version is called. We will look at resizing images as they are drawn in the next section.

The *ship1.png* file we are using is a 32×32 pixel *.png* bitmap, which we have modified from Ari Feldman's excellent SpriteLib. SpriteLib is a free library of pixel-based game sprites that Ari has made available for use in games and books. You can find the entire SpriteLib here: *http://www.flyingyogi.com/fun/spritelib.html*.

The website for this book contains only the files necessary to complete the examples. We have modified Ari's files to fit the needs of this book.

Figure 4-2 shows two copies of the image painted to the canvas. One of the copies has the top-left starting location of 0,0, and the other starts at 50,50.

Figure 4-2. Draw multiple objects with a single source

Resizing an Image Painted to the Canvas

To paint and scale drawn images, we can also pass parameters into the `drawImage()` function. For example, this second version of `drawImage()` takes in an extra two parameters:

```
drawImage(Image, dx, dy, dw, dh)
```

dw and *dh* represent the width and height of the rectangle portion of the canvas where our source image will be painted. If we only want to scale the image to 64×64 or 16×16, we would use the following code:

```
context.drawImage(spaceShip, 0, 0,64,64);
context.drawImage(spaceShip, 0, 0,16,16);
```

Example 4-2 draws various sizes to the canvas.

Example 4-2. Resizing an image as it is drawn

```
function eventShipLoaded() {
    drawScreen();
}

function drawScreen() {

    context.drawImage(spaceShip, 0, 0);
    context.drawImage(spaceShip, 0, 34,32,32);
    context.drawImage(spaceShip, 0, 68,64,64);
    context.drawImage(spaceShip, 0, 140,16,16);
}
```

See Figure 4-3 for the output to this example.

Figure 4-3. Resizing an image as it is drawn

In Example 4-2, we have added a gray box so we can better see the placement of the images on the canvas. The image we placed on the screen can scale in size as it is painted, saving us the calculation and steps necessary to use a matrix transformation on the object. The only caveat is that the scale origin point of reference is the top-left corner of the object. If we used a matrix operation, we could translate the origin point to the center of the object before applying the scale.

We have placed two 32×32 objects on the canvas to show that these two function calls are identical:

```
context.drawImage(spaceShip, 0, 0);
context.drawImage(spaceShip, 0, 34,32,32);
```

Aside from the fact that the second is placed 34 pixels below the first, the extra 32,32 at the end of the second call is unnecessary because it is the original size of the object. This demonstrates that the scale operation does not translate (or move) the object on any axis. The top-left corner of each is 0,0.

Copying Part of an Image to the Canvas

The third set of parameters that can be passed into `drawImage()` allows us to copy an arbitrary rectangle of data from a source image and place it onto the canvas. This image data can be resized as it is placed.

We are going to use a second source image for this set of operations: spaceships that have been laid out on what is called a *tile sheet* (also known as a *sprite sheet*, a *texture sheet*, or by many other names). This type of file layout refers to an image file that is broken up physically into rectangles of data. Usually these rectangles have an equal width and height. The "tiles" or "sprites" we will be using are 32 pixels wide by 32 pixels high, commonly referred to as 32×32 tiles.

Figure 4-4 shows a tile sheet with the grid lines turned on in the drawing application. These grid lines separate each of the tiles on the sheet.

Figure 4-4. The tile sheet inside a drawing program

Figure 4-5 is the actual tile sheet—without grid lines—that we will use for our further examples.

Figure 4-5. The tile sheet exported for use in an application

The structure of the parameters for this third version of the `drawImage()` function looks like this:

```
drawImage(Image, sx, sy, sw, sh, dx, dy, dw, dh)
```

sx and *sy* represent the "source positions" to start copying the source image to the canvas. *sw* and *sh* represent the width and height of the rectangle starting at *sx* and *sy*. That rectangle will be copied to the canvas at "destination" positions *dx* and *dy*. As with the previous `drawImage()` function, *dw* and *dh* represent the newly scaled width and height for the image.

Example 4-3 copies the second version of our spaceship (tile number 2) to the canvas and positions it at 50,50. It also scales the image to 64×64, producing the result shown in Figure 4-6.

Example 4-3. Using all of the drawImage() parameters

```
var tileSheet = new Image();
tileSheet.addEventListener('load', eventShipLoaded , false);

tileSheet.src = "ships.png";

function eventShipLoaded() {
    drawScreen();
}


function drawScreen() {

    //draw a background so we can see the Canvas edges
    context.fillStyle = "#aaaaaa";
```

```
    context.fillRect(0,0,500,500);
    context.drawImage(tileSheet, 32, 0,32,32,50,50,64,64);
}
```

As you can see, we have changed the name of our `Image` instance to `tileSheet` because it represents more than just the source for the single ship image.

Figure 4-6. Using all of the drawImage() parameters

Now, let's use this same concept to simulate animation using the tiles on our tile sheet.

Simple Cell-Based Sprite Animation

With a tile sheet of images, it is relatively simple to create what seems like cell-based or flip-book animation. This technique involves rapidly swapping images over time to simulate animation. The term *flip-book* comes from the age-old technique of drawing individual cells of animation in the top-left corner pages of a book. When the pages are rapidly flipped through, the changes are viewed over time, appearing to create a cartoon. *Cell-based animation* refers to a similar professional technique. Individual samesized cells (or pages) of images are drawn to simulate animation. When played back rapidly with special devices in front of a camera, animated cartoons are recorded.

We can use the `drawImage()` function and the first two tiles on our tile sheet to do the same thing.

Creating an Animation Frame Counter

We can simulate the ship's exhaust firing by rapidly flipping between the first two tiles (or cells) on our tile sheet. To do this, we set up a counter variable, which is how we track the tile we want to paint to the canvas. We will use 0 for the first cell and 1 for the second cell.

We will create a simple integer to count which frame we are displaying on our tile sheet:

```
var counter = 0;
```

Inside drawScreen(), we will increment this value by 1 on each frame. Since we only have two frames, we will need to set it back to 0 when it is greater than 1:

```
counter++;
if (counter >1) {
    counter = 0;
}
```

Or use the nice shortcut:

```
counter ^= 1;
```

Creating a Timer Loop

As it currently stands, our code will only be called a single time. Let's create a simple timer loop that will call the drawScreen() function 10 times a second, or once every 100 milliseconds. A timer loop that is set to run at a certain frame rate is sometimes referred to as a *frame tick* or *timer tick*. Each tick is simply a single iteration of the timer running all the code we put into our drawScreen() function. We will also need a function that starts the timer loop and initiates the tick once the image has preloaded properly. We'll name this function startUp():

```
function eventShipLoaded() {
    startUp();
}

function startUp(){
    setInterval(drawScreen, 100 );
}
```

Changing the Tile to Display

To change the tile to display, we can multiply the counter variable by 32 (the tile width). Since we only have a single row of tiles, we don't have to change the y value:

```
context.drawImage(tileSheet, 32*counter, 0,32,32,50,50,64,64);
```

 We will examine how to use a tile sheet consisting of multiple rows and columns in the next section, "Advanced Cell-Based Animation" on page 132.

Example 4-3 used this same line of code to draw our image. In Example 4-4, it will be placed on the canvas at 50,50 and scaled to 64×64 pixels. Let's look at the entire set of code.

Example 4-4. A simple sprite animation

```
var counter = 0;
var tileSheet = new Image();
tileSheet.addEventListener('load', eventShipLoaded , false);
tileSheet.src = "ships.png";

function eventShipLoaded() {
   startUp();
}

function drawScreen() {

    //draw a background so we can see the Canvas edges
    context.fillStyle = "#aaaaaa";
    context.fillRect(0,0,500,500);
    context.drawImage(tileSheet, 32*counter, 0,32,32,50,50,64,64);
      counter++;
      if (counter >1) {
         counter = 0;
      }
}

 function startUp(){

     setInterval(drawScreen, 100 );
 }
```

When you run this code, you will see the exhaust on the ship turn off and on every 100 milliseconds, creating a simple cell-based animation.

Advanced Cell-Based Animation

In the previous example, we simply flipped back and forth between two tiles on our tile sheet. Next, we are going to create a method that uses a tile sheet to play through a series of images. First, let's look at the new tile sheet, created by using tiles from SpriteLib. Figure 4-7 shows the example sprite sheet, *tanks_sheet.png*; we will refer back to this figure throughout the chapter.

Figure 4-7. Example tile sheet

As you can see, it contains a number of 32×32 tiles that can be used in a game. We will not create an entire game in this chapter, but we will examine how to use these tiles to create a game screen. In Chapter 9, we will create a simple maze-chase game using some of these tiles.

Examining the Tile Sheet

The tile sheet is formatted into a series of tiles starting at the top left. As with a two-dimensional array, the numbering starts at 0—we call this *0 relative*. Moving from left to right and down, each tile will be referenced by a single number index (as opposed to a multidimensional index). The gray square in the top left is tile 0, while the tank at the end of the first row (the rightmost tank) is tile 7. Moving down to the next row, the first tank on the far left of the second row is tile 8, and so on until the final tile on row 3 (the fourth row down when we start numbering at 0) is tile 31. We have four rows with eight columns each, making 32 tiles with indexes numbered 0 to 31.

Creating an Animation Array

Next, we are going to create an array to hold the tiles for the animation. There are two tanks on the tile sheet: one is green and one is blue. Tiles 1-8 are a series that—when played in succession—will make it appear as though the green tank's tracks are moving.

 Remember, the tile sheet starts at tile 0, but we want start with the first tank image at tile number 1.

We will store the tile ids we want to play for the tank in an array:

```
var animationFrames = [1,2,3,4,5,6,7,8];
```

We will use a counter to keep track of the current index of this array:

```
var frameIndex = 0;
```

Choosing the Tile to Display

We will use the frameIndex of the animationFrames array to calculate the 32×32 source rectangle from our tile sheet that we will copy to the canvas. First, we need to find the x and y locations of the top-left corner for the tile we want to copy. To do this, we will create local variables in our drawScreen() function on each iteration (frame) to calculate the position on the tile sheet. The sourceX variable will contain the top-left corner x position, and the sourceY variable will contain the top-left corner y position.

Here is pseudocode for the sourceX calculation:

```
sourceX = integer(current_frame_index modulo
the_number_columns_in_the_tilesheet) * tile_width
```

The modulo (%) operator gives us the remainder of the division calculation. The actual code we will use for this calculation looks like this:

```
var sourceX = Math.floor(animationFrames[frameIndex] % 8) *32;
```

The calculation for the sourceY value is similar, except we divide rather than use the modulo operation:

```
sourceY = integer(current_frame_index divided by
the_number_columns_in_the_tilesheet) *tile_height
```

Here is the actual code we will use for this calculation:

```
var sourceY = Math.floor(animationFrames[frameIndex] / 8) *32;
```

Looping Through the Tiles

We will update the frameIndex value on each frame tick. When frameIndex becomes greater than 7, we will set it back to 0:

```
frameIndex++;
    if (frameIndex == animationFrames.length) {
    frameIndex = 0;
    }
```

The animationFrames.length value is 8. When the frameIndex is equal to 8, we must set it back to 0 to start reading the array values over again, which creates an infinite animation loop.

Drawing the Tile

We will use drawImage() to place the new tile on the screen on each iteration:

```
context.drawImage(tileSheet, sourceX, sourceY,32,32,50,50,32,32);
```

Here, we are passing the calculated sourceX and sourceY values into the drawImage() function. We then pass in the width (32), the height (32), and the location (50,50) to draw the image on the canvas. Example 4-5 shows the full code.

Example 4-5. Advanced sprite animation

```
var tileSheet = new Image();
tileSheet.addEventListener('load', eventShipLoaded , false);

tileSheet.src = "tanks_sheet.png";

var animationFrames = [1,2,3,4,5,6,7,8];
var frameIndex = 0;
```

```
function eventShipLoaded() {
  startUp();
}

function drawScreen() {

  //draw a background so we can see the Canvas edges
  context.fillStyle = "#aaaaaa";
  context.fillRect(0,0,500,500);

  var sourceX = Math.floor(animationFrames[frameIndex] % 8) *32;
  var sourceY = Math.floor(animationFrames[frameIndex] / 8) *32;

  context.drawImage(tileSheet, sourceX, sourceY,32,32,50,50,32,32);

  frameIndex++;
  if (frameIndex ==animationFrames.length) {
     frameIndex=0;
  }

}

function startUp(){

  setInterval(drawScreen, 100 );
}
```

When we run the example, we will see the eight tile cell frames for the tank run in order and then repeat—the only problem is that the tank isn't going anywhere. Let's solve that little dilemma next and drive the tank up the screen.

Moving the Image Across the Canvas

Now that we have the tank tracks animating, let's "move" the tank. By animating the tank tracks and applying a simple movement vector to the tank's position, we can achieve the simulation of animated movement.

To do this, we first need to create variables to hold the current x and y positions of the tank. These represent the top-left corner where the tile from our sheet will be drawn to the canvas. In the previous examples, this number was set at 50 for each, so let's use that value here as well:

```
var x = 50;
var y = 50;
```

We also need a movement vector value for each axis. These are commonly known as deltaX (dx) and deltaY (dy). They represent the "delta" or "change" in the x or y axis position on each iteration. Our tank is currently facing in the "up" position, so we will use -1 for the dy and 0 for the dx:

```
var dx = 0;
var dy = -1;
```

The result is that on each frame tick, our tank will move *one* pixel up on the y-axis and *zero* pixels on the x-axis.

Inside drawScreen() (which is called on each frame tick), we will add the dx and dy values to the x and y values, and then apply them to the drawImage() function:

```
y = y+dy;
x = x+dx;
context.drawImage(tileSheet, sourceX, sourceY,32,32,x,y,32,32);
```

Rather than use the hardcoded 50,50 for the location of the drawImage() call on the canvas, we have replaced it with the current x,y position. Let's examine the entire code in Example 4-6.

Example 4-6. Sprite animation and movement

```
var tileSheet = new Image();
tileSheet.addEventListener('load', eventShipLoaded , false);
tileSheet.src = "tanks_sheet.png";

var animationFrames = [1,2,3,4,5,6,7,8];
var frameIndex = 0;
var dx = 0;
var dy = -1;
var x = 50;
var y = 50;

function eventShipLoaded() {
  startUp();
}

function drawScreen() {

  y = y+dy;
  x = x+dx;

  //draw a background so we can see the Canvas edges
  context.fillStyle = "#aaaaaa";
  context.fillRect(0,0,500,500);

  var sourceX = Math.floor(animationFrames[frameIndex] % 8) *32;
  var sourceY = Math.floor(animationFrames[frameIndex] / 8) *32;

  context.drawImage(tileSheet, sourceX, sourceY,32,32,x,y,32,32);

  frameIndex++;
  if (frameIndex==animationFrames.length) {
     frameIndex=0;
  }

}

function startUp(){
```

```
  setInterval(drawScreen, 100 );
}
```

By running this example, we see the tank move slowly up the canvas while its tracks play through the eight separate tiles of animation.

Our tile sheet only has images of the tank facing in the up position. If we want to have the tank move in other directions, we can do one of two things. The first option is to create more tiles on the tile sheet to represent the left, right, and down positions. However, this method requires much more work and creates a larger source image for the tile sheet. We are going to solve this problem in another way, which we will examine next.

Applying Rotation Transformations to an Image

In the previous section, we created an animation using tiles from a tile sheet. In this section, we will take it one step further and use the Canvas transformation matrix to rotate our image before drawing it to the canvas. This will allow us to use only a single set of animated tiles for all four (or more) rotated directions in which we would like to display our images. Before we write the code, let's examine what it will take to rotate our tank animation from the previous section.

 In Chapter 2, we dove into applying basic transformations when drawing with paths. The same concepts apply to transforming images on the canvas. If you have not read the section "Simple Canvas Transformations" on page 41 in Chapter 2, you might want to review it before reading on.

Canvas Transformation Basics

Although we covered basic Canvas transformations in detail in Chapter 2, let's review what's necessary to transform an individual object on the canvas. Remember, the canvas is a single immediate-mode drawing surface, so any transformations we make are applied to the entire canvas. In our example, we are drawing two objects. First, we draw a gray background rectangle, and then we copy the current tile from our tile sheet to the desired location. These are two discrete objects, but once they are on the canvas, they are both simply collections of pixels painted on the surface. Unlike Flash or other platforms that allow many separate sprites or "movie clips" to occupy the physical space, there is only one such object on Canvas: the *context*.

To compensate for this, we create logical display objects. Both the background and the tank are considered separate logical display objects. If we want to draw the tank but rotate it with a transformation matrix, we must separate the logical drawing operations by using the `save()` and `restore()` Canvas context functions.

Let's look at an example where we rotate the tank 90 degrees so it is facing to the right rather than up.

Step 1: Save the current context to the stack

The `save()` context function will take the current contents of the canvas (in our case the gray background rectangle) and store it away for "safekeeping":

```
context.save();
```

Once we have transformed the tank, we will replace it with the `restore()` function call.

Step 2: Reset the transformation matrix to identity

The next step in transforming an object is to clear the transformation matrix by passing it values that reset it to the identity values:

```
context.setTransform(1,0,0,1,0,0)
```

Step 3: Code the transform algorithm

Each transformation will be slightly different, but usually if you are rotating an object, you will want to translate the matrix to the center point of that object. Our tank will be positioned at 50,50 on the canvas, so we will translate it to 66,66. Since our tank is a 32×32 square tile, we simply add half of 32, or 16, to both the x and y location points:

```
context.translate(x+16, y+16);
```

Next, we need to find the angle in radians for the direction we want the tank to be rotated. For this example, we will choose 90 degrees:

```
var rotation = 90;
var angleInRadians = rotation * Math.PI / 180;
context.rotate(angleInRadians);
```

Step 4: Draw the image

When we draw the image, we must remember that the drawing's point of origin is no longer the 50,50 point from previous examples. Once the transformation matrix has been applied to translate to a new point, that point is now considered the 0,0 origin point for drawing.

This can be confusing at first, but it becomes clear with practice. To draw our image with 50,50 as the top-left coordinate, we must subtract 16 from the current position in both the x and y directions:

```
context.drawImage(tileSheet, sourceX, sourceY,32,32,-16,-16,32,32);
```

Example 4-7 adds in this rotation code to Example 4-4. When you run the example now, you will see the tank facing to the right.

Notice in Example 4-7 that we remove the original call to draw Screen() from the previous examples, and replace it with a new event listener function that is called after the tileSheet has been loaded. The new function is called eventShipLoaded().

Example 4-7. Rotation transformation

```
var tileSheet = new Image();
tileSheet.addEventListener('load', eventShipLoaded , false);

tileSheet.src = "tanks_sheet.png";

var animationFrames = [1,2,3,4,5,6,7,8];
var frameIndex = 0;
var rotation = 90;

var x = 50;
var y = 50;

function eventShipLoaded() {
   drawScreen();
}

function drawScreen() {

   //draw a background so we can see the Canvas edges
   context.fillStyle = "#aaaaaa";
   context.fillRect(0,0,500,500);

   context.save();
   context.setTransform(1,0,0,1,0,0)

   context.translate(x+16, y+16);
   var angleInRadians = rotation * Math.PI / 180;
   context.rotate(angleInRadians);

   var sourceX = Math.floor(animationFrames[frameIndex] % 8) *32;
   var sourceY = Math.floor(animationFrames[frameIndex] / 8) *32;

   context.drawImage(tileSheet, sourceX, sourceY,32,32,-16,-16,32,32);

   context.restore();

}

function eventShipLoaded() {
    drawScreen();
}
```

Figure 4-8 shows the output for this example.

Figure 4-8. Applying a rotation transformation

Let's take this one step further by applying the animation technique from Example 4-5 and looping through the eight tiles while facing the tank at the 90-degree angle.

Animating a Transformed Image

To apply a series of image tiles to the rotated context, we simply have to add back in the frame tick loop code and increment the `frameIndex` variable on each frame tick. Example 4-8 has added this into the code for Example 4-7.

Example 4-8. Animation and rotation

```
var tileSheet = new Image();
tileSheet.addEventListener('load', eventShipLoaded , false);

tileSheet.src = "tanks_sheet.png";

var animationFrames = [1,2,3,4,5,6,7,8];
var frameIndex = 0;
var rotation = 90;
```

```
var x = 50;
var y = 50;

function eventShipLoaded() {
  startUp();
}

function drawScreen() {

  //draw a background so we can see the Canvas edges
  context.fillStyle = "#aaaaaa";
  context.fillRect(0,0,500,500);

  context.save();
  context.setTransform(1,0,0,1,0,0)
  var angleInRadians = rotation * Math.PI / 180;
  context.translate(x+16, y+16)
  context.rotate(angleInRadians);
  var sourceX = Math.floor(animationFrames[frameIndex] % 8) *32;
  var sourceY = Math.floor(animationFrames[frameIndex] / 8) *32;

  context.drawImage(tileSheet, sourceX, sourceY,32,32,-16,-16,32,32);
  context.restore();
  frameIndex++;
  if (frameIndex==animationFrames.length) {
      frameIndex=0;
  }

}

function startUp(){

  setInterval(drawScreen, 100 );
}
```

When you test Example 4-8, you should see that the tank has rotated 90 degrees, and the tank tracks loop through their animation frames.

As we did in Example 4-6, let's move the tank in the direction it is facing. This time, it will move to the right until it goes off the screen. Example 4-9 has added back in the dx and dy movement vectors; notice that dx is now 1, and dy is now 0.

Example 4-9. Rotation, animation, and movement

```
var tileSheet = new Image();
tileSheet.addEventListener('load', eventShipLoaded , false);

tileSheet.src = "tanks_sheet.png";

var animationFrames = [1,2,3,4,5,6,7,8];
var frameIndex = 0;
var rotation = 90;
var x = 50;
var y = 50;
var dx = 1;
```

```
var dy = 0;

function eventShipLoaded() {
  startUp();
}

function drawScreen() {
   x = x+dx;
   y = y+dy;

   //draw a background so we can see the Canvas edges
   context.fillStyle = "#aaaaaa";
   context.fillRect(0,0,500,500);

   context.save();
   context.setTransform(1,0,0,1,0,0)
   var angleInRadians = rotation * Math.PI / 180;
   context.translate(x+16, y+16)
   context.rotate(angleInRadians);
   var sourceX=Math.floor(animationFrames[frameIndex] % 8) *32;
   var sourceY=Math.floor(animationFrames[frameIndex] / 8) *32;

   context.drawImage(tileSheet, sourceX, sourceY,32,32,-16,-16,32,32);
   context.restore();

   frameIndex++;
   if (frameIndex ==animationFrames.length) {
      frameIndex=0;
   }

}

function startUp(){

   setInterval(drawScreen, 100 );
}
```

When Example 4-9 is running, you will see the tank move slowly across the screen to the right. Its tracks animate through the series of tiles from the tile sheet on a plain gray background.

So far, we have only used tiles to simulate sprite-based animated movement. In the next section, we will examine how to use an image tile sheet to create a much more elaborate background using a series of tiles.

Creating a Grid of Tiles

Many games use what is called a *tile-based environment* for backgrounds and level graphics. We are now going to apply the knowledge we have learned from animating an image on the canvas to create the background maze for our hypothetical game: *No Tanks!* We will use the same tile sheet from the previous tank examples, but instead of showing the tank sprite tiles, we will create a maze for the tank to move through. We will not actually cover the game-play portion of the code in this chapter because we want to focus on using images to render the screen. In Chapter 9 we will create a simple game using the type of examples shown here.

Defining a Tile Map

We will use the term *tile map* to refer to a game level or background built from a tile sheet. Take a look back at Figure 4-7—the four row by eight column tile sheet from earlier in this chapter. If we were to create a maze-chase game similar to *Pac-Man*, we could define the maze using tiles from a tile sheet. The sequence of tiles for our game maze would be considered a tile map.

The first tile is a gray square, which we can use for the "road" tiles between the wall tiles. Any tile that a game sprite can move on is referred to as *walkable*. Even though our tanks are not literally walking but driving, the concept is the same. In Chapter 9 we will create a small game using these concepts, but for now, let's concentrate on defining a tile map and displaying it on the canvas.

Our tile map will be a two-dimensional array of tile id numbers. If you recall, the tile id numbers for our tile sheet are in a single dimension, numbering from 0 to 31. Let's say we are going to create a very small game screen consisting of 10 tiles in length and 10 tiles in height. This means we need to define a tile map of 100 individual tiles (10×10). If our tiles are 32 pixels by 32 pixels, we will define a 320×320 game screen.

There are many ways to define a tile map. One simple way is to use a tile map editor program to lay out a grid of tiles, and then export the data to re-create the tile map in JavaScript. This is precisely how we are going to create our tile map.

Creating a Tile Map with Tiled

The program we are going to use, Tiled, is a great tile map editor that is available for Mac OS, Windows, and Linux. Of course, tile maps can be designed by hand, but map creation is much easier if we utilize a program such as Tiled to do some of the legwork for us. Tiled is available for free under the GNU free software license from *http://www .mapeditor.org/*.

 As stated before, you do not need to use this software. Tile maps can be created with other good (and free) software such as Mappy (*http://tile map.co.uk/mappy.php*) and Tile Studio (*http://tilestudio.sourceforge .net/*), and even by hand using MS Paint.

The goal of creating a tile map is to visually lay out a grid of tiles that represents the game screen, and then export the tile ids that represent those tiles. We will use the exported data as a two-dimensional array in our code to build the tile map on the canvas.

Here are the basic steps for creating a simple tile map in Tiled for use in the following section:

1. Create a new tile map from the File menu. When it asks for Orientation, select Orthogonal with a Map Size of 10×10 and a Tile Size of 32×32.

2. From the Map menu, import the *tanks_sheet.png* to be used as the tile set. Select "New tileset" from this menu, and give it any name you want. Browse to find the *tanks_sheet.png* that you downloaded from this book's website. Make sure that Tile Width and Tile Height are both 32; keep the Margin and Spacing both at 0.

3. Select a tile from the tile set on the bottom-right side of the screen. Once selected, you can click and "paint" the tile by selecting a location on the tile map on the top-left side of the screen. Figure 4-9 shows the tile map created for this example.

4. Save the tile map. Tiled uses a plain text file format called *.tmx*. Normally, tile data in Tiled is saved out in a base-64-binary file format; however, we can change this by editing the preferences for Tiled. On a Mac, under the Tiled menu, there should be a Preferences section. (If you are using the software on Windows or Linux, you will find this in the File menu.) When setting the preferences, select CSV in the "Store tile layer data as" drop-down menu. Once you have done this, you can save the file from the File menu.

Here is a look at what the saved *.tmx* file will look like in a text editor:

```
<?xml version="1.0" encoding="UTF-8"?>
<map version="1.0" orientation="orthogonal" width="10" height="10"
        tilewidth="32" tileheight="32">
  <tileset firstgid="1" name="tanks" tilewidth="32" tileheight="32">
  <image source="tanks_sheet.png"/>
  </tileset>
  <layer name="Tile Layer 1" width="10" height="10">
  <data encoding="csv">
32,31,31,31,1,31,31,31,31,32,
1,1,1,1,1,1,1,1,1,1,
32,1,26,1,26,1,26,1,1,32,
32,26,1,1,26,1,1,26,1,32,
32,1,1,1,26,26,1,26,1,32,
32,1,1,26,1,1,1,26,1,32,
32,1,1,1,1,1,1,26,1,32,
1,1,26,1,26,1,26,1,1,1,
32,1,1,1,1,1,1,1,1,32,
32,31,31,31,1,31,31,31,31,32
</data>
</layer>
</map>
```

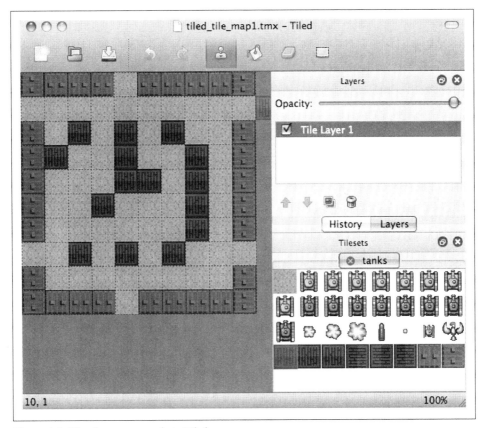

Figure 4-9. The tile map example in Tiled

The data is an XML data set used to load and save tile maps. Because of the open nature of this format and the simple sets of row data for the tile map, we can use this data easily in JavaScript. For now, we are only concerned with the 10 rows of comma-delimited numbers inside the `<data>` node of the XML—we can take those rows of data and create a very simple two-dimensional array to use in our code.

Displaying the Map on the Canvas

The first thing to note about the data from Tiled is that it is *1 relative*, not 0 relative. This means that the tiles are numbered from 1–32 instead of 0–31. We can compensate for this by subtracting one from each value as we transcribe it to our array, or programmatically during our tile sheet drawing operation. We will do it programmatically by creating an offset variable to be used during the draw operation:

```
var mapIndexOffset = -1;
```

Rather than using the `mapIndexOffset` variable, we could loop through the array of data and subtract 1 from each value. This would be done before the game begins, saving the extra processor overload from performing this math operation on each tile when it is displayed.

Map height and width

We also are going to create two variables to give flexibility to our tile map display code. These might seem simple and unnecessary now, but if you get in the habit of using variables for the height and width of the tile map, it will be much easier to change its size in the future.

We will keep track of the width and height based on the number of rows in the map and the number of columns in each row:

```
var mapRows = 10;
var mapCols = 10;
```

Storing the map data

The data that was output from Tiled was a series of rows of numbers starting in the top left and moving left to right, then down when the rightmost column in a row was completed. We can use this data almost exactly as output by placing it in a two-dimensional array:

```
var tileMap = [
       [32,31,31,31,1,31,31,31,31,32]
     , [1,1,1,1,1,1,1,1,1,1]
     , [32,1,26,1,26,1,26,1,1,32]
     , [32,26,1,1,26,1,1,26,1,32]
     , [32,1,1,1,26,26,1,26,1,32]
     , [32,1,1,26,1,1,1,26,1,32]
     , [32,1,1,1,1,1,1,26,1,32]
     , [1,1,26,1,26,1,26,1,1,1]
     , [32,1,1,1,1,1,1,1,1,32]
     , [32,31,31,31,1,31,31,31,31,32]

     ];
```

Displaying the map on the canvas

When we display the tile map, we simply loop through the rows in the `tileMap` array, and then loop through the columns in each row. The `tileID` number at `[row]` `[column]` will be the tile to copy from the tile sheet to the canvas. `row *32` will be the y location to place the tile on the canvas; `col*32` will be the x location to place the tile:

The row, column referencing might seem slightly confusing because row is the *y* direction and column is the *x* direction. We do this because our tiles are organized into a two-dimensional array. The row is always the first subscript when accessing a 2D array.

```
for (var rowCtr=0;rowCtr<mapRows;rowCtr++) {
    for (var colCtr=0;colCtr<mapCols;colCtr++){

        var tileId = tileMap[rowCtr][colCtr]+mapIndexOffset;
        var sourceX = Math.floor(tileId % 8) *32;
        var sourceY = Math.floor(tileId / 8) *32;

        context.drawImage(tileSheet, sourceX,
          sourceY,32,32,colCtr*32,rowCtr*32,32,32);
    }

}
```

We use the `mapRows` and the `mapCols` variables to loop through the data and to paint it to the canvas. This makes it relatively simple to modify the height and width of the tile map without having to find the hardcoded values in the code. We could have also done this with other values such as the tile width and height, as well as the number of tiles per row in the tile sheet (8).

The `sourceX` and `sourceY` values for the tile to copy are found in the same way as in the previous examples. This time, though, we find the `tileId` using the `[rowCtr][colCtr]` two-dimensional lookup, and then adding the `mapIndexOffset`. The offset is a negative number (-1), so this effectively subtracts 1 from each tile map value, resulting in 0-relative map values that are easier to work with. Example 4-10 shows this concept in action, and Figure 4-10 illustrates the results.

Example 4-10. Rotation, animation, and movement

```
var tileSheet = new Image();
tileSheet.addEventListener('load', eventSheetLoaded , false);

tileSheet.src = "tanks_sheet.png";

var mapIndexOffset = -1;
var mapRows = 10;
var mapCols = 10;

var tileMap = [
      [32,31,31,31,1,31,31,31,31,32]
    , [1,1,1,1,1,1,1,1,1,1]
    , [32,1,26,1,26,1,26,1,1,32]
    , [32,26,1,1,26,1,1,26,1,32]
    , [32,1,1,1,26,26,1,26,1,32]
    , [32,1,1,26,1,1,1,26,1,32]
    , [32,1,1,1,1,1,1,26,1,32]
    , [1,1,26,1,26,1,26,1,1,1]
    , [32,1,1,1,1,1,1,1,1,32]
```

```
        ,   [32,31,31,31,1,31,31,31,31,32]
    ];

function eventSheetLoaded() {
    drawScreen()
}

function drawScreen() {
    for (var rowCtr=0;rowCtr<mapRows;rowCtr++) {
        for (var colCtr=0;colCtr<mapCols;colCtr++){

            var tileId = tileMap[rowCtr][colCtr]+mapIndexOffset;
            var sourceX = Math.floor(tileId % 8) *32;
            var sourceY = Math.floor(tileId / 8) *32;

            context.drawImage(tileSheet, sourceX,
            sourceY,32,32,colCtr*32,rowCtr*32,32,32);
        }

    }
}
```

Figure 4-10. The tile map painted on the canvas

Next, we are going to leave the world of tile-based Canvas development (see Chapter 9 for an example of a small game developed with these principles). The final section of this chapter discusses building our own simple tile map editor. But before we get there, let's look at panning around and zooming in and out of an image.

Zooming and Panning an Image

In this section, we will examine some methods to zoom and pan an image on the canvas. The image we are going to use is from a recent vacation to Central California. It is a large *.jpg* file, measuring 3648×2736. Obviously, this is far too large to view in a single canvas, so we will build a simple application allowing us to zoom and pan the image on our 500×500 canvas.

Figure 4-11 is a scaled-down version of this image.

Figure 4-11. A scaled-down version of the image we will zoom and pan

Creating a Window for the Image

The first thing we are going to do is create a logical window, the size of the canvas, where our image will reside. We will use the following two variables to control the dimensions of this window:

```
var windowWidth = 500;
var windowHeight = 500;
```

We will also create two variables to define the current top-left corner for the window. When we move on to the panning examples, we will modify these values to redraw the image based on this location:

```
var windowX = 0;
var windowY = 0;
```

Drawing the Image Window

To draw the image window, we will simply modify the standard `context.drawImage()` function call using the values in the four variables we just defined:

```
context.drawImage(photo, windowX, windowY, windowWidth, windowHeight, 0, 0,
    windowWidth,windowHeight);
```

Let's take a closer look at this for a refresher on how the `drawImage()` function operates. The values are passed in order:

photo
> The image instance we are going to use as our source for painting onto the canvas

windowX
> The top-left x location to start copying from the source image

windowY
> The top-left y location to start copying from the source image

windowWidth
> The width of the rectangle to start copying from the source image

windowHeight
> The height of the rectangle to start copying from the source image

0
> The top-left x destination location for the image on the canvas

0
> The top-left y destination location for the image on the canvas

windowWidth
> The width in pixels for the destination copy (this can be modified to scale the image)

windowHeight
> The height in pixels for the destination copy (this can be modified to scale the image)

When we draw from the image to the canvas, we will be modifying the `windowX` and `windowY` values to create a panning effect. Example 4-11 demonstrates how to get the image onto the canvas with the window location set to 0,0. Figure 4-12 shows an example of the output for Example 4-11.

Example 4-11. Placing an image on the canvas in a logical window

```
var photo = new Image();
photo.addEventListener('load', eventPhotoLoaded , false);

photo.src = "butterfly.jpg";

var windowWidth = 500;
var windowHeight = 500;

var windowX = 0;
var windowY = 0;

function eventPhotoLoaded() {
   drawScreen()
}

function drawScreen(){
  context.drawImage(photo, windowX, windowY, windowWidth, windowHeight,
    0, 0, windowWidth,windowHeight);
}
```

Figure 4-12. An image in a small logical window

Panning the Image

To pan the window across the image, we simply need to modify the windowX and windowY coordinates. In Example 4-12, we will modify the windowX coordinate inside a frame tick interval. During each loop iteration, we will increase the value of windowX by 10. We need to be careful not to go off the far right side of the image, so we will subtract the windowWidth from the image.width, and use the result as the maximum windowX position:

```
windowX+ = 10;
if (windowX>photo.width - windowWidth){
   windowX = photo.width - windowWidth;
}
```

Example 4-12 contains the changes necessary to perform this panning operation.

Example 4-12. Simple image panning

```
var photo = new Image();
photo.addEventListener('load', eventPhotoLoaded , false);

photo.src = "butterfly.jpg";

var windowWidth = 500;
var windowHeight = 500;

var windowX = 0;
var windowY = 0;

function eventPhotoLoaded() {
   startUp();
}

function drawScreen(){

   context.drawImage(photo, windowX, windowY, windowWidth, windowHeight,
      0,0,windowWidth,windowHeight);

   windowX += 10;
   if (windowX>photo.width - windowWidth){
      windowX = photo.width - windowWidth;
   }

}

function startUp(){

   setInterval(drawScreen, 100 );
}
```

When you test Example 4-12, you will see the window pan across the image and stop at the rightmost edge. Next, we will start to implement zooming into this simple example.

Zoom and Pan the Image

To zoom in or out of an image, we need to change the final `width` and `height` values of the `drawImage()` function. Let's examine how we would zoom out to 50% of the original size of the image while panning at the same time. The `drawImage()` function will look like this:

```
context.drawImage(photo, windowX, windowY, windowWidth, windowHeight,
    0, 0, windowWidth*.5,windowHeight*.5);
```

Example 4-13 modifies Example 4-12 and adds in the 50% zoom.

Example 4-13. Pan an image with a preset zoom out

```
var photo = new Image();
photo.addEventListener('load', eventPhotoLoaded , false);

photo.src = "butterfly.jpg";
var windowWidth = 500;
var windowHeight = 500;

var windowX = 0;
var windowY = 0;

function eventPhotoLoaded() {
    startUp();
}

function drawScreen(){

    context.drawImage(photo, windowX, windowY, windowWidth, windowHeight,
        0,0,windowWidth*.5,windowHeight*.5);

    windowX += 10;
    if (windowX>photo.width - windowWidth){
        windowX = photo.width - windowWidth;
    }

}

function startUp(){

    setInterval(drawScreen, 100 );
}
```

When we test this example, we will see that when zoomed out, the image on the canvas is 50% of its original size. To zoom in, we simply change the scale factor from `.5` to a number greater than 1:

```
context.drawImage(photo, windowX, windowY, windowWidth,windowHeight,
    0,0,windowWidth*2,windowHeight*2);
```

Example 4-14 changes this single line from Example 4-13 to zoom in rather than zoom out.

Example 4-14. Pan an image with a preset zoom amount

```
var photo = new Image();
photo.addEventListener('load', eventPhotoLoaded , false);

photo.src = "butterfly.jpg";

var windowWidth = 500;
var windowHeight = 500;

var windowX = 0;
var windowY = 0;


function eventPhotoLoaded() {
   startUp();
}

function drawScreen(){

   context.drawImage(photo, windowX, windowY, windowWidth, windowHeight,
      0,0,windowWidth*2,windowHeight*2);

   windowX += 10;
   if (windowX>photo.width - windowWidth){
      windowX = photo.width - windowWidth;
   }
}

function startUp(){

   setInterval(drawScreen, 100 );
}
```

Application: Controlled Pan and Zoom

Our final example for this section will be a simple application allowing the user to zoom and pan a photo.

The zoom scale

We are going to create a set of variables to handle the current zoom scale, the factor by which the zoom scale is increased or decreased, as well as the maximum and minimum zoom values:

```
var currentScale = .5;
var minScale = .2;
var maxScale = 3;
var scaleIncrement = .1;
```

We will apply these values to the drawImage() function:

```
context.drawImage(photo, windowX, windowY, windowWidth, windowHeight,
   0,0,windowWidth*currentScale,windowHeight*currentScale);
```

Keyboard input

Now we need to create a keyboard listener function. The following function seems to work best in all browsers tested—it's certainly not the only keyboard event listener, but it is tried and true throughout this book:

```
document.onkeydown = function(e){
    e = e?e:window.event;
}
```

 This function utilizes the *ternary operator*. If the statement before the ? is true, the statement following the ? is executed. If it is false, the statement after the : is executed. This is a shorthand version of the classic if/else construct.

We will add a switch/case statement, combining all the functions we have put into the previous zoom and pan examples, along with a new set of code for the *y* direction panning that we have not implemented before. It is very similar to the *x* direction panning: the left arrow key will pan the image to the left; the right arrow key will pan the image to the right:

```
case 38:
      //up
      windowY-=10;
      if (windowY<0){
          windowY = 0;
      }
      break;
case 40:
      //down
      windowY+=10;
      if (windowY>photo.height - windowHeight){
          windowY = photo.height - windowHeight;
      }
      break;
case 37:
      //left
      windowX-=10;
      if (windowX<0){
          windowX = 0;
      }
      break;
case 39:
       //right
      windowX+=10;
      if (windowX>photo.width - windowWidth){
          windowX = photo.width - windowWidth;
      }
      break;
```

We also need to add in two cases for the + and - keys to perform zoom in and zoom out actions:

```
case 109:
    //-
    currentScale-=scaleIncrement;
    if (currentScale<minScale){
        currentScale = minScale;
    }
    break;
case 107:
    //+
    currentScale+=scaleIncrement;
    if (currentScale>maxScale){
        currentScale = maxScale;
    }
```

When the user presses the + or - key, the currentScale variable is either incremented or decremented by the scaleIncrement value. If the new value of currentScale is greater than maxScale or lower than minScale, we set it to maxScale or minScale, respectively.

Example 4-15 puts this entire application together. It doesn't take many lines of code to create the simple interactions.

Example 4-15. Image pan and zoom application

```
var photo = new Image();
photo.addEventListener('load', eventPhotoLoaded , false);

photo.src = "butterfly.jpg";

var windowWidth = 500;
var windowHeight = 500;

var windowX = 0;
var windowY = 0;
var currentScale = .5;
var minScale = .2;
var maxScale = 3;
var scaleIncrement = .1;

function eventPhotoLoaded() {
    startUp();
}

function drawScreen(){

    //draw a background so we can see the Canvas edges
    context.fillStyle = "#ffffff";
    context.fillRect(0,0,500,500);
```

```
        context.drawImage(photo, windowX, windowY, windowWidth, windowHeight,
          0,0,windowWidth*currentScale,windowHeight*currentScale);

}

function startUp(){

    setInterval(drawScreen, 100 );
}

document.onkeydown = function(e){

    e = e?e:window.event;
    console.log(e.keyCode + "down");

    switch (e.keyCode){
        case 38:
            //up
            windowY-=10;
            if (windowY<0){
                windowY = 0;
            }
            break;
        case 40:
            //down
            windowY+=10;
            if (windowY>photo.height - windowHeight){
                windowY = photo.height - windowHeight;
            }
            break;
        case 37:
            //left
            windowX-=10;
            if (windowX<0){
                windowX = 0;
            }
            break;
        case 39:
            //right
            windowX+=10;
            if (windowX>photo.width - windowWidth){
                windowX = photo.width - windowWidth;
            }
            break;
        case 109:
            //-
            currentScale-=scaleIncrement;
            if (currentScale<minScale){
                currentScale = minScale;
            }
            break;
```

```
    case 107:
        //+
        currentScale+=scaleIncrement;
        if (currentScale>maxScale){
            currentScale = maxScale;
        }
    }

}
```

When testing Example 4-15, use the arrow keys to pan across the photo, and the +
and - keys to zoom in and out.

Pixel Manipulation

In this section, we will first examine the Canvas Pixel Manipulation API, and then build
a simple application demonstrating how to manipulate pixels on the canvas in real time.

The Canvas Pixel Manipulation API

The Canvas Pixel Manipulation API gives us the ability to "get," "put," and "change"
individual pixels utilizing what is known as the `CanvasPixelArray` interface. `ImageData`
is the base object type for this manipulation, and an instance of this object is created
with the `createImageData()` function call. Let's start there.

The `createImageData()` function sets aside a portion of memory to store individual
pixels' worth of data based on the following three constructors:

imagedata = context.`createImageData(`*sw, sh)*
> The *sw* and *sh* parameters represent the `width` and `height` values for the Image
> Data object. For example, `imagedata=createImageData(100,100)` would create a
> 100×100 area of memory in which to store pixel data.

imagedata = context.`createImageData(`*imagedata)*
> The *imagedata* parameter represents a separate instance of `ImageData`. This con-
> structor creates a new `ImageData` object with the same width and height as the
> parameter `ImageData`.

imagedata = context.`createImageData()`
> This constructor returns a blank `ImageData` instance.

ImageData attributes

An `ImageData` object contains three attributes:

`ImageData.height`
> This returns the height in pixels of the `ImageData` instance.

`ImageData.width`
> This returns the width in pixels of the `ImageData` instance.

`ImageData.data`

This returns a single dimensional array of pixels representing the image data. Image data is stored with 32-bit color information for each pixel, meaning that every fourth number in this data array starts a new pixel. The four elements in the array represent the red, green, blue, and alpha transparency values of a single pixel.

Getting image data

To retrieve a set of pixel data from the canvas and put it into an `ImageData` instance, we use the `getImageData()` function call:

```
imagedata = context.getImageData(sx, sy, sw, sh)
```

sx, *sy*, *sw*, and *sh* define the location and size of the source rectangle to copy from the canvas to the `ImageData` instance.

 A security error will be thrown if the origin domain of an image file is not the same as the origin domain of the web page. This affects local files (when running on your hard drive rather than on a web server running locally or on a remote server), as most browsers will treat local image files as though they are from a different domain than the web page. When running on a web server, this error will not be thrown with local files. The current version of Safari (5.02) does not throw this error for local files.

Putting image data

To copy the pixels from an `ImageData` instance to the canvas, we use the `putImageData()` function call. There are two different constructors for this call:

```
context.putImageData (imagedata, dx, dy)
context.putImageData (imagedata, dx, dy [, dirtyX, dirtyY,
                      dirtyWidth, dirtyHeight ])
```

The first constructor simply paints the entire `ImageData` instance to the `destinationX` (`dx`) and `destinationY` (`dy`) locations. The second constructor does the same, but allows the passage of a "dirty rectangle," which represents the area of the `ImageData` to paint to the canvas.

Application Tile Stamper

We are going to create a simple application that will allow the user to highlight a box around some pixels on an image, copy them, and then use them as a stamp to paint back to the canvas. It will not be a full-blown editing application by any means—it's just a demonstration of one use of the `ImageData` object.

This application will need to be run from a local or remote web server, as most browsers will throw an exception if an application attempts to call `getImageData()` on a file—even in the same folder on a local machine. The current version of Safari (5.02) does not throw this error.

To create this simple application, we will use the tile sheet from earlier in this chapter. The user will click on a spot on the tile sheet, highlighting a 32×32 square tile. That tile can then be painted onto the bottom section of the canvas. To demonstrate pixel manipulation, we will set the color of the pixels to a new alpha value before they are painted to the screen. This will be the humble beginning to making our own tile map editor.

Once again, we will use the *tanks_sheet.png* file from Figure 4-7.

How ImageData.data is organized

The `ImageData.data` attribute is a single-dimensional array containing four bytes for every pixel in the `ImageData` object. We will be using 32×32 tiles in our example application. A 32×32 tile contains 1,024 pixels (or 1K of data). The `ImageData.data` attribute for an `ImageData` instance that holds a 32×32 image would be 4,096 bytes (or 4K). This is because a separate byte is used to store each of the red, green, blue, and alpha values for each pixel. In our application, we will loop through each pixel and set its alpha value to 128. Here is the code we will use:

```
for (j=3; j< imageData.data.length; j+=4){
    imageData.data[j] = 128;
}
```

We start our loop at 3, which is the fourth attribute in the array. The single-dimensional array contains a continuous set of values for each pixel, so index 3 represents the alpha value for the first pixel (because the array is 0 relative). Our loop then skips to every fourth value in the array and sets it to 128. Once the loop is complete, all pixels will have an alpha value of 128.

As opposed to other Canvas alpha manipulations where the alpha value is between 0 and 1, the alpha value is between 0 and 255 when manipulating it via the pixel color values.

A visual look at our basic application

Figure 4-13 is a screenshot of the simple Tile Stamper application we will create.

Figure 4-13 is running in Safari 5.1 locally. As of this writing, this is the only browser that does not throw an exception when trying to manipulate the pixel data of a locally loaded file when not run on a web server.

Figure 4-13. The Tile Stamper application

The screen is broken up into two sections vertically. The top section is the 256×128 tile sheet; the bottom is a tile map of the same size. The user will select a tile in the top section, and it will be highlighted by a red square. The user can then stamp the selected tile to the tile map drawing area in the lower portion. When a tile is drawn in this lower portion, we will set its alpha value to 128.

Adding mouse events to the canvas

We need to code our application to respond to mouse clicks and to keep track of the current x and y positions of the mouse pointer. We will set up two global application scope variables to store the mouse pointer's current position:

```
var mouseX;
var mouseY;
```

We will also set up two event listener functions and attach them to the theCanvas object:

```
theCanvas.addEventListener("mousemove", onMouseMove, false);
theCanvas.addEventListener("click", onMouseClick, false);
```

In the HTML, we will set up a single Canvas object:

```
<canvas id="canvas" width="256" height="256"  style="position: absolute;
    top: 50px; left: 50px;">
 Your browser does not support HTML5 Canvas.
</canvas>
```

In the JavaScript portion of our code, we will define the canvas:

```
theCanvas = document.getElementById("canvas");
```

Notice that we set the <canvas> position to top: 50px and left: 50px. This will keep the application from being shoved up into the top-left corner of the browser, but it also gives us a chance to demonstrate how to find correct mouse x and y values when the <canvas> tag is not in the top-left corner of the page. The onMouseMove function will make use of this information to offset the mouseX and mouseY values based on the position of the <canvas> tag:

```
function onMouseMove(e) {
    mouseX = e.clientX-theCanvas.offsetLeft;
    mouseY = e.clientY-theCanvas.offsetTop;
}
```

The onMouseClick function will actually do quite a lot in our application. When the mouse button is clicked, this function will determine whether the user clicked on the tile sheet or on the tile map drawing area below it. If the user clicked on the tile sheet, the function will determine which exact tile was clicked. It will then call the highlightTile() function and pass in the id (0–31) of the tile clicked, along with the x and y locations for the top-left corner of the tile.

If the user clicked in the lower portion of the tile map drawing area, this function will again determine which tile the user clicked on, and stamp the current selected tile in that location on the tile map. Here is the function:

```
function onMouseClick(e) {

    if (mouseY < 128){
        //find tile to highlight
        var col = Math.floor(mouseX / 32);
        var row = Math.floor(mouseY / 32);
        var tileId = (row*7)+(col+row);
        highlightTile(tileId,col*32,row*32)
    }else{
        var col = Math.floor(mouseX / 32);
        var row = Math.floor(mouseY / 32);
        context.putImageData(imageData,col*32,row*32);
    }
}
```

Let's take a closer look at the tile sheet click (mouseY < 128).

To determine the tileId of the tile clicked on the tile sheet, we first need to convert the x location of the mouse click to a number from 0–7, and the y location to a number from 0–3. We do this by calling the Math.floor function on the result of the current mouseX or mouseY location, divided by the tile width or height (they are both 32). This will find the row and col of the clicked tile:

```
var col = Math.floor(mouseX / 32);
var row = Math.floor(mouseY / 32)
```

To find the tileId (the 0–31 tile number of the tile sheet) of this row and column combination, we need to use the following calculation:

```
TileId = (row*totalRows-1) + (col+row);
```

The actual calculation, with values for our application, looks like this:

```
var tileId = (row*7)+(col+row);
```

For example, if the user clicks on the point where mouseX = 50 and mouseY = 15, the calculation would work like this:

```
col = Math.floor(50/32);    // col = 1
row = Math.floor(15/32);    // row = 0
tileId = (0*7)+(1+0);       // tileId = 1
```

This position is the second tile on the tile sheet. The onMouseClick() function then passes the tileId and col value multiplied by 32, and the row value multiplied by 32, into the highlightTile() function. This tells the highlightTile() function the exact tileId, row, and col the user clicked.

If the user clicked the tile map drawing area in the lower portion of the screen, the code does the same row and column calculation. However, it then calls the putImage Data() function and passes in the ImageData instance that holds the tile to stamp and the top-left location to place the tile:

```
var col = Math.floor(mouseX / 32);
var row = Math.floor(mouseY / 32);
context.putImageData(imageData,col*32,row*32);
```

The highlightTile() function

The highlightTile() function accepts three parameters:

- The 0–31 tileId of the tile on the tile sheet
- The top-left x coordinate of the tile represented by the tileId
- The top-left y coordinate of the tile represented by the tileId

 The x and y coordinates can be found by passing in the tileId value, but they are needed in the onMouseDown function, so we pass them in from there when calling highlightTile(). This way, we do not need to perform the calculation twice.

The first task highlightTile() tackles is redrawing the tile sheet at the top of the screen:

```
context.fillStyle = "#aaaaaa";
context.fillRect(0,0,256,128);
drawTileSheet();
```

It does this to delete the red box around the current tile, while preparing to draw a new red box around the tile represented by the tileId passed in.

The drawTileSheet() function then paints the *tanks_sheet.png* file to the canvas starting at 0,0:

```
function drawTileSheet(){
    context.drawImage(tileSheet, 0, 0);
}
```

Next, the highlightTile() function copies the new pixel data (with no red line around it yet) from the canvas and places it in the ImageData instance:

```
ImageData = context.getImageData(x,y,32,32);
```

The ImageData variable now contains a copy of the pixel data for the tile from the canvas. We then loop through the pixels in ImageData.data (as described previously in "How ImageData.data is organized" on page 160), and set the alpha value of each to 128.

Finally, now that the ImageData variable contains the correct pixels with the altered alpha values, we can draw the red line around the tile that's been selected to stamp on the tile map:

```
var startX = Math.floor(tileId % 8) *32;
var startY = Math.floor(tileId / 8) *32;
context.strokeStyle = "red";
context.strokeRect(startX,startY,32,32)
```

Example 4-16 is the entire set of code for this application.

Example 4-16. The Tile Stamper application

```
<!doctype html>
<html lang="en">
<head>
<meta charset="UTF-8">
<title>CH4EX16: Tile Stamper Application</title>
<script src="modernizr-1.6.min.js"></script>
<script type="text/javascript">
window.addEventListener('load', eventWindowLoaded, false);
function eventWindowLoaded() {

   canvasApp();

}


function canvasSupport () {
  return Modernizr.canvas;
}

function canvasApp(){

   if (!canvasSupport()) {
        return;
   }else{
      var theCanvas = document.getElementById("canvas");
      var context = theCanvas.getContext("2d");
   }

   var mouseX;
   var mouseY;

   var tileSheet = new Image();
   tileSheet.addEventListener('load', eventSheetLoaded , false);
   tileSheet.src = "tanks_sheet.png";
```

```
var imageData = context.createImageData(32,32);

function eventSheetLoaded() {
    startUp();
}

function startUp(){
    context.fillStyle = "#aaaaaa";
    context.fillRect(0,0,256,256);
    drawTileSheet();
}

function drawTileSheet(){
    context.drawImage(tileSheet, 0, 0);

}

function highlightTile(tileId,x,y){
    context.fillStyle = "#aaaaaa";
    context.fillRect(0,0,256,128);
    drawTileSheet();

    imageData = context.getImageData(x,y,32,32);
    //loop through imageData.data. Set every 4th value to a new value
    for (j=3; j< imageData.data.length; j+=4){
        imageData.data[j]=128;
    }

    var startX = Math.floor(tileId % 8) *32;
    var startY = Math.floor(tileId / 8) *32;
    context.strokeStyle = "red";
    context.strokeRect(startX,startY,32,32)
}

function onMouseMove(e) {
    mouseX = e.clientX-theCanvas.offsetLeft;
    mouseY = e.clientY-theCanvas.offsetTop;

}

function onMouseClick(e) {
    console.log("click: " + mouseX + "," + mouseY);
    if (mouseY < 128){
        //find tile to highlight
        var col = Math.floor(mouseX / 32);
        var row = Math.floor(mouseY / 32)
        var tileId = (row*7)+(col+row);
        highlightTile(tileId,col*32,row*32)
    }else{
        var col = Math.floor(mouseX / 32);
        var row = Math.floor(mouseY / 32);

        context.putImageData(imageData,col*32,row*32);
```

```
      }
   }

   theCanvas.addEventListener("mousemove", onMouseMove, false);
   theCanvas.addEventListener("click", onMouseClick, false);

}

</script>
</head>
<body>
<div>
<canvas id="canvas" width="256" height="256"  style="position: absolute;
    top: 50px; left: 50px;">
 Your browser does not support HTML5 Canvas.
</canvas>
</div>
</body>
</html>
```

 As of this writing, you must run this application from a web server in order to manipulate the local *tanks_sheet.png* file on the canvas. If you are using the Safari browser (version 5.1 as of this writing), you can test the application on a local drive and it will function properly.

Copying from One Canvas to Another

The canvas allows us to use another canvas as the source of a bitmap drawing operation. Let's take a quick look at how we might utilize this functionality.

We will need to modify the base file for this chapter and create an extra <canvas> tag in our HTML. We will name this extra <canvas> element canvas2 (it can be given any id as long as it is not the same id as the first <canvas>). Here is what our HTML <body> will look like now:

```
<body>
<div>
<canvas id="canvas" width="256" height="256"  style="position: absolute;
    top: 50px; left: 50px;">Your browser does not support HTML5 Canvas.</canvas>
<canvas id="canvas2" width="32" height="32"  style="position: absolute;
    top: 256px; left: 50px;">Your browser does not support HTML5 Canvas.</canvas>
</div>
</body>
```

We will place the second <canvas> below the original, and give it a width and height of 32. We will also need to create a new context and internal reference variable for canvas2. Here is the code that will be used to provide a reference to both <canvas> elements:

```
if (!canvasSupport()) {
    return;
```

```
        }else{

            var theCanvas = document.getElementById("canvas");
            var context = theCanvas.getContext("2d");
            var theCanvas2 = document.getElementById("canvas2");
            var context2 = theCanvas2.getContext("2d");

    }
```

Example 4-17 will use the tile sheet image from earlier examples and draw it to the first canvas. It will then copy a 32×32 square from this canvas and place it on the second canvas.

Example 4-17. Copying from one canvas to another

```
<!doctype html>
<html lang="en">
<head>
<meta charset="UTF-8">
<title>CH4EX17: Canvas Copy</title>
<script src="modernizr-1.6.min.js"></script>
<script type="text/javascript">
window.addEventListener('load', eventWindowLoaded, false);
function eventWindowLoaded() {

    canvasApp();

}

function canvasSupport () {

        return Modernizr.canvas;

}

function canvasApp(){
    if (!canvasSupport()) {
        return;
    }else{
        var theCanvas = document.getElementById("canvas");
        var context = theCanvas.getContext("2d");
        var theCanvas2 = document.getElementById("canvas2");
        var context2 = theCanvas2.getContext("2d");
    }

    var tileSheet = new Image();
    tileSheet.addEventListener('load', eventSheetLoaded , false);
    tileSheet.src="tanks_sheet.png";


    function eventSheetLoaded() {

        startUp();
    }
```

```
        function startUp(){
            context.drawImage(tileSheet, 0, 0);
            context2.drawImage(theCanvas, 32, 0,32,32,0,0,32,32);
        }
    }
</script>
</head>
<body>
<div>
<canvas id="canvas" width="256" height="256"  style="position: absolute;
    top: 50px; left: 50px;"> Your browser does not support HTML5 Canvas.</canvas>

<canvas id="canvas2" width="32" height="32"  style="position: absolute;
    top: 256px; left: 50px;">Your browser does not support HTML5 Canvas.</canvas>

</div>
</body>
</html>
```

Figure 4-14 shows the canvas copy functions in operation.

Figure 4-14. An example canvas copy operation

Canvas copy operations can be very useful when creating applications that need to share and copy image data across multiple <div> instances on (and the Canvas object within) a web page. For example, multiple Canvas elements can be spread across a web page, and as the user makes changes to one, the others can be updated. This can be used for fun applications, such as a "minimap" in a game, or even in serious applications, such as stock portfolio charting and personalization features.

What's Next

We covered quite a lot in this chapter, evolving from simply loading images to animating and rotating them. We looked at using tile sheets and tile maps, and then we built some useful applications with Canvas image functions and capabilities. In the first four chapters, we covered most of what Canvas offers as a drawing surface. In the next six chapters, we will cover some more advanced topics, such as applying 2D physics to `Canvas` objects, integrating the HTML5 `<video>` and `<audio>` tags with the `<canvas>` tag, creating games, and looking at some libraries and features that we can use to extend the functionality of HTML5 Canvas, even creating applications for mobile devices.

CHAPTER 5

Math, Physics, and Animation

Impressing users with animation involves more than knowing how to move objects—you also need to know how to move them in ways that users expect. That requires understanding some common algorithms for math-based movement and physics interactions. Simple movement based on points and vectors provides a foundation, and then it's time to create objects that bounce off walls and one another with a bit of friction added to the mix. After that, we will step back and talk about movement that goes beyond straight lines: circles, spirals, and complex Bezier curves. We will then cover how adding gravity can affect movement. Finally, we will finish this chapter by discussing easing and how it can have a positive effect on math-based animations.

Moving in a Straight Line

For the simplest kinds of animations—moving objects in a straight line up and down the canvas—this can take the form of adding a constant value to the x or y position of an object every time it is drawn.

So, to animate graphics, we will need to create an interval and then call a function that will display our updated graphics on every frame. Each example in this chapter will be built in a similar way. The first step is to set up the necessary variables in our canvasApp() function. For this first, basic example of movement, we will create a variable named speed. We will apply this value to the y position of our object on every call to drawScreen(). The x and y variables set up the initial position of the object (a filled circle) we will move down the canvas:

```
var speed = 5;
var y = 10;
var x = 250;
```

After we create the variables, we set up an interval to call the drawScreen() function every 33 milliseconds. This is the loop we need to update our objects and move them around the canvas:

```
setInterval(drawScreen, 33);
```

In the `drawScreen()` function, we update the value of y by adding to it the value of the speed variable:

```
y += speed;
```

Finally, we draw our circle on the canvas. We position it using the current value of x and y. Since y is updated every time the function is called, the circle effectively moves down the canvas:

```
context.fillStyle = "#000000";
context.beginPath();
context.arc(x,y,15,0,Math.PI*2,true);
context.closePath();
context.fill();
```

To move the circle up the screen, we would make speed a negative number. To move it left or right, we would update the x instead of the y variable. To move the circle diagonally, we would update both x and y at the same time.

Example 5-1 shows the complete code needed to create basic movement in a straight line.

Example 5-1. Moving in a straight line

```
<!doctype html>
<html lang="en">
<head>
<meta charset="UTF-8">
<title>CH5EX1: Moving In A Straight Line</title>
<script src="modernizr-1.6.min.js"></script>
<script type="text/javascript">
window.addEventListener('load', eventWindowLoaded, false);
function eventWindowLoaded() {
    canvasApp();

}

function canvasSupport () {
    return Modernizr.canvas;
}

function canvasApp() {

  if (!canvasSupport()) {
        return;
      }

    function  drawScreen () {

      context.fillStyle = '#EEEEEE';
      context.fillRect(0, 0, theCanvas.width, theCanvas.height);
      //Box
      context.strokeStyle = '#000000';
      context.strokeRect(1,  1, theCanvas.width-2, theCanvas.height-2);
```

```
    // Create ball

    y += speed;

    context.fillStyle = "#000000";
    context.beginPath();
    context.arc(x,y,15,0,Math.PI*2,true);
    context.closePath();
    context.fill();

  }

  theCanvas = document.getElementById("canvasOne");
  context = theCanvas.getContext("2d");

  var speed = 5;
  var y = 10;
  var x = 250;

  setInterval(drawScreen, 33);

}

</script>

</head>
<body>
<div style="position: absolute; top: 50px; left: 50px;">

<canvas id="canvasOne" width="500" height="500">
 Your browser does not support HTML5 Canvas.
</canvas>
</div>

</body>
</html>
```

 The basic structure of the HTML for all of the examples in this chapter will follow these rules. In the interest of saving space, we will refrain from discussing this code further, but it will appear in the examples provided.

Moving Between Two Points: The Distance of a Line

Movement based on constant changes to the x or y position of an object works well for some applications, but other times you will need to be more precise. One such instance is when you need to move an object from point A to point B at a constant rate of speed.

In mathematics, a common way to find the length of an unknown line is to use the Pythagorean theorem:

$$A^2 + B^2 = C^2$$

In this equation, C is the unknown side of a triangle when A and B are already known. However, we need to translate this equation into something we can use with the points and pixels we have available on the canvas.

This is a good example of using a mathematical equation in your application. In this case, we want to find the distance of a line, given two points. In English, this equation reads like this:

> The distance equals the square root of the square of the difference between the x value of the second point minus the x value of the first point, plus the square of the difference between the y value of the second point minus the y value of the first point.

You can see this in Equation 5-1. It's much easier to understand in this format.

Equation 5-1. Distance equation

$$d = \sqrt{(x_2 - x_1)^2 + (y_2 - y_1)^2}$$

In the second example, we need to create some new variables in the `canvasApp()` function. We will still use a `speed` variable, just like in the first example, but this time we set it to 5, which means it will move 5 pixels on every call to `drawScreen()`:

```
var speed = 5;
```

We then create a couple dynamic objects—each with an x and a y property—that will represent the two points we want to move between. For this example, we will move our circle from 20,250 to 480,250:

```
var p1 = {x:20,y:250};
var p2 = {x:480,y:250};
```

Now it is time to re-create the distance equation in Equation 5-1. The first step is to calculate the differences between the second and first x and y points:

```
var dx = p2.x - p1.x;
var dy = p2.y - p1.y;
```

To determine the `distance`, we square both the values we just created, add them, and then use the `Math.sqrt()` function to get the square root of the number:

```
var distance = Math.sqrt(dx*dx + dy*dy);
```

Next, we need to use that calculated `distance` in a way that will allow us to move an object a uniform number of pixels from `p1` to `p2`. The first thing we do is calculate how many moves (calls to `drawScreen()`) it will take the object to move at the given value of `speed`. We get this by dividing the `distance` by the `speed`:

```
var moves = distance/speed;
```

Then we find the distance to move both x and y on each call to `drawScreen()`. We name these variables `xunits` and `yunits`:

```
var xunits = (p2.x - p1.x)/moves;
var yunits = (p2.y - p1.y)/moves;
```

Finally, we create a dynamic object named `ball` that holds the x and y value of `p1`...

```
var ball = {x:p1.x, y:p1.y};
```

...and create the interval to call `drawScreen()` every 33 milliseconds:

```
setInterval(drawScreen, 33);
```

Drawing the ball

Let's draw the ball on the screen. In the `drawScreen()` function, we first check to see whether the moves variable is greater than zero. If so, we are still supposed to move the ball across the screen because we have not yet reached `p2`. We decrement moves (moves--) and then update the x and y properties of the ball object by adding the `xunits` to x and `yunits` to y:

```
if (moves > 0 ) {
   moves--;
   ball.x += xunits;
   ball.y += yunits;
}
```

Now that our `values` have been updated, we simply draw the ball at the x and y coordinates specified by the x and y properties, and we are done...that is, until `drawScreen()` is called 33 milliseconds later:

```
context.fillStyle = "#000000";
context.beginPath();
context.arc(ball.x,ball.y,15,0,Math.PI*2,true);
context.closePath();
context.fill();
```

Let's try the example by executing it in a web browser. You can find it in the code distribution as *CH5EX2.html*, or you can type in Example 5-2. Watch the ball move from one point to another. If you update the *x* and *y* values of each point, or change the speed, watch the results. You can do a lot with this very simple example.

Tracing movement: A path of points

For many of the examples in this chapter, we will create a way to trace an object's movement on the canvas by drawing points to show its path. We have done this to help illustrate how objects move. However, in the real world, you would need to remove this functionality so that your application would perform to its potential. This is the only place we will discuss this code, so if you see it listed in any of the later examples in this chapter, refer back to this section to refresh your memory on its functionality.

First, we create an array in `canvasApp()` to hold the set of points we will draw on the canvas:

```
var points = new Array();
```

Next, we load a black 4×4 pixel image, *point.png*, that we will use to display the points on the canvas:

```
var pointImage = new Image();
pointImage.src = "point.png";
```

Whenever we calculate a point for an object we will move, we push that point into the `points` array:

```
points.push({x:ball.x,y:ball.y});
```

On each call to `drawScreen()`, we draw the set of points we have put into the `points` array. Remember, we have to redraw every point each time because the canvas is an immediate-mode display surface that does not retain any information about the images drawn onto it:

```
for (var i = 0; i< points.length; i++) {
   context.drawImage(pointImage, points[i].x, points[i].y,1,1);
}
```

In Figure 5-1, you can see what the ball looks like when moving on a line from one point to another, and also what the `points` path looks like when it is drawn.

 This is the only time in this chapter where we will discuss the `points` path in depth. If you see the points being drawn, you will know how and why we have added that functionality. You should also have enough information to remove the code when necessary.

Figure 5-1. A ball moving from one point to another along the line, with the points drawn for illustration

Example 5-2 is the full code listing for *CH5EX2.html*.

Example 5-2. Moving on a simple line

```
<!doctype html>
<html lang="en">
<head>
<meta charset="UTF-8">
<title>CH5EX2: Moving On A Simple Line</title>
<script src="modernizr-1.6.min.js"></script>
<script type="text/javascript">
window.addEventListener('load', eventWindowLoaded, false);
function eventWindowLoaded() {
    canvasApp();

}

function canvasSupport () {
    return Modernizr.canvas;
```

```
}

function canvasApp() {

  if (!canvasSupport()) {
        return;
      }

  var pointImage = new Image();
  pointImage.src = "point.png";

  function  drawScreen () {

      context.fillStyle = '#EEEEEE';
      context.fillRect(0, 0, theCanvas.width, theCanvas.height);
      //Box
      context.strokeStyle = '#000000';
      context.strokeRect(1,  1, theCanvas.width-2, theCanvas.height-2);

      // Create ball

      if (moves > 0 ) {
         moves--;
         ball.x += xunits;
         ball.y += yunits;
      }

      //Draw points to illustrate path

      points.push({x:ball.x,y:ball.y});

      for (var i = 0; i< points.length; i++) {
         context.drawImage(pointImage, points[i].x, points[i].y,1,1);

      }

      context.fillStyle = "#000000";
      context.beginPath();
      context.arc(ball.x,ball.y,15,0,Math.PI*2,true);
      context.closePath();
      context.fill();

  }
  var speed = 5;
  var p1 = {x:20,y:250};
  var p2 = {x:480,y:250};
  var dx = p2.x - p1.x;
  var dy = p2.y - p1.y;
  var distance = Math.sqrt(dx*dx + dy*dy);
  var moves = distance/speed;
  var xunits = (p2.x - p1.x)/moves;
  var yunits = (p2.y - p1.y)/moves;
  var ball = {x:p1.x, y:p1.y};
  var points = new Array();
```

```
        theCanvas = document.getElementById("canvasOne");
        context = theCanvas.getContext("2d");

        setInterval(drawScreen, 33);

}

</script>

</head>
<body>
<div style="position: absolute; top: 50px; left: 50px;">

<canvas id="canvasOne" width="500" height="500">
 Your browser does not support HTML5 Canvas.
</canvas>
</div>
</body>
</html>
```

Moving on a Vector

Moving between two points is handy, but sometimes you don't have a point to move to, only a point to start from. In cases like this, it can be very useful to create a vector as a means to move your object.

A *vector* is a quantity in physics that has both magnitude and direction. For our purposes, the magnitude will be the speed of the moving object, and the direction will be an angle that the object will move upon.

The good news is that moving on a vector is very similar to moving between two points. In canvasApp(), we first set our speed (magnitude). This is the number of pixels the object will move on every call to drawScreen(). We will set this to 5. We will also set the starting point (p1) for the object to 20,20:

```
var speed = 5;
var p1 = {x:20,y:20};
```

Now, we will set the angle (direction) of movement for our object to 45 degrees. In mathematics, a flat, straight line usually represents the 0 angle, which means a vector with an angle of 45 degrees would be down and to the right on the canvas.

With our angle set, we now need to convert it to radians. Radians are a standard unit of angle measurement, and most mathematical calculations require you to convert an angle into radians before you can use it.

So why not just use radians and forget degrees altogether? Because it is much easier to understand movement in degrees when working with vectors and moving objects on a 2D surface. While a circle has 360 degrees, it has just about 6 radians, which are calculated counterclockwise. This might make perfect sense to mathematicians, but to move objects on a computer screen, angles are much easier. So, we will work with angles, but we still need to convert our 45-degree angle into radians. We do that with a standard formula: `radians = angle * Math.PI/ 180`. And in the code:

```
var angle = 45;
var radians = angle * Math.PI/ 180;
```

Before we can discuss how we calculate the movement of our object along our vector, we need to review a couple trigonometric concepts. These are cosine and sine, and both relate to the arc created by our angle (now converted to radians), if it was drawn outward from the center of the circle.

cosine

    The angle measured counterclockwise from the x-axis (x)

sine

    The vertical coordinate of the arc endpoint (y)

You can see how these values relate to a 45-degree angle in Figure 5-2.

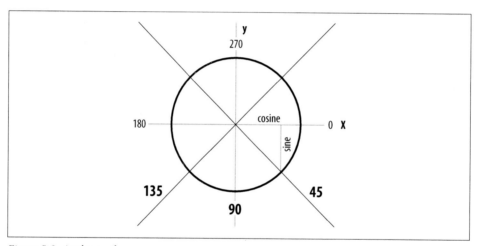

Figure 5-2. Angles on the canvas

This might seem complicated, but there is a very simple way to think about it: cosine usually deals with the x value, and sine usually deals with the y value. We can use sine and cosine to help us calculate movement along our vector.

To calculate the number of pixels to move our object on each call to `drawScreen()` (xunits and yunits), we use the radians (direction) we calculated and speed (magnitude), along with the `Math.cos()` (cosine) and `Math.sin()` (sine) functions of the Java-Script `Math` object:

```
var xunits = Math.cos(radians) * speed;
var yunits = Math.sin(radians) * speed;
```

In drawScreen(), we simply add xunits and yunits to ball.x and ball.y. We don't check to see whether moves has been exhausted because we are not moving to a particular point—we are simply moving along the vector, seemingly forever. In the next section, we will explore what we can do if we want the moving object to change direction when it hits something such as a wall:

```
ball.x += xunits;
ball.y += yunits;
```

Figure 5-3 shows what Example 5-3 looks like when it is executed in a web browser. Recall that the points are drawn for illustr⁀ ⁀n only.

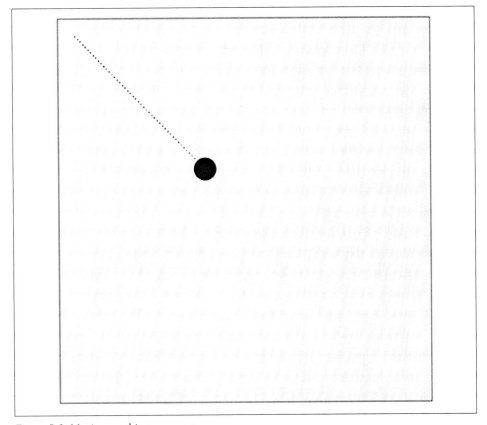

Figure 5-3. Moving an object on a vector

Example 5-3 gives the full code listing.

Example 5-3. Moving on a vector

```
<!doctype html>
<html lang="en">
<head>
<meta charset="UTF-8">
<title>CH5EX3: Moving On A Vector</title>
<script src="modernizr-1.6.min.js"></script>
<script type="text/javascript">
window.addEventListener('load', eventWindowLoaded, false);
function eventWindowLoaded() {
    canvasApp();
}

function canvasSupport () {
    return Modernizr.canvas;
}

function canvasApp() {

  if (!canvasSupport()) {
        return;
      }

  var pointImage = new Image();
  pointImage.src = "point.png";

  function  drawScreen () {

      context.fillStyle = '#EEEEEE';
      context.fillRect(0, 0, theCanvas.width, theCanvas.height);
      //Box
      context.strokeStyle = '#000000';
      context.strokeRect(1,  1, theCanvas.width-2, theCanvas.height-2);

      ball.x += xunits;
      ball.y += yunits;

      //Draw points to illustrate path

      points.push({x:ball.x,y:ball.y});

      for (var i = 0; i< points.length; i++) {
         context.drawImage(pointImage, points[i].x, points[i].y,1,1);
      }

      context.fillStyle = "#000000";
      context.beginPath();
      context.arc(ball.x,ball.y,15,0,Math.PI*2,true);
      context.closePath();
      context.fill();

  }
```

```
        var speed = 5;
        var p1 = {x:20,y:20};
        var angle = 45;
        var radians = angle * Math.PI/ 180;
        var xunits = Math.cos(radians) * speed;
        var yunits = Math.sin(radians) * speed;
        var ball = {x:p1.x, y:p1.y};
        var points = new Array();

        theCanvas = document.getElementById("canvasOne");
        context = theCanvas.getContext("2d");

        setInterval(drawScreen, 33);

}

</script>

</head>
<body>
<div style="position: absolute; top: 50px; left: 50px;">

<canvas id="canvasOne" width="500" height="500">
 Your browser does not support HTML5 Canvas.
</canvas>
</div>
</body>
</html>
```

Bouncing Off Walls

While it's neat that we can create a vector with magnitude and direction and then move an object along it infinitely, it's probably not something you will need to do all that often. Most of the time, you will want to see that object react to the world around it by bouncing off horizontal and vertical walls, for example.

To help you understand how to do this, there is a simple rule in physics. Although this rule is usually applied to rays of light, it can be very useful when animating 2D objects— especially when they are bouncing off horizontal and vertical walls. This rule is known as *the angle of reflection*:

> The angle of incidence is equal to the angle of reflection.

The *angle of incidence* is the angle an object is traveling when it hits the walls, and the *angle of reflection* is the angle it travels after it bounces off the wall.

Figure 5-4 illustrates that when an object hits a wall on a line that forms a 45-degree angle with a perpendicular line drawn to the point of impact, it will bounce off (reflect) at a similar 45-degree angle.

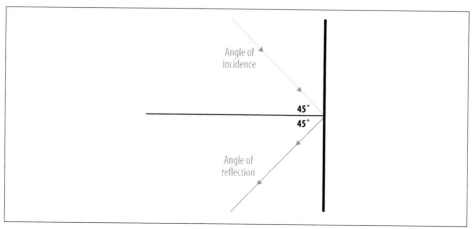

Figure 5-4. Angle of incidence is equal to the angle of reflection

In the next section, we will create a series of examples using this rule to animate objects. The first, Example 5-4, will simply allow a single ball to bounce off the edges of the canvas.

Bouncing a Single Ball

In this first example, we will create a ball traveling on a vector. We will set the speed (magnitude) to 5 and the angle (direction) to 35 degrees. The rest of the variables are identical to those in Example 5-3. We are still moving on a vector, but now we will test to see whether the ball hits a "wall" (the edges of the canvas), in which case it will bounce off, using the rule of the angle of reflection. One big change from the previous vector example is the location in which we initialize the values for radians, xunits, and yunits. Instead of setting them up when we initialize the application in canvasApp(), we save that for a call to a new function named updateBall():

```
var speed = 5;
var p1 = {x:20,y:20};
var angle = 35;
var radians = 0;
var xunits = 0;
var yunits = 0;
var ball = {x:p1.x, y:p1.y};
updateBall();
```

The updateBall() function is called every time we set a new angle for the ball, because we need to recalculate the radians and find new values for xunits and yunits. A new angle is generated when the app starts, as well as every time the ball bounces off a wall:

```
function updateBall() {
    radians = angle * Math.PI/ 180;
    xunits = Math.cos(radians) * speed;
    yunits = Math.sin(radians) * speed;
}
```

In `drawScreen()`, we update the position of the ball, and then draw it on the canvas:

```
ball.x += xunits;
ball.y += yunits;
context.fillStyle = "#000000";
context.beginPath();
context.arc(ball.x,ball.y,15,0,Math.PI*2,true);
context.closePath();
context.fill();
```

Next, we test to see whether the ball has hit a wall before we draw it to the canvas. If the ball hits the right side (`ball.x > the Canvas.width`) or the left side of the canvas (`ball.x < 0`), we set the angle to 180 degrees minus the angle of the vector on which the ball is traveling. This gives us the angle of reflection. Alternatively, if the ball hits the top (`ball.y < 0`) or bottom (`ball.y > theCanvas.height`) of the canvas, we calculate the angle of reflection with 360 degrees minus the angle of the vector on which the ball is traveling:

```
if (ball.x > theCanvas.width || ball.x < 0 ) {
        angle = 180 - angle;
        updateBall();
    } else if (ball.y > theCanvas.height || ball.y < 0) {
        angle = 360 - angle;
        updateBall();
    }
```

That's it. Example 5-4 demonstrates a ball that bounces off walls using the rules of physics. Figure 5-5 illustrates the code.

Example 5-4. Ball bounce

```
<!doctype html>
<html lang="en">
<head>
<meta charset="UTF-8">
<title>CH5EX4: Ball Bounce</title>
<script src="modernizr-1.6.min.js"></script>
<script type="text/javascript">
window.addEventListener('load', eventWindowLoaded, false);
function eventWindowLoaded() {
    canvasApp();
}

function canvasSupport () {
        return Modernizr.canvas;
}
```

```
function canvasApp() {

  if (!canvasSupport()) {
        return;
      }

  function  drawScreen () {
      context.fillStyle = '#EEEEEE';
      context.fillRect(0, 0, theCanvas.width, theCanvas.height);
      //Box
      context.strokeStyle = '#000000';
      context.strokeRect(1,  1, theCanvas.width-2, theCanvas.height-2);
      ball.x += xunits;
      ball.y += yunits;
      context.fillStyle = "#000000";
      context.beginPath();
      context.arc(ball.x,ball.y,15,0,Math.PI*2,true);
      context.closePath();
      context.fill();

      if (ball.x > theCanvas.width || ball.x < 0 ) {
         angle = 180 - angle;
         updateBall();
      } else if (ball.y > theCanvas.height || ball.y < 0) {
         angle = 360 - angle;
         updateBall();
      }

  }

  function updateBall() {
     radians = angle * Math.PI/ 180;
     xunits = Math.cos(radians) * speed;
     yunits = Math.sin(radians) * speed;
  }

  var speed = 5;
  var p1 = {x:20,y:20};
  var angle = 35;
  var radians = 0;
  var xunits = 0;
  var yunits = 0;
  var ball = {x:p1.x, y:p1.y};
  updateBall();

  theCanvas = document.getElementById("canvasOne");
  context = theCanvas.getContext("2d");

  setInterval(drawScreen, 33);

}
```

```
</script>

</head>
<body>
<div style="position: absolute; top: 50px; left: 50px;">

<canvas id="canvasOne" width="500" height="500">
 Your browser does not support HTML5 Canvas.
</canvas>
</div>
</body>
</html>
```

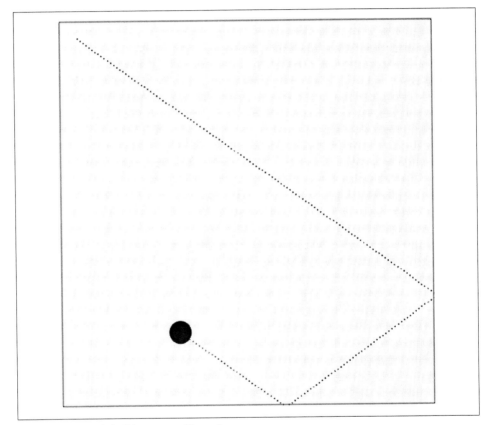

Figure 5-5. A single ball bouncing off a wall

The points on the line are not drawn when executed in the web browser because they slowed down the ball far too much. We left them in Figure 5-5 to illustrate the angles of incidence and reflection.

Multiple Balls Bouncing Off Walls

One ball is cool, but what about 100? Is the code 100 times more complicated? No, not at all. In fact, the code is only slightly more complicated, but it is also more refined. Most programming tasks that require only a single object of a type tend to allow you to be a bit lazy. However, when you need to build an application that must support *n* number of objects, you need to make sure the code will work in many different cases.

In the case of 100 balls bouncing on the canvas, we will need to create a ball object with a few more properties. Recall that the ball object we created previously had only x and y properties, and looked like this:

```
var ball = {x:p1.x, y:p1.y};
```

All the other variables that represented the ball (speed, angle, xunits, yunits) were global in scope to the canvasApp(). We used global variables because we could get away with it. However, because we need to make sure everything works the same way in this app, we make all those values properties of each ball object.

For the multiple-ball-bounce application, we will create an object that holds all the pertinent information about each bouncing ball: x, y, speed, angle, xunits, and yunits. Because we are going to create 100 balls of various sizes, we also add a property named radius, which represents the size of the ball (well, half the size since it *is* a radius):

```
tempBall = {x:tempX,y:tempY,radius:tempRadius, speed:tempSpeed,
    angle:tempAngle, xunits:tempXunits, yunits:tempYunits}
```

Inside canvasApp(), we define some new variables to help manage the multiple balls that will bounce around the canvas:

numBalls
> The number of balls to randomly create

maxSize
> The maximum radius length for any given ball

minSize
> The minimum radius length for any given ball

maxSpeed
> The maximum speed any ball can travel

balls
> An array to hold all of the ball objects we will create

The following code shows the newly defined variables:

```
var numBalls = 100 ;
var maxSize = 8;
var minSize = 5;
var maxSpeed = maxSize+5;
var balls = new Array();
```

We also create a set of temporary variables to hold the values for each ball before we push it into the `balls` array:

```
var tempBall;
var tempX;
var tempY;
var tempSpeed;
var tempAngle;
var tempRadius;
var tempRadians;
var tempXunits;
var tempYunits;
```

Next, in `canvasApp()`, we iterate through a loop to create all the ball objects. Notice how `tempX` and `tempY` are created below. These values represent the ball's starting location on the canvas. We create a random value for each, but we offset it by the size of the ball (`tempRadius*2`). If we did not do that, some of the balls would get "stuck" in a wall when the app starts because their `x` or `y` location would be "through" the wall, but their `speed` would not be enough so that a "bounce" would get them back on the playfield. They would be stuck in bouncing limbo forever (which is kind of sad when you think about it).

When you try this app, you will see that occasionally a ball still gets stuck in a wall. There is a further optimization we need to make to prevent this, but it is a bigger subject than this little iteration. We will talk about it in the section "Multiple Balls Bouncing and Colliding" on page 198.

The `tempSpeed` variable is created by subtracting the value of `tempRadius` from the value of `maxSpeed`, which we created earlier. The `speed` is not random, but it is inversely proportional to the size (radius) of the ball. A larger ball has larger radius, so the value you subtract from `tempSpeed` will be larger, thus making the ball move slower:

When you run *CH5EX4.html* in your web browser, you will notice that this little trick makes the ball appear more "real" because your brain expects larger objects to move slower.

```
for (var i = 0; i < numBalls; i++) {
    tempRadius = Math.floor(Math.random()*maxSize)+minSize;
    tempX = tempRadius*2 + (Math.floor(Math.random()*theCanvas.width)-tempRadius*2);
    tempY = tempRadius*2 + (Math.floor(Math.random()*theCanvas.height)-tempRadius*2);
    tempSpeed = maxSpeed-tempRadius;
    tempAngle = Math.floor(Math.random()*360);
    tempRadians = tempAngle * Math.PI/ 180;
    tempXunits = Math.cos(tempRadians) * tempSpeed;
    tempYunits = Math.sin(tempRadians) * tempSpeed;

    tempBall = {x:tempX,y:tempY,radius:tempRadius, speed:tempSpeed, angle:tempAngle,
        xunits:tempXunits, yunits:tempYunits}
    balls.push(tempBall);
}
```

Now we need to draw the balls onto the canvas. Inside drawScreen(), the code to draw the balls should look very familiar because it is essentially the same code we used for one ball in Example 5-4. We just need to loop through the balls array to render each ball object:

```
for (var i = 0; i <balls.length; i++) {
        ball = balls[i];
        ball.x += ball.xunits;
        ball.y += ball.yunits;

        context.beginPath();
        context.arc(ball.x,ball.y,ball.radius,0,Math.PI*2,true);
        context.closePath();
        context.fill();

        if (ball.x > theCanvas.width || ball.x < 0 ) {
            ball.angle = 180 - ball.angle;
            updateBall(ball);
        } else if (ball.y > theCanvas.height || ball.y < 0) {
            ball.angle = 360 - ball.angle;
            updateBall(ball);
        }
    }
```

When you load Example 5-5 in your web browser, you will see a bunch of balls all moving around the screen independently, as shown in Figure 5-6. For the fun of it, why not change the numBalls variable to 500 or 1,000? What does the canvas look like then?

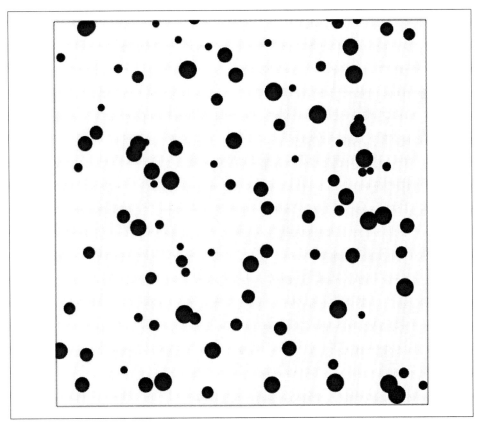

Figure 5-6. Multiple balls of different sizes bouncing off walls

Example 5-5. Multiple ball bounce

```
<!doctype html>
<html lang="en">
<head>
<meta charset="UTF-8">
<title>CH5EX5: Multiple Ball Bounce</title>
<script src="modernizr-1.6.min.js"></script>
<script type="text/javascript">
window.addEventListener('load', eventWindowLoaded, false);
function eventWindowLoaded() {
    canvasApp();
}

function canvasSupport () {
     return Modernizr.canvas;
}

function canvasApp() {
```

```
    if (!canvasSupport()) {
        return;
    }

function  drawScreen () {

    context.fillStyle = '#EEEEEE';
    context.fillRect(0, 0, theCanvas.width, theCanvas.height);

    //Box
    context.strokeStyle = '#000000';
    context.strokeRect(1,  1, theCanvas.width-2, theCanvas.height-2);

    //Place balls
    context.fillStyle = "#000000";
    var ball;

    for (var i = 0; i <balls.length; i++) {
        ball = balls[i];
        ball.x += ball.xunits;
        ball.y += ball.yunits;

        context.beginPath();
        context.arc(ball.x,ball.y,ball.radius,0,Math.PI*2,true);
        context.closePath();
        context.fill();

        if (ball.x > theCanvas.width || ball.x < 0 ) {
            ball.angle = 180 - ball.angle;
            updateBall(ball);
        } else if (ball.y > theCanvas.height || ball.y < 0) {
            ball.angle = 360 - ball.angle;
            updateBall(ball);
        }
    }

}

function updateBall(ball) {

    ball.radians = ball.angle * Math.PI/ 180;
    ball.xunits = Math.cos(ball.radians) * ball.speed;
    ball.yunits = Math.sin(ball.radians) * ball.speed;

}

var numBalls = 100 ;
var maxSize = 8;
var minSize = 5;
var maxSpeed = maxSize+5;
var balls = new Array();
var tempBall;
var tempX;
var tempY;
var tempSpeed;
```

```
    var tempAngle;
    var tempRadius;
    var tempRadians;
    var tempXunits;
    var tempYunits;

    theCanvas = document.getElementById("canvasOne");
    context = theCanvas.getContext("2d");

    for (var i = 0; i < numBalls; i++) {
        tempRadius = Math.floor(Math.random()*maxSize)+minSize;
        tempX = tempRadius*2 + (Math.floor(Math.random()*theCanvas.width)-tempRadius*2);
        tempY = tempRadius*2 + (Math.floor(Math.random()*theCanvas.height)-tempRadius*2);
        tempSpeed = maxSpeed-tempRadius;
        tempAngle = Math.floor(Math.random()*360);
        tempRadians = tempAngle * Math.PI/ 180;
        tempXunits = Math.cos(tempRadians) * tempSpeed;
        tempYunits = Math.sin(tempRadians) * tempSpeed;

        tempBall = {x:tempX,y:tempY,radius:tempRadius, speed:tempSpeed, angle:tempAngle,
            xunits:tempXunits, yunits:tempYunits}
        balls.push(tempBall);
    }

    setInterval(drawScreen, 33);

    }


</script>

</head>
<body>
<div style="position: absolute; top: 50px; left: 50px;">

<canvas id="canvasOne" width="500" height="500">
 Your browser does not support HTML5 Canvas.
</canvas>
</div>
</body>
</html>
```

Multiple Balls Bouncing with a Dynamically Resized Canvas

Before we move on to some more complex interaction among balls, let's try one more thing. Back in Chapter 3, we resized the canvas with some HTML5 form controls to display text in the center of the canvas. Well, let's do the same thing now with the ball example. This will give you a better idea of how we can make objects interact with a dynamically resizing canvas.

First, in the HTML, we create two HTML5 range controls, one for width and one for height, and set their maximum values to 1000. We will use these controls to set the width and height of the canvas at runtime:

```
<form>

Canvas Width:   <input type="range" id="canvasWidth"
        min="0"
        max="1000"
        step="1"
        value="500"/>
<br>
Canvas Height:   <input type="range" id="canvasHeight"
        min="0"
        max="1000"
        step="1"
        value="500"/>
<br>

</form>
```

In canvasApp(), we create the event listeners for the HTML5 form controls. We listen for the change event, which means any time the range control is moved, the event handlers will be called:

```
formElement = document.getElementById("canvasWidth")
formElement.addEventListener('change', canvasWidthChanged, false);

formElement = document.getElementById("canvasHeight")
formElement.addEventListener('change', canvasHeightChanged, false);
```

The event handler functions capture the changes to the range, set theCanvas.width or theCanvas.height, and then call drawScreen() to render the new size. Without a call to drawScreen() here, the canvas will blink when the new size is applied in drawScreen() on the next interval:

```
function canvasWidthChanged(e) {
    var target = e.target;
    theCanvas.width = target.value;
    drawScreen();
}

function canvasHeightChanged(e) {
    var target = e.target;
    theCanvas.height = target.value;
    drawScreen();
}
```

 All of this is explained in gory detail in Chapter 3.

One last thing—let's increase the number of balls set in canvasApp() to 500:

```
var numBalls = 500 ;
```

Now, check out Example 5-6 (*CH5EX6.html* from the code distribution). When you run the code in a web browser, you should see 500 balls bounce around the canvas, as shown in Figure 5-7. When you increase the width or height using the range controls, they continue moving until they hit the new edge of the canvas. If you make the canvas smaller, the balls will be contained within the smaller space. If you adjust the size too rapidly, some balls will be lost off the canvas, but they will reappear when the canvas is resized. Neat, huh?

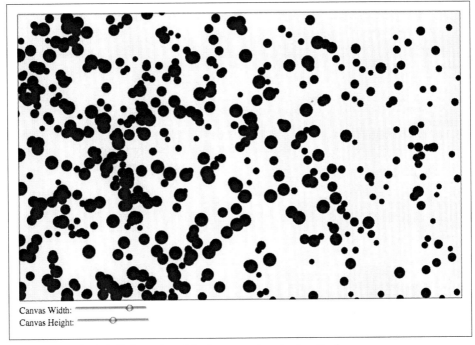

Figure 5-7. Multiple balls bouncing while the canvas is resized on the fly

Example 5-6. Multiple ball bounce with dynamically resized canvas

```
<!doctype html>
<html lang="en">
<head>
<meta charset="UTF-8">
<title>CH5EX6: Multiple Ball Bounce With Resize</title>
<script src="modernizr-1.6.min.js"></script>
<script type="text/javascript">
window.addEventListener('load', eventWindowLoaded, false);
function eventWindowLoaded() {
    canvasApp();
}
```

```
function canvasSupport () {
    return Modernizr.canvas;
}

function canvasApp() {

  if (!canvasSupport()) {
        return;
      }

  formElement = document.getElementById("canvasWidth")
  formElement.addEventListener('change', canvasWidthChanged, false);

  formElement = document.getElementById("canvasHeight")
  formElement.addEventListener('change', canvasHeightChanged, false);

  function  drawScreen () {

      context.fillStyle = '#EEEEEE';
      context.fillRect(0, 0, theCanvas.width, theCanvas.height);
      //Box
      context.strokeStyle = '#000000';
      context.strokeRect(1,  1, theCanvas.width-2, theCanvas.height-2);

      //Place balls
      context.fillStyle = "#000000";
      var ball;

      for (var i = 0; i <balls.length; i++) {
          ball = balls[i];
          ball.x += ball.xunits;
          ball.y += ball.yunits;

          context.beginPath();
          context.arc(ball.x,ball.y,ball.radius,0,Math.PI*2,true);
          context.closePath();
          context.fill();

          if (ball.x > theCanvas.width || ball.x < 0 ) {
              ball.angle = 180 - ball.angle;
              updateBall(ball);
          } else if (ball.y > theCanvas.height || ball.y < 0) {
              ball.angle = 360 - ball.angle;
              updateBall(ball);
          }
      }

  }

  function updateBall(ball) {

      ball.radians = ball.angle * Math.PI/ 180;
      ball.xunits = Math.cos(ball.radians) * ball.speed;
      ball.yunits = Math.sin(ball.radians) * ball.speed;
```

```
        }
        var numBalls = 500 ;
        var maxSize = 8;
        var minSize = 5;
        var maxSpeed = maxSize+5;
        var balls = new Array();
        var tempBall;
        var tempX;
        var tempY;
        var tempSpeed;
        var tempAngle;
        var tempRadius;
        var tempRadians;
        var tempXunits;
        var tempYunits;

        theCanvas = document.getElementById("canvasOne");
        context = theCanvas.getContext("2d");

        for (var i = 0; i < numBalls; i++) {
            tempRadius = Math.floor(Math.random()*maxSize)+minSize;
            tempX = tempRadius*2 + (Math.floor(Math.random()*theCanvas.width)-tempRadius*2);
            tempY = tempRadius*2 + (Math.floor(Math.random()*theCanvas.height)-tempRadius*2);
            tempSpeed = maxSpeed-tempRadius;
            tempAngle = Math.floor(Math.random()*360);
            tempRadians = tempAngle * Math.PI/ 180;
            tempXunits = Math.cos(tempRadians) * tempSpeed;
            tempYunits = Math.sin(tempRadians) * tempSpeed;

            tempBall = {x:tempX,y:tempY,radius:tempRadius, speed:tempSpeed, angle:tempAngle,
                xunits:tempXunits, yunits:tempYunits}
            balls.push(tempBall);
        }

        setInterval(drawScreen, 33);

        function canvasWidthChanged(e) {
            var target = e.target;
            theCanvas.width = target.value;
            drawScreen();
        }

        function canvasHeightChanged(e) {
            var target = e.target;
            theCanvas.height = target.value;
            drawScreen();
        }

    }

</script>

</head>
<body>
```

```
<div style="position: absolute; top: 50px; left: 50px;">

<canvas id="canvasOne" width="500" height="500">
  Your browser does not support HTML5 Canvas.
</canvas>
<form>

Canvas Width:   <input type="range" id="canvasWidth"
        min="0"
        max="1000"
        step="1"
        value="500"/>
  <br>
Canvas Height:   <input type="range" id="canvasHeight"
        min="0"
        max="1000"
        step="1"
        value="500"/>
  <br>

</form>
</div>
</body>
</html>
```

Multiple Balls Bouncing and Colliding

Now it's time to step it up again. Testing balls bouncing off walls is one thing, but what about balls bouncing off one another? We will need to add some pretty intricate code to handle this type of interaction.

Ball interactions in physics

For this example, we are going to create an *elastic collision*, which means that the total kinetic energy of the objects is the same before and after the collision. This is known as the *law of conservation of momentum* (Newton's third law). To do this, we will take the *x* and *y* velocities of two colliding balls, and draw a "line of action" between their centers. This is illustrated in Figure 5-8, which has been adapted from Jobe Makar and Ben Winiarczyk's *Macromedia's Flash MX 2004 Game Design Demystified* (Macromedia Press). Then we will create new x and y velocities for each ball based on this angle and the law of conservation of momentum.

To properly calculate conservation of momentum when balls collide on the canvas, we need to add a new property: mass. Mass is the measurement of how much a ball (or any object) resists any change in its velocity. Because collisions tend to change the velocity of objects, this is an important addition to the ball objects we will use on the canvas.

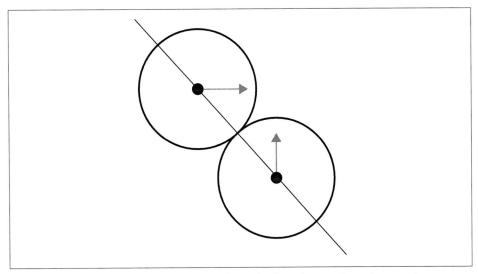

Figure 5-8. Two balls colliding at different angles with a line of action drawn between them

Making sure the balls don't start on top of each other

We will work from the code we created for Example 5-6 (*CH5EX6.html*). The first big change to that code is to make sure the balls don't randomly start on top of one another. If we let them start in the same location, they would be forever intertwined and would spin off into oblivion. To be honest, it looks pretty cool when that happens, but that's not the result we are looking to achieve.

In `canvasApp()`, we set a variable named `tempRadius` to 5. We will use this value as the radius for each ball we create. Next, we create another new variable named `placeOK` and set it to `false`. When this is equal to `true`, we know we have found a place to put a ball that is not on top of another ball.

Next, we enter a `while()` loop that will continue to iterate as long as `placeOK` is `false`. Then, we set all the values for our new ball object:

```
tempRadius = 5;
var placeOK = false;
while (!placeOK) {
tempX = tempRadius*3 + (Math.floor(Math.random()*theCanvas.width)-tempRadius*3);
tempY = tempRadius*3 + (Math.floor(Math.random()*theCanvas.height)-tempRadius*3);
tempSpeed = 4;
tempAngle = Math.floor(Math.random()*360);
tempRadians = tempAngle * Math.PI/ 180;
tempvelocityx = Math.cos(tempRadians) * tempSpeed;
tempvelocityy = Math.sin(tempRadians) * tempSpeed;
```

Now, we need to make a dynamic object out of the values we just created and place that object into the `tempBall` variable. This is where we create a `mass` property for each ball. Again, we do this so that we can calculate the effect when the balls hit one another. For all the balls in this example, the `mass` will be the same—the value of `tempRadius`. We do this because, in our 2D environment, the relative size of each ball is a very simple way to create a value for `mass`. Since the `mass` and `speed` of each ball will be the same, they will affect each other in a similar way. Later, we will show you what happens when we create ball objects with different `mass` values.

Finally, we create `nextX` and `nextY` properties that are equal to `x` and `y`. We will use these values as "look ahead" properties to help alleviate collisions that occur "between" our iterations, which lead to overlapping balls and other oddities:

```
tempBall = {x:tempX,y:tempY, nextX: tempX, nextY: tempY, radius:tempRadius,
    speed:tempSpeed, angle:tempAngle, velocityx:tempvelocityx,
    velocityy:tempvelocityy, mass:tempRadius};
```

Now that we have our new dynamic ball object represented by the `tempBall` variable, we will test to see whether it can be placed at the `tempX` and `tempY` we randomly created for it. We will do this with a call to a new function named `canStartHere()`. If can StartHere() returns `true`, we drop out of the `while()` loop; if not, we start all over again:

```
        placeOK = canStartHere(tempBall);
    }
```

The `canStartHere()` function is very simple. It looks through the `ball` array, testing the new `tempBall` against all existing balls to see whether they overlap. If they do, the function returns `false`; if not, it returns `true`. To test the overlap, we have created another new function: `hitTestCircle()`:

```
function canStartHere(ball) {
    var retval = true;
    for (var i = 0; i <balls.length; i++) {
        if (hitTestCircle(ball, balls[i])) {
            retval = false;
        }
    }
    return retval;
}
```

Circle collision detection

The `hitTestCircle()` function performs a circle/circle collision-detection test to see whether the two circles (each representing a ball) passed as parameters to the function are touching. Because we have been tracking the balls by the center `x` and `y` of their location, this is quite easy to calculate. First, the function finds the distance of the line that connects the center of each circle. We do this using our old friend the Pythagorean theorem $(A^2+B^2 = C^2)$. We use the `nextx` and `nexty` properties of the ball because we want to test the collision before it occurs. (Again, if we test after by using the current `x` and `y` locations, there is a good chance the balls will get stuck together and spin out of control.) We then compare that distance value to the sum of the radius of each ball. If the distance is less than or equal to the sum of the radii, we have a collision. This is a very simple and efficient way to test collisions, and it works especially well with collisions among balls in 2D:

```
function hitTestCircle(ball1,ball2) {
    var retval = false;
    var dx = ball1.nextx - ball2.nextx;
    var dy = ball1.nexty - ball2.nexty;
    var distance = (dx * dx + dy * dy);
    if (distance <= (ball1.radius + ball2.radius) * (ball1.radius + ball2.radius) ) {
        retval = true;
    }
    return retval;
}
```

Figure 5-9 illustrates this code.

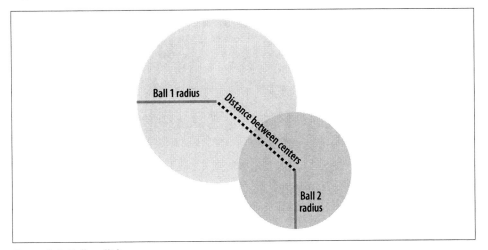

Figure 5-9. Balls colliding

Separating the code in drawScreen()

The next thing we want to do is simplify drawScreen() by separating the code into controllable functions. The idea here is that to test collisions correctly, we need to make sure some of our calculations are done in a particular order. We like to call this an *update-collide-render cycle.*

update()
> Sets the nextx and nexty properties of all the balls in the balls array.

testWalls()
> Tests to see whether the balls have hit one of the walls.

collide()
> Tests collisions among balls. If the balls collide, updates nextx and nexty.

```
render()
```

Makes the x and y properties for each ball equal to nextx and nexty respectively, and then draws them to the canvas.

And here is the code:

```
function  drawScreen () {

    update();
    testWalls();
    collide();
    render();

}
```

Updating positions of objects

The update() function loops through all the balls in the balls array, and updates the nextx and nexty properties with the x and y velocity for each ball. We don't directly update x and y here, because we want to test collisions against walls and other balls before they occur. We will use the nextx and nexty properties for this purpose:

```
function update() {
    for (var i = 0; i <balls.length; i++) {
        ball = balls[i];
        ball.nextx = (ball.x += ball.velocityx);
        ball.nexty = (ball.y += ball.velocityy);
    }
}
```

Better interaction with the walls

We discussed the interactions between balls and walls in the last example, but there is still one issue. Since we move the balls by the x and y location of their center, the balls would move halfway off the canvas before a bounce occurred. To fix this, we add or subtract the radius of the ball object, depending on which walls we are testing. For the right side and bottom of the canvas, we add the radius of the ball when we test the walls. In this way, the ball will appear to bounce exactly when its edge hits a wall. Similarly, we subtract the radius when we test the left side and the top of the canvas, so that the ball does not move off the side before we make it bounce off a wall:

```
function testWalls() {
    var ball;
    var testBall;

    for (var i = 0; i <balls.length; i++) {
        ball = balls[i];

        if (ball.nextx+ball.radius > theCanvas.width) {
            ball.velocityx = ball.velocityx*-1;
            ball.nextx = theCanvas.width - ball.radius;
```

```
    } else if (ball.nextx-ball.radius < 0 ) {
        ball.velocityx = ball.velocityx*-1;
        ball.nextx = ball.radius;

    } else if (ball.nexty+ball.radius > theCanvas.height ) {
        ball.velocityy = ball.velocityy*-1;
        ball.nexty = theCanvas.height - ball.radius;

    } else if(ball.nexty-ball.radius < 0) {
        ball.velocityy = ball.velocityy*-1;
        ball.nexty = ball.radius;
    }

    }

}
```

Collisions with balls

The collide() function tests to see whether any balls have hit one another. This function uses two nested loops, both iterating through the balls array to ensure we test each ball against every other ball. We take the ball from the first loop of the balls array, and place it into the ball variable. Then we loop through balls again, placing each ball in the testBall variable, one at a time. When we have both ball and testBall, we make sure they are not equal to one another. We do this because a ball will always have a false positive collision if we test it against itself. When we are sure they are not the same ball, we call hitTestCircle() to test for a collision. If we find one, we call collide Balls(), and then all hell breaks loose. (OK, not really, but the balls do collide, and some really interesting code gets executed.) See that code here:

```
function collide() {
    var ball;
    var testBall;
    for (var i = 0; i <balls.length; i++) {
        ball = balls[i];
        for (var j = i+1; j < balls.length; j++) {
            testBall = balls[j];
            if (hitTestCircle(ball,testBall)) {
                collideBalls(ball,testBall);
            }
        }
    }
}
```

Ball collisions in depth

So now we get to the most interesting code of this example. We are going to update the properties of each ball so they appear to bounce off one another. Recall that we use the nextx and nexty properties because we want to make sure to test where the balls will be after they are drawn—not where they are right now. This helps keep the balls from overlapping in a way that will make them stick together.

Sometimes the balls will still stick together. This is a common problem when creating collisions among balls. This happens when balls overlap one another before the collision test, and the reaction bounce is not enough to split them apart completely. We have made every attempt to optimize this function for the canvas, but we are sure further optimizations are possible.

The `collideBalls()` function takes two parameters: `ball1` and `ball2`. Both parameters are the `ball` objects that we want to make collide:

```
function collideBalls(ball1,ball2) {
```

First, we need to calculate the difference between the center points of each ball. We store this as `dx` and `dy` (difference x and difference y). This should look familiar because we did something similar when we tested for a collision between the balls. The difference is that now we know they have collided, and we want to know how that collision occurred:

```
var dx = ball1.nextx - ball2.nextx;
var dy = ball1.nexty - ball2.nexty;
```

To do this, we need to find the angle of the collision using the `Math.atan2()` function. This function gives us the angle in radians of the collisions between the two balls. This is the line of action or angle of collision. We need this value so that we can determine how the balls will react when they collide:

```
var collisionAngle = Math.atan2(dy, dx);
```

Next, we calculate the velocity vector for each ball given the x and y velocities that existed before the collision occurred:

```
var speed1 = Math.sqrt(ball1.velocityx * ball1.velocityx +
    ball1.velocityy *   ball1.velocityy);
var speed2 = Math.sqrt(ball2.velocityx * ball2.velocityx +
    ball2.velocityy * ball2.velocityy);
```

Then, we calculate angles (in radians) for each ball given its current velocities:

```
var direction1 = Math.atan2(ball1.velocityy, ball1.velocityx);
var direction2 = Math.atan2(ball2.velocityy, ball2.velocityx);
```

Next, we need to rotate the vectors counterclockwise so that we can plug those values into the equation for conservation of momentum. Basically, we are taking the angle of collision and making it flat so we can bounce the balls, similar to how we bounced balls off the sides of the canvas:

```
var velocityx_1 = speed1 * Math.cos(direction1 - collisionAngle);
var velocityy_1 = speed1 * Math.sin(direction1 - collisionAngle);
var velocityx_2 = speed2 * Math.cos(direction2 - collisionAngle);
var velocityy_2 = speed2 * Math.sin(direction2 - collisionAngle);
```

We take the mass values of each ball and update their x and y velocities based on the law of conservation of momentum. To find the final velocity for both balls, we use the following formulas:

```
velocity1 = ((mass1 - mass2) * velocity1 + 2*mass2 * velocity2) / mass1 + mass2
velocity2 = ((mass2 - mass1) * velocity2 + 2*mass1 * velocity1)/ mass1+ mass2
```

Actually, only the x velocity needs to be updated; the y velocity remains constant:

```
var final_velocityx_1 = ((ball1.mass - ball2.mass) * velocityx_1 +
    (ball2.mass + ball2.mass) * velocityx_2)/(ball1.mass + ball2.mass);
var final_velocityx_2 = ((ball1.mass + ball1.mass) * velocityx_1 +
    (ball2.mass - ball1.mass) * velocityx_2)/(ball1.mass + ball2.mass);

var final_velocityy_1 = velocityy_1;
var final_velocityy_2 = velocityy_2
```

After we have our final velocities, we rotate our angles back again so that the collision angle is preserved:

```
ball1.velocityx = Math.cos(collisionAngle) * final_velocityx_1 +
    Math.cos(collisionAngle + Math.PI/2) * final_velocityy_1;
ball1.velocityy = Math.sin(collisionAngle) * final_velocityx_1 +
    Math.sin(collisionAngle + Math.PI/2) * final_velocityy_1;
ball2.velocityx = Math.cos(collisionAngle) * final_velocityx_2 +
    Math.cos(collisionAngle + Math.PI/2) * final_velocityy_2;
ball2.velocityy = Math.sin(collisionAngle) * final_velocityx_2 +
    Math.sin(collisionAngle + Math.PI/2) * final_velocityy_2;
```

Now, we update nextx and nexty for both balls so can use those values in the render() function—or, for another collision:

```
ball1.nextx = (ball1.nextx += ball1.velocityx);
ball1.nexty = (ball1.nexty += ball1.velocityy);
ball2.nextx = (ball2.nextx += ball2.velocityx);
ball2.nexty = (ball2.nexty += ball2.velocityy);
}
```

 If this is confusing to you, you are not alone. It took some serious effort for us to translate this code from other sources into a working example on HTML5 Canvas. The code here is based on "*Flash Lite Effort - Embedded Systems and Pervasive Computing Lab*" by Felipe Sampaio, available here: *http://wiki.forum.nokia.com/index.php/Collision_for _Balls*. It is also partly based on Jobe Makar and Ben Winiarczyk's work in *Macromedia Flash MX 2004 Game Design Demystified*, and Keith Peters' books on ActionScript animation.

Here is the full code listing for Example 5-7.

Example 5-7. Balls with simple interactions

```
<!doctype html>
<html lang="en">
<head>
```

```
<meta charset="UTF-8">
<title>CH5EX7: Balls With Simple Interactions</title>
<script src="modernizr-1.6.min.js"></script>
<script type="text/javascript">
window.addEventListener('load', eventWindowLoaded, false);
function eventWindowLoaded() {
    canvasApp();

}

function canvasSupport () {
    return Modernizr.canvas;
}

function canvasApp() {

  if (!canvasSupport()) {
        return;
      }

  function  drawScreen () {

      context.fillStyle = '#EEEEEE';
      context.fillRect(0, 0, theCanvas.width, theCanvas.height);
      //Box
      context.strokeStyle = '#000000';
      context.strokeRect(1,  1, theCanvas.width-2, theCanvas.height-2);

      update();
      testWalls();
      collide();
      render();

  }

  function update() {
      for (var i = 0; i <balls.length; i++) {
         ball = balls[i];
         ball.nextx = (ball.x += ball.velocityx);
         ball.nexty = (ball.y += ball.velocityy);
      }

  }

  function testWalls() {
      var ball;
      var testBall;

      for (var i = 0; i <balls.length; i++) {
         ball = balls[i];

         if (ball.nextx+ball.radius > theCanvas.width) {
            ball.velocityx = ball.velocityx*-1;
            ball.nextx = theCanvas.width - ball.radius;
```

```
        } else if (ball.nextx-ball.radius < 0 ) {
            ball.velocityx = ball.velocityx*-1;
            ball.nextx =ball.radius;

        } else if (ball.nexty+ball.radius > theCanvas.height ) {
            ball.velocityy = ball.velocityy*-1;
            ball.nexty = theCanvas.height - ball.radius;

        } else if(ball.nexty-ball.radius < 0) {
            ball.velocityy = ball.velocityy*-1;
            ball.nexty = ball.radius;
        }


    }

}

function render() {
    var ball;
    context.fillStyle = "#000000";
    for (var i = 0; i <balls.length; i++) {
        ball = balls[i];
        ball.x = ball.nextx;
        ball.y = ball.nexty;

        context.beginPath();
        context.arc(ball.x,ball.y,ball.radius,0,Math.PI*2,true);
        context.closePath();
        context.fill();
    }

}

function collide() {
    var ball;
    var testBall;
    for (var i = 0; i <balls.length; i++) {
        ball = balls[i];
        for (var j = i+1; j < balls.length; j++) {
            testBall = balls[j];
            if (hitTestCircle(ball,testBall)) {
                collideBalls(ball,testBall);
            }
        }
    }
}

function hitTestCircle(ball1,ball2) {
    var retval = false;
    var dx = ball1.nextx - ball2.nextx;
    var dy = ball1.nexty - ball2.nexty;
    var distance = (dx * dx + dy * dy);
    if (distance <= (ball1.radius + ball2.radius) * (ball1.radius + ball2.radius) ) {
            retval = true;
```

```
        }
        return retval;
    }

    function collideBalls(ball1,ball2) {

        var dx = ball1.nextx - ball2.nextx;
        var dy = ball1.nexty - ball2.nexty;

        var collisionAngle = Math.atan2(dy, dx);

        var speed1 = Math.sqrt(ball1.velocityx * ball1.velocityx +
            ball1.velocityy * ball1.velocityy);
        var speed2 = Math.sqrt(ball2.velocityx * ball2.velocityx +
            ball2.velocityy * ball2.velocityy);

        var direction1 = Math.atan2(ball1.velocityy, ball1.velocityx);
        var direction2 = Math.atan2(ball2.velocityy, ball2.velocityx);

        var velocityx_1 = speed1 * Math.cos(direction1 - collisionAngle);
        var velocityy_1 = speed1 * Math.sin(direction1 - collisionAngle);
        var velocityx_2 = speed2 * Math.cos(direction2 - collisionAngle);
        var velocityy_2 = speed2 * Math.sin(direction2 - collisionAngle);

        var final_velocityx_1 = ((ball1.mass - ball2.mass) * velocityx_1 +
            (ball2.mass + ball2.mass) * velocityx_2)/(ball1.mass + ball2.mass);
        var final_velocityx_2 = ((ball1.mass + ball1.mass) * velocityx_1 +
            (ball2.mass - ball1.mass) * velocityx_2)/(ball1.mass + ball2.mass);

        var final_velocityy_1 = velocityy_1;
        var final_velocityy_2 = velocityy_2;

        ball1.velocityx = Math.cos(collisionAngle) * final_velocityx_1 +
            Math.cos(collisionAngle + Math.PI/2) * final_velocityy_1;
        ball1.velocityy = Math.sin(collisionAngle) * final_velocityx_1 +
            Math.sin(collisionAngle + Math.PI/2) * final_velocityy_1;
        ball2.velocityx = Math.cos(collisionAngle) * final_velocityx_2 +
            Math.cos(collisionAngle + Math.PI/2) * final_velocityy_2;
        ball2.velocityy = Math.sin(collisionAngle) * final_velocityx_2 +
            Math.sin(collisionAngle + Math.PI/2) * final_velocityy_2;

        ball1.nextx = (ball1.nextx += ball1.velocityx);
        ball1.nexty = (ball1.nexty += ball1.velocityy);
        ball2.nextx = (ball2.nextx += ball2.velocityx);
        ball2.nexty = (ball2.nexty += ball2.velocityy);
    }

var numBalls = 200 ;
var maxSize = 15;
var minSize = 5;
var maxSpeed = maxSize+5;
var balls = new Array();
var tempBall;
var tempX;
var tempY;
```

```
    var tempSpeed;
    var tempAngle;
    var tempRadius;
    var tempRadians;
    var tempvelocityx;
    var tempvelocityy;

    theCanvas = document.getElementById("canvasOne");
    context = theCanvas.getContext("2d");

    for (var i = 0; i < numBalls; i++) {
        tempRadius = 5;
        var placeOK = false;
        while (!placeOK) {
            tempX = tempRadius*3 + (Math.floor(Math.random()*theCanvas.width)-tempRadius*3);
            tempY = tempRadius*3 + (Math.floor(Math.random()*theCanvas.height)-tempRadius*3);
            tempSpeed = 4;
            tempAngle = Math.floor(Math.random()*360);
            tempRadians = tempAngle * Math.PI/ 180;
            tempvelocityx = Math.cos(tempRadians) * tempSpeed;
            tempvelocityy = Math.sin(tempRadians) * tempSpeed;

            tempBall = {x:tempX,y:tempY, nextX: tempX, nextY: tempY, radius:tempRadius,
                speed:tempSpeed, angle:tempAngle, velocityx:tempvelocityx,
                velocityy:tempvelocityy, mass:tempRadius};
            placeOK = canStartHere(tempBall);
        }
        balls.push(tempBall);
    }

    function canStartHere(ball) {
        var retval = true;
        for (var i = 0; i <balls.length; i++) {
            if (hitTestCircle(ball, balls[i])) {
                retval = false;
            }
        }
        return retval;
    }
    setInterval(drawScreen, 33);

}

</script>

</head>
<body>
<div style="position: absolute; top: 50px; left: 50px;">


<canvas id="canvasOne" width="500" height="500">
 Your browser does not support HTML5 Canvas.
</canvas>
</div>
```

```
</body>
</html>
```

Now, when you execute Example 5-7 (*CH5EX7.html*), you will see a bunch of balls of the same size and mass bumping off of each other and the walls of the canvas, as shown in Figure 5-10. When you look at this demo, imagine all the ways you could modify it to do different things. You could create balls with different masses and different speeds, or even create balls that don't move but simply alter the direction of other balls that hit them. In Example 5-8, we will take a slightly different look at this same code and add some new properties to make it more interesting.

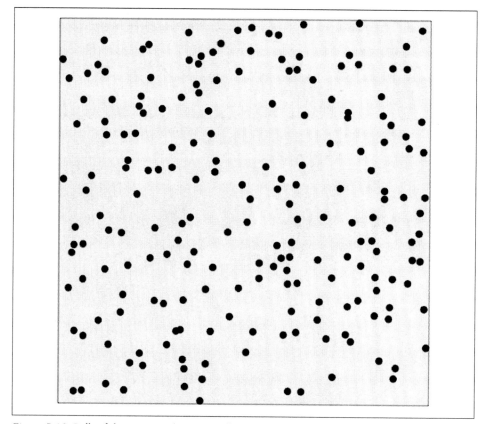

Figure 5-10. Balls of the same size bouncing off one another

Multiple Balls Bouncing with Friction

If we want the balls to slow down and eventually stop, we need to add friction to Example 5-7. For our purposes, simple friction is a value we use to modify the velocity of our objects every time they are drawn to the canvas.

In `canvasApp()`, we now want to create balls of various sizes. In the previous example, the balls were all the same size. It worked, but having balls of different sizes with different masses will create more interesting effects. To do this, we set `minSize` to 3 and `maxSize` to 12, meaning the radii for our balls will range from 3 to 12 pixels. We also add a new property named `friction`. This is a global property, so it will not be applied to each individual ball. We set it to `.01`, which means our balls will degrade their x and y velocities by `.01` pixels per frame (every time `drawScreen()` is called):

```
var numBalls = 50 ;
var maxSize = 12;
var minSize = 3;
var maxSpeed = maxSize+5;
var friction = .01;
```

We will now allow for various ball sizes. The mass of each ball will be different, and balls will have different effects on one another depending on their sizes. Recall that in Example 5-7 we needed a `mass` property so we could calculate conservation of momentum when the balls collided. We are doing the same thing here, but now the masses are different depending on the size:

```
for (var i = 0; i < numBalls; i++) {
    tempRadius = Math.floor(Math.random()*maxSize)+minSize;
```

In `update()`, we apply the `friction` value by calculating the product of the current velocity multiplied by friction, and then subtracting that value from the current velocity. We do this for both the x and y velocities. Why must we do this instead of simply subtracting the friction value from the x and y velocities? Because the x and y velocities are not always proportional to each other. If we simply subtract the friction, we may alter the velocity unintentionally. Instead, we need to subtract a value for the friction that is proportional to the velocity itself, and that value is the product of the velocity multiplied by the `friction` value. This method will give you a smooth degradation of the velocity when the `friction` value is applied:

```
function update() {
    for (var i = 0; i <balls.length; i++) {
        ball = balls[i];
        //Friction
        ball.velocityx = ball.velocityx - ( ball.velocityx*friction);
        ball.velocityy = ball.velocityy - ( ball.velocityy*friction);

        ball.nextx = (ball.x += ball.velocityx);
        ball.nexty = (ball.y += ball.velocityy);
    }

}
```

You can see the full version of this code by executing *CH5EX8.html* from the code distribution, or by typing in Example 5-8. You should notice that the smaller balls have less of an effect on the larger balls when they collide, and vice versa. Also, the balls slow down as they move due to the applied friction.

Example 5-8. Balls with friction

```
<!doctype html>
<html lang="en">
<head>
<meta charset="UTF-8">
<title>CH5EX8: Balls With Friction</title>
<script src="modernizr-1.6.min.js"></script>
<script type="text/javascript">
window.addEventListener('load', eventWindowLoaded, false);
function eventWindowLoaded() {
    canvasApp();

}

function canvasSupport () {
    return Modernizr.canvas;
}

function canvasApp() {

    if (!canvasSupport()) {
        return;
        }

  function  drawScreen () {

       context.fillStyle = '#EEEEEE';
       context.fillRect(0, 0, theCanvas.width, theCanvas.height);
       //Box
       context.strokeStyle = '#000000';
       context.strokeRect(1,  1, theCanvas.width-2, theCanvas.height-2);

       update();
       testWalls();
       collide();
       render();

    }

    function update() {
       for (var i = 0; i <balls.length; i++) {
          ball = balls[i];
          //Friction
          ball.velocityx = ball.velocityx - ( ball.velocityx*friction);
          ball.velocityy = ball.velocityy - ( ball.velocityy*friction);

          ball.nextx = (ball.x += ball.velocityx);
          ball.nexty = (ball.y += ball.velocityy);
       }

    }

    function testWalls() {
       var ball;
       var testBall;
```

```
    for (var i = 0; i <balls.length; i++) {
        ball = balls[i];

        if (ball.nextx+ball.radius > theCanvas.width) {
            ball.velocityx = ball.velocityx*-1;
            ball.nextx = theCanvas.width - ball.radius;

        } else if (ball.nextx-ball.radius < 0 ) {
            ball.velocityx = ball.velocityx*-1;
            ball.nextx = ball.radius;

        } else if (ball.nexty+ball.radius > theCanvas.height ) {
            ball.velocityy = ball.velocityy*-1;
            ball.nexty = theCanvas.height - ball.radius;

        } else if(ball.nexty-ball.radius < 0) {
            ball.velocityy = ball.velocityy*-1;
            ball.nexty = ball.radius;
        }

    }

}

function render() {
    var ball;

    context.fillStyle = "#000000";
    for (var i = 0; i <balls.length; i++) {
        ball = balls[i];
        ball.x = ball.nextx;
        ball.y = ball.nexty;

        context.beginPath();
        context.arc(ball.x,ball.y,ball.radius,0,Math.PI*2,true);
        context.closePath();
        context.fill();
    }

}

function collide() {
    var ball;
    var testBall;
    for (var i = 0; i <balls.length; i++) {
        ball = balls[i];
        for (var j = i+1; j < balls.length; j++) {
            testBall = balls[j];
            if (hitTestCircle(ball,testBall)) {
                collideBalls(ball,testBall);
            }
        }
    }
}
```

```
function hitTestCircle(ball1,ball2) {
    var retval = false;
    var dx = ball1.nextx - ball2.nextx;
    var dy = ball1.nexty - ball2.nexty;
    var distance = (dx * dx + dy * dy);
    if (distance <= (ball1.radius + ball2.radius) * (ball1.radius + ball2.radius) ) {
            retval = true;
       }
     return retval;
  }

function collideBalls(ball1,ball2) {

    var dx = ball1.nextx - ball2.nextx;
    var dy = ball1.nexty - ball2.nexty;

    var collisionAngle = Math.atan2(dy, dx);

    var speed1 = Math.sqrt(ball1.velocityx * ball1.velocityx +
        ball1.velocityy * ball1.velocityy);
    var speed2 = Math.sqrt(ball2.velocityx * ball2.velocityx +
        ball2.velocityy * ball2.velocityy);

    var direction1 = Math.atan2(ball1.velocityy, ball1.velocityx);
    var direction2 = Math.atan2(ball2.velocityy, ball2.velocityx);

    var velocityx_1 = speed1 * Math.cos(direction1 - collisionAngle);
    var velocityy_1 = speed1 * Math.sin(direction1 - collisionAngle);
    var velocityx_2 = speed2 * Math.cos(direction2 - collisionAngle);
    var velocityy_2 = speed2 * Math.sin(direction2 - collisionAngle);

    var final_velocityx_1 = ((ball1.mass - ball2.mass) * velocityx_1 +
        (ball2.mass + ball2.mass) * velocityx_2)/(ball1.mass + ball2.mass);
    var final_velocityx_2 = ((ball1.mass + ball1.mass) * velocityx_1 +
        (ball2.mass - ball1.mass) * velocityx_2)/(ball1.mass + ball2.mass);

    var final_velocityy_1 = velocityy_1;
    var final_velocityy_2 = velocityy_2;

    ball1.velocityx = Math.cos(collisionAngle) * final_velocityx_1 +
        Math.cos(collisionAngle + Math.PI/2) * final_velocityy_1;
    ball1.velocityy = Math.sin(collisionAngle) * final_velocityx_1 +
        Math.sin(collisionAngle + Math.PI/2) * final_velocityy_1;
    ball2.velocityx = Math.cos(collisionAngle) * final_velocityx_2 +
        Math.cos(collisionAngle + Math.PI/2) * final_velocityy_2;
    ball2.velocityy = Math.sin(collisionAngle) * final_velocityx_2 +
        Math.sin(collisionAngle + Math.PI/2) * final_velocityy_2;

    ball1.nextx = (ball1.nextx += ball1.velocityx);
    ball1.nexty = (ball1.nexty += ball1.velocityy);
    ball2.nextx = (ball2.nextx += ball2.velocityx);
    ball2.nexty = (ball2.nexty += ball2.velocityy);
}
var numBalls = 50 ;
```

```
    var maxSize = 12;
    var minSize = 3;
    var maxSpeed = maxSize+5;
    var balls = new Array();
    var tempBall;
    var tempX;
    var tempY;
    var tempSpeed;
    var tempAngle;
    var tempRadius;
    var tempRadians;
    var tempvelocityx;
    var tempvelocityy;
    var friction = .01;

    theCanvas = document.getElementById("canvasOne");
    context = theCanvas.getContext("2d");

    for (var i = 0; i < numBalls; i++) {
        tempRadius = Math.floor(Math.random()*maxSize)+minSize;
        var placeOK = false;
        while (!placeOK) {
            tempX = tempRadius*3 + (Math.floor(Math.random()*theCanvas.width)-tempRadius*3);
            tempY = tempRadius*3 + (Math.floor(Math.random()*theCanvas.height)-tempRadius*3);
            tempSpeed = maxSpeed-tempRadius;
            tempAngle = Math.floor(Math.random()*360);
            tempRadians = tempAngle * Math.PI/ 180;
            tempvelocityx = Math.cos(tempRadians) * tempSpeed;
            tempvelocityy = Math.sin(tempRadians) * tempSpeed;

            tempBall = {x:tempX,y:tempY,radius:tempRadius, speed:tempSpeed, angle:tempAngle,
                velocityx:tempvelocityx, velocityy:tempvelocityy, mass:tempRadius*8,
                nextx: tempX, nexty:tempY};
            placeOK = canStartHere(tempBall);
        }
        balls.push(tempBall);
    }

    function canStartHere(ball) {
        var retval = true;
        for (var i = 0; i <balls.length; i++) {
            if (hitTestCircle(ball, balls[i])) {
                retval = false;
            }
        }
        return retval;
    }
    setInterval(drawScreen, 33);

}

</script>

</head>
<body>
```

```
<div style="position: absolute; top: 50px; left: 50px;">

<canvas id="canvasOne" width="500" height="500">
 Your browser does not support HTML5 Canvas.
</canvas>
</div>
</body>
</html>
```

Figure 5-11 illustrates how this code will look in the browser.

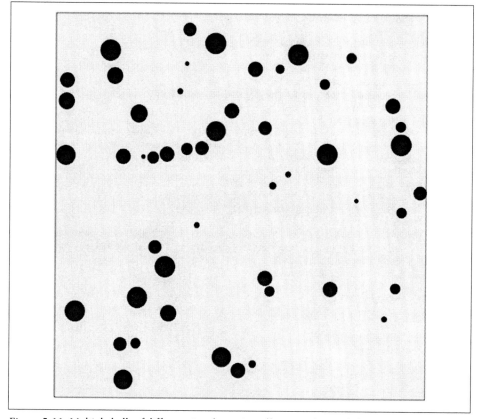

Figure 5-11. Multiple balls of different sizes bouncing off one another with friction applied

Curve and Circular Movement

Whew! Moving and colliding balls on vectors can create some cool effects. However, moving in straight lines is not the only way you might want to move objects. In this section, we will show you some ways to animate objects using circles, spirals, and curves.

Uniform Circular Motion

Uniform circular motion occurs when we move an object along the distinct radius of a defined circle. Once we know the radius, we can use our old friends cosine and sine to find the x and y locations of the moving object. The equations to find the locations of an object moving uniformly on a defined circle are:

```
x = radius * cosine(angle)
y = radius * sine(angle)
```

We will create an example of uniform circular movement with a circle that has a radius of 125, with its center position at 250,250 on the canvas. We will move a ball along that circle, starting at an angle of 0.

In canvasApp(), we will define this circle path as a dynamic object stored in the circle variable. While this object defines the properties of a circle, we will not actually draw this circle on the canvas; rather, it defines only the path on which we will move our ball object:

```
var circle = {centerX:250, centerY:250, radius:125, angle:0}
var ball = {x:0, y:0,speed:.1};
```

In drawScreen(), we will incorporate the equations for uniform circular movement. To do this, we will set the x and y properties of the ball object to the products of the equations, added to the center location of the circle path on the canvas (circle .centerX, circle.centerY):

```
ball.x = circle.centerX + Math.cos(circle.angle) * circle.radius;
ball.y = circle.centerY + Math.sin(circle.angle) * circle.radius;
```

We then add the speed of the ball to the angle of the circle path. This effectively sets the ball to move to a new location the next time drawScreen() is called:

```
circle.angle += ball.speed;
```

Finally, we draw the ball onto the canvas:

```
context.fillStyle = "#000000";
context.beginPath();
context.arc(ball.x,ball.y,15,0,Math.PI*2,true);
context.closePath();
context.fill();
```

You can see what the circle path looks like in Figure 5-12. We have drawn the points on the canvas to illustrate the circle path.

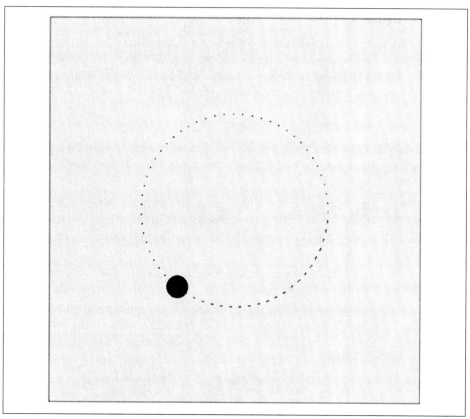

Figure 5-12. Moving an object in a circle

You can easily alter the location and size of the circle path by altering the `radius`, `centerX`, and `centerY` properties of the circle path object.

Example 5-9 shows the code for *CH5EX9.html*.

Example 5-9. Moving in a circle

```
<!doctype html>
<html lang="en">
<head>
<meta charset="UTF-8">
<title>CH5EX9: Moving In A Circle</title>
<script src="modernizr-1.6.min.js"></script>
<script type="text/javascript">
```

```
window.addEventListener('load', eventWindowLoaded, false);
function eventWindowLoaded() {
   canvasApp();

}

function canvasSupport () {
     return Modernizr.canvas;
}

function canvasApp() {

  if (!canvasSupport()) {
        return;
      }

  function  drawScreen () {

      context.fillStyle = '#EEEEEE';
      context.fillRect(0, 0, theCanvas.width, theCanvas.height);
      //Box
      context.strokeStyle = '#000000';
      context.strokeRect(1,  1, theCanvas.width-2, theCanvas.height-2);

      ball.x = circle.centerX + Math.cos(circle.angle) * circle.radius;
      ball.y = circle.centerY + Math.sin(circle.angle) * circle.radius;

      circle.angle += ball.speed;

      context.fillStyle = "#000000";
      context.beginPath();
      context.arc(ball.x,ball.y,15,0,Math.PI*2,true);
      context.closePath();
      context.fill();

  }

  var radius = 100;
  var circle = {centerX:250, centerY:250, radius:125, angle:0}
  var ball = {x:0, y:0,speed:.1};

  theCanvas = document.getElementById("canvasOne");
  context = theCanvas.getContext("2d");

  setInterval(drawScreen, 33);

}

</script>
```

```
</head>
<body>
<div style="position: absolute; top: 50px; left: 50px;">

<canvas id="canvasOne" width="500" height="500">
 Your browser does not support HTML5 Canvas.
</canvas>
</div>
</body>
</html>
```

Moving in a Simple Spiral

There are many complicated ways to move an object on a spiral path. One such way would be to use the Fibonacci sequence, which describes a pattern seen in nature that appears to create perfect spirals. The Fibonacci sequence starts with the number 0, and continues with each subsequent number calculated as the sum of the two previous numbers in the sequence. Each subsequent rotation of the spiral is the sum of the two previous numbers (1, 2, 3, 5, 8, 13, 21, 34, 55, 89...). However, as you might imagine, the math used to create this sequence is quite involved, and it is also difficult to translate to object movement.

For our purposes, we can create a simple spiral by increasing the radius of the circle path on each call to drawScreen(). If we take the code from Example 5-9, we would add a radiusInc variable, which we will use as the value to add the radius movement path of the circle. We create this new variable in canvasApp():

```
var radiusInc = 2;
```

Then, in drawScreen(), we add the following code to increase the radius of the circle every time we move the object:

```
circle.radius += radiusInc;
```

In Figure 5-13, you can see what the resulting spiral looks like (to illustrate the path, this example includes the points).

If you want a tighter spiral, decrease the value of radiusInc. Conversely, if you want a wider spiral, increase the value of radiusInc.

Example 5-10 shows the code for *CH5EX10.html* from the code distribution.

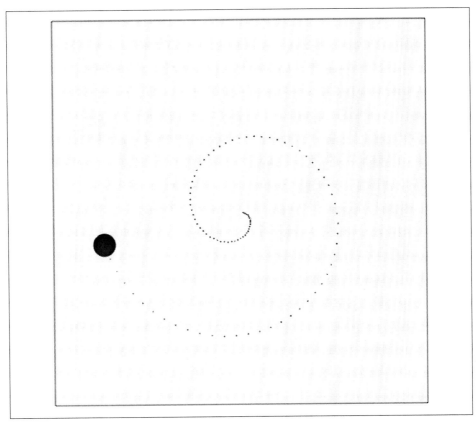

Figure 5-13. Moving an object in a simple spiral pattern

Example 5-10. Moving in a simple geometric spiral

```
<!doctype html>
<html lang="en">
<head>
<meta charset="UTF-8">
<title>CH5EX10: Moving In A Simple Geometric Spiral </title>
<script src="modernizr-1.6.min.js"></script>
<script type="text/javascript">
window.addEventListener('load', eventWindowLoaded, false);
function eventWindowLoaded() {
    canvasApp();

}

function canvasSupport () {
     return Modernizr.canvas;
}


function canvasApp() {
```

```
        if (!canvasSupport()) {
                return;
            }

    var pointImage = new Image();
    pointImage.src = "point.png";
    function  drawScreen () {


        context.fillStyle = '#EEEEEE';
        context.fillRect(0, 0, theCanvas.width, theCanvas.height);
        //Box
        context.strokeStyle = '#000000';
        context.strokeRect(1,  1, theCanvas.width-2, theCanvas.height-2);

        ball.x = circle.centerX + Math.cos(circle.angle) * circle.radius;
        ball.y = circle.centerY + Math.sin(circle.angle) * circle.radius;
        circle.angle += ball.speed;
        circle.radius += radiusInc;

        //Draw points to illustrate path

        points.push({x:ball.x,y:ball.y});

        for (var i = 0; i< points.length; i++) {
            context.drawImage(pointImage, points[i].x, points[i].y,1,1);
        }

        context.fillStyle = "#000000";
        context.beginPath();
        context.arc(ball.x,ball.y,15,0,Math.PI*2,true);
        context.closePath();
        context.fill();

    }

    var radiusInc = 2;
    var circle = {centerX:250, centerY:250, radius:2, angle:0, radiusInc:2}
    var ball = {x:0, y:0,speed:.1};
    var points = new Array();

    theCanvas = document.getElementById("canvasOne");
    context = theCanvas.getContext("2d");

    setInterval(drawScreen, 33);

}

</script>

</head>
<body>
<div style="position: absolute; top: 50px; left: 50px;">
```

```
<canvas id="canvasOne" width="500" height="500">
 Your browser does not support HTML5 Canvas.
</canvas>
</div>
</body>
</html>
```

Cubic Bezier Curve Movement

Cubic Bezier curves can be used to define a movement path for an object. Pierre Bezier first popularized these curves in the 1960s. They are widely used in 2D vector graphics to define smooth curves for drawing, but they can also be used in animation to define a path for motion.

A cubic Bezier curve is created using four distinct points—p0, p1, p2, and p3:

p0
> The starting point of the curve. We will refer to these x and y values as x0 and y0.

p3
> The ending point of the curve. We will refer to these x and y values as x3 and y3.

p1 *and* p2
> The control points for the curve. The curve *does not pass through* these points; instead, the equation uses these points to determine the arc of the curve. We will refer to these x and y values as x0, x1, x2, x3, y0, y1, y2, and y3.

 The usage of the p1 and p2 points is the biggest stumbling block for understanding Bezier curves. The easiest way to understand the relationship between these points and the curve is to draw them on a bitmapped canvas, which we will do several times in this chapter.

After you have the four points, you need to calculate six coefficient values that you will use to find the x and y locations as you move an object on the curve. These coefficients are known as ax, bx, cx, ay, by, and cy. They are calculated as follows:

```
cx = 3 (x1 - x0)
bx = 3 (x2 - x1) - cx
ax = x3 - x0 - cx - bx
cy = 3 (y1 - y0)
by = 3 (y2 - y1) - cy
ay = y3 - y0 - cy - by
```

After you've calculated the six coefficients, you can find the x and y locations based on the changing t value using the following equations. The t value represents movement over time:

```
x(t) = axt3 + bxt2 + cxt + x0
y(t) = ayt3 + byt2 + cyt + y0
```

For our purposes, the t value will be increased by the speed at which we want the object to move. You will notice, though, that this value does not easily equate to the speed values we used elsewhere in this chapter. The reason is that the t value was not created with movement over time for animation in mind. The speed we specify must be smaller than 1 so the movement on the curve will be incremental enough for us to see it as part of the animation. For our example, we will increase t by a speed of .01, so that we will see 100 points on the movement curve (1/100 = .01). This is advantageous because we will know our object has finished moving when the t value is equal to 1.

For Example 5-11 (*CH5EX11.html*), we will start by creating the four points of the Bezier curve in the canvasApp() function:

```
var p0 = {x:60, y:10};
var p1 = {x:70, y:200};
var p2 = {x:125, y:295};
var p3 = {x:350, y:350};
```

We then create a new ball object with a couple differing properties from those in the other examples in this chapter. The speed is .01, which means the object will move 100 points along the curve before it is finished. We start the t value at 0, which means the ball will begin at p0:

```
var ball = {x:0, y:0, speed:.01, t:0};
```

Next, in the drawScreen() function, we calculate the Bezier curve coefficient values (ax, bx, cx, ay, by, cy) based on the four points (p0, p1, p2, p3):

```
var cx = 3 * (p1.x - p0.x)
var bx = 3 * (p2.x - p1.x) - cx;
var ax = p3.x - p0.x - cx - bx;

var cy = 3 * (p1.y - p0.y);
var by = 3 * (p2.y - p1.y) - cy;
var ay = p3.y - p0.y - cy - by;
```

Then, we take our t value and use it with the coefficients to calculate the x and y values for the moving object. First, we get the t value from the ball object, and store it locally so we can use it in our calculations:

```
var t = ball.t;
```

Next, we add the speed to the t value so that we can calculate the next point on the Bezier path:

```
ball.t += ball.speed;
```

Then, we use the t value to calculate the x and y values (xt, yt) using the Bezier curve equations:

```
var xt = ax*(t*t*t) + bx*(t*t) + cx*t + p0.x;
var yt = ay*(t*t*t) + by*(t*t) + cy*t + p0.y;
```

We add the speed to the t value of ball, then check to see whether t is greater than 1. If so, we don't increase it any further because we have finished moving on the curve:

```
ball.t += ball.speed;

if (ball.t > 1) {
    ball.t = 1;
}
```

Finally, when we draw the `ball` object on the canvas, we use the `xt` and `yt` values:

```
context.arc(xt,yt,5,0,Math.PI*2,true);
```

Figure 5-14 shows what Example 5-11 (*CH5EX11.html*) looks like when it is executed in a web browser. In addition to drawing the points of the path using the `points` array, we also draw the four points of the Bezier curve. These illustrate the relationship of the points to the curve itself. Notice that the curve does not pass through `p1` or `p2`.

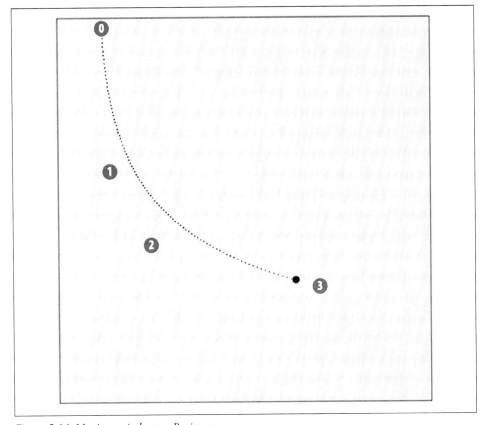

Figure 5-14. Moving a circle on a Bezier curve

Example 5-11 gives the full code listing for *CH5EX11.html*, including the code to draw the Bezier curve points on the canvas. You can find that code in the `drawScreen()` function following the `//draw the points` comment.

Example 5-11. Moving on a cubic Bezier curve

```html
<!doctype html>
<html lang="en">
<head>
<meta charset="UTF-8">
<title>CH5EX11: Moving On A Cubic Bezier Curve </title>
<script src="modernizr-1.6.min.js"></script>
<script type="text/javascript">
window.addEventListener('load', eventWindowLoaded, false);
function eventWindowLoaded() {
   canvasApp();

}
function canvasSupport () {
     return Modernizr.canvas;
}

function canvasApp() {

  if (!canvasSupport()) {
        return;
      }

  var pointImage = new Image();
  pointImage.src = "point.png";

  function  drawScreen () {

      context.fillStyle = '#EEEEEE';
      context.fillRect(0, 0, theCanvas.width, theCanvas.height);
      //Box
      context.strokeStyle = '#000000';
      context.strokeRect(1,  1, theCanvas.width-2, theCanvas.height-2);

      var t = ball.t;

      var cx = 3 * (p1.x - p0.x)
      var bx = 3 * (p2.x - p1.x) - cx;
      var ax = p3.x - p0.x - cx - bx;

      var cy = 3 * (p1.y - p0.y);
      var by = 3 * (p2.y - p1.y) - cy;
      var ay = p3.y - p0.y - cy - by;

      var xt = ax*(t*t*t) + bx*(t*t) + cx*t + p0.x;
      var yt = ay*(t*t*t) + by*(t*t) + cy*t + p0.y;

      ball.t += ball.speed;

      if (ball.t > 1) {
         ball.t = 1;
      }
```

```
//draw the points

context.font ="10px sans";
context.fillStyle = "#FF0000";
context.beginPath();
context.arc(p0.x,p0.y,8,0,Math.PI*2,true);
context.closePath();
context.fill();
context.fillStyle = "#FFFFFF";
context.fillText("0",p0.x-2,p0.y+2);

context.fillStyle = "#FF0000";
context.beginPath();
context.arc(p1.x,p1.y,8,0,Math.PI*2,true);
context.closePath();
context.fill();
context.fillStyle = "#FFFFFF";
context.fillText("1",p1.x-2,p1.y+2);

context.fillStyle = "#FF0000";
context.beginPath();
context.arc(p2.x,p2.y,8,0,Math.PI*2,true);
context.closePath();
context.fill();
context.fillStyle = "#FFFFFF";
context.fillText("2",p2.x-2, p2.y+2);

context.fillStyle = "#FF0000";
context.beginPath();
context.arc(p3.x,p3.y,8,0,Math.PI*2,true);
context.closePath();
context.fill();
context.fillStyle = "#FFFFFF";
context.fillText("3",p3.x-2, p3.y+2);

//Draw points to illustrate path

points.push({x:xt,y:yt});

for (var i = 0; i< points.length; i++) {
   context.drawImage(pointImage, points[i].x, points[i].y,1,1);
}

context.closePath();

//Draw circle moving

context.fillStyle = "#000000";
context.beginPath();
context.arc(xt,yt,5,0,Math.PI*2,true);
context.closePath();
context.fill();

}
```

```
    var p0 = {x:60, y:10};
    var p1 = {x:70, y:200};
    var p2 = {x:125, y:295};
    var p3 = {x:350, y:350};
    var ball = {x:0, y:0, speed:.01, t:0};
    var points = new Array();

    theCanvas = document.getElementById("canvasOne");
    context = theCanvas.getContext("2d");

    setInterval(drawScreen, 33);

}

</script>

</head>
<body>
<div style="position: absolute; top: 50px; left: 50px;">

<canvas id="canvasOne" width="500" height="500">
 Your browser does not support HTML5 Canvas.
</canvas>
</div>
</body>
</html>
```

Moving an Image

Moving an image on a cubic Bezier curve path is just as easy as moving a circular drawing object, as we'll demonstrate in the next two examples. Suppose you are making a game where bullseyes move across the canvas and the player must shoot at them. You could use cubic Bezier curve paths to create new and interesting patterns for the bullseyes to move along.

For this example, we first create a global variable named bullseye, which we will use to hold the *bullseye.png* image that we will load to display on the canvas:

```
    var bullseye;
    function eventWindowLoaded() {
        bullseye = new Image();
        bullseye.src = "bullseye.png"
        bullseye.onload = eventAssetsLoaded;
    }
```

In canvasApp(), we will create a different path for the curve from the one in the first example by setting new values for p0, p1, p2, and p3. Using these values, the bullseye will move on a parabola-like path (Figure 5-15 shows the path of the curve):

```
    var p0 = {x:60, y:10};
    var p1 = {x:150, y:350};
    var p2 = {x:300, y:375};
    var p3 = {x:400, y:20};
```

We also need to create a **player** object that represents the bullseye on the canvas:

```
var player = {x:0, y:0, speed:.01, t:0};
```

In `drawImage()`, after we calculate t, xt, and yt, we draw the image on the canvas:

```
player.x = xt-bullseye.width/2;
    player.y = yt-bullseye.height/2;

    context.drawImage(bullseye,player.x,player.y);
```

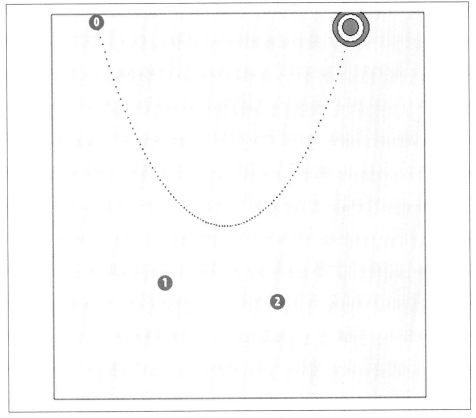

Figure 5-15. Moving an image on a cubic Bezier curve path

The rest of Example 5-12 works just like Example 5-11.

Example 5-12. Moving an image

```
<!doctype html>
<html lang="en">
<head>
<meta charset="UTF-8">
<title>CH5EX12: Moving An Image </title>
<script src="modernizr-1.6.min.js"></script>
```

```
<script type="text/javascript">
window.addEventListener('load', eventWindowLoaded, false);

var bullseye;
function eventWindowLoaded() {
   bullseye = new Image();
   bullseye.src = "bullseye.png"
   bullseye.onload = eventAssetsLoaded;
}

function eventAssetsLoaded() {

   canvasApp();
}

function canvasSupport () {
     return Modernizr.canvas;
}

function canvasApp() {

  if (!canvasSupport()) {
        return;
      }

  var pointImage = new Image();
  pointImage.src = "point.png";
  function  drawScreen () {

      context.fillStyle = '#EEEEEE';
      context.fillRect(0, 0, theCanvas.width, theCanvas.height);
      //Box
      context.strokeStyle = '#000000';
      context.strokeRect(1,  1, theCanvas.width-2, theCanvas.height-2);

      var t = player.t;

      var cx = 3 * (p1.x - p0.x)
      var bx = 3 * (p2.x - p1.x) - cx;
      var ax = p3.x - p0.x - cx - bx;

      var cy = 3 * (p1.y - p0.y);
      var by = 3 * (p2.y - p1.y) - cy;
      var ay = p3.y - p0.y - cy - by;

      var xt = ax*(t*t*t) + bx*(t*t) + cx*t + p0.x;

      var yt = ay*(t*t*t) + by*(t*t) + cy*t + p0.y;

      player.t += player.speed;

      if (player.t > 1) {
         player.t = 1;
      }
```

```
    //draw the points

    context.font = "10px sans";

    context.fillStyle = "#FF0000";
    context.beginPath();
    context.arc(p0.x,p0.y,8,0,Math.PI*2,true);
    context.closePath();
    context.fill();
    context.fillStyle = "#FFFFFF";
    context.fillText("0",p0.x-2,p0.y+2);

    context.fillStyle = "#FF0000";
    context.beginPath();
    context.arc(p1.x,p1.y,8,0,Math.PI*2,true);
    context.closePath();
    context.fill();
    context.fillStyle = "#FFFFFF";
    context.fillText("1",p1.x-2,p1.y+2);

    context.fillStyle = "#FF0000";
    context.beginPath();
    context.arc(p2.x,p2.y,8,0,Math.PI*2,true);
    context.closePath();
    context.fill();
    context.fillStyle = "#FFFFFF";
    context.fillText("2",p2.x-2, p2.y+2);

    context.fillStyle = "#FF0000";
    context.beginPath();
    context.arc(p3.x,p3.y,8,0,Math.PI*2,true);
    context.closePath();
    context.fill();
    context.fillStyle = "#FFFFFF";
    context.fillText("3",p3.x-2, p3.y+2);

    //Draw points to illustrate path

    points.push({x:xt,y:yt});

    for (var i = 0; i< points.length; i++) {
        context.drawImage(pointImage, points[i].x, points[i].y,1,1);
    }

    context.closePath();

    player.x = xt-bullseye.width/2;
    player.y = yt-bullseye.height/2;

    context.drawImage(bullseye,player.x,player.y);

}

var p0 = {x:60, y:10};
var p1 = {x:150, y:350};
```

```
        var p2 = {x:300, y:375};
        var p3 = {x:400, y:20};
        var player = {x:0, y:0, speed:.01, t:0};
        var points = new Array();

        theCanvas = document.getElementById("canvasOne");
        context = theCanvas.getContext("2d");

        setInterval(drawScreen, 33);

    }

    </script>

</head>
<body>
<div style="position: absolute; top: 50px; left: 50px;">

<canvas id="canvasOne" width="500" height="500">
 Your browser does not support HTML5 Canvas.
</canvas>
</div>
</body>
</html>
```

Creating a Cubic Bezier Curve Loop

You can create some very interesting paths using the four points in a cubic Bezier curve. One such effect is a loop. To create a loop, you need to make sure the points form an X, with p0 diagonal from p1, and p2 and p3 on an opposite diagonal from the other two points. p0 and p3 must be closer to the center of the canvas than p1 or p2. Below are the points we will use to create this effect in Example 5-13:

```
    var p0 = {x:150, y:440};
    var p1 = {x:450, y:10};
    var p2 = {x:50, y:10};
    var p3 = {x:325, y:450};
```

Since it is much easier to show than tell when it comes to cubic Bezier curves, look at Figure 5-16. It shows what the looping curve looks like when Example 5-13 is executed in a web browser.

 This effect can only be created with the four points of a cubic Bezier curve. There is also a three-point Bezier curve known as a quadratic Bezier curve. You cannot create loops or S curves with quadratic Bezier curves because the three points are not as precise as the four points of a cubic Bezier curve.

Figure 5-16. Moving an object in a loop using a cubic Bezier curve

Since the code for this example is essentially the same as in Example 5-12 (besides the four points), we have highlighted in bold the changed code in Example 5-13. We have done this to show you that—with relatively simple changes—you can create dramatic animation effects using cubic Bezier curves.

Example 5-13. Bezier curve loop

```
<!doctype html>
<html lang="en">
<head>
<meta charset="UTF-8">
<title>CH5EX13: Bezier Curve Loop </title>
<script src="modernizr-1.6.min.js"></script>
<script type="text/javascript">
window.addEventListener('load', eventWindowLoaded, false);

var bullseye;
function eventWindowLoaded() {
    bullseye = new Image();
    bullseye.src = "bullseye.png"
    bullseye.onload = eventAssetsLoaded;
```

```
}

function eventAssetsLoaded() {

    canvasApp();
}

function canvasSupport () {
    return Modernizr.canvas;
}

function canvasApp() {

    if (!canvasSupport()) {
            return;
        }

  var pointImage = new Image();
  pointImage.src = "point.png";
  function  drawScreen () {

      context.fillStyle = '#EEEEEE';
      context.fillRect(0, 0, theCanvas.width, theCanvas.height);
      //Box
      context.strokeStyle = '#000000';
      context.strokeRect(1,   1, theCanvas.width-2, theCanvas.height-2);

      var t = player.t;

      var cx = 3 * (p1.x - p0.x)
      var bx = 3 * (p2.x - p1.x) - cx;
      var ax = p3.x - p0.x - cx - bx;

      var cy = 3 * (p1.y - p0.y);
      var by = 3 * (p2.y - p1.y) - cy;
      var ay = p3.y - p0.y - cy - by;

      var xt = ax*(t*t*t) + bx*(t*t) + cx*t + p0.x;

      var yt = ay*(t*t*t) + by*(t*t) + cy*t + p0.y;

      player.t += player.speed;

      if (player.t > 1) {
         player.t = 1;
      }
      //draw the points

      context.font = "10px sans";

      context.fillStyle = "#FF0000";
      context.beginPath();
      context.arc(p0.x,p0.y,8,0,Math.PI*2,true);
      context.closePath();
      context.fill();
```

```
        context.fillStyle = "#FFFFFF";
        context.fillText("0",p0.x-2,p0.y+2);

        context.fillStyle = "#FF0000";
        context.beginPath();
        context.arc(p1.x,p1.y,8,0,Math.PI*2,true);
        context.closePath();
        context.fill();
        context.fillStyle = "#FFFFFF";
        context.fillText("1",p1.x-2,p1.y+2);

        context.fillStyle = "#FF0000";
        context.beginPath();
        context.arc(p2.x,p2.y,8,0,Math.PI*2,true);
        context.closePath();
        context.fill();
        context.fillStyle = "#FFFFFF";
        context.fillText("2",p2.x-2, p2.y+2);

        context.fillStyle = "#FF0000";
        context.beginPath();
        context.arc(p3.x,p3.y,8,0,Math.PI*2,true);
        context.closePath();
        context.fill();
        context.fillStyle = "#FFFFFF";
        context.fillText("3",p3.x-2, p3.y+2);

        points.push({x:xt,y:yt});

        for (var i = 0; i< points.length; i++) {
            context.drawImage(pointImage, points[i].x, points[i].y,1,1);
        }

        context.closePath();

        player.x = xt-bullseye.width/2;
        player.y = yt-bullseye.height/2;

        context.drawImage(bullseye,player.x,player.y);

    }

var p0 = {x:150, y:440};
var p1 = {x:450, y:10};
var p2 = {x:50, y:10};
var p3 = {x:325, y:450};
var player = {x:0, y:0, speed:.01, t:0};

var points = new Array();

theCanvas = document.getElementById("canvasOne");
context = theCanvas.getContext("2d");

setInterval(drawScreen, 33);
```

```
      }

  </script>

  </head>
  <body>
  <div style="position: absolute; top: 50px; left: 50px;">

  <canvas id="canvasOne" width="500" height="500">
   Your browser does not support HTML5 Canvas.
  </canvas>
  </div>
  </body>
  </html>
```

Simple Gravity, Elasticity, and Friction

Adding simulated gravity, elasticity, and friction to your objects adds a sense of realism that otherwise would not exist in 2D. These properties are major forces in nature that people feel and understand at nearly every moment of their lives. This means that people who play games expect objects to act in a particular way when these properties are applied. Our job is to simulate those effects as closely as possible, while minimizing the processing power necessary to create them. While there are some very complicated physics equations we could use to create these effects, we will use simplified versions that work well with the limited resources available to HTML5 Canvas in a web browser.

Simple Gravity

A very simple, yet seemingly realistic gravitational effect can be achieved by applying a constant gravity value to the y velocity of an object moving on a vector. To do this, select a value for gravity, such as .1, and then add that value to the y velocity of your object on every call to drawScreen().

For this example, let's simulate a ball with a radius of 15 pixels being shot from a cannon that rests near the bottom of the canvas. The ball will move at a speed of 4 pixels per frame, with an angle of 305 degrees. This means it will move up and to the right on the canvas. If we did not apply any gravity, the ball would simply keep moving on that vector until it left the canvas (actually, it would keep moving, we just would not see it any longer).

You have seen the code to create an effect like this already. In the `canvasApp()` function, we would create the starting variables like this:

```
var speed = 4;
var angle = 305;
var radians = angle * Math.PI/ 180;
var radius = 15;
var vx = Math.cos(radians) * speed;
var vy = Math.sin(radians) * speed;
```

Next, we create the starting point for the ball as `p1`, and then create a dynamic object that holds all the values we created for the `ball` object:

```
var p1 = {x:20,y:theCanvas.width-radius};
var ball = {x:p1.x, y:p1.y, velocityx: vx, velocityy:vy, radius:radius};
```

If we want to add gravity to the application, we would first create a new variable named `gravity` and set it to a constant value of `.1`:

```
var gravity = .1;
```

Next, in the `drawScreen()` function, we apply this gravity value to the `ball` object when it is drawn to the canvas (`ball.velocityy += gravity`). We want the ball to stop moving when it hits the "ground" (the bottom of the canvas), so we test to see whether the y position of the `ball` plus the `radius` of the ball (the outer edge) has passed the bottom of the canvas (`ball.y + ball.radius <= theCanvas.height`). If so, we stop the ball's movement:

```
if (ball.y + ball.radius <= theCanvas.height) {
    ball.velocityy += gravity;
} else {
    ball.velocityx = 0;
    ball.velocityy = 0;
    ball.y = theCanvas.height - ball.radius;

}
```

Next, we apply the constant x velocity and the new y velocity to `ball`, and draw it to the canvas:

```
ball.y += ball.velocityy;
ball.x += ball.velocityx;

context.fillStyle = "#000000";
context.beginPath();
context.arc(ball.x,ball.y,ball.radius,0,Math.PI*2,true);
context.closePath();
context.fill();
```

Figure 5-17 shows what the path looks like when simple gravity is applied to a ball moving on a vector. We have added the points to illustrate the path.

Figure 5-17. Simple gravity with an object moving on a vector

You can test out Example 5-14 with the file *CH5EX14.html* in the code distribution, or type in the full code listing below.

Example 5-14. Simple gravity

```
a<!doctype html>
<html lang="en">
<head>
<meta charset="UTF-8">
<title>CH5EX14: Simple Gravity</title>
<script src="modernizr-1.6.min.js"></script>
<script type="text/javascript">
window.addEventListener('load', eventWindowLoaded, false);
function eventWindowLoaded() {
    canvasApp();
}

function canvasSupport () {
    return Modernizr.canvas;
}
```

```
function canvasApp() {

    if (!canvasSupport()) {
            return;
        }

  function  drawScreen () {

        context.fillStyle = '#EEEEEE';
        context.fillRect(0, 0, theCanvas.width, theCanvas.height);
        //Box
        context.strokeStyle = '#000000';
        context.strokeRect(1,  1, theCanvas.width-2, theCanvas.height-2);

        if (ball.y + ball.radius <= theCanvas.height) {
            ball.velocityy += gravity;
        } else {
            ball.velocityx = 0;
            ball.velocityy = 0;
            ball.y = theCanvas.height - ball.radius;

        }

        ball.y += ball.velocityy;
        ball.x += ball.velocityx;

        context.fillStyle = "#000000";
        context.beginPath();
        context.arc(ball.x,ball.y,ball.radius,0,Math.PI*2,true);
        context.closePath();
        context.fill();

    }
    var speed = 4;

    var gravity = .1;
    var angle = 305;
    var radians = angle * Math.PI/ 180;
    var radius = 15;
    var vx = Math.cos(radians) * speed;
    var vy = Math.sin(radians) * speed;

    theCanvas = document.getElementById("canvasOne");
    context = theCanvas.getContext("2d");

    var p1 = {x:20,y:theCanvas.width-radius};
    var ball = {x:p1.x, y:p1.y, velocityx: vx, velocityy:vy, radius:radius};

    setInterval(drawScreen, 33);

}

</script>
```

```
</head>
<body>
<div style="position: absolute; top: 50px; left: 50px;">

<canvas id="canvasOne" width="500" height="500">
 Your browser does not support HTML5 Canvas.
</canvas>
</div>
</body>
</html>
```

Simple Gravity with a Bounce

The last example showed what a cannonball might look like if it was shot out, landed on a surface, and stuck there with no reaction. However, even a heavy cannonball will bounce when it hits the ground.

To create a bouncing effect we do not have to change the code very much at all. In drawScreen(), we first apply gravity on every frame; then, instead of stopping the ball if it hits the bottom of the canvas, we simply need to reverse the y velocity of ball when it hits the ground.

In *CH5EX14.html* you would replace this code...

```
if (ball.y + ball.radius <= theCanvas.height) {
    ball.velocityy += gravity;
} else {
    ball.velocityx = 0;
    ball.velocityy = 0;
    ball.y = theCanvas.height - ball.radius;
}
```

...with this:

```
ball.velocityy += gravity;
if ((ball.y + ball.radius) > theCanvas.height) {
    ball.velocityy = -(ball.velocityy)
}
```

This code will send the ball bouncing back "up" the canvas. Since it is still traveling on the vector, and gravity is applied every time drawScreen() is called, the ball will eventually come down again as the applied gravity overtakes the reversed y velocity.

Figure 5-18 shows what the cannonball looks like when the bounce is applied.

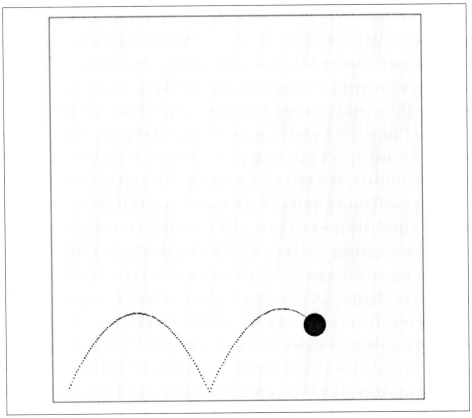

Figure 5-18. A ball moving on a vector with gravity and a bounce applied

 To achieve a nice-looking bounce for this example, we also changed the angle of the vector in `canvasApp()` to 295:

```
var angle = 295;
```

Example 5-15 offers the full code.

Example 5-15. Simple gravity with a bounce

```
<!doctype html>
<html lang="en">
<head>
<meta charset="UTF-8">
<title>CH5EX15: Gravity With A Bounce</title>
<script src="modernizr-1.6.min.js"></script>
<script type="text/javascript">
window.addEventListener('load', eventWindowLoaded, false);
function eventWindowLoaded() {
    canvasApp();
```

```
}

function canvasSupport () {
    return Modernizr.canvas;
}

function canvasApp() {

   if (!canvasSupport()) {
          return;
       }

  function  drawScreen () {

      context.fillStyle = '#EEEEEE';
      context.fillRect(0, 0, theCanvas.width, theCanvas.height);
      //Box
      context.strokeStyle = '#000000';
      context.strokeRect(1,  1, theCanvas.width-2, theCanvas.height-2);

      ball.velocityy  += gravity;

      if ((ball.y + ball.radius) > theCanvas.height) {
         ball.velocityy = -(ball.velocityy)
      }
      ball.y += ball.velocityy;
      ball.x += ball.velocityx;

      context.fillStyle = "#000000";
      context.beginPath();
      context.arc(ball.x,ball.y,ball.radius,0,Math.PI*2,true);
      context.closePath();
      context.fill();

   }
   var speed = 5;

   var gravity = .1;
   var angle = 295;
   var radians = angle * Math.PI/ 180;
   var radius = 15;

   var vx = Math.cos(radians) * speed;
   var vy = Math.sin(radians) * speed;

   theCanvas = document.getElementById("canvasOne");
   context = theCanvas.getContext("2d");

   var p1 = {x:20,y:theCanvas.width-radius};
   var ball = {x:p1.x, y:p1.y, velocityx: vx, velocityy:vy, radius:radius};

   setInterval(drawScreen, 33);

}
```

```
</script>

</head>
<body>
<div style="position: absolute; top: 50px; left: 50px;">

<canvas id="canvasOne" width="500" height="500">
 Your browser does not support HTML5 Canvas.
</canvas>
</div>
</body>
</html>
```

Gravity with Bounce and Applied Simple Elasticity

In physics, the *elasticity* of a bouncing ball refers to how much energy is conserved when a ball bounces off a surface. We already covered a bit about conservation of energy when we discussed balls colliding, but when we are simulating objects falling, we need to take a slightly different path with our code. In Example 5-15, we applied 100% elasticity and the ball bounced forever (actually, this was only implied since we did not consider elasticity at all). However, in real life, balls usually lose some of their energy every time they bounce off a surface. The amount of energy conserved depends on the material the ball is made from, as well as the surface it is bouncing on. For example, a rubber Super Ball is much more elastic than a cannonball and will bounce higher on the first bounce off a surface. Both will bounce higher off a concrete surface than a surface made of thick mud. Eventually, both will come to rest on the surface as all the energy is transferred away from the ball.

We can simulate simple elasticity by applying a constant value to the ball when it bounces off the ground. For this example, we will set the speed of the ball to 6 pixels per frame, and the angle to 285. We will keep our gravity at .1, but set a new variable named elasticity to .5. To make this more straightforward, we will also assume that the surface the ball is bouncing on does not add or subtract from the elasticity of the ball.

In canvasApp() we would set the new properties like this:

```
var speed = 6;
var gravity = .1;
var elasticity = .5;
var angle = 285;
```

We then add the new elasticity property to the ball object because, unlike gravity, elasticity describes a property of an object, not the entire world it resides within. This means that having multiple balls with different values for elasticity would be very easy to implement:

```
var ball = {x:p1.x, y:p1.y, velocityx: vx, velocityy:vy, radius:radius,
    elasticity: elasticity};
```

In the drawScreen() function, we still add the gravity value to the y velocity (velocityy). However, instead of simply reversing the y velocity when the ball hits the bottom of the canvas, we also multiply the y velocity by the elasticity value stored in the ball.elasticity property. This applies the elasticity to the bounce, preserving the y velocity by the percentage value of elasticity for the object:

```
ball.velocityy += gravity;
if ((ball.y + ball.radius) > theCanvas.height) {
    ball.velocityy = -(ball.velocityy)*ball.elasticity;
}
ball.y += ball.velocityy;
ball.x += ball.velocityx;
```

In Figure 5-19 you can see what this application looks like when executed in a web browser.

Figure 5-19. Ball bouncing with elasticity and gravity applied

With gravity applied, the bounce is not exactly as you might expect. Gravity is always pulling down on our object, so the effect of a loss of y velocity due to an elastic bounce is pronounced.

The full code is shown in Example 5-16.

Example 5-16. Simple gravity with bounce and elasticity

```
<!doctype html>
<html lang="en">
<head>
<meta charset="UTF-8">
<title>CH5EX16: Gravity With A Vector With Bounce And Elasticity</title>
<script src="modernizr-1.6.min.js"></script>
<script type="text/javascript">
window.addEventListener('load', eventWindowLoaded, false);
function eventWindowLoaded() {
    canvasApp();

}

function canvasSupport () {
    return Modernizr.canvas;
}

function canvasApp() {

    if (!canvasSupport()) {
        return;
    }

   function  drawScreen () {

        context.fillStyle = '#EEEEEE';
        context.fillRect(0, 0, theCanvas.width, theCanvas.height);
        //Box
        context.strokeStyle = '#000000';
        context.strokeRect(1,  1, theCanvas.width-2, theCanvas.height-2);

        ball.velocityy += gravity;

        if ((ball.y + ball.radius) > theCanvas.height) {
           ball.velocityy = -(ball.velocityy)*ball.elasticity;
        }
        ball.y += ball.velocityy;
        ball.x += ball.velocityx;

        context.fillStyle = "#000000";
        context.beginPath();
        context.arc(ball.x,ball.y,ball.radius,0,Math.PI*2,true);
        context.closePath();
        context.fill();
```

```
    }
    var speed = 6;
    var gravity = .1;
    var elasticity = .5;
    var angle = 285;
    var radians = angle * Math.PI/ 180;
    var radius = 15;

    var vx = Math.cos(radians) * speed;
    var vy = Math.sin(radians) * speed;

    theCanvas = document.getElementById("canvasOne");
    context = theCanvas.getContext("2d");

    var p1 = {x:20,y:theCanvas.width-radius};
    var ball = {x:p1.x, y:p1.y, velocityx: vx, velocityy:vy, radius:radius,
        elasticity: elasticity};

    setInterval(drawScreen, 33);

}

</script>

</head>
<body>
<div style="position: absolute; top: 50px; left: 50px;">

<canvas id="canvasOne" width="500" height="500">
 Your browser does not support HTML5 Canvas.
</canvas>
</div>
</body>
</html>
```

Simple Gravity, Simple Elasticity, and Simple Friction

Now that we have a ball traveling on a vector that is affected by both gravity and elasticity, we have one more element to add to make the animation more realistic. In the previous example, the y velocity was affected by gravity and elasticity, but the ball still traveled on the x-axis without any degradation in velocity. We will fix this issue now by adding friction into the equation.

In physics, *friction* is a force that resists the motion of an object. We have already discussed friction as it applies to colliding balls, and this implementation is similar except that it affects only the x velocity. For our purposes, we will achieve simple friction by degrading the x velocity as gravity degrades the y velocity.

Taking the code from Example 5-16, in canvasApp() we create a new variable named friction. This is the amount of pixels to degrade the x velocity on every frame:

```
    var friction = .008;
```

Notice that the amount is quite small. Friction does not have to be a large value to look realistic—it just needs to be applied uniformly each time `drawScreen()` is called. In `drawScreen()`, we apply `friction` to the x velocity like this:

```
ball.velocityx = ball.velocityx - ( ball.velocityx*friction);
```

This is the same type of proportional application of friction we used with the colliding balls, but again, this time we applied it only to the x velocity.

Figure 5-20 shows what this final version of our application looks like when executed in a web browser.

Figure 5-20. Ball bouncing with gravity, elasticity, and friction applied

Example 5-17 gives the full code for *CH5EX17.html*, the final code of our simple gravity, simple elasticity, and simple friction example.

Example 5-17. Gravity with a vector with bounce friction

```html
<!doctype html>
<html lang="en">
<head>
<meta charset="UTF-8">
<title>CH5EX17: Gravity With A Vector With Bounce Friction</title>
<script src="modernizr-1.6.min.js"></script>
<script type="text/javascript">
window.addEventListener('load', eventWindowLoaded, false);
function eventWindowLoaded() {
   canvasApp();
}

function canvasSupport () {
    return Modernizr.canvas;
}

function canvasApp() {

   if (!canvasSupport()) {
         return;
       }

  function  drawScreen () {

      context.fillStyle = '#EEEEEE';
      context.fillRect(0, 0, theCanvas.width, theCanvas.height);
      //Box
      context.strokeStyle = '#000000';
      context.strokeRect(1,  1, theCanvas.width-2, theCanvas.height-2);

      ball.velocityx = ball.velocityx - ( ball.velocityx*friction);

      ball.velocityy += gravity;

      if ((ball.y + ball.radius) > theCanvas.height) {
         ball.velocityy = -(ball.velocityy)*ball.elasticity;
      }
      ball.y += ball.velocityy;
      ball.x += ball.velocityx;

      context.fillStyle = "#000000";
      context.beginPath();
      context.arc(ball.x,ball.y,ball.radius,0,Math.PI*2,true);
      context.closePath();
      context.fill();

  }
  var speed = 6;
  var gravity = .1;
  var friction = .008;
  var elasticity = .5;
  var angle = 285;
  var radians = angle * Math.PI/ 180;
  var radius = 15;
```

```
    var vx = Math.cos(radians) * speed;
    var vy = Math.sin(radians) * speed;

    theCanvas = document.getElementById("canvasOne");
    context = theCanvas.getContext("2d");

    var p1 = {x:20,y:theCanvas.width-radius};
    var ball = {x:p1.x, y:p1.y, velocityx: vx, velocityy:vy, radius:radius,
        elasticity: elasticity};

    setInterval(drawScreen, 33);

}

</script>

</head>
<body>
<div style="position: absolute; top: 50px; left: 50px;">

<canvas id="canvasOne" width="500" height="500">
 Your browser does not support HTML5 Canvas.
</canvas>
</div>
</body>
</html>
```

Easing

Easing is a technique used in animation to make an object smoothly enter or leave a location. The idea of easing is that instead of uniformly applying movement to every frame of animation, you instead increase (*easing in*) or decrease (*easing out*) the number of pixels you move on each frame. The result is that movement appears to be more realistic and smooth. There are many different ways to create easing animations. We will concentrate on two simple examples that will help pave the way for you to further explore the subject on your own.

Easing Out (Landing the Ship)

The process of easing out refers to easing at the end of an animation: an object moving from one point to another, starting out fast, and slowing down as it reaches the second point. To illustrate the concept, we will use the example of a spaceship landing. A spaceship starts out very fast, applies negative thrust to slow down, and, by the time it reaches the ground, is moving slowly enough to land without incident. If you've ever played the video game *Lunar Lander*, you will understand exactly the type of movement we are trying to accomplish.

To create this easing-out effect, we need to find two distinct points and then move an object between them, slowing down the object in linear fashion as it nears the second point. To achieve this effect, we first calculate the distance between the points. Next, we select a percentage value (easeValue) that we will use to move the object across that distance on each frame. As the distance gets shorter, the amount we move gets shorter as well. This gives the object the appearance of traveling slower and slower as it moves from the starting point to the ending point, as illustrated in Figure 5-21. We have drawn the points to show the easing values as the ship nears the bottom of the screen. Notice that the points get closer and closer until there is almost no distance between them.

Figure 5-21. Spaceship landing (easing out)

Figure 5-21 displays the results of *CH5EX18.html*. Now, let's look at how this example works in detail. First, we will load in the *ship.png* image the same way we have loaded images previously in this chapter:

```
var shipImage;
function eventWindowLoaded() {
    shipImage = new Image();
    shipImage.src = "ship.png"
    shipImage.onload = eventAssetsLoaded;
```

```
    }

    function eventAssetsLoaded() {

        canvasApp();
    }
```

Then in `canvasApp()`, we create a variable named `easeValue`, which represents the percentage to move the ship across the remaining distance between the two points. In our example, it is 5% (.05):

```
    var easeValue = .05;
```

Next, we create our two points. The first point, `p1`, is close to the middle of the canvas on the y-axis, and just above the top (`-20`) on the x-axis. The final point, `p2`, is in the same place on the x-axis, but near the bottom of the canvas (`470`) on the y-axis:

```
    var p1 = {x:240,y:-20};
    var p2 = {x:240,y:470};
```

Finally, we create a dynamic object for the `ship` that holds these values:

```
    var ship = {x:p1.x, y:p1.y, endx: p2.x, endy:p2.y, velocityx:0, velocityy:0};
```

In `drawScreen()`, on every frame, we first find out the distance between the ship and the endpoint by subtracting the current x and y values for the `ship` from the endpoint x and y values. The distance will get shorter on each call to `drawScreen()` as the ship moves farther away from `p1` and gets closer to `p2`. We do this for both x and y even though, in our example, only the y value will change as the spaceship gets closer to `p2`:

```
    var dx = ship.endx - ship.x;
    var dy = ship.endy - ship.y;
```

Once we have the distances, we multiply those values by `easeValue` to get the x and y velocities for the `ship` on this call to `drawScreen()`:

```
    ship.velocityx = dx * easeValue;
    ship.velocityy = dy * easeValue;
```

Finally, we apply those values and draw the spaceship to the canvas:

```
    ship.x += ship.velocityx;
    ship.y += ship.velocityy;
    context.drawImage(shipImage,ship.x,ship.y);
```

You can test this example by executing *CH5EX18.html* from the code distribution in your web browser, or by typing in the full code listing shown in Example 5-18.

Example 5-18. Easing out (landing the ship)

```
<!doctype html>
<html lang="en">
<head>
<meta charset="UTF-8">
<title>CH5EX18:  Easing Out (Landing The Ship)</title>
<script src="modernizr-1.6.min.js"></script>
```

```
<script type="text/javascript">
window.addEventListener('load', eventWindowLoaded, false);
var shipImage;
function eventWindowLoaded() {
   shipImage = new Image();
   shipImage.src = "ship.png"
   shipImage.onload = eventAssetsLoaded;
}

function eventAssetsLoaded() {

   canvasApp();
}

function canvasSupport () {
     return Modernizr.canvas;
}

function canvasApp() {

  if (!canvasSupport()) {
         return;
}

  var pointImage = new Image();
  pointImage.src = "pointwhite.png";
  function  drawScreen () {

     context.fillStyle = '#000000';
     context.fillRect(0, 0, theCanvas.width, theCanvas.height);
     //Box
     context.strokeStyle = '#ffffff';
     context.strokeRect(1,  1, theCanvas.width-2, theCanvas.height-2);
     var dx = ship.endx - ship.x;
     var dy = ship.endy - ship.y;

     ship.velocityx = dx * easeValue;
     ship.velocityy = dy * easeValue;

     ship.x += ship.velocityx;
     ship.y += ship.velocityy;

     //Draw points to illustrate path

     points.push({x:ship.x,y:ship.y});

     for (var i = 0; i< points.length; i++) {
        context.drawImage(pointImage, points[i].x+shipImage.width/2, points[i].y,1,1);
     }

     context.drawImage(shipImage,ship.x,ship.y);

   }
```

```
    var easeValue = .05;
    var p1 = {x:240,y:-20};
    var p2 = {x:240,y:470};

    var ship = {x:p1.x, y:p1.y, endx: p2.x, endy:p2.y, velocityx:0, velocityy:0};
    var points = new Array();

    theCanvas = document.getElementById("canvasOne");
    context = theCanvas.getContext("2d");

    setInterval(drawScreen, 33);

}

</script>

</head>
<body>
<div style="position: absolute; top: 50px; left: 50px;">

<canvas id="canvasOne" width="500" height="500">
 Your browser does not support HTML5 Canvas.
</canvas>
</div>
</body>
</html>
```

 We are showing the points in this example but because the background is black, we load in a white bitmap point image named *pointwhite.png* instead of the all-black image, *point.png*.

Easing In (Taking Off)

Easing in is the opposite of easing out. When an animation *eases in*, it starts slowly and then gets faster and faster. If you have ever seen a video of a space shuttle taking off, you will understand this much better. The thrust builds up as the craft moves slowly, and then gets faster and faster as it moves through the sky. We are going to use this "taking off" example as a way to develop code for an easing-in animation on HTML5 Canvas.

In canvasApp(), we start our code much the same way as in the last example—by creating a variable named easeValue:

```
    var easeValue = .05;
```

However, for easing in, instead of this being a percentage of the remaining distance between two points, it is simply a constant value added to the velocity of the ship on each frame. Figure 5-22 shows what this would look like. We have added the points again to illustrate how the animation speeds up as the ship takes off.

Figure 5-22. Ship taking off (easing in)

First, we set the beginning position of the ship (p1) to the bottom center of the canvas. Then, we set the beginning speed of the ship very low (.5 pixels per frame), and set the angle to 270 (straight up the canvas). We then calculate the x and y velocity values for the ship:

```
var p1 = {x:240,y:470};
var tempSpeed = .5;
var tempAngle = 270 ;
var tempRadians = tempAngle * Math.PI/ 180;
var tempvelocityx = Math.cos(tempRadians) * tempSpeed;
var tempvelocityy  = Math.sin(tempRadians) * tempSpeed;

var ship = {x:p1.x, y:p1.y, velocityx:tempvelocityx, velocityy:tempvelocityy};
```

In drawScreen(), instead of finding the distance between two points, we add the ease Value to the x and y velocities on each frame, and then apply it to the ship x and y values before drawing it to the canvas. This creates a linear increase in speed, resulting in the easing-in effect we want to see:

```
ship.velocityx = ship.velocityx + ( ship.velocityx*easeValue);
ship.velocityy = ship.velocityy + ( ship.velocityy*easeValue);

ship.x += ship.velocityx;
ship.y += ship.velocityy;

context.drawImage(shipImage,ship.x,ship.y);
```

You can see this example by executing *CH5EX19.html* from the code distribution, or by typing in the code listing shown in Example 5-19.

Example 5-19. Easing in (taking off)

```
<!doctype html>
<html lang="en">
<head>
<meta charset="UTF-8">
<title>CH5EX19: Taking Off (Fake Ease In)</title>
<script src="modernizr-1.6.min.js"></script>
<script type="text/javascript">
window.addEventListener('load', eventWindowLoaded, false);
var shipImage;
function eventWindowLoaded() {
    shipImage = new Image();
    shipImage.src = "ship.png"
    shipImage.onload = eventAssetsLoaded;
}

function eventAssetsLoaded() {

    canvasApp();
}

function canvasSupport () {
    return Modernizr.canvas;
}

function canvasApp() {

    if (!canvasSupport()) {
         return;
         }

  var pointImage = new Image();
  pointImage.src = "pointwhite.png";
  function  drawScreen () {

      context.fillStyle = '#000000';
      context.fillRect(0, 0, theCanvas.width, theCanvas.height);
      //Box
      context.strokeStyle = '#ffffff';
      context.strokeRect(1,  1, theCanvas.width-2, theCanvas.height-2);

      ship.velocityx = ship.velocityx + ( ship.velocityx*easeValue);
      ship.velocityy = ship.velocityy + ( ship.velocityy*easeValue);
```

```
                ship.x += ship.velocityx;
                ship.y += ship.velocityy;

                //Draw points to illustrate path

                points.push({x:ship.x,y:ship.y});

                for (var i = 0; i< points.length; i++) {
                    context.drawImage(pointImage, points[i].x+shipImage.width/2, points[i].y,1,1);
                }

                context.drawImage(shipImage,ship.x,ship.y);

            }

        var easeValue = .05;
        var p1 = {x:240,y:470};
        var tempX;
        var tempY;
        var tempSpeed = .5;
        var tempAngle = 270 ;
        var tempRadians = tempAngle * Math.PI/ 180;
        var tempvelocityx = Math.cos(tempRadians) * tempSpeed;
        var tempvelocityy  = Math.sin(tempRadians) * tempSpeed;

        var ship = {x:p1.x, y:p1.y, velocityx:tempvelocityx, velocityy:tempvelocityy};
        var points = new Array();

        theCanvas = document.getElementById("canvasOne");
        context = theCanvas.getContext("2d");

        setInterval(drawScreen, 33);

    }

</script>

</head>
<body>
<div style="position: absolute; top: 50px; left: 50px;">

<canvas id="canvasOne" width="500" height="500">
 Your browser does not support HTML5 Canvas.
</canvas>
</div>
</body>
</html>
```

 For more information on easing, check out Robert Penner's easing equations: *http://www.robertpenner.com/easing/*. These equations have been implemented in jQuery for JavaScript at *http://plugins.jquery.com/ files/jquery.animation.easing.js.txt.*

What's Next?

We have shown you a plethora of examples for how you can use HTML5 Canvas to animate objects using some basic principles of math and physics. However, we have really only begun to scratch the surface of the multitude of ways you can use math and physics in your applications. In the next couple chapters we will switch gears, discussing audio and video, before we start applying many of the concepts we have learned in this book to a couple of in-depth game projects.

CHAPTER 6

Mixing HTML5 Video and Canvas

Using the new `<video>` tag, HTML5 lets sites show video directly in HTML without needing any plug-in technologies. However, the simple `<video>` tag opens up a whole slew of complexities and opportunities for developers. While we can't cover everything related to video in this chapter, we will introduce you to the HTML5 `<video>` tag, and then show you ways in which video can be incorporated and manipulated by HTML5 Canvas.

HTML5 Video Support

HTML5 specifies a new tag, `<video>`, that allows developers to place video directly in an HTML page. With a few simple options, you can autoplay, loop, and add playback controls to the embedded video.

First, let's talk about video format support, which is a very complicated issue. Some video formats are free, and others are licensed. Some formats look better than others, some make smaller file sizes, and some are supported in one browser while others are supported in a different browser. In this chapter we will concentrate on three formats that either have broad support now or promise to have broad support in the future: *.ogg*, *.mp4*, and *.webm*.

We will discuss these video formats in terms of *video codecs*. Each format uses one or more *codecs* to compress and decompress video. Codecs are usually the secret sauce of a video format because compression is the key to making video that, in the wild, can convert very large files into file sizes that can be easily transported on the Internet.

Theora + Vorbis = .ogg

Theora (*http://www.theora.org/*) is an open source, free video codec developed by Xiph.org. Vorbis (*http://www.vorbis.com*) is a free, open source audio codec that is used in conjunction with Theora. Both Theora and Vorbis are stored in an *.ogg* file. *.ogg* files have the broadest support among traditional web browsers, but, unfortunately, not on handheld devices. Many commercial companies (e.g., Apple) have balked at using Theora/Vorbis because they are unsure whether somewhere, someplace, someone might own a patent that covers part of the technology, and thus they might get sued for using it.

 Sometimes technology companies get hit with what is known as a *submarine patent*. This was a patent tactic—available up until 1995 in the U.S.—that allowed a filer to delay the publication of a patent. Because patents were only enforceable for 17 years, if someone filed one but delayed the publications, he could wait years (even decades) until someone else came up with the same idea, then hit that person with a lawsuit.

H.264 + $$$ = .mp4

H.264 is a high-quality video standard that has received the backing of some very big players, such as Apple, Adobe, and Microsoft. However, despite offering high-quality video, it only defines a standard—not a video codec. An organization named MPEG LA owns the intellectual property, and they license it out to software and hardware vendors. Many companies that have implemented H.264 have done so with their own proprietary codecs. As a result, the varying codecs are incompatible with one another, making this a tricky format to use across multiple platforms. H.264 videos have the *.mp4* extension. Most for-profit corporations have implemented support for this format on their platforms, but the developers of open source browsers like Firefox and Opera have not. In late 2010, Google dropped H.264 support in Chrome in favor of WebM.

VP8 + Vorbis = .webm

WebM is a new open source video standard supported by Google, Adobe, Mozilla, and Opera. It is based on the VP8 codec and includes Vorbis (just like Theora) as an audio codec. When YouTube.com (*http://youtube.com*) announced they had converted many of their videos to be HTML5-compatible, one of the formats they used was WebM. Currently, only Google Chrome and Opera support WebM, but broader support should be coming in the future.

To summarize, here is a chart of the video formats supported by various browsers.

Platform	.ogg	.mp4	.webm
Android	X		
Firefox	X		
Chrome	X		X
iPhone		X	
Internet Explorer 9		X	
Opera	X		X
Safari		X	

As you can see, no one format is supported by all browsers or platforms. Because HTML5 Canvas only supports video in the format supported by the browser it is implemented within, we must apply a strategy that uses multiple formats to play video.

Combining All Three

The examples in this chapter will introduce a strategy that may seem crazy at first—using all three formats at once. While this might seem to be more work than necessary, right now it is the only way to ensure broad support across as many platforms as possible. The HTML5 `<video>` tag allows us to specify multiple formats for a single video, and this will help us achieve our goal of broad video support when working with HTML5 Canvas.

Converting Video Formats

Before we get into some video demonstrations, we should discuss video conversions. Since we are going to use *.ogg*, *.mp4*, and *.webm* videos in all our projects, we need to have a way to convert video to these formats. Converting video can be a daunting task for someone unfamiliar with all the existing and competing formats; luckily, there are some great free tools to help us do just that:

Miro Video Converter (http://www.mirovideoconverter.com/)
    This application will quickly convert most video types to *.ogg*, *.mp4*, and *.webm*. It is available for both Windows and Mac.

SUPER © (http://www.erightsoft.com/SUPER.html)
    This is a free video-conversion tool for Windows only that creates *.mp4* and *.ogg* formats. If you can navigate through the maze of screens trying to sell you other products, it can be very useful for video conversions.

HandBrake (http://handbrake.fr/)
> This video-converter application for the Macintosh platform creates *.mp4* and *.ogg* file types.

FFmpeg (http://ffmpeg.org/)
> This is the ultimate cross-platform, command-line tool for doing video conversions. It works in Windows/Mac/Linux and can do nearly any conversion you desire. However, there is no GUI interface, so it can be daunting for beginners. Some of the tools above use FFmpeg as their engine to do video conversions.

Basic HTML5 Video Implementation

In the `<video>` tag's most minimal implementation, it only requires a valid `src` atrribute. For example, if we took a nifty little video of the waves crashing at Muir Beach, California (just north of San Francisco), and we encoded it as an H.264 *.mp4* file, the code might look like this:

```
<video src="muirbeach.mp4" />
```

 To see an example of this basic code, look at the *CH6EX1.html* file in the code distribution.

There are many properties that can be set in an HTML5 video embed. These properties are actually part of the `HTMLMediaElement` interface, implemented by the `HTMLVideo Element` object. Some of the more important properties include:

`src`
> The URL to the video that you want to play.

`autoplay`
> `true` or `false`. Forces the video to play automatically when loaded.

`loop`
> `true` or `false`. Loops the video back to the beginning when it has finished playing (at the time of this writing, this did not work in Firefox).

`volume`
> A number between 0 and 1. Sets the volume level of the playing video.

`poster`
> A URL to an image that will be shown while the video is loading.

There are also some methods of `HTMLVideoElement` that are necessary when playing video in conjunction with JavaScript and Canvas:

`play()`
> A method used to start playing a video.

`pause()`
> A method used to pause a video that is playing.

Additionally, there are some properties you can use to check the status of a video, including:

`duration`
> The length of the video in seconds.

`currentTime`
> The current playing time of the video in seconds. This can be used in conjunction with `duration` for some interesting effects, which we will explore later.

`ended`
> `true` or `false`, depending on whether the video has finished playing.

`muted`
> `true` or `false`. Used to inquire whether the sound of the playing video has been muted.

`paused`
> `true` or `false`. Used to inquire whether the video is currently paused.

 There are even more properties that exist for `HTMLVideoElement`. Check them out at *http://www.w3.org/2010/05/video/mediaevents.html*.

Plain-Vanilla Video Embed

To demonstrate a plain-vanilla embed, we are going to work under our previously established rules for video formats. We will use three formats because no one format will work in every browser. We have created a version of the Muir Beach video as a *.webm*, an *.ogg*, and a *.mp4*. For the rest of this chapter, we will use all three formats in all of our video embeds.

To support all three formats at once, we must use an alternative method for setting the src attribute of the <video> tag. Why? Because we need to specify three different video formats instead of one in our HTML page. To do this, we add <source> tags within the <video> tag:

```
<video id="thevideo"  width="320" height="240">
  <source src="muirbeach.mp4" type='video/mp4; codecs="avc1.42E01E, mp4a.40.2"' >
  <source src="muirbeach.webm"type='video/webm; codecs="vp8, vorbis"' >
  <source src="muirbeach.ogg" type='video/ogg; codecs="theora, vorbis"'>
</video>
```

 We put the *.mp4* file first in the src list because on certain iOS (iPhone, iPad) devices, the browser will not attempt to load any other src type than the first one listed. Since those devices support *.mp4* files, we list them first to get the broadest support for HTML5 video.

When a web browser reads this HTML, it will attempt to load each video in succession. If it does not support one format, it will try the next one. Using this style of embed allows the code in Example 6-1 to execute on all HTML5-compliant browsers.

Also notice that we have set the width and height properties of the video. While these are not necessarily needed (as we saw earlier), it is proper HTML form to include them, and we will need them a bit later when we start to manipulate the video size in code.

Example 6-1. Basic HTML video

```
<!doctype html>
<html lang="en">
<head>
<meta charset="UTF-8">
<title>CH6EX1: Basic HTML5 Video</title>
</head>
<body>
<div>
<video id="thevideo"  width="320" height="240">
  <source src="muirbeach.mp4" type='video/mp4; codecs="avc1.42E01E, mp4a.40.2"' >
  <source src="muirbeach.webm"type='video/webm; codecs="vp8, vorbis"' >
  <source src="muirbeach.ogg" type='video/ogg; codecs="theora, vorbis"'>
</video>
</div>
<div>
(Right-click To Control)
</div>
</body>
</html>
```

Figure 6-1 is an example of the plain-vanilla video embed in an HTML5 page. There are no controls displayed in the default settings, but if you right-click on the video, controls will appear that can be used in conjunction with the embedded video.

(Right click To Control)

Figure 6-1. HTML5 video embed

Video with Controls, Loop, and Autoplay

While a video displayed without controls might suit your needs, most users expect to see some way to control a video. Also, as the developer, you might want a video to play automatically or loop back to the beginning when it finishes. All of these things (if supported in the browser) are very easy to accomplish in HTML5.

Adding controls, looping, and autoplay to an HTML5 video embed is simple. All you need to do is specify the options `controls`, `loop`, and/or `autoplay` in the `<video>` tag, like this:

```
<video autoplay loop controls id="thevideo" width="320" height="240">
 <source src="muirbeach.mp4" type='video/mp4; codecs="avc1.42E01E, mp4a.40.2"' >
 <source src="muirbeach.webm"type='video/webm; codecs="vp8, vorbis"' >
 <source src="muirbeach.ogg" type='video/ogg; codecs="theora, vorbis"'>
</video>
```

 As of this writing, `loop` does not work in Firefox; however, support is expected in version 4.0.

The code to embed our Muir Beach video with controls, loop, and autoplay is in *CH6EX2.html* in the code distribution. Figure 6-2 shows what a video with controls looks like in Google Chrome.

(Autoplay, Loop, Controls)

Figure 6-2. HTML5 video embed with controls

You can see the full code in Example 6-2.

Example 6-2. HTML video with controls, loop, and autoplay

```
<!doctype html>
<html lang="en">
<head>
<meta charset="UTF-8">
<title>CH6EX2: Basic HTML5 Video With Controls</title>
</head>
<body>
<div>
<video autoplay loop controls id="thevideo" width="320" height="240">
 <source src="muirbeach.mp4" type='video/mp4; codecs="avc1.42E01E, mp4a.40.2"' >
 <source src="muirbeach.webm"type='video/webm; codecs="vp8, vorbis"' >
 <source src="muirbeach.ogg" type='video/ogg; codecs="theora, vorbis"'>
</video>
</div>
<div>
(Autoplay, Loop, Controls)
</div>
</body>
</html>
```

Altering the Width and Height of the Video

In our first example, we showed how you could embed a video without changing the default width or height. However, there are many good reasons why you might want to change the default width and height of a video in the HTML page, such as fitting it into a particular part of the page, or enlarging it so it is easier to see. Similar to embedding an image into HTML with the <img> tag, a video will scale to whatever width and height you provide in the <video> tag. Also, like with the <img> tag, this scale does not affect the size of the object downloaded. If the video is 5 megabytes at 640×480, it will still be 5 megabytes when displayed at 180×120—just scaled to fit that size.

In Example 6-3 (*CH6EX3.html*) we have scaled the same video to three different sizes and displayed them on the same page. Figure 6-3 shows what this looks like in HTML (again, rendered in the Google Chrome browser).

Example 6-3. Basic HTML5 video in three sizes

```
<!doctype html>
<html lang="en">
<head>
<meta charset="UTF-8">
<title>CH6EX3: Basic HTML5 Video: 3 Sizes</title>
</head>
<body>
<div>
<video autoplay loop controls  width="640" height="480" id="thevideo">
 <source src="muirbeach.mp4" type='video/mp4; codecs="avc1.42E01E, mp4a.40.2"' >
 <source src="muirbeach.webm"type='video/webm; codecs="vp8, vorbis"' >
 <source src="muirbeach.ogg" type='video/ogg; codecs="theora, vorbis"'>
 <source src="muirbeach.mp4" type='video/mp4; codecs="avc1.42E01E, mp4a.40.2"' >
</video>
</div>
<div>
(640×480)
<div>
<video  autoplay loop controls  width="320" height="240"id="thevideo">
 <source src="muirbeach.mp4" type='video/mp4; codecs="avc1.42E01E, mp4a.40.2"' >
 <source src="muirbeach.webm"type='video/webm; codecs="vp8, vorbis"' >
 <source src="muirbeach.ogg" type='video/ogg; codecs="theora, vorbis"'>
</video>
</div>
<div>
(320×240)
</div>
<div>
<video autoplay loop controls  width="180" height="120"id="thevideo">
 <source src="muirbeach.mp4" type='video/mp4; codecs="avc1.42E01E, mp4a.40.2"' >
 <source src="muirbeach.webm"type='video/webm; codecs="vp8, vorbis"' >
 <source src="muirbeach.ogg" type='video/ogg; codecs="theora, vorbis"'>
</video>
</div>
<div>
(180×120)
</body>
</html>
```

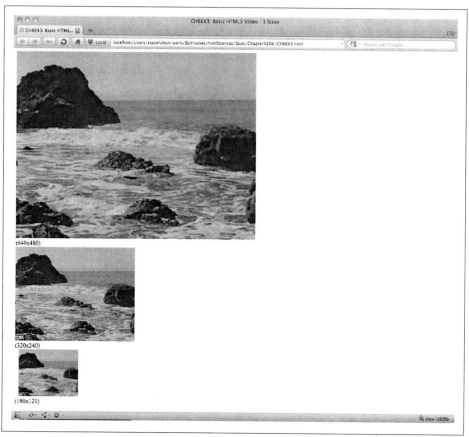

Figure 6-3. Controlling video width and height in the embed

Dynamically scaling a video

Now it is time for a more elaborate (and we think more effective) example of scaling a video. By changing the `width` and `height` attributes of the `<video>` tag, we can scale the video on the fly. While there may be a few practical reasons you would do this in a real-world situation, it is also an effective way to demonstrate some of the power of the HTML5 `<video>` tag.

First, we need to add an HTML5 `range` control to the page:

```
<form>
  Video Size: <input type="range" id="videoSize"
        min="80"
        max="1280"
        step="1"
        value="320"/>
</form>
```

We discussed the details of the range control in Chapter 3, but just to refresh your memory, range is a new form control added to HTML5 that creates a slider of values. We are going to use this slider to set the video size.

 If the browser does not support the range element, a text box will appear that will allow the user to enter text directly.

To capture the change to the video size, we need to add some JavaScript. We create an event listener for the load event that calls the eventWindowLoaded() function when the page loads (this should look very familiar to you by now):

```
window.addEventListener('load', eventWindowLoaded, false);
```

We need to set up a couple things in the eventWindowLoaded() function. First, we need to add an event listener for a change to the videoSize form control we created in the HTML page. A "change" to the control (e.g., someone slides it right or left) will create an event handled by the videoSizeChanged() event handler:

```
var sizeElement = document.getElementById("videoSize")
sizeElement.addEventListener('change', videoSizeChanged, false);
```

Next, we need to create a value that can be used to set both the width and the height of the video at once. This is because we want to keep the proper *aspect ratio* of the video (the ratio of width to height) when the video is resized. To do this, we create the variable widthtoHeightRatio, which is simply the width of the video divided by the height:

```
var widthtoHeightRatio = videoElement.width/videoElement.height;
```

Finally, when the user changes the videoSize range control, the videoSizeChanged() event handler is called. This function sets the width property of the video to the value of the range control (target.value), then sets the height of the video to the same value, and divides by the widthtoHeightRatio value we just created. The effect is that the video resizes while playing. Figure 6-4 captures one moment of that:

```
function videoSizeChanged(e) {

    var target = e.target;
    var videoElement = document.getElementById("theVideo");
    videoElement.width = target.value;
    videoElement.height = target.value/widthtoHeightRatio;

}
```

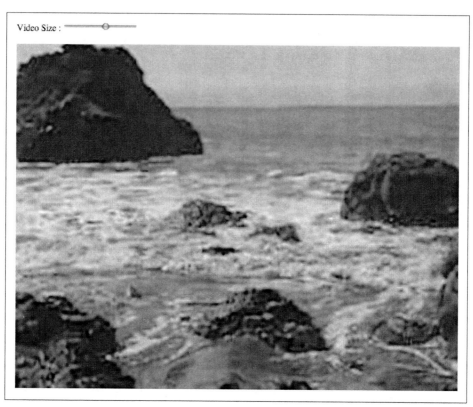

Figure 6-4. Controlling video width and height in JavaScript

Example 6-4 offers the full code listing for this application.

Example 6-4. Basic HTML5 video with resize range control

```
<!doctype html>
<html lang="en">
<head>
<meta charset="UTF-8">
<title>CH6EX4: Basic HTML5 Video With Resize Range Control </title>
<script type="text/javascript">
window.addEventListener('load', eventWindowLoaded, false);
function eventWindowLoaded() {
    var sizeElement = document.getElementById("videoSize")
    sizeElement.addEventListener('change', videoSizeChanged, false);
    var videoElement = document.getElementById("theVideo");
    var widthtoHeightRatio = videoElement.width/videoElement.height;

function videoSizeChanged(e) {
    var target = e.target;
    var videoElement = document.getElementById("theVideo");
    videoElement.width = target.value;
    videoElement.height = target.value/widthtoHeightRatio;
```

```
    }
}

</script>
</head>
<body>
<div>
<form>
 Video Size: <input type="range" id="videoSize"
        min="80"
        max="1280"
        step="1"
        value="320"/>
</form>
  <br>
</div>
<div>
<video autoplay loop controls id="theVideo" width="320" height="240">
 <source src="muirbeach.mp4" type='video/mp4; codecs="avc1.42E01E, mp4a.40.2"' >
 <source src="muirbeach.webm"type='video/webm; codecs="vp8, vorbis"' >
 <source src="muirbeach.ogg" type='video/ogg; codecs="theora, vorbis"'>
</video>
</div>
</body>
</html>
```

Preloading Video in JavaScript

It is often necessary to preload a video before you do anything with it. This is especially true when using video with HTML5 Canvas because many times what you want to do goes beyond the simple act of playing the video.

We are going to leverage the DOM and JavaScript to create a preload architecture that can be reused and expanded upon. We are still not using Canvas, but this process will lead directly to it.

To do this, we must first embed the video in the HTML page in the same way we have done previously in this chapter. However, this time, we are going to add <div> with the id of loadingStatus.

 In practice, you probably would not display the loading status on the HTML page.

This <div> will report the percentage of the video that has loaded when we retrieve it through JavaScript:

```
<div>
<video loop controls id="thevideo" width="320" height="240" preload="auto">
 <source src="muirbeach.mp4" type='video/mp4; codecs="avc1.42E01E, mp4a.40.2"' >
 <source src="muirbeach.webm"type='video/webm; codecs="vp8, vorbis"' >
 <source src="muirbeach.ogg" type='video/ogg; codecs="theora, vorbis"'>
</video>

<div>

<div id="loadingStatus">
0%
</div>
```

In JavaScript, we need to create the same type of eventWindowLoaded() function that we have created many times previously in this book. This function is called when the HTML page has finished loading. In eventWindowLoaded() we need to create two listeners for two more events that are dispatched from the HTMLVideoElement object:

progress
> Dispatched when the video object has updated information about the loading progress of a video. We will use this event to update the percentage text in the loadingStatus <div>.

canplaythrough
> Dispatched when the video has loaded enough that it can play in its entirety. This event will let us know when to start playing the video.

Below is the code that creates the listeners for those events:

```
function eventWindowLoaded() {
    var videoElement = document.getElementById("thevideo");

    videoElement.addEventListener('progress',updateLoadingStatus,false);
    videoElement.addEventListener('canplaythrough',playVideo,false);

}
```

The updateLoadingStatus() function is called when the progress event is dispatched from the video element. This function calculates the percent loaded by calculating the ratio of the already-loaded bytes (videoElement.buffered.end(0)) by the total bytes (videoElement.duration), and dividing that value by 100. That value is then displayed by setting the innerHTML property of the loadingStatus <div>, as shown in Figure 6-5. Remember, this is only for displaying the progress. We still need to do something once the video has loaded.

 At the time of this writing, Firefox did not support the videobuffered property, but this was planned for Firefox version 4.0.

```
function updateLoadingStatus() {

    var loadingStatus = document.getElementById("loadingStatus");
    var videoElement = document.getElementById("thevideo");
    var percentLoaded = parseInt(((videoElement.buffered.end(0) /
        videoElement.duration) * 100));
     document.getElementById("loadingStatus").innerHTML =   percentLoaded + '%';

}
```

100%

Figure 6-5. Preloading a video in JavaScript

The `playVideo()` function is called when the `video` object dispatches a `canplay through` event. `playVideo()` calls the `play()` function of the `video` object, and the video starts to play:

```
function playVideo() {
    var videoElement = document.getElementById("thevideo");
    videoElement.play();

}
```

Example 6-5 gives the full code for preloading video.

Example 6-5. Basic HTML5 preloading video

```
<!doctype html>
<html lang="en">
<head>
<meta charset="UTF-8">
<title>CH6EX5: Basic HTML5 Preloading Video</title>
<script type="text/javascript">
window.addEventListener('load', eventWindowLoaded, false);
function eventWindowLoaded() {
    var videoElement = document.getElementById("thevideo");
```

```
        videoElement.addEventListener('progress',updateLoadingStatus,false);
        videoElement.addEventListener('canplaythrough',playVideo,false);

    }

    function updateLoadingStatus() {

        var loadingStatus = document.getElementById("loadingStatus");
        var videoElement = document.getElementById("thevideo");
        var percentLoaded = parseInt(((videoElement.buffered.end(0) /
            videoElement.duration) * 100));
         document.getElementById("loadingStatus").innerHTML =   percentLoaded + '%';

    }

    function playVideo() {
        var videoElement = document.getElementById("thevideo");
        videoElement.play();

    }
    </script>

    </head>
    <body>
    <div>
    <video loop controls id="thevideo" width="320" height="240" preload="auto">
      <source src="muirbeach.mp4" type='video/mp4; codecs="avc1.42E01E, mp4a.40.2"' >
      <source src="muirbeach.webm"type='video/webm; codecs="vp8, vorbis"' >
      <source src="muirbeach.ogg" type='video/ogg; codecs="theora, vorbis"'>

    </video>

    <div>

    <div id="loadingStatus">
    0%
    </div>

    </div>
    </body>
    </html>
```

A Problem with Events and Embedded Video in HTML5

Now that we have gone through this exercise, we have to give you some bad news. While the code we presented for *CH6EX5.html* works in most HTML5-compliant web browsers, the code stopped working in Google Chrome as we finished up the first draft of this book. This was upsetting because we used Chrome as our primary platform when developing and testing all the book's examples.

With a bit of investigation, we discovered that Chrome was not firing the canplay through or progress events. At the same time, Firefox removed the load event. While these were anecdotal occurrences, they lead to one common truth: *the HTML5 specification is not finished.* This is an obvious but important fact to note. If you are developing for HTML5 or Canvas, you are developing with a moving target.

Specifically in *CH6EX5.html*, we found that the process of embedding the `<video>` tag in the HTML page was the reason why the events weren't firing in Chrome. In order to make this example work in Chrome, you need to add a call to `playVideo()` in the `eventWindowLoaded()` function, like this:

```
function eventWindowLoaded() {
    var videoElement = document.getElementById("thevideo");

    videoElement.addEventListener('progress',updateLoadingStatus,false);
    videoElement.addEventListener('canplaythrough',playVideo,false);
    playVideo()
}
```

However, this code will not solve the core problem: we need a reliable way to know when a video has finished loading so we can use it on the canvas. In Example 6-6, we will show you a way to make that happen.

Video and the Canvas

The HTML `video` object already has a `poster` property for displaying an image before the video starts to play, as well as functions to `autoplay` and `loop`. So why is it necessary to preload the video? Well, as we alluded to in the previous section, simply playing a video is one thing—manipulating it with HTML5 Canvas is quite another. If you want to start manipulating video while it is displayed on the canvas, you first need to make sure it is loaded.

In this section, we will load video and then manipulate it in various ways so you can see how powerful Canvas can be when it is mixed with other HTML5 elements.

Displaying a Video on HTML5 Canvas

First, we must learn the basics of displaying video on HTML5 Canvas. There are a few important things to note that are not immediately obvious when you start working with video and the canvas. We worked through them so you don't have to do it yourself (you're welcome).

Video must still be embedded in HTML

Even though the video is only displayed on HTML5 Canvas, you still need a `<video>` tag in HTML. The key is to put the video in a `<div>` (or a similar construct), and set the `display` CSS style property of that `<div>` to `none` in HTML. This will ensure that while the video is loaded in the page, it is not displayed. If we wrote the code in HTML, it might look like this:

```
<div style="position: absolute; top: 50px; left: 600px; display:none">
 <video loop controls id="thevideo" width="320" height="240" preload="auto">
  <source src="muirbeach.mp4" type='video/mp4; codecs="avc1.42E01E, mp4a.40.2"' >
  <source src="muirbeach.webm"type='video/webm; codecs="vp8, vorbis"' >
  <source src="muirbeach.ogg" type='video/ogg; codecs="theora, vorbis"'>
 </video>
```

However, we already know that we don't want to use an HTML embed. As we stated at the end of the last section, video events do not appear to fire reliably when video elements are embedded in the HTML page. For this reason, we need a new strategy to load video dynamically—we'll create the <div> and <video> elements in JavaScript.

The first thing we do in our JavaScript is add a couple variables to hold references to the dynamic HTML elements we will create. The videoElement variable will hold the dynamically created <video> tag, while videoDiv will hold the dynamically created <div>:

```
var videoElement;
var videoDiv;
```

 We use this method to create global variables throughout this chapter. There are many reasons not to use global variables, but for these simple applications, it's the quickest way to get something on the canvas. If you want to learn a better way to handle loading assets, the last section of Chapter 7 employs a strategy to preload assets without the use of global variables.

Next, we create our dynamic form elements in the eventWindowLoaded() function. First, we use the createElement() method of the document DOM object to create a <video> element and a <div> element, placing references to them in the variables we just created:

```
function eventWindowLoaded() {

    videoElement = document.createElement("video");
    videoDiv = document.createElement('div');
    document.body.appendChild(videoDiv);
```

Next, we add videoElement as a child of videoDiv, essentially putting it inside of that <div> on the HTML page. We then set the style attribute of <div> to display:none;, which will make it invisible on the HTML page. We do this because although we want the video to display on the canvas, we don't want to show it on the HTML page:

```
    videoDiv.appendChild(videoElement);
    videoDiv.setAttribute("style", "display:none;");
```

We then create another new variable named videoType that holds the results of a new function we will create, supportedVideoFormat(). This function returns the file extension of the supported video format for the browser; otherwise, it returns "" (an empty string), which means we alert the user that there is no video support in the app for his browser:

```
var videoType = supportedVideoFormat(videoElement);
if (videoType == "") {
    alert("no video support");
    return;
}
```

Finally, we set the `src` property of the `video` element using the file extension we just received from `supportedVideoFormat()`, and create the event handler for the `canplay through` event:

```
videoElement.setAttribute("src", "muirbeach." + videoType);
videoElement.addEventListener("canplaythrough",videoLoaded,false);

}
```

When the video has finished loading, the `videoLoaded` event handler is called, which in turn calls the `canvasApp()` function:

```
function videoLoaded(event) {

    canvasApp();

}
```

Before the code in the last section will work, we need to define the `supportedVideo Format()` function. The reason for this function is simple: since we are adding `video` objects dynamically to the HTML page, we do not have a way to define multiple `<source>` tags. Instead, we are going to use the `canPlayType()` method of the `video` object to tell us which type of audio file to load.

The `canPlayType()` method takes a single parameter, a MIME type. It returns a text string of `maybe`, `probably`, or nothing (an empty string).

"" (nothing)
  This is returned if the browser knows the type cannot be rendered.

maybe
  This is returned if the browser does not confidently know that the type can be displayed.

probably
  This is returned if the browser knows the type can be displayed using an `audio` or `video` element.

We are going to use these values to determine which media type to load and play. For the sake of this exercise, we will assume that both `maybe` and `probably` equate to yes. If we encounter either result with any of our three MIME types (*video/webm*, *video/ mp4*, *video/ogg*), we will return the extension associated with that MIME type so the sound file can be loaded.

In the function below, `video` represents the instance of `HTMLVideoElement` that we are going to test. The `returnExtension` variable represents that valid extension for the first

MIME type found that has the value of maybe or probably returned from the call to canPlayType():

```
function supportedVideoFormat(video) {
    var returnExtension = "";
    if (video.canPlayType("video/webm") =="probably" ||
        video.canPlayType("video/webm") == "maybe") {
        returnExtension = "webm";
    } else if(video.canPlayType("video/mp4") == "probably" ||
        video.canPlayType("video/mp4") == "maybe") {
        returnExtension = "mp4";
    } else if(video.canPlayType("video/ogg") =="probably" ||
        video.canPlayType("video/ogg") == "maybe") {
        returnExtension = "ogg";
    }

    return returnExtension;

}
```

We do not check for a condition when no valid video format is found and the return value is "". If that is the case, the code that has called this function might need to be written in a way to catch that condition and alter the program execution. We did that with the test of the return value and alert(), which we described previously.

Video is displayed like an image

When you write code to display a video on the canvas, you use the context.draw Image() function, as though you are displaying a static image. Don't go looking for a drawVideo() function in the HTML5 Canvas spec because you won't find it. The following code will display a video stored in a variable named videoElement, displayed at the x,y position of 85,30:

```
context.drawImage(videoElement , 85, 30);
```

However, when you draw a video for the first time, you will notice that it will not move—it stays on the first frame. At first you might think you have done something wrong, but you have not. You just need to add one more thing to make it work.

Set an interval to update the display

Just like when we discussed animation in the previous chapters, a video placed on HTML5 Canvas using drawImage() will not update itself. You need to call draw Image() in some sort of loop to continually update the image with new data from the playing video in the HTML page (hidden or not). To do this, we call the video's play() method, and then use setInterval() to call the drawScreen() function every 33 milliseconds. This will give you about 30 frames per second (FPS). We put this code in our canvasApp() function, which is called after we know the video has loaded:

```
videoElement.play();
setInterval(drawScreen, 33);
```

In `drawScreen()`, we will call `drawImage()` to display the video, but since it will be called every 33 milliseconds, the video will be updated and play on the canvas:

```
function drawScreen () {

    context.drawImage(videoElement , 85, 30);

}
```

Example 6-6 gives the full code for displaying a video on the canvas and updating it using `setInterval()`. Figure 6-6 shows this code in the browser.

Example 6-6. Basic HTML5 loading video onto the canvas

```
<!doctype html>
<html lang="en">
<head>
<meta charset="UTF-8">
<title>CH6EX6: Basic HTML5 Load Video Onto The Canvas</title>
<script src="modernizr-1.6.min.js"></script>
<script type="text/javascript">
window.addEventListener('load', eventWindowLoaded, false);
var videoElement;
var videoDiv;
function eventWindowLoaded() {

    videoElement = document.createElement("video");
    videoDiv = document.createElement('div');
    document.body.appendChild(videoDiv);
    videoDiv.appendChild(videoElement);
    videoDiv.setAttribute("style", "display:none;");
    var videoType = supportedVideoFormat(videoElement);
    if (videoType == "") {
        alert("no video support");
        return;
    }
    videoElement.setAttribute("src", "muirbeach." + videoType);
    videoElement.addEventListener("canplaythrough",videoLoaded,false);

}

function supportedVideoFormat(video) {
    var returnExtension = "";
    if (video.canPlayType("video/webm") =="probably" ||
        video.canPlayType("video/webm") == "maybe") {
            returnExtension = "webm";
    } else if(video.canPlayType("video/mp4") == "probably" ||
        video.canPlayType("video/mp4") == "maybe") {
            returnExtension = "mp4";
    } else if(video.canPlayType("video/ogg") =="probably" ||
        video.canPlayType("video/ogg") == "maybe") {
            returnExtension = "ogg";
    }

    return returnExtension;
```

```
}

function canvasSupport () {
    return Modernizr.canvas;
}

function videoLoaded(event) {

  canvasApp();

}

function canvasApp() {

  if (!canvasSupport()) {
        return;
      }

function  drawScreen () {

     //Background
     context.fillStyle = '#ffffaa';
     context.fillRect(0, 0, theCanvas.width, theCanvas.height);
     //Box
     context.strokeStyle = '#000000';
     context.strokeRect(5,  5, theCanvas.width-10, theCanvas.height-10);
     //video
     context.drawImage(videoElement , 85, 30);

  }

  var theCanvas = document.getElementById("canvasOne");
  var context = theCanvas.getContext("2d");
  videoElement.play();

  setInterval(drawScreen, 33);

}

</script>

</head>
<body>
<div style="position: absolute; top: 50px; left: 50px;">

<canvas id="canvasOne" width="500" height="300">
 Your browser does not support HTML5 Canvas.
</canvas>
</div>
</body>
</html>
```

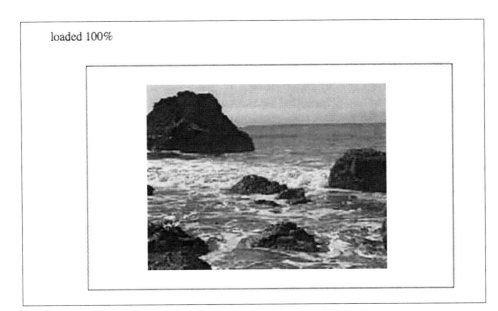

loaded 100%

Figure 6-6. Displaying a video on HTML5 Canvas

HTML5 Video Properties

We have already talked about some properties of HTMLVideoElement (inherited from HTMLMediaElement), but now that we have a video loaded onto the canvas, it would be interesting to see them in action.

In this example, we are going to display seven properties of a playing video, taken from the HTMLVideoElement object: duration, currentTime, loop, autoplay, muted, controls, and volume. Of these, duration, loop, and autoplay will not update because they are set when the video is embedded. Also, since we call the play() function of the video after it is preloaded in JavaScript, autoplay may be set to false, but the video will play anyway. The other properties will update as the video is played.

To display these values on the canvas, we will draw them as text in the drawScreen() function called by setInterval(). Below is the drawScreen() that we have created to display these values:

```
function drawScreen () {

    //Background
    context.fillStyle = '#ffffaa';
    context.fillRect(0, 0, theCanvas.width, theCanvas.height);
    //Box
    context.strokeStyle = '#000000';
    context.strokeRect(5,  5, theCanvas.width-10, theCanvas.height-10);
    //video
    context.drawImage(videoElement , 85, 30);
```

```
// Text
context.fillStyle = "#000000";
context.fillText ("Duration:" + videoElement.duration, 10 ,280);
context.fillText ("Current time:" + videoElement.currentTime, 260 ,280);
context.fillText ("Loop: " + videoElement.loop, 10 ,290);
context.fillText ("Autoplay: " + videoElement.autoplay, 100 ,290);
context.fillText ("Muted: " + videoElement.muted, 180 ,290);
context.fillText ("Controls: " + videoElement.controls, 260 ,290);
context.fillText ("Volume: " + videoElement.volume, 340 ,290);

}
```

Figure 6-7 shows what the attributes look like when displayed on the canvas. Notice that we have placed the <video> embed next to the canvas, and we have *not* set the CSS display style to none. We did this to demonstrate the relationship between the video embedded in the HTML page and the one playing on the canvas. If you roll over the video in the HTML page, you can see the control panel. If you set the volume, you will notice that the volume attribute displayed on the canvas will change. If you pause the embedded video, the video on the canvas will stop playing, and the currentTime value will stop.

This demo should give you a very good idea of the relationship between the video on the canvas and the one embedded with the <video> tag. Even though they are displayed using completely different methods, they are in fact one and the same.

Figure 6-7. Video on the canvas with properties displayed and <video> embed

You can see Example 6-7 in action by executing *CH6EX7.html* from the code distribution.

Example 6-7. Video properties

```
<!doctype html>
<html lang="en">
<head>
<meta charset="UTF-8">
<title>CH6EX7: Video Properties</title>
```

```
<script src="modernizr-1.6.min.js"></script>
<script type="text/javascript">
window.addEventListener('load', eventWindowLoaded, false);
var videoElement;
var videoDiv;
function eventWindowLoaded() {

    videoElement = document.createElement("video");
    var videoDiv = document.createElement('div');
    document.body.appendChild(videoDiv);
    videoDiv.appendChild(videoElement);
    videoDiv.setAttribute("style", "position: absolute; top: 50px; left: 600px; ");
    var videoType = supportedVideoFormat(videoElement);
    if (videoType == "") {
        alert("no video support");
        return;
    }
    videoElement.setAttribute("src", "muirbeach." + videoType);
    videoElement.addEventListener("canplaythrough",videoLoaded,false);

}


function supportedVideoFormat(video) {
    var returnExtension = "";
    if (video.canPlayType("video/webm") =="probably" ||
        video.canPlayType("video/webm") == "maybe") {
            returnExtension = "webm";
    } else if(video.canPlayType("video/mp4") == "probably" ||
        video.canPlayType("video/mp4") == "maybe") {
            returnExtension = "mp4";
    } else if(video.canPlayType("video/ogg") =="probably" ||
        video.canPlayType("video/ogg") == "maybe") {
            returnExtension = "ogg";
    }

    return returnExtension;

}


function canvasSupport () {
        return Modernizr.canvas;
}

function videoLoaded() {
    canvasApp();

}

function canvasApp() {

    if (!canvasSupport()) {
            return;
        }
```

```
function  drawScreen () {

    //Background
    context.fillStyle = '#ffffaa';
    context.fillRect(0, 0, theCanvas.width, theCanvas.height);
    //Box
    context.strokeStyle = '#000000';
    context.strokeRect(5,  5, theCanvas.width-10, theCanvas.height-10);
    //video
    context.drawImage(videoElement , 85, 30);
    // Text
    context.fillStyle = "#000000";
    context.fillText ("Duration:" + videoElement.duration,  10 ,280);
    context.fillText ("Current time:" + videoElement.currentTime,  260 ,280);
    context.fillText ("Loop: " + videoElement.loop,  10 ,290);
    context.fillText ("Autoplay: " + videoElement.autoplay,  100 ,290);
    context.fillText ("Muted: " + videoElement.muted,  180 ,290);
    context.fillText ("Controls: " + videoElement.controls,  260 ,290);
    context.fillText ("Volume: " + videoElement.volume,  340 ,290);

  }

  var theCanvas = document.getElementById("canvasOne");
  var context = theCanvas.getContext("2d");
  videoElement.play();

  setInterval(drawScreen, 33);

}

</script>

</head>
<body>
<div style="position: absolute; top: 50px; left: 50px;">

<canvas id="canvasOne" width="500" height="300">
 Your browser does not support HTML5 Canvas.
</canvas>
</div>
</body>
</html>
```

 You can see all the events and properties for the HTMLVideoElement at *http://www.w3.org/2010/05/video/mediaevents.html.*

Video on the Canvas Examples

In the last section, we learned that the video playing on the canvas and the video embedded with the `<video>` tag are, in fact, the same video. It took a lot more code to play the video on the canvas than it did to embed and play the video in JavaScript. So, this begs the question: *why load video onto the canvas at all?*

Well, sometimes simply displaying a video and playing it is not enough. You might want events to occur as the video is playing, or perhaps you want to use transformations on it, use it in a game, create custom video controls, or animate it and move it on the canvas.

The following five examples will show you in very specific detail why the canvas can be an exciting way to display video.

Using the currentTime Property to Create Video Events

The first way we will use video in conjunction with Canvas is to use the `currentTime` property of a playing video to trigger events. Recall that the `currentTime` property is updated as the video plays, and it shows the video's elapsed running time.

For our example, we are going to create a dynamic object in JavaScript containing the following properties:

time
> The elapsed time to trigger the event

message
> A text message to display on the canvas

x
> The x position of the text message

y
> The y position of the text message

First, we will create an array of these objects and place them into a variable named `messages`. We will then create four events (messages that will appear) that will take place at the elapsed `currentTime` of 0, 1, 4, and 8 seconds:

```
var messages = new Array();
    messages[0] = {time:0,message:"", x:0 ,y:0};
    messages[1] = {time:1,message:"This Is Muir Beach!", x:90 ,y:200};
    messages[2] = {time:4,message:"Look At Those Waves!", x:240 ,y:240};
    messages[3] = {time:8,message:"Look At Those Rocks!", x:100 ,y:100};
```

To display the messages, we will call a `for:next` loop inside our `drawScreen()` function. Inside the loop, we test each message in the `messages` array to see whether the `currentTime` property of the video is greater than the `time` property of the message. If so, we know that it is OK to display the message. We then display the message on the canvas using the `fillStyle` property and `fillText()` function of the Canvas context, producing the results shown in Figure 6-8:

```
for (var i = 0; i < messages.length ; i++) {
        var tempMessage = messages[i];
        if (videoElement.currentTime > tempMessage.time) {
          context.font = "bold 14px sans";
          context.fillStyle = "#FFFF00";
          context.fillText (tempMessage.message,  tempMessage.x ,tempMessage.y);
        }
    }
```

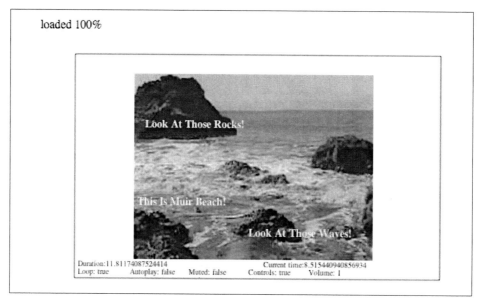

Figure 6-8. Canvas video displaying text overlay events

Of course, this is a very simple way to create events. The various text messages will not disappear after others are created, but that is just a small detail. The point of this exercise is that, with code like this, you could do almost anything with a running video. You could pause the video, show an animation, and then continue once the animation is done. Or you could pause to ask the user for input and then load a different video. Essentially, you can make the video completely interactive in any way you choose. The model for these events could be very similar to the one we just created.

Example 6-8 provides the full code listing for this application.

Example 6-8. Creating simple video events

```
<!doctype html>
<html lang="en">
<head>
<meta charset="UTF-8">
<title>CH6EX8: Creating Simple Video Events</title>
```

```
<script src="modernizr-1.6.min.js"></script>
<script type="text/javascript">
window.addEventListener('load', eventWindowLoaded, false);
var videoElement;
var videoDiv;
function eventWindowLoaded() {

    videoElement = document.createElement("video");
    videoDiv = document.createElement('div');
    document.body.appendChild(videoDiv);
    videoDiv.appendChild(videoElement);
    videoDiv.setAttribute("style", "display:none;");
    var videoType = supportedVideoFormat(videoElement);
    if (videoType == "") {
        alert("no video support");
        return;
    }
    videoElement.setAttribute("src", "muirbeach." + videoType);
    videoElement.addEventListener("canplaythrough",videoLoaded,false);

}
function supportedVideoFormat(video) {
    var returnExtension = "";
    if (video.canPlayType("video/webm") =="probably" ||
        video.canPlayType("video/webm") == "maybe") {
          returnExtension = "webm";
    } else if(video.canPlayType("video/mp4") == "probably" ||
        video.canPlayType("video/mp4") == "maybe") {
          returnExtension = "mp4";
    } else if(video.canPlayType("video/ogg") =="probably" ||
        video.canPlayType("video/ogg") == "maybe") {
          returnExtension = "ogg";
    }

    return returnExtension;

}

function canvasSupport () {
    return Modernizr.canvas;
}


function videoLoaded() {
    canvasApp();

}

function canvasApp() {

  if (!canvasSupport()) {
        return;
      }

  function  drawScreen () {
```

```
        //Background
        context.fillStyle = '#ffffaa';
        context.fillRect(0, 0, theCanvas.width, theCanvas.height);
        //Box
        context.strokeStyle = '#000000';
        context.strokeRect(5,  5, theCanvas.width-10, theCanvas.height-10);
        //video
        context.drawImage(videoElement , 85, 30);
        // Text
        context.fillStyle = "#000000";
        context.font = "10px sans";
        context.fillText ("Duration:" + videoElement.duration,  10 ,280);
        context.fillText ("Current time:" + videoElement.currentTime,  260 ,280);
        context.fillText ("Loop: " + videoElement.loop,  10 ,290);
        context.fillText ("Autoplay: " + videoElement.autoplay,  80 ,290);
        context.fillText ("Muted: " + videoElement.muted,  160 ,290);
        context.fillText ("Controls: " + videoElement.controls,  240 ,290);
        context.fillText ("Volume: " + videoElement.volume,  320 ,290);

        //Display Message
        for (var i =0; i < messages.length ; i++) {
            var tempMessage = messages[i];
            if (videoElement.currentTime > tempMessage.time) {
                context.font = "bold 14px sans";
                context.fillStyle = "#FFFF00";
                context.fillText (tempMessage.message,  tempMessage.x ,tempMessage.y);
            }
        }

    }

    var messages = new Array();
    messages[0] = {time:0,message:"", x:0 ,y:0};
    messages[1] = {time:1,message:"This Is Muir Beach!", x:90 ,y:200};
    messages[2] = {time:4,message:"Look At Those Waves!", x:240 ,y:240};
    messages[3] = {time:8,message:"Look At Those Rocks!", x:100 ,y:100};

    var theCanvas = document.getElementById("canvasOne");
    var context = theCanvas.getContext("2d");
    videoElement.play();

    setInterval(drawScreen, 33);

}

</script>

</head>
<body>
<div style="position: absolute; top: 50px; left: 50px;">

<canvas id="canvasOne" width="500" height="300">
 Your browser does not support HTML5 Canvas.
</canvas>
```

```
</div>
</body>
</html>
```

Canvas Video Transformations: Rotation

Showing a static video on the screen is one thing, but transforming it on the screen using alpha transparency and rotations is quite another. These types of transformations can be easily applied to video on the canvas in much the same way as you would apply them to an image or a drawing object.

In this example, we will create a video that rotates clockwise. To achieve this effect, we first create a variable, rotation, which we will use to hold the current values of the rotation property that we will apply to the video. We create this variable outside of the drawScreen() function, inside canvasApp():

```
var rotation = 0;
```

The drawScreen() function is where all the real action takes place for this example. First, we need to save the current canvas context so we can restore it after we perform the transformation. We covered this in depth in Chapter 2, but here's a quick refresher. Transformations on the canvas are global in nature, which means they affect *everything*. Since the canvas works in immediate mode, there is no stack of objects to manipulate. Instead, we need to save the canvas context before the transformation, apply the transformation, and then restore the saved context afterward.

First, we save it:

```
context.save();
```

Next, we reset the context transformation to the identity, which clears anything that was set previously:

```
context.setTransform(1,0,0,1,0,0);
```

Then we need to set up some variables that will be used for the rotation calculation. The x and y variables set the upper-left location of the video on the canvas. The video Width and videoHeight variables will be used to help rotate the video from the center:

```
var x = 100;
var y = 100;
var videoWidth=320;
var videoHeight=240;
```

Now it is time to use the rotation variable, which represents the angle that we rotated the video on the canvas. It starts at 0, and we will increase it every time drawScreen() is called. However, the context.rotate() method requires an angle to be converted to radians when passed as its lone parameter. The following line of code converts the value in the rotation variable to radians, and stores it in a variable named angleInRadians:

```
var angleInRadians = rotation * Math.PI / 180;
```

We need to find the video's center on the canvas so we can start our rotation from that point. We find the x value by taking our videoX variable and adding half the width of the video. We find the y value by taking our videoY variable and adding half the height of the video. We supply both of those values as parameters to the context.translate() function so the rotation will begin at that point. We need to do this because we are not rotating the video object—we are rotating the entire canvas in relation to the displayed video:

```
context.translate(x+.5*videoWidth, y+.5*videoHeight);
```

The rest of the code is really straightforward. First, we call the rotate() function of the context, passing our angle (converted to radians) to perform the rotation:

```
context.rotate(angleInRadians);
```

Then we call drawImage(), passing the video object, and the x,y positions of where we want the video to be displayed. This is a bit tricky but should make sense. Since we used the context.translate() function to move to the center of the video, we now need to place it in the upper-left corner. To find that corner, we need to subtract half the width to find the x position, and half the height to find the y position:

```
context.drawImage(videoElement ,-.5*videoWidth, -.5*videoHeight);
```

Finally, we restore the canvas we saved before the transformation started, and we update the rotation variable so that we will have a new angle on the next call to drawScreen():

```
context.restore();
rotation++;
```

Now the video should rotate at 1 degree clockwise per call to drawScreen() while fading onto the canvas. You can easily increase the speed of the rotation by changing the value that you input for the rotation variable in the last line in the drawScreen() function.

Here is the code for the final drawScreen() function for this example:

```
function  drawScreen () {

        //Background
        context.fillStyle = '#ffffaa';
        context.fillRect(0, 0, theCanvas.width, theCanvas.height);
        //Box
        context.strokeStyle = '#000000';
        context.strokeRect(5,   5, theCanvas.width-10, theCanvas.height-10);
        //video
        //*** Start rotation calculation
        context.save();
        context.setTransform(1,0,0,1,0,0);

        var angleInRadians = rotation * Math.PI / 180;
        var x = 100;
        var y = 100;
        var videoWidth=320;
        var videoHeight=240;
```

```
            context.translate(x+.5*videoWidth, y+.5*videoHeight);
            context.rotate(angleInRadians);
            //****
            context.drawImage(videoElement ,-.5*videoWidth, -.5*videoHeight);
            //*** restore screen
            context.restore();
            rotation++;
            //***
    }
```

Figure 6-9 shows what the video will look like when rotating on the canvas. You can see the full code for this in Example 6-9.

Figure 6-9. Canvas video rotation

Example 6-9. Rotating a video

```
<!doctype html>
<html lang="en">
<head>
<meta charset="UTF-8">
<title>CH6EX9: Video Rotation Transform</title>
<script src="modernizr-1.6.min.js"></script>
<script type="text/javascript">
window.addEventListener('load', eventWindowLoaded, false);
var videoElement;
var videoDiv;
function eventWindowLoaded() {

    videoElement = document.createElement("video");
    videoDiv = document.createElement('div');
    document.body.appendChild(videoDiv);
    videoDiv.appendChild(videoElement);
    videoDiv.setAttribute("style", "display:none;");
    var videoType = supportedVideoFormat(videoElement);
    if (videoType == "") {
        alert("no video support");
        return;
    }
    videoElement.setAttribute("src", "muirbeach." + videoType);
    videoElement.addEventListener("canplaythrough",videoLoaded,false);

}

function supportedVideoFormat(video) {
    var returnExtension = "";
    if (video.canPlayType("video/webm") =="probably" ||
        video.canPlayType("video/webm") == "maybe") {
            returnExtension = "webm";
    } else if(video.canPlayType("video/mp4") == "probably" ||
        video.canPlayType("video/mp4") == "maybe") {
            returnExtension = "mp4";
    } else if(video.canPlayType("video/ogg") =="probably" ||
        video.canPlayType("video/ogg") == "maybe") {
            returnExtension = "ogg";
    }

    return returnExtension;

}

function canvasSupport () {
    return Modernizr.canvas;
}


function videoLoaded() {
    canvasApp();

}
```

```
function canvasApp() {

  if (!canvasSupport()) {
        return;
      }

  //*** set rotation value
  var rotation = 0;
  //***

  function  drawScreen () {

      //Background
      context.fillStyle = '#ffffaa';
      context.fillRect(0, 0, theCanvas.width, theCanvas.height);
      //Box
      context.strokeStyle = '#000000';
      context.strokeRect(5,  5, theCanvas.width-10, theCanvas.height-10);
      //video
      //*** Start rotation calculation
      context.save();
      context.setTransform(1,0,0,1,0,0);

      var angleInRadians = rotation * Math.PI / 180;
      var x = 100;
      var y = 100;
      var videoWidth=320;
      var videoHeight=240;
      context.translate(x+.5*videoWidth, y+.5*videoHeight);
      context.rotate(angleInRadians);
      //****
      context.drawImage(videoElement ,-.5*videoWidth, -.5*videoHeight);
      //*** restore screen
      context.restore();
      rotation++;
      //***

    }

    var theCanvas = document.getElementById("canvasOne");
    var context = theCanvas.getContext("2d");
    videoElement.setAttribute("loop", "true");      videoElement.play();
    setInterval(drawScreen, 33);

}

</script>

</head>
<body>
<div style="position: absolute; top: 50px; left: 50px;">

<canvas id="canvasOne" width="500" height="500">
 Your browser does not support HTML5 Canvas.
</canvas>
```

```
</div>
</body>
</html>
```

Canvas Video Puzzle

Now we arrive at the most involved example of this section. We are going to create a puzzle game based on the video we have displayed on the canvas, illustrated in Figure 6-10. Here are the steps showing how the game will operate:

1. We will load the video onto the canvas but not display it.
2. We will decide how many parts we want to be in our puzzle.
3. We will create a board array that holds all the puzzle pieces.
4. The pieces will be displayed in a 4×4 grid.
5. We will randomize the pieces on the board to mix up the puzzle.
6. We will add an event listener for the mouse button.
7. We will set an interval to call drawScreen().
8. We will wait for the user to click a puzzle piece.
9. While we are waiting, the various parts of the video will play just as though they were one video.
10. When a user clicks a puzzle piece, it will highlight in yellow.
11. If the user has selected two pieces, we will swap their positions.
12. The user will attempt to put the puzzle back together so she can see the video as it was created.

Setting up the game

To start, we are going to set up some variables that will define the game's playfield. Here is a rundown of the variables and how they will be used:

rows
    The numbers of rows in the grid of puzzle pieces

cols
    The number of columns in the grid of puzzle pieces

xPad
    The space, in pixels, between each column

yPad
    The space, in pixels, between each row

startXOffset
    The number of pixels from the left of the canvas to the location where we will start drawing the grid of puzzle pieces

loaded 100%

Figure 6-10. Video puzzle

startYOffset
> The number of pieces from the top of the canvas to the location where we will start drawing the grid of puzzle pieces

partWidth
> The width of each puzzle piece

partHeight
> The height of each puzzle piece

board
> A two-dimensional array that holds the puzzle pieces

The following code includes values for each variable:

```
var rows = 4;
var cols = 4;
var xPad = 10;
var yPad = 10;
var startXOffset = 10;
var startYOffset = 10;
var partWidth = videoElement.width/cols;
var partHeight = videoElement.height/rows;
var board = new Array();
```

Next we need to initialize the board array and fill it with some dynamic objects that represent each piece of the puzzle. We loop through the number of cols in the board and create rows amount of dynamic objects in each one. The dynamic objects we are creating have these properties:

finalCol

> The final column-resting place of the piece when the puzzle is complete. We use this value to figure out what part of the video cut out to make this piece.

finalRow

> The final row-resting place of the piece when the puzzle is complete. We use this value to figure out what part of the video cut out to make this piece.

selected

> A Boolean that is initially set to `false`. We will use this to see whether we should highlight a piece or switch two pieces when the user clicks a piece.

Notice that we use two nested `for:next` loops to fill the `board` array with these objects. Familiarize yourself with this construct because we use it many times in this game. Two nested loops used like this are particularly useful for games and apps that require a 2D grid in order to be displayed and manipulated:

```
for (var i = 0; i < cols; i++) {
    board[i] = new Array();
    for (var j =0; j < rows; j++) {
        board[i][j] = { finalCol:i,finalRow:j,selected:false };
    }
}
```

Now that we have the `board` array initialized, we call `randomizeBoard()` (we will discuss this function shortly), which mixes up the puzzle by randomly placing the pieces on the screen. We finish the setup section of the game by adding an event listener for the `mouseup` event (when the user releases the mouse button), and by setting an interval to call `drawScreen()` every 33 milliseconds:

```
board = randomizeBoard(board);

theCanvas.addEventListener("mouseup",eventMouseUp, false);

setInterval(drawScreen, 33);
```

Randomizing the puzzle pieces

The `randomizeBoard()` function requires you to pass in the `board` variable so we can operate on it. We've set up the function this way so it will be portable to other applications.

To randomize the puzzle pieces, we first need to set up an array named `newBoard` that will hold the randomized puzzle pieces. `newBoard` will be what we call a *parallel array*. Its purpose is to become the original array—but randomized. We then create a local `cols` variable and initialize it to the length of the `board` array that was passed in to the function, and a local `rows` variable, initialized to the length of the first column—`board[0]`—in the array. This works because all of our rows and columns are the same length, so the number of rows in the first column is the same as all the others. We now have the building blocks required to randomize the pieces:

```
function randomizeBoard(board) {
    var newBoard = new Array();
    var cols = board.length;
    var rows = board[0].length
```

Next, we loop through every column and row, randomly choosing a piece from the board array and moving it into newBoard:

```
for (var i = 0; i < cols; i++) {
```

 We use two nested for:next loops here once again.

Every time we come to an iteration of the outer nested loop, we create a new array that we will fill up in the second nested loop. Then we drop into that nested loop. The found variable will be set to true when we have found a random location to place the piece in the newBoard array. The rndRow and rndCol variables hold the random values we will create to try and find a random location for the puzzle pieces:

```
newBoard[i] = new Array();
        for (var j =0; j < rows; j++) {
            var found = false;
            var rndCol = 0;
            var rndRow = 0;
```

Now we need to find a location in newBoard in which to put the puzzle piece from the board array. We use a while() loop that continues to iterate as long as the found variable is false. To find a piece to move, we randomly choose a row and column, and then use them to see whether that space (board[rndCol][rndRow]) is set to false. If it is not false, we have found a piece to move to the newBoard array. We then set found equal to true so we can get out of the while() loop and move to the next space in newBoard that we need to fill:

```
while (!found) {
    var rndCol = Math.floor(Math.random() * cols);
    var rndRow = Math.floor(Math.random() * rows);
    if (board[rndCol][rndRow] != false) {
        found = true;
    }
}
```

Finally, we move the piece we found in board to the current location we are filling in newBoard. Then, we set the piece in the board array to false so that when we test for the next piece, we won't try to use the same piece we just found. When we are done filling up newBoard, we return it as the newly randomized array of puzzle pieces:

```
newBoard[i][j] = board[rndCol][rndRow];
board[rndCol][rndRow] = false;
}
```

```
        }

        return newBoard;

    }
```

Drawing the screen

The drawScreen() function is the heart of this application. It is called on an interval, and then used to update the video frames and to draw the puzzle pieces on the screen. A good portion of drawScreen() looks like applications we have built many times already in this book. When it begins, we draw the background and a bounding box on the screen:

```
function drawScreen () {

    //Background
    context.fillStyle = '#303030';
    context.fillRect(0, 0, theCanvas.width, theCanvas.height);
    //Box
    context.strokeStyle = '#FFFFFF';
    context.strokeRect(5,  5, theCanvas.width-10, theCanvas.height-10);
```

However, the primary work of this function is—you guessed it—another set of two nested for:next loops that draw the puzzle pieces onto the canvas. This set needs to do three things:

1. Draw a grid of puzzle pieces on the canvas based on their placement in the board two-dimensional array.

2. Find the correct part of the video to render for each piece based on the finalCol and finalRow properties we set in the dynamic object for each piece.

3. Draw a yellow box around the piece that has its selected property set to true.

We start our loop by finding the x and y (imageX, imageY) locations to "cut" the puzzle piece from the video object. We do this by taking the finalRow and finalCol properties of the dynamic piece objects we created, and multiplying them by the partWidth and partHeight, respectively. We then have the origin point (top-left x and y locations) for the piece of the video to display:

```
for (var c = 0; c < cols; c++) {
    for (var r = 0; r < rows; r++) {

        var tempPiece = board[c][r];
        var imageX = tempPiece.finalCol*partWidth;
        var imageY = tempPiece.finalRow*partHeight;
```

Now that we know the origin point of the video we will display for a particular piece of the puzzle, we need to know where it will be placed on the canvas. While the code below might look confusing, it's really just simple arithmetic. To find the x location (placeX) of a piece, multiply the partWidth times the current iterated column (c), then add the current iterated column multiplied by the xPad (the number of pixels between each piece), and add the `startXOffset`, which is the x location of the upper-left corner of the entire board of pieces. Finding `placeY` is very similar, but you use the current row (`r`), `yPad`, and `partHeight` in the calculation:

```
var placeX = c*partWidth+c*xPad+startXOffset;
var placeY = r*partHeight+r*yPad+startYOffset;
```

Now it's time to draw the piece on the canvas. We need to "cut" out the part of the video that we will display for each piece of the puzzle (we won't actually cut anything though). We will again use the `drawImage()` function, as we have many other times already. However, now we use the version of `drawImage()` that accepts nine parameters:

`videoElement`
> The image that we are going to display; in this case, it is the video.

`imageX`
> The x location of the upper-right order of the part of the image to display.

`imageY`
> The y location of the upper-right order of the part of the image to display.

`partWidth`
> The width from the x location of the rectangle to display.

`partHeight`
> The height from the y location of the rectangle to display.

`placeX`
> The x location to place the image on the canvas.

`placeY`
> The y location to place the image on the canvas.

`partWidth`
> The width of the image as displayed on the canvas.

`partHeight`
> The height of the image as displayed on the canvas.

We've already discussed how we calculated most of these values, so it is just a matter of knowing the `drawImage()` API function and plugging in the variables:

```
context.drawImage(videoElement, imageX, imageY, partWidth, partHeight,
    placeX, placeY, partWidth, partHeight);
```

There is one last thing we are going to do in this function. If a puzzle piece is marked as "selected" (the `selected` Boolean property is `true`), we will draw a yellow box around the piece:

```
if (tempPiece.selected) {

    context.strokeStyle = '#FFFF00';
    context.strokeRect( placeX,  placeY, partWidth, partHeight);

}
}
```

```
        }
    }
```

Detecting mouse interactions and the canvas

Recall that back in the canvasApp() function, we set an event listener for the mouseup action with the event handler function set to eventMouseUp. We now need to create that function:

```
theCanvas.addEventListener("mouseup",eventMouseUp, false);
```

The first thing we do in the eventMouseUp() function is test to find the x and y locations of the mouse pointer when the button was pressed. We will use those coordinates to figure out whether the user clicked on any of the puzzle pieces.

Since some browsers support the layerX/layerY properties of the event object, and others support the offsetX/offsetY properties, we need to support both. No matter which one is set, we will use those properties to set our mouseX and mouseY variables to the x and y locations of the mouse pointer:

```
function eventMouseUp(event) {

    var mouseX;
    var mouseY;
    var pieceX;
    var pieceY;
    if ( event.layerX ||  event.layerX == 0) { //Firefox
        mouseX = event.layerX ;
        mouseY = event.layerY;
      } else if (event.offsetX || event.offsetX == 0) { // Opera
        mouseX = event.offsetX;
        mouseY = event.offsetY;
      }
```

Creating hit test point-style collision detection

Now that we know where the user clicked, we need to test whether that location "hits" any of the puzzle pieces. If so, we set the selected property of that piece to true. What we are going to perform is a simple *hit test point*-style hit detection. It will tell us whether the x,y position (*point*) of the mouse is inside (*hits*) any one of the puzzle pieces when the mouse button is clicked.

First, we create a local variable named selectedList that we will use when we need to swap the pieces in the board array. Next, we will use a set of two nested for:next loops to traverse through all the pieces in the board array. Inside the for:next loops, the first thing we do is find the top-left corner x and y points of the current piece pointed to by board[c][r]. We calculate those values and put them into the placeX and placeY variables:

```
var selectedList= new Array();
for (var c = 0; c < cols; c++) {

    for (var r =0; r < rows; r++) {
        pieceX = c*partWidth+c*xPad+startXOffset;
        pieceY = r*partHeight+r*yPad+startYOffset;
```

Next, we use those calculated values to test for a hit test point collision. We do this with a semicomplicated `if:then` statement that tests the following four conditions simultaneously:

`mouseY >= pieceY`
> The mouse pointer lies lower than or equal to the top of the piece.

`mouseY <= pieceY+partHeight`
> The mouse pointer lies above or equal to the bottom of the piece.

`mouseX >= pieceX`
> The mouse pointer lies to the right or equal to the left side of the piece.

`mouseX <= pieceX+partWidth`
> The mouse pointer lies to the left or equal to the right side of the piece.

All of the above conditions must evaluate to `true` for a hit to be registered on any one piece on the board:

```
if ( (mouseY >= pieceY) && (mouseY <= pieceY+partHeight) && (mouseX >= pieceX) &&
    (mouseX <= pieceX+partWidth) ) {
```

If all these conditions are true, we set the selected property of the piece object to `true` if it was already `false`, or we set it to `false` if it was already `true`. This allows the user to "deselect" the selected piece if he has decided not to move it:

```
if ( board[c][r].selected) {
    board[c][r].selected = false;

} else {
    board[c][r].selected = true;

}
}
```

At the end of the nested `for:next` loop, we make sure to test each piece to see whether its `selected` property is `true`. If so, we push it into the `selectedList` local array so we can perform the swap operation on the pieces:

```
if (board[c][r].selected) {
    selectedList.push({col:c,row:r})
}

}

}
```

Swapping two elements in a two-dimensional array

Now we need to test to see whether two pieces have been marked as `selected`. If so, we swap the positions of those pieces. In this way, it appears that the player is clicking on puzzle pieces and changing their locations to try to solve the puzzle.

To achieve the swap, we use a classic *three-way swap* programming construct utilizing a temporary variable, `tempPiece1`, as a placeholder for the values we are going to swap. First, we need to create a couple variables to hold the selected pieces. We will use `selected1` and `selected2` for that purpose. Next, we move the reference to the piece represented by `selected1` into the `tempPiece1` variable:

```
if (selectedList.length == 2) {
        var selected1 = selectedList[0];
        var selected2 = selectedList[1];
        var tempPiece1 = board[selected1.col][selected1.row];
        board[selected1.col][selected1.row] =
```

Next, we move the piece referenced by `selected2` to the location in the `board` array of the piece represented by `selected1` (the first swap). Then we apply the piece referenced in `selected1` to the position represented by `selected2` (the second swap). Finally, now that they are swapped, we make sure to set the `selected` properties of both pieces to `false`:

```
board[selected2.col][selected2.row];
        board[selected2.col][selected2.row] = tempPiece1;
        board[selected1.col][selected1.row].selected = false;
        board[selected2.col][selected2.row].selected = false;
    }

}
```

 This part of the function works because we have limited the number of pieces that can be selected to 2. For a game such as poker, which requires the player to select five cards, you would use a slightly different algorithm that tests for 5 cards instead of 2, and then calculate the value of the hand.

Testing the game

Believe it or not, that is all the code we need to talk about—the rest you have seen many times before. Try running the game (*CH6EX10.html*). When it loads, you should see the video organized in a 16-piece grid. Each part of the video will be playing, just like one of those magic tricks where a woman appears to be separated into multiple boxes but her legs, arms, and head are still moving. In fact, this game is sort of like one of those magic tricks because, in reality, the video was never "cut" in any way. We simply display the parts of the video to make it appear to be cut into 16 independent, moving pieces that can be swapped to re-form the original video.

Example 6-10 shows the full code listing for the Video Puzzle application.

Example 6-10. Video puzzle

```html
<!doctype html>
<html lang="en">
<head>
<meta charset="UTF-8">
<title>CH6EX10: Video Puzzle</title>
<script src="modernizr-1.6.min.js"></script>
<script type="text/javascript">
window.addEventListener('load', eventWindowLoaded, false);
var videoElement;
var videoDiv;
function eventWindowLoaded() {

    videoElement = document.createElement("video");
    videoDiv = document.createElement('div');
    document.body.appendChild(videoDiv);
    videoDiv.appendChild(videoElement);
    videoDiv.setAttribute("style", "display:none;");
    var videoType = supportedVideoFormat(videoElement);
    if (videoType == "") {
        alert("no video support");
        return;
    }
    videoElement.setAttribute("src", "muirbeach." + videoType);
    videoElement.addEventListener("canplaythrough",videoLoaded,false);

}

function supportedVideoFormat(video) {
    var returnExtension = "";
    if (video.canPlayType("video/webm") =="probably" ||
        video.canPlayType("video/webm") == "maybe") {
          returnExtension = "webm";
    } else if(video.canPlayType("video/mp4") == "probably" ||
        video.canPlayType("video/mp4") == "maybe") {
          returnExtension = "mp4";
    } else if(video.canPlayType("video/ogg") =="probably" ||
        video.canPlayType("video/ogg") == "maybe") {
          returnExtension = "ogg";
    }

    return returnExtension;

}

function canvasSupport () {
      return Modernizr.canvas;
}


function videoLoaded() {
    canvasApp();

}
```

```
function canvasApp() {

  if (!canvasSupport()) {
        return;
      }

  function  drawScreen () {

      //Background
      context.fillStyle = '#303030';
      context.fillRect(0, 0, theCanvas.width, theCanvas.height);
      //Box
      context.strokeStyle = '#FFFFFF';
      context.strokeRect(5,  5, theCanvas.width-10, theCanvas.height-10);

      for (var c = 0; c < cols; c++) {
         for (var r = 0; r < rows; r++) {

            var tempPiece = board[c][r];
            var imageX = tempPiece.finalCol*partWidth;
            var imageY = tempPiece.finalRow*partHeight;
            var placeX = c*partWidth+c*xPad+startXOffset;
            var placeY = r*partHeight+r*yPad+startYOffset;
            //context.drawImage(videoElement , imageX, imageY, partWidth, partHeight);
            context.drawImage(videoElement, imageX, imageY, partWidth, partHeight,
                placeX, placeY, partWidth, partHeight);
            if (tempPiece.selected) {

               context.strokeStyle = '#FFFF00';
               context.strokeRect( placeX,  placeY, partWidth, partHeight);

            }
         }
      }

  }

  function randomizeBoard(board) {
      var newBoard = new Array();
      var cols = board.length;
      var rows = board[0].length
      for (var i = 0; i < cols; i++) {
         newBoard[i] = new Array();
         for (var j =0; j < rows; j++) {
            var found = false;
            var rndCol = 0;
            var rndRow = 0;
            while (!found) {
               var rndCol = Math.floor(Math.random() * cols);
               var rndRow = Math.floor(Math.random() * rows);
               if (board[rndCol][rndRow] != false) {
                  found = true;
               }
            }
```

```
            newBoard[i][j] = board[rndCol][rndRow];
            board[rndCol][rndRow] = false;
        }

    }

    return newBoard;

}

function eventMouseUp(event) {

    var mouseX;
    var mouseY;
    var pieceX;
    var pieceY;
    if ( event.layerX ||  event.layerX == 0) { // Firefox
            mouseX = event.layerX ;
        mouseY = event.layerY;
      } else if (event.offsetX || event.offsetX == 0) { // Opera
        mouseX = event.offsetX;
        mouseY = event.offsetY;
      }
    var selectedList= new Array();
    for (var c = 0; c < cols; c++) {

        for (var r =0; r < rows; r++) {
            pieceX = c*partWidth+c*xPad+startXOffset;
            pieceY = r*partHeight+r*yPad+startYOffset;
            if ( (mouseY >= pieceY) && (mouseY <= pieceY+partHeight) &&
                  (mouseX >= pieceX) && (mouseX <= pieceX+partWidth) ) {

                if ( board[c][r].selected) {
                    board[c][r].selected = false;

                } else {
                    board[c][r].selected = true;

                }
            }
            if (board[c][r].selected) {
                selectedList.push({col:c,row:r})
            }

        }

    }
    if (selectedList.length == 2) {
        var selected1 = selectedList[0];
        var selected2 = selectedList[1];
        var tempPiece1 = board[selected1.col][selected1.row];
        board[selected1.col][selected1.row] =  board[selected2.col][selected2.row];
        board[selected2.col][selected2.row] = tempPiece1;
        board[selected1.col][selected1.row].selected = false;
        board[selected2.col][selected2.row].selected = false;
```

```
            }

        }

        var theCanvas = document.getElementById("canvasOne");
        var context = theCanvas.getContext("2d");
        videoElement.play();

        //Puzzle Settings

        var rows = 4;
        var cols = 4;
        var xPad = 10;
        var yPad = 10;
        var startXOffset = 10;
        var startYOffset = 10;
        var partWidth = videoElement.width/cols;
        var partHeight = videoElement.height/rows;
        //320×240
        partWidth = 80;
        partHeight = 60;
        var board = new Array();

        //Initialize Board

        for (var i = 0; i < cols; i++) {
            board[i] = new Array();
            for (var j =0; j < rows; j++) {
                board[i][j] = { finalCol:i,finalRow:j,selected:false };
            }
        }

        board = randomizeBoard(board);

        theCanvas.addEventListener("mouseup",eventMouseUp, false);

        setInterval(drawScreen, 33);

    }

</script>

</head>
<body>
<div style="position: absolute; top: 50px; left: 50px;">

<canvas id="canvasOne" width="370" height="300">
 Your browser does not support HTML5 Canvas.
</canvas>
</div>
</body>
</html>
```

Creating Video Controls on the Canvas

One obvious use of the HTML5 Canvas video display functionality is to create custom video controls to play, pause, stop, etc. You may have already noticed that when a video is rendered on the canvas, it does not retain any of the HTML5 video controls. If you want to create controls on the canvas, you need to make them yourself. Thankfully, we have already learned most everything we need to do this—now we just have to put it all together.

Creating video buttons

We are going to use some video control buttons that were created specifically for this example. Figure 6-11 shows a tile sheet that consists of *off* and *on* states for play, pause, and stop. The top row images are the on state; the bottom row images are the off state.

Figure 6-11. Video control button tile sheet

 We don't use the off state of the stop button in this application, but we included it in case you—the amazing reader and programmer that you are—want to use it later.

We will load this image dynamically onto the canvas, and then place each 32×32 button onto the canvas individually. We use the width and height to calculate which part of the image to display as a control.

Preloading the buttons

The first thing we need to do is preload the button tile sheet. Since we are already testing for the video to preload before we display the canvas, we need a slightly new strategy to preload multiple objects. For this example, we will use a counter variable named loadCount that we will increment each time we detect that an item has loaded. In conjunction with that variable, we will create another named itemsToLoad, which will hold the number of things we are preloading. For this app that number is two: the video and the tile sheet. These two variables are created outside of all functions at the top of our JavaScript:

```
var loadCount = 0;
var itemsToLoad = 2;
```

Along with `videoElement` and `videoDiv`, we also create another new variable, `button Sheet`. This is a reference to the image we load that holds the graphical buttons we will use for the video player interface:

```
var videoElement;
var videoDiv;
var buttonSheet
```

We now must make some updates to our standard `eventWindowLoaded()` function that we have used for most of this chapter. First, we are going to change the `canplay` event handler for the video to a new function, `itemLoaded`:

```
videoElement.addEventListener("canplay",itemLoaded,false);
```

We used the `canplay` event instead of `canplaythrough` because, most of the time, a user wants to start watching a video as soon as enough data has been buffered to play, and not after the entire video has loaded.

Next, we need to load our tile sheet. We create a new `Image` object and set the `src` property to *videobuttons.png*, which is the file shown in Figure 6-11. We also set its `onload` event handler to `itemLoaded`, just like the video:

```
buttonSheet = new Image();
buttonSheet.src = "videobuttons.png";
buttonSheet.onload = itemLoaded;
}
```

Finally, we create the `itemLoaded()` event handler function. When this function is called, we increment the `loadCount` variable and test it against the `itemsToLoad` variable.

 `loadCount` should never be greater than `itemsToLoad` if your application is running correctly. However, we find it safer to limit the use of the strict `==` test if possible. Why? Because if somehow, somewhere, something gets counted twice, the app will never load properly.

If it is equal to or greater than `itemsToLoad`, we call `canvasApp()` to start the application:

```
function itemLoaded() {
    loadCount++;
    if (loadCount >= itemsToLoad) {
        canvasApp();
    }
}
```

Placing the buttons

We need to set some variables in `canvasApp()` that will represent the locations of the three buttons we will display: play, pause, and stop. We start by specifying the standard button width and height as the variables `bW` and `bH`. All the images in the *videobuttons.png* tile sheet are 32×32 pixels, so we will set `bW` and `bH` accordingly. Then, we proceed to create variables that represent the x and y locations of each button: `playX`, playY, pauseX, pauseY, stopX, and stopY. We could use literal values; however, these variables will make a couple of the more complicated calculations easier to swallow:

```
var bW = 32;
var bH = 32;
var playX = 190;
var playY = 300;
var pauseX = 230;
var pauseY = 300;
var stopX = 270
var stopY = 300;
```

In the `drawImage()` function, we need to test for the current state of the playing video and render the buttons accordingly. For this application, we will use the paused state of the video object's attribute to render the buttons properly in their "up" or "down" states.

When a video first loads on the page and is not yet playing, its paused attribute is set to true. When a video is playing, its paused attribute is set to false. Knowing this, we can create the actions for these simple buttons.

First, if we know that the video is not in a paused state, it must be playing, so we display the "down" version of the play button. The "down" position is in the second row on the tile sheet in Figure 6-11. The third parameter of the call to the `drawImage()` function is 32 because that is where the y position of the image we want to display starts on the tile sheet. If paused is true, it means the video is not playing, so we display the "up" version of the play button. It starts at y position 0:

```
if (!videoElement.paused) {
    context.drawImage(buttonSheet, 0,32,bW,bH,playX,playY,bW,bH); //Play Down

} else {
    context.drawImage(buttonSheet, 0,0,bW,bH,playX,playY,bW,bH); //Play up
}
```

Displaying the pause button is simply the opposite of play. If the video paused property is true, we display the "down" version of the pause button. If the video is playing, it means the pause property is false, so we display the "up" version. Notice that the second parameter is 32 because to display the pause buttons in the tile sheet, we need to skip over the play button and start at the x position of the pause button:

```
if (videoElement.paused) {
    context.drawImage(buttonSheet,  32,32,bW,bH,pauseX,pauseY,bW,bH); //down
} else {
    context.drawImage(buttonSheet,  32,0,bW,bH,pauseX,pauseY,bW,bH); // up
}

context.drawImage(buttonSheet,  64,0,bW,bH,stopX,stopY,bW,bH); // Stop up
```

Listening for the button presses

We also need to listen for the mouse button click. This process is very similar to how we accomplished much the same thing in the Video Puzzle application. First, back in the canvasApp() function, we set an event handler, eventMouseUp(), for the mouseup event:

```
theCanvas.addEventListener("mouseup",eventMouseUp, false);
```

The eventMouseUp() function works very similar to the same function we created earlier for Video Puzzle. First, we find the mouse pointer's x and y positions based on the way the browser tracks those values, and we put those values into local mouseX and mouseY variables:

```
function eventMouseUp(event) {

    var mouseX;
    var mouseY;
    if ( event.layerX ||  event.layerX == 0) { // Firefox
        mouseX = event.layerX ;
        mouseY = event.layerY;
      } else if (event.offsetX || event.offsetX == 0) { // Opera
        mouseX = event.offsetX;
        mouseY = event.offsetY;
      }
    //Hit Play
```

Next, we test for a hit test point inside each button by checking the bounds (right, left, top, bottom) on the canvas to see whether the mouse pointer was over any of our buttons when it was clicked. If so, we detect a hit.

First, we test the play button. Notice that those variables we created to represent the upper-left x and y locations of the button (playX and playY) help us make this calculation. They also help us because the names of the buttons self-document what we are trying to accomplish in each test of this function.

If the play button has been clicked, and the video paused property is true, we call the play() function of the video to start playing:

```
//Hit Play
    if ( (mouseY >= playY) && (mouseY <= playY+bH) && (mouseX >= playX) &&
        (mouseX <= playX+bW) ) {
        if (videoElement.paused) {
          videoElement.play();

        }
```

If the stop button was clicked, we set the paused property of the video to true, and set the currentTime property to 0 so that the video will return to the first frame:

```
//Hit Stop

    if ( (mouseY >= stopY) && (mouseY <= stopY+bH) && (mouseX >= stopX) &&
        (mouseX <= stopX+bW) ) {

        videoElement.pause();
        videoElement.currentTime = 0;
    }
```

If the pause button is clicked and the paused property of the video is false, we call the pause() function of the video to—you guessed it—pause the video on the current frame. If the paused property is true, we call the play() function of the video so it will resume playing:

```
//Hit Pause
        if ( (mouseY >= pauseY) && (mouseY <= pauseY+bH) && (mouseX >= pauseX) &&
            (mouseX <= pauseX+bW) ) {

            if (videoElement.paused == false) {
                videoElement.pause();
            } else {
                videoElement.play();
            }

        }
```

Figure 6-12 shows what the canvas looks like when the video is displayed with controls.

You will notice an odd relationship between the play and pause buttons. When one is "on," the other is "off." This is because we have only one property to look at: paused. There is a property named playing that exists in the HTML5 specification, but it did not work in all browsers, so we only used paused. In reality, you could have only one button and swap out the play or paused graphic depending on the paused state. That would make these controls work more like the default HTML video controls.

Figure 6-12. Canvas video player buttons

Example 6-11 shows the full source code for this application.

Example 6-11. Canvas video with controls

```
<!doctype html>
<html lang="en">
<head>
<meta charset="UTF-8">
<title>CH6EX11: Canvas Video With Controls</title>
<script src="modernizr-1.6.min.js"></script>
<script type="text/javascript">
window.addEventListener('load', eventWindowLoaded, false);
var loadCount= 0;
var itemsToLoad = 2;
var videoElement;
var videoDiv;
var buttonSheet

function eventWindowLoaded() {
    videoElement = document.createElement("video");
    videoDiv = document.createElement('div');
    document.body.appendChild(videoDiv);
    videoDiv.appendChild(videoElement);
    videoDiv.setAttribute("style", "display:none;");
    var videoType = supportedVideoFormat(videoElement);
    if (videoType == "") {
        alert("no video support");
        return;
```

```
      }
      videoElement.setAttribute("src", "muirbeach." + videoType);
      videoElement.addEventListener("canplay",itemLoaded,false);
      buttonSheet = new Image();
      buttonSheet.onload = itemLoaded;
      buttonSheet.src = "videobuttons.png";
}

function supportedVideoFormat(video) {
      var returnExtension = "";
      if (video.canPlayType("video/webm") =="probably" ||
          video.canPlayType("video/webm") == "maybe") {
            returnExtension = "webm";
      } else if(video.canPlayType("video/mp4") == "probably" ||
          video.canPlayType("video/mp4") == "maybe") {
            returnExtension = "mp4";
      } else if(video.canPlayType("video/ogg") =="probably" ||
          video.canPlayType("video/ogg") == "maybe") {
            returnExtension = "ogg";
      }

      return returnExtension;

}

function canvasSupport () {
      return Modernizr.canvas;
}
function itemLoaded() {
      loadCount++;
      if (loadCount >= itemsToLoad) {
         canvasApp();
      }


}
function canvasApp() {

      if (!canvasSupport()) {
            return;
          }

      function  drawScreen () {

          //Background
          context.fillStyle = '#ffffaa';
          context.fillRect(0, 0, theCanvas.width, theCanvas.height);
          //Box
          context.strokeStyle = '#000000';
          context.strokeRect(5,  5, theCanvas.width-10, theCanvas.height-10);
          //video
          context.drawImage(videoElement , 85, 30);
          //Draw Buttons
          //Play
```

```
        if (!videoElement.paused) {
           context.drawImage(buttonSheet, 0,32,bW,bH,playX,playY,bW,bH); //Play Down

        } else {
           context.drawImage(buttonSheet, 0,0,bW,bH,playX,playY,bW,bH); //Play up

        }

        if (videoElement.paused) {
           context.drawImage(buttonSheet,  32,32,bW,bH,pauseX,pauseY,bW,bH); // Pause down
        } else {
           context.drawImage(buttonSheet,  32,0,bW,bH,pauseX,pauseY,bW,bH); // Pause up
        }

        context.drawImage(buttonSheet,  64,0,bW,bH,stopX,stopY,bW,bH); // Stop up

}

        function eventMouseUp(event) {

        var mouseX;
        var mouseY;

        if ( event.layerX || event.layerX == 0) { // Firefox
              mouseX = event.layerX ;
           mouseY = event.layerY;
         } else if (event.offsetX || event.offsetX == 0) { // Opera
           mouseX = event.offsetX;
           mouseY = event.offsetY;
         }

        //Hit Play
        if ( (mouseY >= playY) && (mouseY <= playY+bH) && (mouseX >= playX) &&
           (mouseX <= playX+bW) ) {
          if (videoElement.paused) {
             videoElement.play();

          }

        }

        //Hit Stop

        if ( (mouseY >= stopY) && (mouseY <= stopY+bH) && (mouseX >= stopX) &&
           (mouseX <= stopX+bW) ) {

           videoElement.pause();
           videoElement.currentTime = 0;
        }
```

```
            //Hit Pause
        if ( (mouseY >= pauseY) && (mouseY <= pauseY+bH) && (mouseX >= pauseX) &&
              (mouseX <= pauseX+bW) ) {

            if (videoElement.paused == false) {
              videoElement.pause();
            } else {
              videoElement.play();
            }

        }

    }

    var theCanvas = document.getElementById("canvasOne");
    var context = theCanvas.getContext("2d");

    var bW = 32;
    var bH = 32;
    var playX = 190;
    var playY = 300;
    var pauseX = 230;
    var pauseY = 300;
    var stopX = 270
    var stopY = 300;


    theCanvas.addEventListener("mouseup",eventMouseUp, false);

    setInterval(drawScreen, 33);
}

</script>

</head>
<body>
<div style="position: absolute; top: 50px; left: 50px;">

<canvas id="canvasOne" width="500" height="350">
 Your browser does not support HTML5 Canvas.
</canvas>
</div>
</body>
</html>
```

Animation Revisited: Moving Videos

Now we are going to revisit the bouncing balls demo from Chapter 5 to show you how you can achieve the same effect with images and videos. Since we covered this in detail in Example 5-5 (*CH5EX5.html*), we don't need to examine all the code—just the changes that make the videos move.

 Remember that videos are drawn in much the same way as images, so with very few changes this application would work just as well with a static image.

While there are a few other changes, the most important is in the `drawScreen()` function when we draw the videos onto the canvas. Recall that in Chapter 5 we created an array named `balls` and a dynamic object to hold the properties of each ball that looked like this:

```
tempBall = {x:tempX,y:tempY,radius:tempRadius, speed:tempSpeed, angle:tempAngle,
    xunits:tempXunits, yunits:tempYunits}
```

For videos, we will create a similar array, named `videos`, but we will alter the dynamic object:

```
tempvideo = {x:tempX,y:tempY,width:180, height:120, speed:tempSpeed, angle:tempAngle,
    xunits:tempXunits, yunits:tempYunits}
```

The big difference here is that we no longer need a `radius` that represents the size of the ball; instead, we need the `width` and `height` so we can render the video to our desired size in the `drawScreen()` function.

Back in Chapter 5 we used the canvas drawing command to draw balls on the screen like this:

```
context.beginPath();
context.arc(ball.x,ball.y,ball.radius,0,Math.PI*2,true);
context.closePath();
context.fill();
```

To draw videos, we need to change the code:

```
context.drawImage(videoElement, video.x, video.y, video.width, video.height);
```

That is pretty much all you need to do! There are some others changes here (e.g., we start all the videos in the center of the screen before they start moving), but the items mentioned above are the main things you need to concentrate on to move video, not yellow balls, around the screen. Figure 6-13 shows what the example looks like with bouncing videos instead of balls. You can see the full code in Example 6-12.

loaded 100%

Figure 6-13. Canvas video animation demo

Example 6-12. Multiple video bounce

```
<!doctype html>
<html lang="en">
<head>
<meta charset="UTF-8">
<title>CH6EX12: Multiple Video Bounce</title>
<script src="modernizr-1.6.min.js"></script>
<script type="text/javascript">
window.addEventListener('load', eventWindowLoaded, false);

var videoElement;
var videoDiv;
function eventWindowLoaded() {

    videoElement = document.createElement("video");
    var videoDiv = document.createElement('div');
    document.body.appendChild(videoDiv);
```

```
        videoDiv.appendChild(videoElement);
        videoDiv.setAttribute("style", "display:none;");
        var videoType = supportedVideoFormat(videoElement);
        if (videoType == "") {
            alert("no video support");
            return;
        }
        videoElement.setAttribute("src", "muirbeach." + videoType);
        videoElement.addEventListener("canplaythrough",videoLoaded,false);

}

function supportedVideoFormat(video) {
    var returnExtension = "";
    if (video.canPlayType("video/webm") =="probably" ||
        video.canPlayType("video/webm") == "maybe") {
            returnExtension = "webm";
    } else if(video.canPlayType("video/mp4") == "probably" ||
        video.canPlayType("video/mp4") == "maybe") {
            returnExtension = "mp4";
    } else if(video.canPlayType("video/ogg") =="probably" ||
        video.canPlayType("video/ogg") == "maybe") {
            returnExtension = "ogg";
    }

    return returnExtension;

}

function canvasSupport () {
    return Modernizr.canvas;
}

function videoLoaded() {
    canvasApp();

}

function canvasApp() {

  if (!canvasSupport()) {
        return;
      }

  function  drawScreen () {

        context.fillStyle = '#000000';
        context.fillRect(0, 0, theCanvas.width, theCanvas.height);
        //Box
        context.strokeStyle = '#ffffff';
        context.strokeRect(1,  1, theCanvas.width-2, theCanvas.height-2);

        //Place videos
        context.fillStyle = "#FFFF00";
        var video;
```

```
    for (var i =0; i <videos.length; i++) {
       video = videos[i];
       video.x += video.xunits;
       video.y += video.yunits;

       context.drawImage(videoElement ,video.x, video.y, video.width, video.height);

       if (video.x > theCanvas.width-video.width || video.x < 0 ) {
          video.angle = 180 - video.angle;
          updatevideo(video);
       } else if (video.y > theCanvas.height-video.height || video.y < 0) {
          video.angle = 360 - video.angle;
          updatevideo(video);
       }
    }
 }


}

function updatevideo(video) {

   video.radians = video.angle * Math.PI/ 180;
   video.xunits = Math.cos(video.radians) * video.speed;
   video.yunits = Math.sin(video.radians) * video.speed;

}

var numVideos = 12 ;
var maxSpeed = 10;
var videos = new Array();
var tempvideo;
var tempX;
var tempY;
var tempSpeed;
var tempAngle;
var tempRadians;
var tempXunits;
var tempYunits;

var theCanvas = document.getElementById("canvasOne");
var context = theCanvas.getContext("2d");
videoElement.play();

for (var i = 0; i < numVideos; i++) {

   tempX = 160 ;
   tempY = 190 ;
   tempSpeed = 5;
   tempAngle = Math.floor(Math.random()*360);
   tempRadians = tempAngle * Math.PI/ 180;
   tempXunits = Math.cos(tempRadians) * tempSpeed;
   tempYunits = Math.sin(tempRadians) * tempSpeed;
```

```
          tempvideo = {x:tempX,y:tempY,width:180, height:120, speed:tempSpeed, angle:tempAngle,
              xunits:tempXunits, yunits:tempYunits}
          videos.push(tempvideo);
      }

      setInterval(drawScreen, 33);

  }

</script>

</head>
<body>
<div style="position: absolute; top: 50px; left: 50px;">

<canvas id="canvasOne" width="500" height="500">
 Your browser does not support HTML5 Canvas.
</canvas>
</div>
</body>
</html>
```

 The HTML5 video element combined with the canvas is an exciting, emerging area that is being explored on the Web as you read this. One great example of this is the exploding 3D video at CraftyMind.com (*http://craftymind.com*): *http://www.craftymind.com/2010/04/20/blowing-up-html5-video-and-mapping-it-into-3d-space/*.

What's Next?

In this chapter we introduced the HTML `<video>` tag and showed some basic ways that it could be used on an HTML page, including how to manipulate loaded video in numerous ways. While we showed you how to do some pretty cool stuff with the video and HTML5 Canvas, this is really just the tip of the iceberg. We believe that these two very powerful and flexible new features of HTML5 (video and the canvas) will prove to be a very potent combination for web applications of the future. In the next chapter, we will dive into HTML5 audio and how it can be used with applications created on the canvas.

CHAPTER 7

Working with Audio

You can't physically manipulate audio with HTML5 Canvas as directly as you can video, but many canvas applications can use that extra dimension of sound. Audio is represented by the `HTMLAudioElement` object manipulated through JavaScript, and by the `<audio>` tag in HTML5. There is no Canvas API for audio nor, really, is one necessary. However, there are many ways that you might want to use audio with HTML5 Canvas.

The Basic <audio> Tag

The basic usage of the `<audio>` tag in HTML5 is very similar to that of the `<video>` tag. The only required property is `src`, which needs to point to an existing audio file to play in the browser. Of course, it's always nice to show some audio controls on the page, and this can be accomplished using the `controls` Boolean, just as we did with `<video>`.

The code in Example 7-1 will load and play *song1.ogg* in a web browser that supports *.ogg* file playback, as shown in Figure 7-1. (Reminder: not all browsers support all formats.)

Example 7-1. Basic HTML5 audio

```
<!doctype html>
<html lang="en">
<head>
<meta charset="UTF-8">
<title>CH7EX1: Basic HTML5 Audio</title>
</head>
<body>
<div>
<audio src="song1.ogg" controls>
Your browser does not support the audio element.
</audio>
</div>
</body>
</html>
```

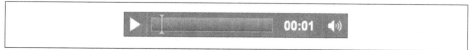

Figure 7-1. The very basic HTML5 <audio> tag

Audio Formats

Similar to video formats, which we learned about in Chapter 6, not every web browser supports every audio format. In fact, audio support appears to be in worse shape than video. As you will soon discover in this chapter, audio is one place where HTML5 needs some serious work. However, we will show you some strategies and workarounds for making audio easier to use in your applications.

Supported Formats

Here is a quick chart to show you which audio formats are supported by which browsers. We are not going to use version numbers here because we assume the latest version of each product:

Platform	.ogg	.mp3	.wav
Chrome	X	X	
Firefox	X		X
Safari		X	X
Opera	X		X
Internet Explorer 9		X	X

The situation is much like that of the `<video>` tag. To support `<audio>` we will need to use multiple separate formats for each piece of audio we want to play. To be on the safe side, we will use three formats: *.mp3*, *.ogg*, and *.wav*.

Audacity

Fortunately, there is a great free audio tool available that will help you convert audio into any format. In our case, we need to convert to *.mp3*, *.ogg*, and *.wav*.

Audacity (*http://audacity.sourceforge.net/*) is an open source, cross-platform project designed to bring sophisticated audio editing to the desktop. The current version works on Mac, Windows, and Linux.

Figure 7-2 shows a sample screen from Audacity. When you load a sound into Audacity, it displays the waveform of the sound. You can manipulate the sound in many ways, including trimming, splitting, and duplicating, and then add effects such as fade, echo, reverse, etc. After editing a sound, you export it to the sound format you would like to create. In our case, that would be *.ogg*, *.wav*, and *.mp3*.

 We don't have the space here to fully describe how to use an audio tool like Audacity, but we do need to give you one caveat: the distributed version of Audacity does not support the export of audio in the *.mp3* format. To export *.mp3* audio, you will need to download the LAME *.mp3* encoder from *http://lame.sourceforge.net/*. LAME is also an open source project.

Figure 7-2. Editing an audio file in Audacity

Example: Using All Three Formats

In Example 7-2, we are going to embed a 40-second song, *song1*, in an HTML5 page and play it. To make sure *song1* can play in as many browsers as possible, we are going to embed it with three different sources. For this example, we are also going to set the `autoplay`, `loop`, and `controls` properties so the song will start automatically, replay when it reaches the end, and display the default browser audio controls. Here is the code to embed *song1*:

```
<audio controls autoplay loop>
<source src="song1.mp3" type="audio/mp3">
<source src="song1.wav" type="audio/wav">
<source src="song1.ogg" type="audio/ogg">
</audio>
```

Just as we did with video, we have placed the audio type with the broadest support for iOS devices first in the list. This is because handheld devices do not do well with multiple embedded sources.

We created *.ogg*, *.wav*, and *.mp3* versions of the song using Audacity. Example 7-2 gives the full code.

Example 7-2. Basic HTML5 audio revisited

```
<!doctype html>
<html lang="en">
<head>
<meta charset="UTF-8">
<title>CH7EX2: Basic HTML5 Audio Revisited</title>
</head>
<body>
<div>
<audio controls autoplay loop>
<source src="song1.mp3" type="audio/mp3">
<source src="song1.ogg" type="audio/ogg">
<source src="song1.wav" type="audio/wav">
Your browser does not support the audio element.
</audio>
</div>
</body>
</html>
```

song1 was created 10 years ago using Sonic Foundry's Acid music-looping software. Acid is an amazing tool for creating soundtracks because it can help even the musically inept (read: us) create songs that sound perfect for games and applications. Acid is now sold by Sony for Windows only. Songs can be created on the Mac in a similar way using GarageBand.

Audio Tag Properties, Functions, and Events

Similar to the `<video>` tag, the `<audio>` tag in HTML5 is based on the HTMLAudio Element DOM object, which is derived from HTMLMediaElement.

Audio Functions

load()
> Starts loading the sound file specified by the src property of the <audio> tag.

play()
> Starts playing the sound file specified by the src property of the <audio> tag. If the file is not ready, it will be loaded.

pause()
> Pauses the playing audio file.

canPlayType()
> Accepts a MIME type as a parameter, and returns the value maybe or probably if the browser can play that type of audio file. It returns "" (an empty string) if it cannot.

Important Audio Properties

There are many properties defined for the audio element in HTML5. We are going to focus on the following because they are the most useful for the applications we will build:

duration
> The total length, in seconds, of the sound represented by the audio object.

currentTime
> The current playing position, in seconds, of the playing audio file.

loop
> true or false: whether the audio clip should start playing at the beginning when currentTime reaches the duration.

autoplay
> true or false: whether the audio should start playing automatically when it has loaded.

muted
> true or false. Setting this to true silences the audio object regardless of volume settings

controls
> true or false. Displays controls for an audio object in an HTML page. Controls will not display on the canvas unless they are created in HTML (for example, with a <div> overlay).

volume
> The volume level of the audio object; the value must be between 0 and 1.

paused
> true or false: whether the audio object is paused. Set with a call to the pause() function.

ended

true or false. Set when an audio object has played through its entire duration.

currentSrc

URL to the source file for the audio object.

preload

Specifies whether the media file should be loaded before the page is displayed. At the time of this writing, this property has not been implemented across all browsers.

 To see which properties and events of the HTMLMediaObject are supported in which browsers, visit *http://www.w3.org/2010/05/video/mediae vents.html.*

Important Audio Events

Many events are defined for the HTML5 audio element. We are going to focus on the following events because they have proven to work when building audio applications:

progress

Raised when the browser is retrieving data while loading the file. (This still has spotty support in browsers, so be careful with it.)

canplaythrough

Raised when the browser calculates that the media element could be played from beginning to end if started immediately.

playing

Set to true when the audio is being played.

volumechange

Set when either the volume property or the muted property changes.

ended

Set when playback reaches the duration of the audio file and the file stops being played.

Loading and Playing the Audio

We are going to use the canplaythrough and progress events to load <audio> before we try to play it. Here is how we embed the audio for *song1*:

```
<audio id="theAudio" controls>
<source src="song1.mp3" type="audio/mp3">
<source src="song1.wav" type="audio/wav">
<source src="song1.ogg" type="audio/ogg">
Your browser does not support the audio element.
</audio>
```

Similar to most of the applications we have built thus far in this book, we will create event handlers for progress and canplaythrough once the window DOM object has finished loading, and then call the load() method of audioElement to force the audio file to start loading:

```
window.addEventListener('load', eventWindowLoaded, false);
function eventWindowLoaded() {
    var audioElement = document.getElementById("theAudio");
    audioElement.addEventListener('progress',updateLoadingStatus,false);
    audioElement.addEventListener('canplaythrough',audioLoaded,false);
    audioElement.load();

}
```

When the canplaythrough event is dispatched, canvasApp() is called. Then, we start playing the audio by retrieving a reference to the audio element in the HTML page through the DOM, with a call to getElementById(). (We will create a variable named audioElement that we will use throughout the canvas application to reference the audio element in the HTML page.) We then call the play() function of audioElement:

```
var audioElement = document.getElementById("theAudio");
audioElement.play();
```

You may be wondering why we didn't use the preload attribute of HTMLAudioElement instead of forcing it to load by listening for the canplaythrough event. There are two reasons for this, and both apply to the video element as well. First, you want to preload so that you are sure the assets you need are available to your program at runtime. Second, preloading ensures that the user will see something useful or interesting while everything is loading. By using the standard preload attribute, you (in theory) force your audio assets to load before the page loads. Because canvas apps are interactive and may require many more assets than those loaded when the page loads, we avoid the preload attribute and load the assets within the application.

Displaying Attributes on the Canvas

Now we are going to display the attribute values of an audio element playing on an HTML page. In this example (*CH7EX3.html*), we are also going to display the audio element in the HTML page so you can see the relationship between what is shown on the canvas and the state of the <audio> tag in the page.

In the drawScreen() function we will add the following code to display the attributes of the audioElement variable:

```
context.fillStyle = "#000000";
context.fillText ("Duration:" + audioElement.duration,  20 ,20);
context.fillText ("Current time:" + audioElement.currentTime,  20 ,40);
context.fillText ("Loop: " + audioElement.loop,  20 ,60);
context.fillText ("Autoplay: " +audioElement.autoplay,  20 ,80);
context.fillText ("Muted: " + audioElement.muted,  20 ,100);
context.fillText ("Controls: " + audioElement.controls,  20 ,120);
context.fillText ("Volume: " + audioElement.volume,  20 ,140);
```

```
context.fillText  ("Paused: " + audioElement.paused,  20 ,160);
context.fillText  ("Ended: " + audioElement.ended,  20 ,180);
context.fillText  ("Source: " + audioElement.currentSrc,  20 ,200);
context.fillText  ("Can Play OGG: " + audioElement.canPlayType("audio/ogg"),
                   20 ,220);
context.fillText  ("Can Play WAV: " + audioElement.canPlayType("audio/wav"),
                   20 ,240);
context.fillText  ("Can Play MP3: " + audioElement.canPlayType("audio/mp3"),
                   20 ,260);
```

You should already be familiar with most of these attributes. When you launch Example 7-3 (*CH7EX3.html*), play with the audio controls in the browser. You will notice that the changes are reflected by the attribute values displayed on the canvas. This is just our first step toward integrating audio with the canvas, but it should give you a good idea of how we will start to use audio elements and manipulate them through JavaScript.

Figure 7-3 shows what this application looks like when it is executed in a web browser.

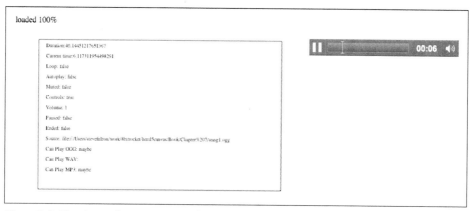

Figure 7-3. Showing audio properties on the canvas

There are also a few attributes displayed at the bottom of this list that we have not discussed. They all come from calls to the canPlayType() function of HTMLAudio Element. We are only displaying these right now, but in Example 7-3 we will make use of this function to help us decide which sound to dynamically load in JavaScript.

Example 7-3. Audio properties and the canvas

```
<!doctype html>
<html lang="en">
<head>
<meta charset="UTF-8">
<title>CH7EX3: Audio Properties And The Canvas</title>
<script src="modernizr-1.6.min.js"></script>
<script type="text/javascript">
window.addEventListener('load', eventWindowLoaded, false);
function eventWindowLoaded() {
```

```
        var audioElement = document.getElementById("theAudio");
        audioElement.addEventListener("progress",updateLoadingStatus,false);
        audioElement.addEventListener("canplaythrough",audioLoaded,false);
        audioElement.load();

}

function canvasSupport () {
        return Modernizr.canvas;
}

function updateLoadingStatus() {
        var loadingStatus = document.getElementById("loadingStatus");
        var audioElement = document.getElementById("theAudio");
        var percentLoaded = parseInt(((audioElement.buffered.end(0) /
            audioElement.duration) * 100));
         document.getElementById("loadingStatus").innerHTML =   'loaded '
            + percentLoaded + '%';


}

function audioLoaded() {

        canvasApp();

}

function canvasApp() {

    if (!canvasSupport()) {
            return;
          }

    function  drawScreen () {


        //Background
        context.fillStyle = "#ffffaa";
        context.fillRect(0, 0, theCanvas.width, theCanvas.height);

        //Box
        context.strokeStyle = "#000000";
        context.strokeRect(5,  5, theCanvas.width-10, theCanvas.height-10);

        // Text
        context.fillStyle  = "#000000";
        context.fillText ("Duration:" + audioElement.duration,  20 ,20);
        context.fillText ("Current time:" + audioElement.currentTime,  20 ,40);
        context.fillText ("Loop: " + audioElement.loop,  20 ,60);
        context.fillText ("Autoplay: " +audioElement.autoplay,  20 ,80);
        context.fillText ("Muted: " + audioElement.muted,  20 ,100);
        context.fillText ("Controls: " + audioElement.controls,  20 ,120);
        context.fillText ("Volume: " + audioElement.volume,  20 ,140);
        context.fillText ("Paused: " + audioElement.paused,  20 ,160);
        context.fillText ("Ended: " + audioElement.ended,  20 ,180);
```

```
            context.fillText ("Source: " + audioElement.currentSrc,  20 ,200);
            context.fillText ("Can Play OGG: " + audioElement.canPlayType("audio/ogg"),
                             20 ,220);
            context.fillText ("Can Play WAV: " + audioElement.canPlayType("audio/wav"),
                             20 ,240);
            context.fillText ("Can Play MP3: " + audioElement.canPlayType("audio/mp3"),
                             20 ,260);

      }

   var theCanvas = document.getElementById("canvasOne");
   var context = theCanvas.getContext("2d");
   var audioElement = document.getElementById("theAudio");
   audioElement.play();

   setInterval(drawScreen, 33);

}

</script>

</head>
<body>
<div style="position: absolute; top: 50px; left: 50px;">

<canvas id="canvasOne" width="500" height="300">
 Your browser does not support HTML5 Canvas.
</canvas>
</div>

<div id="loadingStatus">
0%
</div>

<div style="position: absolute; top: 50px; left: 600px; ">
<audio id="theAudio" controls >
<source src="song1.mp3" type="audio/mp3">
<source src="song1.ogg" type="audio/ogg">
<source src="song1.wav" type="audio/wav">

Your browser does not support the audio element.
</audio>

</div>
</body>
</html>
```

 This process is explained in detail in Chapter 6, where we warned that some browsers do not fire events for embedded <video> tags. That does not appear to be the case for <audio>, but it could happen in the future. We still believe the best bet for loading audio and video is the technique developed in the next section.

Playing a Sound with No Audio Tag

Now that we have a sound playing in an HTML5 page and we are tracking the properties of the audio element on the canvas, it is time to step up their integration. The next step is to do away with the <audio> tag embedded in the HTML page.

If you recall from Chapter 6, we created a video element dynamically in the HTML page and then used the canPlayType() method of the HTMLVideoElement object to figure out what video file type to load for a particular browser. We will do something very similar for audio.

Dynamically Creating an Audio Element in JavaScript

The first step to dynamically creating audio elements is to create a global variable named audioElement. This variable will hold an instance of HTMLAudioElement that we will use in our canvas application. Recall that audio elements in an HTML page are instances of the HTMLAudioElement DOM object. We refer to them as audio objects when embedded in an HTML page, and as instances of HTMLAudioElement when created dynamically in JavaScript. However, they are essentially the same.

 Don't fret if you don't like using global variables. By the end of this chapter, we will show you a way to make these variables local to your canvas application.

Next, we create our event handler for the window load event named eventWindowLoaded(). Inside that function, we call the createElement() function of the DOM document object, passing the value audio as the type of element to create. This will dynamically create an audio object and put it into the DOM. By placing that object in the audioElement variable, we can then dynamically place it onto the HTML page with a call to the appendChild() method of the document.body DOM object:

```
window.addEventListener('load', eventWindowLoaded, false);
var audioElement;
function eventWindowLoaded() {
    audioElement = document.createElement("audio");
    document.body.appendChild(audioElement);
```

However, just having a dynamically created audio element is not enough. We also need to set the src attribute of the HTMLAudioElement object represented by audioElement to a valid audio file to load and play. But the problem is that we don't yet know what type of audio file the current browser supports. We will get that information from a function we will create named supportedAudioFormat(). We will define this function so that it returns a string value representing the extension of the file type we want to load. When we have that extension, we concatenate it with the name of the sound we want to load, and set the src with a call to the setAttribute() method of the HTMLAudioElement object:

```
var audioType = supportedAudioFormat(audioElement);
```

If a valid extension from supportedAudioFormat() is not returned, something has gone wrong and we need to halt execution. To handle this condition in a simple way we create an alert() message and then return from the function, effectively halting execution. While this is not a very robust form of error handling, it will work for the sake of this example:

```
if (audioType == "") {
    alert("no audio support");
    return;
}
audioElement.setAttribute("src", "song1." + audioType);
```

Finally, like we did with video, we will listen for the canplaythrough event of audio Element so that we know when the sound is ready to play:

```
audioElement.addEventListener("canplaythrough",audioLoaded,false);
```

Finding the Supported Audio Format

Before the code in the previous section will work, we need to define the supported AudioFormat() function. Since we are adding audio objects dynamically to the HTML page, we do not have a way to define multiple <source> tags like we can in HTML. Instead, we are going to use the canPlayType() method of the audio object to tell us which type of audio file to load. We already introduced you to the canPlayType() method in Chapter 6, but to refresh your memory, canPlayType() takes a single parameter—a MIME type. It returns a text string of maybe, probably, or "" (nothing). We are going to use these values to figure out which media type to load and play. Just like in Chapter 6, and for the sake of this exercise, we are going to assume that both maybe and probably equate to yes. If we encounter either result with any of our three MIME types (*audio/ogg, audio/wav, audio/mp3*), we will return the extension associated with that MIME type so the sound file can be loaded.

 The next function is essentially the same as the one we created in Chapter 6 to handle video formats. The obvious changes here are with the MIME types for audio.

In the function below, audio represents the instance of HTMLAudioElement that we will test. The returnExtension variable represents that valid extension for the first MIME type found that has the value of maybe or probably returned:

```
function supportedAudioFormat(audio) {
    var returnExtension = "";
    if (audio.canPlayType("audio/ogg") =="probably" ||
        audio.canPlayType("audio/ogg") == "maybe") {
            returnExtension = "ogg";
```

```
        } else if(audio.canPlayType("audio/wav") =="probably" ||
            audio.canPlayType("audio/wav") == "maybe") {
            returnExtension = "wav";
        } else if(audio.canPlayType("audio/mp3") == "probably" ||
            audio.canPlayType("audio/mp3") == "maybe") {
            returnExtension = "mp3";
        }

        return returnExtension;

    }
```

Notice that we do not check for a condition when no valid audio format is found and the return value is *""*. If that is the case, the code that has called this function might need to be written in a way to catch that condition and alter the program execution. We did that with the test of the return value and the alert() message, which we described in the previous section.

 If you want to test the error condition with no valid return value from this function, simply add an extra character to the MIME type (e.g., *audio/oggx*) to make sure an empty string is always returned.

Alternatively, you can use Modernizr to test for audio support. If you have included the Modernizr JavaScript library in your HTML page (as we have done in every application we have written thus far), you can access the static values of *Modernizr.audio.ogg*, *Modernizr.audio.wav*, and *Modernizr.audio.mp3* to test to see whether those types are valid. These are not Booleans—they evaluate to the same probably, maybe, and *""* values that we get from a call to canPlayType(). If you are comfortable using Modernizr for all your tests, you can replace the test in the code with tests of these Modernizr static values.

Playing the Sound

Finally, we get to the point where we can play a sound inside our canvasApp() function. Since we preloaded the sound originally outside the context of this function into a variable with a global scope, we just need to call the play() function audioElement to start playing the sound:

```
    audioElement.play();
```

Figure 7-4 shows what this canvas application will look like when executed in an HTML5-compliant web browser (notice that we have left the display of the audio properties in this application).

Duration:40.14451217651367

Current time:6.914600849151611

Loop: false

Autoplay: false

Muted: false

Controls: false

Volume: 1

Paused: false

Ended: false

Source: file:///Users/stevefulton/work/8bitrocket/html5canvas/Book/Chapter%207/song1.ogg

Can Play OGG: maybe

Can Play WAV:

Can Play MP3: maybe

Figure 7-4. Sound loaded and played "on" the canvas

Look Ma, No Tag!

Now, check out the full application in Example 7-4. Notice that there is no `<audio>` tag defined in the HTML, but the sound still plays. This is our first step toward integrating `HTMLAudioElement` objects with HTML5 Canvas.

Example 7-4. Playing a sound with no tag

```
<!doctype html>
<html lang="en">
<head>
<meta charset="UTF-8">
<title>CH7EX4: Playing A Sound With No Tag</title>
<script src="modernizr-1.6.min.js"></script>
<script type="text/javascript">
window.addEventListener('load', eventWindowLoaded, false);
var audioElement;
function eventWindowLoaded() {

    audioElement = document.createElement("audio");
    document.body.appendChild(audioElement);
    var audioType = supportedAudioFormat(audioElement);
    if (audioType == "") {
        alert("no audio support");
        return;
    }
    audioElement.setAttribute("src", "song1." + audioType);
    audioElement.addEventListener("canplaythrough",audioLoaded,false);

}
```

```javascript
function supportedAudioFormat(audio) {
    var returnExtension = "";
    if (audio.canPlayType("audio/ogg") =="probably" ||
        audio.canPlayType("audio/ogg") == "maybe") {
            returnExtension = "ogg";
    } else if(audio.canPlayType("audio/wav") =="probably" ||
        audio.canPlayType("audio/wav") == "maybe") {
            returnExtension = "wav";
    } else if(audio.canPlayType("audio/mp3") == "probably" ||
        audio.canPlayType("audio/mp3") == "maybe") {
            returnExtension = "mp3";
    }

    return returnExtension;

}

function canvasSupport () {
        return Modernizr.canvas;
}


function audioLoaded(event) {

    canvasApp();

}

function canvasApp() {

    if (!canvasSupport()) {
            return;
          }

    function  drawScreen () {

        //Background
        context.fillStyle = '#ffffaa';
        context.fillRect(0, 0, theCanvas.width, theCanvas.height);

        //Box
        context.strokeStyle = '#000000';
        context.strokeRect(5,  5, theCanvas.width-10, theCanvas.height-10);

        // Text
        context.fillStyle = "#000000";
        context.fillText ("Duration:" + audioElement.duration,  20 ,20);
        context.fillText ("Current time:" + audioElement.currentTime,  20 ,40);
        context.fillText ("Loop: " + audioElement.loop,  20 ,60);
        context.fillText ("Autoplay: " +audioElement.autoplay,  20 ,80);
        context.fillText ("Muted: " + audioElement.muted,  20 ,100);
        context.fillText ("Controls: " + audioElement.controls,  20 ,120);
        context.fillText ("Volume: " + audioElement.volume,  20 ,140);
        context.fillText ("Paused: " + audioElement.paused,  20 ,160);
        context.fillText ("Ended: " + audioElement.ended,  20 ,180);
```

```
        context.fillText  ("Source: " + audioElement.currentSrc,  20 ,200);
        context.fillText  ("Can Play OGG: " + audioElement.canPlayType("audio/ogg"),
                            20 ,220);
        context.fillText  ("Can Play WAV: " + audioElement.canPlayType("audio/wav"),
                            20 ,240);
        context.fillText  ("Can Play MP3: " + audioElement.canPlayType("audio/mp3"),
                            20 ,260);

    }

    var theCanvas = document.getElementById("canvasOne");
    var context = theCanvas.getContext("2d");
    audioElement.play()

    setInterval(drawScreen, 33);

}

</script>

</head>
<body>
<div style="position: absolute; top: 50px; left: 50px;">

<canvas id="canvasOne" width="500" height="300">
 Your browser does not support HTML5 Canvas.
</canvas>
</div>
</body>
</html>
```

Creating a Canvas Audio Player

Now that we can play an audio file directly in an HTML page using the <audio> tag, or through JavaScript by creating a dynamic HTMLAudioElement object, it's time to step up our game. We are going to create an audio player on the canvas that we can use to control dynamically loaded audio files. Why do we want to do this? Well, while the audio controls baked into HTML5-compliant browsers might look decent, it is often necessary for developers to implement a design that more closely matches a particular website. HTML5 Canvas provides a way to create a dynamic set of audio controls with nearly any look-and-feel you desire.

However, this flexibility comes at a cost. HTML5 Canvas does not natively support common GUI controls such as push buttons, toggle buttons, and sliders. So to create a decent audio player, we need to make these types of GUI user controls from scratch. We could create these controls in HTML and JavaScript, but we have already covered communication between HTML and Canvas via form controls several times in this book. You wanted to know how to make HTML5 Canvas apps when you started reading, so we won't pull any punches in this chapter.

Creating Custom User Controls on the Canvas

For this application we are going to create four elements:

Play/pause push button
> The audio file is either playing or is paused. Whichever state it is currently in, we show the other button (i.e., show pause when playing).

A sliding progress bar
> This is a noninteractive slider. It displays how much of the audio track has played and how much is left to play. The movement of this bar needs to be dynamic and based on the `duration` and `currentTime` properties of the `HTMLAudioElement` object.

An interactive volume slider
> We want to create a sliding volume control that the user can manipulate with a click-and-drag operation. This is the trickiest control we will build because Canvas has no native support for click-and-drag.

A loop toggle button
> This is a bonus. Most of the default embedded HTML5 audio players do not have a loop/no-loop toggle button, but we are going to add one. Already, we are outstripping the functionality of standard HTML5!

Figure 7-5 shows the *audiocontrols.png* image that we created. It holds all the images we will use for the audio player. The top row consists of:

- The play state of the play/pause button
- The background of the play slider
- The moving slider we will use for the play and volume sliders

The second row consists of:

- The pause state of the play/pause button
- The background of the volume slider
- The "off" state of the loop button
- The "on" state of the loop button

Figure 7-5. audiocontrols.png

Loading the Button Assets

Since we are going to load in both an audio file and an image file for this application, we need to employ a strategy that will allow us to preload two assets instead of just one. This process is much like the one we employed in Chapter 6 when we created controls for a video. Previously in this chapter, we used a function named audio Loaded() to make sure the audio was loaded before we started use it. However, that strategy will not work when we have two assets to load. We could create two separate event listeners, but then what if we need to load 3, 4, or 10 assets? What we need is a simple way to ensure that we can preload any number of assets before our application executes.

We will start this process by creating some variables that are global in scope to all the functions in the applications. First, outside of all the JavaScript functions, we will create three new variables—loadCount, itemsToLoad, and buttonSheet:

loadCount

This variable will be used as a counter. When an asset has preloaded we will increment this value.

itemsToLoad

This is a numeric value that represents the number of assets we need to load before we can execute the application in the HTML page.

buttonSheet

This variable will hold a reference to the *audiocontrols.png* image shown in Figure 7-5. We will use it to create our audio controls.

Here is the code with values included:

```
var loadCount = 0;
var itemsToLoad = 2;
var buttonSheet;
var audioElement;
```

 To make these variables scope only to the Canvas app and not globally to all of JavaScript, you can encapsulate this code in a function(). The final version of the code in Example 7-6 shows that process.

Inside the eventWindowLoaded() function we now need to set the event handlers for the assets to load. For the audioElement, we will change the handler from audioLoaded to itemLoaded:

```
audioElement.addEventListener("canplaythrough",itemLoaded,false);
```

To load and use the *audiocontrols.png* image, we first create a new Image() object and place a reference to it into the buttonSheet variable. Next, we set the src attribute of the new Image object to the image file we want to load—in this case, *audiocontrols.png*. We then set the onload event handler of the Image object to itemLoaded, which is the same event handler we used for the audio file:

```
buttonSheet = new Image();
buttonSheet.onload = itemLoaded;
buttonSheet.src = "audiocontrols.png";
```

Now we need to create the `itemLoaded()` event handler. This function is quite simple. Every time it is called, we increment the `loadCount` variable. We then test `loadCount` to see whether it is equal to or has surpassed the number of items we want to preload, which is represented by the `itemsToLoad` variable. If so, we call the `canvasApp()` function to start our application:

```
function itemLoaded(event) {

    loadCount++;
    if (loadCount >= itemsToLoad) {
        canvasApp();

    }

}
```

Setting Up the Audio Player Values

Inside the `canvasApp()` function we need to create some values to help us place all the various buttons and sliders on the canvas.

First, `bH` represents the height of all the controls; `bW` represents the width of a standard button (play/pause, loop/not loop):

```
var bW = 32;
var bH = 32;
```

Next, we set the width of the playback area, `playBackW`, and the width of the volume background, `volBackW`. We also set the slider's width (`sliderW`) and height (`sliderH`):

```
var playBackW = 206;
var volBackW = 50;
var sliderW = 10;
var sliderH = 32;
```

We also need a couple variables to represent the x and y locations on the canvas where we will start to build our audio controls. We will define those as `controlStartX` and `controlStartY`:

```
var controlStartX = 25;
var controlStartY = 200;
```

Finally, we need to specify the x and y locations for the play/pause button (`playX`, `playY`), the playing slider background (`playBackX`, `playBackY`), the volume slider background (`volBackX`, `volBackY`), and the location of the loop/no loop toggle button (`loopX`, `loopY`):

```
var playX = controlStartX;
var playY = controlStartY;
var playBackX = controlStartX+bW
```

```
var playBackY = controlStartY;
var volBackX = controlStartX+bW+playBackW;
var volBackY = controlStartY;
var loopX = controlStartX+bW+playBackW+volBackW
var loopY = controlStartY;
```

We are going to use all of these values to help design and add functionality to our audio controls. It may seem like overkill to create so many variables, but when trying to "roll your own" collision detection and drag-and-drop functionality into the canvas, having variable names to manipulate instead of literals makes the job much easier.

Mouse Events

Since we are going to create our own functions for interactivity between the mouse and our custom canvas audio controls, we need to add some event handlers for certain common mouse events.

First, we need to create a couple variables—mouseX and mouseY—that will hold the current x and y locations of the mouse pointer:

```
var mouseX;
var mouseY;
```

Next, we need to create the event handlers. First, we listen for the mouseup event. This event fires when a user stops pressing the mouse button. We will listen for this event when we are trying to determine whether we should stop dragging the volume slider:

```
theCanvas.addEventListener("mouseup",eventMouseUp, false);
```

We also need to listen for the mousedown event to determine whether the play/pause button was pressed, the loop on/off toggle button was pressed, and/or the volume slider was clicked so we can start dragging it:

```
theCanvas.addEventListener("mousedown",eventMouseDown, false);
```

Finally, we listen for mousemove so we can figure out the current x and y locations of the mouse pointer. We use this value to determine whether buttons have been pressed, as well as whether the volume slider has been clicked and/or dragged:

```
theCanvas.addEventListener("mousemove",eventMouseMove, false);
```

Sliding Play Indicator

The sliding play indicator is the simplest control we are going to draw onto the canvas. It is not interactive—it just gives the user a visual indication of how much of the audio clip is left to play.

First of all, in canvasApp() we need to make sure that we call the drawScreen() function on an interval, so our updated controls will be displayed:

```
setInterval(drawScreen, 33);
```

Unlike when displaying video on the canvas, we do not have to call drawScreen() to update the playing audio. In JavaScript, audio plays completely separate from the canvas. Our need to call drawScreen() on an interval is necessary because the audio controls we are creating need to be updated as the audio plays.

In the drawScreen() function we need to draw the slider and background on the canvas. We are going to "cut" all the images we display from the single buttonSheet image we loaded from *audiocontrols.png*. To draw the background, we use the values we set up earlier. We use literals (i.e., 32,0) to locate the starting point of the image because those values do not change on the buttonSheet image. However, we use the variables we created to find the width and height, and to locate the final position of the background on the canvas:

```
context.drawImage(buttonSheet, 32,0,playBackW,bH,playBackX,playBackY,playBackW,bH);
```

Drawing the play slider is only a bit more complicated. Before we draw it, we need to create a variable that represents the relationship between the length of playing audio and the width of slider area. This is so we will know how far on the x-axis to move the slider based on how much of the song has played. This may sound complicated, but it's just a simple fraction. Divide the width of the play background (playBackW) by the duration of the playing audio (audioElement.duration). We will store that ratio in sliderIncrement and use it to place the play slider on the canvas:

```
var slideIncrement = playBackW/audioElement.duration;
```

Now we need to calculate the x position of the slider. The x position is the sum of the slider's starting position (the place on the canvas where the controls start plus the width of the play/pause button: controlStartX+bW) plus the audio's current play position. We calculate the play position by taking the ratio we just created, sliderIncrement, and multiplying it by the current play time of the audio clip (audioElement.currentTime). That's it!

```
var sliderX = (playBackW,bH,controlStartX+bW) +
    (slideIncrement*audioElement.currentTime);
```

Now all we need to do is draw the image onto the canvas, and then test to see whether the audio clip has ended. If it has ended, we put the play position back to the beginning of the playback area and call audioElement.pause() to pause the audio clip. That is, unless the loop property is sent, in which case we start playing the audio clip from the beginning by setting the currentTime property to 0:

```
context.drawImage(buttonSheet, 238,0,sliderW,bH,sliderX,controlStartY,sliderW,bH);

if (audioElement.ended && !audioElement.loop) {
    audioElement.currentTime = 0;
    audioElement.pause();
}
```

This leads us right into our next topic, handling the play/pause button.

Play/Pause Push Button: Hit Test Point Revisited

The first thing we need to do when implementing the play/pause button is create the event handler for the mousemove event. The function really is just the standard cross-browser code we introduced earlier in the book for tracking the mouse position, depending on which properties the DOM in browsers supports: layerX/layerY or offsetX/offsetY. This function is called every time the mouse is moved on the canvas to update the mouseX and mouseY variables. Those variables are scoped to canvasApp() so all functions defined inside of it can access them:

```
function eventMouseMove(event) {
    if ( event.layerX ||  event.layerX == 0) { // Firefox
        mouseX = event.layerX ;
      mouseY = event.layerY;
    } else if (event.offsetX || event.offsetX == 0) { // Opera
      mouseX = event.offsetX;
      mouseY = event.offsetY;
    }

}
```

Now we need to create the eventMouseUp() handler function. This function is called when the user releases the mouse button after clicking. Why *after* and not when the mouse is clicked? Well, one reason is because we generally use the mousedown event for the start of a "dragging" operation, which we will show you shortly.

The heart of this function is a hit test point-style collision detection check for the buttons. We discussed this in depth in Chapter 6 when we created the buttons for the video puzzle game (*CH6EX10.html*). Notice that here we are using the variables we create to represent the x and y locations of the button (playX, playY) and the width and height of a button (bW, bH) to form the bounds of the area we will test. If the mouse pointer is within those bounds, we know the button has been clicked:

```
function eventMouseUp(event) {

if ( (mouseY >= playY) && (mouseY <= playY+bH) && (mouseX >= playX) &&
    (mouseX <= playX+bW) ) {
```

 If you had images stacked on top of one another, you would need to store some kind of stacking value or z-index to know which item was on top and was clicked at any one time. Because the canvas works in immediate mode, you would have to "roll your own" just like the other functionality we have discussed.

After a hit is detected, we need to determine whether we are going to call the play() or pause() method of the HTMLAudioElement object represented by the audioElement variable. To figure out which method to call, we simply test to see whether the audio is paused by checking the audioElement.paused property. If so, we call the play() method; if not, we call pause(). Recall that the HTMLAudioElement.paused property is set to `true` if the audio is not playing, regardless of whether the `paused()` function was called. This means that when the application starts but we have not set `autoplay`, we can easily display the proper button (play or pause) just by testing this property:

```
if (audioElement.paused) {
    audioElement.play();

} else {
    audioElement.pause();

}

    }
}
```

Now, in `drawScreen()` we need to choose which button to display: the one representing play (green triangle) or pause (two horizontal boxes). The play button is displayed when the audio is paused, and the pause button is displayed when the audio is playing. This button is a "call to action," so it displays what will happen when you click on it, not the status of the audio element that is playing. This *inverse relationship* exists because it is the standard way audio players work.

If the `audioElement` is paused, we display the graphic from the top row of the *audio-controls.png* image represented by `buttonSheet` (see Figure 7-5). If it is not paused, we display the button on the second row right below it. Since that button starts at the y position of `32`, we use that literal value in the call to `drawImage()`:

```
if (audioElement.paused) {
    context.drawImage(buttonSheet, 0,0,bW,bH,playX,playY,bW,bH);//show play

} else {
    context.drawImage(buttonSheet, 0,32,bW,bH,playX,playY,bW,bH); //show pause

}
```

 Again, we could have represented the literal values of locations in the `buttonSheet` with variables, but we decided to use literals to show you the difference between how we specify `buttonSheet` pixel locations, and how we calculate widths and distances for placing those elements.

Loop/No Loop Toggle Button

Implementing the loop/no loop toggle button is nearly identical to implementing the play/pause button. In Figure 7-5, you can see that the last two buttons on the bottom row represent the "on" and "off" states of the loop/no loop button. Unlike the play/pause button, this button shows the "state" of looping: the lighter, 3D-looking "out" button is displayed when the audio is not set to loop. The inverse, darker button is displayed when the audio is set to loop (because it looks like the button has been pressed).

In the `eventMouseUp()` function, we need to add support for loop/no loop. First, we test for a hit test point on the button with the current location of the mouse pointer. This is identical to the test we did for the play/pause button, except that we use `loopX` and `loopY` to find the current location of the loop/no loop button.

Next, we check the value of `audioElement.loop`. We need to update the value to the opposite of the current setting. If `loop` is `true`, we set it to `false`; if it is `false`, we set it to `true`:

```
if ( (mouseY >=loopY) && (mouseY <= loopY+bH) && (mouseX >= loopX) &&
    (mouseX <= loopX+bW) ) {
  if (audioElement.loop) {
        audioElement.loop = false;

    } else {
        audioElement.loop = true;

    }
```

Finally, in `drawScreen()` we will display the proper part of the `buttonSheet` image for whichever state of loop/no loop is currently set. Unlike play/pause, we display the "off" state when `loop` is `false` and the "on" state when it is set to `true` because, again, there is not an inverse relationship to the states of the button:

```
if (audioElement.loop) {
        context.drawImage(buttonSheet, 114,32,bW,bH,loopX,loopY,bW,bH);//loop

    } else {
        context.drawImage(buttonSheet, 82,32,bW,bH,loopX,loopY,bW,bH); // no loop
    }
```

Click-and-Drag Volume Slider

So now we make it to the last, but certainly not least, piece of functionality for the audio player: the volume slider. The volume slider is an interactive control allowing the user to manipulate it by sliding it right or left to control the volume of the playing audio element. Before we create the volume slider, we need to define some boundaries for its usage:

- The slider never moves on the y-axis; it will always keep a constant y value.
- The farther the volume slider is to the right (the greater the x value), the higher the volume.
- The slider moves on the x-axis but is bounded by the starting x value of the volume slider image—`volumeSliderStart` on the left and `volumeSliderEnd` on the right.
- When the user clicks on the volume slider, we will assume that the user wants to set the volume, so we will start "dragging" the slider. This means that if the user moves the mouse on the x-axis, we will move the slider accordingly.

- When the user takes his finger off the mouse button, we will assume that he no longer wishes to set the volume, and we still stop "dragging" the slider.
- The volume will be set based on the slider's position on the x-axis in relation to the `volumeSliderStart` plus a ratio (`volumeIncrement`) that we create describing how much volume to increase or decrease based on where the slider rests.

Volume slider variables

OK, now that we have thoroughly confused you, let's talk about the process in depth. First, we start with the `canvasApp()` function. In `canvasApp()` we need to set up some variables to set the rules we defined in the list above.

The starting x position for the volume slider is `volumeSliderStart`. When the application starts, it is equal to the x position of the volume background, or `volBackX`. This means it will start at the leftmost edge of the volume slider where the `volume` will be set to 0. We will update this to the correct position based on the `volume` as soon as we calculate that value:

```
var volumeSliderStart = volBackX;
```

The final x position for the volume slider is `volumeSliderEnd`, which is the rightmost position. It is the position where the volume will be set to 100% (or 1). This position lies at the x position of `volumeSliderStart` plus the width of the volume slider background (`volBackW`), less the width of the volume slider itself (`sliderW`):

```
var volumeSliderEnd = volumeSliderStart + volBackW - sliderW;
```

`volumeSliderX` and `volumeSliderY` are the slider's x and y positions on the canvas. The y position is the same as the other elements in the audio player, `controlStartY`. However, the x position is calculated in quite a different way. First, we take the value of `volumeSliderStart` and add the difference between slider volume background width and the slider width (`volBackW - sliderW`), multiplied by the `volume` property of the `audioElement`, which is a number between 0 and 1. This will give us the position relative to the starting point from which we want to draw the volume slider for any given volume setting:

```
var volumeSliderX  = volumeSliderStart + (audioElement.volume*
    (volBackW - sliderW));
var volumeSliderY  = controlStartY;
```

Next, we create the `volumeSliderDrag` variable, which we will use as a switch to tell us whether the volume slider is being dragged by the user at any given moment:

```
var volumeSliderDrag = false;
```

Finally, we create the `volumeIncrement` variable. This variable tells us how much volume to increase or decrease on the `audioElement.volume` property based on where the slider is positioned on the volume background. Since the maximum value of the volume is 1, we simply find the total width that the volume slider can move on the x-axis (`volBackW - sliderW`) and divide 1 by that value. This will give us a product that we can multiply by the x position of the slider, relative to volumeSliderStart, to give us the volume we should set for the audioElement:

```
var volumeIncrement = 1/(volBackW - sliderW);
```

Volume slider functionality

Now that we have discussed the variables we need for the volume slider, we will talk about how we use them in the various functions of the audio player. The good news is that the implementation is simple now that you know how the variables work.

In the eventMouseDown() handler, we perform a hit test point-style test, just like we did with the play/pause and loop/no loop buttons to see whether the volume slider was clicked. If so, we set the volumeSliderDrag variable to true. This means that the volume slider will now to move to the x position of the mouse when we call drawScreen():

```
function eventMouseDown(event) {

if ( (mouseY >= volumeSliderY) && (mouseY <=volumeSliderY+sliderH) &&
    (mouseX >= volumeSliderX) && (mouseX <= volumeSliderX+sliderW) ) {
        volumeSliderDrag = true;

    }

}
```

In the eventMouseUp() handler, we test to see whether the volumeSliderDrag is set to true. If so, it means that the user has released the mouse button and no longer wants to drag the volume slider. We set volumeSliderDrag to false so the slider will not move with the mouse:

```
if (volumeSliderDrag) {
        volumeSliderDrag = false;
    }
```

In drawScreen() we actually put the pixels to the canvas, so to speak, with the volume slider. First, we draw the background image from buttonSheet:

```
//vol Background
        context.drawImage(buttonSheet, 32,32,volBackW,bH,volBackX,volBackY,volBackW,bH);
```

Next, we check to see whether volumeSliderDrag is true. If so, we make the volume SliderX variable equal to the mouse's x position. Then, we drop in a couple more tests to determine whether the x position of the volume slider falls outside the bounds of the volume background. These two tests make sure that the volume slider does not move past the rightmost or leftmost sides of the volume slider background, and in turn, the volume property of audioElement is not calculated to be more than 1 or less than 0:

```
if (volumeSliderDrag) {
    volumeSliderX = mouseX;
    if (volumeSliderX > volumeSliderEnd) {
        volumeSliderX = volumeSliderEnd;
    }
```

```
    if (volumeSliderX < volumeSliderStart) {
        volumeSliderX = volumeSliderStart;
    }
```

If the `volumeSliderDrag` is `false`, we still need an x position at which to draw the slider graphic. We get this the same way we calculated the `volumeSliderX` when we initialized the variable in the `canvasApp()` function:

```
} else {
    volumeSliderX = volumeSliderStart + (audioElement.volume*
    (volBackW -sliderW));
}
```

Finally, we draw the slider onto the canvas:

```
context.drawImage(buttonSheet, 238,0,sliderW,bH,volumeSliderX,
    volumeSliderY, sliderW,bH);
audioElement.volume = (volumeSliderX-volumeSliderStart) * volumeIncrement;
```

Figure 7-6 displays the custom controls in the browser.

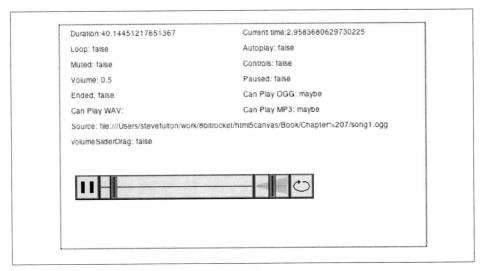

Figure 7-6. Canvas sound player with custom controls

So there you have it. You can test the audio player as *CH7EX5.html* in the source code. The full code listing for the HTML5 Canvas audio player is shown in Example 7-5.

Example 7-5. A custom audio player on the canvas

```
<!doctype html>
<html lang="en">
<head>
<meta charset="UTF-8">
<title>CH7EX5: A Custom Sound Player On The Canvas</title>
<script src="modernizr-1.6.min.js"></script>
<script type="text/javascript">
```

```
window.addEventListener('load', eventWindowLoaded, false);
var loadCount = 0;
var itemsToLoad = 2;
var buttonSheet;
var audioElement;
function eventWindowLoaded() {

    audioElement = document.createElement("audio");
    document.body.appendChild(audioElement);
    var audioType = supportedAudioFormat(audioElement);
    if (audioType == "") {
        alert("no audio support");
        return;
    }
    audioElement.setAttribute("src", "song1." + audioType);
    audioElement.addEventListener("canplaythrough",itemLoaded,false);

    buttonSheet = new Image();
    buttonSheet.onload = itemLoaded;
    buttonSheet.src = "audiocontrols.png";

}

function supportedAudioFormat(audio) {
    var returnExtension = "";
    if (audio.canPlayType("audio/ogg") =="probably" ||
        audio.canPlayType("audio/ogg") == "maybe") {
            returnExtension = "ogg";
    } else if(audio.canPlayType("audio/wav") =="probably" ||
        audio.canPlayType("audio/wav") == "maybe") {
            returnExtension = "wav";
    } else if(audio.canPlayType("audio/mp3") == "probably" ||
        audio.canPlayType("audio/mp3") == "maybe") {
            returnExtension = "mp3";
    }

    return returnExtension;

}

function canvasSupport () {
    return Modernizr.canvas;
}

function itemLoaded(event) {

    loadCount++;
    if (loadCount >= itemsToLoad) {
        canvasApp();

    }

}

function canvasApp() {
```

```
if (!canvasSupport()) {
        return;
    }

function  drawScreen () {

    //Background

    context.fillStyle = "#ffffaa";
    context.fillRect(0, 0, theCanvas.width, theCanvas.height);

    //Box
    context.strokeStyle = "#000000";
    context.strokeRect(5,  5, theCanvas.width-10, theCanvas.height-10);

    // Text
    context.fillStyle = "#000000";
    context.fillText ("Duration:" + audioElement.duration,  20 ,20);
    context.fillText ("Current time:" + audioElement.currentTime,  250 ,20);
    context.fillText ("Loop: " + audioElement.loop,  20 ,40);
    context.fillText ("Autoplay: " +audioElement.autoplay,  250 ,40);
    context.fillText ("Muted: " + audioElement.muted,  20 ,60);
    context.fillText ("Controls: " + audioElement.controls,  250 ,60);
    context.fillText ("Volume: " + audioElement.volume,  20 ,80);
    context.fillText ("Paused: " + audioElement.paused,  250 ,80);
    context.fillText ("Ended: " + audioElement.ended,  20 ,100);
    context.fillText ("Can Play OGG: " + audioElement.canPlayType("audio/ogg"),
                      250 ,100);
    context.fillText ("Can Play WAV: " + audioElement.canPlayType("audio/wav"),
                      20 ,120);
    context.fillText ("Can Play MP3: " + audioElement.canPlayType("audio/mp3"),
                      250 ,120);
    context.fillText ("Source: " + audioElement.currentSrc, 20 ,140);
    context.fillText ("volumeSliderDrag: " + volumeSliderDrag, 20 ,160);

    //Draw Controls

    //play or pause

    if (audioElement.paused) {
       context.drawImage(buttonSheet, 0,0,bW,bH,playX,playY,bW,bH);//show play

    } else {
       context.drawImage(buttonSheet, 0,32,bW,bH,playX,playY,bW,bH); //show pause

    }

    //loop

    if (audioElement.loop) {
       context.drawImage(buttonSheet, 114,32,bW,bH,loopX,loopY,bW,bH);//show loop
    } else {
       context.drawImage(buttonSheet, 82,32,bW,bH,loopX,loopY,bW,bH); //show no loop
    }
```

```
//play background
context.drawImage(buttonSheet, 32,0,playBackW,bH,playBackX,playBackY,playBackW,bH);

//vol Background
context.drawImage(buttonSheet, 32,32,volBackW,bH,volBackX,volBackY,volBackW,bH);

//play slider
var slideIncrement = playBackW/audioElement.duration;
var sliderX = (playBackW,bH,controlStartX+bW) +
    (slideIncrement*audioElement.currentTime);
context.drawImage(buttonSheet, 238,0,sliderW,bH,sliderX,controlStartY,sliderW,bH);

//Go back to start
if (audioElement.ended && !audioElement.loop) {
    audioElement.currentTime = 0;
    audioElement.pause();
}

//Volume slider
//Test Volume Drag

if (volumeSliderDrag) {
    volumeSliderX = mouseX;
    if (volumeSliderX > volumeSliderEnd) {
        volumeSliderX = volumeSliderEnd;
    }
    if (volumeSliderX < volumeSliderStart) {
        volumeSliderX = volumeSliderStart;
    }
} else {
    volumeSliderX = volumeSliderStart + (audioElement.volume*(volBackW -sliderW));
}

context.drawImage(buttonSheet, 238,0,sliderW,bH,volumeSliderX,volumeSliderY,
    sliderW,bH);
audioElement.volume = (volumeSliderX-volumeSliderStart) * volumeIncrement;

}

function eventMouseDown(event) {

    //Hit Volume Slider
    if ( (mouseY >= volumeSliderY) && (mouseY <=volumeSliderY+sliderH) &&
        (mouseX >= volumeSliderX) && (mouseX <= volumeSliderX+sliderW) ) {
        volumeSliderDrag = true;

    }

}

function eventMouseMove(event) {
    if ( event.layerX ||  event.layerX == 0) {
        mouseX = event.layerX ;
        mouseY = event.layerY;
```

```
        } else if (event.offsetX || event.offsetX == 0) {
          mouseX = event.offsetX;
         mouseY = event.offsetY;
        }

}

function eventMouseUp(event) {

    //Hit Play
    if ( (mouseY >= playY) && (mouseY <= playY+bH) && (mouseX >= playX) &&
        (mouseX <= playX+bW) ) {
      if (audioElement.paused) {
         audioElement.play();

      } else {
         audioElement.pause();

      }

    }

    //Hit loop
    if ( (mouseY >=loopY) && (mouseY <= loopY+bH) && (mouseX >= loopX) &&
        (mouseX <= loopX+bW) ) {
      if (audioElement.loop) {
         audioElement.loop=false;

      } else {
         audioElement.loop = true;

      }

    }

    if (volumeSliderDrag) {
       volumeSliderDrag = false;
    }

}

var theCanvas = document.getElementById("canvasOne");
var context = theCanvas.getContext("2d");

var bW = 32;
var bH = 32;
var playBackW = 206;
var volBackW = 50;
var sliderW = 10;
var sliderH = 32;
var controlStartX = 25;
var controlStartY =200;
var playX = controlStartX;
var playY = controlStartY;
var playBackX = controlStartX+bW;
```

```
    var playBackY = controlStartY;
    var volBackX = controlStartX+bW+playBackW;
    var volBackY = controlStartY;
    var loopX = controlStartX+bW+playBackW+volBackW;
    var loopY = controlStartY;
    var mouseX;
    var mouseY;

    theCanvas.addEventListener("mouseup",eventMouseUp, false);
    theCanvas.addEventListener("mousedown",eventMouseDown, false);
    theCanvas.addEventListener("mousemove",eventMouseMove, false);

    audioElement.play();
    audioElement.loop = false;
    audioElement.volume = .5;
    var volumeSliderStart = volBackX;
    var volumeSliderEnd = volumeSliderStart + volBackW -sliderW;
    var volumeSliderX = volumeSliderStart + (audioElement.volume*(volBackW -sliderW));
    var volumeSliderY = controlStartY;
    var volumeSliderDrag = false;
    var volumeIncrement = 1/(volBackW -sliderW);

    setInterval(drawScreen, 33);

}

</script>

</head>
<body>
<div style="position: absolute; top: 50px; left: 50px;">

<canvas id="canvasOne" width="500" height="300">
 Your browser does not support HTML5 Canvas.
</canvas>
</div>
</body>
</html>
```

Case Study in Audio: Space Raiders Game

If we were writing a book about standard HTML5, we might be able to stop here and continue on with another topic. However, there is a lot more to playing audio in an application than simply getting a song to play and tracking its progress. In the last part of this chapter, we will look at a case study: *Space Raiders*. We will iterate through several ideas and attempts to get audio working in an efficient way in conjunction with action on HTML5 Canvas.

Why Sounds in Apps Are Different: Event Sounds

Why make a game as an example for playing sounds in HTML5? Well, a game is a perfect example because it is difficult to predict how many sounds might be playing at any one time.

If you can imagine, games are some of the most demanding applications when it comes to sound. In most games, sounds are played based on user interactions, and those interactions are usually both asynchronous and unpredictable. Because of those factors, we need to create a strategy for playing sounds that is flexible and resource-efficient.

To demonstrate how tricky sounds can be when using JavaScript and HTML5 with a canvas game, we will iterate this game several times until we have a working model.

Here are some assumptions we will make regarding sound in *Space Raiders* based on what we know about the HTML5 `audio` object.

1. After loading a sound, you can make another object with the same source and "load" it without having to wait for it to load. (Flash sort of works this way.)
2. Playing sounds locally is the same as playing them on a remotely hosted web page.

It turns out that both of these assumptions are *wrong*. As we continue through this case study, we will show you why, as well as how to accommodate them.

Since this is not a chapter about making games, *Space Raiders* is only going to be a façade. In Hollywood, a façade is a structure built for filming, containing only the parts the camera will see. For example, a building façade might have only the front wall and windows—with nothing behind them. *Space Raiders* is like this because we are only going to create the parts necessary to include the dynamic sounds we will be using. It will be most of a game, leading you into Chapters 8 and 9, which take a deep dive into making complete games with HTML5 Canvas.

Iterations

In this case study, we will create four iterations of *Space Raiders*. Each one will attempt to solve a dynamic audio problem in a different way. First, we will show you the basics of the *Space Raiders* game structure, and then we will discuss how to solve the audio problem.

Space Raiders Game Structure

Space Raiders is an iconic action game where a swarm of alien invaders attack from the top of the screen, and the player's job is to defend the world. The raiders move in horizontal lines near the top of the screen. When each raider reaches the side of the playfield, it moves down the screen and then switches direction.

The player controls a spaceship by moving the mouse, and fires missiles using the left mouse button. We need to play a "shoot" sound every time the player fires a missile. When the missiles hit the enemy space raiders, we need to remove them from the screen, and then play an "explosion" sound. We are not limiting the number of shots the player can fire, which means that there could be any number of shoot and explode sounds playing simultaneously. Our goal is to manage all these dynamic sounds.

State machine

This game runs using a very simple state machine. A *state machine* is a construct that allows an application to exist in only one state at a time, which means it is only doing one thing. This kind of construct is great for single-player games because it removes the need to hold a bunch of Booleans describing what is going on at any one moment.

Space Raiders has four states plus a variable named `appState` that holds the value of the current state. Those states include:

STATE_INIT
> A state to set up the loading of assets:

```
const STATE_INIT = 10;
```

STATE_LOADING
> A wait state that has the application sleep until all assets have been loaded:

```
const STATE_LOADING = 20;
```

STATE_RESET
> A state to set up the initial game values:

```
const STATE_RESET = 30;
```

STATE_PLAYING
> A state that handles all game-play logic:

```
const STATE_PLAYING = 40;
```

 A final game of this type might have a few more states, such as STATE_END_GAME and STATE_NEXT_LEVEL, but our case study does not require them.

The heart of our state machine is the `run()` function, which is called on an interval every 33 milliseconds. The `appState` variable determines what function to call at any given time using a `switch()` statement. `appState` is updated to a different state any time the program is ready to move on and do something else. The process of calling a function such as `run()` on an interval and switching states is commonly known as a *game loop*:

```
function run() {
    switch(appState) {
```

```
        case STATE_INIT:
          initApp();
          break;
        case STATE_LOADING:
          //wait for call backs
          break;
        case STATE_RESET:
          resetApp();
          break;
        case STATE_PLAYING:
          drawScreen();
          break;

    }
  }
```

Initializing the game: no global variables

Now that we know a bit about the state machine construct we will use for this game, it's time to set up the preload for our assets. As we mentioned previously, this game has two sounds, shoot and explode, but it also has three images: a player, an alien, and a missile.

Remember how we kept saying we'd do away with global variables in these applications? Well, here's where it happens. With the state machine, we now have a mechanism to allow our application to wait for loading assets instead of leveraging only the DOM's window load event.

In the canvasApp() function, we set up the following variables to use in the game.

The appState variable holds the current state constant:

```
var appState = STATE_INIT;
```

We use the loadCount and itemsToLoad variables in exactly the same way we used them in the audio player application—except here we will be loading more items:

```
var loadCount= 0;
var itemsToLoad = 0;
```

The variables alienImage, missileImage, and playerImage will hold the loaded images we use in the game:

```
var alienImage = new Image();
var missileImage = new Image();
var playerImage = new Image();
```

explodeSound and shootSound will hold the references to the HTMLAudioElement objects we will load:

```
var explodeSound ;
var shootSound;
```

The audioType variable will hold the extension of the valid audio file type for the browser displaying the application:

```
var audioType;
```

The `mouseX` and `mouseY` variables will hold the current `x` and `y` location of the mouse:

```
var mouseX;
var mouseY;
```

The `player` variable will hold a dynamic object with the `x` and `y` location of the player ship (controlled with the mouse):

```
var player = {x:250,y:475};
```

Both the `aliens` and `missiles` arrays will hold lists of dynamic objects for displaying aliens and missiles on the canvas:

```
var aliens = new Array();
var missiles = new Array();
```

The next five constants set the number of aliens (`ALIEN_ROWS`, `ALIEN_COLS`), their starting location (`ALIEN_START_X`, `ALIEN_START_Y`), and their spacing on screen (`ALIEN_SPACING`):

```
const ALIEN_START_X = 25;
const ALIEN_START_Y = 25;
const ALIEN_ROWS = 5;
const ALIEN_COLS = 8;
const ALIEN_SPACING = 40;
```

Also in the `canvasApp()` function, we need to set up event handlers for `mouseup` and `mousemove`. To create the game loop, we need to set up our interval to call the `run()` function:

```
theCanvas.addEventListener("mouseup",eventMouseUp, false);
theCanvas.addEventListener("mousemove",eventMouseMove, false);

setInterval(run, 33);
```

At this point, `run()` will be called and our game loop will start by calling the function associated with the value of `appState`.

Preloading all assets without global variables

We just showed that the `appState` variable was initialized to `STATE_INIT`, which means that when the `run()` function is called for the first time, the `initApp()` function will be called. The good news (at least for this discussion) is that `initApp()` does very little that we have not already seen—it just does it in the context of the Canvas application. The result? Now we don't need any global variables.

In the code below, notice that we are using the same strategy. We have a single event handler for all loaded assets (`itemLoaded()`),we set `itemsToLoad` to 5 (three graphics and two sounds), and we set the `appState` to `STATE_LOADING` at the end of the function. The rest of the code is all simple review:

```
function initApp() {
    loadCount=0;
    itemsToLoad = 5;
```

```
explodeSound = document.createElement("audio");
document.body.appendChild(explodeSound);
audioType = supportedAudioFormat(explodeSound);
explodeSound.setAttribute("src", "explode1." + audioType);
explodeSound.addEventListener("canplaythrough",itemLoaded,false);

shootSound = document.createElement("audio");
document.body.appendChild(shootSound);
shootSound.setAttribute("src", "shoot1." + audioType);
shootSound.addEventListener("canplaythrough",itemLoaded,false);

alienImage = new Image();
alienImage.onload = itemLoaded;
alienImage.src = "alien.png";
playerImage = new Image();
playerImage.onload = itemLoaded;
playerImage.src = "player.png";
missileImage = new Image();
missileImage.onload = itemLoaded;
missileImage.src = "missile.png"; appState = STATE_LOADING;
}
```

If you recall, STATE_LOADING does nothing in our run() function; it just waits for all events to occur. The action here is handled by the itemLoaded() event handler, which works exactly like the itemLoaded() function we wrote for the audio player, except that it has two additional functions:

1. It must remove the event listeners from the two sound objects we created. This is because, in some browsers, calling the play() method of an HTMLAudioElement object—or changing the src attribute of an HTMLAudioElement object—initiates a load operation, which will then call the itemLoaded event handler a second time. This will cause unexpected results in your application. Furthermore, it is always a good idea to remove unneeded event handlers from your objects.

2. We set the appState to STATE_RESET, which will initialize the game the next time the run() function is called on the interval.

Here is the code with the two additional functions:

```
function itemLoaded(event) {

    loadCount++;
    if (loadCount >= itemsToLoad) {

        shootSound.removeEventListener("canplaythrough",itemLoaded, false);
        explodeSound.removeEventListener("canplaythrough",itemLoaded,false);

        appState = STATE_RESET;

    }

}
```

Resetting the game

In the run() function, the STATE_RESET state calls the resetApp() function, which in turn calls startLevel(). It also sets the volume of our two sounds to 50% (.5) before setting the appState to STATE_PLAYING:

```
function resetApp() {

    startLevel();
    shootSound.volume = .5;
    explodeSound.volume = .5;
    appState = STATE_PLAYING;

}
```

The startLevel() function traverses through two nested for:next loops, creating the rows of aliens by column. Each time we create an alien, we push a dynamic object into the aliens array with the following properties:

speed
    The number of pixels the aliens will move left or right on each call to drawScreen().

x
    The starting x position of the alien on the screen. This value is set by the column (c) multiplied by ALIEN_SPACING, added to ALIEN_START_X.

y
    The starting y position of the alien on the screen. This is set by the row (r) multiplied by ALIEN_SPACING, added to ALIEN_START_X.

width
    The width of the alien image.

height
    The height of the alien image.

Here is the code for the startLevel() function:

```
function startLevel() {

    for (var r = 0; r < ALIEN_ROWS; r++) {
        for( var c= 0; c < ALIEN_COLS; c++) {
            aliens.push({speed:2,x:ALIEN_START_X+c*ALIEN_SPACING, y:ALIEN_START_Y+r*
                ALIEN_SPACING,width:alienImage.width, height:alienImage.height});
        }
    }
}
```

Mouse control

Before we talk about the game play itself, let's quickly discuss mouse event handlers, which will collect all user input for the game. When the player moves the mouse, the eventMouseMove() handler is called. This function operates just like the same function we created for the audio player, except for the last two lines. Those two lines set the x and y properties of the `player` object we created back in the variable definition section of `canvasApp()`. We will use these two properties to position the `playerImage` on the canvas in the `drawScreen()` function:

```
function eventMouseMove(event) {
    if ( event.layerX || event.layerX == 0) { // Firefox
        mouseX = event.layerX ;
      mouseY = event.layerY;
    } else if (event.offsetX || event.offsetX == 0) { // Opera
      mouseX = event.offsetX;
      mouseY = event.offsetY;
    }
    player.x = mouseX;
    player.y = mouseY;

}
```

The `eventMouseUp()` handler is called when the player presses and releases the left mouse button. When this event occurs, a missile will fire. The `missile` object is almost identical to the `alien` object, as it includes `speed`, `x`, `y`, `width`, and `height` properties. Since the player is firing the missile, we set the missile's `x` and `y` positions to the center of the player's ship on the x-axis (`player.x+.5*playerImage.width`), and to the y position of the player's ship, minus the height of the missile (`player.y - missileImage.height`):

```
function eventMouseUp(event) {

    missiles.push({speed:5, x: player.x+.5*playerImage.width,
        y:player.y-missileImage.height,width:missileImage.width,
        height:missileImage.height});
```

Next is the first really critical line of code for the subject at hand: audio. For this first iteration of *Space Raiders*, we simply call the `play()` function of `shootSound`. This will play the shoot sound as often as the player presses the left mouse button (in theory):

```
    shootSound.play();
}
```

Bounding box collision detection

Before we get to the main part of the game logic, we should discuss bounding box collision detection. We need to detect collisions between the missiles the player fires and the aliens the player is firing upon. To do this, we will create a function that tests to see whether two objects are overlapping. For lack of a better name, we call this function `hitTest()`.

The type of hit test we are going to perform is called a bounding box collision test. This means that we are going to ignore the intricate details of the bitmapped graphics and simply test to see whether an invisible "box" drawn around the bounds of each object overlaps with a similar box drawn around the other objects.

Recall that both the `alien` and `missile` dynamic objects were created with similar properties: `x`, `y`, `width`, `height`. This was so the `hitTest()` function could test them as generic objects, unspecific to the type of on-screen object that they represent. This means that we can add any other type of object to this game (boss alien, power-ups, enemy missiles, etc.), and if it is created with similar properties, we can use the same function to test collisions against it.

The function works by finding the top, left, bottom, and right values for each object, and then testing to see whether any of those values overlap. Bounding box collision detection will be discussed in detail in Chapter 8, but we just wanted to give you a preview of what it looks like for *Space Raiders*:

```
function hitTest(image1,image2) {
    r1left = image1.x;
    r1top = image1.y;
    r1right = image1.x + image1.width;
    r1bottom = image1.y + image1.height;
    r2left = image2.x;
    r2top = image2.y;
    r2right = image2.x + image2.width;
    r2bottom = image2.y + image2.height;
    retval = false;

    if ( (r1left > r2right) || (r1right < r2left) || (r1bottom < r2top) ||
        (r1top > r2bottom) ) {
      retval = false;
    } else {
      retval = true;
    }


    return retval;
}
```

Playing the game

Now the game is ready to play. STATE_PLAYING calls the drawScreen() function, which is the heart of *Space Raiders*. The first part of this function simply moves the missiles and aliens on the screen. Moving the missiles is quite easy. We loop through the array (backward), updating the y property of each with the speed property. If they move off the top of the screen, we remove them from the array. We move through the array backward so that we can splice() array elements out of the array and not affect loop length. If we did not do this, elements would be skipped after we splice() the array:

```
for (var i=missiles.length-1; i>= 0;i--) {
    missiles[i].y -= missiles[i].speed;
    if (missiles[i].y < (0-missiles[i].height)) {
        missiles.splice(i,1);
    }

}
```

Drawing the aliens is similar to drawing missiles—with a few exceptions. Aliens move left and right, and when they reach the side of the canvas, they move down 20 pixels and then reverse direction. To achieve the reversal in direction, multiply the speed property by -1. If the aliens are moving to the right (speed = 2), this will make the speed = -2, which will subtract from the x position and move the aliens to the left. If the aliens hit the left side of the canvas, the speed property will again be multiplied by -1 (-2 * -1), which will equal 2. The alien will then move to the right because 2 will be added to the x value for the alien each time drawScreen() is called:

```
//Move Aliens
    for (var i=aliens.length-1; i>= 0;i--) {
        aliens[i].x += aliens[i].speed;
        if (aliens[i].x > (theCanvas.width-aliens[i].width) || aliens[i].x < 0) {
            aliens[i].speed *= -1;
            aliens[i].y += 20;
        }
        if (aliens[i].y > theCanvas.height) {
            aliens.splice(i,1);
        }

    }
```

The next step in drawScreen() is to detect collisions between the aliens and the missiles. This part of the code loops through the missiles array backward while nesting a loop through the aliens array. It will test every missile against every alien to determine whether there is a collision. Since we have already covered the hitTest() function, we only need to discuss what happens if a collision is detected. First, we call the play() function of the explodeSound. This is the second critical line of code in this iteration of *Space Raiders*, as it plays (or attempts to play) the explosion sound every time a collision is detected. After that, it splices the alien and missile objects out of their respective arrays, and then breaks out of the nested for:next loop. If there are no aliens left to shoot, we set the appState to STATE_RESET, which will add more aliens to the canvas so the player can continue shooting:

```
missile: for (var i=missiles.length-1; i>= 0;i--) {
        var tempMissile = missiles[i]
        for (var j=aliens.length-1; j>= 0;j--) {
            var tempAlien =aliens[j];
            if (hitTest(tempMissile,tempAlien)) {
                explodeSound.play();
                missiles.splice(i,1);
                aliens.splice(j,1);
                break missile;
            }
        }

        if (aliens.length <=0) {
            appState = STATE_RESET;
        }
    }
```

The last few lines of code in drawScreen() loop through the missiles and aliens arrays, and draw them onto the canvas. This is done using the drawImage() method of the context object, and the x and y properties we calculated earlier. Finally, it draws the playerImage on the canvas, and the function is finished:

```
//Draw Missiles
        for (var i=missiles.length-1; i>= 0;i--) {
            context.drawImage(missileImage,missiles[i].x,missiles[i].y);

        }
//draw aliens
        for (var i=aliens.length-1; i>= 0;i--) {
            context.drawImage(alienImage,aliens[i].x,aliens[i].y);

        }

//Draw Player
        context.drawImage(playerImage,player.x,player.y);
```

Like we stated previously, *Space Raiders* is not a full game. We have only implemented enough to get the player to shoot missiles so we can play the shoot sound, and to detect collisions so we can play the explode sound.

Iteration #1: Playing Sounds Using a Single Object

We just described the first iteration of the dynamic audio code. It works by attempting to call the play() function of both shootSound and explodeSound as often as necessary. This appears to work at first, but if you listen carefully (and this is apparent on some browsers more than others), the sounds start to play "off," or not play at all. This is because we are using a single object and attempting to play and replay the same sound over and over. A single HTMLAudioElement was not designed to operate this way. You can test this example in the code distribution by running *CH7EX6.html* in your HTML5-compliant web browser. Press the fire button as quickly as possible and listen to when and how the sounds play. After a bit, they start to play at the wrong time, don't finish, or don't play at all. Figure 7-7 shows what the first iteration of *Space Raiders* looks like in a web browser.

Iteration #2: Creating Unlimited Dynamic Sound Objects

So, we almost got what we wanted with the first iteration, but we ran into some oddities when calling the play() function on a single HTMLAudioElement multiple times before the sound had finished playing.

For our second iteration, we are going to try something different. Let's see what happens when you simply create a new HTMLAudioElement object every time you want to play a sound. If this doesn't sound like an efficient use of memory or resources in the web browser, you are a keen observer. It's actually a horrible idea. However, let's proceed just to see what happens.

Figure 7-7. Space Raiders playing sounds from two objects

In `canvasApp()`, we will create a couple constants that represent the filenames of the sounds we want to play, but without the associated extension. We will still retrieve the extension with a call to `supportedAudioFormat()`, just as we did in the first iteration, and store that value in the `audioType` variable.

We will also create an array named `sounds` that we will use to hold all the `HTMLAudio Element` objects we create. This array will tell us how many objects we have created so we can visually see when all hell breaks loose:

```
const SOUND_EXPLODE = "explode1";
const SOUND_SHOOT  = "shoot1";
var sounds = new Array();
```

Instead of calling the play() function of each sound directly, we are going to create a function named playSound(). This function accepts two parameters:

sound

One of the constants we created above that contains the name of the sound file

volume

A number between 0 and 1 that represents the volume of the sound to play

The function here creates a new sound object every time it is called by calling the createElement() function of the document DOM object. It then sets the properties (src, loop, volume) and attempts to play the sound. Just for fun, let's push the object into the sounds array:

```
function playSound(sound,volume) {
    var tempSound = document.createElement("audio");
    tempSound.setAttribute("src", sound + "." + audioType);
    tempSound.loop = false;
    tempSound.volume = volume;
    tempSound.play();
    sounds.push(tempSound);
}
```

To play the sounds, we call playSound(), passing the proper parameters.

The call in eventMouseUp() looks like this:

```
playSound(SOUND_SHOOT,.5);
```

And in drawScreen() it looks like this:

```
playSound(SOUND_EXPLODE,.5);
```

To display on the canvas how many sounds we have created, we add this code to the drawScreen() function:

```
context.fillStyle  = "#FFFFFF";
context.fillText  ("Active Sounds: " + sounds.length,  200 ,480);
```

Now, go ahead and try this example (*CH7EX7.html* in the code distribution). Figure 7-8 shows what *Space Raiders* iteration #2 looks like. Notice we have added some display text at the bottom of the screen to show how many sounds are in the sounds array. You will discover two issues with this iteration:

1. The sounds play with almost no pauses when loaded from a local drive. But when the page is loaded from a remote website, there is a defined pause before each sound is loaded and played.

2. The number of sound objects created is a huge problem. For some browsers, such as Chrome, the number of active sounds caps out at about 50. After that, no sounds play at all.

Figure 7-8. Space Raiders creating sounds on the fly

Iteration #3: Creating a Sound Pool

So, now we know we don't want to play an HTMLAudioElement repeatedly, or create unlimited sound objects on the fly. However, what if we cap the number of audio objects we create, and put those objects in a pool so we can use them over and over? This will save us memory, and after the sounds are loaded, we shouldn't see any loading pause before they are played, right?

We will implement a solution that uses HTMLAudioElement objects as general-purpose sound objects. We will keep a pool of them, and change the src attribute to whatever sound we want to play. This appears to be an elegant solution that reuses as much as possible, in addition to giving us a lot of flexibility as to which sounds we want to play.

In canvasApp(), we will create a new constant named MAX_SOUNDS. This will represent the maximum number of sound objects we can create at any one time. We will also rename our sounds array to soundPool to better describe its purpose:

```
const MAX_SOUNDS = 8;
var soundPool = new Array();
```

The big change here is the playSound() function. It uses the same parameters as the one from iteration #2, but the functionality is very different:

```
function playSound(sound,volume) {
```

The first half of the function loops through the soundPool array to see whether any of the HTMLAudioElement objects in the pool are available to play a sound. We determine this by checking the ended property. Since only HTMLAudioElement objects that have previously been used to play a sound are put into the pool, the ended property will be set to true once the sound has finished playing. By replaying sounds that have finished, we remove the issue of trying to reuse an HTMLAudioElement object to play a sound while it is already in use:

```
var soundFound = false;
var soundIndex = 0;
var tempSound;

if (soundPool.length> 0) {
    while (!soundFound && soundIndex < soundPool.length) {

        var tSound = soundPool[soundIndex];

        if (tSound.ended) {
            soundFound = true;
        } else {
            soundIndex++;
        }

    }
}
if (soundFound) {
    tempSound = soundPool[soundIndex];
    tempSound.setAttribute("src", sound + "." + audioType);
    tempSound.loop = false;
    tempSound.volume = volume;
    tempSound.play();
```

If we don't find a sound, and the size of the pool is less than MAX_SOUNDS, we go ahead and create a new HTMLAudioElement, call its play() function, and push it into the sound pool. This keeps the pool from getting too large, while making sure there are not too many HTMLAudioElement objects in the browser at any one time:

```
} else if (soundPool.length < MAX_SOUNDS){
    tempSound = document.createElement("audio");
    tempSound.setAttribute("src", sound + "." + audioType);
    tempSound.volume = volume;
    tempSound.play();
    soundPool.push(tempSound);
}

}
```

You can go ahead and try this iteration by loading *CH7EX8.html* in your HTML5-compliant web browser. In this case, it works! You hear every sound, and the browser doesn't die like it would with iteration #2.

Unfortunately, there are some issues. On some browsers, there is still a pause before a sound plays, just like with iteration #2. Again, this happens more often when the page is loaded from an external website than when it is loaded locally in a web browser.

The worst manifestation of this comes in Google Chrome, where the sounds pause every time they are played. Also, in Firefox, the src doesn't change for all the objects, making the shoot sound play when the explode sound should play, and vice versa.

Uh-oh, it looks like we need another iteration. Figure 7-9 shows *Space Raiders* playing with a pool size governed by MAX_SOUNDS.

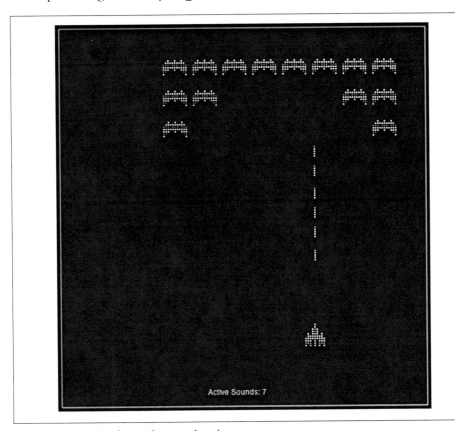

Figure 7-9. Space Raiders with a sound pool

Iteration #4: Reusing Preloaded Sounds

Even though the code in iteration #3 was pretty clean, it simply did not work for us. Instead, we need to compromise and implement a solution that is less elegant, but that works to play sounds nearly every time they are needed. This solution must also work both locally and when loaded from a website.

For this final iteration, we are going to use a sound pool just like in iteration #3, but it will operate in a different way. We will not reuse sound objects for different sound files. Instead, we will load all our sounds up front, and simply play a sound object that is currently not being used. In effect, we will "prime the pump," creating three sound objects for each of our two sounds for a total of six sound objects when we start the application. While this may not seem like the perfect solution, it appears to work fairly well in all browsers and plays sounds in the most effective way.

In canvasApp(), we set our MAX_SOUNDS constant to 6. We could make it higher, but for this example we will limit it to the number of sounds we will create and preload:

```
const MAX_SOUNDS = 6;
```

We then create six variables to hold our HTMLAudioElement objects: three for the explode sound...

```
var explodeSound ;
var explodeSound2 ;
var explodeSound3 ;
```

...and three for the shoot sound:

```
var shootSound;
var shootSound2;
var shootSound3;
```

In the initApp() function, we preload all of these sound objects. Yes, we load the same object multiple times:

```
explodeSound = document.createElement("audio");
document.body.appendChild(explodeSound);
audioType = supportedAudioFormat(explodeSound);
explodeSound.setAttribute("src", "explode1." + audioType);
explodeSound.addEventListener("canplaythrough",itemLoaded,false);

explodeSound2 = document.createElement("audio");
document.body.appendChild(explodeSound2);
explodeSound2.setAttribute("src", "explode1." + audioType);
explodeSound2.addEventListener("canplaythrough",itemLoaded,false);

explodeSound3 = document.createElement("audio");
document.body.appendChild(explodeSound3);
explodeSound3.setAttribute("src", "explode1." + audioType);
explodeSound3.addEventListener("canplaythrough",itemLoaded,false);

shootSound = document.createElement("audio");
document.body.appendChild(shootSound);
```

```
shootSound.setAttribute("src", "shoot1." + audioType);
shootSound.addEventListener("canplaythrough",itemLoaded,false);

shootSound2 = document.createElement("audio");
document.body.appendChild(shootSound2);
shootSound2.setAttribute("src", "shoot1." + audioType);
shootSound2.addEventListener("canplaythrough",itemLoaded,false);

shootSound3 = document.createElement("audio");
document.body.appendChild(shootSound3);
shootSound3.setAttribute("src", "shoot1." + audioType);
shootSound3.addEventListener("canplaythrough",itemLoaded,false);
```

In the itemLoaded() function, we remove the event listeners for all six loaded sounds:

```
shootSound.removeEventListener("canplaythrough",itemLoaded, false);
shootSound2.removeEventListener("canplaythrough",itemLoaded, false);
shootSound3.removeEventListener("canplaythrough",itemLoaded, false);
explodeSound.removeEventListener("canplaythrough",itemLoaded,false);
explodeSound2.removeEventListener("canplaythrough",itemLoaded,false);
explodeSound3.removeEventListener("canplaythrough",itemLoaded,false);
```

Then, we push each sound into our soundPool array. However, this time, we push them as dynamic objects so we can set the following properties, which don't exist in the HTMLAudioElement object:

name

The name of the sound file to play (again, without the extension).

element

The reference to the HTMLAudioElement object.

played

A Boolean that tells us whether this sound has played once or not. We need this property because we are putting all of these sound objects into our array, but they have not been played yet. That means their ended property has not yet been set to true. The played property tells us whether the sound is ready to play—that is, it has not been played yet. We will set this to true after we play the sound once:

```
soundPool.push({name:"explode1", element:explodeSound, played:false});
soundPool.push({name:"explode1", element:explodeSound2, played:false});
soundPool.push({name:"explode1", element:explodeSound3, played:false});
soundPool.push({name:"shoot1", element:shootSound, played:false});
soundPool.push({name:"shoot1", element:shootSound2, played:false});
soundPool.push({name:"shoot1", element:shootSound3, played:false});
```

Now we need to make a change in our resetApp() function. This change is to support sounds playing in Chrome, which appears to be the only browser that has a slight issue with loading sounds in this manner. The first time you play a sound in Chrome, there is a pause before it starts. To alleviate this, we play each sound type once but set the volume to 0. This will make sure a sound is loaded and ready to play the first time we call playSound() in Chrome:

```
function resetApp() {

    playSound(SOUND_EXPLODE,0);
    playSound(SOUND_SHOOT,0);
    startLevel();
    appState = STATE_PLAYING;


}
```

The playSound() function operates in a similar way to iteration #3. It loops through the soundPool array looking for a sound that it can play. However, in this version, we check to see whether the HTMLAudioElement has ended (tSound.element.ended) or if it has not been played (!tSound.played) yet. We also check whether the value in the sound parameter matches the name property of the sound object in soundPool (tSound.name == sound):

```
function playSound(sound,volume) {

        var soundFound = false;
        var soundIndex = 0;
        var tempSound;

        if (soundPool.length > 0) {
            while (!soundFound && soundIndex < soundPool.length) {

                var tSound = soundPool[soundIndex];
                if ((tSound.element.ended || !tSound.played) && tSound.name == sound) {
                    soundFound = true;
                    tSound.played = true;
                } else {
                    soundIndex++;
                }

            }
        }
```

Using this method, we play a sound only if it has not been played, it has ended, and it already has the sound file loaded that we need to play. There is no pause to load (most of the time), and sounds play at pretty much the time we need them to play. If we need more sounds, we can load more up front, or set MAX_SOUNDS to a number greater than the number of preloaded sounds. If we do that, we will create new sound objects on the fly (although this might still give you a pause when loading from a web server):

```
    if (soundFound) {
            tempSound = soundPool[soundIndex].element;
            tempSound.volume = volume;
            tempSound.play();

        } else if (soundPool.length < MAX_SOUNDS){
            tempSound = document.createElement("audio");
            tempSound.setAttribute("src", sound + "." + audioType);
```

```
        tempSound.volume = volume;
        tempSound.play();
        soundPool.push({name:sound, element:tempSound, type:audioType, played:true});
    }
```

Go ahead and try this code. It is *CH7EX9.html* in the code distribution, or you can type in the program listing.

Other stuff you could do to improve the game

Since the next couple chapters introduce game concepts, we really shouldn't go much further with *Space Raiders*. Still, if you were going to finish this game, these are the things you might consider doing:

1. Add a score.
2. Increase the aliens' speed on each new level.
3. Collision-detect the aliens and the player.
4. Make an object pool for missiles and aliens.
5. Slow down firing with a `wait()` state or frame counter.
6. Add explosions.
7. Include a title sequence, level sequence, and end game sequence.
8. Add a looping soundtrack.

The final code for Space Raiders

Example 7-6 shows the final code for the *Space Raiders* game (*CH7EX9.html*).

Example 7-6. Space Raiders with optimized dynamic network sound and state loader

```
<!doctype html>
<html lang="en">
<head>
<meta charset="UTF-8">
<title>CH7EX9: Space Raiders With Optimized Dynamic Network Sound And State Loader</title>
<script src="modernizr-1.6.min.js"></script>
<script type="text/javascript">
window.addEventListener('load', eventWindowLoaded, false);

function eventWindowLoaded() {

    canvasApp();

}

function supportedAudioFormat(audio) {
    var returnExtension = "";
    if (audio.canPlayType("audio/ogg") =="probably" ||
        audio.canPlayType("audio/ogg") == "maybe") {
        returnExtension = "ogg";
```

```
        } else if(audio.canPlayType("audio/wav") =="probably" ||
            audio.canPlayType("audio/wav") == "maybe") {
                returnExtension = "wav";
        } else if(audio.canPlayType("audio/mp3") == "probably" ||
            audio.canPlayType("audio/mp3") == "maybe") {
                returnExtension = "mp3";
        }

    return returnExtension;

}

function canvasSupport () {
        return Modernizr.canvas;
}

function canvasApp() {

    const STATE_INIT  = 10;
    const STATE_LOADING = 20;
    const STATE_RESET  = 30;
    const STATE_PLAYING = 40;
    var appState = STATE_INIT;
    var loadCount= 0;
    var itemsToLoad = 0;
    var alienImage = new Image();
    var missileImage = new Image();
    var playerImage = new Image();

    const SOUND_EXPLODE = "explode1";
    const SOUND_SHOOT  = "shoot1";
    const MAX_SOUNDS = 6;
    var soundPool = new Array();
    var explodeSound ;
    var explodeSound2 ;
    var explodeSound3 ;
    var shootSound;
    var shootSound2;
    var shootSound3;
    var audioType;

    var mouseX;
    var mouseY;
    var player = {x:250,y:475};
    var aliens = new Array();
    var missiles = new Array();

    const ALIEN_START_X = 25;
    const ALIEN_START_Y = 25;
    const ALIEN_ROWS = 5;
    const ALIEN_COLS = 8;
    const ALIEN_SPACING = 40;
```

```
    if (!canvasSupport()) {
        return;
      }

  var theCanvas = document.getElementById("canvasOne");
  var context = theCanvas.getContext("2d");

function itemLoaded(event) {

 loadCount++;
 if (loadCount >= itemsToLoad) {

    shootSound.removeEventListener("canplaythrough",itemLoaded, false);
    shootSound2.removeEventListener("canplaythrough",itemLoaded, false);
    shootSound3.removeEventListener("canplaythrough",itemLoaded, false);
    explodeSound.removeEventListener("canplaythrough",itemLoaded,false);
    explodeSound2.removeEventListener("canplaythrough",itemLoaded,false);
    explodeSound3.removeEventListener("canplaythrough",itemLoaded,false);
    soundPool.push({name:"explode1", element:explodeSound, played:false});
    soundPool.push({name:"explode1", element:explodeSound2, played:false});
    soundPool.push({name:"explode1", element:explodeSound3, played:false});
    soundPool.push({name:"shoot1", element:shootSound, played:false});
    soundPool.push({name:"shoot1", element:shootSound2, played:false});
    soundPool.push({name:"shoot1", element:shootSound3, played:false});

    appState = STATE_RESET;

  }

}

function initApp() {
 loadCount=0;
 itemsToLoad = 9;
 explodeSound = document.createElement("audio");
 document.body.appendChild(explodeSound);
 audioType = supportedAudioFormat(explodeSound);
 explodeSound.setAttribute("src", "explode1." + audioType);
 explodeSound.addEventListener("canplaythrough",itemLoaded,false);

 explodeSound2 = document.createElement("audio");
 document.body.appendChild(explodeSound2);
 explodeSound2.setAttribute("src", "explode1." + audioType);
 explodeSound2.addEventListener("canplaythrough",itemLoaded,false);

 explodeSound3 = document.createElement("audio");
 document.body.appendChild(explodeSound3);
 explodeSound3.setAttribute("src", "explode1." + audioType);
 explodeSound3.addEventListener("canplaythrough",itemLoaded,false);

 shootSound = document.createElement("audio");
 document.body.appendChild(shootSound);
 shootSound.setAttribute("src", "shoot1." + audioType);
 shootSound.addEventListener("canplaythrough",itemLoaded,false);
```

```
shootSound2 = document.createElement("audio");
document.body.appendChild(shootSound2);
shootSound2.setAttribute("src", "shoot1." + audioType);
shootSound2.addEventListener("canplaythrough",itemLoaded,false);

shootSound3 = document.createElement("audio");
document.body.appendChild(shootSound3);
shootSound3.setAttribute("src", "shoot1." + audioType);
shootSound3.addEventListener("canplaythrough",itemLoaded,false);

alienImage = new Image();
alienImage.onload = itemLoaded;
alienImage.src = "alien.png";
playerImage = new Image();
playerImage.onload = itemLoaded;
playerImage.src = "player.png";
missileImage = new Image();
missileImage.onload = itemLoaded;
missileImage.src = "missile.png";
appState = STATE_LOADING;
}

function startLevel() {

    for (var r = 0; r < ALIEN_ROWS; r++) {
       for( var c= 0; c < ALIEN_COLS; c++) {
          aliens.push({speed:2,x:ALIEN_START_X+c*ALIEN_SPACING, y:ALIEN_START_Y+r*
             ALIEN_SPACING,width:alienImage.width, height:alienImage.height});
       }
    }
}

function resetApp() {

 playSound(SOUND_EXPLODE,0);
 playSound(SOUND_SHOOT,0);
 startLevel();
 appState = STATE_PLAYING;

}

function  drawScreen () {

    //Move missiles
    for (var i=missiles.length-1; i>= 0;i--) {
       missiles[i].y -= missiles[i].speed;
       if (missiles[i].y < (0-missiles[i].height)) {
          missiles.splice(i,1);
       }

    }

    //Move Aliens
    for (var i=aliens.length-1; i>= 0;i--) {
       aliens[i].x += aliens[i].speed;
```

```
        if (aliens[i].x > (theCanvas.width-aliens[i].width) || aliens[i].x < 0) {
            aliens[i].speed *= -1;
            aliens[i].y += 20;
        }
        if (aliens[i].y > theCanvas.height) {
            aliens.splice(i,1);
        }

    }

    //Detect Collisions
    missile: for (var i=missiles.length-1; i>= 0;i--) {
        var tempMissile = missiles[i]
        for (var j=aliens.length-1; j>= 0;j--) {
            var tempAlien =aliens[j];
            if (hitTest(tempMissile,tempAlien)) {
                playSound(SOUND_EXPLODE,.5);
                missiles.splice(i,1);
                aliens.splice(j,1);
                break missile;
            }
        }

        if (aliens.length <=0) {
            appState = STATE_RESET;
        }
    }

    //Background
    context.fillStyle = "#000000";
    context.fillRect(0, 0, theCanvas.width, theCanvas.height);
    //Box
    context.strokeStyle = "#EEEEEE";
    context.strokeRect(5,  5, theCanvas.width-10, theCanvas.height-10);

    //Draw Player
    context.drawImage(playerImage,player.x,player.y);

    //Draw Missiles
    for (var i=missiles.length-1; i>= 0;i--) {
        context.drawImage(missileImage,missiles[i].x,missiles[i].y);

    }

    //draw aliens
    for (var i=aliens.length-1; i>= 0;i--) {
        context.drawImage(alienImage,aliens[i].x,aliens[i].y);

    }

    //Draw Text
    context.fillStyle = "#FFFFFF";
    context.fillText ("Active Sounds: " + soundPool.length,  200 ,480);

}
```

```
function hitTest(image1,image2) {
  r1left = image1.x;
  r1top = image1.y;
  r1right = image1.x + image1.width;
  r1bottom = image1.y + image1.height;
  r2left = image2.x;
  r2top = image2.y;
  r2right = image2.x + image2.width;
  r2bottom = image2.y + image2.height;
  retval = false;

  if ( (r1left > r2right) || (r1right < r2left) || (r1bottom < r2top) ||
       (r1top > r2bottom) ) {
    retval = false;
  } else {
    retval = true;
  }

  return retval;
}

function eventMouseMove(event) {
  if ( event.layerX ||  event.layerX == 0) { // Firefox
      mouseX = event.layerX ;
    mouseY = event.layerY;
   } else if (event.offsetX || event.offsetX == 0) { // Opera
     mouseX = event.offsetX;
    mouseY = event.offsetY;
   }

  player.x = mouseX;
  player.y = mouseY;

}

function eventMouseUp(event) {

  missiles.push({speed:5, x: player.x+.5*playerImage.width,
    y:player.y-missileImage.height,width:missileImage.width,
    height:missileImage.height});

  playSound(SOUND_SHOOT,.5);
}

function playSound(sound,volume) {

  var soundFound = false;
  var soundIndex = 0;
  var tempSound;

  if (soundPool.length> 0) {
    while (!soundFound && soundIndex < soundPool.length) {
```

```
            var tSound = soundPool[soundIndex];
            if ((tSound.element.ended || !tSound.played) && tSound.name == sound) {
                soundFound = true;
                tSound.played = true;
            } else {
                soundIndex++;
            }

        }
    }
    if (soundFound) {
        tempSound = soundPool[soundIndex].element;
        tempSound.volume = volume;
        tempSound.play();

    } else if (soundPool.length < MAX_SOUNDS){
        tempSound = document.createElement("audio");
        tempSound.setAttribute("src", sound + "." + audioType);
        tempSound.volume = volume;
        tempSound.play();
        soundPool.push({name:sound, element:tempSound, type:audioType, played:true});
    }

}

function run() {
    switch(appState) {
    case STATE_INIT:
        initApp();
        break;
    case STATE_LOADING:
        //wait for call backs
        break;
    case STATE_RESET:
        resetApp();
        break;
    case STATE_PLAYING:
        drawScreen();
        break;
    }

}

theCanvas.addEventListener("mouseup",eventMouseUp, false);
theCanvas.addEventListener("mousemove",eventMouseMove, false);

setInterval(run, 33);

}


</script>
</head>
```

```
<body>
<div style="position: absolute; top: 50px; left: 50px;">

<canvas id="canvasOne" width="500" height="500">
 Your browser does not support HTML5 Canvas.
</canvas>
</div>
</body>
</html>
```

What's Next

Since this is not a book about the HTML5 `<audio>` tag, we did not cover every aspect of that new feature. Instead, we focused on the elements of `audio` that could be used with HTML5 Canvas. We created two in-depth applications that make use of sound with HTML5 Canvas in very different ways: an audio player that plays one song, and a game that plays many sounds dynamically. During that process we learned that audio in HTML, while being a wonderful new feature, is not without its pitfalls and gotchas.

In the next two chapters we will expand upon the last section we presented here, and discuss how to implement games on HTML5 Canvas.

CHAPTER 8

Canvas Game Essentials

Games are the reason why many of us initially became interested in computers, and they continue to be a major driving force that pushes computer technology to new heights. In this chapter, we will examine how to build a mini game framework that can be used to create games on the canvas. We will explore many of the core building blocks associated with game development and apply them to HTML5 Canvas with the JavaScript API.

We don't have the space to cover every type of game you might want to create, but we will discuss many elementary and intermediate topics necessary for most games. At the end of this chapter, we will have a basic clone of Atari's classic *Asteroids* game. We will step through the creation of this game by first applying some of the techniques for drawing and transformations specific to our game's visual objects. This will help get our feet wet by taking some of the techniques we covered in previous chapters and applying them to an arcade game application. Next, we will create a basic game framework that can be applied to any game we want to make on the canvas. Following this, we will dive into some game techniques and algorithms, and finally, we will apply everything we have covered to create the finished product.

Why Games in HTML5?

Playing games in a browser has become one of the most popular activities for Internet users. HTML5 Canvas gives web developers an API to directly manage drawing to a specific area of the browser. This functionality makes game development in JavaScript much more powerful than ever before.

Canvas Compared to Flash

We've covered this topic in earlier chapters, but we expect that a large portion of readers might have previously developed games in Flash. If so, you will find that Canvas offers similar functionality in certain areas, but lacks some of the more refined features of Flash.

No Flash timeline

There is no frame-based timeline for animation intrinsic to Canvas. This means that we will need to code all of our animations using images and/or paths, and apply our own frame-based updates.

No display list

Flash AS3 offers the very powerful idea of an object display list; a developer can add hundreds of individual physical display objects to the game screen. HTML5 Canvas has only a single display object (the canvas itself).

What Does Canvas Offer?

Even though Canvas lacks some of the features that make the Flash platform very nice for game development, it also has some strengths.

A powerful single stage

HTML5 Canvas is closely akin to the Flash Stage. It is a rectangular piece of screen real estate that can be manipulated programmatically. Advanced Flash developers might recognize the canvas as a close cousin to both the `BitmapData` and `Shape` objects in ActionScript. We can draw directly to the canvas with paths and images, and transform them on the fly.

Logical display objects

Canvas gives us a single physical display object, but we can create any number of logical display objects. We will use JavaScript objects to hold all of the logical data and methods we need to draw and transform our logical game objects to the physical canvas.

Our Basic Game HTML5 File

Before we start to develop our arcade game, let's look at Example 8-1, the most basic HTML file we will use in this chapter (*CH8EX1.html*). We'll start by using the basic HTML5 template we defined in Chapter 1. Our canvas will be a 200×200 square.

Example 8-1. The Basic HTML file for Chapter 8

```
<!doctype html>
<html lang="en">
<head>
<meta charset="UTF-8">
<title>CH8EX1: Filled Screen With Some Text</title>
<script type="text/javascript">
   window.addEventListener('load', eventWindowLoaded, false);
   function eventWindowLoaded() {
      canvasApp();
   }
   function canvasApp(){
      var theCanvas = document.getElementById("canvas");
```

```
        if (!theCanvas || !theCanvas.getContext) {
            return;
        }
        var context = theCanvas.getContext("2d");
        if (!context) {
            return;
        }
        drawScreen();
        function drawScreen() {
            context.fillStyle = '#ffaaaa';
            context.fillRect(0, 0, 200, 200);
            context.fillStyle = '#000000';
            context.font = '20px _sans';
            context.textBaseline = 'top';
            context.fillText  ("Canvas!", 0, 0);
        }
    }
</script>
</head>
    <body>
        <div style="position: absolute; top: 50px; left: 50px;">
            <canvas id="canvas" width="200" height="200">
            Your browser does not support HTML5 Canvas.
            </canvas>
        </div>
    </body>
</html>
```

This example will do nothing more than place a 200×200 gray box on the canvas and write "Canvas!" starting at 0,0. We will be replacing the drawScreen() function for most of the next few examples. Figure 8-1 illustrates Example 8-1.

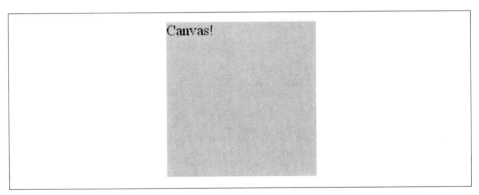

Figure 8-1. The basic HTML file for Chapter 8

Next, we will begin to make our *Asteroids*-like game, which we've named *Geo Blaster Basic*. See Figure 8-7 for an example of the final game in action.

Our Game's Design

We are not going to assume that everyone who reads this chapter knows of or understands Atari's classic arcade game *Asteroids*. So, let's start by taking a peek at *Asteroids'* game-play elements.

Asteroids, designed by Ed Logg and Lyle Rains, was released by Atari in 1979. The game pitted a lone triangular two-dimensional vector spaceship (the player ship) against screen after screen of asteroid rocks that needed to be dodged and destroyed. Every so often a space saucer would enter the screen attempting to destroy the player ship.

All asteroids started the game as large rocks; once they were hit, they would split into two medium-sized rocks. When hit by a player missile, these medium-sized rocks would then split into two small rocks. The small rocks would simply be destroyed when hit (small was the final size for all asteroids).

When the player destroyed all the asteroids, a new screen of more and slightly faster asteroids would appear. This went on until the player exhausted his three ships. At each 10,000-point score mark, the player was awarded an extra ship.

All of the game objects moved (thrusting, rotating, and/or floating) freely across the entire screen, which represented a slice of space as a flat plane. When an object went off the side of the screen, it would reappear on the opposite side, in warp-like fashion.

Game Graphics: Drawing with Paths

Let's jump into game development on Canvas by first taking a look at some of the graphics we will use in our game. This will help give us a visual feel for what type of code we will need to implement.

Needed Assets

For our *Asteroids*-like game, *Geo Blaster Basic*, we will need some very simple game graphics, including:

- A solid black background.
- A player ship that will rotate and thrust (move on a vector) across the game screen. There will be two frames of animation for this ship: a "static" frame and a "thrust" frame.
- A saucer that flies across the screen and shoots at the player.
- Some "rocks" for the player to shoot. We will use a simple square as our rock.

There are two different methods we can employ to draw the graphics for our game: bitmap images or paths. For the game in this chapter, we will focus on using paths. In Chapter 9, we will explore how to manipulate bitmap images for our game graphics.

Using Paths to Draw the Game's Main Character

Paths offer us a very simple but powerful way to mimic the vector look of the classic *Asteroids* game. We could use bitmap images for this purpose, but in this chapter we are going to focus on creating our game in code with no external assets. Let's take a look at the two frames of animation we will create for our player ship.

The static player ship (frame 1)

The main frame of the player ship will be drawn with paths on a 20×20 grid, as shown in Figure 8-2.

Figure 8-2. The player ship

Using the basic HTML file presented in Example 8-1, we can simply swap the `drawScreen()` function with the code in Example 8-2 to draw the ship.

Example 8-2. Drawing the player ship

```
function drawScreen() {
   // draw background and text
   context.fillStyle = '#000000';
   context.fillRect(0, 0, 200, 200);
   context.fillStyle = '#ffffff';
   context.font = '20px _sans';
   context.textBaseline = 'top';
   context.fillText ("Player Ship - Static", 0, 180);

   //drawShip
   context.strokeStyle = '#ffffff';
   context.beginPath();
   context.moveTo(10,0);
   context.lineTo(19,19);
   context.lineTo(10,9);
   context.moveTo(9,9);
   context.lineTo(0,19);
   context.lineTo(9,0);

   context.stroke();
   context.closePath();
}
```

We are drawing to the upper-left corner of the screen starting at 0,0. Figure 8-3 shows what this will look like.

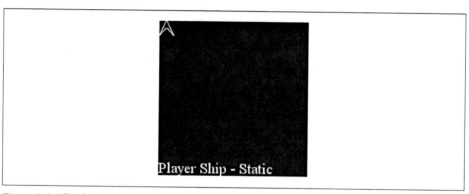

Figure 8-3. The player ship on the canvas

The ship with thrust engaged (frame 2)

Now let's take a look at the second frame of animation for the player ship, which is shown in Figure 8-4.

Figure 8-4. The player ship with thrust engaged

The `drawScreen()` function code to add this extra "thrust" graphic is very simple; see Example 8-3.

Example 8-3. Drawing the player ship with thrust

```
function drawScreen() {
   // draw background and text
   context.fillStyle = '#000000';
   context.fillRect(0, 0, 200, 200);
   context.fillStyle = '#ffffff';
   context.font = '20px _sans';
   context.textBaseline = 'top';
   context.fillText  ("Player Ship - Thrust", 0, 180);

   //drawShip
   context.strokeStyle = '#ffffff';
   context.beginPath();
   context.moveTo(10,0);
   context.lineTo(19,19);
   context.lineTo(10,9);
   context.moveTo(9,9);
   context.lineTo(0,19);
   context.lineTo(9,0);

   //draw thrust
   context.moveTo(8,13);
   context.lineTo(11,13);
   context.moveTo(9,14);
   context.lineTo(9,18);
   context.moveTo(10,14);
   context.lineTo(10,18);

   context.stroke();
   context.closePath();
}
```

Animating on the Canvas

The player ship we just created has two frames (static and thrust), but we can only display a single frame at a time. Our game will need to switch out the frame of animation based on the state of the player ship, and it will need to run on a timer so this animation can occur. Let's take a quick look at the code necessary to create our game timer.

Game Timer Loop

Games on HTML5 Canvas require the use of the repeated update/render loop to simulate animation. We do this by using the `setInterval()` JavaScript function, which will repeatedly call a function of our choosing at millisecond intervals. Each second of game/animation time is made up of 1,000 milliseconds. If we want our game to run at 30 update/render cycles per second, we call this a 30 frames per second (FPS) rate. To run our interval at 30 FPS, we first need to divide 1,000 by 30. The result is the number of milliseconds in each interval:

```
const FRAME_RATE = 30;
var intervalTime = 1000/FRAME_RATE;
setInterval(drawScreen, intervalTime );
```

By calling the drawScreen() function repeatedly on each interval, we can simulate animation.

 Sometimes we will refer to each of the frame intervals as a *frame tick*.

The Player Ship State Changes

We simply need to switch between the static and thrust states to simulate the animation. Let's take a look at the full HTML file to do this. In Example 8-4, we will start to place canvasApp class-level variables in a new section just above the drawScreen() function. This will be the location going forward for all variables needing a global scope inside the canvasApp() object.

Example 8-4. The player ship state changes for thrust animation

```
<!doctype html>
<html lang="en">
<head>
<meta charset="UTF-8">
<title>CH8EX4: Ship Animation Loop</title>
<script type="text/javascript">
window.addEventListener('load', eventWindowLoaded, false);
function eventWindowLoaded() {

    canvasApp();
}

function canvasApp(){

    var theCanvas = document.getElementById("canvas");
    if (!theCanvas || !theCanvas.getContext) {
        return;
    }

    var context = theCanvas.getContext("2d");

    if (!context) {
        return;
    }

    //canvasApp level variables
    var shipState = 0; //0 = static, 1 = thrust
```

```
   function drawScreen() {
      //update the shipState
      shipState++;
      if (shipState >1) {
          shipState=0;
      }

      // draw background and text
      context.fillStyle = '#000000';
      context.fillRect(0, 0, 200, 200);
      context.fillStyle = '#ffffff';
      context.font = '20px _sans';
      context.textBaseline = 'top';
      context.fillText  ("Player Ship - animate", 0, 180);

      //drawShip
      context.strokeStyle = '#ffffff';
      context.beginPath();
      context.moveTo(10,0);
      context.lineTo(19,19);
      context.lineTo(10,9);
      context.moveTo(9,9);
      context.lineTo(0,19);
      context.lineTo(9,0);

      if (shipState==1) {
          //draw thrust
          context.moveTo(8,13);
          context.lineTo(11,13);
          context.moveTo(9,14);
          context.lineTo(9,18);
          context.moveTo(10,14);
          context.lineTo(10,18);
      }

       context.stroke();
       context.closePath();
      }

      const FRAME_RATE = 40;
      var intervalTime = 1000/FRAME_RATE;
      setInterval(drawScreen, intervalTime );

}

</script>
</head>
<body>
<div style="position: absolute; top: 50px; left: 50px;">

<canvas id="canvas" width="200" height="200">
 Your browser does not support HTML5 Canvas.
</canvas>
</div>
```

```
</body>
</html>
```

When we run Example 8-4 we will see the player ship in the upper-left corner of the canvas. The static and thrust states will alternate on each frame.

Applying Transformations to Game Graphics

Our game will probably have many individual logical display objects that need to be updated on a single frame tick. We can make use of the Canvas stack (`save()` and `restore()` functions), and use the transformation matrix to ensure the final output affects only the current object we are working on—not the entire canvas.

The Canvas Stack

The Canvas state can be saved to a stack and retrieved. This is important when we are transforming and animating game objects because we want our transformations to affect only the current game object and not the entire canvas. The basic workflow for using the Canvas stack in a game looks like this:

1. Save the current canvas to the stack.
2. Transform and draw the game object.
3. Retrieve the saved canvas from the stack.

As an example, let's set up a basic rotation for our player ship. We will rotate it by 1 degree on each frame. Since we are currently drawing the player ship in the top-left corner of the canvas, we are going to move it to a new location. We do this because the basic rotation will use the top-left corner of the ship as the *registration point*: the axis location used for rotation and scale operations. So, if we kept the ship at the 0,0 location and rotated it by its top-left corner, you would not see it half the time because its location would be off the top and left edges of the canvas. Instead, we will place the ship at 50,50.

We will be using the same HTML code as in Example 8-4, changing out only the `drawCanvas()` function. To simplify this example, we will remove the `shipState` variable and concentrate on the static state only. We will be adding in three new variables above the `drawCanvas()` function:

```
var rotation = 0; - holds the current rotation of the player ship
var x = 50; - holds the x location to start drawing the player ship
var y = 50; - holds the y location to start drawing the player ship
```

Example 8-5 gives the full code.

Example 8-5. Rotating an image

```
//canvasApp level variables
    var rotation = 0;
    var x = 50;
    var y = 50;

    function drawScreen() {

        // draw background and text
        context.fillStyle = '#000000';
        context.fillRect(0, 0, 200, 200);
        context.fillStyle = '#ffffff';
        context.font = '20px _sans';
        context.textBaseline = 'top';
        context.fillText ("Player Ship - rotate", 0, 180);

        //transformation
        var angleInRadians = rotation * Math.PI / 180;
        context.save(); //save current state in stack
        context.setTransform(1,0,0,1,0,0); // reset to identity

        //translate the canvas origin to the center of the player
        context.translate(x,y);
        context.rotate(angleInRadians);

        //drawShip
        context.strokeStyle = '#ffffff';
        context.beginPath();
        context.moveTo(10,0);
        context.lineTo(19,19);
        context.lineTo(10,9);
        context.moveTo(9,9);
        context.lineTo(0,19);
        context.lineTo(9,0);

        context.stroke();
        context.closePath();

        //restore context
        context.restore(); //pop old state on to screen

        //add to rotation
        rotation++;
    }
```

As you can see, the player ship rotates clockwise one degree at a time. As we've mentioned many times already, we must convert from degrees to radians because the context.rotate() transformations use radians for calculations. In the next section, we'll take a deeper look at some of the transformations we will use in our *Geo Blaster Basic* game.

Game Graphic Transformations

As we saw in the previous section, we can easily rotate a game graphic at the top-left corner by using the `context.rotate()` transformation. However, our game will need to rotate objects at the center rather than the top-left corner. To do this, we must change the transformation point to the center of our game graphic object.

Rotating the Player Ship from the Center

The code to rotate the player ship from its center point is almost exactly like the code used to rotate it at the top-left corner. What we need to modify is the point of the translation. In Example 8-5, we placed the immediate-mode drawing context at the x and y coordinates of our game object (50,50). This had the effect of rotating the object from the top-left corner. Now we must move the translation to the center of our object:

```
context.translate(x+.5*width,y+.5*height);
```

 The `width` and `height` variables represent attributes of our drawn player ship. We will create these attributes in Example 8-6.

This is not the only change we need to make; we also need to draw our ship as though it is the center point. To do this, we will subtract half the `width` from each x attribute in our path draw sequence, and half the `height` from each y attribute:

```
context.moveTo(10-.5*width,0-.5*height);
context.lineTo(19-.5*width,19-.5*height);
```

As you can see, it might get a little confusing trying to draw coordinates in this manner. It is also slightly more processor-intensive than using constants. In that case, we would simply hardcode in the needed values. Remember, the `width` and `height` attributes of our ship are both `20`. The hardcoded version would look something like this:

```
context.moveTo(0,-10);  //10-10, 0-10
context.lineTo(9,9); //19-10, 19-10
```

The method where we use the calculated values (using the `width` and `height` variables) is much more flexible, while the hardcoded method is much less processor-intensive. Example 8-6 contains all the code to use either method. We have commented out the calculated version of the code.

Example 8-6. Rotating an image from its center point

```
//canvasApp level variables
   var rotation = 0;
   var x = 50;
   var y = 50;
```

```
var width = 20;
var height = 20;

function drawScreen() {
    // draw background and text
    context.fillStyle = '#000000';
    context.fillRect(0, 0, 200, 200);
    context.fillStyle = '#ffffff';
    context.font = '20px _sans';
    context.textBaseline = 'top';
    context.fillText ("Player Ship - rotate", 0, 180);

    //transformation
    var angleInRadians = rotation * Math.PI / 180;
    context.save(); //save current state in stack
    context.setTransform(1,0,0,1,0,0); // reset to identity

    //translate the canvas origin to the center of the player
    context.translate(x+.5*width,y+.5*height);
    context.rotate(angleInRadians);

    //drawShip

    context.strokeStyle = '#ffffff';
    context.beginPath();

    //hardcoding in locations
    context.moveTo(0,-10);
    context.lineTo(9,9);
    context.lineTo(0,-1);
    context.moveTo(-1,-1);
    context.lineTo(-10,9);
    context.lineTo(-1,-10);

    /*
    //using the width and height to calculate
    context.moveTo(10-.5*width,0-.5*height);
    context.lineTo(19-.5*width,19-.5*height);
    context.lineTo(10-.5*width,9-.5*height);
    context.moveTo(9-.5*width,9-.5*height);
    context.lineTo(0-.5*width,19-.5*height);
    context.lineTo(9-.5*width,0-.5*height);
    */

    context.stroke();
    context.closePath();

    //restore context
    context.restore(); //pop old state on to screen

    //add to rotation
    rotation++;

}
```

Alpha Fading the Player Ship

When a new player ship in *Geo Blaster Basic* enters the game screen, we will have it fade from transparent to opaque. Example 8-7 shows how we will create this transformation in our game.

Using the context.globalAlpha attribute

To use the `context.globalAlpha` attribute of the canvas, we simply set it to a number between 0 and 1 before we draw the game graphics. We will create a new variable in our code called `alpha`, which will hold the current alpha value for our player ship. We will increase it by .01 until it reaches 1. When we actually create our game we will stop it at 1 and then start the game level. However, for this demo, we will just repeat it over and over.

Example 8-7. Alpha fading to the player ship

```
//canvasApp level variables
    var x = 50;
    var y = 50;
    var width = 20;
    var height = 20;
    var alpha = 0;
    context.globalAlpha  = 1;

    function drawScreen() {

        context.globalAlpha = 1;
        context.fillStyle = '#000000';
        context.fillRect(0, 0, 200, 200);
        context.fillStyle = '#ffffff';
        context.font = '20px _sans';
        context.textBaseline = 'top';
        context.fillText ("Player Ship - alpha", 0, 180);
        context.globalAlpha = alpha;
        context.save(); //save current state in stack
        context.setTransform(1,0,0,1,0,0); // reset to identity

        //translate the canvas origin to the center of the player
        context.translate(x+.5*width,y+.5*height);

        //drawShip
        context.strokeStyle = '#ffffff';
        context.beginPath();

        //hardcoding in locations
        context.moveTo(0,-10);
        context.lineTo(9,9);
        context.lineTo(0,-1);
        context.moveTo(-1,-1);
        context.lineTo(-10,9);
        context.lineTo(-1,-10);
```

```
        context.stroke();
        context.closePath();

        //restore context
        context.restore(); //pop old state on to screen

        //add to rotation
        alpha+=.01;
        if (alpha > 1) {
        alpha=0;
        }
    }
}
```

Game Object Physics and Animation

All of our game objects will move on a two-dimensional plane. We will use basic directional movement vectors to calculate the change in the x and y coordinates for each game object. At its very basic level, we will be updating the delta x (dx) and delta y (dy) of each of our game objects on each frame to simulate movement. These dx and dy values will be based on the angle and direction in which we want the object to move. All of our logical display objects will add their respective dx and dy values to their x and y values on each frame of animation. The player ship will not use strict dx and dy because it needs to be able to float and turn independently. Let's take a closer look at the player movement now.

How Our Player Ship Will Move

Our player ship will change its angle of center axis rotation when the game player presses the left and right arrow keys. When the game player presses the up arrow key, the player ship will accelerate (thrust) in the angle it is facing. Because there is no friction applied to the ship, it will continue to float in the current accelerated angle until a different angle of acceleration is applied. This happens when the game player rotates to a new angle and presses the up (thrust) key once again.

The difference between facing and moving

Our player ship can rotate to the direction it is facing while it is moving in a different direction. For this reason, we cannot simply use classic dx and dy values to represent the movement vector on the x and y axes. We must keep both sets of values for the ship at all times. When the player rotates the ship but does not thrust it, we need to draw the ship in the new rotated angle. All missile projectiles the ship fires must also move in the direction the ship is facing. On the x-axis, we will name this value facingX; on the y-axis, it's facingY. movingX and movingY values will handle moving the ship in the direction it was pointed in when the thrust was applied. All four values are needed to thrust the ship in a new direction. Let's take a look at this next.

Thrusting in the rotated direction

Once the ship is rotated to the desired direction, the player can thrust it forward by pressing the up arrow key. This thrust will accelerate the player ship only while the key is pressed. Since we know the rotation of the ship, we can easily calculate the angle of the rotation. We will then add new movingX and movingY values to the ship's x and y attributes to move it forward.

First, we must change the rotation value from degrees to radians:

```
var angleInRadians = rotation * Math.PI / 180;
```

You have seen this before—it's identical to how we calculated the rotation transformation before it was applied to the player ship.

Once we have the angle of the ship's rotation, we must calculate the facingX and facingY values for this current direction. We only do this when we are going to thrust because it is an expensive calculation, processor-wise. We could calculate these each time the player changes the ship's rotation, but doing so would add unnecessary processor overhead:

```
facingX = Math.cos(angleInRadians);
facingY = Math.sin(angleInRadians);
```

Once we have values on the x and y axes that represent the direction the player ship is currently facing, we can calculate the new movingX and movingY values for the player:

```
movingX = movingX+thrustAcceleration*facingX;
movingY = movingY+thrustAcceleration*facingY;
```

To apply these new values to the player ship's current position, we need to add them to its current x and y positions. *This does not occur only when the player presses the up key.* If it did, the player ship would not float; it would only move when the key was pressed. We must modify the x and y values on each frame with the movingX and movingY values:

```
x = x+movingX;
y = y+movingY;
```

Redrawing the player ship to start at angle 0

As you may recall, when we first drew the image for our player ship, we had the point end (the top) of the ship pointing up. We did this for ease of drawing, but it's not really the best direction in which to draw our ship when we intend to apply calculations for rotational thrust. The pointing-up direction is actually the -90 (or 270) degree angle. If we want to leave everything the way it currently is, we will need to modify the angleIn Radians calculation to look like this:

```
var angleInRadians = (Math.PI * (player.rotation -90 ))/ 180;
```

This is some ugly code, but it works fine if we want our player ship to be pointing up before we apply rotation transformations. A better method is to keep the current `angleInRadians` calculation but draw the ship pointing in the actual angle 0 direction (to the right). Figure 8-5 shows how we would draw this.

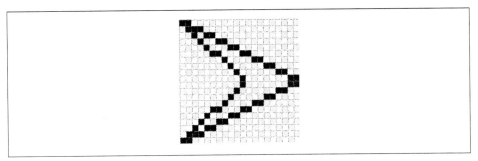

Figure 8-5. The player ship drawn at the 0 degree rotation

The drawing code for this direction would be modified to look like this:

```
//facing right
context.moveTo(-10,-10);
context.lineTo(10,0);
context.moveTo(10,1);
context.lineTo(-10,10);
context.lineTo(1,1);
context.moveTo(1,-1);
context.lineTo(-10,-10);
```

Controlling the Player Ship with the Keyboard

We will add in two keyboard events and an array object to hold the state of each key press. This will allow the player to hold down a key and have it repeat without a pause. Arcade games require this type of key-press response.

The array to hold our key presses

An array will hold the `true` or `false` value for each `keyCode` associated with key events. The `keyCode` will be the index of the array that will receive the `true` or `false` value:

```
var keyPressList = [];
```

The key events

We will use separate events for both key down and key up. The key down event will put a `true` value in the `keyPressList` array at the index associated with the event's `keyCode`. Conversely, the key up event will place a `false` in that array index:

```
document.onkeydown = function(e){

    e=e?e:window.event;
    //ConsoleLog.log(e.keyCode + "down");
    keyPressList[e.keyCode] = true;
}

document.onkeyup = function(e){
//document.body.onkeyup=function(e){
    e = e?e:window.event;
    //ConsoleLog.log(e.keyCode + "up");
    keyPressList[e.keyCode] = false;
};
```

Evaluating key presses

Our game will need to include code to look for true (or false) values in the keyPress
List array, and use those values to apply game logic:

```
if (keyPressList[38]==true){
    //thrust
    var angleInRadians = player.rotation * Math.PI / 180;
    facingX = Math.cos(angleInRadians);
    facingY = Math.sin(angleInRadians);

    movingX = movingX+thurstAcceleration*facingX;
    movingY = movingY+thurstAcceleration*facingY;
}

if (keyPressList[37]==true) {
    //rotate counterclockwise
    rotation-=rotationalVelocity;
}

if (keyPressList[39]==true) {
    //rotate clockwise
    rotation+=rotationalVelocity;;
}
```

Let's add this code to our current set of rotation examples and test it out. We have
made some major changes, so Example 8-8 presents the entire HTML file once again.

Example 8-8. Controlling the player ship

```
<!doctype html>
<html lang="en">
<head>
<meta charset="UTF-8">
<title>CH8EX8: Ship Turn With Keys</title>
<script type="text/javascript">
window.addEventListener('load', eventWindowLoaded, false);
function eventWindowLoaded() {

    canvasApp();
```

```
}

function canvasApp(){

    var theCanvas = document.getElementById("canvas");
    if (!theCanvas || !theCanvas.getContext) {
       return;
    }

    var context = theCanvas.getContext("2d");

    if (!context) {
       return;
    }

    //canvasApp level variables

    var rotation = 0;
    var x = 50;
    var y = 50;
    var facingX = 0;
    var facingY = 0;
    var movingX = 0;
    var movingY = 0;
    var width = 20;
    var height = 20;
    var rotationalVelocity = 5; //how many degrees to turn the ship
    var thrustAcceleration = .03;
    var keyPressList = [];
    function drawScreen() {

    //check keys

    if (keyPressList[38]==true){
       //thrust
        var angleInRadians = rotation * Math.PI / 180;
        facingX = Math.cos(angleInRadians);
        facingY = Math.sin(angleInRadians);

        movingX = movingX+thrustAcceleration*facingX;
        movingY = movingY+thrustAcceleration*facingY;

    }

    if (keyPressList[37]==true) {
        //rotate counterclockwise
        rotation -= rotationalVelocity;
    }

    if (keyPressList[39]==true) {
        //rotate clockwise
        rotation += rotationalVelocity;;
    }
```

```
    x = x+movingX;
    y = y+movingY;

    // draw background and text
    context.fillStyle = '#000000';
    context.fillRect(0, 0, 200, 200);
    context.fillStyle = '#ffffff';
    context.font = '20px _sans';
    context.textBaseline = 'top';
    context.fillText ("Player Ship - key turn", 0, 180);

    //transformation
    var angleInRadians = rotation * Math.PI / 180;
    context.save(); //save current state in stack
    context.setTransform(1,0,0,1,0,0); // reset to identity

    //translate the canvas origin to the center of the player
    context.translate(x+.5*width,y+.5*height);
    context.rotate(angleInRadians);

    //drawShip

    context.strokeStyle = '#ffffff';
    context.beginPath();

    //hardcoding in locations
    //facing right
    context.moveTo(-10,-10);
    context.lineTo(10,0);
    context.moveTo(10,1);
    context.lineTo(-10,10);
    context.lineTo(1,1);
    context.moveTo(1,-1);
    context.lineTo(-10,-10);

    context.stroke();
    context.closePath();

    //restore context
    context.restore(); //pop old state on to screen
    }

    const FRAME_RATE = 40;
    var intervalTime = 1000/FRAME_RATE;
    setInterval(drawScreen, intervalTime );

    document.onkeydown = function(e){
        e = e?e:window.event;
        //ConsoleLog.log(e.keyCode + "down");
        keyPressList[e.keyCode] = true;
    }

    document.onkeyup = function(e){
        //document.body.onkeyup = function(e){
        e = e?e:window.event;
```

```
        //ConsoleLog.log(e.keyCode + "up");
        keyPressList[e.keyCode] = false;
    };

}


</script>
</head>
<body>
<div style="position: absolute; top: 50px; left: 50px;">
<canvas id="canvas" width="200" height="200">
 Your browser does not support HTML5 Canvas.
</canvas>
</div>
</body>
</html>
```

Once this file is run in a browser, you should be able to press the left and right keys to rotate the ship on its center axis. If you press the up key, the ship will move in the direction it is facing.

Giving the Player Ship a Maximum Velocity

If you play with the code in Example 8-8, you will notice two problems:

1. The ship can go off the sides of the screen and get lost.
2. The ship has no maximum speed.

We'll resolve the first issue when we start to code the complete game, but for now, let's look at how to apply a maximum velocity to our current movement code. Suppose we give our player ship a maximum acceleration of 2 pixels per frame. It's easy to calculate the current velocity if we are only moving in the four primary directions: up, down, right, left. When we are moving left or right, the movingY value will always be 0. If we are moving up or down, the movingX value will always be 0. The current velocity we are moving on one axis would be easy to compare to the maximum velocity.

But in our game, we are almost always moving in the *x* and *y* directions at the same time. To calculate the current velocity and compare it to a maximum velocity, we must use a bit more math.

First, let's assume that we will add a maximum velocity variable to our game:

```
    var maxVelocity = 2;
```

Next, we must make sure to calculate and compare the maxVelocity to the current velocity *before* we calculate the new movingX and movingY values. We will do this with local variables used to store the new values for movingX and movingY before they are applied:

```
    var movingXNew = movingX+thrustAcceleration*facingX;
    var movingYNew = movingY+thrustAcceleration*facingY;
```

The current velocity of our ship is the square root of movingXNew^2 + movingYNew^2:

```
var currentVelocity = Math.sqrt ((movingXNew*movingXNew) + (movingXNew*movingXNew));
```

If the currentVelocity is less than the maxVelocity, we set the movingX and movingY values:

```
if (currentVelocity < maxVelocity) {
    movingX = movingXNew;
    movingY = movingYNew;
}
```

A Basic Game Framework

Now that we have gotten our feet wet (so to speak) by taking a peek at some of the graphics, transformations, and basic physics we will use in our game, let's look at how we will structure a simple framework for all games we might want to create on HTML5 Canvas. We will begin by creating a simple state machine using constant variables. Next, we will introduce our game timer interval function to this structure, and finally, we will create a simple reusable object that will display the current frame rate our game is running in. Let's get started.

The Game State Machine

A state machine is a programming construct that allows for our game to be in only a single application state at any one time. We will create a state machine for our game, called *application state*, which will include seven basic states (we will use constants to refer to these states):

- GAME_STATE_TITLE
- GAME_STATE_NEW_GAME
- GAME_STATE_NEW_LEVEL
- GAME_STATE_PLAYER_START
- GAME_STATE_PLAY_LEVEL
- GAME_STATE_PLAYER_DIE
- GAME_STATE_GAME_OVER

We will create a function object for each state that will contain game logic necessary for the state to function and to change to a new state when appropriate. By doing this, we can use the same structure for each game we create by simply changing out the content of each *state function* (as we will refer to them).

Let's take a look at a very basic version of this in action. We will use a function reference variable called currentGameStateFunction, as well as an integer variable called current GameState that will hold the current application state constant value:

```
var currentGameState = 0;
var currentGameStateFunction = null;
```

We will create a function called `switchAppState()` that will be called only when we want to switch to a new state:

```
function switchGameState(newState) {
    currentGameState = newState;
    switch (currentState) {

        case GAME_STATE_TITLE:
            currentGameStateFunction = gameStateTitle;
            break;

        case GAME_STATE_PLAY_LEVEL:
            currentGameStateFunctionappStatePlayeLevel;
            break;

        case GAME_STATE_GAME_OVER:
            currentGameStateFunction = gameStateGameOver;
            break;

    }

}
```

We will call the `runGame()` function repeatedly in the `setInterval()` method. `run Game()` will call the `currentGameStateFunction` reference variable on each frame tick. This allows us to easily change the function called by `runGame()` based on changes in the application state:

```
setInterval(runGame, intervalTime );

function runGame(){
    currentGameStateFunction();
}
```

Let's look at the complete code. We will create some shell functions for the various application state functions. Before the application starts, we will call the `switchGame State()` function, and pass in the constant value for the new function we want as the `currentGameStateFunction`:

```
//*** application start
    switchGameState(GAME_STATE_TITLE);
```

In Example 8-9, we will use the `GAME_STATE_TITLE` state to draw a simple title screen that will be redrawn on each frame tick.

Example 8-9. The tile screen state

```
<script type="text/javascript">
window.addEventListener('load', eventWindowLoaded, false);
function eventWindowLoaded() {

    canvasApp();
```

```
}

    function canvasApp(){

    var theCanvas = document.getElementById("canvas");
    if (!theCanvas || !theCanvas.getContext) {
       return;
    }

    var context = theCanvas.getContext("2d");

    if (!context) {
       return;
    }

    //application states

    const GAME_STATE_TITLE = 0;
    const GAME_STATE_NEW_LEVEL = 1;
    const GAME_STATE_GAME_OVER = 2;

    var currentGameState = 0;
    var currentGameStateFunction = null;

    function switchGameState(newState) {
       currentGameState = newState;
       switch (currentGameState) {

          case GAME_STATE_TITLE:
              currentGameStateFunction = gameStateTitle;
              break;

          case GAME_STATE_PLAY_LEVEL:
              currentGameStateFunctionappStatePlayeLevel;
              break;

          case GAME_STATE_GAME_OVER:
              currentGameStateFunction = gameStateGameOver;
              break;

       }

    }

    function gameStateTitle() {
       ConsoleLog.log("appStateTitle");
       // draw background and text
       context.fillStyle = '#000000';
          context.fillRect(0, 0, 200, 200);
       context.fillStyle = '#ffffff';
       context.font = '20px _sans';
       context.textBaseline = 'top';
       context.fillText  ("Title Screen", 50, 90);
```

```
    }

    function gameStatePlayLevel() {
        ConsoleLog.log("appStateGamePlay");
    }

    function gameStateGameOver() {
        ConsoleLog.log("appStateGameOver");
    }

    function runGame(){
        currentGameStateFunction();
    }

    //*** application start
    switchGameState(GAME_STATE_TITLE);

    //**** application loop
    const FRAME_RATE = 40;
    var intervalTime = 1000/FRAME_RATE;
    setInterval(runGame, intervalTime );

}

//***** object prototypes *****

//*** consoleLog util object
//create constructor
function ConsoleLog(){

}

//create function that will be added to the class
console_log = function(message) {
    if(typeof(console) !== 'undefined' && console != null) {
        console.log(message);
    }
}
//add class/static function to class by assignment
ConsoleLog.log = console_log;

//*** end console log object

</script>
```

 Example 8-9 added in the ConsoleLog object from the previous chapters. We will continue to use this utility to create helpful debug messages in the JavaScript log window of the browser.

We will continue to explore the application state machine, and then create one for our game logic states in the upcoming section, "Putting It All Together" on page 407.

The Update/Render (Repeat) Cycle

In any of our application states, we might need to employ animation and screen updates. We will handle these updates by separating our code into distinct update() and render() operations. For example, as you might recall, the player ship can move around the game screen, and when the player presses the up arrow key, the ship's thrust frame of animation will be displayed rather than its static frame. In the previous examples, we contained all the code that updates the properties of the ship, as well as the code that actually draws the ship, in a single function called drawScreen(). Starting with Example 8-10, we will rid ourselves of this simple drawScreen() function and instead employ update() and render() functions separately. We will also separate out the code that checks for the game-specific key presses into a checkKeys() function.

Let's reexamine the contents of the drawScreen() function from Example 8-8, but this time break the function up into separate functions for each set of tasks, as shown in Example 8-10.

Example 8-10. Splitting the update and render cycles

```
function gameStatePlayLevel() {
   checkKeys();
   update();
   render();
}

function checkKeys() {

   //check keys

   if (keyPressList[38]==true){
      //thrust
      var angleInRadians = rotation * Math.PI / 180;
      facingX = Math.cos(angleInRadians);
      facingY = Math.sin(angleInRadians);

      movingX = movingX+thrustAcceleration*facingX;
      movingY = movingY+thrustAcceleration*facingY;

   }

   if (keyPressList[37]==true) {
      //rotate counterclockwise
      rotation-=rotationalVelocity;
   }

   if (keyPressList[39]==true) {
      //rotate clockwise
      rotation+=rotationalVelocity;;
   }
}

function update() {
```

```
        x = x+movingX;
        y = y+movingY;
}

function render() {
    //draw background and text
    context.fillStyle = '#000000';
    context.fillRect(0, 0, 200, 200);
    context.fillStyle = '#ffffff';
    context.font = '20px _sans';
    context.textBaseline = 'top';
    context.fillText  ("render/update", 0, 180);

    //transformation
    var angleInRadians = rotation * Math.PI / 180;
    context.save(); //save current state in stack
    context.setTransform(1,0,0,1,0,0); // reset to identity

    //translate the canvas origin to the center of the player
    context.translate(x+.5*width,y+.5*height);
    context.rotate(angleInRadians);

    //drawShip

    context.strokeStyle = '#ffffff';
    context.beginPath();

    //hardcoding in locations
    //facing right
    context.moveTo(-10,-10);
    context.lineTo(10,0);
    context.moveTo(10,1);
    context.lineTo(-10,10);
    context.lineTo(1,1);
    context.moveTo(1,-1);
    context.lineTo(-10,-10);

    context.stroke();
    context.closePath();

    //restore context
    context.restore(); //pop old state on to screen
}

const FRAME_RATE = 40;
var intervalTime = 1000/FRAME_RATE;
setInterval(appStateGamePlay, intervalTime );
```

We left out the entire application state machine from Example 8-9 to save space. In Example 8-10, we are simply showing what the gameStatePlayLevel() function might look like.

In the section "Putting It All Together" on page 407, we will go into this in greater detail as we start to build out the entire application.

The FrameRateCounter Object Prototype

Arcade games such as *Asteroids* and *Geo Blaster Basic* rely on fast processing and screen updates to ensure all game-object rendering and game-play logic are delivered to the player at a reliable rate. One way to tell whether your game is performing up to par is to employ the use of a frame rate per second (FPS) counter. Below is a simple one that can be reused in any game you create on the canvas:

```
//*** FrameRateCounter  object prototype
function FrameRateCounter() {

    this.lastFrameCount = 0;
    var dateTemp = new Date();
    this.frameLast = dateTemp.getTime();
    delete dateTemp;
    this.frameCtr = 0;
}

FrameRateCounter.prototype.countFrames=function() {
    var dateTemp = new Date();
    this.frameCtr++;

    if (dateTemp.getTime() >=this.frameLast+1000) {
        ConsoleLog.log("frame event");
        this.lastFrameCount = this.frameCtr;
        this.frameLast = dateTemp.getTime();
        this.frameCtr = 0;
    }

    delete dateTemp;
}
```

Our game will create an instance of this object and call the `countFrames()` function on each frame tick in our `update()` function. We will write out the current frame rate in our `render()` function.

Example 8-11 shows these functions by adding code to Example 8-10. Make sure you add the definition of the `FrameRateCounter` prototype object to the code in Example 8-10 under the `canvasApp()` function but before the final `<script>` tag. Alternatively, you can place it in its own `<script\>` tags, or in a separate *.js* file and set the URL as the `src=` value of a `<script>` tag. For simplicity's sake, we will keep all our code in a single file.

Example 8-11 contains the definition for our `FrameRateCounter` object prototype, as well as the code changes to Example 8-10 that are necessary to implement it.

Example 8-11. The FrameRateCounter is added

```
function update() {
    x = x+movingX;
    y = y+movingY;
    frameRateCounter.countFrames();
}
```

```
function render() {
    // draw background and text
    context.fillStyle = '#000000';
    context.fillRect(0, 0, 200, 200);
    context.fillStyle = '#ffffff';
    context.font = '20px _sans';
    context.textBaseline = 'top';
    context.fillText ("FPS:" + frameRateCounter.lastFrameCount, 0, 180);

    //...Leave everything else from Example 8-10 intact here
}

frameRateCounter = new FrameRateCounter();
const FRAME_RATE = 40;
var intervalTime = 1000/FRAME_RATE;
setInterval(runGame, intervalTime );
```

Putting It All Together

We are now ready to start coding our game. First, we will look at the structure of the game and some of the ideas behind the various algorithms we will employ to create it. After that, we will present the full source code for *Geo Blaster Basic*.

Geo Blaster Game Structure

The structure of the game application is very similar to the structure we started to build earlier in this chapter. Let's take a closer look at the state functions and how they will work together.

Game application states

Our game will have seven distinct game application states. We will store these in constants:

```
const GAME_STATE_TITLE = 0;
const GAME_STATE_NEW_GAME = 1;
const GAME_STATE_NEW_LEVEL = 2;
const GAME_STATE_PLAYER_START = 3;
const GAME_STATE_PLAY_LEVEL = 4;
const GAME_STATE_PLAYER_DIE = 5;
const GAME_STATE_GAME_OVER = 6;
```

Game application state functions

Each individual state will have an associated function that will be called on each frame tick. Let's look at the functionality for each:

`gameStateTitle()`

Displays the title screen text and waits for the space bar to be pressed before the game starts.

`gameStateNewGame()`

Sets up all the defaults for a new game. All of the arrays for holding display objects are reinitialized—the game `level` is reset to 0, and the game `score` is set to 0.

`gameStateNewLevel()`

Increases the `level` value by one, and then sets the "game knob" values to control the level difficulty. See the upcoming section "Level Knobs" on page 415 for details.

`gameStatePlayerStart()`

Fades the player graphic onto the screen from 0 alpha to 1. Once this is complete, level play will start.

`gameStatePlayLevel()`

Controls the play of the game level. It calls the `update()` and `render()` functions, as well as the functions for evaluating keyboard input for player ship control.

`gameStatePlayerDie()`

Starts up an explosion at the location where the player ship was when it was hit by a rock, saucer, or saucer missile. Once the explosion is complete (all particles in the explosion have exhausted their individual life values), it sets the move to the `GAME_STATE_PLAYER_START` state.

`gameStateGameOver()`

Displays the "Game Over" screen, and starts a new game when the space bar is pressed.

Game application functions

Aside from the game application state functions, there are a number of functions we need for the game to run. Each state function will call these functions as needed:

`resetPlayer()`

Resets the player to the center of the game screen and readies it for game play.

`checkForExtraShip()`

Checks to see whether the player should be awarded an extra ship. See the section "Awarding the Player Extra Ships" on page 416 for details on this algorithm.

`checkForEndOfLevel()`

Checks to see whether all the rocks have been destroyed on a given level and, if so, starts up a new level. See the section "Level and Game End" on page 415 for details on this algorithm.

`fillBackground()`

Fills the canvas with the background color on each frame tick.

setTextStyle()

Sets the base text style before text is written to the game screen.

renderScoreBoard()

Is called on each frame tick. It displays the updated score, number of ships remaining, and the current FPS for the game.

checkKeys()

Checks the keyPressList array, and then modifies the player ship attributes based on the values found to be true.

update()

Is called from GAME_STATE_PLAY_LEVEL. It in turn calls the update() function for each individual display object array.

Individual display object update() functions

The unique functions listed below update each different type of display object. These functions (with the exception of updatePlayer()) will loop through the respective array of objects associated with its type of display object, and update the x and y values with dx and dy values. The updateSaucer() function contains the logic necessary to check whether to create a new saucer, and whether any current saucers on the screen should fire a missile at the player.

- updatePlayer()
- updatePlayerMissiles()
- updateRocks()
- updateSaucers()
- updateSaucerMissiles()
- updateParticles()

render()

Is called from GAME_STATE_PLAY_LEVEL. It in turn calls the render() function for each individual display object array.

Individual display object render() functions

Like the update() functions, the unique functions listed below render each different type of display object. Again, with the exception of the render Player() object (because there is only a single player ship), each of these functions will loop through the array of objects associated with its type and draw them to the game screen. As we saw when drawing the player ship earlier in this chapter, we will draw each object by moving and translating the canvas to the point at which we want to draw our logical object. We will then transform our object (if necessary) and paint the paths to the game screen.

- renderPlayer()
- renderPlayerMissiles()
- renderRocks()

- renderSaucers()
- renderSaucerMissiles()
- renderParticles()

checkCollisions()

Loops through the individual game display objects and checks them for collisions. See the section "Applying Collision Detection" on page 417 for a detailed discussion of this topic.

firePlayerMissile()

Creates a playerMissile object at the center of the player ship and fires it in the direction the player ship is facing.

fireSaucerMissile()

Creates a saucerMissile object at the center of the saucer and fires it in the direction of the player ship.

playerDie()

Creates an explosion for the player by calling createExplode(), as well as changing the game application state to GAME_STATE_PLAYER_DIE.

createExplode()

Accepts in the location for the explosion to start and the number of particles for the explosion.

boundingBoxCollide()

Determines whether the rectangular box that encompasses an object's width and height is overlapping the bounding box of another object. It takes in two logical display objects as parameters, and returns true if they are overlapping and false if they are not. See the section "Applying Collision Detection" on page 417 for details on this function.

splitRock()

Accepts in the scale and x and y starting points for two new rocks that will be created if a large or medium rock is destroyed.

addToScore()

Accepts in a value to add to the player's score.

Geo Blaster Global Game Variables

Now let's look at the entire set of game application scope variables needed for our game.

Variables that control screen flow

These variables will be used when the title and "Game Over" screens first appear. They will be set to true once the screen is drawn. When these variables are true, the screens will look for the space bar to be pressed before moving on to the next application state:

```
var titleStarted = false;
var gameOverStarted = false;
```

Game environment variables

These variables set up the necessary defaults for a new game. We will discuss the extraShipAtEach and extraShipsEarned in the section, "Awarding the Player Extra Ships" on page 416:

```
var score = 0;
var level = 0;
var extraShipAtEach = 10000;
var extraShipsEarned = 0;
var playerShips = 3;
```

Playfield variables

These variables set up the maximum and minimum x and y coordinates for the game stage:

```
var xMin = 0;
var xMax = 400;
var yMin = 0;
var yMax = 400;
```

Score value variables

These variables set the score value for each of the objects the player can destroy:

```
var bigRockScore = 50;
var medRockScore = 75;
var smlRockScore = 100;
var saucerScore = 300;
```

Rock size constants

These variables set up some human-readable values for the three rock sizes, allowing us to simply use the constant instead of a literal value. We can then change the literal value if needed:

```
const ROCK_SCALE_LARGE = 1;
const ROCK_SCALE_MEDIUM = 2;
const ROCK_SCALE_SMALL = 3;
```

Logical display objects

These variables set up the single player object and arrays to hold the various other logical display objects for our game. See the upcoming sections "The player Object" and "Arrays of Logical Display Objects" on page 412 for further details on each:

```
var player = {};
var rocks = [];
var saucers = [];
var playerMissiles = [];
var particles = []
var saucerMissiles = [];
```

Level-specific variables

The level-specific variables handle the difficulty settings when the game level increases. See the section "Level Knobs" on page 415 for more details on how these are used:

```
var levelRockMaxSpeedAdjust = 1;
var levelSaucerMax = 1;
var levelSaucerOccurrenceRate = 25
var levelSaucerSpeed = 1;
var levelSaucerFireDelay = 300;
var levelSaucerFireRate = 30;
var levelSaucerMissileSpeed = 1;
```

The player Object

The `player` object contains many of the variables we encountered earlier in this chapter when we discussed animating, rotating, and moving the player ship about the game screen. We have also added in three new variables that you have not seen before:

```
player.maxVelocity = 5;
player.width = 20;
player.height = 20;
player.halfWidth = 10;
player.halfHeight = 10;
player.rotationalVelocity = 5
player.thrustAcceleration = .05;
player.missileFrameDelay = 5;
player.thrust = false;
```

The new variables are `halfWidth`, `halfHeight`, and `missileFrameDelay`. `halfWidth` and `halfHeight` simply store half the width and half the height values, so these need not be calculated on each frame tick in multiple locations inside the code. The `missileFrame Delay` variable contains the number of frame ticks the game will count between firing player missiles. This way, the player cannot simply fire a steady stream of ordnance and destroy everything with little difficulty.

The `player.thrust` variable will be set to `true` when the player presses the up key.

Geo Blaster Game Algorithms

The game source code covers a lot of ground that we did not touch on earlier in this chapter. Let's discuss some of those topics now; the rest will be covered in detail in Chapter 9.

Arrays of Logical Display Objects

We have used arrays to hold all our logical display objects, and we have an array for each type of object (`rocks`, `saucers`, `playerMissiles`, `saucerMissiles`, and `particles`).

Each logical display object is a simple object instance. We have created a separate function to draw and update each of our objects.

 The use of an object class prototype similar to `FrameRateCounter` can be implemented easily for the various display object types. To conserve space, we have not implemented them in this game. However, these objects would allow us to separate the update and draw code from the current common functions, and then place that code into the individual object prototypes. We have included a Rock prototype at the end of this chapter as an example (see Example 8-13).

You will notice that saucers and rocks are drawn with points in the same manner as the player ship.

Rocks

The rocks will be simple squares that rotate clockwise or counterclockwise. The rock instances will be in the `rocks` array. When a new level starts, these will all be created in the upper-right corner of the game screen.

Here are the variable attributes of a `rock` object:

```
newRock.scale = 1;
newRock.width = 50;
newRock.height = 50;
newRock.halfWidth = 25;
newRock.halfHeight = 25;
newRock.x
newRock.y
newRock.dx
newRock.dy
newRock.scoreValue = bigRockScore;
newRock.rotation = 0;
```

The rock scale will be set to one of the three rock-scale constants discussed earlier. `halfWidth` and `halfHeight` will be set based on the scale, and they will be used in calculations in the same manner as the player object versions. The `dx` and `dy` values represent the values to apply to the x and y axes when updating the rock on each frame tick.

Saucers

Unlike Atari's *Asteroids* game, which has both small and large saucers, we are only going to have one size in *Geo Blaster Basic*. It will be stored in the `saucers` array. On a 28×13 grid (using paths), it looks like Figure 8-6.

Figure 8-6. The saucer design

The variable attributes of the saucer object are very similar to the attributes of a rock object, although without the rock scale attribute. Also, saucers don't have a rotation; it is always set at 0. The saucer also contains variables that are updated on each new level to make the game more challenging for the player. Here are those variables, which will be discussed in more detail in the upcoming section "Level Knobs":

```
newSaucer.fireRate = levelSaucerFireRate;
newSaucer.fireDelay = levelSaucerFireDelay;
newSaucer.fireDelayCount = 0;
newSaucer.missileSpeed = levelSaucerMissileSpeed;
```

Missiles

Both the player missiles and saucer missiles will be 2×2-pixel blocks. They will be stored in the playerMissiles and saucerMissiles arrays, respectively.

The objects are very simple. They contain enough attributes to move them across the game screen and to calculate life values:

```
newPlayerMissile.dx = 5*Math.cos(Math.PI*(player.rotation)/180);
newPlayerMissile.dy = 5*Math.sin(Math.PI*(player.rotation)/180);
newPlayerMissile.x = player.x+player.halfWidth;
newPlayerMissile.y = player.y+player.halfHeight;
newPlayerMissile.life = 60;
newPlayerMissile.lifeCtr = 0;
newPlayerMissile.width = 2;
newPlayerMissile.height = 2;
```

Explosions and particles

When a rock, saucer, or the player ship is destroyed, that object explodes into a series of particles. The createExplode() function creates this so-called particle explosion. Particles are simply individual logical display objects with their own life, dx, and dy values. Randomly generating these values makes each explosion appear to be unique. Particles will be stored in the particles array.

Like missiles, particle objects are rather simple. They also contain enough information to move them across the screen and to calculate their life span in frame ticks:

```
newParticle.dx = Math.random()*3;
newParticle.dy = Math.random()*3;
newParticle.life = Math.floor(Math.random()*30+30);
```

```
newParticle.lifeCtr = 0;
newParticle.x = x;
newParticle.y = y;
```

Level Knobs

Even though we never show the level number to the game player, we are adjusting the difficulty every time a screen of rocks is cleared. We do this by increasing the level variable by 1 and then recalculating these values before the level begins. We refer to the variance in level difficulty as *knobs*, which refers to dials or switches. Here are the variables we will use for these knobs:

level+3
> Number of rocks

levelRockMaxSpeedAdjust = level*.25;
> Rock max speed

levelSaucerMax = 1+Math.floor(level/10);
> Number of simultaneous saucers

levelSaucerOccurrenceRate = 10+3*level;
> Percent chance a saucer will appear

levelSaucerSpeed = 1+.5*level;
> Saucer speed

levelSaucerFireDelay = 120-10*level;
> Delay between saucer missiles

levelSaucerFireRate = 20+3*level;
> Percent chance a saucer will fire at the player

levelSaucerMissileSpeed = 1+.2*level;
> Speed of saucer missiles

Level and Game End

We need to check for game and level end so we can transition to either a new game or to the next level.

Level end

We will check for level end on each frame tick. The function to do so will look like this:

```
function checkForEndOfLevel(){
    if (rocks.length==0) {
        switchGameState(GAME_STATE_NEW_LEVEL);
    }
}
```

Once the rocks array length is 0, we switch the state to GAME_STATE_NEW_LEVEL.

Game end

We do not need to check for the end of the game on each frame tick. We only need to check when the player loses a ship. We do this inside the gameStatePlayerDie() function:

```
function gameStatePlayerDie(){
    if (particles.length >0 || playerMissiles.length>0) {
        fillBackground();
        renderScoreBoard();
        updateRocks();
        updateSaucers();
        updateParticles();
        updateSaucerMissiles();
        updatePlayerMissiles();
        renderRocks();
        renderSaucers();
        renderParticles();
        renderSaucerMissiles();
        renderPlayerMissiles();
        frameRateCounter.countFrames();

    }else{
        playerShips--;
        if (playerShips<1) {
            switchGameState(GAME_STATE_GAME_OVER);
        }else{
            resetPlayer();
            switchGameState(GAME_STATE_PLAYER_START);
        }
    }
}
```

This is the state function that is called on each frame tick during the GAME_STATE_PLAYER_DIE state. First, it checks to see that there are no longer any particles on the screen. This ensures that the game will not end until the player ship has finished exploding. We also check to make sure that all the player's missiles have finished their lives. We do this so we can check for collisions between the playerMissiles, and for rocks against saucers. This way the player might earn an extra ship before player Ships-- is called.

Once the particles and missiles have all left the game screen, we subtract 1 from the playerShips variable and then switch to GAME_STATE_GAME_OVER if the playerShips number is less than 1.

Awarding the Player Extra Ships

We want to award the player extra ships at regular intervals based on her score. We do this by setting an amount of points that the game player must achieve to earn a new ship—this also helps us keep a count of the number of ships earned:

```
function checkForExtraShip() {
    if (Math.floor(score/extraShipAtEach) > extraShipsEarned) {
        playerShips++
        extraShipsEarned++;
    }
}
```

We call this function on each frame tick. The player earns an extra ship if the score/ extraShipAtEach variable (with the decimals stripped off) is greater than the number of ships earned. In our game, we have set the extraShipAtEach value to 10000. When the game starts, extraShipsEarned is 0. When the player's score is 10000 or more, score/ extraShipAtEach will equal 1, which is greater than the extraShipsEarned value of 0. An extra ship is given to the player, and the extraShipsEarned value is increased by 1.

Applying Collision Detection

We will be checking the bounding box around each object when we do our collision detection. A bounding box is the smallest rectangle that will encompass all four corners of a game logic object. We have created a function for this purpose:

```
function boundingBoxCollide(object1, object2) {

    var left1 = object1.x;
    var left2 = object2.x;
    var right1 = object1.x + object1.width;
    var right2 = object2.x + object2.width;
    var top1 = object1.y;
    var top2 = object2.y;
    var bottom1 = object1.y + object1.height;
    var bottom2 = object2.y + object2.height;

    if (bottom1 < top2) return(false);
    if (top1 > bottom2) return(false);

    if (right1 < left2) return(false);
    if (left1 > right2) return(false);

    return(true);

};
```

We can pass any two of our game objects into this function as long as each contains x, y, width, and height attributes. If the two objects are overlapping, the function will return true. If not, it will return false.

The checkCollision() function for *Geo Blaster Basic* is quite involved. The full code listing is given in Example 8-12. Rather than reprint it here, let's examine some of the basic concepts.

One thing you will notice is the use of "labels" next to the for loop constructs. Using labels such as in the following line can help streamline collision detection:

```
rocks: for (var rockCtr=rocksLength;rockCtr>=0;rockCtr--){
```

We will need to loop through each of the various object types that must be checked against one another. But we do not want to check an object that was previously destroyed against other objects. To ensure we do the fewest amount of collision checks necessary, we have implemented a routine that employs label and break statements.

Here is the logic behind the routine:

1. Create a rocks: label and then start to loop through the rocks array.

2. Create a missiles: label inside the rocks iteration, and loop through the player Missiles array.

3. Do a bounding box collision detection between the last rock and the last missile. Notice that we loop starting at the end of each array so that we can remove elements (when collisions occur) in the array without affecting array members that have not been checked yet.

4. If a rock and a missile collide, remove them from their respective arrays, and then call break rocks and then break missiles. We must break back to the next element in an array for any object type that is removed.

5. Continue looping through the missiles until they have all been checked against the current rock (unless break rocks was fired off for a rock/missile collision).

6. Check each saucer, each saucer missile, and the player against each of the rocks. The player does not need a label because there is only a single instance of the player. The saucers and saucerMissiles will follow the same logic as missiles. If there is a collision between one and a rock, break back to their respective labels after removing the objects from their respective arrays.

7. Once we have checked the rocks against all the other game objects, check the playerMissiles against the saucers using the same basic logic of loop labels, looping backward through the arrays, and breaking back to the labels once objects are removed.

8. Check the saucerMissiles against the player in the same manner.

Over the years, we have found this to be a powerful way to check multiple objects' arrays against one another. It certainly is not the only way to do so. If you are not comfortable using loop labels, you can employ a method such as the following:

1. Add a Boolean hit attribute to each object and set it to false when an object is created.

2. Loop through the rocks and check them against the other game objects. This time the direction (forward or backward) through the loops does not matter.

3. Before calling the boundingBoxCollide() function, be sure that each object's hit attribute is false. If not, skip the collision check.

4. If the two objects collide, set each object's hit attribute to true. There is no need to remove objects from the arrays at this time.

5. Loop though `playerMissiles` and check against the `saucers`, and then loop through the `saucers` to check against the `player`.

6. When all the collision-detection routines are complete, reloop through each object array (backward this time) and remove all the objects with `true` as a `hit` attribute.

We have used both methods—and variations—on each. While the second method is a little cleaner, this final loop through all of the objects might add more processor overhead when dealing with a large number of objects. We will leave the implementation of this second method to you as an exercise, in case you wish to test it.

The Geo Blaster Basic Full Source

Example 8-12 shows the entire set of code for our game. You can download this and the entire set of example files from the book's website.

Example 8-12. The Geo Blaster Basic full source listing

```
<!doctype html>
<html lang="en">
<head>
<meta charset="UTF-8">
<title>Geo Blaster Basic Game</title>
<script type="text/javascript">
window.addEventListener('load', eventWindowLoaded, false);
function eventWindowLoaded() {
        canvasApp();
}

function canvasApp(){
    var theCanvas = document.getElementById("canvas");
    if (!theCanvas || !theCanvas.getContext) {
        return;
    }

    var context = theCanvas.getContext("2d");

    if (!context) {
        return;
    }

    //application states
    const GAME_STATE_TITLE = 0;
    const GAME_STATE_NEW_GAME = 1;
    const GAME_STATE_NEW_LEVEL = 2;
    const GAME_STATE_PLAYER_START = 3;
    const GAME_STATE_PLAY_LEVEL = 4;
    const GAME_STATE_PLAYER_DIE = 5;
    const GAME_STATE_GAME_OVER = 6;
    var currentGameState = 0;
    var currentGameStateFunction = null;
```

```
//title screen
var titleStarted = false;

//gameover screen
var gameOverStarted = false;

//objects for game play

//game environment
var score = 0;
var level = 0;
var extraShipAtEach = 10000;
var extraShipsEarned = 0;
var playerShips = 3;

//playfield
var xMin = 0;
var xMax = 400;
var yMin = 0;
var yMax = 400;

//score values
var bigRockScore = 50;
var medRockScore = 75;
var smlRockScore = 100;
var saucerScore = 300;

//rock scale constants
const ROCK_SCALE_LARGE = 1;
const ROCK_SCALE_MEDIUM = 2;
const ROCK_SCALE_SMALL = 3;

//create game objects and arrays
var player = {};
var rocks = [];
var saucers = [];
var playerMissiles = [];
var particles = []
var saucerMissiles = [];

//level specific
var levelRockMaxSpeedAdjust = 1;
var levelSaucerMax = 1;
var levelSaucerOccurrenceRate = 25;
var levelSaucerSpeed = 1;
var levelSaucerFireDelay = 300;
var levelSaucerFireRate = 30;
var levelSaucerMissileSpeed = 1;

//keyPresses
var keyPressList = [];

function runGame(){
    currentGameStateFunction();
}
```

```
function switchGameState(newState) {
    currentGameState = newState;
    switch (currentGameState) {

        case GAME_STATE_TITLE:
            currentGameStateFunction = gameStateTitle;
            break;
        case GAME_STATE_NEW_GAME:
            currentGameStateFunction = gameStateNewGame;
            break;
        case GAME_STATE_NEW_LEVEL:
            currentGameStateFunction = gameStateNewLevel;
            break;
        case GAME_STATE_PLAYER_START:
            currentGameStateFunction = gameStatePlayerStart;
            break;
        case GAME_STATE_PLAY_LEVEL:
            currentGameStateFunction = gameStatePlayLevel;
            break;
        case GAME_STATE_PLAYER_DIE:
            currentGameStateFunction = gameStatePlayerDie;
            break;

        case GAME_STATE_GAME_OVER:
            currentGameStateFunction = gameStateGameOver;
            break;

    }

}

function gameStateTitle() {
    if (titleStarted !=true){
        fillBackground();
        setTextStyle();
        context.fillText  ("Geo Blaster Basic", 130, 70);
        context.fillText  ("Press Space To Play", 120, 140);

        titleStarted = true;
    }else{
        //wait for space key click
        if (keyPressList[32]==true){
            ConsoleLog.log("space pressed");
            switchGameState(GAME_STATE_NEW_GAME);
            titleStarted = false;

        }
    }
}

function gameStateNewGame(){
    ConsoleLog.log("gameStateNewGame")
    //set up new game
    level = 0;
```

```
    score = 0;
    playerShips = 3;
    player.maxVelocity = 5;
    player.width = 20;
    player.height = 20;
    player.halfWidth = 10;
    player.halfHeight = 10;
    player.rotationalVelocity = 5; //how many degrees to turn the ship
    player.thrustAcceleration = .05;
    player.missileFrameDelay = 5;
    player.thrust = false;

    fillBackground();
    renderScoreBoard();
    switchGameState(GAME_STATE_NEW_LEVEL)

}

function gameStateNewLevel(){
    rocks = [];
    saucers = [];
    playerMissiles = [];
    particles = [];
    saucerMissiles = [];
    level++;
    levelRockMaxSpeedAdjust = level*.25;
    if (levelRockMaxSpeedAdjust > 3){
        levelRockMaxSpeed = 3;
    }

    levelSaucerMax = 1+Math.floor(level/10);
    if (levelSaucerMax > 5){
        levelSaucerMax = 5;
    }
    levelSaucerOccurrenceRate = 10+3*level;
    if (levelSaucerOccurrenceRate > 35){
        levelSaucerOccurrenceRate = 35;
    }
    levelSaucerSpeed = 1+.5*level;
    if (levelSaucerSpeed>5){
        levelSaucerSpeed = 5;
    }
    levelSaucerFireDelay = 120-10*level;
    if (levelSaucerFireDelay<20) {
        levelSaucerFireDelay = 20;
    }

    levelSaucerFireRate = 20 + 3*level;
    if (levelSaucerFireRate<50) {
        levelSaucerFireRate = 50;
    }

    levelSaucerMissileSpeed = 1+.2*level;
    if (levelSaucerMissileSpeed > 4){
        levelSaucerMissileSpeed = 4;
```

```
    }
    //create level rocks
    for (var newRockctr=0;newRockctr<level+3;newRockctr++){
       var newRock={};

       newRock.scale = 1;
       //scale
       //1 = large
       //2 = medium
       //3 = small
       //these will be used as the divisor for the new size
       //50/1 = 50
       //50/2 = 25
       //50/3 = 16
       newRock.width = 50;
       newRock.height = 50;
       newRock.halfWidth = 25;
       newRock.halfHeight = 25;

       //start all new rocks in upper left for ship safety
       newRock.x = Math.floor(Math.random()*50);

       //ConsoleLog.log("newRock.x=" + newRock.x);
       newRock.y = Math.floor(Math.random()*50);

       //ConsoleLog.log("newRock.y=" + newRock.y);
       newRock.dx = (Math.random()*2)+levelRockMaxSpeedAdjust;
       if (Math.random()<.5){
          newRock.dx*=-1;
       }

       newRock.dy = (Math.random()*2)+levelRockMaxSpeedAdjust;
       if (Math.random()<.5){
          newRock.dy*=-1;
       }

       //rotation speed and direction
       newRock.rotationInc = (Math.random()*5)+1;

       if (Math.random()<.5){
          newRock.rotationInc*=-1;
       }

       newRock.scoreValue = bigRockScore;
       newRock.rotation = 0;

       rocks.push(newRock);
       //ConsoleLog.log("rock created rotationInc=" + newRock.rotationInc);
    }
    resetPlayer();
    switchGameState(GAME_STATE_PLAYER_START);

}
```

```
function gameStatePlayerStart(){
   fillBackground();
   renderScoreBoard();
   if (player.alpha < 1){
      player.alpha += .02;
      context.globalAlpha = player.alpha;
   }else{
      switchGameState(GAME_STATE_PLAY_LEVEL);
   }

   renderPlayerShip(player.x, player.y,270,1);
   context.globalAlpha = 1;
   updateRocks();
   renderRocks();
}

function gameStatePlayLevel(){
   checkKeys();
   update();
   render();
   checkCollisions();
   checkForExtraShip();
   checkForEndOfLevel();
   frameRateCounter.countFrames();
}

function resetPlayer() {
   player.rotation = 270;
   player.x = .5*xMax;
   player.y = .5*yMax;
   player.facingX = 0;
   player.facingY = 0;
   player.movingX = 0;
   player.movingY = 0;
   player.alpha = 0;
   player.missileFrameCount = 0;
}

function checkForExtraShip() {
   if (Math.floor(score/extraShipAtEach) > extraShipsEarned) {
      playerShips++
      extraShipsEarned++;
   }
}

function checkForEndOfLevel(){
   if (rocks.length==0) {
      switchGameState(GAME_STATE_NEW_LEVEL);
   }
}

function gameStatePlayerDie(){
   if (particles.length >0 || playerMissiles.length>0) {
      fillBackground();
      renderScoreBoard();
```

```
            updateRocks();
            updateSaucers();
            updateParticles();
            updateSaucerMissiles();
            updatePlayerMissiles();
            renderRocks();
            renderSaucers();
            renderParticles();
            renderSaucerMissiles();
            renderPlayerMissiles();
            frameRateCounter.countFrames();

        }else{
            playerShips--;
            if (playerShips<1) {
                switchGameState(GAME_STATE_GAME_OVER);
            }else{
                resetPlayer();
                switchGameState(GAME_STATE_PLAYER_START);
            }
        }
    }
}

function gameStateGameOver() {
    //ConsoleLog.log("Game Over State");
    if (gameOverStarted !=true){
        fillBackground();
        renderScoreBoard();
        setTextStyle();
        context.fillText  ("Game Over!", 150, 70);
        context.fillText  ("Press Space To Play", 120, 140);

        gameOverStarted = true;
    }else{
        //wait for space key click
        if (keyPressList[32]==true){
            ConsoleLog.log("space pressed");
            switchGameState(GAME_STATE_TITLE);
            gameOverStarted = false;

        }
    }
}

function fillBackground() {
    // draw background and text
    context.fillStyle = '#000000';
    context.fillRect(xMin, yMin, xMax, yMax);

}

function setTextStyle() {
    context.fillStyle = '#ffffff';
    context.font = '15px _sans';
    context.textBaseline = 'top';
```

```
}

function renderScoreBoard() {

   context.fillStyle = "#ffffff";
   context.fillText('Score ' + score, 10, 20);
   renderPlayerShip(200,16,270,.75)
   context.fillText('X ' + playerShips, 220, 20);

   context.fillText('FPS: ' + frameRateCounter.lastFrameCount, 300,20)

}

function checkKeys() {
   //check keys

   if (keyPressList[38]==true){
   //thrust
      var angleInRadians = player.rotation * Math.PI / 180;
      player.facingX = Math.cos(angleInRadians);
      player.facingY = Math.sin(angleInRadians);

      var movingXNew = player.movingX+player.thrustAcceleration*player.facingX;
      var movingYNew = player.movingY+player.thrustAcceleration*player.facingY;

      var currentVelocity = Math.sqrt ((movingXNew*movingXNew)
       + (movingXNew*movingXNew));

      if (currentVelocity < player.maxVelocity) {
         player.movingX = movingXNew;
         player.movingY = movingYNew;
      }
      player.thrust = true;


   }else{
      player.thrust = false;
   }

   if (keyPressList[37]==true) {
   //rotate counterclockwise
      player.rotation -= player.rotationalVelocity;

   }

   if (keyPressList[39]==true) {
   //rotate clockwise
      player.rotation += player.rotationalVelocity;;
   }

   if (keyPressList[32]==true) {
      //ConsoleLog.log("player.missileFrameCount=" + player.missileFrameCount);
      //ConsoleLog.log("player.missileFrameDelay=" + player.missileFrameDelay);
```

```
        if (player.missileFrameCount>player.missileFrameDelay){
            firePlayerMissile();
            player.missileFrameCount = 0;

        }
    }
}

function update() {
    updatePlayer();
    updatePlayerMissiles();
    updateRocks();
    updateSaucers();
    updateSaucerMissiles();
    updateParticles();
}

function render() {
    fillBackground();
    renderScoreBoard();
    renderPlayerShip(player.x,player.y,player.rotation,1);
    renderPlayerMissiles();
    renderRocks();
    renderSaucers();
    renderSaucerMissiles();
    renderParticles();
}

function updatePlayer() {
    player.missileFrameCount++;

    player.x += player.movingX;
    player.y += player.movingY;

    if (player.x > xMax) {
        player.x =- player.width;
    }else if (player.x<-player.width){
        player.x = xMax;
    }

    if (player.y > yMax) {
        player.y =- player.height;
    }else if (player.y<-player.height){
        player.y = yMax;
    }
}

function updatePlayerMissiles() {
    var tempPlayerMissile= {};
    var playerMissileLength = playerMissiles.length-1;
    //ConsoleLog.log("update playerMissileLength=" + playerMissileLength);

    for (var playerMissileCtr=playerMissileLength;
        playerMissileCtr>=0;playerMissileCtr--){
```

```
        //ConsoleLog.log("update player missile" + playerMissileCtr)
        tempPlayerMissile = playerMissiles[playerMissileCtr];
        tempPlayerMissile.x += tempPlayerMissile.dx;
        tempPlayerMissile.y += tempPlayerMissile.dy;
        if (tempPlayerMissile.x > xMax) {
            tempPlayerMissile.x =- tempPlayerMissile.width;
        }else if (tempPlayerMissile.x<-tempPlayerMissile.width){
            tempPlayerMissile.x = xMax;
        }

        if (tempPlayerMissile.y > yMax) {
            tempPlayerMissile.y =- tempPlayerMissile.height;
        }else if (tempPlayerMissile.y<-tempPlayerMissile.height){
            tempPlayerMissile.y = yMax;
        }

        tempPlayerMissile.lifeCtr++;
        if (tempPlayerMissile.lifeCtr > tempPlayerMissile.life){
            //ConsoleLog.log("removing player missile");
            playerMissiles.splice(playerMissileCtr,1)
            tempPlayerMissile = null;
        }
    }
  }
}

function updateRocks(){

    var tempRock = {};
    var rocksLength = rocks.length-1;
    //ConsoleLog.log("update rocks length=" + rocksLength);
    for (var rockCtr=rocksLength;rockCtr>=0;rockCtr--){
        tempRock = rocks[rockCtr]
        tempRock.x += tempRock.dx;
        tempRock.y += tempRock.dy;
        tempRock.rotation += tempRock.rotationInc;
        //ConsoleLog.log("rock rotationInc="+ tempRock.rotationInc)
        //ConsoleLog.log("rock rotation="+ tempRock.rotation)
        if (tempRock.x > xMax) {
            tempRock.x = xMin-tempRock.width;
        }else if (tempRock.x<xMin-tempRock.width){
            tempRock.x = xMax;
        }

        if (tempRock.y > yMax) {
            tempRock.y = yMin-tempRock.width;
        }else if (tempRock.y<yMin-tempRock.width){
            tempRock.y = yMax;
        }

        //ConsoleLog.log("update rock "+ rockCtr)
    }
}

function updateSaucers() {
    //first check to see if we want to add a saucer
```

```
if (saucers.length< levelSaucerMax){
    if (Math.floor(Math.random()*100)<=levelSaucerOccurrenceRate){
        //ConsoleLog.log("create saucer")
        var newSaucer = {};

        newSaucer.width = 28;
        newSaucer.height = 13;
        newSaucer.halfHeight = 6.5;
        newSaucer.halfWidth = 14;
        newSaucer.scoreValue = saucerScore;
        newSaucer.fireRate = levelSaucerFireRate;
        newSaucer.fireDelay = levelSaucerFireDelay;
        newSaucer.fireDelayCount = 0;
        newSaucer.missileSpeed = levelSaucerMissileSpeed;
        newSaucer.dy = (Math.random()*2);
        if (Math.floor(Math.random)*2==1){
            newSaucer.dy*=-1;
        }

        //choose betweeen left or right edge to start
        if (Math.floor(Math.random()*2)==1){
            //start on right and go left
            newSaucer.x = 450;
            newSaucer.dx=-1*levelSaucerSpeed;

        }else{
            //left to right
            newSaucer.x=-50;
            newSaucer.dx = levelSaucerSpeed;
        }

        newSaucer.missileSpeed = levelSaucerMissileSpeed;
        newSaucer.fireDelay = levelSaucerFireDelay;
        newSaucer.fireRate = levelSaucerFireRate;
        newSaucer.y = Math.floor(Math.random()*400);

        saucers.push(newSaucer);
    }

}

var tempSaucer = {};
var saucerLength = saucers.length-1;
//ConsoleLog.log("update rocks length=" + rocksLength);
for (var saucerCtr=saucerLength;saucerCtr>=0;saucerCtr--){
    tempSaucer = saucers[saucerCtr];

    //should saucer fire
    tempSaucer.fireDelayCount++;

    if (Math.floor(Math.random()*100) <=tempSaucer.fireRate
        && tempSaucer.fireDelayCount>tempSaucer.fireDelay ){
```

```
            fireSaucerMissile(tempSaucer)
            tempSaucer.fireDelayCount= 0;
        }

        var remove = false;
        tempSaucer.x += tempSaucer.dx;
        tempSaucer.y += tempSaucer.dy;

        //remove saucers on left and right edges
        if (tempSaucer.dx > 0 && tempSaucer.x >xMax){
            remove = true;
        }else if (tempSaucer.dx <0 &&tempSaucer.x<xMin-tempSaucer.width){
            remove = true;
        }

        //bounce saucers off over vertical edges
        if (tempSaucer.y > yMax || tempSaucer.y<yMin-tempSaucer.width) {
            tempSaucer.dy*=-1
        }

        if (remove==true) {
            //remove the saucer
            ConsoleLog.log("saucer removed")
            saucers.splice(saucerCtr,1);
            tempSaucer = null;
        }

    }
}

function updateSaucerMissiles() {
    var tempSaucerMissile = {};
    var saucerMissileLength = saucerMissiles.length-1;

    for (var saucerMissileCtr=saucerMissileLength;
        saucerMissileCtr>=0;saucerMissileCtr--){

        //ConsoleLog.log("update player missile" + playerMissileCtr)
        tempSaucerMissile = saucerMissiles[saucerMissileCtr];
        tempSaucerMissile.x += tempSaucerMissile.dx;
        tempSaucerMissile.y += tempSaucerMissile.dy;
        if (tempSaucerMissile.x > xMax) {
            tempSaucerMissile.x=-tempSaucerMissile.width;
        }else if (tempSaucerMissile.x<-tempSaucerMissile.width){
            tempSaucerMissile.x = xMax;
        }

        if (tempSaucerMissile.y > yMax) {
            tempSaucerMissile.y=-tempSaucerMissile.height;
        }else if (tempSaucerMissile.y<-tempSaucerMissile.height){
            tempSaucerMissile.y = yMax;
        }

        tempSaucerMissile.lifeCtr++;
        if (tempSaucerMissile.lifeCtr > tempSaucerMissile.life){
```

```
            //remove
            saucerMissiles.splice(saucerMissileCtr,1)
            tempSaucerMissile = null;
        }
    }
}

function updateParticles() {
    var tempParticle = {};
    var particleLength = particles.length-1;
    //ConsoleLog.log("particle=" + particleLength)
    for (var particleCtr=particleLength;particleCtr>=0;particleCtr--){
        var remove = false;
        tempParticle = particles[particleCtr];
        tempParticle.x += tempParticle.dx;
        tempParticle.y += tempParticle.dy;

        tempParticle.lifeCtr++;
        //ConsoleLog.log("particle.lifeCtr=" + tempParticle.lifeCtr);

        //try{
        if (tempParticle.lifeCtr > tempParticle.life){
            remove = true;

        } else if ((tempParticle.x > xMax) || (tempParticle.x<xMin)
          || (tempParticle.y > yMax) || (tempParticle.y<yMin)){

            remove = true;

        }
        //}
        //catch(err) {
        //    ConsoleLog.log ("error in particle");
        //    ConsoleLog.log("particle:" + particleCtr);

        //}

        if (remove) {
            particles.splice(particleCtr,1);
            tempParticle = null;
        }

    }
}

function renderPlayerShip(x,y,rotation, scale) {
    //transformation
    var angleInRadians = rotation * Math.PI / 180;
    context.save(); //save current state in stack
    context.setTransform(1,0,0,1,0,0); // reset to identity

    //translate the canvas origin to the center of the player
    context.translate(x+player.halfWidth,y+player.halfHeight);
    context.rotate(angleInRadians);
    context.scale(scale,scale);
```

```
//drawShip
context.strokeStyle = '#ffffff';
context.beginPath();

//hardcoding in locations
//facing right
context.moveTo(-10,-10);
context.lineTo(10,0);
context.moveTo(10,1);
context.lineTo(-10,10);
context.lineTo(1,1);
context.moveTo(1,-1);
context.lineTo(-10,-10);

if (player.thrust==true && scale==1) {
//check for scale==1 for ship indicator does not display with thrust
    context.moveTo(-4,-2);
    context.lineTo(-4,1);
    context.moveTo(-5,-1);
    context.lineTo(-10,-1);
    context.moveTo(-5,0);
    context.lineTo(-10,0);
}
context.stroke();
context.closePath();

//restore context
context.restore(); //pop old state on to screen
}

function renderPlayerMissiles() {
    var tempPlayerMissile = {};
    var playerMissileLength = playerMissiles.length-1;
    //ConsoleLog.log("render playerMissileLength=" + playerMissileLength);

    for (var playerMissileCtr=playerMissileLength;
        playerMissileCtr>=0;playerMissileCtr--){

        //ConsoleLog.log("draw player missile " + playerMissileCtr)
        tempPlayerMissile = playerMissiles[playerMissileCtr];
        context.save(); //save current state in stack
        context.setTransform(1,0,0,1,0,0); // reset to identity

        //translate the canvas origin to the center of the player
        context.translate(tempPlayerMissile.x+1,tempPlayerMissile.y+1);
        context.strokeStyle = '#ffffff';

        context.beginPath();

        //draw everything offset by 1/2. Zero Relative 1/2 is 15
        context.moveTo(-1,-1);
        context.lineTo(1,-1);
        context.lineTo(1,1);
        context.lineTo(-1,1);
```

```
        context.lineTo(-1,-1);
        context.stroke();
        context.closePath();
        context.restore(); //pop old state on to screen
    }
}

function renderRocks() {
    var tempRock = {};
    var rocksLength = rocks.length-1;
    for (var rockCtr=rocksLength;rockCtr>=0;rockCtr--){

        tempRock = rocks[rockCtr];
        var angleInRadians  = tempRock.rotation * Math.PI / 180;
        //ConsoleLog.log("render rock rotation"+(tempRock.rotation));
        context.save(); //save current state in stack
        context.setTransform(1,0,0,1,0,0); // reset to identity

        //translate the canvas origin to the center of the player
        context.translate(tempRock.x+tempRock.halfWidth,
                          tempRock.y+tempRock.halfHeight);

        //ConsoleLog.log("render rock x"+(tempRock.x+tempRock.halfWidth));
        //ConsoleLog.log("render rock y"+(tempRock.y+tempRock.halfHeight));
        context.rotate(angleInRadians);
        context.strokeStyle = '#ffffff';

        context.beginPath();

        //draw everything offset by 1/2.
        //Zero Relative 1/2 is if .5*width -1. Same for height

        context.moveTo(-(tempRock.halfWidth-1),-(tempRock.halfHeight-1));
        context.lineTo((tempRock.halfWidth-1),-(tempRock.halfHeight-1));
        context.lineTo((tempRock.halfWidth-1),(tempRock.halfHeight-1));
        context.lineTo(-(tempRock.halfWidth-1),(tempRock.halfHeight-1));
        context.lineTo(-(tempRock.halfWidth-1),-(tempRock.halfHeight-1));

        context.stroke();
        context.closePath();
        context.restore(); //pop old state on to screen

    }
}

function renderSaucers() {
    var tempSaucer = {};
    var saucerLength = saucers.length-1;
    for (var saucerCtr=saucerLength;saucerCtr>=0;saucerCtr--){
        //ConsoleLog.log("saucer: " + saucerCtr);
        tempSaucer = saucers[saucerCtr];

        context.save(); //save current state in stack
        context.setTransform(1,0,0,1,0,0); // reset to identity
```

```
        //translate the canvas origin to the center of the player
        //context.translate(this.x+halfWidth,this.y+halfHeight);
        context.translate(tempSaucer.x,tempSaucer.y);
        context.strokeStyle = '#ffffff';

        context.beginPath();

        //did not move to middle because it is drawn in exact space

        context.moveTo(4,0);
        context.lineTo(9,0);
        context.lineTo(12,3);
        context.lineTo(13,3);
        context.moveTo(13,4);
        context.lineTo(10,7);
        context.lineTo(3,7);
        context.lineTo(1,5);
        context.lineTo(12,5);
        context.moveTo(0,4);
        context.lineTo(0,3);
        context.lineTo(13,3);
        context.moveTo(5,1);
        context.lineTo(5,2);
        context.moveTo(8,1);
        context.lineTo(8,2);
        context.moveTo(2,2);
        context.lineTo(4,0);

        context.stroke();
        context.closePath();
        context.restore(); //pop old state on to screen
    }
}

function renderSaucerMissiles() {
    var tempSaucerMissile = {};
    var saucerMissileLength = saucerMissiles.length-1;
    //ConsoleLog.log("saucerMissiles= " + saucerMissiles.length)

    for (var saucerMissileCtr=saucerMissileLength;
        saucerMissileCtr>=0;saucerMissileCtr--){

        //ConsoleLog.log("draw player missile " + playerMissileCtr)
        tempSaucerMissile = saucerMissiles[saucerMissileCtr];
        context.save(); //save current state in stack
        context.setTransform(1,0,0,1,0,0); // reset to identity

        //translate the canvas origin to the center of the player
        context.translate(tempSaucerMissile.x+1,tempSaucerMissile.y+1);
        context.strokeStyle = '#ffffff';

        context.beginPath();

        //draw everything offset by 1/2. Zero Relative 1/2 is 15
        context.moveTo(-1,-1);
```

```
            context.lineTo(1,-1);
            context.lineTo(1,1);
            context.lineTo(-1,1);
            context.lineTo(-1,-1);
            context.stroke();
            context.closePath();
            context.restore(); //pop old state on to screen


    }
}

function renderParticles() {

    var tempParticle = {};
    var particleLength = particles.length-1;
    for (var particleCtr=particleLength;particleCtr>=0;particleCtr--){
        tempParticle = particles[particleCtr];
        context.save(); //save current state in stack
        context.setTransform(1,0,0,1,0,0); // reset to identity

        //translate the canvas origin to the center of the player
        context.translate(tempParticle.x,tempParticle.y);
        context.strokeStyle = '#ffffff';

        context.beginPath();

        //draw everything offset by 1/2. Zero Relative 1/2 is 15
        context.moveTo(0,0);
        context.lineTo(1,1);
        context.stroke();
        context.closePath();
        context.restore(); //pop old state on to screen


    }

}

function checkCollisions() {

    //loop through rocks then missiles. There will always be rocks and a ship,
    //but there will not always be missiles.

    var tempRock = {};
    var rocksLength = rocks.length-1;
    var tempPlayerMissile = {};
    var playerMissileLength = playerMissiles.length-1;
    var saucerLength = saucers.length-1;
    var tempSaucer = {};
    var saucerMissileLength = saucerMissiles.length-1;

    rocks: for (var rockCtr=rocksLength;rockCtr>=0;rockCtr--){
        tempRock = rocks[rockCtr];

        missiles:for (var playerMissileCtr=playerMissileLength;
            playerMissileCtr>=0;playerMissileCtr--){
```

```
            tempPlayerMissile = playerMissiles[playerMissileCtr];

        if (boundingBoxCollide(tempRock,tempPlayerMissile)){
            //ConsoleLog.log("hit rock");

            createExplode(tempRock.x+tempRock.halfWidth,
            tempRock.y+tempRock.halfHeight,10);

            if (tempRock.scale<3) {
                splitRock(tempRock.scale+1, tempRock.x, tempRock.y);
            }
            addToScore(tempRock.scoreValue);
            playerMissiles.splice(playerMissileCtr,1);
            tempPlayerMissile = null;

            rocks.splice(rockCtr,1);
            tempRock = null;


            break rocks;
            break missiles;
        }
    }

    saucers:for (var saucerCtr=saucerLength;saucerCtr>=0;saucerCtr--){
        tempSaucer = saucers[saucerCtr];

        if (boundingBoxCollide(tempRock,tempSaucer)){
            //ConsoleLog.log("hit rock");
            createExplode(tempSaucer.x+tempSaucer.halfWidth,
                          tempSaucer.y+tempSaucer.halfHeight,10);

            createExplode(tempRock.x+tempRock.halfWidth,
                          tempRock.y+tempRock.halfHeight,10);

            if (tempRock.scale<3) {
                splitRock(tempRock.scale+1, tempRock.x, tempRock.y);
            }

            saucers.splice(saucerCtr,1);
            tempSaucer = null;

            rocks.splice(rockCtr,1);
            tempRock = null;

            break rocks;
            break saucers;
        }
    }
}
//saucer missiles against rocks
//this is done here so we don't have to loop
//through rocks again as it would probably
//be the biggest array
```

```
saucerMissiles:for (var saucerMissileCtr=saucerMissileLength;
    saucerMissileCtr>=0;saucerMissileCtr--){

    tempSaucerMissile = saucerMissiles[saucerMissileCtr];

    if (boundingBoxCollide(tempRock,tempSaucerMissile)){
        //ConsoleLog.log("hit rock");

        createExplode(tempRock.x+tempRock.halfWidth,
        tempRock.y+tempRock.halfHeight,10);
        if (tempRock.scale<3) {
            splitRock(tempRock.scale+1, tempRock.x, tempRock.y);
        }

        saucerMissiles.splice(saucerCtr,1);
        tempSaucerMissile = null;

        rocks.splice(rockCtr,1);
        tempRock = null;

        break rocks;
        break saucerMissiles;
    }
}

//check player aginst rocks

if (boundingBoxCollide(tempRock,player)){
    //ConsoleLog.log("hit player");
    createExplode(tempRock.x+tempRock.halfWidth,tempRock.halfHeight,10);
    addToScore(tempRock.scoreValue);
    if (tempRock.scale<3) {
        splitRock(tempRock.scale+1, tempRock.x, tempRock.y);
    }
    rocks.splice(rockCtr,1);
    tempRock = null;

    playerDie();
}
}

//now check player against saucers and then saucers against player missiles
//and finally player against saucer missiles

playerMissileLength = playerMissiles.length-1;
saucerLength = saucers.length-1;
saucers:for (var saucerCtr=saucerLength;saucerCtr>=0;saucerCtr--){
    tempSaucer = saucers[saucerCtr];

    missiles:for (var playerMissileCtr=playerMissileLength;
            playerMissileCtr>=0;playerMissileCtr--){

        tempPlayerMissile = playerMissiles[playerMissileCtr];
```

```
            if (boundingBoxCollide(tempSaucer,tempPlayerMissile)){
            //ConsoleLog.log("hit rock");

                createExplode(tempSaucer.x+tempSaucer.halfWidth,
                            tempSaucer.y+tempSaucer.halfHeight,10);

                addToScore(tempSaucer.scoreValue);

                playerMissiles.splice(playerMissileCtr,1);
                tempPlayerMissile = null;

                saucers.splice(saucerCtr,1);
                tempSaucer = null;

                break saucers;
                break missiles;
            }
        }

    //player against saucers
    if (boundingBoxCollide(tempSaucer,player)){
        ConsoleLog.log("hit player");
        createExplode(tempSaucer.x+16,tempSaucer.y+16,10);
        addToScore(tempSaucer.scoreValue);

        saucers.splice(rockCtr,1);
        tempSaucer = null;

        playerDie();
    }
}

//saucerMissiles against player
saucerMissileLength = saucerMissiles.length-1;

saucerMissiles:for (var saucerMissileCtr=saucerMissileLength;
    saucerMissileCtr>=0;saucerMissileCtr--){

    tempSaucerMissile = saucerMissiles[saucerMissileCtr];

    if (boundingBoxCollide(player,tempSaucerMissile)){
        ConsoleLog.log("saucer missile hit player");

        playerDie();
        saucerMissiles.splice(saucerCtr,1);
        tempSaucerMissile = null;

        break saucerMissiles;
    }
}
}

function firePlayerMissile(){
    //ConsoleLog.log("fire playerMissile");
    var newPlayerMissile = {};
```

```
        newPlayerMissile.dx = 5*Math.cos(Math.PI*(player.rotation)/180);
        newPlayerMissile.dy = 5*Math.sin(Math.PI*(player.rotation)/180);
        newPlayerMissile.x = player.x+player.halfWidth;
        newPlayerMissile.y = player.y+player.halfHeight;
        newPlayerMissile.life = 60;
        newPlayerMissile.lifeCtr = 0;
        newPlayerMissile.width = 2;
        newPlayerMissile.height = 2;
        playerMissiles.push(newPlayerMissile);
}

function fireSaucerMissile(saucer) {
        var newSaucerMissile = {};
        newSaucerMissile.x = saucer.x+.5*saucer.width;
        newSaucerMissile.y = saucer.y+.5*saucer.height;

        newSaucerMissile.width = 2;
        newSaucerMissile.height = 2;
        newSaucerMissile.speed = saucer.missileSpeed;

        //ConsoleLog.log("saucer fire");
        //fire at player from small saucer
        var diffx = player.x-saucer.x;
        var diffy = player.y-saucer.y;
        var radians = Math.atan2(diffy, diffx);
        var degrees = 360 * radians / (2 * Math.PI);
        newSaucerMissile.dx = saucer.missileSpeed*Math.cos(Math.PI*(degrees)/180);
        newSaucerMissile.dy = saucer.missileSpeed*Math.sin(Math.PI*(degrees)/180);
        newSaucerMissile.life = 160;
        newSaucerMissile.lifeCtr = 0;
        saucerMissiles.push(newSaucerMissile);
}

function playerDie() {
        ConsoleLog.log("player die");
        createExplode(player.x+player.halfWidth, player.y+player.halfWidth,50);
        switchGameState(GAME_STATE_PLAYER_DIE);

}

function createExplode(x,y,num) {
        //create 10 particles
        for (var partCtr=0;partCtr<num;partCtr++){
            var newParticle = new Object();
            newParticle.dx = Math.random()*3;
                if (Math.random()<.5){
                    newParticle.dx*=-1;
                }
            newParticle.dy = Math.random()*3;
            if (Math.random()<.5){
                newParticle.dy*=-1;
            }

            newParticle.life = Math.floor(Math.random()*30+30);
            newParticle.lifeCtr = 0;
```

```
            newParticle.x = x;
            newParticle.y = y;
            //ConsoleLog.log("newParticle.life=" + newParticle.life);
            particles.push(newParticle);
        }

    }

    function boundingBoxCollide(object1, object2) {

        var left1 = object1.x;
        var left2 = object2.x;
        var right1 = object1.x + object1.width;
        var right2 = object2.x + object2.width;
        var top1 = object1.y;
        var top2 = object2.y;
        var bottom1 = object1.y + object1.height;
        var bottom2 = object2.y + object2.height;

        if (bottom1 < top2) return(false);
        if (top1 > bottom2) return(false);

        if (right1 < left2) return(false);
        if (left1 > right2) return(false);

        return(true);

    };

    function splitRock(scale,x,y){
        for (var newRockctr=0;newRockctr<2;newRockctr++){
            var newRock = {};
            //ConsoleLog.log("split rock");

            if (scale==2){
                newRock.scoreValue = medRockScore;
                newRock.width = 25;
                newRock.height = 25;
                newRock.halfWidth = 12.5;
                newRock.halfHeight = 12.5;

            }else {
                newRock.scoreValue = smlRockScore;
                newRock.width = 16;
                newRock.height = 16;
                newRock.halfWidth = 8;
                newRock.halfHeight = 8;
            }

            newRock.scale = scale;
            newRock.x = x;
            newRock.y = y;
            newRock.dx = Math.random()*3;
            if (Math.random()<.5){
                newRock.dx*=-1;
```

```
        }
        newRock.dy = Math.random()*3;
        if (Math.random()<.5){
            newRock.dy*=-1;
        }
        newRock.rotationInc = (Math.random()*5)+1;
        if (Math.random()<.5){
            newRock.rotationInc*=-1;
        }
        newRock.rotation = 0;
        ConsoleLog.log("new rock scale"+(newRock.scale));
        rocks.push(newRock);

    }

}

function addToScore(value){
    score+=value;
}

document.onkeydown = function(e){

    e = e?e:window.event;
    //ConsoleLog.log(e.keyCode + "down");
    keyPressList[e.keyCode] = true;
}

document.onkeyup = function(e){
//document.body.onkeyup = function(e){
    e = e?e:window.event;
    //ConsoleLog.log(e.keyCode + "up");
    keyPressList[e.keyCode] = false;
};

//*** application start
switchGameState(GAME_STATE_TITLE);
frameRateCounter = new FrameRateCounter();
//**** application loop
const FRAME_RATE = 40;
var intervalTime = 1000/FRAME_RATE;
setInterval(runGame, intervalTime );

}

//***** object prototypes *****

//*** consoleLog util object
//create constructor
function ConsoleLog(){

}
```

```
//create function that will be added to the class
console_log = function(message) {
   if(typeof(console) !== 'undefined' && console != null) {
      console.log(message);
   }
}
//add class/static function to class by assignment
ConsoleLog.log = console_log;

//*** end console log object

//*** FrameRateCounter  object prototype
function FrameRateCounter() {

   this.lastFrameCount = 0;
   var dateTemp = new Date();
   this.frameLast = dateTemp.getTime();
   delete dateTemp;
   this.frameCtr = 0;
}

FrameRateCounter.prototype.countFrames = function() {
   var dateTemp = new Date();
   this.frameCtr++;

   if (dateTemp.getTime() >=this.frameLast+1000) {
      ConsoleLog.log("frame event");
      this.lastFrameCount = this.frameCtr;
      this.frameLast = dateTemp.getTime();
      this.frameCtr = 0;
   }

   delete dateTemp;
}
</script>
</head>
<body>
<div style="position: absolute; top: 50px; left: 50px;">
<canvas id="canvas" width="400" height="400">
 Your browser does not support HTML5 Canvas.
</canvas>
</div>
</body>
</html>
```

Figure 8-7 shows a screenshot of the game in action.

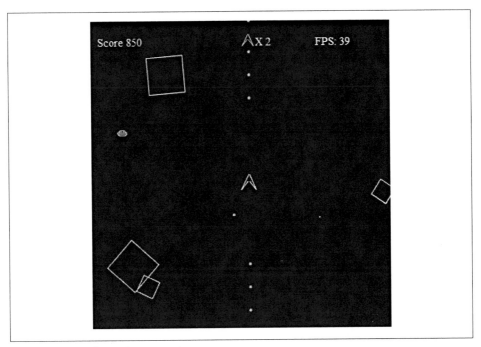

Figure 8-7. Geo Blaster Basic in action

Rock Object Prototype

To conserve space, we did not create separate object prototypes for the various display objects in this game. However, Example 8-13 is a Rock prototype object that can be used in a game such as *Geo Blaster Basic*.

Example 8-13. The Rock.js prototype

```
//*** Rock Object Prototype

function Rock(scale, type) {

    //scale
    //1 = large
    //2 = medium
    //3 = small
    //these will be used as the divisor for the new size
    //50/1 = 50
    //50/2 = 25
    //50/3 = 16

    this.scale = scale;
    if (this.scale <1 || this.scale >3){
        this.scale=1;
    }
```

```
        this.type = type;
        this.dx = 0;
        this.dy = 0;
        this.x = 0;
        this.y = 0;
        this.rotation = 0;
        this.rotationInc = 0;
        this.scoreValue = 0;

        //ConsoleLog.log("create rock. Scale=" + this.scale);
        switch(this.scale){

            case 1:
                this.width = 50;
                this.height = 50;
                break;
            case 2:
                this.width = 25;
                this.height = 25;
                break;
            case 3:
                this.width = 16;
                this.height = 16;
                break;
        }

}

Rock.prototype.update = function(xmin,xmax,ymin,ymax) {
    this.x += this.dx;
    this.y += this.dy;
    this.rotation += this.rotationInc;
    if (this.x > xmax) {
        this.x = xmin-this.width;
    }else if (this.x<xmin-this.width){
        this.x = xmax;
    }

    if (this.y > ymax) {
        this.y = ymin-this.width;
    }else if (this.y<ymin-this.width){
        this.y = ymax;
    }
}

Rock.prototype.draw = function(context) {

    var angleInRadians = this.rotation * Math.PI / 180;
    var halfWidth = Math.floor(this.width*.5); //used to find center of object
    var halfHeight = Math.floor(this.height*.5)// used to find center of object
    context.save(); //save current state in stack
    context.setTransform(1,0,0,1,0,0); // reset to identity
```

```
//translate the canvas origin to the center of the player
context.translate(this.x+halfWidth,this.y+halfHeight);
context.rotate(angleInRadians);
context.strokeStyle = '#ffffff';

context.beginPath();

//draw everything offset by 1/2. Zero Relative 1/2 is if .5*width -1. Same for height

context.moveTo(-(halfWidth-1),-(halfHeight-1));
context.lineTo((halfWidth-1),-(halfHeight-1));
context.lineTo((halfWidth-1),(halfHeight-1));
context.lineTo(-(halfWidth-1),(halfHeight-1));
context.lineTo(-(halfWidth-1),-(halfHeight-1));

context.stroke();
context.closePath();
context.restore(); //pop old state on to screen

}

//*** end Rock Class
```

What's Next

We covered quite a bit in this chapter. HTML5 Canvas might lack some of the more refined features common to web game development platforms such as Flash, but it contains powerful tools for manipulating the screen in immediate mode. These features allow us to create a game application with many individual logical display objects— even though each canvas can support only a single physical display object (the canvas itself).

In Chapter 9 we will explore some more advanced game topics, such as replacing paths with bitmap images, creating object pools, and adding a sound manager. We'll extend the game we built in this chapter and create a new turn-based strategy game.

Combining Bitmaps and Sound

Geo Blaster Basic was constructed using pure paths for drawing. In its creation, we began to cover some game-application-related topics, such as basic collision detection and state machines. In this chapter, we will focus on using bitmaps and tile sheets for our game graphics, and we will also add sound using techniques introduced in Chapter 7.

Along the way, we will update the `FrameRateCounter` from Chapter 8 by adding in a "step timer." We will also examine how we can eliminate the use of a tile sheet for rotations by precreating an array of `imageData` instances using the `getImageData()` and `putImageData()` Canvas functions.

In the second half of this chapter, we will create another small turn-based strategy game using bitmaps. This game will be roughly based on the classic computer game *Daleks*.

Geo Blaster Extended

We will create a new game, *Geo Blaster Extended*, by adding bitmaps and sound to the *Geo Blaster Basic* game from Chapter 8. Much of the game logic will be the same, but adding bitmaps to replace paths will enable us to optimize the game for rendering. Optimized rendering is very important when you are targeting limited-processor devices, such as mobile phones. We will also add sound to *Geo Blaster Extended*, and apply an object pool to the particles used for game explosions. Figure 9-1 shows an example screen of the finished game.

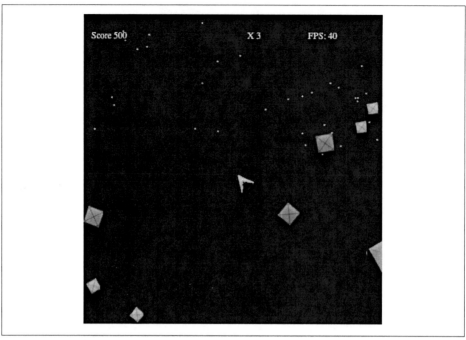

Figure 9-1. Geo Blaster Extended

First, let's look at the tile sheets we will use for our new game.

Geo Blaster Tile Sheet

In Chapter 4, we examined applying bitmap graphics to the canvas, and we explored using tile sheet methods to render images. In Chapter 8, we drew all our game graphics as paths and transformed them on the fly. In this chapter, we will apply the concepts from Chapter 4 to optimizing the rendering of the *Geo Blaster Basic* game. We will do this by prerendering all of our game graphics and transformations as bitmaps. We will then use these bitmaps instead of paths and the immediate-mode transformations that were necessary in Chapter 8 to create *Geo Blaster Extended*.

Figure 9-2 shows one of the tile sheets we will use for this game (*ship_tiles.png*).

These tiles are the 36 rotations for our player ship. We are "canning" the rotations in a tile sheet to avoid spending processor cycles transforming them on each frame tick as we draw them to the canvas.

Figure 9-2. The ship_tiles.png tile sheet

Figure 9-3 shows a second set of tiles for the ship with the "thruster" firing (*ship_tiles2.png*). We will use this set to depict the ship when the user is pressing the up arrow key.

Figure 9-3. The ship_tiles2.png tile sheet

The next three sets of tiles are for the rocks that the player will destroy. We have three sheets for these: *largerocks.png* (Figure 9-4), *mediumrocks.png* (Figure 9-5), and *smallrocks.png* (Figure 9-6).

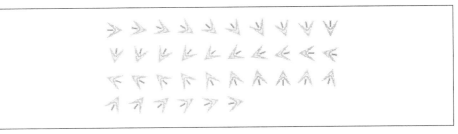

Figure 9-4. The largerocks.png tile sheet

Figure 9-5. The mediumrocks.png tile sheet

Figure 9-6. The smallrocks.png tile sheet

These three tile sheets only need to be five tiles each. Since the rock is a square, we can simply repeat the five frames to simulate rotation in either the clockwise or counter-clockwise direction.

The saucer that attempts to shoot the player is a single tile, *saucer.png*, shown in Figure 9-7.

Figure 9-7. The saucer.png tile

Finally, *parts.png* (Figure 9-8), is a tiny 8×2 tile sheet that contains four 2×2 "particle" tiles. These will be used for the explosions and missiles fired by the player and the saucer.

Figure 9-8. The parts.png tile sheet

You cannot see the colors in a black-and-white printed book, but you can view them by downloading the files from this book's website. The first tile is green, and it will be used for the small rock and saucer explosions. The second tile is light blue, and it will depict the player's missiles and the player explosion. The third tile is reddish pink (salmon, if you will), and it will illustrate the large rock explosions. The final, purple tile will be used for the medium rock explosions.

Now that we have our tiles in place, let's look at the methods we will use to transform *Geo Blaster Basic*'s immediate-mode path, rendering it to *Geo Blaster Extended*'s tile-based bitmap.

Refresher: Calculating the tile source location

In Chapter 4, we examined the method to calculate a tile's location on a tile sheet if we know the single-dimension id of that tile. Let's briefly look back at this, as it will be reused to render all the tiles for the games in this chapter.

Given that we have a tile sheet such as *ship_tiles.png*, we can locate the tile we want to display with a simple math trick.

ship_tiles.png is a 36-tile animation with the player ship starting in the 0-degree angle, or "pointing right" direction. Each of the remaining 35 tiles displays the ship rotating in 10-degree increments.

If we would like to display tile 19 (the ship pointing to the left, or in the 190-degree angle), we first need to find the x and y coordinates for the top-left corner of the tile, by calculating sourceX and sourceY.

Here is pseudocode for the sourceX calculation:

```
sourceX = integer(current_frame_index modulo
the_number_columns_in_the_tilesheet) * tile_width
```

The modulo (%) operator will return the remainder of the division calculation. Below is the actual code (with variables replaced with literals) we will use for this calculation:

```
var sourceX = Math.floor(19 % 10) *32;
```

The result is x = 9*32 = 288;.

The calculation for the sourceY value is similar except we divide rather than use the modulo operator:

```
sourceY = integer(current_frame_index divided by
the_number_columns_in_the_tilesheet) *tile_height
```

Here's the actual code we will use for this calculation:

```
var sourceY = Math.floor(19 / 10) *32;
```

This works out to y = 1*32 = 32;. So, the top-left location on the *ship_tiles.png* from which to start copying pixels is 288,32.

To actually copy this to the canvas, we will use this statement:

```
context.drawImage(shipTiles, sourceX, sourceY,32,32,player.x,player.y,32,32);
```

In Chapter 8, we needed quite a lot of code to draw and translate the player ship at the current rotation. When we use a tile sheet, this code is reduced considerably.

Here is the code we will use to render the player ship. It will replace the render Player() function in Example 8-12 in Chapter 8:

```
function renderPlayerShip(x,y,rotation, scale) {
    //transformation
    context.save(); //save current state in stack
    context.globalAlpha = parseFloat(player.alpha);
    var angleInRadians = rotation * Math.PI / 180;
    var sourceX = Math.floor((player.rotation/10) % 10) * 32;
    var sourceY = Math.floor((player.rotation/10) /10) *32;
    if (player.thrust){
        context.drawImage(shipTiles2, sourceX, sourceY, 32, 32,
            player.x,player.y,32,32);
    }else{
        context.drawImage(shipTiles, sourceX, sourceY, 32, 32,
        player.x,player.y,32,32);
    }

    //restore context
    context.restore(); //pop old state on to screen

    context.globalAlpha = 1;

}
```

You will find the entire source code for *Geo Blaster Extended* (Example 9-1) later, in "Geo Blaster Extended Full Source" on page 468.

The `renderPlayer()` function divides the `player.rotation` by 10 to determine which of the 36 tiles in the `shipTiles` image instance to display on the canvas. If the player is in "thrust" mode, the `shipTiles2` image is used instead of `shipTiles`.

This works because we have set the ship to rotate by 10 degrees with each press of the left or right arrow key. In Chapter 8's version of the game, we set this to 5 degrees. If we had created a 72-frame tile sheet, with the player ship rotated in 5-degree increments, we could have kept the `player.rotationalVelocity` at 5. For *Geo Blaster Extended*, we only drew 36 tiles for the player ship, so we are using the value 10 for the rotational velocity. There certainly is no reason why we could not use 72 or even 360 frames for the player ship rotation tiles. This is only limited by creative imagination (and patience with a drawing tool).

Let's look at the `rotationalVelocity` value assigned earlier in the `gameStateNewGame()` function:

```
function gameStateNewGame(){
    ConsoleLog.log("gameStateNewGame")
    //setup new game
    level = 0;
    score = 0;
    playerShips = 3;
    player.maxVelocity = 5;
    player.width = 32;
    player.height = 32;
    player.halfWidth = 16;
    player.halfHeight = 16;
    player.hitWidth = 24;
    player.hitHeight = 24;
    player.rotationalVelocity = 10; //how many degrees to turn the ship
    player.thrustAcceleration = .05;
    player.missileFrameDelay = 5;
    player.thrust = false;
    player.alpha = 1;
    player.rotation = 0;
    player.x = 0;
    player.y = 0;

    fillBackground();
    renderScoreBoard();
    switchGameState(GAME_STATE_NEW_LEVEL)

}
```

Other new player attributes

Along with the change in the rotational velocity, we have also modified the player's `width` and `height` attributes. These are both now 32, which is the same as the tile width and height. If you look at the first frame of the *ship_tiles.png* tile sheet, you will see that the player ship does not fill the entire 32×32 tile. It is centered in the middle, taking up roughly 24×24 of the tile, which leaves enough space around the edges of the tile to eliminate clipping when the ship is rotated. We also used this concept when we created the rock rotations.

The extra pixels of padding added to eliminate clipping during frame rotation poses a small problem for collision detection. In the Chapter 8 version of the game, we used the `width` and `height` values for bounding box collision detection. We will not use those values in this new version because we have created two new variables to use for collision detection: `hitWidth` and `hitHeight`. Instead of setting these values to 32, they are 24. This new smaller value makes our collision detection more accurate than if we used the entire tile width and height.

The new boundingBoxCollide() algorithm

All the other game objects will also have new `hitWidth` and `hitHeight` attributes. We will modify the `boundingBoxCollide()` function from *Geo Blaster Basic* to use these new values for all collision testing:

```
function boundingBoxCollide(object1, object2) {

    var left1 = object1.x;
    var left2 = object2.x;
    var right1 = object1.x + object1.hitWidth;
    var right2 = object2.x + object2.hitWidth;
    var top1 = object1.y;
    var top2 = object2.y;
    var bottom1 = object1.y + object1.hitHeight;
    var bottom2 = object2.y + object2.hitHeight;

    if (bottom1 < top2) return(false);
    if (top1 > bottom2) return(false);

    if (right1 < left2) return(false);
    if (left1 > right2) return(false);

    return(true);

}
```

Next, we will take a quick look at how we will use these same ideas to render the rest of the game objects with the new tile sheets.

Rendering the Other Game Objects

The rocks, saucers, missiles, and particles will all be rendered in a manner similar to the method implemented for the player ship. Let's first look at the code for the saucer's render function.

Rendering the saucers

The saucers do not have a multiple-cell tile sheet, but to be consistent, we will render them as though they do. This will allow us to add more animation tiles for the saucers later:

```
function renderSaucers() {
    var tempSaucer = {};
    var saucerLength = saucers.length-1;
    for (var saucerCtr=saucerLength;saucerCtr>=0;saucerCtr--){
        //ConsoleLog.log("saucer: " + saucerCtr);
        tempSaucer = saucers[saucerCtr];

        context.save(); //save current state in stack
        var sourceX = 0;
        var sourceY = 0;
        context.drawImage(saucerTiles, sourceX, sourceY, 30, 15,
        tempSaucer.x,tempSaucer.y,30,15);
        context.restore(); //pop old state on to screen
    }
}
```

There is no need to actually calculate the `sourceX` and `sourceY` values for the saucer because the saucer is only a single tile. In this instance, we can just set them to 0. We have hardcoded the `saucer.width` (30) and `saucer.height` (15) as an example, but with all the rest of the game objects, we will use the object `width` and `height` attributes rather than literals.

Next, let's look at the rock rendering, which varies slightly from both the player ship and the saucers.

Rendering the rocks

The rock tiles are contained inside three separate tile sheets based on their size (large, medium, and small), and we have used only five tiles for each rock. The rocks are square with a symmetrical pattern, so we only need to precreate a single quarter-turn rotation for each of the three sizes.

Here is the `renderRocks()` function. Notice that we must "switch" based on the scale of the rock (1=large, 2=medium, 3=small) to choose the right tile sheet to render:

```
function renderRocks() {
    var tempRock = {};
    var rocksLength = rocks.length-1;
    for (var rockCtr=rocksLength;rockCtr>=0;rockCtr--){
        context.save(); //save current state in stack
```

```
tempRock = rocks[rockCtr];
var sourceX = Math.floor((tempRock.rotation) % 5) * tempRock.width;
var sourceY = Math.floor((tempRock.rotation) /5) *tempRock.height;

switch(tempRock.scale){
    case 1:
    context.drawImage(largeRockTiles, sourceX, sourceY,
     tempRock.width,tempRock.height,tempRock.x,tempRock.y,
     tempRock.width,tempRock.height);
    break;
    case 2:
    context.drawImage(mediumRockTiles, sourceX,
     sourceY,tempRock.width,tempRock.height,tempRock.x,tempRock.y,
     tempRock.width,tempRock.height);
    break;
    case 3:
    context.drawImage(smallRockTiles, sourceX,
     sourceY,tempRock.width,tempRock.height,tempRock.x,tempRock.y,
     tempRock.width,tempRock.height);
    break;

}

context.restore(); //pop old state on to screen

    }
}
```

In the renderRocks() function, we are no longer using the rock.rotation attribute as the angle of rotation as we did in *Geo Blaster Basic*. Instead, we have repurposed the rotation attribute to represent the tile id (0–4) of the current tile on the tile sheet to render.

In the Chapter 8 version, we were able to simulate faster or slower speeds for the rock rotations by simply giving each rock a random rotationInc value. This value, either negative for counterclockwise or positive for clockwise, was added to the rotation attribute on each frame. In this new tilesheet-based version, we only have five frames of animation, so we don't want to skip frames because it will look choppy. Instead, we are going to add two new attributes to each rock: animationCount and animationDelay.

The animationDelay will represent the number of frames between each tile change for a given rock. The animationCount variable will restart at 0 after each tile frame change and will increase by 1 on each subsequent frame tick. When animationCount is greater than animationDelay, the rock.rotation value will be increased (clockwise) or decreased (counterclockwise). Here is the new code that we will have in our updateRocks() function:

```
tempRock.animationCount++;
    if (tempRock.animationCount > tempRock.animationDelay){
        tempRock.animationCount = 0;
        tempRock.rotation += tempRock.rotationInc;
```

```
      if (tempRock.rotation > 4){
         tempRock.rotation = 0;
      }else if (tempRock.rotation <0){
         tempRock.rotation = 4;
      }
   }
```

You will notice that we have hardcoded the values 4 and 0 into the tile id maximum
and minimum checks. We could have just as easily used a constant or two variables for
this purpose.

Rendering the missiles

Both the player missiles and saucer missiles are rendered in the same manner. For each,
we simply need to know the tile id on the four-tile `particleTiles` image representing
the tile we want to display. For the player missiles, this tile id is 1; for the saucer missile,
the tile id is 0.

Let's take a quick look at both of these functions:

```
function renderPlayerMissiles() {
   var tempPlayerMissile = {};
   var playerMissileLength = playerMissiles.length-1;
   //ConsoleLog.log("render playerMissileLength=" + playerMissileLength);
   for (var playerMissileCtr=playerMissileLength; playerMissileCtr>=0;
    playerMissileCtr--){

   //ConsoleLog.log("draw player missile " + playerMissileCtr)
   tempPlayerMissile = playerMissiles[playerMissileCtr];
   context.save(); //save current state in stack
   var sourceX = Math.floor(1 % 4) * tempPlayerMissile.width;
   var sourceY = Math.floor(1 / 4) * tempPlayerMissile.height;

   context.drawImage(particleTiles, sourceX, sourceY,
    tempPlayerMissile.width,tempPlayerMissile.height,
    tempPlayerMissile.x,tempPlayerMissile.y,tempPlayerMissile.width,
    tempPlayerMissile.height);

   context.restore(); //pop old state on to screen
   }
   }

function renderSaucerMissiles() {
   var tempSaucerMissile = {};
   var saucerMissileLength = saucerMissiles.length-1;
   //ConsoleLog.log("saucerMissiles= " + saucerMissiles.length)
   for (var saucerMissileCtr=saucerMissileLength;
   saucerMissileCtr >= 0;saucerMissileCtr--){
   //ConsoleLog.log("draw player missile " + playerMissileCtr)
   tempSaucerMissile = saucerMissiles[saucerMissileCtr];
   context.save(); //save current state in stack
   var sourceX = Math.floor(0 % 4) * tempSaucerMissile.width;
   var sourceY = Math.floor(0 / 4) * tempSaucerMissile.height;
```

```
context.drawImage(particleTiles, sourceX, sourceY,
 tempSaucerMissile.width,tempSaucerMissile.height,
 tempSaucerMissile.x,tempSaucerMissile.y,tempSaucerMissile.width,
 tempSaucerMissile.height);

context.restore(); //pop old state on to screen

}
}
```

The particle explosion will also be rendered using a bitmap tile sheet, and its code will be very similar to the code for the projectiles. Let's examine the particles next.

Rendering the particles

The particles will use the same four-tile *parts.png* file (as shown in Figure 9-8) that rendered the projectiles. The *Geo Blaster Basic* game from Chapter 8 used only a single white particle for all explosions. We replace the `createExplode()` function from this previous game with a new one that will be able to use a different-colored particle for each type of explosion. This way the rocks, saucers, and player ship can all have unique colored explosions.

The new `createExplode()` function will handle this by adding a final `type` parameter to its parameter list. Let's look at the code:

```
function createExplode(x,y,num,type) {

    playSound(SOUND_EXPLODE,.5);
    for (var partCtr=0;partCtr<num;partCtr++){
       if (particlePool.length > 0){
         newParticle = particlePool.pop();
       newParticle.dx = Math.random()*3;
       if (Math.random()<.5){
          newParticle.dx *= -1;
       }
       newParticle.dy = Math.random()*3;
       if (Math.random()<.5){
       newParticle.dy *= -1;
       }

       newParticle.life = Math.floor(Math.random()*30+30);
       newParticle.lifeCtr = 0;
       newParticle.x = x;
       newParticle.width = 2;
       newParticle.height = 2;
       newParticle.y = y;
       newParticle.type = type;
       //ConsoleLog.log("newParticle.life=" + newParticle.life);
       particles.push(newParticle);
       }

    }

}
```

As the particle objects are created in createExplode(), we added a new type attribute to them. When an explosion is triggered in the checkCollisions() function, the call to createExplode() will now include this type value based on the object that was destroyed. Each rock already has a scale parameter that varies from 1 to 3 based on its size. We will use those as our base type value to pass in for the rocks. Now we only need type values for the player and the saucer. For the saucer we will use 0, and for the player we will use 4. We pulled these id values out of the air. We very well could have used 99 for the saucer and 200 for the player. We just could not use 1, 2, or 3 because those values are used for the rocks. The type breakdown looks like this:

- Saucer: type=0
- Large rock: type=1
- Medium rock: type=2
- Small rock: type=3
- Player: type=4

This type value will need to be used in a switch statement inside the render Particles() function to determine which of the four tiles to render for a given particle. Let's examine this function now:

```
function renderParticles() {

    var tempParticle = {};
    var particleLength = particles.length-1;
    for (var particleCtr=particleLength;particleCtr>=0;particleCtr--){
        tempParticle = particles[particleCtr];
        context.save(); //save current state in stack

        var tile;

        console.log("part type=" + tempParticle.type)
        switch(tempParticle.type){
            case 0: // saucer
              tile = 0;
              break;
            case 1: //large rock
              tile = 2
              break;
            case 2: //medium rock
              tile = 3;
              break;
            case 3: //small rock
              tile = 0;
              break;
            case 4: //player
              tile = 1;
              break;

    }
```

```
            var sourceX = Math.floor(tile % 4) * tempParticle.width;
            var sourceY = Math.floor(tile / 4) * tempParticle.height;

            context.drawImage(particleTiles, sourceX, sourceY,
            tempParticle.width, tempParticle.height, tempParticle.x,
            tempParticle.y,tempParticle.width,tempParticle.height);

            context.restore(); //pop old state on to screen


        }
```

In `checkCollisions()`, we will need to pass the `type` parameter to the `createExplode()` function so the `type` can be assigned to the particles in the explosion. Here is an example of a `createExplode()` function call used for a rock instance:

```
createExplode(tempRock.x+tempRock.halfWidth,tempRock.y+tempRock.halfHeight,
    10,tempRock.scale);
```

We pass the `tempRock.scale` as the final parameter because we are using the rock's scale as the `type`.

For a saucer:

```
createExplode(tempSaucer.x+tempSaucer.halfWidth,
    tempSaucer.y+tempSaucer.halfHeight,10,0);
```

For the saucers and the player, we will pass a number literal into the `createExplode()` function. In the saucer's case, we pass in a 1. For the player ship, we pass in a 4:

```
createExplode(player.x+player.halfWidth, player.y+player.halfWidth,50,4);
```

Note that the `createExplode()` function call for the player is in the `playerDie()` function, which is called from `checkCollisions()`.

 After we discuss adding sound and a particle pool to this game, we will present the entire set of code (Example 9-1), replacing the *Geo Blaster Basic* code. There will be no need to make the changes to the individual functions.

Adding Sound

In Chapter 7, we covered everything we need to know to add robust sound management to our canvas applications. If you are unfamiliar with the concepts presented in Chapter 7, please review that chapter first. In this chapter, we will cover only the code necessary to include sound in our game.

Arcade games need to play many sounds simultaneously, and sometimes those sounds play very rapidly in succession. In Chapter 7, we used the HTML5 `<audio>` tag to create a pool of sounds, solving the problems associated with playing the same sound instance multiple times.

As of this writing, the Opera browser in Windows offers the best support for playing sounds. If you are having trouble with the sound in this game, any other sound example in the book, or in your own games, please test them out in the Opera browser.

The sounds for our game

We will be adding three sounds to our game:

- A sound for when the player shoots a projectile (*shoot1.mp3, .ogg, .wav*)
- A sound for explosions (*explode1.mp3, .ogg, .wav*)
- A sound for when the saucer shoots a projectile (*saucershoot.mp3, .ogg, .wav*)

In the file download for this chapter, we have provided each of the three sounds in three different formats: *.wav, .ogg,* and *.mp3.*

Adding sound instances and management variables to the game

In the variable definition section of our game code, we will create variables to work with the sound manager code from Chapter 7. We will create three instances of each sound that goes into our pool:

```
var explodeSound;
var explodeSound2;
var explodeSound3;
var shootSound;
var shootSound2;
var shootSound3;
var saucershootSound;
var saucershootSound2;
var saucershootSound3;
```

We also need to create an array to hold our pool of sounds:

```
var soundPool = new Array();
```

To control which sound we want to play, we will assign a constant string to each, and to play the sound, we only ever need to use the constant. This way, we can change the sound names easily, which will help in refactoring code if we want to modify the sounds at a later time:

```
const SOUND_EXPLODE = "explode1";
    const SOUND_SHOOT = "shoot1";
    const SOUND_SAUCER_SHOOT = "saucershoot"
```

Finally, we need a variable called `audioType`, which we will use to reference the current file type (*.ogg, .mp3,* or *.wav*) by the sound manager code.

Loading in sounds and tile sheet assets

In Chapter 7, we used a function to load all of the game assets while our state machine waited in an idle state. We will add this code to our game in a function called game StateInit():

```
function gameStateInit() {
    loadCount = 0;
    itemsToLoad  = 16;

    explodeSound = document.createElement("audio");
    document.body.appendChild(explodeSound);
    audioType = supportedAudioFormat(explodeSound);
    explodeSound.setAttribute("src", "explode1." + audioType);
    explodeSound.addEventListener("canplaythrough",itemLoaded,false);

    explodeSound2 = document.createElement("audio");
    document.body.appendChild(explodeSound2);
    explodeSound2.setAttribute("src", "explode1." + audioType);
    explodeSound2.addEventListener("canplaythrough",itemLoaded,false);

    explodeSound3 = document.createElement("audio");
    document.body.appendChild(explodeSound3);
    explodeSound3.setAttribute("src", "explode1." + audioType);
    explodeSound3.addEventListener("canplaythrough",itemLoaded,false);

    shootSound = document.createElement("audio");
    audioType = supportedAudioFormat(shootSound);
    document.body.appendChild(shootSound);
    shootSound.setAttribute("src", "shoot1." + audioType);
    shootSound.addEventListener("canplaythrough",itemLoaded,false);

    shootSound2 = document.createElement("audio");
    document.body.appendChild(shootSound2);
    shootSound2.setAttribute("src", "shoot1." + audioType);
    shootSound2.addEventListener("canplaythrough",itemLoaded,false);

    shootSound3 = document.createElement("audio");
    document.body.appendChild(shootSound3);
    shootSound3.setAttribute("src", "shoot1." + audioType);
    shootSound3.addEventListener("canplaythrough",itemLoaded,false);

    saucershootSound = document.createElement("audio");
    audioType = supportedAudioFormat(saucershootSound);
    document.body.appendChild(saucershootSound);
    saucershootSound.setAttribute("src", "saucershoot." + audioType);
    saucershootSound.addEventListener("canplaythrough",itemLoaded,false);

    saucershootSound2 = document.createElement("audio");
    document.body.appendChild(saucershootSound2);
    saucershootSound2.setAttribute("src", "saucershoot." + audioType);
    saucershootSound2.addEventListener("canplaythrough",itemLoaded,false);

    saucershootSound3 = document.createElement("audio");
    document.body.appendChild(saucershootSound3);
```

```
saucershootSound3.setAttribute("src", "saucershoot." + audioType);
saucershootSound3.addEventListener("canplaythrough",itemLoaded,false);

shipTiles = new Image();
shipTiles.src = "ship_tiles.png";
shipTiles.onload = itemLoaded;

shipTiles2 = new Image();
shipTiles2.src = "ship_tiles2.png";
shipTiles2.onload = itemLoaded;

saucerTiles= new Image();
saucerTiles.src = "saucer.png";
saucerTiles.onload = itemLoaded;

largeRockTiles = new Image();
largeRockTiles.src = "largerocks.png";
largeRockTiles.onload = itemLoaded;

mediumRockTiles = new Image();
mediumRockTiles.src = "mediumrocks.png";
mediumRockTiles.onload = itemLoaded;

smallRockTiles = new Image();
smallRockTiles.src = "smallrocks.png";
smallRockTiles.onload = itemLoaded;

particleTiles = new Image();
particleTiles.src = "parts.png";
particleTiles.onload = itemLoaded;

switchGameState(GAME_STATE_WAIT_FOR_LOAD);

}
```

Notice that we must create and preload three separate instances of each sound, even though they share the same sound file (or files). In this function, we also load in our tile sheets. The application scope itemsToLoad variable will be used to check against the application scope loadCount variable in the load event callback itemLoaded() function, which is shared by all assets to be loaded. This will make it easy for the application to change state so that it can start playing the game when all assets have loaded. Let's briefly look at the itemLoaded() function now:

```
function itemLoaded(event) {

loadCount++;
//console.log("loading:" + loadCount)
if (loadCount >= itemsToLoad) {

    shootSound.removeEventListener("canplaythrough",itemLoaded, false);
    shootSound2.removeEventListener("canplaythrough",itemLoaded, false);
    shootSound3.removeEventListener("canplaythrough",itemLoaded, false);
    explodeSound.removeEventListener("canplaythrough",itemLoaded,false);
    explodeSound2.removeEventListener("canplaythrough",itemLoaded,false);
```

```
explodeSound3.removeEventListener("canplaythrough",itemLoaded,false);
saucershootSound.removeEventListener("canplaythrough",itemLoaded,false);
saucershootSound2.removeEventListener("canplaythrough",itemLoaded,false);
saucershootSound3.removeEventListener("canplaythrough",itemLoaded,false);

soundPool.push({name:"explode1", element:explodeSound, played:false});
soundPool.push({name:"explode1", element:explodeSound2, played:false});
soundPool.push({name:"explode1", element:explodeSound3, played:false});
soundPool.push({name:"shoot1", element:shootSound, played:false});
soundPool.push({name:"shoot1", element:shootSound2, played:false});
soundPool.push({name:"shoot1", element:shootSound3, played:false});
soundPool.push({name:"saucershoot", element:saucershootSound,
 played:false});
soundPool.push({name:"saucershoot", element:saucershootSound2,
 played:false});
soundPool.push({name:"saucershoot", element:saucershootSound3,
 played:false});

switchGameState(GAME_STATE_TITLE)
   }

 }
```

In this function, we first remove the event listener from each loaded item, then add the sounds to our sound pool. Finally, we call the `switchGameState()` to send the game to the title screen.

Playing sounds

Sounds will be played using the `playSound()` function from Chapter 7. We will not reprint that function here, but it will be in Example 9-1 where we give the entire set of code for the game. We will call the `playSound()` function at various instances in our code to play the needed sounds. For example, the `createExplode()` function presented earlier in this chapter included this line:

```
playSound(SOUND_EXPLODE,.5);
```

When we want to play a sound instance from the pool, we call the `playSound()` function and pass in the constants representing the sound and the volume for the sound. If an instance of the sound is available in the pool, it will be used and the sound will play.

Now, let's move on to another type of application pool—the object pool.

Pooling Object Instances

We have looked at object pools as they relate to sounds, but we have not applied this concept to our game objects. Object pooling is a technique designed to save processing time, so it is very applicable to an arcade game application such as the one we are building. By pooling object instances, we avoid the sometimes processor-intensive task of creating object instances on the fly during game execution. This is especially applicable to our particle explosions, as we create multiple objects on the same frame tick.

On a lower-powered platform, such as a handheld device, object pooling can help increase frame rate.

Object pooling in Geo Blaster Extended

In our game, we will apply the pooling concept to the explosion particles. Of course, we can extend this concept to rocks, projectiles, saucers, and any other type of object that requires multiple instances. For this example, though, let's focus on the particles. As we will see, adding pooling in JavaScript is a relatively simple but powerful technique.

Adding pooling variables to our game

We will need to add four application scope variables to our game to make use of pooling for our game particle:

```
var particlePool = [];
    var maxParticles = 200;
    var newParticle;
    var tempParticle;
```

The `particlePool` array will hold the list of `particle` object instances that are waiting to be used. When `createExplode()` needs to use a particle, it will first look to see whether any are available in this array. If one is available, it will be "popped" off the top of the `particlePool` stack and placed in the application scope `newParticle` variable—which is a reference to the pooled particle. The `createExplode()` function will set the properties of the `newParticle`, and then "push" it to the end of the existing `particles` array.

Once a particle's life has been exhausted, the `updateParticles()` function will splice the particle from the `particles` array and push it back into the `particlePool` array. We have created the `tempParticle` reference to alleviate the `updateParticles()` function's need to create this instance on each frame tick.

The `maxParticles` value will be used in a new function called `createObjectPools()`. We will call this function in the `gameStateInit()` state function before we create the sound and tile sheet loading events.

Let's take a look at the `createObjectPools()` function now:

```
function createObjectPools(){
    for (var ctr=0;ctr<maxParticles;ctr++){
        var newParticle = {};
        particlePool.push(newParticle)
    }
    console.log("particlePool=" + particlePool.length)
}
```

As you can see, we simply iterate from 0 to 1 less than the `maxParticles` value, and place a generic object instance at each element in the pool. When a particle is needed, the `createExplode()` function will look to see whether `particlePool.length` is greater than 0. If a particle is available, it will be added to the `particles` array after its attributes are set. If no particle is available, none will be used.

 This functionality can be extended to add a particle as needed to the pool when none is available. We have not added that functionality to our example, but it is common in some pooling algorithms.

Here is the newly modified `createExplode()` function in its entirety:

```
function createExplode(x,y,num,type) {

    playSound(SOUND_EXPLODE,.5);
    for (var partCtr=0;partCtr<num;partCtr++){
        if (particlePool.length > 0){

        newParticle = particlePool.pop();
        newParticle.dx = Math.random()*3;
        if (Math.random()<.5){
            newParticle.dx* = -1;
        }
        newParticle.dy = Math.random()*3;
        if (Math.random()<.5){
        newParticle.dy* = -1;
        }

        newParticle.life = Math.floor(Math.random()*30+30);
        newParticle.lifeCtr = 0;
        newParticle.x = x;
        newParticle.width = 2;
        newParticle.height = 2;
        newParticle.y = y;
        newParticle.type = type;
        //ConsoleLog.log("newParticle.life=" + newParticle.life);
        particles.push(newParticle);
        }

    }

}
```

The `updateParticles()` function will loop through the `particles` instances, update the attributes of each, and then check to see whether the particle's life has been exhausted. If it has, the function will place the particle back in the pool. Here is the code we will add to `updateParticles()` to replenish the pool:

```
if (remove) {
    particlePool.push(tempParticle)
    particles.splice(particleCtr,1)

}
```

Adding in a Step Timer

In Chapter 8, we created a simple FrameRateCounter object prototype that was used to display the current frame rate as the game was running. We are going to extend the functionality of this counter to add in a "step timer." The step timer will use the time difference calculated between frames to create a "step factor." This step factor will be used when updating the positions of the objects on the canvas. The result will be smoother rendering of the game objects when there are drops in frame rate, as well as keeping relatively consistent game play on browsers and systems that cannot maintain the frame rate needed to play the game effectively.

How the step timer works

We will update the constructor function for FrameRateCounter to accept in a new single parameter called fps. This value will represent the frames per second that we want our game to run:

```
function FrameRateCounter(fps) {
    if (fps == undefined){
        this.fps = 40
    }else{
        this.fps = fps
    }
}
```

If no fps value is passed in, the value 40 will be used.

We will also add in two new object-level scope variables to calculate the step in our step timer:

```
this.lastTime = dateTemp.getTime();
this.step = 1;
```

The lastTime variable will contain the time in which the previous frame completed its work.

We calculate the step by comparing the current time value with the lastTime value on each frame tick. This calculation will occur in the FrameRateCounter countFrames() function:

```
FrameRateCounter.prototype.countFrames=function() {

    var dateTemp = new Date();

    var timeDifference = dateTemp.getTime()-this.lastTime;
    this.step = (timeDifference/1000)*this.fps;
    this.lastTime = dateTemp.getTime();
```

The local timeDifference value is calculated by subtracting the lastTime value from the current time (represented by the dateTemp.getTime() return value).

To calculate the step value, divide the timeDifference by 1000 (the number of milliseconds in a single second), and multiply the result by the desired frame rate. If the

---

game is running with no surplus or no deficit in time between frame ticks, the step value will be 1. If the current frame tick took longer than a single frame to finish, the value will be greater than 1 (a deficit). If the current frame took less time than a single frame, the step value will be less than 1 (a surplus).

For example, if the last frame took too long to process, the current frame will compensate by moving each object a little bit more than the step value of 1. Let's illustrate this with a simple example.

Let's say we want the saucer to move five pixels to the right on each frame tick. This would be a dx value of 5.

For this example, we will also say that our desired frame rate is 40 FPS. This means that we want each frame tick to use up 25 milliseconds (1000/40 = 25).

Let's also suppose that the timeDifference between the current frame and the last frame is 26 milliseconds. Our game is running at a deficit of 1 millisecond per frame—this means that the game processing is taking more time than we want it to.

To calculate the step value, divide the timeDifference by 1000: 26/1000 = .026.

We multiply this value by the desired fps for our game: .026 * 40 = 1.04

Our step value is 1.04 for the current frame. Because of the deficit in processing time, we want to move each game object slightly more than a frame so there is no surplus or deficit. In the case of no surplus or deficit, the step value would be 1. If there is a surplus, the step value would be less than 1.

This step value will be multiplied to the changes in movement vectors for each object in the update functions. This allows the game to keep a relatively smooth look even when there are fluctuations in the frame rate. In addition, the game will update the screen in a relatively consistent manner across the various browsers and systems, resulting in game play that is relatively consistent for each user.

Here are the new movement vector calculations for each object:

player

```
        player.x += player.movingX*frameRateCounter.step;
        player.y += player.movingY*frameRateCounter.step;
```

playerMissiles

```
        tempPlayerMissile.x += tempPlayerMissile.dx*frameRateCounter.step;
        tempPlayerMissile.y += tempPlayerMissile.dy*frameRateCounter.step;
```

rocks

```
        tempRock.x += tempRock.dx*frameRateCounter.step;
        tempRock.y += tempRock.dy*frameRateCounter.step;
```

saucers

```
        tempSaucer.x += tempSaucer.dx*frameRateCounter.step;
        tempSaucer.y += tempSaucer.dy*frameRateCounter.step;
```

saucerMissiles

```
        tempSaucerMissile.x += tempSaucerMissile.dx*frameRateCounter.step;
        tempSaucerMissile.y += tempSaucerMissile.dy*frameRateCounter.step;
```

particles

```
        tempParticle.x += tempParticle.dx*frameRateCounter.step;
        tempParticle.y += tempParticle.dy*frameRateCounter.step;
```

We have now covered all of the major changes to turn *Geo Blaster Basic* into *Geo Blaster Extended*. Let's look at Example 9-1, which has the entire code for the final game.

Geo Blaster Extended Full Source

Example 9-1. Geo Blaster Extended full source code listing

```html
<!doctype html>
<html lang="en">
<head>
<meta charset="UTF-8">
<title>CH9EX1: Geo Blaster Extended</title>
<script src="modernizr-1.6.min.js"></script>
<script type="text/javascript">
window.addEventListener('load', eventWindowLoaded, false);
function eventWindowLoaded() {

    canvasApp();

}

function canvasSupport () {
    return Modernizr.canvas;
}

function supportedAudioFormat(audio) {
    var returnExtension = "";
    if (audio.canPlayType("audio/ogg") =="probably" ||
        audio.canPlayType("audio/ogg") == "maybe") {
        returnExtension = "ogg";
    } else if(audio.canPlayType("audio/wav") =="probably" ||
        audio.canPlayType("audio/wav") == "maybe") {
        returnExtension = "wav";
    } else if(audio.canPlayType("audio/wav") == "probably" ||
        audio.canPlayType("audio/wav") == "maybe") {
        returnExtension = "mp3";
    }

    return returnExtension;
```

```
}

function canvasApp(){

    if (!canvasSupport()) {
          return;
      }else{
         theCanvas = document.getElementById("canvas");
         context = theCanvas.getContext("2d");
    }

    //sounds
    const SOUND_EXPLODE = "explode1";
    const SOUND_SHOOT = "shoot1";
    const SOUND_SAUCER_SHOOT = "saucershoot"
    const MAX_SOUNDS = 9;
    var soundPool = new Array();
    var explodeSound;
    var explodeSound2;
    var explodeSound3;
    var shootSound;
    var shootSound2;
    var shootSound3;
    var saucershootSound;
    var saucershootSound2;
    var saucershootSound3;
    var audioType;

    //application states
    const GAME_STATE_INIT = 0;
    const GAME_STATE_WAIT_FOR_LOAD = 5;
    const GAME_STATE_TITLE = 10;
    const GAME_STATE_NEW_GAME = 20;
    const GAME_STATE_NEW_LEVEL = 30;
    const GAME_STATE_PLAYER_START = 40;
    const GAME_STATE_PLAY_LEVEL = 50;
    const GAME_STATE_PLAYER_DIE = 60;
    const GAME_STATE_GAME_OVER = 70;
    var currentGameState = 0;
    var currentGameStateFunction = null;

    //title screen
    var titleStarted = false;

    //game over screen
    var gameOverStarted = false;

    //objects for game play

    //game environment
    var score = 0;
    var level = 0;
```

```
var extraShipAtEach = 10000;
var extraShipsEarned = 0;
var playerShips = 3;

//playfield
var xMin = 0;
var xMax = 400;
var yMin = 0;
var yMax = 400;

//score values
var bigRockScore = 50;
var medRockScore = 75;
var smlRockScore = 100;
var saucerScore = 300;

//rock scale constants
const ROCK_SCALE_LARGE = 1;
const ROCK_SCALE_MEDIUM = 2;
const ROCK_SCALE_SMALL = 3;

//create game objects and arrays
var player = {};
var rocks = [];
var saucers = [];
var playerMissiles = [];
var particles = [];
var saucerMissiles = [];
var particlePool = [];
var maxParticles = 200;
var newParticle;
var tempParticle;

//level specific
var levelRockMaxSpeedAdjust = 1;
var levelSaucerMax = 1;
var levelSaucerOccurrenceRate = 25;
var levelSaucerSpeed = 1;
var levelSaucerFireDelay = 300;
var levelSaucerFireRate = 30;
var levelSaucerMissileSpeed = 1;

//keyPresses
var keyPressList=[];

//tile sheets
var shipTiles;
var shipTiles2;
var saucerTiles;
var largeRockTiles;
var mediumRockTiles;
var smallRockTiles;
var particleTiles;

 function itemLoaded(event) {
```

```
        loadCount++;
        //console.log("loading:" + loadCount)
        if (loadCount >= itemsToLoad) {

            shootSound.removeEventListener("canplaythrough",itemLoaded, false);
            shootSound2.removeEventListener("canplaythrough",itemLoaded, false);
            shootSound3.removeEventListener("canplaythrough",itemLoaded, false);
            explodeSound.removeEventListener("canplaythrough",itemLoaded,false);
            explodeSound2.removeEventListener("canplaythrough",itemLoaded,false);
            explodeSound3.removeEventListener("canplaythrough",itemLoaded,false);
            saucershootSound.removeEventListener("canplaythrough",itemLoaded,false);
            saucershootSound2.removeEventListener("canplaythrough",itemLoaded,
             false);
            saucershootSound3.removeEventListener("canplaythrough",itemLoaded,
             false);

            soundPool.push({name:"explode1", element:explodeSound, played:false});
            soundPool.push({name:"explode1", element:explodeSound2, played:false});
            soundPool.push({name:"explode1", element:explodeSound3, played:false});
            soundPool.push({name:"shoot1", element:shootSound, played:false});
            soundPool.push({name:"shoot1", element:shootSound2, played:false});
            soundPool.push({name:"shoot1", element:shootSound3, played:false});
            soundPool.push({name:"saucershoot", element:saucershootSound,
             played:false});
            soundPool.push({name:"saucershoot", element:saucershootSound2,
             played:false});
            soundPool.push({name:"saucershoot", element:saucershootSound3,
             played:false});

            switchGameState(GAME_STATE_TITLE)

        }

    }
    function playSound(sound,volume) {
        ConsoleLog.log("play sound" + sound);
        var soundFound = false;
        var soundIndex = 0;
        var tempSound;

        if (soundPool.length> 0) {
            while (!soundFound && soundIndex < soundPool.length) {

                var tSound = soundPool[soundIndex];
                if ((tSound.element.ended || !tSound.played) && tSound.name == sound) {
                    soundFound = true;
                    tSound.played = true;
                } else {
                    soundIndex++;
                }

            }
        }
```

```
        if (soundFound) {
            ConsoleLog.log("sound found");
            tempSound = soundPool[soundIndex].element;
            //tempSound.setAttribute("src", sound + "." + audioType);
            //tempSound.loop = false;
            //tempSound.volume = volume;
            tempSound.play();

        } else if (soundPool.length < MAX_SOUNDS){
            ConsoleLog.log("sound not found");
            tempSound = document.createElement("audio");
            tempSound.setAttribute("src", sound + "." + audioType);
            tempSound.volume = volume;
            tempSound.play();
            soundPool.push({name:sound, element:tempSound, type:audioType,
             played:true});
        }

    }
}
function runGame(){
    currentGameStateFunction();
}

function switchGameState(newState) {
    currentGameState = newState;
    switch (currentGameState) {

        case GAME_STATE_INIT:
            currentGameStateFunction = gameStateInit;
            break;
        case GAME_STATE_WAIT_FOR_LOAD:
            currentGameStateFunction = gameStateWaitForLoad;
            break;
        case GAME_STATE_TITLE:
            currentGameStateFunction = gameStateTitle;
            break;
        case GAME_STATE_NEW_GAME:
            currentGameStateFunction = gameStateNewGame;
            break;
        case GAME_STATE_NEW_LEVEL:
            currentGameStateFunction = gameStateNewLevel;
            break;
        case GAME_STATE_PLAYER_START:
            currentGameStateFunction = gameStatePlayerStart;
            break;
        case GAME_STATE_PLAY_LEVEL:
            currentGameStateFunction = gameStatePlayLevel;
            break;
        case GAME_STATE_PLAYER_DIE:
            currentGameStateFunction = gameStatePlayerDie;
            break;
        case GAME_STATE_GAME_OVER:
            currentGameStateFunction = gameStateGameOver;
            break;
```

```
      }

   }

   function gameStateWaitForLoad(){
      //do nothing while loading events occur
      console.log("doing nothing...")
   }

   function createObjectPools(){
      for (var ctr=0;ctr<maxParticles;ctr++){
         var newParticle = {};
         particlePool.push(newParticle)
      }
      console.log("particlePool=" + particlePool.length)
   }

   function gameStateInit() {
      createObjectPools();

      loadCount = 0;
      itemsToLoad = 16;

      explodeSound = document.createElement("audio");
      document.body.appendChild(explodeSound);
      audioType = supportedAudioFormat(explodeSound);
      explodeSound.setAttribute("src", "explode1." + audioType);
      explodeSound.addEventListener("canplaythrough",itemLoaded,false);

      explodeSound2 = document.createElement("audio");
      document.body.appendChild(explodeSound2);
      explodeSound2.setAttribute("src", "explode1." + audioType);
      explodeSound2.addEventListener("canplaythrough",itemLoaded,false);

      explodeSound3 = document.createElement("audio");
      document.body.appendChild(explodeSound3);
      explodeSound3.setAttribute("src", "explode1." + audioType);
      explodeSound3.addEventListener("canplaythrough",itemLoaded,false);

      shootSound = document.createElement("audio");
      audioType = supportedAudioFormat(shootSound);
      document.body.appendChild(shootSound);
      shootSound.setAttribute("src", "shoot1." + audioType);
      shootSound.addEventListener("canplaythrough",itemLoaded,false);

      shootSound2 = document.createElement("audio");
      document.body.appendChild(shootSound2);
      shootSound2.setAttribute("src", "shoot1." + audioType);
      shootSound2.addEventListener("canplaythrough",itemLoaded,false);

      shootSound3 = document.createElement("audio");
      document.body.appendChild(shootSound3);
      shootSound3.setAttribute("src", "shoot1." + audioType);
      shootSound3.addEventListener("canplaythrough",itemLoaded,false);
```

```
    saucershootSound = document.createElement("audio");
    audioType = supportedAudioFormat(saucershootSound);
    document.body.appendChild(saucershootSound);
    saucershootSound.setAttribute("src", "saucershoot." + audioType);
    saucershootSound.addEventListener("canplaythrough",itemLoaded,false);

    saucershootSound2 = document.createElement("audio");
    document.body.appendChild(saucershootSound2);
    saucershootSound2.setAttribute("src", "saucershoot." + audioType);
    saucershootSound2.addEventListener("canplaythrough",itemLoaded,false);

    saucershootSound3 = document.createElement("audio");
    document.body.appendChild(saucershootSound3);
    saucershootSound3.setAttribute("src", "saucershoot." + audioType);
    saucershootSound3.addEventListener("canplaythrough",itemLoaded,false);

    shipTiles = new Image();
    shipTiles.src = "ship_tiles.png";
    shipTiles.onload = itemLoaded;

    shipTiles2 = new Image();
    shipTiles2.src = "ship_tiles2.png";
    shipTiles2.onload = itemLoaded;

    saucerTiles= new Image();
    saucerTiles.src = "saucer.png";
    saucerTiles.onload = itemLoaded;

    largeRockTiles = new Image();
    largeRockTiles.src = "largerocks.png";
    largeRockTiles.onload = itemLoaded;

    mediumRockTiles = new Image();
    mediumRockTiles.src = "mediumrocks.png";
    mediumRockTiles.onload = itemLoaded;

    smallRockTiles = new Image();
    smallRockTiles.src = "smallrocks.png";
    smallRockTiles.onload = itemLoaded;

    particleTiles = new Image();
    particleTiles.src = "parts.png";
    particleTiles.onload = itemLoaded;

    switchGameState(GAME_STATE_WAIT_FOR_LOAD);
}

function gameStateTitle() {
    if (titleStarted !=true){
        fillBackground();
        setTextStyleTitle();
        context.fillText  ("Geo Blaster X-ten-d", 120, 70);
```

```
        setTextStyle();
        context.fillText  ("Press Space To Play", 130, 140);

        setTextStyleCredits();
        context.fillText  ("An HTML5 Example Game", 125, 200);
        context.fillText  ("From our upcoming HTML5 Canvas", 100, 215);
        context.fillText  ("book on O'Reilly Press", 130, 230);

        context.fillText  ("Game Code - Jeff Fulton", 130, 260);
        context.fillText  ("Sound Manager - Steve Fulton", 120, 275);


        titleStarted = true;
    }else{
        //wait for space key click
        if (keyPressList[32]==true){
            ConsoleLog.log("space pressed");
            switchGameState(GAME_STATE_NEW_GAME);
            titleStarted = false;

        }

    }

}

function gameStateNewGame(){
    ConsoleLog.log("gameStateNewGame")
    //set up new game
    level = 0;
    score = 0;
    playerShips = 3;
    player.maxVelocity = 5;
    player.width = 32;
    player.height = 32;
    player.halfWidth = 16;
    player.halfHeight = 16;
    player.hitWidth = 24;
    player.hitHeight = 24;
    player.rotationalVelocity = 10; //how many degrees to turn the ship
    player.thrustAcceleration = .05;
    player.missileFrameDelay = 5;
    player.thrust = false;
    player.alpha = 1;
    player.rotation = 0;
    player.x = 0;
    player.y = 0;

    fillBackground();
    renderScoreBoard();
    switchGameState(GAME_STATE_NEW_LEVEL)

}
```

```
function gameStateNewLevel(){
    rocks = [];
    saucers = [];
    playerMissiles = [];
    particles = [];
    saucerMissiles = [];
    level++;
    levelRockMaxSpeedAdjust = level*.25;
    if (levelRockMaxSpeedAdjust > 3){
        levelRockMaxSpeed = 3;
    }

    levelSaucerMax = 1+Math.floor(level/10);
    if (levelSaucerMax > 5){
        levelSaucerMax = 5;
    }
    levelSaucerOccurrenceRate = 10+3*level;
    if (levelSaucerOccurrenceRate > 35){
        levelSaucerOccurrenceRate = 35;
    }
    levelSaucerSpeed = 1+.5*level;
    if (levelSaucerSpeed>5){
        levelSaucerSpeed = 5;
    }
    levelSaucerFireDelay = 120-10*level;
    if (levelSaucerFireDelay<20) {
        levelSaucerFireDelay = 20;
    }

    levelSaucerFireRate = 20 + 3*level;
    if (levelSaucerFireRate<50) {
        levelSaucerFireRate = 50;
    }

    levelSaucerMissileSpeed = 1+.2*level;
    if (levelSaucerMissileSpeed > 4){
        levelSaucerMissileSpeed = 4;
    }
    //create level rocks
    for (var newRockctr=0;newRockctr<level+3;newRockctr++){
        var newRock = {};

        newRock.scale = 1;
        //scale
        //1 = large
        //2 = medium
        //3 = small
        //these will be used as the divisor for the new size
        //50/1 = 50
        //50/2 = 25
        //50/3 = 16
        newRock.width = 64;
        newRock.height = 64;
        newRock.halfWidth = 32;
        newRock.halfHeight = 32;
```

```
        newRock.hitWidth = 48;
        newRock.hitHeight = 48;

        //start all new rocks in upper left for ship safety
        newRock.x = Math.floor(Math.random()*50);
        //ConsoleLog.log("newRock.x=" + newRock.x);
        newRock.y = Math.floor(Math.random()*50);
        //ConsoleLog.log("newRock.y=" + newRock.y);
        newRock.dx = (Math.random()*2)+levelRockMaxSpeedAdjust;
        if (Math.random()<.5){
            newRock.dx *= -1;
        }
        newRock.dy=(Math.random()*2)+levelRockMaxSpeedAdjust;
        if (Math.random()<.5){
            newRock.dy *= -1;
        }
        //rotation speed and direction

        if (Math.random()<.5){
            newRock.rotationInc = -1;
        }else{
            newRock.rotationInc = 1;
        }

        newRock.animationDelay = Math.floor(Math.random()*3+1);
        newRock.animationCount = 0;

        newRock.scoreValue = bigRockScore;
        newRock.rotation = 0;

        rocks.push(newRock);
        //ConsoleLog.log("rock created rotationInc=" + newRock.rotationInc);
    }
    resetPlayer();
    switchGameState(GAME_STATE_PLAYER_START);

}

function gameStatePlayerStart(){

    fillBackground();
    renderScoreBoard();
    if (player.alpha < 1){
        player.alpha += .01;

        ConsoleLog.log("player.alpha=" + context.globalAlpha)
    }else{
        switchGameState(GAME_STATE_PLAY_LEVEL);
        player.safe = false; // added chapter 9

    }

    //renderPlayerShip(player.x, player.y,270,1);
    context.globalAlpha = 1;
```

```
    //new in chapter 9
    checkKeys();
    update();
    render(); //added chapter 9
    checkCollisions();
    checkForExtraShip();
    checkForEndOfLevel();
    frameRateCounter.countFrames();

}

function gameStatePlayLevel(){
    checkKeys();
    update();
    render();
    checkCollisions();
    checkForExtraShip();
    checkForEndOfLevel();
    frameRateCounter.countFrames();

}

function resetPlayer() {
    player.rotation = 270;
    player.x = .5*xMax;
    player.y = .5*yMax;
    player.facingX = 0;
    player.facingY = 0;
    player.movingX = 0;
    player.movingY = 0;
    player.alpha = 0;
    player.missileFrameCount = 0;
    //added chapter 9
    player.safe = true;
}

function checkForExtraShip() {
    if (Math.floor(score/extraShipAtEach) > extraShipsEarned) {
        playerShips++
        extraShipsEarned++;
    }
}

function checkForEndOfLevel(){
    if (rocks.length==0) {
        switchGameState(GAME_STATE_NEW_LEVEL);
    }
}

function gameStatePlayerDie(){
    if (particles.length >0 || playerMissiles.length>0) {
        fillBackground();
        renderScoreBoard();
        updateRocks();
        updateSaucers();
```

```
            updateParticles();
            updateSaucerMissiles();
            updatePlayerMissiles();
            renderRocks();
            renderSaucers();
            renderParticles();
            renderSaucerMissiles();
            renderPlayerMissiles();
            frameRateCounter.countFrames();

    }else{
            playerShips--;
            if (playerShips<1) {
                switchGameState(GAME_STATE_GAME_OVER);
            }else{
                //resetPlayer();
                switchGameState(GAME_STATE_PLAYER_START);
            }
        }
    }
}

function gameStateGameOver() {
    //ConsoleLog.log("Game Over State");
    if (gameOverStarted !=true){
        fillBackground();
        renderScoreBoard();
        setTextStyle();
        context.fillText  ("Game Over!", 160, 70);
        context.fillText  ("Press Space To Play", 130, 140);

        gameOverStarted = true;
    }else{
        //wait for space key click
        if (keyPressList[32]==true){
            ConsoleLog.log("space pressed");
            switchGameState(GAME_STATE_TITLE);
            gameOverStarted = false;

        }

    }
}

function fillBackground() {
    // draw background and text
    context.fillStyle = '#000000';
    context.fillRect(xMin, yMin, xMax, yMax);

}

function setTextStyle() {
    context.fillStyle = '#ffffff';
    context.font = '15px _sans';
    context.textBaseline = 'top';
}
```

```
function setTextStyleTitle() {
    context.fillStyle  = '#54ebeb';
    context.font = '20px _sans';
    context.textBaseline = 'top';
}

function setTextStyleCredits() {
    context.fillStyle = '#ffffff';
    context.font = '12px _sans';
    context.textBaseline = 'top';
}

function renderScoreBoard() {

    context.fillStyle = "#ffffff";
    context.fillText('Score ' + score, 10, 20);
    renderPlayerShip(200,16,270,.75)
    context.fillText('X ' + playerShips, 220, 20);

    context.fillText('FPS: ' + frameRateCounter.lastFrameCount, 300,20)

}

function checkKeys() {
    //check keys

    if (keyPressList[38]==true){
    //thrust
        var angleInRadians = player.rotation * Math.PI / 180;
        player.facingX = Math.cos(angleInRadians);
        player.facingY = Math.sin(angleInRadians);

        var movingXNew = player.movingX+player.thrustAcceleration*player.facingX;
        var movingYNew = player.movingY+player.thrustAcceleration*player.facingY;

        var currentVelocity = Math.sqrt ((movingXNew*movingXNew) +
        (movingXNew*movingXNew));

        if (currentVelocity < player.maxVelocity) {
            player.movingX = movingXNew;
            player.movingY = movingYNew;
        }
        player.thrust = true;

    }else{
        player.thrust = false;
    }

    if (keyPressList[37]==true) {
        //rotate counterclockwise
        player.rotation -= player.rotationalVelocity;
        if (player.rotation <0) {
            player.rotation = 350
        }
```

```
      }

   if (keyPressList[39]==true) {
      //rotate clockwise
      player.rotation += player.rotationalVelocity;
      if (player.rotation >350) {
         player.rotation = 10
      }
   }

   if (keyPressList[32]==true) {
         if (player.missileFrameCount>player.missileFrameDelay){
         playSound(SOUND_SHOOT,.5);
         firePlayerMissile();
         player.missileFrameCount = 0;

      }
   }
}

function update() {
   updatePlayer();
   updatePlayerMissiles();
   updateRocks();
   updateSaucers();
   updateSaucerMissiles();
   updateParticles();
}

function render() {
   fillBackground();
   renderScoreBoard();
   renderPlayerShip(player.x,player.y,player.rotation,1);
   renderPlayerMissiles();
   renderRocks();
   renderSaucers();
   renderSaucerMissiles();
   renderParticles();
}

function updatePlayer() {
   player.missileFrameCount++;

   player.x += player.movingX*frameRateCounter.step;
   player.y += player.movingY*frameRateCounter.step;

   if (player.x > xMax) {
      player.x =- player.width;
   }else if (player.x<-player.width){
      player.x = xMax;
   }

   if (player.y > yMax) {
      player.y =- player.height;
```

```
        }else if (player.y<-player.height){
            player.y = yMax;
        }
    }

    function updatePlayerMissiles() {
        var tempPlayerMissile = {};
        var playerMissileLength=playerMissiles.length-1;
        //ConsoleLog.log("update playerMissileLength=" + playerMissileLength);
        for (var playerMissileCtr=playerMissileLength;playerMissileCtr>=0;
         playerMissileCtr--){
            //ConsoleLog.log("update player missile" + playerMissileCtr)
            tempPlayerMissile = playerMissiles[playerMissileCtr];
            tempPlayerMissile.x += tempPlayerMissile.dx*frameRateCounter.step;;
            tempPlayerMissile.y += tempPlayerMissile.dy*frameRateCounter.step;;
            if (tempPlayerMissile.x > xMax) {
                tempPlayerMissile.x =- tempPlayerMissile.width;
            }else if (tempPlayerMissile.x<-tempPlayerMissile.width){
                tempPlayerMissile.x = xMax;
            }

            if (tempPlayerMissile.y > yMax) {
                tempPlayerMissile.y =- tempPlayerMissile.height;
            }else if (tempPlayerMissile.y<-tempPlayerMissile.height){
                tempPlayerMissile.y = yMax;
            }

            tempPlayerMissile.lifeCtr++;
            if (tempPlayerMissile.lifeCtr > tempPlayerMissile.life){
                //ConsoleLog.log("removing player missile");
                playerMissiles.splice(playerMissileCtr,1)
                tempPlayerMissile = null;
            }
        }
    }

    function updateRocks(){

        var tempRock = {};
        var rocksLength = rocks.length-1;
        //ConsoleLog.log("update rocks length=" + rocksLength);
        for (var rockCtr=rocksLength;rockCtr>=0;rockCtr--){
            tempRock = rocks[rockCtr]
            tempRock.x += tempRock.dx*frameRateCounter.step;
            tempRock.y += tempRock.dy*frameRateCounter.step;

            tempRock.animationCount++;
            if (tempRock.animationCount > tempRock.animationDelay){
                tempRock.animationCount = 0;
                tempRock.rotation += tempRock.rotationInc;

                if (tempRock.rotation > 4){
                    tempRock.rotation = 0;
                }else if (tempRock.rotation <0){
                    tempRock.rotation = 4;
```

```
        }
    }

    if (tempRock.x > xMax) {
        tempRock.x = xMin-tempRock.width;
    }else if (tempRock.x<xMin-tempRock.width){
        tempRock.x = xMax;
    }

    if (tempRock.y > yMax) {
        tempRock.y = yMin-tempRock.width;
    }else if (tempRock.y<yMin-tempRock.width){
        tempRock.y = yMax;
    }

    //ConsoleLog.log("update rock "+ rockCtr)
    }
}

function updateSaucers() {
    //first check to see if we want to add a saucer

    if (saucers.length< levelSaucerMax){
        if (Math.floor(Math.random()*100)<=levelSaucerOccurrenceRate){
            //ConsoleLog.log("create saucer")
            var newSaucer = {};

            newSaucer.width = 30;
            newSaucer.height = 13;
            newSaucer.halfHeight = 6.5;
            newSaucer.halfWidth = 15;
            newSaucer.hitWidth = 30;
            newSaucer.hitHeight = 13;
            newSaucer.scoreValue = saucerScore;
            newSaucer.fireRate = levelSaucerFireRate;
            newSaucer.fireDelay = levelSaucerFireDelay;
            newSaucer.fireDelayCount = 0;
            newSaucer.missileSpeed = levelSaucerMissileSpeed;
            newSaucer.dy = (Math.random()*2);
            if (Math.floor(Math.random)*2==1){
                newSaucer.dy *= -1;
            }

            //choose betweeen left or right edge to start
            if (Math.floor(Math.random()*2)==1){
                //start on right and go left
                newSaucer.x = 450;
                newSaucer.dx = -1*levelSaucerSpeed;

            }else{
                //left to right
                newSaucer.x = -50;
                newSaucer.dx = levelSaucerSpeed;
            }
```

```
            newSaucer.missileSpeed = levelSaucerMissileSpeed;
            newSaucer.fireDelay = levelSaucerFireDelay;
            newSaucer.fireRate = levelSaucerFireRate;
            newSaucer.y = Math.floor(Math.random()*400);

            saucers.push(newSaucer);
        }

    }

    var tempSaucer = {};
    var saucerLength = saucers.length-1;
    //ConsoleLog.log("update rocks length=" + rocksLength);
    for (var saucerCtr=saucerLength;saucerCtr>=0;saucerCtr--){
        tempSaucer = saucers[saucerCtr];

        //should saucer fire
        tempSaucer.fireDelayCount++;
        if (Math.floor(Math.random()*100) <=tempSaucer.fireRate &&
         tempSaucer.fireDelayCount>tempSaucer.fireDelay ){
            playSound(SOUND_SAUCER_SHOOT,.5);
            fireSaucerMissile(tempSaucer)
            tempSaucer.fireDelayCount=0;
        }

        var remove = false;
        tempSaucer.x += tempSaucer.dx*frameRateCounter.step;
        tempSaucer.y += tempSaucer.dy*frameRateCounter.step;

        //remove saucers on left and right edges
        if (tempSaucer.dx > 0 && tempSaucer.x >xMax){
            remove = true;
        }else if (tempSaucer.dx <0 &&tempSaucer.x<xMin-tempSaucer.width){
            remove = true;
        }

        //bounce saucers off over vertical edges
        if (tempSaucer.y > yMax || tempSaucer.y<yMin-tempSaucer.width) {
            tempSaucer.dy *= -1
        }


        if (remove==true) {
            //remove the saucer
            ConsoleLog.log("saucer removed")
            saucers.splice(saucerCtr,1);
            tempSaucer = null;
        }

    }

}
```

```
function updateSaucerMissiles() {
    var tempSaucerMissile = {};
    var saucerMissileLength = saucerMissiles.length-1;
    for (var saucerMissileCtr = saucerMissileLength;saucerMissileCtr>=0;
     saucerMissileCtr--){
        //ConsoleLog.log("update player missile" + playerMissileCtr)
        tempSaucerMissile = saucerMissiles[saucerMissileCtr];
        tempSaucerMissile.x += tempSaucerMissile.dx*frameRateCounter.step;
        tempSaucerMissile.y += tempSaucerMissile.dy*frameRateCounter.step;
        if (tempSaucerMissile.x > xMax) {
            tempSaucerMissile.x =- tempSaucerMissile.width;
        }else if (tempSaucerMissile.x<-tempSaucerMissile.width){
            tempSaucerMissile.x = xMax;
        }

        if (tempSaucerMissile.y > yMax) {
            tempSaucerMissile.y =- tempSaucerMissile.height;
        }else if (tempSaucerMissile.y<-tempSaucerMissile.height){
            tempSaucerMissile.y = yMax;
        }

        tempSaucerMissile.lifeCtr++;
        if (tempSaucerMissile.lifeCtr > tempSaucerMissile.life){
            //remove
            saucerMissiles.splice(saucerMissileCtr,1)
            tempSaucerMissile = null;
        }
    }
}

function updateParticles() {

    var particleLength=particles.length-1;
    ConsoleLog.log("particle=" + particleLength)
    ConsoleLog.log("particlePool=" + particlePool.length)
    for (var particleCtr=particleLength;particleCtr>=0;particleCtr--){
        var remove = false;
        tempParticle = particles[particleCtr];
        tempParticle.x += tempParticle.dx*frameRateCounter.step;
        tempParticle.y += tempParticle.dy*frameRateCounter.step;

        tempParticle.lifeCtr++;

        if (tempParticle.lifeCtr > tempParticle.life){
            remove = true;

        } else if ((tempParticle.x > xMax) || (tempParticle.x<xMin)
            || (tempParticle.y > yMax) || (tempParticle.y<yMin)){
            remove=true;

        }
```

```
        if (remove) {
            particlePool.push(tempParticle)
            particles.splice(particleCtr,1)

        }

    }

}

function renderPlayerShip(x,y,rotation, scale) {
    //transformation
    context.save(); //save current state in stack
    context.globalAlpha = parseFloat(player.alpha);
    var angleInRadians = rotation * Math.PI / 180;
    var sourceX = Math.floor((player.rotation/10) % 10) * 32;
    var sourceY = Math.floor((player.rotation/10) /10) *32;
    if (player.thrust){
        context.drawImage(shipTiles2, sourceX, sourceY, 32,32,
          player.x,player.y,32,32);
    }else{
        context.drawImage(shipTiles, sourceX, sourceY, 32,32,
          player.x,player.y,32,32);
    }

    //restore context
    context.restore(); //pop old state on to screen

    context.globalAlpha = 1;

}

function renderPlayerMissiles() {
    var tempPlayerMissile = {};
    var playerMissileLength=playerMissiles.length-1;
    //ConsoleLog.log("render playerMissileLength=" + playerMissileLength);
    for (var playerMissileCtr=playerMissileLength;playerMissileCtr>=0;
      playerMissileCtr--){
        //ConsoleLog.log("draw player missile " + playerMissileCtr)
        tempPlayerMissile = playerMissiles[playerMissileCtr];
        context.save(); //save current state in stack
        var sourceX=Math.floor(1 % 4) * tempPlayerMissile.width;
        var sourceY=Math.floor(1 / 4) * tempPlayerMissile.height;

        context.drawImage(particleTiles, sourceX, sourceY,
          tempPlayerMissile.width,tempPlayerMissile.height,
          tempPlayerMissile.x,tempPlayerMissile.y,
          tempPlayerMissile.width,tempPlayerMissile.height);

        context.restore(); //pop old state on to screen
    }
}
```

```
function renderRocks() {
    var tempRock = {};
    var rocksLength = rocks.length-1;
    for (var rockCtr = rocksLength;rockCtr>=0;rockCtr--){
        context.save(); //save current state in stack
        tempRock = rocks[rockCtr];
        var sourceX = Math.floor((tempRock.rotation) % 5) * tempRock.width;
        var sourceY = Math.floor((tempRock.rotation) /5) *tempRock.height;

        switch(tempRock.scale){
            case 1:
                context.drawImage(largeRockTiles, sourceX, sourceY,
                 tempRock.width,tempRock.height,tempRock.x,tempRock.y,
                 tempRock.width,tempRock.height);
                break;
            case 2:
                context.drawImage(mediumRockTiles, sourceX,
                 sourceY,tempRock.width,tempRock.height,tempRock.x,tempRock.y,
                 tempRock.width,tempRock.height);
                break;
            case 3:
                context.drawImage(smallRockTiles, sourceX,
                 sourceY,tempRock.width,tempRock.height,tempRock.x,tempRock.y,
                 tempRock.width,tempRock.height);
                break;

        }
        context.restore(); //pop old state on to screen

    }
}

function renderSaucers() {
    var tempSaucer = {};
    var saucerLength = saucers.length-1;
    for (var saucerCtr = saucerLength;saucerCtr>=0;saucerCtr--){
        //ConsoleLog.log("saucer: " + saucerCtr);
        tempSaucer = saucers[saucerCtr];

        context.save(); //save current state in stack
        var sourceX = 0;
        var sourceY = 0;
        context.drawImage(saucerTiles, sourceX, sourceY, 30,15,
         tempSaucer.x,tempSaucer.y,30,15);
        context.restore(); //pop old state on to screen
    }
}
function renderSaucerMissiles() {
    var tempSaucerMissile = {};
    var saucerMissileLength = saucerMissiles.length-1;
    //ConsoleLog.log("saucerMissiles= " + saucerMissiles.length)
    for (var saucerMissileCtr=saucerMissileLength;saucerMissileCtr>=0;
     saucerMissileCtr--){
        //ConsoleLog.log("draw player missile " + playerMissileCtr)
        tempSaucerMissile = saucerMissiles[saucerMissileCtr];
```

```
            context.save(); //save current state in stack
            var sourceX = Math.floor(0 % 4) * tempSaucerMissile.width;
            var sourceY = Math.floor(0 / 4) * tempSaucerMissile.height;

            context.drawImage(particleTiles, sourceX, sourceY,
             tempSaucerMissile.width,tempSaucerMissile.height,
             tempSaucerMissile.x,tempSaucerMissile.y,tempSaucerMissile.width,
             tempSaucerMissile.height);

            context.restore(); //pop old state on to screen

        }
    }

function renderParticles() {

    var tempParticle = {};
    var particleLength = particles.length-1;
    for (var particleCtr=particleLength;particleCtr>=0;particleCtr--){
        tempParticle = particles[particleCtr];
        context.save(); //save current state in stack

        var tile;

        //console.log("part type=" + tempParticle.type)
        switch(tempParticle.type){
            case 0: // saucer
                tile = 0;
                break;
            case 1: //large rock
                tile = 2
                break;
            case 2: //medium rock
                tile = 3;
                break;
            case 3: //small rock
                tile = 0;
                break;
            case 4: //player
                tile = 1;
                break;

        }

        var sourceX = Math.floor(tile % 4) * tempParticle.width;
        var sourceY = Math.floor(tile / 4) * tempParticle.height;

        context.drawImage(particleTiles, sourceX, sourceY,
         tempParticle.width,tempParticle.height,tempParticle.x,
         tempParticle.y,tempParticle.width,tempParticle.height);

        context.restore(); //pop old state on to screen

    }
}
```

```
function checkCollisions() {

    //loop through rocks then missiles.
    //There will always be rocks and a ship,
    //but there will not always be missiles.
    var tempRock = {};
    var rocksLength = rocks.length-1;
    var tempPlayerMissile = {};
    var playerMissileLength = playerMissiles.length-1;
    var saucerLength = saucers.length-1;
    var tempSaucer = {};
    var saucerMissileLength = saucerMissiles.length-1;

    rocks: for (var rockCtr=rocksLength;rockCtr>=0;rockCtr--){
        tempRock = rocks[rockCtr];

        missiles:for (var playerMissileCtr=playerMissileLength;
         playerMissileCtr>=0;playerMissileCtr--){
            tempPlayerMissile = playerMissiles[playerMissileCtr];

            if (boundingBoxCollide(tempRock,tempPlayerMissile)){
                //ConsoleLog.log("hit rock");
                createExplode(tempRock.x+tempRock.halfWidth,
                 tempRock.y+tempRock.halfHeight,10,tempRock.scale);
                if (tempRock.scale<3) {
                    splitRock(tempRock.scale+1, tempRock.x, tempRock.y);
                }
                addToScore(tempRock.scoreValue);
                playerMissiles.splice(playerMissileCtr,1);
                tempPlayerMissile = null;


                rocks.splice(rockCtr,1);
                tempRock = null;

                break rocks;
                break missiles;
            }
        }

        saucers:for (var saucerCtr=saucerLength;saucerCtr>=0;saucerCtr--){
            tempSaucer = saucers[saucerCtr];

            if (boundingBoxCollide(tempRock,tempSaucer)){
                //ConsoleLog.log("hit rock");
                createExplode(tempSaucer.x+tempSaucer.halfWidth,
                 tempSaucer.y+tempSaucer.halfHeight,10,0);
                createExplode(tempRock.x+tempRock.halfWidth,
                 tempRock.y+tempRock.halfHeight,10,tempRock.scale);

                if (tempRock.scale<3) {
                    splitRock(tempRock.scale+1, tempRock.x, tempRock.y);
                }
```

```
                    saucers.splice(saucerCtr,1);
                    tempSaucer = null;

                    rocks.splice(rockCtr,1);
                    tempRock = null;

                    break rocks;
                    break saucers;
                }
            }
    //saucer missiles against rocks
    //this is done here so we don't have to loop through
    //rocks again as it would probably
    //be the biggest array
    saucerMissiles:for (var saucerMissileCtr=saucerMissileLength;
                    saucerMissileCtr>=0;saucerMissileCtr--){

        tempSaucerMissile = saucerMissiles[saucerMissileCtr];
        if (boundingBoxCollide(tempRock,tempSaucerMissile)){
            //ConsoleLog.log("hit rock");

            createExplode(tempRock.x+tempRock.halfWidth,
             tempRock.y+tempRock.halfHeight,10,tempRock.scale);
            if (tempRock.scale<3) {
                splitRock(tempRock.scale+1, tempRock.x, tempRock.y);
            }

            saucerMissiles.splice(saucerCtr,1);
            tempSaucerMissile = null;

            rocks.splice(rockCtr,1);
            tempRock = null;

            break rocks;
            break saucerMissiles;
        }
    }

    //check player against rocks

    if (boundingBoxCollide(tempRock,player) && player.safe==false){
        //ConsoleLog.log("hit player");
        createExplode(tempRock.x+tempRock.halfWidth,
         tempRock.halfHeight,10,tempRock.scale);
        addToScore(tempRock.scoreValue);
        if (tempRock.scale<3) {
            splitRock(tempRock.scale+1, tempRock.x, tempRock.y);
        }
        rocks.splice(rockCtr,1);
        tempRock=null;

        playerDie();
    }

}
```

```
//now check player against saucers and then saucers against player missiles
//and finally player against saucer missiles
playerMissileLength = playerMissiles.length-1;
saucerLength = saucers.length-1;
saucers:for (var saucerCtr=saucerLength;saucerCtr>=0;saucerCtr--){
    tempSaucer = saucers[saucerCtr];

    missiles:for (var playerMissileCtr=playerMissileLength;
     playerMissileCtr>=0;playerMissileCtr--){

    tempPlayerMissile = playerMissiles[playerMissileCtr];

        if (boundingBoxCollide(tempSaucer,tempPlayerMissile)){
            //ConsoleLog.log("hit rock");
            createExplode(tempSaucer.x+tempSaucer.halfWidth,
             tempSaucer.y+tempSaucer.halfHeight,10,0);
            addToScore(tempSaucer.scoreValue);

            playerMissiles.splice(playerMissileCtr,1);
            tempPlayerMissile = null;

            saucers.splice(saucerCtr,1);
            tempSaucer = null;

            break saucers;
            break missiles;
        }
    }

    //player against saucers
    if (boundingBoxCollide(tempSaucer,player) & player.safe==false){
        ConsoleLog.log("hit player");
        createExplode(tempSaucer.x+16,tempSaucer.y+16,10,tempRock.scale);
        addToScore(tempSaucer.scoreValue);

        saucers.splice(rockCtr,1);
        tempSaucer = null;

        playerDie();
    }
}

//saucerMissiles against player
saucerMissileLength = saucerMissiles.length-1;

saucerMissiles:for (var saucerMissileCtr=saucerMissileLength;
                saucerMissileCtr>=0;saucerMissileCtr--){

    tempSaucerMissile = saucerMissiles[saucerMissileCtr];

    if (boundingBoxCollide(player,tempSaucerMissile) & player.safe==false){
        ConsoleLog.log("saucer missile hit player");

        playerDie();
```

```
            saucerMissiles.splice(saucerCtr,1);
            tempSaucerMissile = null;

            break saucerMissiles;
        }
    }

}

function firePlayerMissile(){

    //ConsoleLog.log("fire playerMissile");
    var newPlayerMissile = {};
    newPlayerMissile.dx = 5*Math.cos(Math.PI*(player.rotation)/180);
    newPlayerMissile.dy = 5*Math.sin(Math.PI*(player.rotation)/180);
    newPlayerMissile.x = player.x+player.halfWidth;
    newPlayerMissile.y = player.y+player.halfHeight;
    newPlayerMissile.life = 60;
    newPlayerMissile.lifeCtr = 0;
    newPlayerMissile.width = 2;
    newPlayerMissile.height = 2;
    newPlayerMissile.hitHeight = 2;
    newPlayerMissile.hitWidth = 2;
    playerMissiles.push(newPlayerMissile);
}

function fireSaucerMissile(saucer) {
    var newSaucerMissile = {};
    newSaucerMissile.x = saucer.x+.5*saucer.width;
    newSaucerMissile.y = saucer.y+.5*saucer.height;
    newSaucerMissile.width = 2;
    newSaucerMissile.height = 2;
    newSaucerMissile.hitHeight = 2;
    newSaucerMissile.hitWidth = 2;
    newSaucerMissile.speed = saucer.missileSpeed;

    //ConsoleLog.log("saucer fire");
    //fire at player from small saucer
    var diffx = player.x-saucer.x;
    var diffy = player.y-saucer.y;
    var radians = Math.atan2(diffy, diffx);
    var degrees = 360 * radians / (2 * Math.PI);
    newSaucerMissile.dx = saucer.missileSpeed*Math.cos(Math.PI*(degrees)/180);
    newSaucerMissile.dy = saucer.missileSpeed*Math.sin(Math.PI*(degrees)/180);
    newSaucerMissile.life = 160;
    newSaucerMissile.lifeCtr = 0;
    saucerMissiles.push(newSaucerMissile);
}

function playerDie() {

    ConsoleLog.log("player die");
    createExplode(player.x+player.halfWidth, player.y+player.halfWidth,50,4);
    resetPlayer();
    switchGameState(GAME_STATE_PLAYER_DIE);
```

```
}

function createExplode(x,y,num,type) {

    playSound(SOUND_EXPLODE,.5);
    for (var partCtr=0;partCtr<num;partCtr++){
        if (particlePool.length > 0){

            newParticle = particlePool.pop();
        newParticle.dx = Math.random()*3;
            if (Math.random()<.5){
                newParticle.dx *= -1;
            }
        newParticle.dy = Math.random()*3;
        if (Math.random()<.5){
            newParticle.dy *= -1;
        }

        newParticle.life = Math.floor(Math.random()*30+30);
        newParticle.lifeCtr = 0;
        newParticle.x = x;
        newParticle.width = 2;
        newParticle.height = 2;
        newParticle.y = y;
        newParticle.type = type;
        //ConsoleLog.log("newParticle.life=" + newParticle.life);
        particles.push(newParticle);
        }

    }

}

function boundingBoxCollide(object1, object2) {

    var left1 = object1.x;
    var left2 = object2.x;
    var right1 = object1.x + object1.hitWidth;
    var right2 = object2.x + object2.hitWidth;
    var top1 = object1.y;
    var top2 = object2.y;
    var bottom1 = object1.y + object1.hitHeight;
    var bottom2 = object2.y + object2.hitHeight;

    if (bottom1 < top2) return(false);
    if (top1 > bottom2) return(false);

    if (right1 < left2) return(false);
    if (left1 > right2) return(false);

    return(true);

};
```

```
function splitRock(scale,x,y){
    for (var newRockctr=0;newRockctr<2;newRockctr++){
        var newRock = {};
        //ConsoleLog.log("split rock");

        if (scale==2){
            newRock.scoreValue = medRockScore;
            newRock.width = 32;
            newRock.height = 32;
            newRock.halfWidth = 16;
            newRock.halfHeight = 16;
            newRock.hitWidth = 24;
            newRock.hitHeight = 24;

        }else {
            newRock.scoreValue = smlRockScore;
            newRock.width = 24;
            newRock.height = 24;
            newRock.halfWidth = 12;
            newRock.halfHeight = 12;
            newRock.hitWidth = 16;
            newRock.hitHeight = 16;
        }

        newRock.scale = scale;
        newRock.x = x;
        newRock.y = y;
        newRock.dx = Math.random()*3;
        if (Math.random()<.5){
            newRock.dx *= -1;
        }
        newRock.dy = Math.random()*3;
        if (Math.random()<.5){
            newRock.dy *= -1;
        }
        if (Math.random()<.5){
            newRock.rotationInc = -1;
        }else{
            newRock.rotationInc = 1;
        }

        newRock.animationDelay = Math.floor(Math.random()*3+1);
        newRock.animationCount = 0;

        newRock.rotation = 0;
        ConsoleLog.log("new rock scale"+(newRock.scale));
        rocks.push(newRock);

    }

}
```

```
   function addToScore(value){
      score += value;
   }

   document.onkeydown = function(e){

      e = e?e:window.event;
      //ConsoleLog.log(e.keyCode + "down");
      keyPressList[e.keyCode] = true;
   }

   document.onkeyup = function(e){
   //document.body.onkeyup = function(e){
      e = e?e:window.event;
      //ConsoleLog.log(e.keyCode + "up");
      keyPressList[e.keyCode] =  false;
   };



   //*** application start

      switchGameState(GAME_STATE_INIT);
      const FRAME_RATE = 40;
      frameRateCounter = new FrameRateCounter(FRAME_RATE);
      //**** application loop
      var intervalTime = 1000/FRAME_RATE;
      setInterval(runGame, intervalTime );

}

//***** object prototypes *****

//*** consoleLog util object
//create constructor
function ConsoleLog(){

}

//create function that will be added to the class
console_log = function(message) {
   if(typeof(console) !== 'undefined' && console != null) {
      console.log(message);
   }
}
//add class/static function to class by assignment
ConsoleLog.log = console_log;

//*** end console log object

//***  new FrameRateCounter object prototype
```

```
function FrameRateCounter(fps) {
    if (fps == undefined){

        this.fps = 40
    }else{
        this.fps = fps
    }

    this.lastFrameCount = 0;
    var dateTemp = new Date();
    this.frameLast = dateTemp.getTime();
    delete dateTemp;
    this.frameCtr = 0;
    this.lastTime = dateTemp.getTime();

    this.step = 1;

}


FrameRateCounter.prototype.countFrames = function() {

    var dateTemp = new Date();
    var timeDifference = dateTemp.getTime()-this.lastTime;
    this.step = (timeDifference/1000)*this.fps;
    this.lastTime = dateTemp.getTime();
    this.frameCtr++;

    if (dateTemp.getTime() >=this.frameLast+1000) {
        ConsoleLog.log("frame event");
        this.lastFrameCount = this.frameCtr;
        this.frameCtr = 0;
        this.frameLast = dateTemp.getTime();
    }
    delete dateTemp;

}
</script>
</head>
<body>
<div style="position: absolute; top: 50px; left: 50px;">

<canvas id="canvas" width="400" height="400">
 Your browser does not support HTML5 Canvas.
</canvas>

</div>
</body>
</html>
```

Creating a Dynamic Tile Sheet at Runtime

In Chapter 4, we briefly examined two principles we can use to help eliminate the need to precreate rotations of objects in tile sheets. Creating these types of tile sheets can be cumbersome and use up valuable time that's better spent elsewhere in the project.

The idea will be to take a single image of a game object (e.g., the first tile in the medium rock tile sheet), create a "dynamic tile sheet" at runtime, and store it in an array rather than using the prerendered image rotation tiles.

To accomplish this, we need to make use of a second canvas, as well as the getImage Data() and putImageData() Canvas functions. If you recall from Chapter 4, getImage Data() will throw a security error if the HTML page using it is not on a web server.

Currently, only the Safari browser will not throw this error if the file is used on a local filesystem. For this reason, we have separated this functionality from the *Geo Blaster Extended* game and will simply demonstrate how it could be used instead of replacing all the tile sheets in the game with this type of prerendering.

We will start by creating two <canvas> elements on our HTML page:

```
<body>
<div>
<canvas id="canvas" width="256" height="256" style="position: absolute; top:
50px; left: 50px;">
 Your browser does not support HTML5 Canvas.
</canvas>

<canvas id="canvas2" width="32" height="32"  style="position: absolute; top:
 256px; left: 50px;">
 Your browser does not support HTML5 Canvas.
</canvas>
</div>
</body>
```

The first <canvas>, named canvas, will represent our hypothetical game screen, which will be used to display the precached dynamic tile sheet animation.

The second <canvas>, named canvas2, will be used as a drawing surface to create the dynamic tile frames for our tile sheet.

We will need to separate context instances in the JavaScript, one for each <canvas>:

```
var theCanvas = document.getElementById("canvas");
var context = theCanvas.getContext("2d");
var theCanvas2 = document.getElementById("canvas2");
var context2= theCanvas2.getContext("2d");
```

We will use the *mediumrocks.png* file (Figure 9-9) from the *Geo Blaster Extended* game as our source for the dynamic tile sheet. Don't let this confuse you. We are not going to use all five tiles on this tile sheet—only the first tile.

Figure 9-9. The mediumrocks.png tile sheet

In *Geo Blaster Extended*, we used all five tiles to create a simulated rotation animation. Here, we will only use the first tile. We will draw this first tile and rotate it on the Canvas2 by 10 degrees, and then copy the current imageData pixels from this canvas to an array of imageData instances, called rotationImageArray.

We will then repeat this process by rotating theCanvas2 by 10 more degrees and in a loop until we have 36 individual frames of imageData representing the rotation animation for our medium rock in an array:

```
var rotationImageArray = [];
var animationFrame = 0;
var tileSheet = new Image();
tileSheet.addEventListener('load', eventSheetLoaded , false);
tileSheet.src = "mediumrocks.png";
```

The rotationImageArray variable will hold the generated imageData instances, which we will create by using a rotation transformation on theCanvas2.

The animationFrame is used when redisplaying the rotation animation frames in rotationImageArray back to the first theCanvas to demo the animation.

When the tileSheet is loaded, the eventSheetLoaded() function is called, which in turn calls the startup() function. The startup() function will use a loop to create the 36 frames of animation:

```
function startUp(){

    for (var ctr=0;ctr<360;ctr+=10){
      context2.fillStyle = "#ffffff";
      context2.fillRect(0,0,32,32);
      context2.save();
      context2.setTransform(1,0,0,1,0,0)
      var angleInRadians = ctr * Math.PI / 180;
      context2.translate(16, 16);
      context2.rotate(angleInRadians);
      context2.drawImage(tileSheet, 0, 0,32,32,-16,-16,32,32);
      context2.restore();
      var imagedata = context2.getImageData(0, 0, 32, 32)
      rotationImageArray.push(imagedata);
    }
    setInterval(drawScreen, 100 );
  }
```

This loop first clears theCanvas2 with a white color, and then saves it to the stack. We then translate to the center of our object and rotate the canvas by the current ctr value (an increment of 10). Next, we draw the first tile from *mediumrocks.png* and save the result into a new local imageData instance using the getImageData() function.

This is the place where the security error will be thrown if the domain of the image and the domain of the HTML file are not the same. On a local machine (not running on a local web server, but from the filesystem), this error will be thrown on all browsers but Safari (currently).

Finally, the new `imageData` is pushed into the `rotationImageArray`. When the loop is complete, we set up an interval to run and call the `drawScreen()` function every 100 milliseconds.

To display the animation on the first canvas, we use this timer loop interval and call `putImageData()` to draw each frame in succession, creating the simulation of animation. As with the tile sheet, we didn't have to use 36 frames of animation, we could use just five. Naturally, the animation is much smoother with more frames. But this process shows how easy it is to create simple transformation animations "on the fly" rather than precreating them in image files:

```
function drawScreen() {

        //context.fillStyle = "#ffffff";
        //context.fillRect(50,50,32,32);
        context.putImageData(rotationImageArray[animationFrame],50,50);
        animationFrame++;
        if (animationFrame ==rotationImageArray.length){
            animationFrame=0;
        }
}
```

Example 9-2 shows the entire code.

Example 9-2. A dynamic tile sheet example

```
<!doctype html>
<html lang="en">
<head>
<meta charset="UTF-8">
<title>CH9EX2: Canvas Copy</title>
<script src="modernizr-1.6.min.js"></script>
<script type="text/javascript">
window.addEventListener('load', eventWindowLoaded, false);
function eventWindowLoaded() {
    canvasApp();
}

function canvasSupport () {
    return Modernizr.canvas;
}

function canvasApp(){

    if (!canvasSupport()) {
            return;
```

```
        }else{
          var theCanvas = document.getElementById("canvas");
          var context = theCanvas.getContext("2d");

          var theCanvas2 = document.getElementById("canvas2");
          var context2= theCanvas2.getContext("2d");
        }
      var rotationImageArray = []
      var tileSheet = new Image();
      var animationFrame = 0;
      tileSheet.addEventListener('load', eventSheetLoaded , false);
      tileSheet.src = "mediumrocks.png";
      function eventSheetLoaded() {
          startUp();
      }

      function startUp(){
        //context.drawImage(tileSheet, 0, 0);
        //context2.drawImage(theCanvas, 0, 0,32,32,0,0,32,32);

        for (var ctr=0;ctr<360;ctr+=10){
          context2.fillStyle="#ffffff";
          context2.fillRect(0,0,32,32);

          context2.save();
          context2.setTransform(1,0,0,1,0,0)
          var angleInRadians = ctr * Math.PI / 180;
          context2.translate(16, 16)
          context2.rotate(angleInRadians);
          context2.drawImage(tileSheet, 0, 0,32,32,-16,-16,32,32);
          context2.restore();

          var imagedata = context2.getImageData(0, 0, 32, 32);

          rotationImageArray.push(imagedata);
        }
        setInterval(drawScreen, 100 );
      }

      function drawScreen() {
        //context.fillStyle="#ffffff";
        //context.fillRect(50,50,32,32);
        context.putImageData(rotationImageArray[animationFrame],50,50);
        animationFrame++;
        if (animationFrame ==rotationImageArray.length){
          animationFrame = 0;
        }
      }

    }

</script>
</head>
<body>
<div>
```

```
<canvas id="canvas" width="256" height="256" style="position: absolute; top:
  50px; left: 50px;">
  Your browser does not support the HTML 5 Canvas.
</canvas>

<canvas id="canvas2" width="32" height="32" style="position: absolute; top:
  256px; left: 50px;">
  Your browser does not support HTML5 Canvas.
</canvas>

</div>
</body>
</html>
```

In the rest of the chapter, we will look at creating a simple tile-based game using some of the techniques first discussed in Chapter 4.

A Simple Tile-Based Game

Let's move from *Asteroids* to another classic game genre, the tile-based maze-chase game. When you're discussing early tile-based games, undoubtedly *Pac-Man* enters the conversation. *Pac-Man* was one of the first commercially successful tile-based games, although it certainly was not the first of its kind. The maze-chase genre was actually well covered by budding game developers before microcomputers were even thought possible. Many minicomputer and mainframe tile-based games, such as *Daleks*, were crafted in the '60s and '70s. In this section, we will create a simple turn-based maze-chase game. Our game, *Micro Tank Maze*, will be based loosely on *Daleks*, but we will use the tank sprites from Chapter 4. Figure 9-10 is a screenshot from the finished game.

Micro Tank Maze Description

Micro Tank Maze is a simple turn-based strategy game played on a 15×15 tile-based grid. At the beginning of each game, the player (the green tank), 20 enemy tanks (the blue tanks), 25 wall tiles, and a single goal tile (the phoenix) are randomly placed on the grid. The rest of the grid is simply "road" tiles on which the tanks move. The player is tasked with getting to the goal object without running into any walls or any of the enemy tanks. On each turn, the player and all enemy tanks will move a single space (tile) on the grid. Neither the player nor the enemy tanks can move off the grid edges. If the player runs into a wall tile or an enemy tank, his game is over. If an enemy tank runs into a wall or another tank, it is destroyed and removed from the game board. If an enemy tank runs into the player tank, it and the player are destroyed. If the player hits the goal tile without an enemy tank also hitting the tile on the same turn, the player wins.

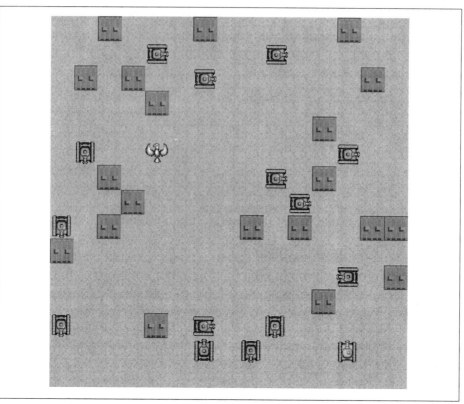

Figure 9-10. Micro Tank Maze in action

Game progression

Each time the player collects the goal object and wins the game, the next game will start with one more enemy tank (up to 50 enemy tanks). The ultimate goal of the game is to see how many times you (the player) can win before your tank is finally destroyed. The game will keep a session-based high score, and even if you lose, you always start from the last completed level.

This is a simple game, and much more can be added to it to enhance the gaming experience. In this chapter, though, we want to cover the basics of creating a tile-based game on HTML5 Canvas. By combining what we have learned throughout this book, you should have enough skill and knowledge to extend this simple contest into a much more robust game-play experience.

Game strategy

The player must try to reach the goal while avoiding the enemy tanks. The enemy will follow or chase the player to a fault. Most of the time (75%), each enemy tank will stupidly follow the player, even if that means moving into a wall and destroying itself.

The player then has the advantage of intelligence to compensate for the large number of tanks the enemy employs. The other 25% of the time, an enemy tank will randomly choose a direction to move in.

Now, let's get into the game by looking at the tile sheet we will be using.

The Tile Sheet for Our Game

Make sure you've read Chapter 4 and the Chapter 8 section "A Basic Game Framework" on page 400 before moving on. Even though *Micro Tank Maze* is a relatively simple game, it is still quite a few lines of code. We'll hit the major points, but we don't have space to discuss every detail.

The tile sheet (*tanks_sheet.png*) we are going to use will look very familiar if you've read Chapter 4. Figure 9-11 shows *tanks_sheet.png*.

Figure 9-11. The Micro Tank Maze tile sheet

We will be using only a very small portion of these tiles for *Micro Tank Maze*.

Road tile
> This is the tile on which the player and the enemy tanks can move. Tile 0, the road tile, is in the top-left corner.

Wall tile
> The wall tile will cause any tank moving on it to be destroyed. Tile 30, the second to last tile on the sheet, will be the wall tile.

Goal tile
> This is the tile the player must reach to win the game. It is the last tile in the second to last row (the phoenix).

Player tiles
> The player will be made up of the first eight green tank tiles. Each tile will be used to simulate the tank treads moving from tile to tile.

Enemy tiles
> The enemy will be made up of the second eight blue tank tiles. These tiles will be used to animate the tank treads as it moves from tile to tile.

Our game code will store the tile ids needed for each of these game objects in application scope variables:

```
var playerTiles = [1,2,3,4,5,6,7,8];
var enemyTiles = [9,10,11,12,13,14,15,16];
var roadTile = 0;
var wallTile = 30;
var goalTile = 23;
var explodeTiles = [17,18,19,18,17];
```

The tile sheet will be loaded into an application scope `Image` instance and given the name `tileSheet`:

```
var tileSheet;
```

In the application's initialization state, we will load in and assign the `Image` instance:

```
tileSheet = new Image();
tileSheet.src = "tanks_sheet.png";
```

Next, we will examine the setup of the game playfield.

The Playfield

The game playfield will be a 15×15 grid of 32×32 tiles. This is a total of 225 tiles with a width and height of 480 pixels each. Every time we start a new game, all the objects will be placed randomly onto the grid. The `playField[]` array will hold 15 row arrays each with 15 columns. This gives us 225 tiles that can be easily accessed with the simple `playField[row][col]` syntax.

Creating the board

We will first place a road tile on each of the 225 `playField` array locations. We then randomly place all of the wall tiles (these will actually replace some of the road tiles at locations in the `playField` array).

Next, we randomly place all of the enemy tank tiles. Unlike the wall tiles, the tank tiles will *not* replace road tiles in the `playField` array. Instead, they will be placed into an array of their own called `enemy`. To ensure that neither the player nor the goal object occupies the same tile space as the enemy tanks, we will create another array called `items`.

The `items` array will also be a 15×15 two-dimensional array of rows and columns, which can be considered the "second" layer of playfield data. Unlike the `playField` array, it will only be used to make sure no two objects (player, enemy, or goal) occupy the same space while building the playfield. We must do this because the player and enemy objects are not added to the `playField` array.

Once we have placed the enemy, we will randomly place the player at a spot that is not currently occupied by an enemy or a wall. Finally, we will place the goal tile in a spot not taken by the player, a wall, or an enemy tank.

The code for this will be in the createPlayField() function. If you would like to review it now, go to the section "Micro Tank Maze Complete Game Code" on page 516 (Example 9-3).

All the data about the playField will be stored in application scope variables:

```
//playfield
var playField = [];
var items = [];
var xMin = 0;
var xMax = 480;
var yMin = 0;
var yMax = 480;
```

To create the playField, the game code will need to know the maximum number of each type of tile. These will also be application scope variables:

```
var wallMax = 20;
var playerMax = 1;
var enemyMax = 20;
var goalMax = 1;
```

The Player

The player and all of its current attributes will be contained in the player object. Even a game as simple as *Micro Tank Maze* requires quite a few attributes. Here is a list and description of each:

player.row
> The current row on the 15×15 playField grid where the player resides.

player.col
> The current column on the 15×15 playField grid where the player resides.

player.nextRow
> The row the player will move to next, after a successful key press in that direction.

player.nextCol
> The column the player will move to next, after a successful key press in that direction.

player.currentTile
> The id of the current tile used to display the player from the playerTiles array.

player.rotation
> The player starts pointed up, so this will be the 0 rotation. When the player moves in one of the four basic directions, this rotation will change and will be used to move the player in the direction it is facing.

player.speed
> The number of pixels the player object will move on each frame tick.

`player.destinationX`

The final x location for the 32×32 `player` object while it is moving to a new tile. It represents the top-left corner x location for this new location. During the player movement and animation phase of the game, this value determines when the player has arrived at its new x-axis location.

`player.destinationY`

The final y location for the 32×32 `player` object while it is moving to a new tile. It represents the top-left corner y location for this new location. During the player movement and animation phase of the game, this value determines when the player has arrived at its new y-axis location.

`player.x`

The current x location of the top-left corner of the 32×32 player object.

`player.y`

The current y location of the top-left corner of the 32×32 player object.

`player.dx`

The player's change in x direction on each frame tick while it is animating. This will be -1, 0, or 1, depending on the direction in which the player is moving.

`player.dy`

The player's change in y direction on each frame tick while it is animating. This will be -1, 0, or 1, depending on the direction in which the player is moving.

`player.hit`

Set to true when the player moves to a new square that is occupied by an enemy tank or a wall.

`player.dead`

When `player.hit` is true, it will be replaced on the `playField` by an explosion sprite. With `dead` set to true, it will not be rendered to the game screen.

`player.win`

Set to true if the player collects the goal object.

The enemy and the player share many of the same attributes, as they both use the same type of calculations to move about the grid. Now let's examine how the enemy object is constructed.

The Enemy

Each enemy object will have its own set of attributes that are very similar to those of the player. Like the player, each enemy will be an object instance.

Here is the code from the `createPlayField()` function that sets up the attributes for a new enemy object:

```
EnemyLocationFound = true;
var tempEnemy = {};
tempEnemy.row = randRow;
```

```
tempEnemy.col = randCol;
tempEnemy.nextRow = 0;
tempEnemy.nextCol = 0;
tempEnemy.currentTile = 0;
tempEnemy.rotation = 0;
tempEnemy.x = tempEnemy.col*32;
tempEnemy.y = tempEnemy.row*32;
tempEnemy.speed = 2;
tempEnemy.destinationX = 0;
tempEnemy.destinationY = 0;
tempEnemy.dx = 0;
tempEnemy.dy = 0;
tempEnemy.hit = false;
tempEnemy.dead = false;
tempEnemy.moveComplete = false;
enemy.push(tempEnemy);
items[randRow][randCol] = 1;
```

There are a couple extra things worth pointing out in this code. The first is that each enemy object needs an attribute called moveComplete. This is used in the animate Enemy() game state function. When the entire enemy battalion has moved to its new location, the game will transition to the next game state. This is discussed in detail in the next section "Turn-Based Game Flow and the State Machine".

Also, notice that the new enemy objects are added to the enemy array, as well as to the items multidimensional array. This ensures that the player and the goal cannot be placed on to an enemy location. Once the enemy moves from its initial location, the playField array will still have a road tile to show in its place. We call the player and the enemy "moving object" tiles because they can move about the game board. When they move, they must "uncover" the road tile in the spot they were in before moving.

Now let's take a quick look at the goal tile to solidify your understanding of the difference between the playField and the moving object tiles.

The Goal

The tile id of the goal tile will be stored in the playField array along with the road and wall tiles. It is not considered a separate item because, unlike the player and enemy objects, it does not need to move. As we have described previously, since the enemy and player tiles move on top of the playfield, they are considered moving items and not part of the playfield.

The Explosions

The explosion tiles are unique. They will be rendered on top of the playfield when an enemy tank or the player's hit attribute has been set to true. The explosion tiles will animate through a list of five tiles and then be removed from the game screen. Again, tiles for the explosion are set in the explodeTiles array:

```
var explodeTiles = [17,18,19,18,17];
```

Next, we will examine the entire game flow and state machine to give you an overall look at how the game logic is designed.

Turn-Based Game Flow and the State Machine

Our game logic and flow is separated into 16 discrete states. The entire application runs on a 40 frames per second interval timer:

```
switchGameState(GAME_STATE_INIT);
const FRAME_RATE = 40;
var intervalTime = 1000/FRAME_RATE;
setInterval(runGame, intervalTime )
```

As with the other games, in Chapter 8 and earlier in this chapter, we will use a function reference state machine to run our current game state. The switchGameState() function will be used to transition to a new game state. Let's begin by discussing this function briefly, and then moving through the rest of the game functions.

 We will not reprint each line of code or dissect it in detail here. Use this section as a guide for perusing the entire set of game code included at the end of this chapter (in Example 9-3). By now, you have seen most of the code and ideas used to create this game logic. We will break out the new ideas and code in the sections that follow.

GAME_STATE_INIT

This state loads in the assets we need for our game. We are loading in only a single tile sheet and no sounds for *Micro Tank Maze*.

After the initial load, it sends the state machine to the GAME_STATE_WAIT_FOR_LOAD state until the load event has occurred.

GAME_STATE_WAIT_FOR_LOAD

This state simply makes sure that all the items in GAME_STATE_INIT have loaded properly. It then sends the state machine to the GAME_STATE_TITLE state.

GAME_STATE_TITLE

This state shows the title screen and then waits for the space bar to be pressed. When this happens, it sends the state machine to GAME_STATE_NEW_GAME.

GAME_STATE_NEW_GAME

This state resets all of the game arrays and objects and then calls the createPlay Field() function. The createPlayField() function creates the playField and enemy arrays for the new game, as well as sets the player object's starting location. Once it has finished, it calls the `renderPlayField()` function a single time to display the initial board on the game screen.

Once this completes, the state machine is now ready to start the real game loop. This is done by moving the game state machine to the `GAME_STATE_WAIT_FOR_PLAYER_MOVE` state.

GAME_STATE_WAIT_FOR_PLAYER_MOVE

This state waits for the player to press one of the four arrow buttons. Once the player has done so, the switch statement checks to see which arrow was pressed. Based on the direction pressed, the `checkBounds()` function is called.

 This state contains a bit of the new code for tile movement logic that we have not seen previously in this book. See the upcoming section "Simple Tile Movement Logic Overview" on page 512 for more details on these concepts.

The `checkBounds()` function accepts in three parameters:

- The number to increment the row the player is currently in
- The number to increment the column the player is currently in
- The object being tested (either the player or one of the enemy tanks)

The sole purpose of this function is to determine whether the object being tested can move in the desired direction. In this game, the only illegal moves are off the side of the screen. In games such as *Pac-Man*, this would check to make sure that the tile was not a wall tile. Our game does not do this because we want the player and the enemy objects to be able to move mistakenly onto the wall tiles (and be destroyed).

If a valid move is found for the player in the direction pressed, the `setPlayerDestination()` function is called. This function simply sets the `player.destinationX` and `player.destinationY` attributes based on the new tile location.

`checkBounds()` sets the `player.nextRow` and `player.nextCol` attributes. The `setPlayerDestination()` function multiplies the `player.nextRow` and the `player.nextCol` by the tile size (32) to determine the `player.destinationX` and `player.destinationY` attributes. These will be used to move the player to its new location.

`GAME_STATE_ANIMATE_PLAYER` is then set as the current game state.

GAME_STATE_ANIMATE_PLAYER

This function moves the player to its `destinationX` and `destinationY` locations. Since this is a turn-based game, we don't have to do any other processing while this movement is occurring.

On each iteration, the player.currentTile is incremented by 1. This will change the tile that is rendered to be the next tile in the playerTiles array. When destinationX and destinationY are equal to the x and y values for the player, the movement and animation stop, and the game state is changed to the GAME_STATE_EVALUATE_PLAYER_MOVE state.

GAME_STATE_EVALUATE_PLAYER_MOVE

Now that the player has been moved to the next tile, the player.row and player.col attributes are set to player.nextRow and player.nextCol, respectively.

Next, if the player is on a goal tile, the player.win attribute will be set to true. If the player is on a wall tile, the player.hit will be set to true.

We then loop though all of the enemy objects and see whether any occupy the same tile as the player. If they do, both the player and the enemy hit attributes are set to true.

Next, we move the game to the GAME_STATE_ENEMY_MOVE state.

GAME_STATE_ENEMY_MOVE

This state uses the homegrown chase AI—discussed in "Simple Homegrown AI Overview" on page 515—to choose a direction in which to move each enemy tank. It does this by looping through all the tanks and applying the logic to them individually.

This function first uses a little tile-based math to determine where the player is in relation to an enemy tank. It then creates an array of directions to test based on these calculations. It stores these as string values in a variable called directionsToTest.

Next, it uses the chanceRandomMovement value (25%) to determine whether it will use the list of directions it just compiled, or whether it will throw them out and simply choose a random direction to move in.

In either case, it must check all of the available directions (either in the list of directionsToMove or in all four directions for random movement) to see which is the first that will not move the tank off the side of the screen.

Once it has the direction to move in, it sets the destinationX and destinationY values of the enemy tank using the same tile size * x and tile size * y trick used for the player.

Finally, it sets the game state to GAME_STATE_ANIMATE_ENEMY.

GAME_STATE_ANIMATE_ENEMY

Like GAME_STATE_ANIMATE_PLAYER, this state moves and animates the tank to its new location represented by its destinationX and destinationY values. It must do this for each of the enemy tanks, so it uses the enemyMoveCompleteCount variable to keep count of how many of the enemy tanks have finished their moves.

When all the enemy tanks have completed their moves, the game state is changed to the GAME_STATE_EVALUATE_ENEMY_MOVE state.

GAME_STATE_EVALUATE_ENEMY_MOVE

Like GAME_STATE_EVALUATE_PLAYER_MOVE, this state looks at the location of each tank to determine which ones need to be destroyed.

If a tank occupies the same tile as the player, a wall, or another tank, the tank is "to be destroyed". If the player and enemy tank occupy the same tile, the player is also "to be destroyed". This "to be destroyed" state is set by placing true in the hit attribute of the enemy tank or the player.

The game is then moved to the GAME_STATE_EVALUATE_OUTCOME state.

GAME_STATE_EVALUATE_OUTCOME

This function looks at each of the enemy tanks and the player tank to determine which have a hit attribute set to true. If any do, that tank's dead attribute is set to true, and an explosion is created by calling createExplode() and passing in the object instance (player or enemy tank). In the case of the enemy, a dead enemy is also removed from the enemy array.

The GAME_STATE_ANIMATE_EXPLODE state is called next.

GAME_STATE_ANIMATE_EXPLODE

If the explosions array length is greater than 0, this function loops through each instance and animates them using the explodeTiles array. Each explosion instance is removed from the explosions array after it finishes its animation. When the explosions array length is 0, the game moves to the GAME_STATE_CHECK_FOR_GAME_OVER state.

GAME_STATE_CHECK_FOR_GAME_OVER

This state will first check to see whether the player is dead, and then check to see whether he has won. That means that the player cannot win if an enemy tank makes it to the goal on the same try as the player.

If the player has lost, the state changes to GAME_STATE_PLAYER_LOSE; if the player has won, it moves to the GAME_STATE_PLAYER_WIN state. If neither of those has occurred, the game is set to GAME_STATE_WAIT_FOR_PLAYER_MOVE. This starts the game loop iteration over, and the player begins her next turn.

GAME_STATE_PLAYER_WIN

If the player wins, the maxEnemy is increased for the next game. The player's score is also checked against the current session high score to determine whether a new high score has been achieved. This state waits for a space bar press and then moves to the GAME_STATE_NEW_GAME state.

GAME_STATE_PLAYER_LOSE

The player's score is checked against the current session high score to determine whether a new high score has been achieved. This state waits for a space bar press and then moves to the GAME_STATE_NEW_GAME state.

Simple Tile Movement Logic Overview

Micro Tank Maze employs simple tile-to-tile movement using the "center of a tile" logic. This logic relies on making calculations once the game character has reached the center of a tile. The origin point of our game character tiles is the top-left corner. Because of this, we can easily calculate that a game character is in the center of a tile when its x and y coordinates are equal to the destination tile's x and y coordinates.

When the user presses a movement key (up, down, right, or left arrow), we first must check whether the player is trying to move to a "legal" tile on the playField. In *Micro Tank Maze*, all tiles are legal. The only illegal moves are off the edges of the board. So, if the player wants to move up, down, left, or right, we must first check the tile in that direction based on the key pressed in the gameStateWaitForPlayerMove() function. Here is the switch statement used to determine whether the player pressed an arrow key:

```
if (keyPressList[38]==true){
    //up
    if (checkBounds(-1,0, player)){
    setPlayerDestination();
    }
}else if (keyPressList[37]==true) {
    //left
    if (checkBounds(0,-1, player)){
    setPlayerDestination();
    }
}else if (keyPressList[39]==true) {
    //right
    if (checkBounds(0,1, player)){
    setPlayerDestination();
    }
}else if  (keyPressList[40]==true){
    //down
    if (checkBounds(1,0, player)){
    setPlayerDestination();
    }
}
```

Notice that the checkBounds() function takes a row increment and then a column increment to test. It is important to note that we don't access tiles in the same manner that we would access pixels on the screen. Tiles in the playField array are accessed by addressing the vertical (row) and then the horizontal (column) (using [row][column], not [column][row]). This is because a simple array is organized into a set of rows. Each row has a set of 15 columns. Therefore, we do not access a tile in the playField using the [horizontal][vertical] coordinates. Instead, we use the [row][column] syntax that simple arrays use to powerful and elegant effect.

In the checkBounds() function, enter the row increment, then the column increment, and then the object to be tested. If this is a legal move, the checkBounds() function sets the nextRow and nextCol to be row+rowInc and col+colInc, respectively:

```
function checkBounds(rowInc, colInc, object){
    object.nextRow = object.row+rowInc;
    object.nextCol = object.col+colInc;

    if (object.nextCol >=0 && object.nextCol<15 &&
     object.nextRow>=0 && object.nextRow<15){
        object.dx = colInc;
        object.dy = rowInc;

        if (colInc==1){
        object.rotation = 90;
        }else if (colInc==-1){
        object.rotation = 270;
        }else if (rowInc==-1){
        object.rotation = 0;
        }else if (rowInc==1){
        object.rotation = 180;
        }

        return(true);

    }else{
        object.nextRow = object.row;
        object.nextCol = object.col;
        return(false);

    }

}
```

If the move is legal, the dx (delta, or change in x) and dy (delta, or change in y) are set to the colInc and rowInc, respectively.

The animatePlayer() function is called next. Its job is to move the player object to its new location while running through its animation frames. Here is the code from the animatePlayer() function:

```
player.x += player.dx*player.speed;
player.currentTile++;
```

```
if (player.currentTile==playerTiles.length){
    player.currentTile = 0;
}
renderPlayField();
if (player.x==player.destinationX && player.y==player.destinationY){
    switchGameState(GAME_STATE_EVALUATE_PLAYER_MOVE);
}
```

First, the `player` object's `x` and `y` locations are increased by the `player.speed` * `player.dx` (or `dy`). The tile size is `32`, so we must use a speed value that is evenly divided into `32`. The values 1, 2, 4, 8, 16, and 32 are all valid.

This function also runs though the `playerTiles` array on each game loop iteration. This will render the tank tracks moving, simulating a smooth ride from one tile to the next.

Next, let's take a closer look at how we render the `playField`.

Rendering Logic Overview

Each time the game renders objects to the screen, it runs through the entire `render()` function. It does this to ensure that even the nonmoving objects are rendered back to the game screen. The `render()` function looks like this:

```
function renderPlayField() {
    fillBackground();
    drawPlayField();
    drawPlayer();
    drawEnemy();
    drawExplosions();
}
```

First, we draw the plain black background, then we draw the `playField`, and after that we draw the game objects. `drawPlayField()` draws the map of tiles to the game screen. This function is similar to the functions in Chapter 4, but with some additions for our game. Let's review how it is organized:

```
function drawPlayField(){
    for (rowCtr=0;rowCtr<15;rowCtr++){

        for (colCtr=0;colCtr<15;colCtr++) {
        var sourceX = Math.floor((playField[rowCtr][colCtr]) % 8) * 32;
        var sourceY = Math.floor((playField[rowCtr][colCtr]) /8) *32;

        if (playField[rowCtr][colCtr] != roadTile){
            context.drawImage(tileSheet, 0, 0,32,32,colCtr*32,rowCtr*32,32,32);
        }
        context.drawImage(tileSheet, sourceX, sourceY, 32,32,
          colCtr*32,rowCtr*32,32,32);
          }
    }
}
```

The drawPlayField() function loops through the rows in the playField array, and then through each column inside each row. If the tile id number at playField[rowCtr][colCtr] is a road tile, it simply paints that tile at the correct location on the play Field. If the tile id is a game object (not a road tile), it first paints a road tile in that spot and then paints the object tile in that spot.

Simple Homegrown AI Overview

The enemy tanks chase the player object based on a set of simple rules. We have coded those rules into the gameStateEnemyMove() function, which is one of the longest and most complicated functions in this book. Let's first step through the logic used to create the function, and then you can examine it in Example 9-3.

This function starts by looping through the enemy array. It must determine a new tile location on which to move each enemy. To do so, it follows some simple rules that determine the order in which the testBounds() function will test the movement directions:

1. First, it tests to see whether the player is closer to the enemy vertically or horizontally.
2. If vertically, and the player is above the enemy, it places up and then down into the directionsToTest array.
3. If vertically, and the player is below the enemy, it places down and then up into the directionsToTest array.

> The up and then down, or down and then up, directions are pushed into the directionsTest array to simplify the AI. The logic here is if the player is "up" from the enemy, but the enemy is blocked by an object, the enemy will try the opposite direction first. In our game, there will be no instance where an object blocks the direction the enemy tank wants to move in. This is because the only illegal direction is trying to move off the bounds of the screen. If we add tiles to our playfield that "block" the enemy, this entire set of AI code suddenly becomes very useful and necessary. We have included this entire "homegrown chase AI" in our game in case more of these tile types are added.

4. It then looks to see where to add the left and right directions. It does this based on which way will put it closer to the player.
5. If the horizontal direction and not the vertical direction is the shortest, it runs through the same type of logic, but this time using left and then right, then up and then down.
6. When this is complete, all four directions will be in the directionsToTest array.

Next, the logic finds a number between 0 and 99, and checks to see whether it is less than the chanceRandomEnemyMovement value. If it is, it will ignore the directionsToTest array and simply try to find a random direction to move in. In either case, all the directions (either in the directionsToTest array or in order up, down, left, and right) are tested until the testBounds() function returns true.

That's all there is to this code. In Example 9-3, you will find the entire set of code for this game.

Micro Tank Maze Complete Game Code

Example 9-3. Micro Tank Maze full source code listing

```
<!doctype html>
<html lang="en">
<head>
<meta charset="UTF-8">
<title>CH(EX3: Micro Tank Maze Game</title>
<script src="modernizr-1.6.min.js"></script>
<script type="text/javascript">
window.addEventListener('load', eventWindowLoaded, false);
function eventWindowLoaded() {

    canvasApp();
}

function canvasSupport () {
return Modernizr.canvas;
}

function canvasApp(){

    if (!canvasSupport()) {
          return;
      }else{
        theCanvas = document.getElementById("canvas");
        context = theCanvas.getContext("2d");
    }

    //application states
    const GAME_STATE_INIT = 0;
    const GAME_STATE_WAIT_FOR_LOAD = 10;
    const GAME_STATE_TITLE = 20;
    const GAME_STATE_NEW_GAME = 30;
    const GAME_STATE_WAIT_FOR_PLAYER_MOVE = 40;
    const GAME_STATE_ANIMATE_PLAYER = 50;
    const GAME_STATE_EVALUATE_PLAYER_MOVE = 60;
    const GAME_STATE_ENEMY_MOVE = 70;
    const GAME_STATE_ANIMATE_ENEMY = 80;
    const GAME_STATE_EVALUATE_ENEMY_MOVE = 90;
    const GAME_STATE_EVALUATE_OUTCOME = 100;
    const GAME_STATE_ANIMATE_EXPLODE = 110;
    const GAME_STATE_CHECK_FOR_GAME_OVER = 120;
```

```
const GAME_STATE_PLAYER_WIN = 130;
const GAME_STATE_PLAYER_LOSE = 140;
const GAME_STATE_GAME_OVER = 150;

var currentGameState = 0;
var currentGameStateFunction = null;

//loading
var loadCount = 0;
var itemsToLoad  = 1;

//keyPresses
var keyPressList = [];

var tileSheet;

var mapRows = 15;
var mapCols = 15;

//playfield
var playField = [];
var items = [];
var xMin = 0;
var xMax = 480;
var yMin = 0;
var yMax = 480;

//tiles
var playerTiles = [1,2,3,4,5,6,7,8];
var enemyTiles = [9,10,11,12,13,14,15,16];
var roadTile = 0;
var wallTile = 30;
var goalTile = 23;
var explodeTiles = [17,18,19,18,17];

var wallMax = 20;
var playerMax = 1;
var enemyMax = 20;
var goalMax = 1;

var enemyMoveCompleteCount=0;

//objects
var player = {};
var enemy = [];
var explosions = [];

//screens
var screenStarted = false;
var score = 0;
var enemyScore = 10;
var goalScore = 50;
var highScore = 0;

var chanceRandomEnemyMovement = 25;
```

```
function runGame(){
   currentGameStateFunction();
}

function switchGameState(newState) {
   currentGameState = newState;
   switch (currentGameState) {

      case GAME_STATE_INIT:
         currentGameStateFunction = gameStateInit;
         break;
      case GAME_STATE_WAIT_FOR_LOAD:
         currentGameStateFunction = gameStateWaitForLoad;
         break;
      case GAME_STATE_TITLE:
         currentGameStateFunction = gameStateTitle;
         break;
      case GAME_STATE_NEW_GAME:
         currentGameStateFunction = gameStateNewGame;
         break;
      case GAME_STATE_WAIT_FOR_PLAYER_MOVE:
         currentGameStateFunction = gameStateWaitForPlayerMove;
         break;
      case GAME_STATE_ANIMATE_PLAYER:
         currentGameStateFunction = gameStateAnimatePlayer;
         break;
      case GAME_STATE_EVALUATE_PLAYER_MOVE:
         currentGameStateFunction = gameStateEvaluatePlayerMove;
         break;
      case GAME_STATE_ENEMY_MOVE:
         currentGameStateFunction = gameStateEnemyMove;
         break;
      case GAME_STATE_ANIMATE_ENEMY:
         currentGameStateFunction = gameStateAnimateEnemy;
         break;
      case GAME_STATE_EVALUATE_ENEMY_MOVE:
         currentGameStateFunction = gameStateEvaluateEnemyMove;
         break;
      case GAME_STATE_EVALUATE_OUTCOME:
         currentGameStateFunction = gameStateEvaluateOutcome;
         break;
      case GAME_STATE_ANIMATE_EXPLODE:
         currentGameStateFunction = gameStateAnimateExplode;
         break;
      case GAME_STATE_CHECK_FOR_GAME_OVER:
         currentGameStateFunction = gameStateCheckForGameOver;
         break;
      case GAME_STATE_PLAYER_WIN:
         currentGameStateFunction = gameStatePlayerWin;
         break;
      case GAME_STATE_PLAYER_LOSE:
         currentGameStateFunction = gameStatePlayerLose;
         break;
```

```
        }
    }

function gameStateWaitForLoad(){
    //do nothing while loading events occur
    //console.log("doing nothing...")
}

function gameStateInit() {

    tileSheet = new Image();
    tileSheet.src = "tanks_sheet.png";
    tileSheet.onload = itemLoaded;

    switchGameState(GAME_STATE_WAIT_FOR_LOAD);

}

 function itemLoaded(event) {

    loadCount++;
    ////console.log("loading:" + loadCount)
    if (loadCount >= itemsToLoad) {

        switchGameState(GAME_STATE_TITLE)

    }

}

function gameStateTitle() {
    if (screenStarted !=true){
        fillBackground();
        setTextStyleTitle();
        context.fillText  ("Micro Tank Maze", 160, 70);
        context.fillText  ("Press Space To Play", 150, 140);

        screenStarted = true;
    }else{
        //wait for space key click
        if (keyPressList[32]==true){
            //console.log("space pressed");
            switchGameState(GAME_STATE_NEW_GAME);
            screenStarted = false;

        }

    }

}

 function gameStatePlayerWin(){

    if (!screenStarted){
```

```
        score += goalScore;
        fillBackground();
        setTextStyleTitle();
        context.fillText  ("YOU WON THE GAME!", 135, 70);
        context.fillText  ("Final Score: " + score, 150, 100);
        context.fillText  ("Number of enemy: " + enemyMax, 150,130);

        if (score > highScore){
           highScore = score;
           context.fillText  ("NEW HIGH SCORE!", 150,160);
        }

        context.fillText  ("High Score: " + score, 150, 190);

        screenStarted = true;

        enemyMax++;
        if (enemyMax >50){
           enemyMax = 50;
        }
        context.fillText  ("Number of enemy for next game: " +
          enemyMax, 100,220);

        context.fillText  ("Press Space To Play", 150, 300);

    }else{
       //wait for space key click
       if (keyPressList[32]==true){
          //console.log("space pressed");
          switchGameState(GAME_STATE_NEW_GAME);
          screenStarted = false;

       }

    }

}

function gameStatePlayerLose(){
    if (!screenStarted){
       fillBackground();
       setTextStyleTitle();
       context.fillText  ("SORRY, YOU LOST THE GAME!", 100, 70);
       context.fillText  ("Final Score: " + score, 150, 100);
       context.fillText  ("Number of enemy: " + enemyMax, 150,130);

       if (score > highScore){
          highScore = score;
          context.fillText  ("NEW HIGH SCORE!", 150,160);
       }

       context.fillText  ("High Score: " + score, 150, 190);

       screenStarted = true;
```

```
            context.fillText  ("Number of enemy for next game: " +
              enemyMax, 100,220);
            context.fillText  ("Press Space To Play", 150, 300);
        }else{
            //wait for space key click
            if (keyPressList[32]==true){
                //console.log("space pressed");
                switchGameState(GAME_STATE_NEW_GAME);
                screenStarted = false;

            }

        }

}

function gameStateNewGame(){
    score = 0;
    enemy = [];
    explosions = [];
    playField = [];
    items = [];
    resetPlayer();
    createPlayField();
    renderPlayField();

    switchGameState(GAME_STATE_WAIT_FOR_PLAYER_MOVE);

}

function createPlayField(){
    var wallCount = 0;
    var playerCount = 0;
    var enemyCount = 0;
    var goalCount = 0;
    var roadCount = 0;

    //fill with road
    for (var rowCtr=0;rowCtr<15;rowCtr++){
        var tempRow = [];
        for (colCtr=0;colCtr<15;colCtr++) {
            tempRow.push(roadTile)
        }

        playField.push(tempRow);

    }
    //console.log("playField=" + playField);

    //create items array
    for (rowCtr=0;rowCtr<15;rowCtr++){
        var tempRow = [];
        for (colCtr=0;colCtr<15;colCtr++) {
            tempRow.push(0);
```

```
        }
        items.push(tempRow);

    }

    var randRow;
    var randCol;
    //placewalls
    for (var wallCtr=0;wallCtr<wallMax;wallCtr++){
        var wallLocationFound = false;
        while(!wallLocationFound){
            randRow = Math.floor(Math.random()*15);
            randCol = Math.floor(Math.random()*15);
            if (playField[randRow][randCol]==roadTile){
                playField[randRow][randCol] = wallTile;
                wallLocationFound = true;
            }
        }
    }

    //place enemy
    for (var enemyCtr=0;enemyCtr<enemyMax;enemyCtr++){
        var enemyLocationFound = false;
        while(!enemyLocationFound){
            randRow = Math.floor(Math.random()*15);
            randCol = Math.floor(Math.random()*15);
            if (playField[randRow][randCol]==roadTile){
                enemyLocationFound = true;
                var tempEnemy = {};
                tempEnemy.row = randRow;
                tempEnemy.col = randCol;
                tempEnemy.nextRow = 0;
                tempEnemy.nextCol = 0;
                tempEnemy.currentTile = 0;
                tempEnemy.rotation = 0;
                tempEnemy.x = tempEnemy.col*32;
                tempEnemy.y = tempEnemy.row*32;
                tempEnemy.speed = 2;
                tempEnemy.destinationX = 0;
                tempEnemy.destinationY = 0;
                tempEnemy.dx = 0;
                tempEnemy.dy = 0;
                tempEnemy.hit = false;
                tempEnemy.dead = false;
                tempEnemy.moveComplete = false;
                enemy.push(tempEnemy);
                items[randRow][randCol] = 1;
            }
        }
    }

    //place player
    var playerLocationFound = false;
    while(!playerLocationFound){
```

```
            randRow = Math.floor(Math.random()*15);
            randCol = Math.floor(Math.random()*15);
            if (playField[randRow][randCol]==roadTile &&
             items[randRow][randCol]==0){
                playerLocationFound = true;
                player.col = randCol;
                player.row = randRow;
                player.x = player.col*32;
                player.y = player.row*32;
                items[randRow][randCol] = 1;
            }
        }

    //place goal
    var goalLocationFound = false;
    while(!goalLocationFound){
        randRow = Math.floor(Math.random()*15);
        randCol = Math.floor(Math.random()*15);
        if (playField[randRow][randCol]==roadTile &&
         items[randRow][randCol]==0){
            playField[randRow][randCol] = goalTile;
            goalLocationFound = true;
        }
    }

    //console.log("playField=" + playField);

}

function resetPlayer(){
    player.row = 0;
    player.col = 0;
    player.nextRow = 0;
    player.nextCol = 0;
    player.currentTile = 0;
    player.rotation = 0;
    player.speed = 2;
    player.destinationX = 0;
    player.destinationY = 0;
    player.x = 0;
    player.y = 0;
    player.dx = 0;
    player.dy = 0;
    player.hit = false;
    player.dead = false;
    player.win = false;
}

function gameStateWaitForPlayerMove() {
    if (keyPressList[38]==true){
        //up
        if (checkBounds(-1,0, player)){
            setPlayerDestination();
```

```
        }
      }else if (keyPressList[37]==true) {
         //left
         if (checkBounds(0,-1, player)){
            setPlayerDestination();
         }
      }else if (keyPressList[39]==true) {
         //right
         if (checkBounds(0,1, player)){
            setPlayerDestination();
         }
      }else if  (keyPressList[40]==true){
         //down
         if (checkBounds(1,0, player)){
            setPlayerDestination();
         }
      }
   }
}

function setPlayerDestination(){
   player.destinationX = player.nextCol*32;
   player.destinationY = player.nextRow*32;
   switchGameState(GAME_STATE_ANIMATE_PLAYER);
}

function checkBounds(rowInc, colInc, object){
   object.nextRow = object.row+rowInc;
   object.nextCol = object.col+colInc;

   if (object.nextCol >=0 && object.nextCol<15 &&
    object.nextRow>=0 && object.nextRow<15){
      object.dx = colInc;
      object.dy = rowInc;

      if (colInc==1){
         object.rotation = 90;
      }else if (colInc==-1){
         object.rotation = 270;
      }else if (rowInc==-1){
         object.rotation = 0;
      }else if (rowInc==1){
         object.rotation = 180;
      }

      return(true);

   }else{
      object.nextRow = object.row;
      object.nextCol = object.col;
      return(false);

   }

}
```

```
function gameStateAnimatePlayer(){
   player.x += player.dx*player.speed;
   player.y += player.dy*player.speed;
   player.currentTile++;
   if (player.currentTile==playerTiles.length){
      player.currentTile = 0;
   }
   renderPlayField();
   if (player.x==player.destinationX && player.y==player.destinationY){
      switchGameState(GAME_STATE_EVALUATE_PLAYER_MOVE);
   }

}

function gameStateEvaluatePlayerMove(){
   player.row = player.nextRow;
   player.col = player.nextCol;

   if (playField[player.row][player.col]==wallTile){
      player.hit = true;
   }else if (playField[player.row][player.col]==goalTile){
      player.win = true;
   }

   for (var eCtr=enemy.length-1;eCtr>=0;eCtr--){
      if (player.row==enemy[eCtr].row && player.col==enemy[eCtr].col){
         enemy[eCtr].hit = true;
         player.hit = true;
      }
   }

   switchGameState(GAME_STATE_ENEMY_MOVE);

}

function gameStateEnemyMove(){
   for (var eCtr=0;eCtr<enemy.length;eCtr++){
      var tempEnemy = enemy[eCtr];
      if (!tempEnemy.hit){

         var directionsToTest=[];
         var hDiff = tempEnemy.col - player.col;
         var vDiff = tempEnemy.row - player.row;

         if (Math.abs(vDiff) < Math.abs(hDiff)){
            if (vDiff > 0){
               directionsToTest.push("up");
               directionsToTest.push("down");
            }else if (vDiff <0){
               directionsToTest.push("down");
               directionsToTest.push("up");
            }
```

```
        if (hDiff >0){
            directionsToTest.push("left");
            directionsToTest.push("right");
        }else if (hDiff <0){
            directionsToTest.push("right");
            directionsToTest.push("left");
        }
    }else if (Math.abs(hDiff) < Math.abs(vDiff)) {
        if (hDiff >0){
            directionsToTest.push("left");
            directionsToTest.push("right");
        }else if (hDiff<0){
            directionsToTest.push("right");
            directionsToTest.push("left");
        }else if (vDiff > 0){
            directionsToTest.push("up");
            directionsToTest.push("down");
        }else if (vDiff <0){
            directionsToTest.push("down");
            directionsToTest.push("up");
        }
    }else if (Math.abs(hDiff) == Math.abs(vDiff)) {
        //make an educated random guess
        if (Math.floor(Math.random()*2)==0){
            //try vertical first
            if (vDiff >0){
                directionsToTest.push("up");
                directionsToTest.push("down");
            }else if (vDiff<0){
                directionsToTest.push("down");
                directionsToTest.push("up");
            }
        }else{
            //try vertical first
            if (hDiff >0){
                directionsToTest.push("left");
                directionsToTest.push("right");
            }else if (hDiff<0){
                directionsToTest.push("right");
                directionsToTest.push("left");
            }
        }
    }
}
var chooseRandom = false;
var moveFound = false;
var movePtr = 0;
var move;

if (Math.floor(Math.random()*100)> chanceRandomEnemyMovement){

    //not random movement

    while(!moveFound){

        move = directionsToTest[movePtr];
```

```
    switch(move){
        case "up":
            if (checkBounds(-1,0,tempEnemy)){
                moveFound = true;

            }
            break;

        case "down":
            if (checkBounds(1,0,tempEnemy)){
                moveFound = true;

            }
            break;

        case "left":
            if (checkBounds(0,-1, tempEnemy)){
                moveFound = true;

            }
            break;
        case "right":
            if (checkBounds(0,1,tempEnemy)){
                moveFound = true;

            }
            break
    }

    movePtr++
    if (movePtr==directionsToTest.length){
        //do not move if no move found
        //this should be impossible
        chooseRandom = true;

    }
}

}else{
    chooseRandom = true;
}
    //pick random direction to test;
if (chooseRandom) {

    while(!moveFound){
        switch(Math.floor(Math.random()*4)){
            case 0:
                if (checkBounds(-1,0,tempEnemy)){
                    moveFound = true;

                }else{

                }
                break;
```

```
                case 1:
                    if (checkBounds(1,0,tempEnemy)){
                        moveFound = true;

                    }else{

                    }
                    break;

                case 2:
                    if (checkBounds(0,-1, tempEnemy)){
                        moveFound = true;

                    }else{

                    }
                    break;
                case 3:
                    if (checkBounds(0,1,tempEnemy)){
                        moveFound = true;

                    }else{

                    }
                    break
            }
        }

    }


        tempEnemy.destinationX = tempEnemy.nextCol*32;
        tempEnemy.destinationY = tempEnemy.nextRow*32;


    }else{
        tempEnemy.nextCol = tempEnemy.col;
        tempEnemy.nextRow = tempEnemy.row;
        tempEnemy.destinationX = tempEnemy.nextCol*32;
        tempEnemy.destinationY = tempEnemy.nextRow*32;
    }


    }
    switchGameState(GAME_STATE_ANIMATE_ENEMY);
}

function gameStateAnimateEnemy(){
    for (var eCtr=enemy.length-1;eCtr>=0;eCtr--){
        var tempEnemy = enemy[eCtr];

        if (!tempEnemy.moveComplete){
```

```
            tempEnemy.x += tempEnemy.dx*tempEnemy.speed;
            tempEnemy.y += tempEnemy.dy*tempEnemy.speed;
            tempEnemy.currentTile++;
            if (tempEnemy.currentTile==enemyTiles.length){
               tempEnemy.currentTile = 0;
            }
            renderPlayField();
            if (tempEnemy.x==tempEnemy.destinationX &&
             tempEnemy.y==tempEnemy.destinationY){
               tempEnemy.moveComplete = true;
               enemyMoveCompleteCount++;
            }
         }
      }

   if (enemyMoveCompleteCount >= enemy.length){
      enemyMoveCompleteCount = 0;
      for (var eCtr=0;eCtr<enemy.length;eCtr++){
         var tempEnemy = enemy[eCtr];
         tempEnemy.moveComplete = false;
      }
      switchGameState(GAME_STATE_EVALUATE_ENEMY_MOVE);

   }

}

function gameStateEvaluateEnemyMove(){
   for (var eCtr=enemy.length-1;eCtr>=0;eCtr--){
      var tempEnemy = enemy[eCtr];
      tempEnemy.row = tempEnemy.nextRow;
      tempEnemy.col = tempEnemy.nextCol;

      if (playField[tempEnemy.row][tempEnemy.col]==wallTile){
         tempEnemy.hit = true;
      }

      if (player.row==tempEnemy.row && player.col==tempEnemy.col){
         tempEnemy.hit = true;
         player.hit = true;

      }

      //check against other enemy
      for (var eCtr2=enemy.length-1;eCtr2>=0;eCtr2--){
         var tempEnemy2 = enemy[eCtr2];

         if (tempEnemy.row==tempEnemy2.row &&
          tempEnemy.col==tempEnemy2.col && eCtr != eCtr2){
            tempEnemy.hit = true;
            tempEnemy2.hit = true;
         }

      }
```

```
        }
        switchGameState(GAME_STATE_EVALUATE_OUTCOME);
    }

    function gameStateEvaluateOutcome(){
        if (player.hit){
            player.dead = true;
            createExplode(player);
        }

        for (var eCtr=enemy.length-1;eCtr>=0;eCtr--){
            var tempEnemy = enemy[eCtr];
            if (tempEnemy.hit){
                score += enemyScore;
                tempEnemy.dead  = true;
                createExplode(tempEnemy)
                enemy.splice(eCtr,1);
                tempEnemy = null;
            }
        }

        switchGameState(GAME_STATE_ANIMATE_EXPLODE);
    }

    function createExplode(object){
        var newExplode = {};
        newExplode.currentTile = 0;
        newExplode.row = object.row;
        newExplode.col = object.com;
        newExplode.x = object.x;
        newExplode.y = object.y;
          newExplode.rotation = 0;
        explosions.push(newExplode);
    }


    function gameStateAnimateExplode(){
        for (var eCtr=explosions.length-1;eCtr>=0;eCtr--){
            var tempExplosion = explosions[eCtr];
            renderPlayField();
            tempExplosion.currentTile++;
            if (tempExplosion.currentTile == explodeTiles.length){
                explosions.splice(eCtr,1);
                tempExplode = null;
            }
        }

        if (explosions.length==0){
            switchGameState(GAME_STATE_CHECK_FOR_GAME_OVER);
        }
    }

    function gameStateCheckForGameOver() {
        if (player.dead){
            switchGameState(GAME_STATE_PLAYER_LOSE);
```

```
        }else if (player.win){
            switchGameState(GAME_STATE_PLAYER_WIN)
        }else{
            switchGameState(GAME_STATE_WAIT_FOR_PLAYER_MOVE);
        }
}

function drawPlayField(){
    for (rowCtr=0;rowCtr<15;rowCtr++){

        for (colCtr=0;colCtr<15;colCtr++) {
            var sourceX = Math.floor((playField[rowCtr][colCtr]) % 8) * 32;
            var sourceY = Math.floor((playField[rowCtr][colCtr]) /8) *32;

            if (playField[rowCtr][colCtr] != roadTile){
                context.drawImage(tileSheet, 0, 0,32,32, colCtr*32,
                    rowCtr*32,32,32);
            }
            context.drawImage(tileSheet, sourceX, sourceY,32,32,
              colCtr*32,rowCtr*32,32,32);
        }
    }
}

function drawPlayer(){
    if (!player.dead){
        context.save();

        context.setTransform(1,0,0,1,0,0);
        context.translate(player.x+16, player.y+16);
        var angleInRadians = player.rotation * Math.PI / 180;
        context.rotate(angleInRadians);

        var sourceX = Math.floor(playerTiles[player.currentTile] % 8) * 32;
        var sourceY = Math.floor(playerTiles[player.currentTile] /8) *32;

        context.drawImage(tileSheet, sourceX, sourceY,32,32,-16,-16,32,32);

        context.restore();
    }

}

function drawEnemy(){
    for (var eCtr=enemy.length-1;eCtr>=0;eCtr--){
        tempEnemy = enemy[eCtr];
        if (!tempEnemy.dead){
            context.save();

            context.setTransform(1,0,0,1,0,0);
            context.translate(tempEnemy.x+16, tempEnemy.y+16);
            var angleInRadians = tempEnemy.rotation * Math.PI / 180;
            context.rotate(angleInRadians);
```

```
                var sourceX = Math.floor(enemyTiles[tempEnemy.currentTile] % 8) * 32;
                var sourceY = Math.floor(enemyTiles[tempEnemy.currentTile] /8) *32;

                context.drawImage(tileSheet, sourceX, sourceY,32,32,-16,-16,32,32);

                context.restore();
            }
        }
    }

    function drawExplosions(){
        for (var eCtr=explosions.length-1;eCtr>=0;eCtr--){
            tempExplosion = explosions[eCtr];

            context.save();

            var sourceX = Math.floor(explodeTiles[tempExplosion.currentTile]
             % 8) * 32;
            var sourceY = Math.floor(explodeTiles[tempExplosion.currentTile] /8) *32;

            context.drawImage(tileSheet, sourceX, sourceY,32,32,
             tempExplosion.x,tempExplosion.y,32,32);

            context.restore();

        }
    }

    function fillBackground() {
        // draw background and text
        context.fillStyle = '#000000';
        context.fillRect(xMin, yMin, xMax, yMax);

    }

    function setTextStyleTitle() {
        context.fillStyle = '#54ebeb';
        context.font = '20px _sans';
        context.textBaseline = 'top';
    }

    function renderPlayField() {
        fillBackground();
        drawPlayField();
        drawPlayer();
        drawEnemy();
        drawExplosions();

    }

    document.onkeydown = function(e){

        e = e?e:window.event;
        keyPressList[e.keyCode]=true;
    }
```

```
   document.onkeyup = function(e){
   //document.body.onkeyup = function(e){
      e = e?e:window.event;
      keyPressList[e.keyCode] = false;
   };

//*** application start
   switchGameState(GAME_STATE_INIT);
   const FRAME_RATE = 40;
   frameRateCounter = new FrameRateCounter(FRAME_RATE);
   //**** application loop
   var intervalTime = 1000/FRAME_RATE;
   setInterval(runGame, intervalTime );

}

//***  new FrameRateCounter   object prototype

function FrameRateCounter(fps) {
   if (fps == undefined){
      this.fps = 40
   }else{
      this.fps = fps
   }
   this.lastFrameCount = 0;
   var dateTemp = new Date();

   this.frameLast = dateTemp.getTime();
   delete dateTemp;
   this.frameCtr = 0;
   this.lastTime = dateTemp.getTime();
   this.step = 1;
}
FrameRateCounter.prototype.countFrames=function() {

   var dateTemp = new Date();
   var timeDifference = dateTemp.getTime()-this.lastTime;
   this.step = (timeDifference/1000)*this.fps;
   this.lastTime = dateTemp.getTime();
   //console.log("step=",this.step)
   this.frameCtr++;

   if (dateTemp.getTime() >=this.frameLast+1000) {
      ConsoleLog.log("frame event");
      this.lastFrameCount = this.frameCtr;
      this.frameCtr = 0;
      this.frameLast = dateTemp.getTime();
   }
   delete dateTemp;

}

</script>
</head>
```

```
<body>
<div style="position: absolute; top: 50px; left: 50px;">
<canvas id="canvas" width="480" height="480">
 Your browser does not support HTML5 Canvas.
</canvas>
</body>
</html>
```

What's Next

Throughout this entire book, we have used game- and entertainment-related subjects to demonstrate canvas application building concepts. Over these last two chapters, we've sped up the game discussion and covered many game concepts directly by creating two unique games and optimizing a third with bitmaps and object pooling. In doing so, we have applied many of the concepts from the earlier chapters in full-blown game applications. The techniques used to create a game on Canvas can be applied to almost any canvas application from image viewers to stock charting. The sky is really the limit, as the canvas allows the developer a full suite of powerful low-level capabilities that can be molded into any application.

In Chapter 10, we will look at porting a simple game from the canvas into a native iPhone application.

Mobilizing Games with PhoneGap

Going Mobile!

Nowadays it seems that everyone is making, planning to make, or thinking of making applications for mobile devices. Mobile is the next great (or maybe actually the current) place to make money by selling applications. The Apple iPhone is currently one of the most popular personal communication devices, and the iTunes Store gives budding application developers a place to show and sell the fruits of their labor. Apple separates their application-development platforms into three categories: Desktop (OS X), Browser (Safari), and iPhone/iPad/iPod Touch (iOS).

Most iOS applications, especially games, are written in Objective-C and compiled directly to the platform using the Xcode IDE. This is a large barrier to entry to develop native applications, as Objective-C is not widely used on platforms other than Apple devices. Up until early 2010, Objective-C/Xcode was the only viable development system for targeting iOS development.

In this chapter, we will "port" our HTML5 Canvas application to the iPhone using a technology called PhoneGap. PhoneGap allows an HTML application to run natively on an iPhone by packaging the application as a Safari Mobile "app." This app can be run from the iPhone interface, and it will look and act like an app compiled in Objective-C. Applications packaged with PhoneGap can even be sold in the iTunes Store.

 Other third-party tools can be used to create iOS applications and games. For example, Unity (*http://unity3d.com/*) is a powerful game-development platform that can target iOS. In addition, there are tools such as Ansca's Corona SDK (*http://www.anscamobile.com/*) that use scripting languages to harness the power of the platform.

Introducing PhoneGap

PhoneGap is an open source development tool created by Nitobi (*http://www.nitobi.com*) that acts as a software bridge between standards-based HTML development and several mobile platforms. Using PhoneGap, the HTML5 Canvas developer has access to the various hardware APIs for supported devices through an *abstraction layer*. This software interface allows the same code to be used to target features common among various devices—such as geolocation, touch screens, microphones, and other hardware capabilities—so that separate code does not need to be written for each device.

 You will need an Intel-based Macintosh running Xcode to be able to compile a PhoneGap project. There currently is no development platform for Windows that will allow compiling Safari Mobile applications to the iOS platform with an Objective-C wrapper.

We won't target too many specific iPhone features in this chapter. In the allotted space, we will cover the basics needed to take a simple application and get it up and running in the iPhone simulator, and then onto a physical device. We will then implement an accelerometer feature into our application.

 For further reading, Jonathan Stark's *Building iPhone Apps with HTML, CSS, and JavaScript* (O'Reilly) covers PhoneGap and hardware feature API integration in detail. If you'd rather try this with Android, explore the similar *Building Android Apps with HTML, CSS, and JavaScript* (O'Reilly), also by Jonathan Stark, which applies PhoneGap to create applications for Android.

The Application

The application we are going to create is a simple *BS Bingo* game. BS Bingo was designed on paper well before mobile devices were available. This cynical game concept is based on the feeling (by some) that the typical business workplace has been overtaken with *Dilbert-* or *Office Space*-esque annoying corporate jargon and doublespeak. This doublespeak seems to have deeply rooted itself in the workplace over the last 20 years, mostly to the annoyance of software developers (such as ourselves).

In the pen-and-paper version of the game, each player brings a "bingo card" to a meeting where he expects to hear a lot of this corporate doublespeak. The bingo card is a 5×5 grid, and each of the 25 squares is filled with one of the annoying words or jargon phrases. During the meeting, each player marks off squares as the words or phrases are said aloud by the unsuspecting (and not playing) members of the meeting. When a player has a full column of his card marked off, he is supposed to jump up from the meeting table and yell "BS!"

Whether this game was ever widely played (or even played at all) is a debatable urban legend, but the simple concept of clicking squares to highlight them makes for a useful piece of code that we can build easily and then port to the iPhone. We are not even going to build the entire game here; we will leave extending it into a full application (possibly adding multiplayer, which is discussed in Chapter 11) for you, the reader.

The Code

Example 10-1 gives the code for our game. We'll discuss the various functions in the next section before we move on to installing, modifying, and testing it in Xcode using PhoneGap. This version of the game will work fine on a Safari desktop browser. We will highlight the modifications necessary to port it to the iPhone in the next section.

Example 10-1. BSBingo.html full source listing

```
<!doctype html>
 <html lang="en">
 <head>
     <meta charset="UTF-8">

<title>BS Bingo</title>
<script src="modernizr-1.6.min.js"></script>
<script src="TextButton.js"></script>
<script src="ConsoleLog.js"></script>
<script type="text/javascript">

window.addEventListener('load', eventWindowLoaded, false);
function eventWindowLoaded() {

    canvasApp();

}

function canvasSupport () {
    return Modernizr.canvas;
}

function canvasApp(){

    if (!canvasSupport()) {
          return;
      }else{
        theCanvas = document.getElementById("canvas");
         context = theCanvas.getContext("2d");
    }

    var bingoCard = [];
    var buttons = [];

    var standardJargonList = [];
    var tempButton = {};
    var clickSound;
```

```
function initLists(){

    standardJargonList=[
    "Actionable", "Assessment" ,"Bandwidth", "Benchmark",
    "Best\nPractices", "Bottle neck" , "Change\nManagement",  "Coach",
    "Competitive\nAdvantage", "Constraints", "Core\nCompetencies",
    "Core values", "Critical\nthinking", "Cutting\nedge",
    "Dashboard", "Deliverables", "Enterprise","Gatekeeper",
    "Individual\nContributor", "Leadership", "Matrix\norganisation",
    "Metrics", "Milestones", "Momentum", "Moving target",
    "Initiative","Partnership", "Process", "Process\nmanagement",
    "Re-engineer", "Requirements", "Rightsize", "Seat at\nthe table",
    "Tentpole", " Silo", "Standards", "State of the art",
    "Supply chain", "Synergy","Teamwork", "Thought\nleader",
    "Touchpoints", "Value\nadded", "Drink the\nKool Aid",
    "Baked In", "Champion", "Circle Back", "Dialogue", "Emerge",
    "Enhance", "Evolve", "Execute", "Facilitate" ,"Incentivise",
    "Leverage", "Partner", "Spearhead", "Strategize","Synergise",
    "Throw\na\nCurve", "Touch Base", "Outside\nthe\nBox",
    "Opportunity", "Open Door\nPolicy","Win-Win\n(Anything)",
    "Risk\n(Anything)","Proactive","Reactive","Buy-In",
    "Paradigm\nShift","Task-Oriented","Empower","Team\nPlayer",
    "Enterprise\nWide","Globalization","Localization",
    "Mission-critical", "Magic\nQuadrant","Agile\n(Anything)",
    "Waterfall","Outsourcing","Off-Shoring","Blue Sky",
    "20/20 \nindsight","Low\nHanging\nFruit","10,000\nFoot View",
    "Take\nOwnership","Ramp up", "Out of\nthe Box", "24x7",
    "Fast Track", "Out of\nthe Loop", "In the\nLoop","Touch Base",
    "Mindset", "Game Plan", "Bring to \nthe Table", "Drill Down",
    "Elevator\nSpeech", "Level the\nPlaying field",
    "Ping\n(Someone)","Pushback","Retool", "Take Away",
    "Life-Time\nValue", "Thought\nLeadership", "Up Sell"
    ];

}

function initButtons(){
    buttons = [
        [

        new TextButton(0,0,"Button
            0,0",85,50,gr,"#000000","#ffff00","#000000"),

        new TextButton(92,0,"Button
            0,1",85,50,gr,"#000000","#ffff00","#000000"),

        new TextButton(184,0,"Button
            0,2",85,50,gr,"#000000","#ffff00","#000000"),

        new TextButton(276,0,"Button
            0,3",85,50,gr,"#000000","#ffff00","#000000"),

        new TextButton(368,0,"Button
            0,4",85,50,gr,"#000000","#ffff00","#000000")
```

```
    ],

    [

     new TextButton(0,57,"Button
         1,0",85,50,gr,"#000000","#ffff00","#000000"),

     new TextButton(92,57,"Button
         1,1",85,50,gr,"#000000","#ffff00","#000000"),

     new TextButton(184,57,"Button
         1,2",85,50,gr,"#000000","#ffff00","#000000"),

     new TextButton(276,57,"Button
         1,3",85,50,gr,"#000000","#ffff00","#000000"),

     new TextButton(368,57,"Button
         1,4",85,50,gr,"#000000","#ffff00","#000000")

    ],

    [

     new TextButton(0,114,"Button
         2,0",85,50,gr,"#000000","#ffff00","#000000"),

     new TextButton(92,114,"Button
         2,1",85,50,gr,"#000000","#ffff00","#000000"),

     new TextButton(184,114,"Button
         2,2",85,50,gr,"#000000","#ffff00","#000000"),

     new TextButton(276,114,"Button
         2,3",85,50,gr,"#000000","#ffff00","#000000"),

     new TextButton(368,114,"Button
         2,4",85,50,gr,"#000000","#ffff00","#000000")

    ],

    [

     new TextButton(0,171,"Button
         3,0",85,50,gr,"#000000","#ffff00","#000000"),

     new TextButton(92,171,"Button
         3,1",85,50,gr,"#000000","#ffff00","#000000"),

     new TextButton(184,171,"Button
         3,2",85,50,gr,"#000000","#ffff00","#000000"),

     new TextButton(276,171,"Button
         3,3",85,50,gr,"#000000","#ffff00","#000000"),
```

```
                 new TextButton(368,171,"Button
                    3,4",85,50,gr,"#000000","#ffff00","#000000")

             ],

             [

               new TextButton(0,228,"Button
                  4,0",85,50,gr,"#000000","#ffff00","#000000"),

               new TextButton(92,228,"Button
                  4,1",85,50,gr,"#000000","#ffff00","#000000"),

               new TextButton(184,228,"Button
                  4,2",85,50,gr,"#000000","#ffff00","#000000"),

               new TextButton(276,228,"Button
                  4,3",85,50,gr,"#000000","#ffff00","#000000"),

               new TextButton(368,228,"Button
                  4,4",85,50,gr,"#000000","#ffff00","#000000")

             ]
          ];
   }

   function initSounds(){
      clickSound = document.getElementById('clicksound');
   }

   function chooseButtonsForCard(){
      //copy jargon into temp array
      var tempArray = [];
      for (var arrayctr=0;arrayctr<standardJargonList.length;arrayctr++){
         tempArray.push(standardJargonList[arrayctr]);
      }

      for (var ctr1=0;ctr1<buttons.length;ctr1++){

         for (var ctr2=0; ctr2<buttons[ctr1].length;ctr2++){
            var randInt = Math.floor(Math.random()*tempArray.length)
            buttons[ctr1][ctr2].text = tempArray[randInt];
            tempArray.splice(randInt,1)
         }
      }

   }



   function drawScreen() {
      //ConsoleLog.log("standardAcronymList="+standardAcronymList.length);
      //ConsoleLog.log("standardJargonList="+standardJargonList.length);
      for (var ctr1=0;ctr1<buttons.length;ctr1++){
         ConsoleLog.log("ctr1="+ctr1)
```

```
            for (var ctr2=0; ctr2<buttons[ctr1].length;ctr2++){
                ConsoleLog.log("ctr2="+ctr2)
                buttons[ctr1][ctr2].draw(context);
            }
        }

    }

    function onMouseClick(e) {

        //select case through states and then the locations of
        //buttons in those states
        mouseX = e.clientX-theCanvas.offsetLeft;
        mouseY = e.clientY-theCanvas.offsetTop;
        ConsoleLog.log("click " + mouseX + "," + mouseY);
        //find the button clicked

        var col = Math.floor(mouseX/92);
        var row = Math.floor(mouseY/57);

        console.log("row",row,"col", col);
        tempButton = buttons[row][col];
        clickSound.play();
        tempButton.pressDown();
        tempButton.draw(context);

    }

    function onMouseMove(e) {
        mouseX = e.clientX-theCanvas.offsetLeft;
        mouseY = e.clientY-theCanvas.offsetTop;

        //ConsoleLog.log("move: " + mouseX + "," + mouseY);
    }

        //**** start application
    var gr = context.createLinearGradient(0, 0, 85, 50);

    // Add the color stops.
    gr.addColorStop(0,'#ffffff');
        gr.addColorStop(.5,'#bbbbbb');
    gr.addColorStop(1,'#777777');

    theCanvas.addEventListener("mousemove", onMouseMove, false);
    theCanvas.addEventListener("click", onMouseClick, false);

    initSounds();
    initButtons();
    initLists();
    chooseButtonsForCard();
    drawScreen();

}

</script>
```

```
</head>
<body>
<div style="position: absolute; top: 0px; left: 0px;">
<canvas id="canvas" width="570" height="418">
 Your browser does not support HTML5 Canvas.
</canvas>
<audio id ="clicksound"  preload="auto">
   <source src="click.mp3" type="audio/mpeg" />

Your browser does not support the audio element.
</audio>
</div>
</body>
</html>
```

Name this file *BSBingo.html* and save it in a folder. If you are going to follow along and create the example project, you will also want to create a folder to hold the project files.

Examining the Code for BSBingo.html

 When designing an application for the iPhone using PhoneGap, we are actually targeting the Safari Mobile browser. This means we can make concessions rather than having to target all available HTML5-compatible devices. You will notice this especially when we discuss <audio> tag usage.

The TextButton.js file

Our BS Bingo game will be played on a grid of 25 squares. We created a class (an object prototype, actually) called *TextButton.js* to help us create buttons with the text, as well as a "press" state we can use to show that the button has been clicked. You will want to save this file in the project folder along with the *BSBingo.html* file. Here is the code for this file:

```
function TextButton(x,y,text, width, height, backColor, strokeColor,
  overColor, textColor){
    this.x = x;
    this.y = y;
    this.text = text;
    this.width = width;
    this.height = height;
    this.backColor = backColor;
    this.strokeColor = strokeColor;
    this.overColor = overColor;
    this.textColor = textColor;
    this.press = false;
}

TextButton.prototype.pressDown=function() {
    if (this.press==true){
        this.press = false;
```

```
    }else{
        this.press = true;
    }
}

TextButton.prototype.draw = function(context){

    context.save();
    context.setTransform(1,0,0,1,0,0); // reset to identity
    context.translate(this.x, this.y);

    context.shadowOffsetX = 3;
    context.shadowOffsetY = 3;
    context.shadowBlur = 3;
    context.shadowColor = "#222222";

    context.lineWidth = 4;
    context.lineJoin = 'round';
    context.strokeStyle = this.strokeColor;

    if (this.press==true){
        context.fillStyle = this.overColor;
    }else{
        context.fillStyle = this.backColor;
    }

    context.strokeRect(0, 0, this.width,this.height);
    context.fillRect(0, 0, this.width,this.height);

    //text
    context.shadowOffsetX = 1;
    context.shadowOffsetY = 1;
    context.shadowBlur = 1;
    context.shadowColor = "#ffffff";
    context.font = "14px serif"
    context.fillStyle = this.textColor;
    context.textAlign = "center";
    context.textBaseline = "middle";
    var metrics = context.measureText(this.text)
    var textWidth = metrics.width;
    var xPosition = this.width/2;
    var yPosition = (this.height/2);

    var splitText = this.text.split('\n');
    var verticalSpacing = 14;
    console.log("text=" + this.text)
    console.log("text split length=" + splitText.length)

    for (var ctr1=0; ctr1<splitText.length;ctr1++) {
        context.fillText ( splitText[ctr1],  xPosition,
        yPosition+ (ctr1*verticalSpacing));
    }

    context.restore();
}
```

This object prototype contains functions for creating, drawing, and clicking a gray square button with black text on it. When clicked, the button will be drawn with a yellow background. We have covered all these drawing functions earlier in this book, so they will look familiar to you if you have read those chapters. If you have not, it's especially a good idea to read Chapter 2, which covers drawing and shading objects drawn with paths.

Let's now take a quick look at the functions we have created in *BSBingo.html*.

The initLists() function

The first game-related function you will encounter is `initLists()`. For our simple game implementation, we have created a single list of words based on some common business jargon. The `standardJargonList` application scope variable will contain a single-dimension array of words that will be placed randomly on the player's bingo card. We can add more types of lists if we would like to target other types of jargon-speak, such as pure IT process-speak, marketing-speak, or even sports- or geek-speak.

The initButtons() function

This function creates a grid of 25 `TextButton` instances, 85 pixels in width and 25 in height. These are stored in the application scope `buttons` two-dimensional array so they can be accessed via the `[row][column]` syntax.

The initSounds() function

The `initSounds()` function needs to initialize only a single sound referenced in an HTML5 `<audio>` tag. Since we are targeting the iOS platform, we need to provide only a single *.mp3*-formatted sound. We do not need *.ogg* or *.wav* because we are not targeting any other browsers. Here is the HTML5 `<audio>` tag:

```
<audio id="clicksound" preload="auto">
    <source src="click.mp3" type="audio/mpeg" />
  Your browser does not support the audio element.
</audio>
```

The chooseButtonsForCard() function

This function creates a local array called `tempArray` and fills it with the contents of the `standardJargonList`. Next, it randomly chooses an element from the `tempArray` for each of the 25 row/column combinations on the bingo card. As it selects a word, it splices it from the `tempArray` so it cannot be selected again, leaving the card with no duplicates.

The drawScreen() function

This function loops through the buttons two-dimensional array and draws the initial 25 buttons with text onto the canvas.

The onMouseClick() function

When the user clicks the mouse on the game screen, this event listener function determines which of the 25 squares was clicked. It calls the appropriate TextButton instance's pressDown() function and then its draw() function, passing in the context.

The onMouseMove() function

When the mouse is moved, this event listener function will set the mouseX and mouseY values to the current mouse position on the canvas.

The Application Code

Once all the functions and the TextButton object prototype are created, the actual application code is very simple. Because this is a completely event-based application, we don't need a main loop. We also have not put in any other states or buttons, such as a title screen or a reset button. This makes the app less user-friendly, but it is fine for this simple example. It also makes the application code very simple:

```
//**** start application
    var gr = context.createLinearGradient(0, 0, 100, 100);

    // Add the color stops.
    gr.addColorStop(0,'#ffffff');
    gr.addColorStop(.5,'#bbbbbb');
    gr.addColorStop(1,'#777777');

    theCanvas.addEventListener("mousemove", onMouseMove, false);
    theCanvas.addEventListener("click", onMouseClick, false);
    initSounds();
    initButtons();
    initLists();
    chooseButtonsForCard();
    drawScreen();
```

First, we create a shared linear gradient that can be used by all the TextButton instances. Next, we add the mouse event listeners for click and move. Finally, we run through our functions to set up the card, and then we simply wait for the user to click a button. That's all there is to it. We haven't even added a way to announce that the player has won. Extending this into a full-fledged application would be very simple, so we leave this task up to the reader if you have the desire to do so.

Figure 10-1 shows the screen for the finished application.

Buy-In	Touch Base	Elevator Speech	Agile (Anything)	Critical thinking
Re-engineer	Individual Contributor	Synergy	Enhance	Localization
Level the Playing field	Up Sell	Moving target	Ramp up	Strategize
Momentum	Out of the Box	Teamwork	Change Management	Enterprise Wide
Globalization	Retool	State of the art	10,000 Foot View	Assessment

Figure 10-1. BS Bingo in Safari Desktop Edition

Next, we will look at how to use PhoneGap to turn this simple game into a native iOS application.

Creating the iOS Application with PhoneGap

You will need to install and set up two tools to get an iOS application up and running on your iOS device simulator: Xcode, a free application development IDE from Apple, and PhoneGap. Let's start with Xcode.

Installing Xcode

Xcode actually comes packaged on the installable operating system DVD for Snow Leopard, but this version will not be as up-to-date as the version available on the Apple developer website.

First, you will want to visit the iOS Developer Center: *http://developer.apple.com/dev center/ios/index.action*. Once there, you can create a free user account, which you will need to download Xcode and the latest iOS developer SDK. You will also need to create a paid account if you would like to test or deploy on a physical device and/or sell your application in the iTunes Store. You do not need a paid account to build and test your application in the SDK and the included iOS device simulators.

Download and install the latest version of Xcode and the iOS SDK. This is a large download (3.5 GB at the time of this writing). See Figure 10-2.

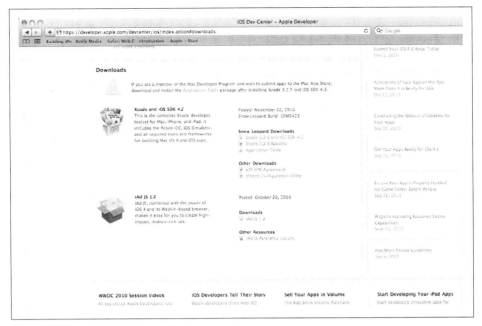

Figure 10-2. Download the iOS SDK

Once these are downloaded (most likely to your Downloads folder), start the Xcode installer. The file will be named similar to *xcode_3.2.3_and_ios_sdk_4.0.2.dmg*. Run the package installer to set up Xcode and the development kit on your computer.

> Once installed (using the default location), Xcode can be found in the Developer folder on your main storage drive.

Installing PhoneGap

Download PhoneGap from *https://github.com/phonegap/phonegap*, choosing the ZIP file option, as shown in Figure 10-3.

The file will most likely be saved into your Mac Downloads folder. Unpack this ZIP file in a safe location, such as the desktop.

Inside the ZIP, you will find a series of folders for various devices. We are interested in the iOS folder. Figure 10-4 illustrates this folder structure.

Figure 10-3. Download PhoneGap

Figure 10-4. PhoneGap folder structure

In the iOS folder there will be an installer with a name similar to *PhoneGapLibInstaller.pkg*. Open this to start the install process.

After the install, you will be given the latest install notes. It is important to read them carefully as they give great information, including the latest tips for getting started with PhoneGap. For example, after this installation, the notes read as follows:

> To get started creating PhoneGap projects, launch Xcode, then under the File menu, select "New Project...".
>
> Navigate to the section "User Templates", select PhoneGap, then in the right pane, select "PhoneGap-based Application".
>
> Select the "Choose..." button, name your project and choose the location where you want the new project to be.
>
> That's it! Modify the contents of the "www" directory to add your HTML, CSS and JavaScript.
>
> iPad:
>
> Go to your project folder and launch the "[projectname]-iPad" Xcode project. You will need the 3.2 iPhone OS SDK.
>
> *http://www.phonegap.com*
>
> *http://github.com/phonegap*

In the next section, we will follow these directions closely to get BS Bingo into a PhoneGap Xcode project.

Creating the BS Bingo PhoneGap Project in Xcode

To begin, launch Xcode and create a new PhoneGap project. See Figure 10-5 for an example of the New Project screen.

Select the PhoneGap-based application and click the Choose button.

You will next be asked to save the project in a location and give it a name. We will use the name *chapter10_bs_bingo*.

You will be presented with a screen that resembles Figure 10-6.

On the lefthand side, you will find a folder called "www". This is the most important folder because it is where we will place all of the files for our game. Before we do that, we need to make sure that the SDK is set to the correct version. In the top left, you might see a drop-down with the words "Base SDK Missing" (as shown in Figure 10-6). This means that we will not be able to build and compile our game until we choose an SDK.

Figure 10-5. Xcode New Project screen

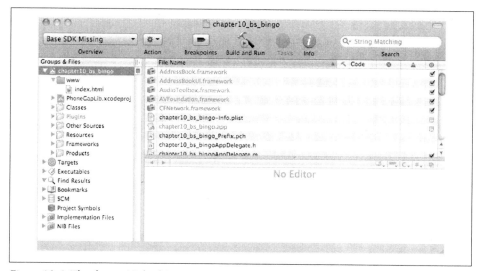

Figure 10-6. The chapter10_bs_bingo project

The Base SDK Missing message simply indicates that the default SDK is not the current version installed. In the [Project] drop-down menu, you will find a menu item called Edit Project Settings. Click this and you will see a screen similar to Figure 10-7.

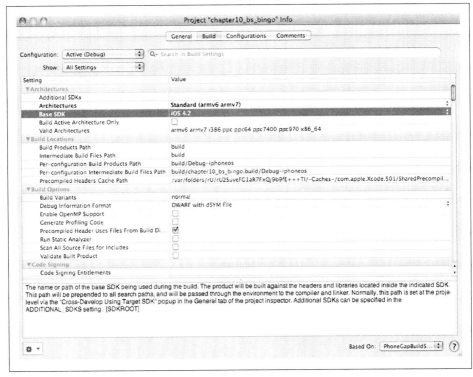

Figure 10-7. Select the correct Base SDK

Make sure that you select an SDK that is present on your machine (4.2 is the latest as of this writing).

Close this window and click on the Base SDK Missing drop-down, and be sure to select the Simulator option rather than the Device option. See Figure 10-8 for an example of this screen.

Testing the New Blank Application in the Simulator

We are now ready to build our first application and see it in the simulator. We have not added any of our own code yet (though we will in the next section), so we will be testing the contents of the *index.html* file in the project's www folder. Simply click the "Build and Run" button at the top of the IDE. If everything is set up properly, the simulator will come up with a blank screen, as shown in Figure 10-9.

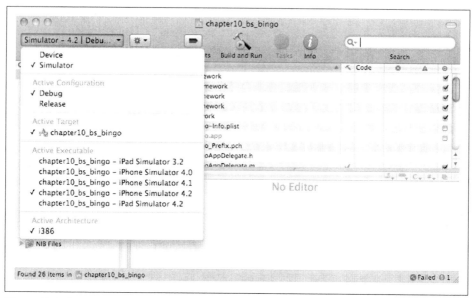

Figure 10-8. Setting up an app to run in the simulator

Figure 10-9. A basic app running in the simulator

For a single second you will see the PhoneGap banner show up on the screen. We will customize this banner for our own game shortly.

Integrating BS Bingo into the Project

We are now going to copy code from the *BSBingo.html* file we created earlier into the *index.html* file in our project.

First we will copy our JavaScript include files and add them under the *phonegap.js* script include. We will not need the *modernizer.js* file, as we will assume the iOS platform can use HTML5 Canvas:

```
<script type="text/javascript" charset="utf-8" src="phonegap.js"></script>
<script src="TextButton.js"></script>
<script src="ConsoleLog.js"></script>
```

The *phonegap.js* file should already be included in the www folder, along with *index.html*. It is part of the project template and is needed for all PhoneGap iOS applications.

Next, we will need to add the call to start our application into the `deviceReady()` function:

```
/*When this function is called, PhoneGap has been initialized and is ready to roll*/
    function onDeviceReady()
    {
        // do your thing!
        canvasApp();
    }
```

We can now replace the rest of the `script` code in the file with our code.

 At this step, don't replace from the <body> tag down to the end of the <html>. Just add the game code inside the <script> tags. You can use the existing <script></script> tags; if you do, be careful not to copy them from *BSBingo.html*.

Make sure that the first few lines look like this because we are removing the check for Canvas support:

```
function canvasApp(){

    theCanvas = document.getElementById("canvas");
    context = theCanvas.getContext("2d");
    var bingoCard = [];

    var buttons = [];

    var standardJargonList = [];

    var tempButton = {};

    var clickSound;
```

Notice that we have removed this set of code:

```
if (!canvasSupport()) {
    return;

}else{

    theCanvas = document.getElementById("canvas");

    context = theCanvas.getContext("2d");

}
```

We have replaced it with just the following since we no longer need to check whether the device can use the canvas (we must assume it can):

```
theCanvas = document.getElementById("canvas");
context = theCanvas.getContext("2d");
```

We have also deleted the canvasSupport() function, as it is not needed. We will next copy the rest of the code, including our HTML, and replace everything in the *index.html* file.

We need to make sure that the current opening <body> tag remains in *index.html*. It should look like this:

```
</head>
<body onload="onBodyLoad()">
```

The next step is to replace the rest of the file with HTML code from *BSBingo.html*:

```
<div style="position: absolute; top: 0px; left: 0px;">
<canvas id="canvas" width="570" height="418">

 Your browser does not support HTML5 Canvas.

</canvas>

<audio id ="clicksound"  preload="auto">
<source src="click.mp3" type="audio/mpeg" />

Your browser does not support the audio element.
</audio>
</div>
</body>
</html>
```

We now have enough code to do a preliminary test of our game in the simulator.

We will first need to move our files into the project folder. Take *TextButton.js*, *ConsoleLog.js*, and *click.mp3* and move them to the www folder on the disk. The project in Xcode will now reflect the new files, as seen in Figure 10-10.

Figure 10-10. The project www file listing

You will see that we have added the *BSBingo.html* file to the www folder. This is not *necessary*, but it makes it easier to edit and copy code into the *index.html* file.

Setting the Orientation

It is important to note that Safari Mobile and iOS applications render the screen in different ways. A Safari Mobile application can be set to automatically scale to fit in the iOS device's window, while a pure iOS application needs to be coded to fit the size of the target device. If an application targeted to the iOS platform is taller or wider than the device, the application will automatically be put into "scroll" mode.

We set the width of our application to be 570 and the height to be 418. The height will fit fine in either Landscape or Portrait orientation, but the width will only fit in Landscape (without scrolling). For this reason, we will want our application to run in Landscape mode only.

To set the application to default to Landscape and not allow Portrait, we must make some changes to a file called *chapter10_bs_bingo-info.plist*, which is in the root folder (the parent of the www folder) for our project.

Open this file and you will see settings called "Supported interface orientations" and "Supported interface orientations (iPad)". You will want to be sure to have four entries in each that allow only the "Landscape (left home button)" value. See Figure 10-11 for an example.

 The iPad entries are only necessary if you are targeting that platform. There is a separate PhoneGap project created by the template for iPad-targeted projects.

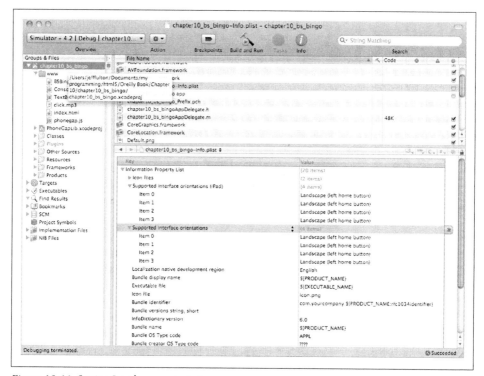

Figure 10-11. Setting Landscape orientation

Next, we will customize the banner and icon for our application.

Changing the Banner and Icon

We have the option of changing the startup banner and "desktop" icon for our application to customized graphics.

In the root folder of our project, we will customize two image files. *default.png* is the banner image that shows up when the application starts. *icon.png* is the "desktop" icon that remains on the iOS device just like any other installed application.

Our icon is a 57×75 image called *bingo_icon.png* (see Figure 10-12).

Figure 10-12. The BS Bingo icon.png customization

The startup banner is a 320×460 image, which we will name *startup.png*. It will look like Figure 10-13.

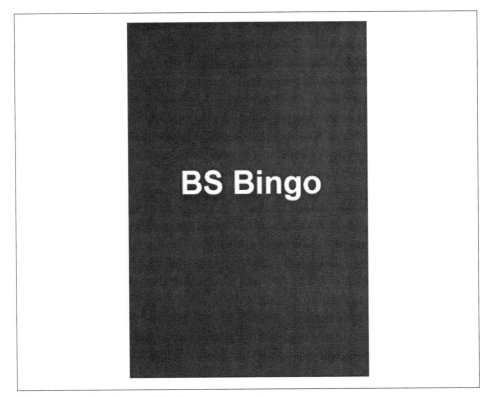

Figure 10-13. The BS Bingo default.png customization

Now we need to replace the existing *default.png* and *icon.png* files with these new images.

Once you change these files in the project, you should be able to explore the root project folder in Xcode and see the new images. Figure 10-14 illustrates the root folder for our project.

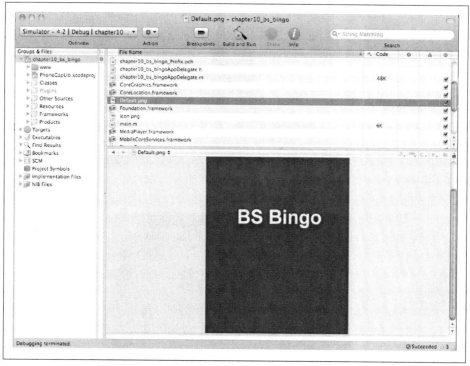

Figure 10-14. The BS Bingo root folder

Included in the source for this chapter is the full Xcode project with all of these changes ready to be made and compiled.

We are ready to test on the iPhone simulator. If you have any problems or questions up to this point, you can always examine the source files on this book's download site.

Testing on the Simulator

Our project is set to target the iPhone (not iPad). Before we test, we must make sure that we target that platform in the simulator. To do this, choose the iPhone simulator from the SDK drop-down menu at the top left of the Xcode screen, as shown in Figure 10-15.

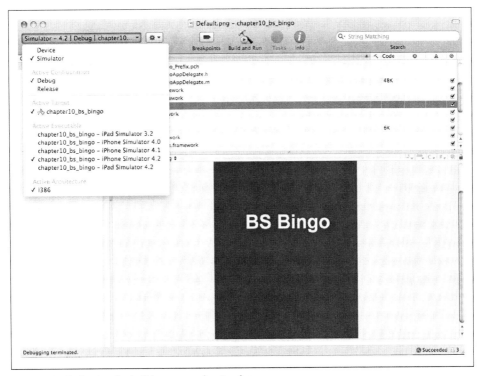

Figure 10-15. Setting the build target to the simulator

 The PhoneGap template has created a second project file, called *chapter10_bs_bingo-iPad.xcodeproj*, to target the iPad.

Once this is set, click on the "Build and Run" icon at the top center of this screen.

You should see the simulator fire up, show the custom banner image oriented to Landscape mode, and present the game, as shown in Figure 10-16.

If you click on the buttons, the simulator will even play the *click.mp3* file we included. When the iPhone "control button" is clicked (the big black circle on the left), the game will exit to the iOS "desktop." On the desktop, the custom *icon.png* will wait to be clicked once again, as shown in Figure 10-17.

Figure 10-16. BS Bingo running in the simulator

Figure 10-17. The BS Bingo iOS desktop icon

 You will notice that the iPhone simulator has made our plain icon look much better by adding a bevel and highlighting. There is no need for you to create anything other than a plain image, as the phone takes care of the rest.

Adding in an iPhone "Gesture"

The PhoneGap API allows us to add in control over various iOS features, such as vibrate, geolocation, and accelerometer. We will target one of these features by adding code that will wipe our board clean and create a fresh new game when the phone is shaken.

To do this, we will look for changes to the device's physical location in space (using JavaScript), and then simply call our existing chooseButtonsForCard() and drawScreen() functions to refresh the card.

First, we need to add a single line to the chooseButtonsForCard() function that will set all the buttons instances' press attributes to false:

```
function chooseButtonsForCard(){
    //copy jargon into temp array
    var tempArray = [];
    for (var arrayctr=0;arrayctr<standardJargonList.length;arrayctr++){
        tempArray.push(standardJargonList[arrayctr]);
    }

    for (var ctr1=0;ctr1<buttons.length;ctr1++){

        for (var ctr2=0; ctr2<buttons[ctr1].length;ctr2++){
            var randInt = Math.floor(Math.random()*tempArray.length)
            buttons[ctr1][ctr2].text = tempArray[randInt];
            buttons[ctr1][ctr2].press = false;
            tempArray.splice(randInt,1);
        }
    }

}
```

Next, we need to add a function that will listen for the iOS "shake" event, and then refresh the card.

Apple makes it pretty easy to test for changes in the x, y, and z coordinate spaces of an iOS device (and PhoneGap makes it even easier), but acting on this information is a little tricky and will require the use of an actual device for testing.

 At the time of this writing, a PhoneGap Adobe AIR iPhone simulator was available that goes beyond the limited shake gestures available in the SDK simulator. If you do not have a device to test with, we recommend trying this emulator. It can be found at *http://blogs.nitobi.com/yohei/2009/04/01/phonegap-air-simulator-in-development/*.

Adding the Gesture Functions to index.html

Inside the canvasApp() function, we will need to add a series of functions and a variable to use in testing the iPhone's accelerometer, which detects movement in our application.

Example 10-2 shows the code necessary to do this. Notice we are placing it under the current application start code (the new code is in bold).

Example 10-2. The gesture code added to BS Bingo

```
theCanvas.addEventListener("mousemove", onMouseMove, false);
theCanvas.addEventListener("click", onMouseClick, false);
initSounds();
initButtons();
initLists();
chooseButtonsForCard();
drawScreen();

var accelerationWatchId = null;

startAccelerationWatch();

function startAccelerationWatch() {

    // Update acceleration every 3 seconds
    var options = { frequency: 100 };

    accelerationWatchId = navigator.accelerometer.watchAcceleration
    (onSuccess, onError, options);
}

function stopAccelerationWatch() {
    if (accelerationWatchId) {
        navigator.accelerometer.clearWatch(accelerationWatchId);
        accelerationWatchIdD = null;
    }
}

function onSuccess(acceleration) {

    if (Math.abs(acceleration.x) > 2 || Math.abs(acceleration.y)>2
    || Math.abs(acceleration.z)>2) {
    alert('Acceleration X: ' + acceleration.x + '\n' +
        'Acceleration Y: ' + acceleration.y + '\n' +
        'Acceleration Z: ' + acceleration.z + '\n' +
        'Timestamp: '     + acceleration.timestamp + '\n');
        stopAccelerationWatch()
        chooseButtonsForCard();
        drawScreen();
        startAccelerationWatch();
    }

}

// onError: Failed to get the acceleration
//
function onError() {
    alert('onError!');
}
```

The new code begins with the `var accelerationWatchId = null;` variable setting. We have created a `startAccelerationWatch()` function, which will call the `onSuccess()` function every 100 milliseconds.

The `onSuccess()` function receives the "acceleration" values from the API, which consist of delta changes to the x, y, and z of the device. These values are set to 0,0,0 when the application begins.

On each 100-millisecond interval, these values are checked. If any is 2 units greater (in either the positive or negative direction) from the 0 beginning values, we fire off an `alert` and then call our functions to reset the card. First, we call the `stopAcceleration Watch()` function, which acts as a reset for the location of the device in physical space. Next, we call the `chooseButtonsForCard()` and `drawScreen()` functions. Finally, we set up the watch again with `startAccelerationWatch()`.

 For the most detailed and up-to-date information on integrating PhoneGap with iOS and other device features, visit the PhoneGap documentation website. Most of the information for this example is based off the explanation and examples found at *http://docs.phonegap.com/ phonegap_accelerometer_accelerometer.md.html*.

Testing on a Device

Before we can test the application on an actual device, we need to "provision" the device. To do this, we will need the device, a paid iOS developer account, and a development Mac computer all synced up into a single provisioning profile. This necessary process is not for the faint of heart.

Step 1: Launch the Provisioning Assistant

Begin by visiting the Developer Provisioning Assistant (*http://developer.apple.com/ iphone*) and logging in with your paid iOS developer ID. Once logged in, click on the link for the "iOS Provisioning Portal" (currently in the upper-right side menu). There should be a button called "Launch the Provisioning Assistant." Click on this button and follow all the on-screen instructions.

Step 2: Find the device's Unique ID

You will be asked to find the Unique ID of your physical device. This is found by plugging the device into your computer, and then looking up the ID in Xcode. In the Window→Organizer Information window, you will see a list of the attached devices. The ID will be a long alphanumeric string next to the word Identifier.

Step 3: Generate a Certificate Signing Request

When asked by the Provisioning Assistant, input this ID value. You will next be asked to "Generate a Certificate Signing Request", which involves the Apple Keychain. Follow all the on-screen dialogs carefully because this can be a confusing process. You will need to open the Keychain Access application in the Applications→Utilities folder on your machine, and then follow the on-screen instructions from the Provisioning Assistant.

Step 4: Locate saved Certificate Signing Request File

This will save a Certificate Signing Request File to your desktop. In the next step, the Provisioning Assistant will need to find this file, so it is important to remember where you save the request.

After you find the file, the assistant will ask you to name your profile. This will generate a file that you must download and install on your Mac.

Step 5: Drag provisioning file into Xcode Organizer window

With the location of the downloaded file handy, plug in your device (if it isn't already plugged in), and open up the Xcode Window→Organizer once again. Simply drag the .mobileProvision file into the Organizer window, and it will set up the profile in Xcode automatically.

Step 6: Set up certificates with the Keychain

Next, you will be asked to download and install development certificates that match this profile. Save the .cer file and double-click it to add it to the Keychain Access list.

You should now see both Public and Private keys paired together with your developer account name inside the Keychain Access provisioning list.

Success

Whew! That certainly was not simple, but the Provisioning Assistant is very easy to use as long as you follow each step carefully. We are now ready to test the application on a physical device.

Using Xcode to Target a Test Device

We will need to change the build profile to target the attached device rather than the simulator. To do this, we simply change the drop-down in the upper left from Simulator to Device, as shown in Figure 10-18.

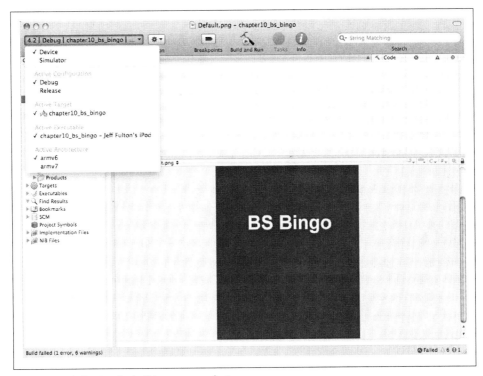

Figure 10-18. Setting the build target to a device

After all that, now it is time to click the "Build and Run" icon.

After a few seconds, the application will initialize and show up on the device like a normal iOS application.

When running the app on a device, you will be able to click the buttons, hear the sounds, and see the buttons change color. When you want to reset the card, give the device a good shake to see the alert box with the current location offsets for the accelerometer. Click the OK button, and the card will reset.

Beyond the Canvas

A nice set of tools and frameworks are available (with more emerging every day) that can help transform the look and feel of HTML or an HTML5 application (not necessarily just on Canvas) into an iPhone-like application. These can be used in conjunction with a canvas app to provide a seamless iPhone look and feel for the user.

If you would like to explore mobile functionality further, we recommend the following technologies, which can be combined with PhoneGap to create very powerful mobile applications:

jQTouch

jQTouch (*http://www.jqtouch.com/*) is a framework that makes use of jQuery to target mobile-device-specific features across platforms that use WebKit (iOS, Palm, Nexus, etc.).

jQuery Mobile Framework

The jQuery Mobile Framework (*http://jquerymobile.com/*) is another jQuery-based mobile framework for building cross-platform applications. It can be used to create a unified user interface across mobile platforms.

What's Next

As you can see, HTML5 Canvas is a powerful and easy way to target native apps across a variety of mobile devices. In this chapter, we built a small game to run in the Safari browser, and then installed PhoneGap and modified the application to run on the iPhone simulator using an Xcode project template. Once the simulation was successful, we added in a device-specific accelerometer feature, and then provisioned a physical device for testing. Finally, we were able to see our completed application running on an actual iOS device.

In Chapter 11, we will look at applying multiplayer capabilities to a canvas application using ElectroServer, and we'll even take a small tour of 3D in Canvas.

Further Explorations

There are many emerging technologies and frameworks that can help take HTML5 Canvas into rarely explored areas. In this chapter, we will cover a couple of those areas: using Canvas for 3D with WebGL, and using Canvas for multiplayer applications. Both of these areas are still experimental, requiring you to either download beta/developer versions of browsers, or launch browsers using command-line switches so you can turn various technologies off and on.

This chapter is structured a bit differently. The discussions are focused on giving you some tools and information about these new and emerging areas for Canvas. While we will offer code, examples, and some explanation, it's geared more toward getting you started on the path to learning than on teaching you how every detail works. We have structured these two topics in this way for one very simple reason: *they are incomplete*. With APIs, libraries, locations, browsers, names, etc., all subject to change, we are not comfortable presenting these topics as finished and ready to go. You need to approach this chapter knowing that things are bound to go wrong or change frequently.

Having said that, even though these topics are experimental, that does not mean you cannot use them right now, nor does it mean they are not useful or capable of doing very cool things. You just need to be aware of the pitfalls before treading forward.

3D with WebGL

The 2D capabilities of HTML5 Canvas are impressive, but what about 3D? There is no "production" 3D context available in the standard version of any web browser at this time. However, the best support for a 3D context will probably come in the form of WebGL.

What Is WebGL?

WebGL is a JavaScript API that gives programmers access to the 3D hardware on the user's machine. Currently, it is only supported by the debug/development versions of Opera, Firefox, and Chrome. The API is managed by Kronos, the same organization that manages OpenGL. In fact, much of WebGL is similar to programming in OpenGL. This is both good and bad. It's good because it's a standard programming interface that is recognizable to many developers, but bad because it is not as easy to learn as the 2D Canvas context.

How Do I Test WebGL?

First, you need to find a web browser that supports WebGL. When trying to run a WebGL application, a browser that does not support WebGL might give a message like the one shown in Figure 11-1.

Figure 11-1. Trying to run WebGL in a standard web browser

 Chromium, the open source version of Chrome, will display WebGL. You can download the latest development build of Chromium from *http://build.chromium.org/f/chromium/continuous/*.

Once you have a browser that can display WebGL, you need to write the code to make it happen. You start that process by accessing the WebGL context instead of the Canvas 2d context. So, instead of this code, which we have used throughout this book:

```
context = theCanvas.getContext("2d");
```

We reference the `experimental-webgl` context, like this:

```
gl = theCanvas.getContext("experimental-webgl");
```

How Do I Learn More About WebGL?

The best place to learn about WebGL is at *http://learningwebgl.com/*. This site has an FAQ, a blog, and some helpful low-level lessons on how to create apps using WebGL. You can also find a ton of great content about WebGL at *http://developer.mozilla.org*.

One warning, though: programming WebGL is not for the uninitiated. Although WebGL is based on OpenGL, it is still a very low-level API, meaning you will need to create everything by hand. At the end of this section, we will guide you toward some higher-level libraries that should make this process a bit easier.

What Does a WebGL Application Look Like?

Now we are going to show you a WebGL application demo that rotates a 3D cube on Canvas (see Figure 11-2). Since we are not experts in 3D graphics, we will forgo our practice of describing every line of code in the example; instead, we will highlight interesting sections of code to help you understand what is happening.

This demo is based on Lesson 4 from Giles Thomas's Learning WebGL website (*http://learningwebgl.com/blog/?p=370*). While this is only one short demo, it should give you a very good idea of how to structure and build code for a WebGL application.

 Much of this code has been adapted from the work of Giles Thomas with his expressed, written permission.

JavaScript libraries

First, we add some JavaScript libraries. Modernizr 1.6 includes a test for WebGL support in a web browser. This version was freshly released, but it could be updated with new features at any time (in fact, at the time of this writing, this had been updated to version 1.7). It is necessary to make sure you have the most recent versions of your libraries:

```
<script src="modernizr-1.6.min.js"></script>
```

We now need to include some JavaScript libraries to assist with our application. *sylvester.js* and *glUtils.as* are two libraries that you will find included for most apps that use WebGL. *sylvester.js* (*http://sylvester.jcoglan.com/*) is a library that helps when performing vector and matrix math calculations in JavaScript. *glUtils.as* is an extension for *sylvester.js*, specifically for helping with math related to WebGL:

```
<script type="text/javascript" src="sylvester.js"></script>
<script type="text/javascript" src="glUtils.js"></script>
```

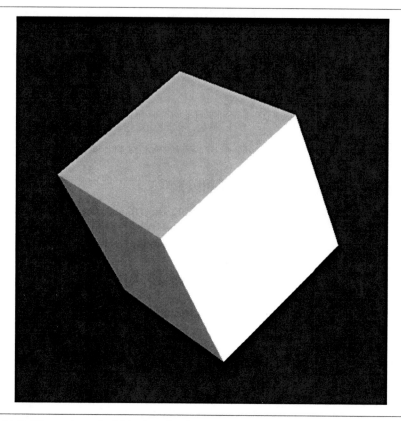

Figure 11-2. 3D rotating cube (CH11EX1.html)

Shaders

Shaders are pieces of code that run directly on a graphics card. They describe how a *scene*—how you refer to a 3D canvas when working with WebGL—should be rendered. Many of these little programs perform mathematical transformations that would otherwise run very slowly in JavaScript. In fact, we are pointing these out because they are *not* JavaScript; they are written in a way that WebGL can understand. These sections of code will be read in like text files and passed to the graphics hardware. Full discussions of topics like shaders are far out of scope for this little section of the book, but we will tell you a bit about each one of them to help set the tone for what comes next.

The first shader below is a *fragment shader*, which tells the graphics card that we will be using floating-point numbers and blended colors. The second shader is the *vertex shader*. It works with the vertices (defined points in 3D space used to create 3D objects) and will be used for every vertex we draw onto the Canvas 3D context:

```
<script id="shader-fs" type="x-shader/x-fragment">
  #ifdef GL_ES
  precision highp float;
  #endif

  varying vec4 vColor;

  void main(void) {
    gl_FragColor = vColor;
  }
</script>

<script id="shader-vs" type="x-shader/x-vertex">
  attribute vec3 aVertexPosition;
  attribute vec4 aVertexColor;

  uniform mat4 uMVMatrix;
  uniform mat4 uPMatrix;

  varying vec4 vColor;

  void main(void) {
    gl_Position = uPMatrix * uMVMatrix * vec4(aVertexPosition, 1.0);
    vColor = aVertexColor;
  }
</script>
```

Testing for WebGL support with Modernizr

The structure of the code in this example is much like the other applications we have
written in this book. However, it has been modified to work with the specific needs of
the 3D context. In the canvasApp() function, we need to test to see whether the browser
has WebGL support. This is easily accomplished by using the Modernizr.webgl static
constant in Modernizr 1.6:

```
if ( !webglSupport()) {
    alert("Unable to initialize WebGL");
    return;
}
function webglSupport() {
    return Modernizr.webgl;
}
```

Initialization in canvasApp()

In canvasApp() we still get a context, but this time it is the experimental-webgl context.
Also, just like in our other apps, we still call drawScreen() on an interval to render the
canvas:

```
var theCanvas = document.getElementById("canvasOne");
webGLContext = theCanvas.getContext("experimental-webgl");

setInterval(drawScreen, 33);
```

However, there is additional code in `canvasApp()` required to set up the application to rotate the cube. A couple of the most important initialization steps are the calls to `initShaders()` and `initBuffers()`:

```
initShaders();
initBuffers();
```

The `initShaders()` function itself calls a function named `getShader()` to load in the text of the `shader` programs we have already defined. You can see the code for these functions in the code listing a bit later in Example 11-1.

 You can learn about the shaders used in this program in "Lesson 2—Adding colour" on the LearningWebGL website: *http://learningwebgl.com/blog/?p=134.*

Once we have loaded the `shader` programs, we need to create the buffers. *Buffers* refer to space in the video card's memory that we set aside to hold the geometry describing our 3D objects. In our case, we need to create buffers to describe the cube we will rotate on the canvas. We do this in `initBuffers()`.

The `initBuffers()` function contains a lot of code, but we'll discuss only a couple very interesting sections. The first is the Vertex Position buffer, which describes the vertices that make up the sides of the cube:

```
webGLContext.bindBuffer(webGLContext.ARRAY_BUFFER, cubeVertexPositionBuffer);
        vertices = [
        // Front face
        -1.0, -1.0,  1.0,
         1.0, -1.0,  1.0,
         1.0,  1.0,  1.0,
        -1.0,  1.0,  1.0,

        // Back face
        -1.0, -1.0, -1.0,
        -1.0,  1.0, -1.0,
         1.0,  1.0, -1.0,
         1.0, -1.0, -1.0,

        // Top face
        -1.0,  1.0, -1.0,
        -1.0,  1.0,  1.0,
         1.0,  1.0,  1.0,
         1.0,  1.0, -1.0,

        // Bottom face
        -1.0, -1.0, -1.0,
         1.0, -1.0, -1.0,
         1.0, -1.0,  1.0,
        -1.0, -1.0,  1.0,
```

```
        // Right face
         1.0, -1.0, -1.0,
         1.0,  1.0, -1.0,
         1.0,  1.0,  1.0,
         1.0, -1.0,  1.0,

        // Left face
        -1.0, -1.0, -1.0,
        -1.0, -1.0,  1.0,
        -1.0,  1.0,  1.0,
        -1.0,  1.0, -1.0,
      ];
```

The Vertex Color buffer holds information about the color that will appear on each side of the cube. These values are set as percentages of RBGA values (red, green, blue, alpha):

```
webGLContext.bindBuffer(webGLContext.ARRAY_BUFFER, cubeVertexColorBuffer);
      var colors = [
        [1.0, 1.0, 1.0, 1.0],    // Front face
        [0.9, 0.0, 0.0, 1.0],    // Back face
        [0.6, 0.6, 0.6, 1.0],    // Top face
        [0.6, 0.0, 0.0, 1.0],    // Bottom face
        [0.3 ,0.0, 0.0, 1.0],    // Right face
        [0.3, 0.3, 0.3, 1.0],    // Left face
      ];
```

The Vertex Index buffer is kind of like a map that builds the object (our cube) based on the colors specified in Vertex Color (the order of these elements) and the vertices specified in the Vertex Position buffer. Each of these sets of three values represents a triangle that will be drawn onto the 3D context:

```
webGLContext.bindBuffer(webGLContext.ELEMENT_ARRAY_BUFFER, cubeVertexIndexBuffer);
      var cubeVertexIndices = [
        0, 1, 2,     0, 2, 3,    // Front face
        4, 5, 6,     4, 6, 7,    // Back face
        8, 9, 10,    8, 10, 11,  // Top face
        12, 13, 14,  12, 14, 15, // Bottom face
        16, 17, 18,  16, 18, 19, // Right face
        20, 21, 22,  20, 22, 23  // Left face
      ]
```

Again, there is more code in initBuffers() than we described here, but start with these three sections when you want to play with the code and make your own objects.

Animating the cube

Now that you know a bit about creating an object in WebGL, let's learn about animating the cube on the canvas. Similar to what we did in the 2D context, we use the drawScreen() function to position, draw, and animate objects in the 3D context. The first thing we do here is set up the viewport, which defines the canvas' view of the 3D scene. Next, we clear the canvas and then set up the perspective. The perspective has four parameters:

Field of view

The angle at which we will view the 3D scene (25 degrees).

Width-to-height ratio

The radio of width to height of the current size of the canvas (500×500).

Minimum units

The smallest unit size away from our viewport we want to display (0.1).

Maximum units

The furthest unit size away from our viewport that we want to see (100.0).

```
function drawScreen() {

    webGLContext.viewport(0, 0, webGLContext.viewportWidth,
        webGLContext.viewportHeight);
    webGLContext.clear(webGLContext.COLOR_BUFFER_BIT |
        webGLContext.DEPTH_BUFFER_BIT);

    perspective(25, (webGLContext.viewportWidth / webGLContext.viewportHeight),
        0.1, 100.0);
```

Next, we move to the center of the 3D scene, calling `loadIdentity()` so we can start drawing. We then call `mvTranslate()`, passing the locations on the x, y, and z axes to draw the cube. To rotate the cube, we call a function named `mvPushMatrix()`, and later `mvPopMatrix()`, which is similar to how we called `context.save()` and `context.restore()` when rotating objects on the 2D canvas. The call to `mvRotate()` then makes the cube rotate from the center, tilted up and to the right:

```
loadIdentity();

mvTranslate([0, 0.0, -10.0])

mvPushMatrix();
mvRotate(rotateCube, [0, .5, .5]);
```

Next, we draw the cube by binding the buffers that hold the vertices and color information that we set up earlier for the cube's sides. We then draw each side, made up of two triangles each:

```
webGLContext.bindBuffer(webGLContext.ARRAY_BUFFER, cubeVertexPositionBuffer);
webGLContext.vertexAttribPointer(shaderProgram.vertexPositionAttribute,
    cubeVertexPositionBuffer.itemSize, webGLContext.FLOAT, false, 0, 0);

webGLContext.bindBuffer(webGLContext.ARRAY_BUFFER, cubeVertexColorBuffer);
webGLContext.vertexAttribPointer(shaderProgram.vertexColorAttribute,
    cubeVertexColorBuffer.itemSize, webGLContext.FLOAT, false, 0, 0);

webGLContext.bindBuffer(webGLContext.ELEMENT_ARRAY_BUFFER, cubeVertexIndexBuffer);
setMatrixUniforms();
```

```
webGLContext.drawElements(webGLContext.TRIANGLES, cubeVertexIndexBuffer.numItems,
    webGLContext.UNSIGNED_SHORT, 0);

mvPopMatrix();
```

Finally, we increase the `rotateCube` variable so that the next time `drawScreen()` is called, the cube will be updated with a new angle. The code below adds 2 degrees to the rotation angle each time `drawScreen()` is called:

```
rotateCube += 2;

}
```

Full Code Listing

Example 11-1 gives the full code listing for *CH11EX1.html*. Notice that many of the code styles and constructs we have used over the past 10 chapters are still in place in this application. Besides the obvious inclusion of code related directly to WebGL, this application operates essentially the same way as the other apps we discussed in this book.

Example 11-1. WebGL test

```
<!doctype html>
<html lang="en">
<head>
<meta charset="UTF-8">
<title>CH11EX1: WebGL Test </title>
<script src="modernizr-1.6.min.js"></script>
<script type="text/javascript" src="sylvester.js"></script>
<script type="text/javascript" src="glUtils.js"></script>

<script id="shader-fs" type="x-shader/x-fragment">
    #ifdef GL_ES
    precision highp float;
    #endif

    varying vec4 vColor;

    void main(void) {
      gl_FragColor = vColor;
    }
</script>

<script id="shader-vs" type="x-shader/x-vertex">
    attribute vec3 aVertexPosition;
    attribute vec4 aVertexColor;

    uniform mat4 uMVMatrix;
    uniform mat4 uPMatrix;

    varying vec4 vColor;
```

```
    void main(void) {
      gl_Position = uPMatrix * uMVMatrix * vec4(aVertexPosition, 1.0);
      vColor = aVertexColor;
    }
</script>

<script type="text/javascript">
window.addEventListener("load", eventWindowLoaded, false);

function eventWindowLoaded () {
   canvasApp();
}

function canvasSupport () {
   return Modernizr.canvas;
}

function webglSupport() {
   return Modernizr.webgl;
}
function canvasApp () {

function drawScreen() {

    webGLContext.viewport(0, 0, webGLContext.viewportWidth,
        webGLContext.viewportHeight);
    webGLContext.clear(webGLContext.COLOR_BUFFER_BIT | webGLContext.DEPTH_BUFFER_BIT);

    perspective(25, (webGLContext.viewportWidth / webGLContext.viewportHeight),
        0.1, 100.0);
    loadIdentity();

    mvTranslate([0, 0.0, -10.0])

    mvPushMatrix();
    mvRotate(rotateCube, [0, .5, .5]);

    webGLContext.bindBuffer(webGLContext.ARRAY_BUFFER, cubeVertexPositionBuffer);
    webGLContext.vertexAttribPointer(shaderProgram.vertexPositionAttribute,
        cubeVertexPositionBuffer.itemSize, webGLContext.FLOAT, false, 0, 0);

    webGLContext.bindBuffer(webGLContext.ARRAY_BUFFER, cubeVertexColorBuffer);
    webGLContext.vertexAttribPointer(shaderProgram.vertexColorAttribute,
        cubeVertexColorBuffer.itemSize, webGLContext.FLOAT, false, 0, 0);

    webGLContext.bindBuffer(webGLContext.ELEMENT_ARRAY_BUFFER, cubeVertexIndexBuffer);
    setMatrixUniforms();
    webGLContext.drawElements(webGLContext.TRIANGLES, cubeVertexIndexBuffer.numItems,
        webGLContext.UNSIGNED_SHORT, 0);

    mvPopMatrix();
    rotateCube += 2;

    }
```

```
    if (!canvasSupport() ) {
        alert("Unable to initialize Canvas");
        return;
    }

    if ( !webglSupport()) {
        alert("Unable to initialize WebGL");
        return;
    }

    var webGLContext;
    var rotateCube = 0;

    var theCanvas = document.getElementById("canvasOne");
    webGLContext =theCanvas.getContext("experimental-webgl");
    webGLContext.viewportWidth =theCanvas.width;
    webGLContext.viewportHeight = theCanvas.height;

    initShaders()
    initBuffers();

    webGLContext.clearColor(0.0, 0.0, 0.0, 1.0);
    webGLContext.clearDepth(1.0);
    webGLContext.enable(webGLContext.DEPTH_TEST);
    webGLContext.depthFunc(webGLContext.LEQUAL);

    setInterval(drawScreen, 33);

function getShader(webglcontext, id) {
    var shaderScript = document.getElementById(id);
    if (!shaderScript) {
      return null;
    }

    var str = "";
    var scriptChild = shaderScript.firstChild;
    while (scriptChild) {
      if (scriptChild.nodeType == 3) {
       str += scriptChild.textContent;
      }
      scriptChild = scriptChild.nextSibling;
    }

    var shader;
    if (shaderScript.type == "x-shader/x-fragment") {
      shader = webGLContext.createShader(webGLContext.FRAGMENT_SHADER);
    } else if (shaderScript.type == "x-shader/x-vertex") {
      shader = webGLContext.createShader(webGLContext.VERTEX_SHADER);
    } else {
      return null;
    }

    webGLContext.shaderSource(shader, str);
    webGLContext.compileShader(shader);
```

```
    if (!webGLContext.getShaderParameter(shader, webGLContext.COMPILE_STATUS)) {
      alert(webGLContext.getShaderInfoLog(shader));
      return null;
    }

    return shader;
  }

  var shaderProgram;
function initShaders() {
    var fragmentShader = getShader(webGLContext, "shader-fs");
    var vertexShader = getShader(webGLContext, "shader-vs");

    shaderProgram = webGLContext.createProgram();
    webGLContext.attachShader(shaderProgram, vertexShader);
    webGLContext.attachShader(shaderProgram, fragmentShader);
    webGLContext.linkProgram(shaderProgram);

    if (!webGLContext.getProgramParameter(shaderProgram, webGLContext.LINK_STATUS)) {
      alert("Could not initialize shaders");
    }

    webGLContext.useProgram(shaderProgram);

    shaderProgram.vertexPositionAttribute = webGLContext.getAttribLocation
        (shaderProgram, "aVertexPosition");
    webGLContext.enableVertexAttribArray(shaderProgram.vertexPositionAttribute);

    shaderProgram.vertexColorAttribute = webGLContext.getAttribLocation
        (shaderProgram, "aVertexColor");
    webGLContext.enableVertexAttribArray(shaderProgram.vertexColorAttribute);

    shaderProgram.pMatrixUniform = webGLContext.getUniformLocation
        (shaderProgram, "uPMatrix");
    shaderProgram.mvMatrixUniform = webGLContext.getUniformLocation
        (shaderProgram, "uMVMatrix");
  }

  var mvMatrix;
  var mvMatrixStack = [];

function mvPushMatrix(matrix) {
    if (matrix) {
      mvMatrixStack.push(matrix.dup());
      mvMatrix = matrix.dup();
    } else {
      mvMatrixStack.push(mvMatrix.dup());
    }
  }

function mvPopMatrix() {
    if (mvMatrixStack.length == 0) {
      throw "Invalid popMatrix!";
    }
```

```
    mvMatrix = mvMatrixStack.pop();
    return mvMatrix;
  }

function loadIdentity() {
    mvMatrix = Matrix.I(4);
  }

function multMatrix(matrix) {
    mvMatrix = mvMatrix.x(matrix);
  }

function mvTranslate(vector) {
    var matrix = Matrix.Translation($V([vector[0], vector[1], vector[2]])).ensure4x4();
    multMatrix(matrix);
  }

function mvRotate(angle, vector) {
    var radians = angle * Math.PI / 180.0;
    var matrix = Matrix.Rotation(radians, $V([vector[0],
        vector[1], vector[2]])).ensure4x4();
    multMatrix(matrix);
  }

  var pMatrix;
  function perspective(fovy, aspect, znear, zfar) {
    pMatrix = makePerspective(fovy, aspect, znear, zfar);
  }

function setMatrixUniforms() {
    webGLContext.uniformMatrix4fv(shaderProgram.pMatrixUniform, false,
        new Float32Array(pMatrix.flatten()));
    webGLContext.uniformMatrix4fv(shaderProgram.mvMatrixUniform, false,
        new Float32Array(mvMatrix.flatten()));
  }

  var cubeVertexPositionBuffer;
  var cubeVertexColorBuffer;
  var cubeVertexIndexBuffer;
function initBuffers() {

    cubeVertexPositionBuffer = webGLContext.createBuffer();
    webGLContext.bindBuffer(webGLContext.ARRAY_BUFFER, cubeVertexPositionBuffer);
    vertices = [
      // Front face
      -1.0, -1.0,  1.0,
       1.0, -1.0,  1.0,
       1.0,  1.0,  1.0,
      -1.0,  1.0,  1.0,

      // Back face
      -1.0, -1.0, -1.0,
      -1.0,  1.0, -1.0,
       1.0,  1.0, -1.0,
```

```
    1.0, -1.0, -1.0,

  // Top face
  -1.0,  1.0, -1.0,
  -1.0,  1.0,  1.0,
   1.0,  1.0,  1.0,
   1.0,  1.0, -1.0,

  // Bottom face
  -1.0, -1.0, -1.0,
   1.0, -1.0, -1.0,
   1.0, -1.0,  1.0,
  -1.0, -1.0,  1.0,

  // Right face
   1.0, -1.0, -1.0,
   1.0,  1.0, -1.0,
   1.0,  1.0,  1.0,
   1.0, -1.0,  1.0,

  // Left face
  -1.0, -1.0, -1.0,
  -1.0, -1.0,  1.0,
  -1.0,  1.0,  1.0,
  -1.0,  1.0, -1.0,
];
webGLContext.bufferData(webGLContext.ARRAY_BUFFER, new Float32Array(vertices),
    webGLContext.STATIC_DRAW);
cubeVertexPositionBuffer.itemSize = 3;
cubeVertexPositionBuffer.numItems = 24;

cubeVertexColorBuffer = webGLContext.createBuffer();
webGLContext.bindBuffer(webGLContext.ARRAY_BUFFER, cubeVertexColorBuffer);
var colors = [
  [1.0, 1.0, 1.0, 1.0],    // Front face
  [0.9, 0.0, 0.0, 1.0],    // Back face
  [0.6, 0.6, 0.6, 1.0],    // Top face
  [0.6, 0.0, 0.0, 1.0],    // Bottom face
  [0.3 ,0.0, 0.0, 1.0],    // Right face
  [0.3, 0.3, 0.3, 1.0],    // Left face
];

var unpackedColors = []
for (var i in colors) {
  var color = colors[i];
  for (var j=0; j < 4; j++) {
   unpackedColors = unpackedColors.concat(color);
  }
}
webGLContext.bufferData(webGLContext.ARRAY_BUFFER, new Float32Array(unpackedColors),
    webGLContext.STATIC_DRAW);
cubeVertexColorBuffer.itemSize = 4;
cubeVertexColorBuffer.numItems = 24;

cubeVertexIndexBuffer = webGLContext.createBuffer();
```

```
webGLContext.bindBuffer(webGLContext.ELEMENT_ARRAY_BUFFER, cubeVertexIndexBuffer);
var cubeVertexIndices = [
  0, 1, 2,      0, 2, 3,     // Front face
  4, 5, 6,      4, 6, 7,     // Back face
  8, 9, 10,     8, 10, 11,   // Top face
  12, 13, 14,   12, 14, 15,  // Bottom face
  16, 17, 18,   16, 18, 19,  // Right face
  20, 21, 22,   20, 22, 23   // Left face
]
webGLContext.bufferData(webGLContext.ELEMENT_ARRAY_BUFFER,
    new Uint16Array(cubeVertexIndices), webGLContext.STATIC_DRAW);
cubeVertexIndexBuffer.itemSize = 1;
cubeVertexIndexBuffer.numItems = 36;

  }

}

</script>
</head>
<body>
<div style="position: absolute; top: 50px; left: 50px;">
<canvas id="canvasOne" width="500" height="500">
 Your browser does not support HTML5 Canvas or WebGLContext.
</canvas>
</div>
</body>
</html>
```

Further Explorations with WebGL

Obviously, we cannot teach you all about WebGL in this chapter. We opted to include this demo and short discussion to introduce you to WebGL and show you what it looks like. In reality, a full discussion of WebGL, even the basic concepts, could take up an entire volume.

If you are interested in WebGL, we strongly recommend you consult *http://learning webgl.com* for more examples and the latest information about this exciting yet still experimental context for HTML5 Canvas.

WebGL JavaScript Libraries

At the start of this section, we promised to show you some libraries that can be used with WebGL to make it easier to develop applications. Here are some of the more interesting libraries and projects.

Google O3D

Google's O3D library (*http://code.google.com/p/o3d/*) was once a browser plug-in but has now been released as a standalone JavaScript library for WebGL. The examples of using O3D with JavaScript—including a fairly spectacular 3D pool game—are very impressive. O3D allows you to load COLLADA 3D models created with Google SketchUp (as well as other 3D packages).

The required code looks about as complex as straight WebGL code, so while this is very powerful, you might want to look at some of the other libraries here first if you are just starting out.

GLGE

"WebGL for the lazy" is the tagline for this JavaScript library (*http://www.glge.org/*). The author of the library, Paul Brunt, says this about GLGE:

> The aim of GLGE is to mask the involved nature of WebGL from the web developer, who can then spend his/her time creating richer content for the Web.

This is a high-level API that is still in development. Just like O3D, it has the ability to load COLLADA models. Applications written with GLGE are created with a combination of XML and JavaScript. It looks very promising.

C3DL

The tagline for C3DL (*http://www.c3dl.org/*) is "WebGL made easy!" C3DL, or "Canvas 3D JS Library," is similar to GLGE, but it seems to have a head start thanks to a larger API and more support. This library also appears to be slanted toward games, as a real-time strategy (RTS) and an arcade game are featured as its more prominent demos. The library supports COLLADA models, and the code also appears very straightforward to implement.

SpiderGL

"3D Graphics for Next-Generation WWW" is how SpiderGL (*http://spidergl.org/*) bills itself to the world. This library appears to be very similar to GLGE and C3DL, except that the demos focus more on lighting, color, and textures than on games and applications. It also supports COLLADA models.

SceneJS

SceneJS (*http://scenejs.org/*) is geared toward rendering 3D scenes built as COLLADA JSON models in WebGL. You can also define and manipulate 3D scenes. Loading and rendering the models is a straightforward process, and the results are quite impressive.

CopperLicht

This commercial library (*http://www.ambiera.com/copperlicht/*) advertises itself as the "fast WebGL JavaScript 3D Engine." All the demos are game-oriented, and the library supports many commercial 3D formats. It has both collision detection and physics built in. The demos are fast and are fun to play. This library appears to be centered around loading and using external 3D assets, so if that is what you are looking for, this might be your best choice.

Multiplayer Applications with ElectroServer 5

The extended HTML5 specification includes an API for what is known as *WebSockets*. Socket communications allow a client application to remain constantly connected to a server-aide application. This type of communication can be especially useful for chat, multiplayer games, e-learning applications, and multiuser whiteboards, as well as many others. At this point, WebSockets is just a promise with very little support beyond test and development builds of web browsers. In fact, security concerns have halted some implementations and slowed others. However, this does not mean you cannot make use of socket-server applications with HTML5 Canvas.

Because Flash has built-in support for communication via sockets, its applications have had the ability to open socket communications with server-side applications for many years. HTML, on the other hand, has never had the ability to reliably communicate to a socket server without performing some sleight of hand, usually involving constant polling by the web browser for new information from the web server.

ElectroServer from Electrotank was one of the first reliable socket-server applications built to communicate with Flash clients. Over the past couple years, ElectroServer has been updated with APIs for iOS, C#, C++, and now JavaScript. This first iteration of the ElectroServer JavaScript API does not use WebSockets, but instead implements JavaScript polling. However, with the availability of ElectroServer's simplified JavaScript API, you can still start to write multiplayer applications using HTML5 Canvas.

 While this portion of the chapter is specific to ElectroServer, many of the multiplayer/multiuser concepts are applicable to other technologies as well.

Installing ElectroServer

To get started with multiplayer development using HTML5 Canvas and the Electro-Server socket server, you first need to download the free, 25-user version of the software from Electrotank. You can download the appropriate version for your operating system (Windows, Mac, Linux) at *http://www.electrotank.com/resources/downloads.html*.

 There are some installation prerequisites, such as having Java version 1.6. For detailed installation instructions for every OS, visit *http://www .electrotank.com/docs/es5/manual/index.html?operating_system.htm*.

The install package includes the server software, client APIs, documentation, and sample applications. Once you have installed the server software, you should have a folder named something like "Electroserver_5_x_" on your computer. We used Mac OS X for this test, so this folder was created inside the Mac Applications folder. On Windows, it will be created in the location you specify upon installation.

Starting the server

Once you have the files installed, you need to start the ElectroServer socket server by finding the installation directory and executing the file *Start_ElectroServer_5_0_1*. (Note: the three numbers at the end of this file will change as the version is upgraded, but the concept will remain the same.)

When ElectroServer starts, you should see a screen similar to Figure 11-3.

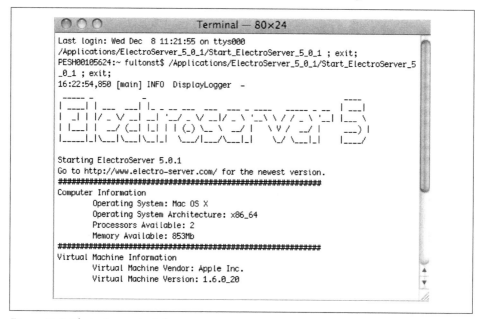

Figure 11-3. ElectroServer started

The server will run on your local machine for testing purposes. However, for any real-world application, you will need to install a production version of the software on a web server.

The ElectroServer admin tool

Because ElectroServer is a socket server, it listens on a specified port for communication from the JavaScript client using one of the supported protocols. ElectroServer supports multiple protocols, but we need to make sure we are using the *BinaryHTTP* protocol for the JavaScript API. The default port for BinaryHTTP in ElectroServer is 8989.

When the ElectroServer JavaScript API is updated to support Web-Sockets, the port and protocol will likely be different.

There is a nifty admin tool for ElectroServer that allows you to view and modify all the supported protocols and ports, as well as many other cool features of the socket server. In the */admin* directory of the install folder, you should find both an installer for an Adobe AIR admin tool (named something like *es5-airadmin-5.0.0.air*), and a */webadmin* directory with an HTML file named *webadmin.html*. Either one will work for this exercise.

In order for the admin console to display properly, the server needs to be started.

When you launch the admin tool, you will be asked to supply a username and password. The default is `administrator` and `password`, unless you changed them upon installation.

Once you log in, click the Server Management button on the top menu, and then the Gateways option from the side menu. You should see a screen that looks similar to Figure 11-4.

This screen shows you the port settings for each protocol that ElectroServer supports. For the JavaScript API, we are most interested in the BinaryHTTP setting, which you can see is set to port 8989.

The JavaScript API

Besides starting ElectroServer, you will also need the JavaScript API so you can begin building Canvas apps that connect to the server. You should be able to find the Java-Script API in the */apis/client/javascript* directory of the folder in which you installed ElectroServer (this name might change in the final version). The API should be named *ElectroServer-5-Client-JavaScript.js*.

The Basic Architecture of a Socket-Server Application

Now that you have ElectroServer ready to go, and you have the JavaScript API, it is time to learn a bit about how socket-server-based multiplayer/multiuser applications are designed. Using a socket server means you are creating an application that relies on a client for input from a user, as well as relying on a server to distribute that input to other users who are connected to the first user.

A good example of this is a chat application. Most chat applications require a user to enter a *room* (a logical space in which people are "chatting," i.e., exchanging messages),

Figure 11-4. ElectroServer ports and protocols

where that user can see the messages of other people in the same virtual space. In that room, the client is "connected" to those other users. However, it is usually not a direct connection (e.g., peer-to-peer), but instead a connection through a port to a socket server.

The socket server acts as the traffic cop for the chat messages. It listens on a port (in our case, 8989) for messages coming in from the clients. Those messages need to be formatted in a way that the server can understand so it can process them. The JavaScript API we will use performs this formatting for our client applications.

When the socket server receives a message from the client, it routes the various text messages sent by each client back out to the other clients in the room. However, it can also do much more by using server-side processing, such as hold the list of current messages, so people entering the room while the chat is ongoing can see what has been said previously, scan chat messages for swear words, award points to users for their input, or anything else you can dream up.

When the server finally processes the message and sends it back, the client then processes that message. In the case of the chat, that processing usually involves displaying the message on the canvas.

The Basic Architecture of an ElectroServer Application

ElectroServer acts very much like the socket-server application we described in the previous section. It listens on specified ports for different protocols; when messages arrive, they are routed back to the connected clients.

However, ElectroServer has some specific features that we should discuss. Some of these exist on other socket-server platforms, while some don't. However, much of this discussion will still be applicable to other socket servers once they make JavaScript APIs available.

Client

The client for an ElectroServer application is a program written in one of the API-supported language platforms, including Flash ActionScript 2, Flash ActionScript 3, Java, Objective-C, C#/.NET, and now JavaScript. The client is the application, which the user will manipulate to send messages through the API to ElectroServer. This is usually a game, a chat room, a virtual world, or some other kind of multiuser social or communication application.

All the communication with ElectroServer is *event*-based. The client application uses the JavaScript API to send events, and the client defines event handlers that listen for messages from ElectroServer. All of these messages and events are communicated through the API, which in turn is communicating through port 8989 using the BinaryHTTP protocol (at least for our examples).

Zones, rooms, and games

When a user first connects to ElectroServer, she needs to join or create a *zone*, which is simply a collection of rooms. If the user tries to create a zone that already exists, she will be added to that zone without creating a new one.

After entering a zone, the user needs to join a room in that zone. If a user attempts to create a new room that already exists, she will be added to that room instead.

 Beyond zones and rooms, ElectroServer also offers a GameManager API that allows you to further segment users into specific instances of a game that is being played. We do not get this granular for the examples in this chapter.

Extensions

Extensions are server-side code modules that can process data sent by clients before that data is sent back to other clients. Extensions can also process and create their own events. For many games, the extension contains much of the game logic, relying on the clients for displaying and gathering user input.

At the very minimum, an extension contains what is known as a *plug-in*. A plug-in is a code module written in ActionScript 1 (basically JavaScript) or Java that can be instantiated and scoped to a room. For example, if you were making a card game, you would want a card game plug-in on the server to handle things like shuffling the deck and making sure the correct player wins a hand. In this way, the server holds the true state of the game. Using an extension helps keep a game flowing and lessens the users' ability to cheat. For the simple examples in this chapter, we will not be using any server-side extensions. However, if you delve further into ElectroServer or other socket-server applications, you should make sure to learn as much as possible about them.

Creating a Chat Application with ElectroServer

As an example, we are going to create a single chat application using the ElectroServer JavaScript API. Users will submit a chat message through an HTML form, and the displayed chat will be in HTML5 Canvas. We are also going to create and display some messages from ElectroServer so you can see the status of the connection to the server.

Establishing a connection to ElectroServer

First, a client application is written so that it includes the ElectroServer JavaScript API:

```
<script src="ElectroServer-5-Client-JavaScript.js"></script>
```

The client application makes a connection to ElectroServer running on a server at a specific URL, listening on a specific port, using a specific protocol. For our examples, this will be localhost, 8989, and BinaryHTTP, respectively.

We need to use these values to make a connection from the client to the server. We do this by first creating an instance of the ElectroServer object, and then calling its methods. We start by creating an instance of an ElectroServer server connection named server. We then configure a new variable named availableConnection with the previous properties we described, then add it to the server variable with a call to the method addAvailableConnection(). We will create all of this code inside our canvasApp() function:

```
var server = new ElectroServer.Server("server1");
var availableConnection = new ElectroServer.AvailableConnection
    ("localhost", 8989, ElectroServer.TransportType.BinaryHTTP);
server.addAvailableConnection(availableConnection);
```

Now, we need to use the server variable we just configured to establish a connection to ElectroServer. We do this by setting a new variable, es, as an instance of the class ElectroServer. We then call its initialize() method and add the server we just configured to the es object by calling the addServer() method of the ElectroServer server engine property:

```
var es = new ElectroServer();
es.initialize();
es.engine.addServer(server);
```

We are almost ready to try to connect to ElectroServer. First though, we need to create some event handlers for ElectroServer events. Remember when we told you that all the communication with ElectroServer is done through creating and listening for events? This is where that process begins. We need to listen for the following events: ConnectionResponse, LoginResponse, JoinRoomEvent, JoinZoneEvent, ConnectionAttemptResponse, and PublicMessageEvent:

```
es.engine.addEventListener(MessageType.ConnectionResponse, onConnectionResponse);
es.engine.addEventListener(MessageType.LoginResponse, onLoginResponse);
es.engine.addEventListener(MessageType.JoinRoomEvent, onJoinRoomEvent);
es.engine.addEventListener(MessageType.JoinZoneEvent, onJoinZoneEvent);
es.engine.addEventListener(MessageType.ConnectionAttemptResponse,
    onConnectionAttemptResponse);
es.engine.addEventListener(MessageType.PublicMessageEvent, onPublicMessageEvent);
```

Finally, once we have everything ready, we call the connect method of the Electro Server object, and wait for events to be handled by the event listener functions we have just established:

```
es.engine.connect();
```

When the ElectroServer API object tries to connect to an ElectroServer server, a ConnectionAttemptResponse event will be fired back to the client from the server. We handle that event with the onConnectionAttemptResponse() event handler. For our application, we don't do anything with this event, except create a status message for it that we will display. The statusMessages variable is an array of messages that we keep around to display back as debug information for our chat application. We will discuss this briefly in the next section:

```
function onConnectionAttemptResponse(event) {
  statusMessages.push("connection attempt response!!");
}
```

At this point, the client waits for a ConnectionResponse event to be sent back from the ElectroServer server. When the client application receives a ConnectionResponse event, it handles it with the onConnectionResponse() event handler. Once the connection is established, the client then attempts to log on to the server. To make a logon attempt, we need a username. We will create a random username, but it could come from an account on a web server, a form field or cookie, Facebook Connect, or any other location or service you might have available.

After we have a username, we create a LoginRequest() object, set the userName property, and then call the send() method of the es.engine object. This is how we will send all messages to ElectroServer from this point forward:

```
function onConnectionResponse(event) {
    statusMessages.push("Connect Successful?: "+event.successful);
    var r = new LoginRequest();
    r.userName = "CanvasUser_" + Math.floor(Math.random() * 1000);
    es.engine.send(r);
}
```

When ElectroServer responds from the `LoginRequest`, it is time to join a `zone` and a `room`. Recall that any user connected to ElectroServer needs to belong to a `room`, and every `room` belongs to a `zone`. Therefore, we need to make a user belong to one of each, which we accomplish with a `CreateRoomRequest()`. We set the `zoneName` property to `TestZoneChat`, and the `roomName` property to `TestRoomChat`. If either of these do not already exist, they will be created by the server. If they do exist, the user will be added to them. We then send the message to ElectroServer:

```
function onLoginResponse(event) {
    statusMessages.push("Login Successful?: "+event.successful);

    username = event.userName;

    var crr = new CreateRoomRequest();
    crr.zoneName = "TestZoneChat";
    crr.roomName = "TestRoomChat";

    es.engine.send(crr);
}
```

We still need to wait for a couple responses from ElectroServer events that come back through the API via port 8989. We know we have to join a `zone`, and we handle the event with the function `onJoinZoneEvent()`, but we don't need to do anything with it:

```
function onJoinZoneEvent(event) {
    statusMessages.push("joined a zone");
}
```

The most important event we are waiting to handle is `JoinRoomEvent`. When we receive this event, we know that we have joined both a `zone` and a `room`, and the application is ready to run. For the chat application, this means the user can start typing and sending messages. First, we set the `_room` variable equal to the `Room` object, which was returned by the event from `ElectroServer`. We will use this variable for our further communications with `ElectroServer`. The other thing we do in this function is set an HTML `<div>` with the id of `inputForm`, which is made visible by changing its style. The `inputForm` `<div>` is invisible when the page loads. We do this so the user won't send chat messages before the connection to `ElectroServer` is established. Now that everything is ready to go, we display the `inputForm` `<div>` so chatting can start:

```
function onJoinRoomEvent(event) {
        statusMessages.push("joined a room");
        _room = es.managerHelper.zoneManager.zoneById
            (event.zoneId).roomById(event.roomId);
        var formElement = document.getElementById("inputForm");
        formElement.setAttribute("style", "display:true");
    }
```

Creating the chat functionality

Now that we have established a connection to ElectroServer and joined a zone and a room, the chat application can start.

First, let's talk a bit about a few more variables we have created in our `canvasApp()` function, which we must scope to the rest of the chat application. The `status Messages` array will hold a set of messages that we want to keep about the connection to `ElectroServer`. We will display these in a box on the right side of the canvas. The `chatMessages` array holds all the messages users have sent into the chat room. The `username` variable holds the name of the user who is running the Canvas application, and `_room` is a reference to the `room` object that user has joined:

```
var statusMessages = new Array();
var chatMessages = new Array();
var username;
var _room;
```

The HTML page holds a `<form>` that we will use to collect the chat messages from the user. It contains a text box for the user to type into (the id of `textBox`), and a button with the id of `sendChat`. This is the same form that was invisible until we received the `JoinRoomEvent` event:

```
<form>
<input id="textBox" placeholder="your text" />
<input type="button" id ="sendChat" value="Send"/>
</form>
```

In `canvasApp()`, we set up an event listener for when the user clicks the `sendChat` button. When a click event occurs, the function `sendMessage` handles the event:

```
var formElement = document.getElementById("sendChat");
formElement.addEventListener('click', sendMessage, false);
```

The `sendMessage()` function is one of the most important functions in this application. This is where we create a couple very critical objects for communicating with Electro-Server. The first is a `PublicMessageRequest`, which is one of several types we can make to the ElectroServer socket server. Others include a `PrivateMessageRequest` and a `PluginMessageRequest`. A `PublicMessageRequest` is a message that will be sent to everyone in the room. We send that data using an `EsObject`, which is native to the ElectroServer API. It allows you to create and access ad hoc data elements for any type of information you want to send to other users in the same room.

 For a full discussion of `EsObject` and `ElectroServer` events, see the ElectroServer documentation. It is installed with the server on your local machine in *[your install folder]//documentation/html/index.html* *.

For this simple chat example, we want to send the chat message the user typed and submitted. To do this, we will use the `setString()` method of `EsObject`. This method takes two parameters: the text you want to send, and an identifier you can use to access the text. We also set another element named `type`, which will tell us what kind of message we are sending. We do this because in a more complicated application, you may send all sorts of messages and need a way to identify what they are so you can process them.

Once we have configured our `PublicMessageEvent` with the `roomId`, the `zoneId`, and the `EsObject`, we call `es.engine.send(pmr)` to send it to the rest of the room:

```
function sendMessage(event) {
    var formElement = document.getElementById("textBox");
    var pmr = new PublicMessageRequest();
    pmr.message = "";
    pmr.roomId = _room.id;
    pmr.zoneId = _room.zoneId;
    var esob = new ElectroServer.EsObject();
    esob.setString("message", formElement.value);
    esob.setString("type","chatmessage");
    pmr.esObject = esob;
    es.engine.send(pmr);
    statusMessages.push("message sent")
}
```

Notice that we did not print the user's chat message to the canvas when it was submitted. Instead, we will wait for the `PublicMessageEvent` to return from Electro Server, and then handle it like all the other chats. This keeps the interface clean, while preserving a create event/handle event processing model across the entire application.

After the socket server processes the chat message, it is broadcast out to all the users in the room. All the users must create an event handler for a `PublicMessageEvent` so they can receive and process the message; we have created the `onPublicMessageEvent` handler for this purpose. This function is very simple. It checks the `type` `EsObject` variable we set to see whether it is a `chatmessage`. If so, it pushes a string that includes the user who submitted the message (`event.userName`) and the message itself (`esob.get String("message")`) into the `chatMessages` array. This is what will be displayed on the canvas:

```
function onPublicMessageEvent(event) {

    var esob = event.esObject;
    statusMessages.push("message received")
    if (esob.getString("type") == "chatmessage") {

        chatMessages.push(event.userName + ":" + esob.getString("message"));

    }

}
```

Now, all that remains is to display the messages that we have collected. We do this (where else?) in `drawScreen()`. For both the `statusMessages` and `chatMessages` arrays, we need to display the "current" 22 messages (if we have 22), and start them at the y position of 15 pixels. We only display the last 22 messages so both the chat and the status messages will appear to scroll up the screen as more chatting and status messages are generated:

```
var starty = 15;
var maxMessages = 22;
```

If the array is larger than maxMessages, we display only the latest 22. To find those messages, we set a new variable named starti to the length of the statusMessages array, subtracted by the value in maxMessages. This gives us the index into the array of the first message we want to display. We do the exact same thing for the chatMessages array:

```
//status box
    context.strokeStyle = '#000000';
      context.strokeRect(345,  10, 145, 285);
          var starti = 0;

          if (statusMessages.length > maxMessages) {
              starti = (statusMessages.length) - maxMessages;

          }
          for (var i = starti;i< statusMessages.length;i++) {
              context.fillText  (statusMessages[i], 350, starty );
              starty+=12;
//chat box
          context.strokeStyle = '#000000';
          context.strokeRect(10,  10, 335, 285);

          starti = 0;
          lastMessage = chatMessages.length-1;
          if (chatMessages.length > maxMessages) {
              starti = (chatMessages.length) - maxMessages;
          }
          starty = 15;
          for (var i = starti;i< chatMessages.length;i++) {
              context.fillText  (chatMessages[i], 10, starty );
              starty+=12;
          }
      }
}
```

That's it! We've finished developing our multiuser chat application.

Testing the Application in Google Chrome

To test the current ElectroServer JavaScript API, you need to start Google Chrome with web security disabled. The method of doing this varies by OS, but on Mac OS X, you can open a Terminal session and execute the following command (which will open Chrome if you have it in your Applications folder):

```
/Applications/Google\ Chrome.app/Contents/MacOS/Google\ Chrome --disable-web-security
```

On a Windows PC, input a command similar to this from a command prompt or from a .bat file:

```
"C:\Program Files (x86)\Google\Chrome\Application\chrome.exe" --disable-web-security
```

Obviously this is not a workable solution for a production application. As Electrotank (and other companies who make similar products) continue to improve the functionality of their APIs and add support for HTML5 WebSockets, this limitation should disappear.

The best way to test a multiplayer application on your own development machine is to open two web browsers, or two web browser windows, at the same time. When you look at *CH11EX2.html* in Google Chrome using this method, you should see something that looks like Figure 11-5.

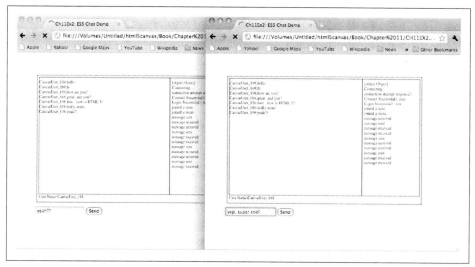

Figure 11-5. ElectroServer chat demo on the canvas with JavaScript API

The full source code is listed in Example 11-2.

Example 11-2. ES5 chat demo

```html
<!doctype html>
<html lang="en">
<head>
<meta charset="UTF-8">
<title>CH11EX2: ES5 Chat Demo</title>
<script src="modernizr-1.6.min.js"></script>
<script src="ElectroServer-5-Client-JavaScript.js"></script>
<script type="text/javascript">
window.addEventListener("load", eventWindowLoaded, false);

    function eventWindowLoaded () {
        canvasApp();
}
```

```
    function canvasSupport () {
        return Modernizr.canvas;
}

    function canvasApp () {

        if (!canvasSupport()) {
          return;
        }

      var theCanvas = document.getElementById("canvasOne");
      var context = theCanvas.getContext("2d");

      var formElement = document.getElementById("sendChat");
      formElement.addEventListener('click', sendMessage, false);

    function drawScreen() {
        //background
        context.fillStyle = "#ffffaa";
        context.fillRect(0, 0, 500, 320);

        context.fillStyle = "#000000";
        context.font = "10px _sans";
        context.textBaseline = "top";

        //box
        context.strokeStyle = '#000000';
        context.strokeRect(5,  5, 490, 310);

        var starty = 15;
        var maxMessages = 22;


        //status box
        context.strokeStyle = '#000000';
        context.strokeRect(345,  10, 145, 285);
        var starti = 0;

        if (statusMessages.length > maxMessages) {
              starti = (statusMessages.length) - maxMessages;

        }
        for (var i = starti;i< statusMessages.length;i++) {
           context.fillText  (statusMessages[i], 350, starty );
           starty+=12;
        }

        //chat box
        context.strokeStyle = '#000000';
        context.strokeRect(10,  10, 335, 285);

        starti = 0;
        lastMessage = chatMessages.length-1;
        if (chatMessages.length > maxMessages) {
              starti = (chatMessages.length) - maxMessages;
```

```
        }
        starty = 15;
        for (var i = starti;i< chatMessages.length;i++) {
            context.fillText (chatMessages[i], 10, starty );
            starty+=12;
        }

        context.fillText ("User Name:" + username, 10, 295 );

    }

    var statusMessages = new Array();
    var chatMessages = new Array();

    var server = new ElectroServer.Server("server1");

    statusMessages.push(server);

    var availableConnection = new ElectroServer.AvailableConnection
        ("localhost", 8989, ElectroServer.TransportType.BinaryHTTP);

    server.addAvailableConnection(availableConnection);

    var es = new ElectroServer();
    es.initialize();

    var username;
    var _room;

    es.engine.addServer(server);

    es.engine.addEventListener(MessageType.ConnectionResponse, onConnectionResponse);
    es.engine.addEventListener(MessageType.LoginResponse, onLoginResponse);
    es.engine.addEventListener(MessageType.JoinRoomEvent, onJoinRoomEvent);
    es.engine.addEventListener(MessageType.JoinZoneEvent, onJoinZoneEvent);
    es.engine.addEventListener(MessageType.ConnectionAttemptResponse,
        onConnectionAttemptResponse);
    es.engine.addEventListener(MessageType.PublicMessageEvent, onPublicMessageEvent);

    es.engine.connect();

    statusMessages.push("Connecting...");

    setInterval(drawScreen, 33);

function onConnectionAttemptResponse(event) {
    statusMessages.push("connection attempt response!!");
    }

function onJoinRoomEvent(event) {
    statusMessages.push("joined a room");
    _room = es.managerHelper.zoneManager.zoneById
        (event.zoneId).roomById(event.roomId);
    var formElement = document.getElementById("inputForm");
    formElement.setAttribute("style", "display:true");
```

```
        }

    function onJoinZoneEvent(event) {
        statusMessages.push("joined a zone");


    }

    function onConnectionResponse(event) {
        statusMessages.push("Connect Successful?: "+event.successful);
        var r = new LoginRequest();
        r.userName = "CanvasUser_" + Math.floor(Math.random() * 1000);
        es.engine.send(r);
    }

    function onLoginResponse(event) {
        statusMessages.push("Login Successful?: "+event.successful);

        username = event.userName;

        var crr = new CreateRoomRequest();
        crr.zoneName = "TestZoneChat";
        crr.roomName = "TestRoomChat";

        es.engine.send(crr);
    }

    function sendMessage(event) {
        var formElement = document.getElementById("textBox");
        var pmr = new PublicMessageRequest();
        pmr.message = "";
        pmr.roomId = _room.id;
        pmr.zoneId = _room.zoneId;
        var esob = new ElectroServer.EsObject();
        esob.setString("message", formElement.value);
        esob.setString("type","chatmessage");
        pmr.esObject = esob;
        es.engine.send(pmr);
        statusMessages.push("message sent")


    }

    function onPublicMessageEvent(event) {

        var esob = event.esObject;
        statusMessages.push("message received")
        if (esob.getString("type") == "chatmessage") {

            chatMessages.push(event.userName + ":" + esob.getString("message"));

        }

    }

}
```

```
</script>
</head>
<body>
<div style="position: absolute; top: 50px; left: 50px;">
<canvas id="canvasOne" width="500" height="320">
 Your browser does not support HTML5 Canvas.
</canvas>
<div id="inputForm"  style="display:none;">
<form>
<input id="textBox" placeholder="your text" />
<input type="button" id ="sendChat" value="Send"/>
</form>
</div>

</div>
</body>
</html>
```

Further Explorations with ElectroServer

Displaying text on HTML5 Canvas is interesting, but as we have shown you in this book, you can do much more. Let's add some graphics to the previous demo. We have added a second application for you to peruse, named *CH11EX3.html*. This application adds the bouncing ball demo app from Chapter 5 to the chat application we just created. It allows chatters to "send" bouncing balls to each other by clicking on the canvas.

The heart of the app is simply another use of the `EsObject` from the chat application, which is created when the user clicks on the canvas. This `EsObject` adds information about a `ball` that one user created for the others in the room:

```
function eventMouseUp(event) {
    var mouseX;
    var mouseY;
    if (event.layerX ||  event.layerX == 0) { // Firefox
        mouseX = event.layerX ;
        mouseY = event.layerY;
    } else if (event.offsetX || event.offsetX == 0) { // Opera
        mouseX = event.offsetX;
        mouseY = event.offsetY;
    }
    ballcounter++;
    var maxSize = 8;
    var minSize = 5;
    var maxSpeed = maxSize+5;
    var tempRadius = Math.floor(Math.random()*maxSize)+minSize;
    var tempX = mouseX;
    var tempY = mouseY;
    var tempSpeed = maxSpeed-tempRadius;
    var tempAngle = Math.floor(Math.random()*360);
    var tempRadians = tempAngle * Math.PI/ 180;
    var tempvelocityx = Math.cos(tempRadians) * tempSpeed;
    var tempvelocityy = Math.sin(tempRadians) * tempSpeed;
    var pmr = new PublicMessageRequest();
```

```
pmr.message = "";
pmr.roomId = _room.id;
pmr.zoneId = _room.zoneId;
var esob = new ElectroServer.EsObject();
esob.setFloat("tempX",tempX );
esob.setFloat("tempY",tempY );
esob.setFloat("tempRadius",tempRadius );
esob.setFloat("tempSpeed",tempSpeed );
esob.setFloat("tempAngle",tempAngle );
esob.setFloat("velocityx",tempvelocityx );
esob.setFloat("velocityy",tempvelocityy );
esob.setString("usercolor",usercolor );
esob.setString("ballname",username+ballcounter);
esob.setString("type", "newball");
pmr.esObject = esob;
es.engine.send(pmr);
statusMessages.push("send ball");

}
```

When a user connected in the same room receives this public message, we handle the
newball event in a similar manner to how we handled the chat text, by using the on
PublicMessageEvent() function. When the function sees an event with the type new
ball, it calls createNetBall(). The createNetBall() function creates ball objects to
bounce around the canvas, much like the ones we created in Chapter 5:

```
function onPublicMessageEvent(event) {
    statusMessages.push("message received")
    var esob = event.esObject;
    if (esob.getString("type") == "chatmessage") {
     chatMessages.push(event.userName + ":" + esob.getString("message"));
    } else if (esob.getString("type") == "newball") {
        statusMessages.push("create ball")
        createNetBall(esob.getFloat("tempX"),esob.getFloat("tempY"),
            esob.getFloat("tempSpeed"),esob.getFloat("tempAngle"),
            esob.getFloat("tempRadius"),esob.getFloat("velocityx"),
            esob.getFloat("velocityy"),event.userName,esob.getString("usercolor"),
            esob.getString("ballname") );
    }

}

function createNetBall(tempX,tempY,tempSpeed,tempAngle,tempRadius,tempvelocityx,
                    tempvelocityy, user, usercolor, ballname) {

    tempBall = {x:tempX,y:tempY,radius:tempRadius, speed:tempSpeed, angle:tempAngle,
        velocityx:tempvelocityx, velocityy:tempvelocityy,nextx:tempX, nexty:tempY,
        mass:tempRadius, usercolor:usercolor, ballname:ballname}
    balls.push(tempBall);
    }
```

Figure 11-6 shows what this demo looks like when users click the mouse button to send
balls to other users. The colors of the balls are assigned randomly.

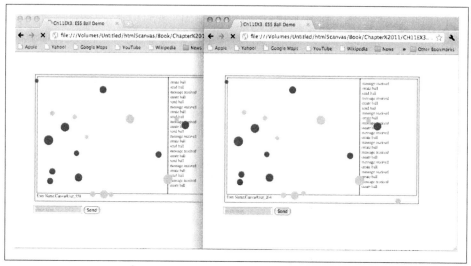

Figure 11-6. ElectroServer chat ball demo

Example 11-3 gives the full set of code for *CH11EX3.html*.

Example 11-3. ES5 ball demo

```
<!doctype html>
<html lang="en">
<head>
<meta charset="UTF-8">
<title>CH11EX3: ES5 Ball Demo</title>
<script src="modernizr-1.6.min.js"></script>
<script src="ElectroServer-5-Client-JavaScript.js"></script>
<script type="text/javascript">
window.addEventListener("load", eventWindowLoaded, false);

function eventWindowLoaded () {
    canvasApp();
}

function canvasSupport () {
    return Modernizr.canvas;
}

function canvasApp () {

    if (!canvasSupport()) {
      return;
    }

    var theCanvas = document.getElementById("canvasOne");
    var context = theCanvas.getContext("2d");
```

```
var formElement = document.getElementById("sendChat");
formElement.addEventListener('click', sendMessage, false);

  function drawScreen() {
   //background
   context.fillStyle = "#ffffaa";
   context.fillRect(0, 0, 500, 320);

   context.fillStyle = "#000000";
   context.font = "10px _sans";
   context.textBaseline = "top";

   //box
   context.strokeStyle = '#000000';
   context.strokeRect(5,  5, 490, 310);

   var starty = 15;
   var maxMessages = 22;

   //status box
   context.strokeStyle = '#000000';
   context.strokeRect(345,  10, 145, 285);
   var starti = 0;

   if (statusMessages.length > maxMessages) {
      starti = (statusMessages.length) - maxMessages;

   }
   for (var i = starti;i< statusMessages.length;i++) {
      context.fillText  (statusMessages[i], 350, starty );
      starty+=12;
   }

   //chat box
   context.strokeStyle = '#000000';
   context.strokeRect(10,  10, 335, 285);

   starti = 0;
   lastMessage = chatMessages.length-1;
   if (chatMessages.length > maxMessages) {
      starti = (chatMessages.length) - maxMessages;
   }
   starty = 15;
   for (var i = starti;i< chatMessages.length;i++) {
      context.fillText  (chatMessages[i], 10, starty );
      starty+=12;
   }

   context.fillText  ("User Name:" + username, 10, 295 );

   update();
   testWalls();
   render();

  }
```

```
 function updateBall(ball) {
   ball.radians = ball.angle * Math.PI/ 180;
   ball.velocityx = Math.cos(ball.radians) * ball.speed;
   ball.velocityy = Math.sin(ball.radians) * ball.speed;

}

var statusMessages = new Array();
var chatMessages = new Array();

var server = new ElectroServer.Server("server1");

statusMessages.push(server);

var availableConnection = new ElectroServer.AvailableConnection
    ("localhost", 8989, ElectroServer.TransportType.BinaryHTTP);

server.addAvailableConnection(availableConnection);

var es = new ElectroServer();
es.initialize();

var username;
var usercolor;
var _room;
var ballcounter = 0;

es.engine.addServer(server);

es.engine.addEventListener(MessageType.ConnectionResponse, onConnectionResponse);
es.engine.addEventListener(MessageType.LoginResponse, onLoginResponse);
es.engine.addEventListener(MessageType.JoinRoomEvent, onJoinRoomEvent);
es.engine.addEventListener(MessageType.JoinZoneEvent, onJoinZoneEvent);
es.engine.addEventListener(MessageType.ConnectionAttemptResponse,
    onConnectionAttemptResponse);
es.engine.addEventListener(MessageType.PublicMessageEvent, onPublicMessageEvent);

es.engine.connect();


statusMessages.push("Connecting...");


var balls = new Array();

theCanvas.addEventListener("mouseup",eventMouseUp, false);

var friction = 0;

setInterval(drawScreen, 33);

function eventMouseUp(event) {
   var mouseX;
   var mouseY;
```

```
        if ( event.layerX || event.layerX == 0) { // Firefox
            mouseX = event.layerX ;
            mouseY = event.layerY;
        } else if (event.offsetX || event.offsetX == 0) { // Opera
            mouseX = event.offsetX;
            mouseY = event.offsetY;
        }
        ballcounter++;
        var maxSize = 8;
        var minSize = 5;
        var maxSpeed = maxSize+5;
        var tempRadius = Math.floor(Math.random()*maxSize)+minSize;
        var tempX = mouseX;
        var tempY = mouseY;
        var tempSpeed = maxSpeed-tempRadius;
        var tempAngle = Math.floor(Math.random()*360);
        var tempRadians = tempAngle * Math.PI/ 180;
        var tempvelocityx = Math.cos(tempRadians) * tempSpeed;
        var tempvelocityy = Math.sin(tempRadians) * tempSpeed;
        var pmr = new PublicMessageRequest();
        pmr.message = "";
        pmr.roomId = _room.id;
         pmr.zoneId = _room.zoneId;
        var esob = new ElectroServer.EsObject();
        esob.setFloat("tempX",tempX );
        esob.setFloat("tempY",tempY );
        esob.setFloat("tempRadius",tempRadius );
        esob.setFloat("tempSpeed",tempSpeed );
        esob.setFloat("tempAngle",tempAngle );
        esob.setFloat("velocityx",tempvelocityx );
        esob.setFloat("velocityy",tempvelocityy );
        esob.setString("usercolor",usercolor );
        esob.setString("ballname",username+ballcounter);
        esob.setString("type", "newball");
        pmr.esObject = esob;
        es.engine.send(pmr);
        statusMessages.push("send ball");

    }

    function createNetBall(tempX,tempY,tempSpeed,tempAngle,tempRadius,tempvelocityx,
                        tempvelocityy, user, usercolor, ballname) {

        tempBall = {x:tempX,y:tempY,radius:tempRadius, speed:tempSpeed,
            angle:tempAngle, velocityx:tempvelocityx, velocityy:tempvelocityy,
            nextx:tempX, nexty:tempY, mass:tempRadius, usercolor:usercolor,
            ballname:ballname}
        balls.push(tempBall);
    }

    function onConnectionAttemptResponse(event) {
        statusMessages.push("connection attempt response!!");
    }
```

```
function onJoinRoomEvent(event) {
    statusMessages.push("joined a room");
    _room = es.managerHelper.zoneManager.zoneById
        (event.zoneId).roomById(event.roomId);
    var formElement = document.getElementById("inputForm");
    formElement.setAttribute("style", "display:true");
}

function onJoinZoneEvent(event) {
    statusMessages.push("joined a zone");

}

function onConnectionResponse(event) {
    statusMessages.push("Connect Successful?: "+event.successful);
    var r = new LoginRequest();
    r.userName = "CanvasUser_" + Math.floor(Math.random() * 1000);
    es.engine.send(r);
}

function onLoginResponse(event) {
    statusMessages.push("Login Successful?: "+event.successful);

    username = event.userName;
    usercolor = "#"+(Math.random()*0xFFFFFF<<0).toString(16);

    var crr = new CreateRoomRequest();
    crr.zoneName = "TestZoneCuesors";
    crr.roomName = "TestRoomCursors";

    es.engine.send(crr);

}

function sendMessage(event) {
    var formElement = document.getElementById("textBox");
    var pmr = new PublicMessageRequest();
    pmr.message = "";
    pmr.roomId = _room.id;
    pmr.zoneId = _room.zoneId;
    var esob = new ElectroServer.EsObject();
    esob.setString("message", formElement.value);
    esob.setString("type","chatmessage");
    pmr.esObject = esob;
    es.engine.send(pmr);
    statusMessages.push("message sent")

}

function onPublicMessageEvent(event) {
    statusMessages.push("message received")
    var esob = event.esObject;

    if (esob.getString("type") == "chatmessage") {
```

```
        chatMessages.push(event.userName + ":" + esob.getString("message"));

    } else if (esob.getString("type") == "newball") {
        statusMessages.push("create ball")
        createNetBall(esob.getFloat("tempX"),esob.getFloat("tempY"),
            esob.getFloat("tempSpeed"),esob.getFloat("tempAngle"),
            esob.getFloat("tempRadius"),esob.getFloat("velocityx"),
            esob.getFloat("velocityy"),event.userName,esob.getString("usercolor"),
            esob.getString("ballname") );
    }

}


function update() {
    for (var i =0; i <balls.length; i++) {
        ball = balls[i];
        //Friction
        ball.velocityx = ball.velocityx - ( ball.velocityx*friction);
        ball.velocityy = ball.velocityy - ( ball.velocityy*friction);

        ball.nextx = (ball.x += ball.velocityx);
        ball.nexty = (ball.y += ball.velocityy);
    }

}

function testWalls() {
    var ball;
    var testBall;

    for (var i = 0; i <balls.length; i++) {
        ball = balls[i];

        if (ball.nextx+ball.radius > theCanvas.width) {
            ball.velocityx = ball.velocityx*-1;
            ball.nextx = theCanvas.width - ball.radius;

        } else if (ball.nextx-ball.radius < 0 ) {
            ball.velocityx = ball.velocityx*-1;
            ball.nextx = ball.radius;

        } else if (ball.nexty+ball.radius > theCanvas.height ) {
            ball.velocityy = ball.velocityy*-1;
            ball.nexty = theCanvas.height - ball.radius;

        } else if(ball.nexty-ball.radius < 0) {
            ball.velocityy = ball.velocityy*-1;
            ball.nexty = ball.radius;
        }

    }

}
```

```
            function render() {
                var ball;

                for (var i =0; i <balls.length; i++) {

                    ball = balls[i];
                    ball.x = ball.nextx;
                    ball.y = ball.nexty;
                    context.fillStyle = ball.usercolor;
                    context.beginPath();
                    context.arc(ball.x,ball.y,ball.radius,0,Math.PI*2,true);
                    context.closePath();
                    context.fill();
                }

            }

        }


</script>
</head>
<body>
<div style="position: absolute; top: 50px; left: 50px;">
<canvas id="canvasOne" width="500" height="320">
 Your browser does not support HTML5 Canvas.
</canvas>
<div id="inputForm"   style="display:none;">
<form>
<input id="textBox" placeholder="your text" />
<input type="button" id ="sendChat" value="Send"/>
</form>
</div>

</div>
</body>
</html>
```

This Is Just the Tip of the Iceberg

There is much more you can do with ElectroServer than what we showed you in this chapter. Sending and receiving PublicMessage events can only get you so far when designing multiuser/multiplayer applications.

To start designing multiplayer applications seriously, you will need to delve into the extension and plug-in architecture of ElectroServer, as well as explore plug-in events, which are used to communicate to the server portion of an application. We suggest you check out *http://www.electrotank.com/es5.html* for more information about the socket server. You can also read *ActionScript for Multiplayer Games and Virtual Worlds* by Jobe Makar (New Riders). Even though it centers on Flash and an earlier version of

---

ElectroServer, the architectural information about designing apps for a socket server is well worth your time.

At the same time, ElectroServer can be used with technologies other than Canvas (Flash, iOS, etc.), so Canvas will be able to communicate with other socket servers via JavaScript and WebSockets. We chose to base this example on ElectroServer because it allowed us to create a full application for you to test and work through. Other libraries and tools are bound to appear very soon that can work with canvas; for example, the SmartFoxServer Ajax API. Still in beta, this API uses the Google Web Toolkit to connect to the SmartFox socket server through an Ajax connection in JavaScript. This library requires the SmartFoxServer BlueBox add-on module. In theory, this means SmartFoxServer could be used in conjunction with Canvas right now.

Conclusion

Over the past 11 chapters, you have been immersed in the world of HTML5 Canvas. We have given you dozens of examples and applications to work from and through so you can start building your own creations. From simple text displays to high-performance games, we have showed you many ways to bring some of the magic of previous RIA (Rich Internet Application) technologies into the plug-in-*less* browser experience.

We offered many strategies for integrating Canvas with other HTML5 technologies, as well as techniques for handling text, displaying graphics, scrolling bitmaps, creating animation, detecting multiple types of collisions, embedding and manipulating video, playing music, handling sound effects, creating user interfaces, optimizing code, and preparing apps for mobile platforms. We even introduced you to the future of 3D and multiuser applications directly in the web browser.

The true future, though, is up to you. HTML5 and Canvas are dynamic topics that are still in a rapid state of change and adoption. While this book is a good starting point, you will need to keep abreast of new changes to the technology. Visit our website, *http://www.8bitrocket.com*, for news and updates on HTML5 Canvas.

O'Reilly also has several books that you might find useful, including:

- *HTML5: Up and Running* by Mark Pilgrim
- *Supercharged JavaScript Graphics* by Raffaele Cecco

If you are interested in learning how some of the game-development techniques described in this book (as well as many others) can be applied to Flash, check out our other most recent book, *The Essential Guide to Flash Games* (friendsofED).

There is a real paradigm shift occurring right now on the Web. For most of the first decade of the 21st century, Java, Flash, Silverlight, and other plug-in RIA technologies dominated application development and design. At the time, there appeared to be no better solution for the development of rich applications in a web browser than to bolt on technology that was not native to the browser.

The emergence of the "connected apps" culture is changing this. Every platform—from phones to TVs, e-readers to tablets, wireless printers to desktop PCs—is targeted for web-enabled applications sold or distributed through an app store. In many ways, these apps are replacing RIA applications, or at the very least offering a compelling new platform for their development and distribution.

Where RIA technologies of the past—like Java, Flash, and Silverlight—could target nearly all web browsers and PCs, they are having trouble finding a true foothold in the area of connected apps (especially on platforms where they are restricted from running, like iOS). This is where HTML5 Canvas can really make a difference. With true cross-platform execution, applications run in the web browser (or compiled with technologies like PhoneGap) can be made available to the widest audience possible. Soon these applications will be enhanced with 3D graphics and have the ability to communicate with one another via technologies like the ElectroServer socket server. One can envision a day in the near future where technology platforms fade away, and the web-connected app world simply works, regardless of screen or location. This is the promise of HTML5—especially HTML5 Canvas. So, now that you have the tools to begin, what do you plan to build?

Index

Symbols

- (minus sign), -- (decrement) operator, 175
2D context, 1
    and current state, 15
    retrieving, 11
3D with WebGL, 567–583
    JavaScript libraries used with WebGL, 581
    resources for learning about WebGL, 569
    rotating cube application, 569
        adding JavaScript libraries, 569
        animating the cube, 573
        complete code, 575–581
        initialization in canvasApp( ), 571
        shaders, 570
        testing for WebGL support, 571
    testing WebGL, 568
? (question mark), ?: ternary operator, 155

A

accelerometer (iPhone), 561
    adding gesture to BS Bingo game (example), 561–563
addColorStop( ) method, CanvasGradient objects, 100
addEventListener( ) method, window objects, 7, 19
alignment, text, 86–90
    centering text with TextMetrics, width property, 72
    handling in Text Arranger (example), 87–90
    horizontal, 87
    setting vertical alignment with textBaseline property, 11

vertical, 86
vertically centering text on canvas, 72
alpha values
    alpha fading player ship (game example), 392
    globalAlpha property, 39
        using with text, 94
    manipulating via pixel color values, 160
    rgba colors, 52
angle of incidence, 183
angle of reflection, 183
angles
    defined in radians for drawing arcs, 34
    direction of movement on a vector, 179
    measurement in radians, 42
animations
    adding step timer to FrameRateCounter object prototype, 466–468
    advanced cell-based animation, 132–137
    bouncing off walls, 183–216
        multiple balls, 188–193
        multiple balls bouncing with friction, 210–216
        multiple balls colliding, 198–210
        multiple balls with dynamically resized canvas, 193–198
        single ball, 184–188
    Canvas compared to Flash, 379
    combining rotation, animation, and movement, 141–142
        displaying tile map on canvas, 147
    combining with rotation transformations, 140
    curve and circular movement, 216–236

We'd like to hear your suggestions for improving our indexes. Send email to *index@oreilly.com*.

About the Authors

Steve Fulton is an RIA and web game developer who has been cultivating an audience for news, stories, blogs, and tutorials about Flash, Silverlight, and now the HTML5 Canvas at his website, *http://www.8bitrocket.com*, for the past 3½ years. He has one of the highest Alexa rankings among Flash game developers' blogs. Steve has worked as a web development manager at Mattel Toys for the past 14 years, helping to create Mattel's extensive online presence.

Jeff Fulton has been creating games and RIAs for the past 17 years. He is currently a Senior Game Engineer at Zynga, having previously plied his trade at Mattel Toys and freelanced for his own consulting company, 8bitrocket Studios. Jeff has previously co-authored (with his brother Steve) a book on advanced Flash game development, and currently runs a popular and successful blog site, *http://www.8bitrocket.com*, which focuses on Flash, HTML5, Silverlight, and retro gaming.

Colophon

The animal on the cover of *HTML5 Canvas* is the New Zealand kaka (*Nestor meridionalis*), a parrot endemic to that country. The kaka's name comes from the Maori word for parrot (a duplication of the word *kā*, Maori for "to screech"). It is part of the Strigopidae family, which diverged from other parrots 80–100 million years ago when the landmass that is now New Zealand broke apart from the supercontinent Gondwana. A defining characteristic of this family of parrots is the bristles on their tongues, which are used to collect nectar.

A medium-sized parrot about 18 inches in length, the kaka is stocky and has a short, square tail. Its feathers are primarily olive-brown, with brighter splashes of crimson on the underwings and rump. It also has yellow-brown spots on its cheeks and a gray crown. It possesses the sharp curved beak common to many parrot species, which it uses to pry seeds loose from cones and dig up insects. The kaka also eats fruit, berries, nectar, and flowers.

These birds are primarily arboreal, living in the canopies of New Zealand forests. Very social creatures, kakas live in large flocks that sometimes include other local parrot species as well. In winter, breeding pairs build nests in hollow trees, and lay a clutch of two to four eggs. Both parents help feed their young.

The kaka is currently endangered due to deforestation, predators, and competition for food with non-native species. The closely related kea and kakapo parrots are facing similar challenges—and in fact, two species within the *Nestor* genus have already gone extinct (most recently in 1851).

The cover image is from Cassell's *Natural History*. The cover font is Adobe ITC Garamond. The text font is Linotype Birka; the heading font is Adobe Myriad Condensed; and the code font is LucasFont's TheSansMonoCondensed.

Get even more for your money.

Join the O'Reilly Community, and register the O'Reilly books you own. It's free, and you'll get:

- $4.99 ebook upgrade offer
- 40% upgrade offer on O'Reilly print books
- Membership discounts on books and events
- Free lifetime updates to ebooks and videos
- Multiple ebook formats, DRM FREE
- Participation in the O'Reilly community
- Newsletters
- Account management
- 100% Satisfaction Guarantee

Signing up is easy:

1. **Go to: oreilly.com/go/register**
2. **Create an O'Reilly login.**
3. **Provide your address.**
4. **Register your books.**

Note: English-language books only

To order books online:
oreilly.com/store

For questions about products or an order:
orders@oreilly.com

To sign up to get topic-specific email announcements and/or news about upcoming books, conferences, special offers, and new technologies:
elists@oreilly.com

For technical questions about book content:
booktech@oreilly.com

To submit new book proposals to our editors:
proposals@oreilly.com

O'Reilly books are available in multiple DRM-free ebook formats. For more information:
oreilly.com/ebooks

O'REILLY®

Spreading the knowledge of innovators   oreilly.com

The information you need, when and where you need it.

With Safari Books Online, you can:

Access the contents of thousands of technology and business books

- Quickly search over 7000 books and certification guides
- Download whole books or chapters in PDF format, at no extra cost, to print or read on the go
- Copy and paste code
- Save up to 35% on O'Reilly print books
- **New!** Access mobile-friendly books directly from cell phones and mobile devices

Stay up-to-date on emerging topics before the books are published

- Get on-demand access to evolving manuscripts.
- Interact directly with authors of upcoming books

Explore thousands of hours of video on technology and design topics

- Learn from expert video tutorials
- Watch and replay recorded conference sessions

O'REILLY®

CPSIA information can be obtained at www.ICGtesting.com

260731BV00001BA/47-2500/P

9 781449 393908